A Critical Introduction to Intellectual Property Law

This highly accessible and engaging introduction to IP law encourages readers to critically evaluate the ownership of intangible goods. The rigorous pedagogy, featuring many real-world cases, both historical and up to date, full colour images, discussion exercises, end-of-chapter questions and activities, allows readers to engage fully with the philosophical concepts foundational of the subject, while also enabling them to independently analyse key cases, texts and materials relevant to IP law in the contemporary world. This innovative textbook, written by one of the leading authorities on the subject, is the ideal route to a full understanding of copyright, patents, designs, trade marks, passing off, remedies and litigation for undergraduate and beginning graduate students in IP law.

PATRICK GOOLD is a reader in law at the City University of London, and a Senior Fellow of the Higher Education Academy. He has received numerous awards for teaching and has been shortlisted for the HE Innovate Award for most innovative approach to widening participation in the curriculum. He is a leading theorist on IP law, the author of *IP Accidents* (Cambridge 2022), and the co-editor of *The Cambridge Handbook of Investment-Driven Intellectual Property* (Cambridge 2023).

A Critical Introduction to Intellectual Property Law

Texts, Cases and Materials

Patrick R Goold
The City Law School

Shaftesbury Road, Cambridge CB2 8EA, United Kingdom

One Liberty Plaza, 20th Floor, New York, NY 10006, USA

477 Williamstown Road, Port Melbourne, VIC 3207, Australia

314–321, 3rd Floor, Plot 3, Splendor Forum, Jasola District Centre, New Delhi – 110025, India

103 Penang Road, #05–06/07, Visioncrest Commercial, Singapore 238467

Cambridge University Press is part of Cambridge University Press & Assessment, a department of the University of Cambridge.

We share the University's mission to contribute to society through the pursuit of education, learning and research at the highest international levels of excellence.

www.cambridge.org
Information on this title: www.cambridge.org/highereducation/isbn/9781009182287

DOI: 10.1017/9781009182294

© Cambridge University Press & Assessment 2024

This publication is in copyright. Subject to statutory exception and to the provisions of relevant collective licensing agreements, no reproduction of any part may take place without the written permission of Cambridge University Press & Assessment.

First published 2024

Printed in Great Britain by CPI Group (UK) Ltd, Croydon CR0 4YY

A catalogue record for this publication is available from the British Library

Library of Congress Cataloging-in-Publication data
Names: Goold, Patrick Russell, 1987– author.
Title: A critical introduction to intellectual property law : texts, cases, and materials / Patrick R. Goold, The City Law School.
Description: Cambridge, United Kingdom ; New York, NY : Cambridge University Press, 2024 | Includes bibliographical references and index.
Identifiers: LCCN 2023050838 (print) | LCCN 2023050839 (ebook) | ISBN 9781009182287 (hardback) | ISBN 9781009182270 (paperback) | ISBN 9781009182294 (ebook)
Subjects: LCSH: Intellectual property. | Copyright. | Patent laws and legislation. | Trademarks–Law and legislation.
Classification: LCC K1401 .G66 2024 (print) | LCC K1401 (ebook) | DDC 346.04/8–dc23/eng/20231031
LC record available at https://lccn.loc.gov/2023050838
LC ebook record available at https://lccn.loc.gov/2023050839

ISBN 978-1-009-18228-7 Hardback
ISBN 978-1-009-18227-0 Paperback

Additional resources for this publication at www.cambridge.org/goold

Cambridge University Press & Assessment has no responsibility for the persistence or accuracy of URLs for external or third-party internet websites referred to in this publication and does not guarantee that any content on such websites is, or will remain, accurate or appropriate.

Contents

List of Figures	page *xi*
List of Tables	*xiii*
List of Boxes	*xiv*
Acknowledgements	*xix*
Table of Cases	*xx*
Table of Legislation	*xxviii*
List of Abbreviations	*xxx*

1 Introduction to Intellectual Property — **1**

1.1 THREE QUESTIONS — **1**
1.1.1 The Metaphysical Question — 1
1.1.2 The Conceptual Question — 4
1.1.3 The Normative Question — 6

1.2 ARGUING ABOUT IP — **8**

1.3 JURISDICTION — **10**

1.4 SCOPE — **11**

1.5 BOOK FEATURES — **11**

1.6 SELF-ASSESSMENT — **12**
Self-Assessment Answers — 12

PART I COPYRIGHT — **15**

2 Copyright I: Foundations of Copyright Law — **17**

2.1 CREATING COPYRIGHT — **17**
2.1.1 Precursors to Copyright — 18
2.1.2 The Statute of Anne — 20

2.2 ARGUMENTS FOR COPYRIGHT — **24**
2.2.1 The Labour Argument — 25
2.2.1.1 Problems with the Labour Argument — 29

2.2.2 The Utilitarian Argument — 32
2.2.2.1 Problems with the Utilitarian Argument — 35

2.2.3 The Personality Argument — 38
2.2.3.1 Problems with the Personality Argument — 40

2.3 THE INTERNATIONALISATION OF COPYRIGHT — **41**

2.4 SUMMARY — **44**

2.5 SELF-ASSESSMENT — **44**
Activity Discussion — 45
Self-Assessment Answers — 47

3 Copyright II: Subject Matter — **49**

3.1 TWENTIETH-CENTURY UK SUBJECT MATTER — **50**
3.1.1 Works — 50
3.1.2 Original — 53
3.1.3 A Closed List — 59
3.1.3.1 Literary — 60
3.1.3.2 Dramatic — 63
3.1.3.3 Musical — 65
3.1.3.4 Artistic — 69
3.1.3.5 LDMA as a Group — 74
3.1.4 Non-Original 'Works' — 74

3.2 EUROPEAN INFLUENCES — **75**
3.2.1 Original Works — 76
3.2.2 An Open List — 80
3.2.3 Non-Original Works — 81
3.2.4 No Formalities — 81

3.3 SUMMARY — **82**

3.4 SELF-ASSESSMENT 82

Activity Discussion 83
Self-Assessment Answers 84

4 Copyright III: Rights 86

4.1 ECONOMIC RIGHTS 86
4.1.1 Reproduction Right 87
    4.1.1.1 Copying 88
    4.1.1.2 Substantial Part 93
    4.1.1.3 Any Material Form 98
4.1.2 Distribution Right 99
4.1.3 Rental and Lending Right 103
4.1.4 Performance Right 103
4.1.5 Communication Right 104
4.1.6 Adaptation Right 113

4.2 MORAL RIGHTS 114
4.2.1 The Integrity Right 116
4.2.2 The Attribution and False
    Attribution Rights 119

4.3 DURATION 120

4.4 OWNERSHIP 122
4.4.1 First Ownership 123
4.4.2 Assignment, Licence, Waiver 123

4.5 SUMMARY 126

4.6 SELF-ASSESSMENT 126

Activity Discussion 127
Self-Assessment Answers 128

5 Copyright IV: Exceptions 131

5.1 FAIR DEALING 133
5.1.1 Statutory Purposes 133
    5.1.1.1 Parody, Caricature
    or Pastiche 136
    5.1.1.2 Criticism or Review 144
    5.1.1.3 Quotation 144
    5.1.1.4 Reporting
    Current Events 146
    5.1.1.5 Non-Commercial
    Research or Private
    Study 147

    5.1.2 Fairness 147
    5.1.3 Sufficient Acknowledgment 151

5.2 TEMPORARY COPIES 151

5.3 PERSONAL COPYING FOR PRIVATE USE 155

5.4 DISCLOSURE IN THE PUBLIC INTEREST 157

5.5 TEXT AND DATA ANALYSIS 159

5.6 SUMMARY 162

5.7 SELF-ASSESSMENT 163

Activity Discussion 163
Self-Assessment Answers 165

PART II PATENTS 167

6 Patents I: Foundations of Patent Law 169

6.1 INVENTING PATENTS 170
6.1.1 Patents as Industrial Policy 171
6.1.2 Hostility to Monopolies 173
6.1.3 The Statute of Monopolies 175
6.1.4 The Patent Controversy in the
    Nineteenth Century 178

6.2 ARGUMENTS FOR PATENTS 180
6.2.1 The Personality
    Argument Revisited 181
6.2.2 The Labour
    Argument Revisited 182
6.2.3 The Utilitarian Arguments 184
    6.2.3.1 Invention 184
    6.2.3.2 Disclosure 188
    6.2.3.3 Development 190

6.3 REGISTRATION 193
6.3.1 Patent Specification 193
6.3.2 Registration Process 200
6.3.3 Entitlement 201

6.4 THE INTERNATIONALISATION OF PATENTS 203
6.4.1 Paris Convention 203
6.4.2 European Patent Convention and
    Patent Cooperation Treaty 204

6.4.3 TRIPS	205
6.4.4 European Union Influence	205

6.5 SUMMARY — 207
6.6 SELF-ASSESSMENT — 207
Activity Discussion — 208
Self-Assessment Answers — 209

7 Patents II: Patentability — 212
7.1 INVENTIONS — 212
7.2 NOT INVENTIONS — 215
7.2.1 Discoveries	217
7.2.2 Computer Programs	222
7.2.3 Business Methods	226
7.2.4 Presentation of Information	228
7.2.5 Mental Acts	230

7.3 EXCLUDED INVENTIONS — 232
7.3.1 Public Policy and Morality	232
7.3.2 Plants and Animals	240
7.3.3 Methods of Veterinary and Medical Treatment	243

7.4 SUMMARY — 244
7.5 SELF-ASSESSMENT — 244
Activity Discussion — 245
Self-Assessment Answers — 246

8 Patents III: Patentability (Continued) — 248
8.1 NOVELTY — 249
8.1.1 State of the Art	249
8.1.2 PSITA	251
8.1.3 Enabling Disclosure	252
8.1.4 Novelty of Purpose	257

8.2 INVENTIVE STEP — 260
8.2.1 The Inventive Step Standard	261
8.2.2 Secondary Evidence	267

8.3 INDUSTRIAL APPLICATION — 271
8.4 INTERNAL REQUIREMENTS — 274
8.4.1 Sufficiency of Disclosure	275
8.4.2 Claims	280

8.5 SUMMARY — 282
8.6 SELF-ASSESSMENT — 282
Activity Discussion — 283
Self-Assessment Answers — 284

9 Patents IV: Scope — 286
9.1 THE PATENT RIGHT — 286
9.2 CLAIM CONSTRUCTION — 288
9.2.1 Purposive Construction	290
9.2.2 Doctrine of Equivalents	297
9.2.3 The New British Approach: *Actavis*	300

9.3 EXCEPTIONS — 304
9.3.1 Experimental Use	305
9.3.2 Private Use and Prior Use	308

9.4 COMPULSORY LICENSING — 308
9.4.1 International Provision	308
9.4.2 UK Provision	314
9.4.2.1 General	314
9.4.2.2 Crown Use	315

9.5 SUMMARY — 317
9.6 SELF-ASSESSMENT — 318
Activity Discussion — 319
Self-Assessment Answers — 320

PART III DESIGNS — 323

10 Designs I: Foundations of Design Law — 325
10.1 DESIGNING DESIGNS — 327
10.1.1 Inauspicious Beginnings	327
10.1.2 Demarcation	329
10.1.3 Cumulation	332

10.2 ARGUMENTS FOR DESIGN RIGHTS — 335
10.3 SUMMARY — 338
10.4 SELF-ASSESSMENT — 338
Activity Discussion — 339
Self-Assessment Answers — 340

11 Designs II: Contemporary Design Rights 341

11.1 REGISTERED DESIGN RIGHT 342
11.1.1 Registration 342
11.1.2 Subject Matter 342
    11.1.2.1 Appearance 343
    11.1.2.2 Product 345
11.1.3 Excluded Subject Matter 345
11.1.4 Grounds for Invalidity 346
    11.1.4.1 Novelty 347
    11.1.4.2 Individual Character 349
11.1.5 Scope 350

11.2 UNREGISTERED DESIGN RIGHT 353
11.2.1 Subject Matter 354
11.2.2 Excluded Subject Matter 356
    11.2.2.1 Method or Principle of Construction 356
    11.2.2.2 Must Fit and Must Match 357
    11.2.2.3 Surface Decorations 358
11.2.3 Originality 359
11.2.4 Scope 361

11.3 SUPPLEMENTARY UNREGISTERED DESIGN RIGHT 362

11.4 COPYRIGHT FOR DESIGNS 363
11.4.1 Subject Matter 363
    11.4.1.1 Twentieth-Century UK Subject Matter 363
    11.4.1.2 European Influences 367
11.4.2 Scope 368
    11.4.2.1 Section 52 368
    11.4.2.2 Section 51 369

11.5 SUMMARY 371

11.6 SELF-ASSESSMENT 371
Activity Discussion 372
Self-Assessment Answers 372

PART IV TRADE MARKS AND PASSING OFF 375

12 Trade Marks I: Foundations of Trade Marks and Passing Off 377

12.1 SIGN FUNCTIONS 378
12.1.1 Signs as Badges of Origin 379
12.1.2 Signs as Adverts 380
12.1.3 Signs as Quality Indicators 382
12.1.4 Signs as Identity 383

12.2 MANUFACTURING TRADE MARKS 385
12.2.1 The Action of Deceit 385
12.2.2 The Trade Mark as Property 388
12.2.3 Protecting Functions beyond Origin 390
12.2.4 The Functionalist Metaphysics of Trade Marks 396

12.3 ARGUMENTS FOR TRADE MARKS 397
12.3.1 Utilitarian Argument 397
    12.3.1.1 Monopolies and Monopolistic Competition 397
    12.3.1.2 The Pro-Competitive Effects of Trade Marks 399
12.3.2 Free Riding 402

12.4 REGISTRATION 405

12.5 THE INTERNATIONALISATION OF TRADE MARKS 407

12.6 SUMMARY 409

12.7 SELF-ASSESSMENT 409
Activity Discussion 410
Self-Assessment Answers 411

13 Trade Marks II: Absolute Grounds for Refusal 413

13.1 SIGNS 413
13.1.1 Signs 414

13.1.2 Capable of Representation	416	
13.1.3 Capable of Distinguishing	421	

13.2 CONDITIONALLY REGISTRABLE SIGNS — 422

13.2.1 Devoid of a Distinctive Character — 423
13.2.2 Descriptive — 428
13.2.3 Customary — 432
13.2.4 Acquired Distinctiveness — 432

13.3 UNREGISTRABLE SIGNS — 438

13.3.1 Shapes with Excluded Functionality — 439
    13.3.1.1 Nature of the Goods — 439
    13.3.1.2 Technical Result — 441
    13.3.1.3 Substantial Value — 443
13.3.2 Public Policy or Morality — 446
13.3.3 Deceptive Marks — 449
13.3.4 Specially Protected Emblems — 449
13.3.5 Bad Faith — 450

13.4 SUMMARY — 452

13.5 SELF-ASSESSMENT — 452

Activity Discussion — 453
Self-Assessment Answers — 454

14 Trade Marks III: Scope — 456

14.1 RELATIVE GROUNDS FOR REFUSAL — 456

14.1.1 Double Identity — 456
14.1.2 Confusing Similarity — 457
14.1.3 Free Riding or Dilution — 463
    14.1.3.1 Reputation — 465
    14.1.3.2 Similarity — 466
    14.1.3.3 Unfair Advantage, Detrimental to Distinctive Character or Repute — 469
    14.1.3.4 Without Due Cause — 474

14.2 INFRINGEMENT — 477

14.3 DEFENCES — 485

14.3.1 Use of Registered Mark — 485
14.3.2 Uses in Accordance with Honest Practices — 486
    14.3.2.1 Name or Address — 486
    14.3.2.2 Descriptive Use — 486
    14.3.2.3 Nominative or Referential Use — 488
    14.3.2.4 Honest Practices — 490
14.3.3 Exhaustion — 491

14.4 SUMMARY — 494

14.5 SELF-ASSESSMENT — 494

Activity Discussion — 495
Self-Assessment Answers — 495

15 Passing Off — 497

15.1 GOODWILL — 498

15.2 MISREPRESENTATION — 503

15.2.1 Misrepresentation of Origin — 503
15.2.2 Misrepresentation of Quality — 507

15.3 DAMAGE — 512

15.4 SUMMARY — 516

15.5 SELF-ASSESSMENT — 516

Activity Discussion — 516
Self-Assessment Answers — 517

PART V REMEDIES AND LITIGATION — 519

16 Remedies and Litigation — 521

16.1 FINAL INJUNCTIONS — 521

16.2 MONETARY REMEDIES — 528

16.2.1 Monetary Damages — 529
16.2.2 Account of Profits — 540

16.3 ADDITIONAL REMEDIES — 543

16.3.1 Punitive Damages and Criminal Sanctions — 543

16.3.2 Delivery Up	544	**16.7 SELF-ASSESSMENT**	**555**
16.3.3 Stopping Imports	548	Activity Discussion	556
16.4 PRETRIAL RELIEF	**548**	Self-Assessment Answers	556
16.4.1 Interim Injunctions	548		
16.4.2 Evidentiary Orders	551	**17 Epilogue**	**558**
16.5 UNJUSTIFIED THREATS	**554**		
16.6 SUMMARY	**555**	*Glossary*	*561*
		Index	*568*

Figures

1.1	Vincent van Gogh, *Starry Night* (1889)	page 2
1.2	Theory of monopoly	7
2.1	The printing press	18
2.2	Statute of Anne 1710	23
2.3	Sarah Bernhardt as Hamlet	29
2.4	'The Pirate Publisher', *Puck Magazine*	42
3.1	William Hill's betting coupon	56
3.2	An extract from University of London's exam papers	60
3.3	Original de Lalande *Te Deum Laudamus* score (1684)	67
3.4	Oasis's *Be Here Now* cover art	70
3.5	Original stormtrooper helmet	72
4.1	The chorus in 'Oh Why' ((a)); the hook in Shape ((b))	89
4.2	'Ixia' created by Helen Burke ((a)); Marguerite created by Jane Ibbotson ((b))	93
4.3	Protests against the Directive on Copyright in the Digital Single Market (2019) took place in numerous European cities, including Berlin	104
5.1	The Vandersteen comic ((a)); the Deckmyn comic ((b))	138
6.1	Christiansen's Toy Building Brick	170
6.2	Venetian Senate Act 1474	173
6.3	Statute of Monopolies 1624	177
6.4	Patent specification for James Puckle's invention 'the autocannon'	179
6.5	Christiansen minifigures Patent	194
6.6	UK patent registration	200
6.7	The patent bargain	207
7.1	DNA function	218
7.2	*Mus musculus* taxonomy	241
8.1	The evolution of toy bricks	250
8.2	Berumda-rigged sail ((a)); Square-rigged sails ((b))	261
8.3	Wind-propelled vehicle, technical drawing	262
8.4	The Sawyer and Mann incandescent light	276
8.5	Antibody structure displaying variable part	278
9.1	ATC brick	287
9.2	Catnic lintel ((a)); Hill & Smith lintel ((b))	291
9.3	Epilady ((a)); Epilady helical spring ((b)); Lady Remington rubber rod ((c))	295
9.4	The *Improver* questions	296
9.5	*Actavis* standard	302
9.6	Modified *Improver* questions	303

9.7	A sceptical view of the patent bargain	317
10.1	The Trunki. Community design right representation	326
11.1	Two versions of the Kiddee Case	343
11.2	The Rodeo	347
11.3	Trunki Mark I	354
11.4	Trunki Mark II	358
11.5	Interlego design drawing	365
11.6	Stein lamp base	371
12.1	A figurative sign used by the Coca-Cola Company	378
12.2	A 3D sign used by the Coca-Cola Company	396
12.3	UK trade mark registration	406
13.1	London Taxi Corp trade mark registration	426
13.2	Windsurfing Chiemsee trade mark registration	428
13.3	Kit Kat shape	433
13.4	Coca-Cola bottle shape without fluting	435
13.5	Tripp Trapp trade mark registration	440
13.6	Philips trade mark registration	442
13.7	Gömböc	444
13.8	Rock icon	452
14.1	Puma sign ((a)); Sabel sign ((b))	458
14.2	Specsavers sign ((a)); Asda sign ((b))	462
14.3	Lancôme Miracle signs ((a)); Bellure Pink Wonder ((b))	469
15.1	Jiff Lemon ((a)); ReaLemon ((b))	504

Tables

4.1	The CDPA's economic rights	page 87
4.2	The similarities and differences between Ixia and Marguerite	94
4.3	The CDPA's moral rights	114
4.4	Licences	124
5.1	The CDPA's exceptions	132
5.2	Fair dealing statutory purposes	134
5.3	Copyright's associated rights	162
9.1	Patent infringing acts	287

Boxes

1.1	Abraham Drassinower, *What's Wrong with Copying?* (Harvard UP 2015)	page 3
1.2	Thomas C Grey, 'The Disintegration of Property' (1980) Nomos XII: Property	4
1.3	Ruth Towse, *Textbook of Cultural Economics* (2nd edn, CUP 2019)	6
1.4	Peter Smith, *An Introduction to Formal Logic* (CUP 2003)	8
1.5	Peter Smith, *An Introduction to Formal Logic* (CUP 2003)	9
2.1	John Locke's 'Memorandum on the Licensing Act 1662'	19
2.2	Daniel Defoe, *An Essay on the Regulation of the Press* (1704)	21
2.3	Daniel Defoe, *An Essay on the Regulation of the Press* (1704)	21
2.4	Statute of Anne 1710	23
2.5	John Locke, *Two Treatises of Government* (1690)	26
2.6	Robert Merges, *Justifying Intellectual Property* (Harvard UP 2011)	28
2.7	Robert Nozick, *Anarchy, State, and Utopia* (Basic Books 1974)	30
2.8	Seana Valentine Shiffrin, 'Lockean Arguments for Private Intellectual Property' in Stephen R Munzer (ed), *New Essays in the Legal and Political Theory of Property* (CUP 2001)	31
2.9	Oren Bracha and Talha Syed, 'Beyond Efficiency: Consequences Sensitive Theories of Copyright' (2014) 29 Berkeley Tech LJ	33
2.10	Robert Merges, *Justifying Intellectual Property* (Harvard UP 2011)	36
2.11	Stephen Breyer, 'The Uneasy Case for Copyright: A Study of Copyright in Books, Photocopies, and Computer Programs' (1970) 84 Harv L Rev	37
2.12	Georg Wilhelm Friedrich Hegel, *Elements of Philosophy of Right* (1821)	39
3.1	Cheng Lim Saw, 'Protecting the Sound of Silence in 4'33: A Timely Revisit of Basic Principles in Copyright Law' (2005) 27 EIPR	65
Case 3.1	*Donoghue v Allied Newspapers Limited* [1938] 1 Ch 106	51
Case 3.2	*Walter v Lane* [1900] AC 539	54
Case 3.3	*Ladbroke (Football) Ltd v William Hill (Football) Ltd* [1964] 1 WLR 273	56
Case 3.4	*University of London Press, Limited v University Tutorial Press, Limited* [1916] 2 Ch 601	60
Case 3.5	*Exxon Corporation and Others v Exxon Insurance Consultants International Ltd* [1982] Ch 119	61
Case 3.6	*Green v Broadcasting Corp of New Zealand* [1989] RPC 700	64
Case 3.7	*Sawkins v Hyperion Records Ltd* [2005] EWCA Civ 565	66
Case 3.8	*Creation Records Limited and Others v News Group Newspapers Ltd* [1997] EMLR 444	69
Case 3.9	*Lucasfilm Ltd and others v Ainsworth and another* [2011] UKSC 39	72
Case 3.10	*Levola Hengelo BV v Smilde Foods BV*, Case C-310/17, EU:C:2018:899	76
Case 3.11	*Eva-Maria Painer v Standard Verlags GmbH*, Case C-145/10 [2012] ECDR (6) 89 (ECJ)	78
4.1	Peter Baldwin, *The Copyright Wars: Three Centuries of Trans-Atlantic Battle* (Princeton UP 2014)	115

Case 4.1	*Sheeran v Chokri* [2022] EWHC 827 (Ch)	89
Case 4.2	*Designers Guild Ltd v Russell Williams (Textiles) Ltd* [2001] 1 WLR 2416	93
Case 4.3	*Nederlands Uitgeversverbnd, Groep Algemene Uitgevers v Tom Kabinet Internet BV*, C-263/18 (2019) (CJEU)	100
Case 4.4	*TuneIn Inc v Warner Music UK Ltd* [2021] EWCA Civ 441	105
Case 4.5	*GS Media BV v Sanoma Media Netherlands BV and others*, C-160/15 (2016) (CJEU)	112
Case 4.6	*Confetti Records v Warner Music UK Ltd* [2003] EMLR 35	116
Case 4.7	*Sawkins v Hyperion Records Ltd* [2005] EWCA Civ 565	119
Case 4.8	*Eldred v Ashcroft* 537 US 186 (2003), Brief of 17 Economists	121
5.1	*Digital Opportunity: A Review of Intellectual Property and Growth* (Dept for Business, Innovation & Skills 2011)	134
5.2	Artificial Intelligence and Intellectual Property: Copyright and Patents: Government Response to Consultation (28 June 2022)	160
Case 5.1	*Shazam v Only Fools the Dining Experience* [2022] EWHC 1379 (IPEC)	137
Case 5.2	*Pelham GmbH v Ralf Hütter and Florian Schneider-Esleben*, Case C-476/17, EU:C:2019:624	144
Case 5.3	*England & Wales Cricket Board v Tixdaq & Fanatix* [2016] EWHC 575 (Ch)	146
Case 5.4	*Public Relations Consultants Association Limited v The Newspaper Licensing Agency Limited and others* [2013] UKSC 18.	152
Case 5.5	*Stichting Brein v Jack Frederik Wullems (Filmspeler)*, Case C-527/15 (ECJ)	153
Case 5.6	*R (on the application of British Academy of Songwriters, Composers and Authors) v Secretary of State for Business, Innovation & Skills* [2015] EWHC 1723 (Admin)	155
Case 5.7	*Ashdown v Telegraph Group* [2002] Ch 149	157
6.1	Christine MacLeod, *Inventing the Industrial Revolution: The English Patent System, 1660–1800* (CUP 1988)	171
6.2	Venetian Senate Act 1474	172
6.3	Christine MacLeod, *Inventing the Industrial Revolution: The English Patent System, 1660–1800* (CUP 1988)	173
6.4	Christine MacLeod, *Inventing the Industrial Revolution: The English Patent System, 1660–1800* (CUP 1988)	176
6.5	Statute of Monopolies 1624, s 6	177
6.6	Fritz Machlup and Edith Penrose, 'The Patent Controversy in the Nineteenth Century' (1950) 10 Journal of Economic History	179
6.7	Thomas Jefferson, Letter to Isaac McPherson (13 August 1813) in Andrew A Lipscomb and Albert Ellery Bergh (eds), *The Writings of Thomas Jefferson*, vol 13 (Thomas Jefferson Memorial Association 1904)	182
6.8	Jeremy Bentham, 'A Manual of Political Economy' in John Bowring (ed), *The Works of Jeremy Bentham*, vol 3 (1843)	184
6.9	Michele Boldrin and David K Levine, 'The Case against Patents' (2013) 27(1) Journal of Economic Perspectives	186
6.10	Petra Moser, 'Patents and Innovation: Evidence from Economic History' (2013) 27 Journal of Economic Perspectives	187
6.11	Frtiz Machlup and Edith Penrose, 'The Patent Controversy in the Nineteenth Century' (1950) 10 Journal of Economic History	188

6.12	Robert P Merges and Richard R Nelson, 'On the Complex Economics of Patent Scope' (1990) 90 Colum L Rev	190
6.13	*Thaler v Comptroller-General of Patents, Designs and Trademarks* [2021] EWCA Civ 1374	201
Case 6.1	*Darcy v Allein* (1601) 77 ER 1260	174
7.1	Talha Syed, 'Reconstructing Patent Eligibility' (2021) 70 Am U L Rev	213
7.2	Justine Pila, *The Subject Matter of Intellectual Property* (OUP 2017)	214
7.3	EPO Opposition Division	219
Case 7.1	*Howard Florey/Relaxin* [1995] EPOR 541	218
Case 7.2	*Association for Molecular Pathology et al v Myriad Genetics Inc et al* 596 US 576 (2013) (US)	220
Case 7.3	*Pension Benefits Systems Partnership/Controlling Pension Benefits Systems*, T931/95 [2002] EPOR	223
Case 7.4	*Symbian Limited v Comptroller General of Patents* [2008] EWCA Civ 1066	224
Case 7.5	*Hitachi/Auction method* (T258/03) [2004] EPOR 55	226
Case 7.6	*Gemstar-TV Guide International Inc v Virgin Media Ltd* [2009] EWHC 3068 (Ch)	228
Case 7.7	*Halliburton Energy Service's Patent Application* [2011] EWCH 2508 (Pat)	230
Case 7.8	*Harvard/Transgenic Animals*, T315/03 (2006) OJ EPO 15	234
Case 7.9	*Plant Genetic Systems* [1995] OJ EPO 545	237
Case 8.1	*Synthon BV v SmithKline Beecham plc* [2005] UKHL 59	252
Case 8.2	*Merrell Dow v Norton* [1996] RPC 76 (HL)	254
Case 8.3	*Mobil/Friction Reducing Additive*, G2/88 [1990] OJ EPO 114	258
Case 8.4	*Windsurfing International v Tabor Marine* [1985] RPC 59 (CA)	261
Case 8.5	*Hospira v Genentech* [2016] EWCA Civ 780	265
Case 8.6	*Haberman v Jackel International* [1999] FSR 683	267
Case 8.7	*Human Genome Sciences v Eli Lilly* [2011] USKC 51	271
Case 8.8	*Regeneron Pharmaceuticals Inc v Kymab Ltd* [2020] UKSC 27	277
Case 9.1	*Catnic Components Ltd v Hill & Smith Ltd* [1982] RPC 183 (HL)	291
Case 9.2	*Graver Tank & MFG Co, Inc v Linde Air Products Co*, 339 US 605 (1950) (USA)	298
Case 9.3	*Actavis v Eli Lilly* [2017] UKSC 48	300
Case 9.4	*CoreValve Inc v Edwards Lifesciences* [2009] EWHC 6 (Pat)	305
Case 9.5	*Bayer v Natco*, Indian Intellectual Property Appellate Board OA/35/2012/PT/MUM (4 March 2013) (India)	310
10.1	Lionel Bently, 'The Design/Copyright Conflict in the United Kingdom: A History' in Estelle Derclaye, *The Copyright/Design Interface* (CUP 2018)	327
10.2	Lionel Bently, 'The Design/Copyright Conflict in the United Kingdom: A History' in Estelle Derclaye, *The Copyright/Design Interface* (CUP 2018)	329
10.3	Lionel Bently, 'The Design/Copyright Conflict in the United Kingdom: A History' in Estelle Derclaye, *The Copyright/Design Interface* (CUP 2018)	329
10.4	Lionel Bently, 'The Design/Copyright Conflict in the United Kingdom: A History' in Estelle Derclaye, *The Copyright/Design Interface* (CUP 2018)	330
10.5	Lionel Bently, 'The Design/Copyright Conflict in the United Kingdom: A History' in Estelle Derclaye, *The Copyright/Design Interface* (CUP 2018)	332

10.6	Kal Raustiala and Christopher Sprigman, 'The Piracy Paradox: Innovation and Intellectual Property in Fashion Design' (2006) 92 Virginia L Rev	336
Case 10.1	*Gorham Mfg Co v White* 81 US 511 (1872) (US)	336
11.1	Trunki clasp design	357
11.2	Inside of the Trunki	360
11.3	Lionel Bently, 'The Design/Copyright Conflict in the United Kingdom: A History' in Estelle Derclaye (ed), *The Copyright/Design Interface* (CUP 2018)	369
Case 11.1	*Magmatic ('Trunki') v PMS International Group* [2013] EWHC 1925 (Pat) revd in *PMS International Group v Magmatic ('Trunki')* [2014] EWCA Civ 181, affd in [2016] UKSC 12	343
Case 11.2	*Interlego AG v Tyco Industries* [1989] AC 217	365
12.1	Thomas Drescher, 'The Transformation and Evolution of Trademarks: From Signals to Symbols to Myth' (1992) 82 TM Rep	379
12.2	Thomas Drescher, 'The Transformation and Evolution of Trademarks: From Signals to Symbols to Myth' (1992) 82 TM Rep	380
12.3	Thomas Drescher, 'The Transformation and Evolution of Trademarks: From Signals to Symbols to Myth' (1992) 82 TM Rep	381
12.4	Thomas Drescher, 'The Transformation and Evolution of Trademarks: From Signals to Symbols to Myth' (1992) 82 TM Rep	382
12.5	Thomas Drescher, 'The Transformation and Evolution of Trademarks: From Signals to Symbols to Myth' (1992) 82 TM Rep	383
12.6	Lionel Bently, 'From Communication to Thing: Historical Aspects of the Conceptualisation of Trade Marks as Property' in Graeme Dinwoodie and Mark Janis (eds), *Trademark Law and Theory: A Handbook of Contemporary Research* (Edward Elgar 2008)	388
12.7	Frank Schechter, 'The Rational Basis of Trade Mark Protection' (1927) 40 Harv L Rev	391
12.8	Frank Schechter, 'The Rational Basis of Trade Mark Protection' (1927) 40 Harv L Rev	392
12.9	Frank Schechter, 'The Rational Basis of Trade Mark Protection' (1927) 40 Harv L Rev	393
12.10	Rebecca Tushnet, 'Gone in 60 Milliseconds: Trademark Law and Cognitive Science' (2008) 86 Tex L Rev	395
12.11	Nicholas Economides, 'The Economics of Trademarks' (1988) 78 TM Rep	397
12.12	William M Landes and Richard A Posner, 'Trade Mark Law: An Economic Perspective' (1987) Journal of Law and Economics	400
12.13	Robert Nozick, *Anarchy, State and Utopia* (Basic Books [1974] 2013)	403
Case 12.1	*Croft v Day* (1843) 7 Beavan 84	386
Case 13.1	*Dyson Ltd v Registrar of Trade Marks*, Case C-321/03 [2007] ECR I–687	414
Case 13.2	*Ralf Sieckmann v Deutsches Patent-und Markenamt*, Case C-273/00 [2002] ECR I–11737	417
Case 13.3	*Libertel Groep BV v Benelux-Merkenbureau*, Case C-104/01 [2003] ECR I–3793	418
Case 13.4	*Société des Produits Nestlé SA v Cadbury UK Ltd* [2013] EWCA Civ 1174	420
Case 13.5	*London Taxi Corp v Frazer-Nash Research Ltd* [2017] EWCA Civ 1729	425
Case 13.6	*Windsurfing Chiemsee Produktions und Vertriebs GmbH v Boots und Segelzubehör Walter Huber*, Joined Cases C-108/97 and C-109/97, EU:C:1999:230, [1999] ECR I-2779	428
Case 13.7	*Proctor & Gamble Co v Office for Harmonization in the Internal Market (Trade Marks and Designs) (OHIM)*, Case C-383/99 P	430

Case 13.8	*Société des Produits Nestlé SA v Cadbury UK Ltd* [2017] EWCA Civ 358	433
Case 13.9	*The Coca-Cola Corporation v Office for Harmonization in the Internal Market (Trade Marks and Designs) (OHIM)*, Case T-411/14, EU:T:2016:94	435
Case 13.10	*Hauck GmbH & Co KG v Stokke A/S*, Case C-205/13, EU:C:2014:322	439
Case 13.11	*Koninklijke Philips v Remington*, Case 299/99 [2002] ECR I–5475	442
Case 13.12	*Gömböc Kutató, Szolgáltató és Kereskedelmi Kft. v Szellemi Tulajdon Nemzeti Hivatala*, Case C-237/19, EU:C:2020:296	444
Case 13.13	*Constantin Film Produktion v EUIPO*, Case C-240/18, EU:C:2020:118	446
Case 13.14	*Sky v SkyKick*, Case C-371/18, EU:C:2020:45	450
Case 14.1	*Sabel BV v Puma, Rudolf Dassler Sport*, Case C-251/95 [1997] ECR I–6191	457
Case 14.2	*Canon Kabushiki Kaisha v Metro-Goldwyn-Mayer Inc* [1999] 1 CMLR 77	459
Case 14.3	*Specsavers Intl Healthcare v Asda Stores* [2010] EWHC 2035 (Ch), affirmed in part in [2012] EWCA Civ 24	461
Case 14.4	*General Motors Corporation v Yplon*, Case C-375/97 [1999] ECR I–5421	465
Case 14.5	*Intel Corp v CPM UK*, Case C-252/07 [2008] ECR I–8823	467
Case 14.6	*L'Oréal v Bellure*, Case C-487/07 [2009] ECR I–5185, [2010] EWCA Civ 535	469
Case 14.7	*Interflora v Marks & Spencer*, Case C-323/09 [2011] ECR I–8625	474
Case 14.8	*Arsenal v Reed*, Case C-206/01 [2002] ECR I–10273	477
Case 14.9	*Google France v Louis Vuitton*, Cases C-236/08–238/08 [2010] ECR I–2417	482
Case 14.10	*Mitsubishi v Duma Forklifts*, Case C-129/17, EU:C:2018:594	484
Case 14.11	*Hölterhoff v Freiesleben*, Case C-2/00 [2002] ECR I–4187	487
Case 14.12	*New Kids on the Block v News America Publishing, Inc* 971 F.2d 302 (1992) (US)	489
Case 14.13	*L'Oréal v eBay International*, Case C-324/09 [2011] ECR I–6011	491
Case 15.1	*Starbucks (HK) Limited and another (Appellants) v British Sky Broadcasting Group plc and others (Respondents)* [2015] UKSC 31	498
Case 15.2	*Reckitt & Colman Products Ltd v Borden Inc (No 3)* [1990] 1 WLR 491 (1990)	503
Case 15.3	*AG Spalding Brothers v AW Gamage, Ltd* [1915] All ER Rep 147	507
Case 15.4	*Erven Warnink BV v J Townend & Sons (Hull) Ltd* [1979] AC 731 (1979)	509
Case 15.5	*Lego v Lemelstrich* [1983] FSR 155	513
Case 16.1	*eBay v MercExchange LLC*, 547 US 388 (2006) (US)	522
Case 16.2	*Evalve Inc v Edwards Lifescience* [2020] EWHC 513 (Pat)	525
Case 16.3	*General Tire v Firestone* [1975] 1 WLR 819	529
Case 16.4	*Fabio v LPC Group* [2012] EWHC 911 (Ch)	534
Case 16.5	*Henderson v All Around the World* [2014] EWHC 3087 (IPEC)	539
Case 16.6	*Potton v Yorkclose* [1990] FSR 11	541
Case 16.7	*Merck Canada v Sigma (No 2)* [2013] EWCA Civ 326	544
Case 16.8	*American Cyanamid Co (No 1) v Ethicon Ltd* [1975] AC 396	548
Case 16.9	*Anton Piller KG v Manufacturing Processes Ltd* [1976] Ch 55	552
17.1	Mark A Lemley, 'Faith-Based Intellectual Property' (2015) 62 UCLA L Rev	559

Acknowledgements

Writing this book was quite the journey. I would like to thank everyone at Cambridge University Press for making the journey possible. I am particularly grateful to Helen Shannon for keeping me on track and guiding the book's development. Along the way, a fleet of colleagues in the IP community provided assistance, sometimes without even realising it. The list includes Graeme Dinwoodie, Shubha Ghosh, Oren Bracha, Talha Syed, David Simon, Marc Mimler, Enrico Bonadio, Luke McDonagh, Estelle Derclaye and a team of anonymous reviewers. I also thank Kyla Allyna Donnelly for her research assistance, and my colleagues at City for their support.

But the greatest appreciation is reserved for my family and my partner, Lisa Dresser. Thank you for putting up with all the missed evenings, weekends and holidays while I worked on this project. A special acknowledgement goes to my little dog Archibald who demanded to sit on my lap and 'help' me write.

Table of Cases

A Fulton v Totes Isotoner (UK) [2003] EWCA Civ 1514, [2004] RPC (16) 301 373

Actavis v Eli Lilly [2017] UKSC 48 .... 294, 296, 300–4, 321, 563

Adam Opel v Autec, Case C-48/05 [2007] ECR I–1017 .... 488, 496

Adidas-Salomon AG and Adidas Benelux BV v Fitnessworld, Case C-408/01 [2003] ECR I–12537, [2004] 1 CMLR (4) 448 .... 467, 468, 496

Aerotel Ltd (A Company Incorporated Under the Laws of Israel) v Telco Holdings Ltd, Telco Global Distribution Ltd, Telco Global Ltd [2006] EWCA Civ 1371 .... 216, 217, 225, 231, 247

AG Spalding Brothers v AW Gamage, Ltd [1915[ALL ER Rep 147 .... 412, 499 507, 518

American Cyanamid Co (No 1) v Ethicon Ltd [1975] AC 396 548–49

AMP Inc v Utilux Pty Ltd [1971] FSR 572 .... 333, 364

Anton Piller KG v Manufacturing Processes Ltd [1976] Ch 55 .... 552–53 556, 566

Arsenal v Reed, Case C-206/01 [2002] ECR I–10273 .... 477–78, 481, 496

Arsenal Football Club Plc v Matthew Reed [2002] EWHC 2695 (Ch) 493

Artistic Upholstery v Art Forma (Furniture) [1999] 4 All ER 277 518

Ashdown v Telegraph Group [2002] Ch 149 .... 157–58, 165

AssiDoman Multipack (formerly Multipack Wraparound Systems) v Mead Corp [1995] FSR 225 321

Association for Molecular Pathology et al v Myriad Genetics Inc et al 596 US 576 (2013) (US) 220–21

Azumi Ltd v Zuma's Choice Pet Products Ltd [2017] EWHC 609 (IPEC) 474, 496

Bach v Longman (1777) 2 Cowp 623 85

Baigent v Random House [2007] EWCA Civ 247 52

Balmoral [1999] RPC 297 496

Barnsley Brewery Co v RBNB [1997] FSR 462 518

BASF/Metal Refining, Case T-24/81 [1979–85] B EPOR 354 285

Basic Trademark [2005] RPC 611 455

Bayer Co v United Drug Co 272 F 505 (SDNY 1921) (US) 454

Bayer v Natco, Indian Intellectual Property Appellate Board OA/35/2012/PT/MUM (4 March 2013) (India) 310–14

Bayerische Motorenwerke v Ronald Karel Deenik, Case C-63/97 [1999]
ECR I–905 496
Best-Lock (Europe) Ltd v OHIM, Lego Juris A/S, Case T-395/14,
EU:T:2015:380, affd Case C-451/15P, EU:C:2016:269 455
Biogen v Medeva [1997] RPC 1 .... 253, 266, 277, 285
Blue IP v KCS Herr-Voss [2004] EWHC 97 (Ch) 496
Bobbs-Merrill Co v Straus 210 U.S. 339 (1908) (US) 129
Boulton and Watt v Bull (1795) 126 ER 651 .... 210, 285
Bridgeport Music v Dimension Films 410 F3d 792 (US) 97
Britain and Others v Hank Brothers (1902) 86 LT 765 330
British Leyland v Armstrong [1986] AC 577 334
British Sugar v Robertson [1996] RPC 281 496

Caffé Nero, Case T-29/16, EU:T:2016:635 .... 449, 455
Cain Cellars v OHIM, Case T-304/05 [2007] ECR II–113 454
Campina Melkunie v Benelux-Merkenbureau, Case C-265/00 [2004] ECR
I–1699 454
Canon Kabushiki Kaisha v Metro-Goldwyn-Mayer Inc, Case C-39/97 [1998]
ECR I–5507 .... 463, 496
Canon Kabushiki Kaisha v Metro-Goldwyn-Mayer Inc [1999]
1 CMLR 77 459–60
Cass Ire civ, 5 December 2006: RIDA 1/2007, 359 129
Catnic Components Ltd v Hill & Smith Ltd [1982] RPC 183 (HL) 291–95
299, 301, 303, 318, 321
Chiron v Murex (No 12) [1996] RPC 535 285
Clark v Associated Newspapers (1998) 1 WLR 1558 120
Claudia Oberhauser v OHIM, Case T-6/01 [2002] ECR II–4335 496
Coca-Cola Corporation v Office for Harmonization in the Internal Market
(Trade Marks and Designs) (OHIM), Case T-411/14, EU:T:2016:94 ... 435–36
Cofemel – Sociedade de Vestuário SA v G-Star Raw CV, Case C-683/17,
EU:C:2019:721 .... 80, 137, 367–68
Confetti Records v Warner Music UK Ltd [2003] EMLR 35 116–18
Constantin Film Produktion v EUIPO, Case C-240/18, EU:C:2020:118 ... 446–49
CoreValve Inc v Edwards Lifesciences [2009] EWHC 6 (Pat) 305–7
Coventry v Lawrence [2014] UKSC 13 .... 525, 526
Creation Records Limited and others v News Group Newspapers Ltd [1997]
EMLR 444 .... 69–70, 74
Croft v Day (1843) 7 Beavan 84 .... 386–88, 456

Darcy v Allein (1601) 77 ER 1260 ('The Case of Monopolies') 174, 176, 254
Deckman v Vandersteen, Case C-201/13, EU:C:2014:2132 138
Designers Guild Ltd v Russell Williams (Textiles) Ltd [2001]
1 WLR 2416 93–95

Deutsche Grammophon GmbH v Metro GmbH, Case C-78/70 [1971]
ECR 487 129
Doceram v CeramTec, Case C-395/16, EU:C:2018:172 373
Donaldson v Becket (1774) 2 Brown's Parl Cases (2d ed) 129, 1 Eng Rep
837; 4 Burr 2408, 98 Eng Rep 257; 17 Cobbett's Parl Hist 953 24
Donoghue v Allied Newspapers Limited [1938] 1 Ch 106 .... 51–52, 53
Dyson Ltd v Registrar of Trade Marks, Case C-321/03 [2007]
ECR I–687 414–16
Dyson v Registrar of Trade Marks [2003] EWHC 1062 (Ch) 454

eBay v MercExchange LLC 547 US 388 (2006) (US) 519, 522–24
Edelsten v Edelsten (1863) 1 De G & Sm 18, 46 ER 72 389
Eldred v Ashcroft 537 US 186 (2003) 121–22
Electric and Musical Industries Ltd v Lissen Ltd (1938) 56 RPC 23 321
Elizabeth Florence Emanuel v Continental Shelf 138, Case C-259/04 [2006]
ECR I–3089 455
Elvis Presley Trade Marks [1997] RPC 543 454
England & Wales Cricket Board v Tixdaq & Fanatix [2016] EWHC
575 (Ch) 146–47, 151
Entick v Carrington (1765) 2 Wils KB 275 553
Erven Warnink BV v J Townend & Sons (Hull) Ltd [1979]
AC 731 (1979) 500, 509–10
Evalve Inc v Edwards Lifescience [2020] EWHC 513 (Pat) 525–26, 528
Eva-Maria Painer v Standard Verlags GmbH, Case C-145/10 [2012]
ECDR (6) 89 (ECJ) 78–79
Exxon Corporation and Others v Exxon Insurance Consultants International
Ltd [1982] Ch 119 61–62

Fabio v LPC Group [2012] EWHC 911 (Ch) 534–35
Farmers Build v Carier Bulk Materials Handling [1999] RPC 461 373
FCUK [2007] RPC 1 455
Feist Publications, Inc v Rural Telephone Service Co, Inc, 499 US 340
(1991) (US) 129
Flos SpA v Semararo Case e Famiglia SpA, Case C-168/09, [2011]
ECR I–181 .... 368, 370, 373
Folsom v Marsh (CCD Mass 1841) 9 F Cas 342 12
Fraud Music Company v Ford Motor Company, BL O/504/13 496
Fromageries Bel SA v J Sainsbury plc [2019] EWHC 3454 (Ch) 454
Funke Medien v Bundesrepublik Deutschland, Case C-469/17,
EU:C:2019:623 165

Gemstar v Virgin [2011] EWCA Civ 302 226
Gemstar-TV Guide International Inc v Virgin Media Ltd [2009] EWHC
3068 (Ch) 228–29

Genentech/t-PA, Case T-923/92 [1996] EPOR 275 285

General Motors Corporation v Yplon, Case C-375/97 [1999] ECR
I–5421 .... 465–66, 468

General Tire v Firestone [1975] 1 WLR 819 .... 529–30, 532, 534, 543

George Hensher Ltd v Restawile Upholstery (Lancs) Ltd [1976] AC 64 71

Ghazilian's Application [2002] RPC 628 455

Gillette v LA-Laboratories, Case C-228/03 [2005] ECR I–2337 .... 489, 490

Gömböc Kutató, Szolgáltató és Kereskedelmi Kft. v Szellemi Tulajdon Nemzeti
Hivatala, Case C-237/19, EU:C:2020:296 .... 444–45, 453

Google France v Louis Vuitton, Cases C-236/08–238/08 [2010] ECR
I–2417 .... 476, 482–83

Gorham Mfg Co v White 81 US 511 (1872) (US) 336

Graver Tank & MFG Co, Inc v Linde Air Products Co, 339 US 605
(1950) (USA) 298–99

Green v Broadcasting Corp of New Zealand [1989] RPC 700 .... 64–65, 74

Groente en fruit, R 595/2012–3 (18 February 2013) 373

GS Media BV v Sanoma Media Netherlands BV and others, Case C-160/15
(2016) (CJEU) 108, 109, 112–13, 128

Gyles v Wilcox (1740) 26 ER 489 .... 88, 133

Haberman v Jackel International [1999] FSR 683 267–69

Halliburton Energy Service's Patent Application [2011] EWCH
2508 (Pat) 230–31

Harries v Air King Prod. Co, 183 F.2d 158, 162 (2d Cir. 1950) (US) 285

Harms v Martans [1927] 1 Ch 526 129

Harvard/Transgenic Animals, Case T-315/03 (2006) OJ EPO 15 234–37
240, 242

Hauck GmbH & Co KG v Stokke A/S, Case C-205/13,
EU:C:2014:322 .... 439–40, 444, 445

Hearst Holdings v AVELA [2014] EWHC 439 (Ch) 496

Henderson v All Around the World [2014] EWHC 3087 (IPEC) 539–40

Heptulla v Orient Longman [1989] 1 FSR 598 High Court (India) 84

Hitachi/Auction method, Case T-258/03 [2004] EPOR 55 226–27

Hölterhoff v Freiesleben, Case C-2/00 [2002] ECR I–4187 487–88

Hornblower & Maberly v Boulton, 101 Eng Rep 1285 (KB 1799) 210

Hospira v Genentech [2016] EWCA Civ 780 265–67

Hotel Cipriani v Cipriani (Grosvenor Street) [2010] ECWA Civ 110 486

Howard Florey/Relaxin [1995] EPOR 541 .... 218–20, 238, 245, 246

HTC Europe v Apple [2012] EWHC 1789 (Pat) 229

Human Genome Sciences v Eli Lilly [2011] USKC 51 .... 271–74, 283, 284

ICI/Containers, Case T-26/81 [1982] OJ EPO 211 285

Improver Corp v Remington Consumer Products [1990] FSR 181 .... 295, 296
297, 301, 304

Incandescent Lamp Patent, 159 US 465 (1895) 285
Infopaq International v Danske Dagblades Forening, Case C-5/08 [2009]
    ECR I–6569 (ECJ) 77, 78, 79, 85, 368, 373
Intel Corp v CPM UK, Case C-252/07 [2008] ECR I–8823 .... 467–68, 470
Interflora v Marks & Spencer, Case C-323/09 [2011] ECR I–8625
    (AG Jääskinen) 496
Interflora v Marks & Spencer, Case C-323/09 [2011] ECR I–8625 474–76
                                                                         482
Interlego AG v Tyco Industries [1989] AC 217 .... 365–66, 368
IRC v Muller and Co's Margarine Ltd [1901] AC 217 410

Jennings v Stephens (1936) Ch 469 104
JG v Samford (1584) (unreported) 412

Kirin-Amgen v Hoechst [2004] UKHL 46 296
Kirin-Amgen v Transkaryotic Therapies [2002] EWCA Civ 1096 285
Koninklijke Philips v Remington, Case C-299/99 [2002] ECR I–5475 442–43

La Chemise Lacoste v Baker Street Clothing [2011] RPC (5) 165(AP) 496
Ladbroke (Football) Ltd v William Hill (Football) Ltd [1964]
    1 WLR 273 .... 56–58, 80, 84, 95
La Mafia Franchises v EUIPO, Case T-1/17, EU:T:2018:146 455
Land Nordrhein-Westfalen v Dirk Renckhoff, Case C-161/17,
    EU:C:2018:634 129
Lego v Lemelstrich [1983] FSR 155 513–15
Lego Juris A/S v OHIM, Case C-48/09P [2010] ECR I–8403
    (Grand Chamber) 440–41
Leidseplein Beheer v Red Bull, Case C-65/12, EU:C:2014:49 476
Levola Hengelo BV v Smilde Foods BV, Case C-310/17,
    EU:C:2018:899 .... 76–77, 80, 137, 367
Liardet v Johnson (1780) 5 July 210
Libertel Groep BV v Benelux-Merkenbureau, Case C-104/01 [2003] ECR
    I–3793 .... 416, 418–19, 424
Linde A, Winward Industries, Rado Watch, Cases C-53/01, C-54/01,
    and C-55/01 [2003] ECR I–3161 454
Lindt, Case C-529/07 [2009] ECR I–4893 .... 451, 455
London Taxi Corp v Frazer-Nash Research Ltd [2017] EWCA
    Civ 1729 425–27
L'Oréal v Bellure, Case C-487/07 [2009] ECR I–5185 .... 469–71, 475
L'Oréal SA v Bellure NV [2010] EWCA Civ 535 496
L'Oréal v eBay International, Case C-324/09 [2011] ECR I–6011 491–93
Lucasfilm Ltd and others v Ainsworth and another [2011] UKSC 39 72–74
                                                                   364, 367, 370

Magmatic ('Trunki') v PMS International Group [2013] EWHC 1925 (Pat) 343–45, 354
Martin v Kogan [2019] EWCA Civ 1645 129
Masterman's Design Application [1991] RPC 89 373
Matratzen Concord GmbH v OHIM, Case T-6/01 [2002] ECR II–4335 496
Merchandising Corporation v Harpbond [1971] 2 All E.R. 657 71
Merck Canada v Sigma (No. 2) [2013] EWCA Civ 326 544–45
Merrell Dow v Norton [1996] RPC 76 (HL) 254–57
Merrill Lynch's Application [1989] 4 WLUK 219 .... 225, 228
Millar v Taylor (1769) 4 Burr 2303, 98 ER 201 24
Millington v Fox (1838) 3 My & Cr 338, 40 ER 956 389
Mitsubishi v Duma Forklifts, Case C-129/17, EU:C:2018:594 484–85
Mobil/Friction reducing additive, G2/88 [1990] OJ EPO 114 258–59

Nederlands Uitgeversverbnd, Groep Algemene Uitgevers v Tom Kabinet Internet BV, Case C-263/18 (2019) (CJEU) 100–1
Nestlé v Mars [2003] EWCA Civ 1072, [2003] ETMR (101) 1335 454
New Kids on the Block v News America Publishing, Inc 971 F 2d 302 (1992) (US) 489–90
Newspaper Licensing Agency v Marks & Spencer [2000] 4 All ER 239 165
Nichols v Universal Pictures Corporation, 45 F2d 119 at 122 (2d Cir 1930) (US) 84
Noah v Shubha (1991) FSR 14 123
Norowzian v Arks (No 2) [2000] EMLR 67, 73 85
NTP v Research in Motion 261 F Supp 2d 423 (ED Va 2002) (US) 521–22

PAKI Logistics v OHIM, Case C-526/09 455
Pelham GmbH v Ralf Hütter and Florian Schneider-Esleben, Case C-476/17, EU:C:2019:624 .... 97, 140, 141, 144–45
Pension Benefits Systems Partnership/Controlling pension benefits systems, Case T-931/95 [2002] EPOR 52 .... 215, 223
Pfizer v Ministry of Health [1964] Ch 614 316
Philips/Public availability of documents on the World Wide Web, Case T-1553/06 [2012] EPOR 383 285
Plant Genetic Systems [1995] OJ EPO 545 .... 236–40, 242
PLG Research Limited Another v Ardon International Limited [1995] FSR 116 321
PMS International Group v Magmatic ('Trunki') [2014] EWCA Civ 181 343–45
PMS International Group v Magmatic ('Trunki') [2016] UKSC 12 373
Pope v Curll (1741) 2 Atk 342 129
Portakabin v Primakabin, Case C-558/08 [2010] ECR I–6963 496
Portakabin, R 789/2001-3 455

Positec Power Tools v Husqvarna [2016] EWHC 1061 (Pat), [2016]
FSR (29) 798 285

Potton v Yorkclose [1990] FSR 11 541–42

Pozzoli SpA v BDMO SA [2007] EWCA Civ 588 285

Proctor & Gamble Co v Office for Harmonization in the Internal Market
(Trade Marks and Designs) (OHIM), Case C-383/99 P 430–31

Public Relations Consultants Association Limited v The Newspaper
Licensing Agency Limited and others [2013] UKSC 18 152–53

R (on the application of British Academy of Songwriters, Composers and
Authors) v Secretary of State for Business, Innovation & Skills [2015]
EWHC 1723 (Admin) 155–57

R v Carter [1983] FSR 303 (CA) 544

Ralf Sieckmann v Deutsches Patent-und Markenamt, Case C-273/00 [2002]
ECR I–11737 417–18

Reckitt & Colman Products Ltd v Borden Inc (No 3) [1990] 1 WLR
491 (1990) 497, 500, 503–7

Regeneron Pharmaceuticals Inc v Kymab Ltd [2020] UKSC 27 277–80

Robin v Classic FM (1998) ECC 488 124

Sabel BV v Puma, Rudolf Dassler Sport, Case C-251/95 [1997] ECR
I–6191 .... 457–60, 463, 495

Sawkins v Hyperion Records Ltd [2005] EWCA Civ 565 ...... 66–68, 119–20

Schneidmesser, I BGH, (2002) 33 IIC 873 321

Schütz v Werit [2013] UKSC 16 320

Shazam v Only Fools The Dining Experience [2022] EWHC
1379 (IPEC) 137–41, 149–50, 164

Sheeran v Chokri [2022] EWHC 827 (Ch) 89–92

Shelfer v City of London Electric Lighting Co [1895] 1 Ch 287 525

Sky v SkyKick, Case C-371/18, EU:C:2020:45 450–51

Sky Ltd (formerly Sky plc) v Skykick UK Ltd [2021] EWCA Civ 1131 455

Société des Produits Nestlé SA Appellant v Cadbury UK Ltd [2017]
EWCA Civ 358 433–35

Société des Produits Nestlé SA v Cadbury UK Ltd [2013] EWCA
Civ 1174 420–21

Société des Produits Nestlé v Mars ('Have a Break') [2004] FSR (2) 16 454

Specsavers Int'l Healthcare v Asda Stores [2012] EWCA Civ 24 461–63
468

Starbucks (HK) Limited and another (Appellants) v British Sky Broadcasting
Group PLC and others (Respondents) [2015] UKSC 31 498–99

Stichting Brein v Jack Frederik Wullems (Filmspeler), Case C-527/15
(ECJ) 153–54

Storck v OHIM, Case C-25/05 P [2006] ECR I-5719 454

Svensson v Retriever Sverige AB, Case C-466/12, EU:C:2014:76 ... 109, 110, 111

Symbian Limited v Comptroller General of Patents [2008] EWCA
    Civ 1066 .... 217, 224–25
Synthon BV v SmithKline Beecham plc [2005] UKHL 59 .... 252–53, 275

Temple Island Collections Ltd v New English Teas [2012] EWPCC 1 80
Thaler v Commissioner of Patents [2021] FCA 879 210
Thaler v Commissioner of Patents [2022] HCA Trans 199 210
Thaler v Comptroller General of Patents Trade Marks and Designs [2021]
    EWCA Civ 1374 201–3
TuneIn Inc v Warner Music UK Ltd [2021] EWCA Civ 441 105
Two identities/COMVIK, Case T-0641/00 285

University of London Press, Limited v University Tutorial Press, Limited
    [1916] 2 Ch 601 .... 58, 60–62
UsedSoft, Case C-128/11, EU:C:2012:407 .... 101–2, 128

Vereniging Openbare Bibliotheken (VOB) v Sichting Leenrecht,
    Case C-174/15 .... 103, 129

Walter v Lane [1900] AC 539 .... 53, 54–55, 57, 58, 80, 83
Websphere Trade Mark [2004] EWHC 529 (Ch), [2004] FSR (39) 796 457
Windsurfing Chiemsee Produktions und Vertriebs GmbH v Boots und
    Segelzubehör Walter Huber, Joined Cases C-108/97 and C-109/97,
    EU:C:1999:230, [1999] ECR I-2779 .... 428–30, 443
Windsurfing International v Tabor Marine [1985] RPC 59 (CA) 261–64, 267
Wine Oh!'s Application, R 1074/2005–4 [2006] ETMR (95) 1319 455
Wood v Capita Insurance Services Ltd [2017] 2 WLR 1095 321
Wrigley (Doublemint), Case C-191/01P [2003] ECR I–13447 454

Table of Legislation

Agreement on Trade Related Aspects of IP Rights (1994) (TRIPS Agreement)

Berne Convention for the Protection of Literary and Artistic Works, 1886

Copyright Act (1976) 17 USC, s 101 (US)

Copyright Act 1911

Copyright Act 1956

Copyright Act 2007, s 19 (Israel)

Copyright of Designs Act 1839, 2 Vict, c 17

Copyright, Designs and Patents Act 1988

Council Regulation of 12 December 2001 on Community designs (Community Design Regulation (CDR)) 6/2002/EC

Customs (Enforcement of Intellectual Property Rights) (Amendment) (EU Exit) Regulations 2019 (SI 2019/514)

Design Copyright Act 1968

Designs Act 1842, 5 & 6 Vict, c 100

Directive (EU) 2015/2436 of the European Parliament and of the Council of 16 December 2015 to approximate the laws of the Member States relating to trade marks. Regulation (EU) 2017/1001 of the European Parliament and of the Council of 14 June 2017 on the European Union trade mark

Directive 2001/29/EC of the European Parliament and of the Council of 22 May 2001 on the harmonisation of certain aspects of copyright and related rights in the information society ('Information Society Directive')

Directive 92/100/EEC Council of 27 November 1992 on rental right and lending right and on certain rights related to copyright in the field of intellectual property No L 346/62

Directive 98/44/EC of the European Parliament and of the Council of 6 July 1998 on the legal protection of biotechnological inventions.

Directive of 13 October 1998 on the legal protection of designs 98/71/EC

Dramatic Literary Property Act 1833

European Patent Convention (1973) (as updated 2000)

First Council Directive 89/104/EEC of 21 December 1988 to approximate the laws of the Member States relating to trade marks. Council Regulation (EC) No 40/94 of 20 December 1993 on the Community trade mark

Hague Agreement concerning International Registration of Industrial Designs (1925)

International Convention for the Protection of New Varieties of Plants (UPOV) 1961 (as amended 1991)

Madrid Agreement on the International Registration of Marks (1891)

Ordinance for the Regulating of Printing 1643 (renewed in 1662)

Paris Convention for the Protection of Industrial Property (1883)

Paris Convention for the Protection of Industrial Property (as amended 28 September 1979)

Patent Act 1790 (US)

Patent Law Amendment Act 1852

Patents Act 1949

Patents Act 1977

Patents (Amendment) (EU Exit) Regulations 2019

Plant Varieties Act 1997

Protocol Relating to the Madrid Agreement Concerning the International Registration of Marks 1989

Registered Designs Act 1949

Regulation No 608/2013/EU concerning customs enforcement of intellectual property rights and repealing Council Regulation 1383/2003/EC (Border Measures Regulation (BMR))

Sonny Bono Copyright Term Extension Act (1998) 17 USC

Statute of Anne 1710 (An Act for the Encouragement of Learning, by Vesting the Copies of Printed Books in the Authors or Purchasers of such Copies, during the Times therein mention)

Statute of Monopolies 1624

Supplementary Protection Certificates (Amendment) (EU Exit) Regulations 2020)

Town and Country Planning Act 1947 (as amended by Planning and Compulsory Purchase Act 2004)

Trade Mark Act 1994

Trade Mark Registration Act 1875

Transfer of Property Act (1882)

Venetian Senate Act 1474

World Intellectual Property Organization Copyright Treaty (1996)

Abbreviations

AC	Appeal Cases
All ER	All England Reports
CDPA	Copyright, Designs and Patents Act 1988
CJEU	Court of Justice of the European Union
EBA	Enlarged Board of Appeals [EPO]
EPO	European Patent Office
EUTM	European Union Trade Mark
EWHC	High Court of Justice of England and Wales
IPEC	Intellectual Property Enterprise Court
IPQ	Intellectual Property Quarterly
LJ	law journal
L Rev	law review
PA	Patents Act 1977
RDA	Registered Designs Act 1949
TBA	Technical Board of Appeals [EPO]
TMA	Trade Mark Act 1994
TMD 2015	Directive (EU) 2015/2436 of the European Parliament and of the Council of 16 December 2015 to approximate the laws of the Member States relating to trade marks [2015] OJ L 336/1
TM Rep	*Trademark Reporter*
TRIPS	Agreement on Trade-Related Aspects of Intellectual Property Rights 1994
UKSC	UK Supreme Court Decisions
WIPO	World Intellectual Property Organization
WTO	World Trade Organization

1

Introduction to Intellectual Property

Students are typically introduced to intellectual property (IP) law as an elective module within the second or third year of an LLB degree. All LLB degrees are regulated by the UK Quality Assurance Agency (QAA) Framework for Higher Education.[1] The QAA Framework requires students to develop a systematic understanding of, and an ability to analyse and evaluate arguments within, their field. This book helps students achieve the QAA outcomes by developing an independent critical understanding of IP law.

1.1 THREE QUESTIONS

What is IP? A simple definition is that IP is property in things that are intellectual. But this simple definition raises three questions: the metaphysical, conceptual and normative questions. Understanding these questions is foundational. To study IP law without appreciating these three questions is to be like 'an assembly of blind men disputing about colours', as philosopher Jeremy Bentham once said of IP lawyers.[2]

1.1.1 The Metaphysical Question

If IP is property in intellectual things, then what are 'intellectual things'? To illustrate the problem, consider Vincent van Gogh's the *Starry Night* (Figure 1.1). The Dutch painter, Vincent van Gogh, led an unhappy life.[3] He sold only one painting during his lifetime and suffered from severe mental illness including hallucinations. Van Gogh created the *Starry Night* in 1889 in Saint-Remy-de-Provence in France. In that year, van Gogh suffered a mental breakdown, cut off one of his ears and was committed to an asylum. From the

> Metaphysics is the study of the fundamental nature of reality.

Figure 1.1. Vincent van Gogh, *Starry Night* (1889). Museum of Modern Art, New York, USA. (Photo by Art Images via Getty Images)

barred windows of his cell, he could see the night sky and was moved to paint what he saw. The result is one of the world's most beloved artworks.

Is the *Starry Night* a thing? Of course, the canvas on which it is painted is a thing. And the paint van Gogh applied to the canvas is also a thing. But IP lawyers are not concerned with those **tangible** things that can be touched and felt. Instead, IP law is about something far more intriguing: the image of the *Starry Night* itself. We are interested in the curious notion that there is some **intangible** phenomenon called the *Starry Night*; something that cannot be touched, and that exists independently of the canvas and paint. The question is whether this intangible phenomenon is a thing?

A phenomenon is an event or thing in the world that can be observed through human senses.

What might seem like an abstract philosophical question has real-world importance. For hundreds of years, lawyers have disagreed about whether intangible phenomena like the *Starry Night* are things. The prevailing modern view is that such phenomena are things. As such, there is nothing particularly different between the *Starry Night* and other things – like a house, a car or a mobile phone. Furthermore, just like a house, a car or a mobile phone, the *Starry Night* is a thing that can be owned. The *Starry Night* can be someone's property.

But not all lawyers agree. As the scholar Abraham Drassinower argues, not all intangible phenomena are things (Box 1.1). Imagine, for example, that you and a friend have a nice long conversation over coffee. Is your conversation a thing? Can your conversation be owned? Drassinower argues that the *Starry Night*, like a conversation, is not a thing at all, but an act.

> ## BOX 1.1 ABRAHAM DRASSINOWER, *WHAT'S WRONG WITH COPYING?* (HARVARD UP 2015)
>
> While it is true that copyright protects the form of expression, it is important to observe that this does not mean that copyright protects expression as some kind of proprietary object – whether intangible or otherwise – exclusively held by its author... A work is not a thing but an act: at issue is the work not as a noun but as a verb. An author does not hold her expression as an object of ownership to the disposition of which she has exclusive rights. Copyright infringement is neither conversion nor theft. It is less a matter of disposing of an object than of repeating or reproducing an act of authorship without authorization. This is why to infringe the right attendant on the work is to repeat it or to reproduce it – i.e., to copy it – but not to create it independently. Either we insist on grasping the work as a communicative act, or we jettison the defense of independent creation from copyright doctrine.
>
> (pp. 61–62)

Professor Drassinower is the Chair in Legal, Ethical, and Cultural Implications of Technological Innovation at the University of Toronto.

Drassinower uses a range of terms – 'copyright', 'independent creation', 'expression', etc. – which are explained later in the book. For now, it is enough to reflect on his central argument: that the *Starry Night* is not a thing at all, but something entirely different.

The reason why the *Starry Night* feels different is because it is a **public good**. A **good** is a phenomenon which is valuable in some way.[4] **Private goods** are goods that are '**excludable**' and '**rivalrous**'.[5] Your mobile phone is a private good. It is excludable because you can easily stop other people from using it: you can lock your phone in a desk drawer or protect it with a password so that only you can use it. Your phone is also rivalrous because if you are using it, no one else can use it at the same time. But the *Starry Night* is not at all like that. The *Starry Night* is non-excludable and non-rivalrous. People use the image all the time in films, on TV shows, on coffee mugs, posters, and more. It is not only very hard to stop this use, but all this use can happen at the same time. Therefore, if the *Starry Night* is a thing, it must be a very different type of thing from houses, cars or mobile phones.

Other public goods include clean air, the rule of law and national defence; none of which are things naturally susceptible to ownership.

Nevertheless, if you are amenable to the idea that the *Starry Night* is a thing, the next question is: what makes it an 'intellectual' thing? There are many intangible phenomena in this world – stocks and shares, gravity, love – and not all are 'IP'. What is the characteristic of the *Starry Night* that makes it IP, that is lacking from other intangibles, like debt or one's reputation? And on what side of the line do phenomena like the words 'Coca-Cola' or the text and images generated by artificial intelligence fall?

Because of these deep philosophical questions, IP law was once called the 'metaphysics of law' by one influential American judge.[6] Together, this book refers to these related issues about the nature of intellectual things as the metaphysical question. The metaphysical question features prominently in Chapters 3, 7, 8 and 13.

1.1.2 The Conceptual Question

A concept is an abstract idea. Concepts are the fundamental building blocks of thought. Property is one example of a concept.

Is IP really property? Of course, some like to think it is. European Union (EU) law calls IP an 'integral part of property'.[7] UK statutes refer to IP rights as 'property rights'.[8] Judges call piracy 'theft' and 'stealing'.[9] But are they right? These legal labels are not determinative. I can call my dog a cat; it does not make him so. Instead, answering this question requires some deeper conceptual thinking. We need to know: (1) what is 'property' and (2) what is 'IP'.

What, then, is property? In Box 1.2, Thomas Grey introduces two possible answers to that question: property as **exclusive control** over a thing, and property as a **bundle of rights**.

BOX 1.2 THOMAS C GREY, 'THE DISINTEGRATION OF PROPERTY' (1980) NOMOS XII: PROPERTY 69

In the English-speaking countries today, the conception of property held by the specialist (the lawyer or economist) is quite different from that held by the ordinary person.[10] Most people, including most specialists in their unprofessional moments, conceive of property as things that are owned by persons. To own property is to have exclusive control of something – to be able to use it as one wishes, to sell it, give it away, leave it idle, or destroy it. Legal restraints on the free use of one's property are conceived as departures from an ideal conception of full ownership.

Professor Grey is the Nelson Bowman Sweitzer and Marie B Sweitzer Professor of Law, Emiratus, at Stanford Law School.

By contrast, the theory of property rights held by the modern specialist tends both to dissolve the notion of ownership and to eliminate any necessary connection between property rights and things. Consider ownership first. The specialist fragments the robust unitary conception of ownership into a more shadowy 'bundle of rights'. Thus, a thing can be owned by more than one person, in which case it becomes necessary to focus on the particular limited rights each of the co-owners has with respect to the thing. Further, the notion that full ownership includes rights to do as you wish with what you own suggests that you might sell off particular aspects of your control – rights to certain uses, to profits from the thing, and so on. Finally, rights of use, profit, and the like can be parceled out along a temporal dimension as well – you might sell your control over your property for tomorrow to one person, for the next day to another, and so on.

(p. 69)

It was not always so. At the high point of classical liberal thought, around the end of the eighteenth century, the idea of private property stood at the center of the conceptual scheme of lawyers and political theorists. Thus, Blackstone wrote: 'There is nothing which so generally strikes the imagination, and engages the affections of mankind, as the right of property'... Thus, Blackstone described property as 'that sole and despotic dominion which one man claims and exercises over the external things of the world, in total exclusion of the right of any other individual in the universe'. And, in perfect concord, the French Civil Code defined property as 'the right of enjoying and disposing of things in the most absolute manner'.

(p. 73)

Sir William Blackstone (1723–80) was one of England's most significant lawyers. The definition of property given here is today sometimes known as **'Blackstonian property'**. The definition appears in his famous treatise, *Commentaries on the Laws of England* (1765).

The idea of property as exclusive control of a thing is intuitively familiar to many. According to that idea, if X owns a plot of land called Blackacre, then X alone can decide what happens to that estate. If Y tries to enter Blackacre without X's permission, then X can tell Y to 'get out'. If Z wants to buy the estate, and X does not want to sell, then X can simply say 'sorry, no deal'. Indeed, without these powers, we might question whether X really owns Blackacre at all. Exclusive control is, perhaps, essential to what property is.

However, not all agree that property is exclusive control of a thing. In reality, X does not have exclusive control over Blackacre. X cannot tell Y to 'get out' if Y has an easement permitting them to walk across the estate.[11] X cannot say 'sorry, no deal' to Z, if Z is a member of the government with a valid compulsory purchase order.[12] To those who view property as exclusive control, such limits to X's control might be deviations from the ideal of property.[13] But, to others, they show that exclusive control is not essential to property. Even though X does not have exclusive control over Blackacre, X does have property because he has a certain relationship to Blackacre. What property is, therefore, is the bundle of rights that together X, Y and Z hold in respect to Blackacre.

The 'what is property?' question is slightly beyond the scope of this book. Students will need to consider this question in tandem with their study of other property subjects like land law and trusts law. Instead, the book focuses primarily on the second question: what is IP? Is IP the exclusive control over intellectual things? Or is IP a 'bundle of rights'? Does the law give anyone exclusive control over how the *Starry Night* is used? Or does the law merely give van Gogh certain limited rights therein, while also giving rights to the wider public – such as the right to be inspired by, or to poke fun at, van Gogh's masterpiece?

As discussed in Chapters 4, 5, 9, 14 and 16, what IP truly is remains debatable. To some, IP law is simply an assortment of various legal rights; rights that can be granted, shaped and revoked by Parliament and the courts, as necessary. But, to others, IP is something more powerful, immutable and absolute: the exclusive control over an intellectual thing. Whether IP is really property, then, depends not only on what property is, but also on how one understands the contemporary IP system.

1.1.3   The Normative Question

A question is 'normative' when it is about how the world ought *to be, as opposed to how the world currently is.*

Finally, and most importantly of all, is the normative question. Why should intellectual things be property? After all, granting property rights over intellectual things has some bad consequences.

A market is a system through which goods are transferred between people.

Economists distinguish between two types of markets: **perfect competition** and **monopoly**.[14] A perfectly competitive market is, among other things, one where there are multiple sellers of a good. By contrast, a monopolistic market is one in which there exists only one seller of a good.

Normally, monopolies are viewed as bad things to be avoided. In a perfectly competitive market, if a seller tries to increase the price of their goods, their customers will simply switch to someone else selling the good at a cheaper price. But this does not happen in a monopolistic market. Free from competition, a monopolist can raise prices, knowing that their customers cannot simply switch to a cheaper seller. This ability to keep prices high – known as **market power** – means that some consumers can no longer afford the good and must go without. Monopolies therefore harm consumers.

Granting property rights over intellectual things creates monopolies. Consider, for example, a market for flowerpots. Imagine that one pot maker designs an attractive new shape for their pots. That shape is an intangible phenomenon, much like the *Starry Night*: we can touch and feel the clay from which the pot is made, but we cannot touch and feel a mere *shape*. But what happens to the price of pots when someone owns the shape and can stop others from copying it? In Box 1.3, economist Ruth Towse explains.

BOX 1.3 RUTH TOWSE, *TEXTBOOK OF CULTURAL ECONOMICS* (2ND EDN, CUP 2019)

Professor Ruth Towse is Professor of Economics of Creative Industries at Bournemouth University.

Neoclassical theory of monopoly and competition can be summed up in a well-known diagram.[15] As the sole supplier to the market for this particular good, say of a brand name designer pottery, the market demand and the firm's demand schedule are the same thing – D in [Figure 1.2].

Related to demand is marginal revenue (MR), the increase in total revenue as one more unit of output is sold. The firm has the objective of maximizing profit, where profit is the excess of revenue over costs, and it therefore chooses the output at which the difference between total revenue and total cost is greatest, which is where marginal cost (MC) is equal to marginal revenue (MR). In [Figure 1.2], that corresponds to output Q_B and Price P_B.

> The firm's 'demand schedule' is the quantity of goods (i.e. pots) consumers will buy from the firm at a given price. If the price is high, consumers will buy fewer pots. If the price is low, they will buy more. Accordingly, the demand schedule slopes down.

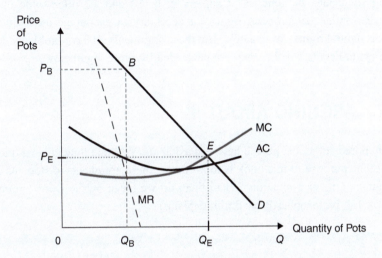

Figure 1.2. Theory of monopoly.
Source: Ruth Towse, *Textbook of Cultural Economics* (2nd edn, CUP 2019) 130, with minor amendments by Patrick Goold.

If the market consisted of competing firms, say ones producing identical pots, instead of by a monopoly supplier... Point E would be the result, with a market price P_E and market supply of Q_E. At point E, the MC = MR rule also applies two competitive firms but now marginal revenue is the price per item because each pot sells at the same price. Comparison of the two position shows that the price P_E would be lower and the output Q_E greater in a competitive market than in a monopoly and it demonstrates the 'social cost' or **deadweight loss** of monopoly; in this case, the monopoly is due to brand names of designer pots but it could be due to a copyright or trademark or other 'barrier to entry'. The demonstration that consumers are worse off with monopoly is the basis for the promotion of competition by economists and that is achieved by the regulation of monopoly (antitrust) by competition law.

(p. 130)

> 'Revenue' is the money earned by the firm. 'Cost' is the money required to produce the good.

The more powerful IP rights are, the worse the problem is. If someone has 'exclusive control' over how the *Starry Night* is used, then anyone who wants to use the image – to put it in a new film or documentary for example – will need to pay the owner a high price to do so. Some people will not be able to afford the price and must go without. This problem can be called the **problem of monopoly**, i.e., the fact that monopolies result in higher prices, and therefore less use and enjoyment of, the intellectual things.

Why, therefore, should society recognise property in intellectual things when doing so creates monopolies? Chapters 2, 6, 10 and 12 offer some answers. Lawyers argue that property rights are necessary to encourage creativity, or to protect natural rights, for example. But these arguments all have problems. It is for students to decide whether they are persuaded by those arguments.

1.2   ARGUING ABOUT IP

For hundreds of years, people have argued about the three fundamental questions of IP. The purpose of this book is to introduce these arguments to students and to encourage critical evaluation. What, then, do we mean by the word 'argument'? In Box 1.4, philosopher Peter Smith explains.

Peter Smith was a lecturer in logic at the University of Cambridge.

> ### BOX 1.4 PETER SMITH, *AN INTRODUCTION TO FORMAL LOGIC* (CUP 2003)
>
> By 'argument' we mean a chain of reasoning, short or long, in support of some conclusion.[16] So we must distinguish arguments from mere disagreements and disputes. The children who shout at each other 'You did', 'I didn't', 'Oh yes, you did', 'Oh no, I didn't' are certainly disagreeing: but they are not *arguing* in our sense – they are not yet giving any reasons in support of one claim or the other.
>
> Reason-giving arguments are the very stuff of all serious inquiry, whether it is philosophy or physics, economics or experimental psychology. Of course, we also deploy recent arguments in the course of everyday, street-level inquiry into the likely winner of next month's election, the best place to train as a lawyer or what explains our team's losing streak. We want our opinions to be true; that means that we should aim to have good reasons backing up our opinions, so raising the chances of getting things right. This in turn means that we have an interest in being skillful reasoners, using arguments which really do support their conclusions.
>
> (p. 1)

This chapter has already considered one argument: we have briefly considered Drassinower's argument that creative works are not things that can be owned. But most of the arguments in this book do not come from professional academics;

instead, most are written by judges and are found in case law. Judges are called upon every year to decide what kind of intangible phenomena should be owned, how much control to give IP owners, and why such control is necessary. The written decisions issued by judges are arguments in the sense described by Smith: they are a set of reasons that seek to support a conclusion. The rules and principles of IP law – or what we call the 'doctrine' – are the conclusions that judges seek to support through reason. In a legal system based on parliamentary supremacy and *stare decisis*, the conclusions reached by Parliament and courts become binding law.

Understanding these arguments is necessary but not sufficient. Independent critical thinkers also need the ability to analyse and evaluate those arguments. Great IP lawyers need an ability to deconstruct the arguments into their component parts, and to evaluate their soundness. How then does one analyse or evaluate an argument? In Box 1.5, Peter Smith explains.

BOX 1.5 PETER SMITH, *AN INTRODUCTION TO FORMAL LOGIC* (CUP 2003)

Logic, then, is concerned with evaluating stretches of reasoning. Take this really simple example, and call it argument A. Suppose you hold

(1) All philosophers are eccentric.

I then introduce you to Jack, telling you that he's a philosopher. So you come to believe

(2) Jack is a philosopher.

Putting these two thoughts together, you can obviously draw the conclusion

(3) Jack is eccentric.

This little bit of reasoning can now be evaluated along two quite independent dimensions.

First, we can ask whether the *premises* (1) and (2) are true: are the 'inputs' to your reasoning correct? (1) in fact looks very disputable. And maybe Jack's reflective skills are so limited that we'd want to dispute the truth of (2) as well.

Second, we can ask about the quality of the *inference* from the premises (1) and (2) to the conclusion (3). In this case, the movement of thought from premises (1) and (2) to conclusion (3) is surely absolutely compelling. We have agreed that it may be open to question whether one and two are both true. However, if (1) and (2) are granted to be true... then (3) has got to be true too.

In brief, it is one thing to consider whether an argument starts from true premises; it is another thing entirely to consider whether it moves on by reliable inferential steps. To be sure, we normally want our arguments to pass muster on both counts. We want to start from true

> premises and to move by steps which give us good reasons to accept the target conclusion. But the crucial point to emphasise is that these are distinguishable aims.
>
> (pp. 1–2)

The book's purpose is not to teach formal logical analysis and evaluation of the sort described by Smith. Nevertheless, some understanding of argument is essential. If we wish to become independent critical thinkers about IP law, it is not enough to understand the conclusions that judges reach; we also need the ability to identify premises and test inferences.

Finally, some of the arguments presented in the book do not come from legal academics, or judges, but instead come from me, Patrick Goold. In a book that encourages critical thinking about IP law, it would be disingenuous to not occasionally introduce and defend my own conclusions. These arguments are not held out, however, as indisputable truth. Any arguments that I offer must be evaluated with the same rigour that is employed when evaluating the arguments presented by judges.

1.3 JURISDICTION

This book focuses primarily on how UK lawyers have answered the three fundamental questions. Over time, UK lawyers have created a unique body of IP doctrine that understands intangible phenomena as things that can be owned, grants powerful property rights in relation to those things, and claims that such property is normatively justified. The resulting law is philosophically and politically contentious.

There are two situations where the book looks to arguments developed outside of the UK. The first situation concerns the EU. As part of the EU from 1973 to 2020, the UK accepted the principle of EU supremacy. Accepting the EU supremacy principle meant that EU regulations, directives and case law became binding UK law. Accordingly, much modern UK IP doctrine is EU made. The regulations, directives and case law made prior to the legally effective Brexit date (30 December 2020) is 'retained law' and remains binding UK law unless the UK chooses to depart therefrom.[17] There are important questions about how UK law should interpret retained law post-Brexit; this question is the focus of EU law modules and books.

Second, arguments developed outside of the UK are introduced occasionally to provide points of comparison. In the UK legal system, foreign law is a type of 'persuasive precedent'.[18] Our system actively encourages lawyers to understand how other countries have answered the fundamental questions of IP, and to consider whether those arguments are persuasive. This book accordingly introduces foreign law when such law has developed interesting arguments in relation to the fundamental questions.

1.4 SCOPE

This book has been designed with a target audience in mind: students studying IP law for the first time with approximately 150–300 hours to spend reading. This is commonly the amount of time dedicated to independent study in an undergraduate IP module. As many will appreciate already, 150–300 hours is not a lot of time. A commonly held piece of wisdom is that 10,000 hours of practice is required to become an expert in a field.[19] With limited time for study, one must adopt clear objectives and a strategy that best facilitates the achievement of those objectives.

The purpose of this book is to provide students with a critical introduction to IP law. To that end, the book does not introduce students to every IP case. Instead, it delivers a systematic overview of the subject, highlighting key cases and materials to illustrate the arguments. Some of the materials are short, others are long, depending on the nature of the arguments. Some areas of law are summarised to leave more space for the foundational questions. And some cases are omitted altogether to provide room for critical thinking exercises. For, as the old proverb goes, 'if you give a man a fish, you feed him for a day. If you teach a man to fish, you feed him for a lifetime'. And, when the full philosophical depth of IP law is appreciated, it becomes a subject that can sustain one intellectually for a lifetime.

1.5 BOOK FEATURES

It is always preferable to read an argument directly, rather than rely solely on third-party accounts. Accordingly, this book is composed of primary sources, such as extracts from judicial decisions, academic monographs and journal articles. These sources are accompanied by activities and self-assessment questions. These features are designed to help students grasp the intricacies of the arguments and to encourage critical evaluation. Along the way, the sidebar provides important contextual information. Words in bold appear in a glossary at the end. Students who want further readings will find a list of resources in the online companion.

1.6 SELF-ASSESSMENT

Before moving on, try to answer the following questions to consolidate your learning.

1. Which of the following is the best definition of a 'public good'?
   a. A good that is excludable and non-rivalrous.
   b. A good that is non-excludable and non-rivalrous.
   c. A good that is non-excludable and rivalrous.
   d. A good that is excludable and rivalrous.
2. When the seller of a good has market power, which of the following consequences is likely to occur? Select one or more.
   a. The seller will sell the good at a price higher than would be set in a perfectly competitive market.
   b. The seller will sell the good at a price that is lower than would be set in a perfectly competitive market.
   c. Consumers will consume a smaller quantity of the good than they would in a perfectly competitive market.
   d. Consumers will consume a higher quantity of the good than they would in a perfectly competitive market.

SELF-ASSESSMENT ANSWERS

1. **Correct answer: b.** Answer **d.** describes the characteristics of a 'private good'. Answers **a.** and **c.** relate to types of goods not directly relevant to IP law; these are sometimes known as club goods, toll goods and common pool goods.
2. **Correct answer: a.** and **c.** Insulation from competition creates market power (i.e. the ability to increase prices and restrict output). It is likely that the seller will use this ability because, as explained by Ruth Towse, monopoly pricing maximises the profits the seller earns (even though they sell a lower quantity!).

Notes

1 QAA, 'UK Quality Code for Higher Education, Part A: Setting and Maintaining Academic Standards' (October 2014) <https://www.qaa.ac.uk/docs/qaa/quality-code/qualifications-frameworks.pdf> (accessed 8 December 2023).

2 *Manual of Political Economy* (first published in 1800, W Stark ed, 1952) 265.

3 Steven Naifeh and Gregory White Smith, *Van Gogh: The Life* (Random House Group 2012) 744–72.

4 Alfred Marshall, *Principles of Economics* (Macmillan 1890) ch 2, §1.

5 Paul A Samuelson, 'The Pure Theory of Public Expenditure' (1954) 36(4) Review of Economics and Statistics, 387–89.

6 *Folsom v Marsh* (CCD Mass 1841) 9 FCas 342, 344–45 (per Story J).

7 Directive 2001/29/EC of the European Parliament and of the Council of 22 May 2001 on the harmonisation of certain aspects of copyright and related rights in the information society ('Information Society Directive') Recital 9.

8 Copyright, Designs and Patents Act 1988, s 1(1); Patents Act 1977, s 30(1). Registered Designs Act 1949, s 15(A); Trade Mark Act 1994, s 2(1).

9 See eg *R v Carter* [1993] FSR 303, 304 (per Jowitt J).

10 Thomas C Grey, 'The Disintegration of Property' (1980) Nomos XII: Property 69, reproduced with permission from New York UP.

11 *Re Ellenborough Park* [1956] Ch 131.

12 Town and Country Planning Act 1947, Pt 4 (as amended by Planning and Compulsory Purchase Act 2004, Pt 8).

13 Richard A Epstein, 'The Disintegration of Intellectual Property? A Classical Liberal Response to a Premature Obituary' (2010) 62 Stan L Rev 455.

14 Léon Walras, *Elements of Pure Economics* (first published in French in 1874, William Jaffé tr, 1954).

15 Ruth Towse, *Textbook of Cultural Economics* (2nd edn, CUP 2019) reproduced with permission of the Licensor through PLSclear.

16 Peter Smith, *An Introduction to Formal Logic* (CUP 2003) reproduced with permission of the Licensor through PLSclear.

17 Agreement on the Withdrawal of the United Kingdom of Great Britain and Northern Ireland from the European Union and the European Atomic Energy Community (2020) CP 219.

18 See Thomas H Bingham, *Widening Horizons: The Influence of Comparative Law and International Law on Domestic Law* (CUP 2010).

19 Malcolm Gladwell, *Outliers: The Story of Success* (Little, Brown & Co 2008).

FIGURE ACKNOWLEDGEMENTS

1.1 Museum of Modern Art, New York, USA. (Photo by Art Images via Getty Images)

1.2 Ruth Towse, *Textbook of Cultural Economics* (2nd edn, CUP 2019) 130, with minor amendments by Patrick Goold

Part I

Copyright

The principle of copyright is this. It is a tax on readers for the purpose of giving a bounty to writers. The tax is an exceedingly bad one...
I admit, however, the necessity of giving a bounty to genius and learning. In order to give such a bounty, I willingly submit even to this severe and burdensome tax.

—Thomas Babington Macaulay MP, First Speech to the House of Commons on Copyright
5 February 1841

2

Copyright I: Foundations of Copyright Law

Copyright is a property right in original work. Through copyright, works like van Gogh's *Starry Night* (Figure 1.1) become privately owned. Yet, the idea of owning works is a curious one. The notion raises the three questions introduced in Chapter 1: are works things that can be owned? Does anyone really own those things? And why should they be owned at all? After all, it was not always the case that works were property. The history of copyright is a story about how society gradually accepted the idea of property in works.

Chapter 3 discusses the metaphysical question of how copyright lawyers came to understand 'works' as things that can be owned. Chapters 4 and 5 discuss whether copyright really is a property right. But we start in this chapter with the normative question: why should works be property? To use the language of Thomas Macaulay in the opening quote, why should the law tax readers in this way? As we will see, this question has attracted considerable attention from lawyers, authors and philosophers for over three hundred years.

2.1   CREATING COPYRIGHT

The story of copyright begins with the story of books. During the early medieval period, copying books was a highly laborious task. Once an author wrote a manuscript, subsequent copies of the manuscript could only be reproduced through the very time-consuming process of copying by hand. Scribes would painstakingly copy manuscripts by hand and either keep those copies in libraries or sell them to wealthy individuals. As the process was laborious, only a limited number of copied manuscripts could feasibly be produced.

This chapter contains public sector information licensed under the Open Government Licence v3.0.

Figure 2.1 The printing press. Gutenberg printing the first page of the Bible, 1439. After a nineteenth-century print.
(Photo by Universal History Archive/Universal Images Group via Getty Images)

Johannes Gutenberg (*c*.1400–68) was a goldsmith, inventor, printer and publisher. Despite devising one of the world's most influential inventions, much of his life remains a mystery.

Around 1440 in Germany, Johannes Gutenberg invented the printing press. The printing press made the copying process easier and quicker. Figure 2.1 displays a version of the Gutenberg printing press. The wooden block in the centre (point A) is called the 'press', and functions much like a big stamp. To use the machine, the printer would arrange stencil letters on the underside of the press and dip them in ink. Underneath the press, the printer would place a blank sheet of paper. Finally, the printer would turn the handle (point B), pushing the press down onto the paper. The lettering would be imprinted upon the paper. If the stencils used mimicked the words from a manuscript (for example a page from a book), then the printer could use the machine to duplicate hundreds of manuscripts in reasonably rapid succession.

Gutenberg's printing press ushered in the '**printing revolution**'. The revolution made it easier for knowledge and information to spread between people, and enabled European society to move out of the Middle Ages and into the Enlightenment. But, at the same time, the printing revolution created a series of challenges for governments. Responding to these challenges put society on a path towards the creation of modern copyright law.

2.1.1 Precursors to Copyright

The most immediate challenge the printing press presented to governments was the threat of sedition. The printing press enabled individuals to print and distribute pamphlets and books that were critical of the state. In turn, governments sought to regulate the use of the printing press.

Parliament passed An Ordinance for the Regulating of Printing – also known as the Licensing Order – in 1643; later renewed in 1662. Under the terms of the order, control of printing was granted to a guild called the Stationers' Company (first established in the 15th century). The Stationers were a collective of printers and booksellers. To print material, members of the guild had first to obtain permission (also known as a 'licence') from the Company. The Stationers' acted as a censor and refused to permit material that would offend the government.

In return for acting as censors, the Stationers enjoyed a monopoly over the book trade. After a bookseller obtained permission, the Stationers would not permit anyone else in the realm to print the same book, or import copies of the book from another country. As discussed in Section 1.1.3, exercising this control reduced the level of competition the bookseller faced: no other bookseller could sell the same material at a cheaper price. Insulated from competition, the authorised bookseller enjoyed market power and could keep the price of the material high. Thus, while the Licensing Order was a form of censorship for the British state, it was primarily a financial tool for the Stationers.

The Licensing Order was highly contentious because it restricted freedom of expression. In a famous memorandum, the British philosopher John Locke wrote: 'I know not why a man should not have liberty to print whatever he would speak.'[1] But Locke's trouble with the Licensing Order was not purely related to its potential to censor speech. Locke was also troubled by the monopoly that the law gave to the Stationers. As Box 2.1 demonstrates, Locke particularly disliked the fact that members of the Stationers could obtain a monopoly over the printing of old books (or 'classical' books) such as those written by the ancient Roman or Greek authors.

The Stationers' Company still exists today and is located near St Paul's Cathedral in London. The nature of their work is quite different in the modern era. (Image reproduced with permission of the Stationers' Company)

BOX 2.1 JOHN LOCKE'S 'MEMORANDUM ON THE LICENSING ACT 1662' (REPRINTED IN LORD KING, *THE LIFE OF JOHN LOCKE, WITH EXTRACTS FROM HIS CORRESPONDENCE, JOURNALS AND COMMON PLACE BOOKS*, VOL 1 (HENRY COLDUM & RICHARD BENTLY 1830) 373–87)

By this clause, the Company of Stationers have a monopoly of all the classical authors; and scholars cannot, but at excessive rates, have the fair and correct edition of those books printed beyond seas. For the Company of Stationers have obtained from the Crown a patent to print all, or at least the greatest part, of the classic authors, upon pretence, as I hear, that they should be well and truly printed; whereas they are by them scandalously ill printed, both for letter, paper, and correctness, and scarce one tolerable edition is made by them of any one of them. Whenever any of these books of better editions are imported from beyond seas, the Company seizes them, and makes the importers pay 6s. 8d. for each book so imported, or

John Locke (1632–1704) was one of England's most important philosophers. His arguments remain highly important in IP law. (Photo by Stock Montage/Getty Images)

else they confiscate them, unless they are so bountiful as to let the importer compound with them at a lower rate. . . .

Upon occasion of this instance of the classic authors, I demand whether, if another act for printing should be made, it be not reasonable that nobody should have any peculiar right in any book which has been in print fifty years, but any one as well as another might have the liberty to print it; for by such titles as these, which lie dormant, and hinder others, many good books come quite to be lost. But be that determined as it will, in regard of those authors who now write and sell their copies to booksellers, this certainly is very absurd at first sight, that any person or company should now have a title to the printing of the works of Tully, Caesar, or Livy, who lived so many ages since, in exclusion of any other; nor can there be any reason in nature why I might not print them as well as the Company of Stationers, if I thought fit. This liberty, to any one, of printing them, is certainly the way to have them the cheaper and the better.

(pp. 378–80)

ACTIVITY 2.1

Read Locke's extract. As you read, try to answer the following two questions:
  a. What, in Locke's view, was the problem with allowing the Stationers to control the printing of the works of 'classical authors'?
  b. Does Locke say that no one should ever have rights in relation to books?
  Turn to the end of the chapter for discussion.

2.1.2 The Statute of Anne

In 1695, the Licensing Order expired, and so began a period in which society reconsidered its attitude to printing and the free press. Citizens were now free to print whatever they desired without first obtaining permission from the Stationers' Company. Not everyone saw this liberty as an unqualified good, however. Some advocated a return to the system of prepublication licensing. Among that group were the Stationers who, because of the lapse of the Licensing Order, had lost their monopoly over the book trade. Between 1695 and 1705, there were approximately thirteen attempts to reintroduce a statutory regulation of the press.[2]

Against this backdrop, Daniel Defoe wrote an influential pamphlet called *An Essay on the Regulation of the Press* in 1704. Like Locke before him, Defoe argued that the state ought not to determine what could or could not be published. The second paragraph of his essay powerfully explains his opposition to such censorship.

> ### BOX 2.2 DANIEL DEFOE, *AN ESSAY ON THE REGULATION OF THE PRESS* (1704) (REPRINTED BY THE LUTTRELL SOCIETY (BLACKWELL 1958))
>
> To put a general stop to publick Printing, would be a check to Learning, a Prohibition of Knowledge, and make Instruction Contraband: And as Printing has been own'd to be the most useful Invention ever found out, in order to polish the Learned World, make men Polite, and encrease the Knowledge of Letters, and thereby all useful Arts and Sciences; so the high Perfection of Human Knowledge must be at a stand, Improvements stop, and the Knowledge of Letters decay in the Kingdom, if a general Interruption should be put to the Press.
>
> (p. 3)

Daniel Defoe (*c*.1660–1731) was an English writer, journalist and merchant. His most famous novel is *Robinson Crusoe* published in 1707. Defoe had previously been imprisoned for publishing seditious material. (Photo by Stock Montage/Getty Images)

According to Defoe, reintroducing a system of prepublication censorship would have significant social consequences. Resurrecting the Licensing Order would produce a 'check to Learning' and a 'Prohibition of Knowledge' which would stand in the way of the 'Perfection of Human Knowledge' and the 'useful Arts and Sciences'.

Equally however, Defoe did not believe that printers should be able to print whatever they wanted. In fact, Defoe's desire to advance human knowledge also caused him to advocate a new law giving authors the exclusive privilege to print their works.

> ### BOX 2.3 DANIEL DEFOE, *AN ESSAY ON THE REGULATION OF THE PRESS* (1704) (REPRINTED BY THE LUTTRELL SOCIETY (BLACKWELL 1958))
>
> This Law would also put a Stop to a certain sort of Thieving which is now in full practice in *England*, and which no Law extends to punish, *viz.* some Printers and Booksellers printing Copies none of their own.
>
> This is really a most injurious piece of Violence, and a Grievance to all Mankind; for it not only robs their Neighbour of their just Right, but it robs Men of the due Reward of Industry, the Prize of Learning, and the Benefit of their Studies; in the next Place, it robs the Reader, by

Defoe discusses abridgements in the last paragraph. Abridgements are slightly shorter (or abbreviated) versions of original books. We will see this concept again in Section 4.1.1.

> printing Copies of other Men uncorrect and imperfect, making surreptitious and spurious Collections, and innumerable Errors, by which the Design of the Author is often inverted, conceal'd, or destroy'd, and the Information the World would reap by a curious and well studied Discourse, is dwindled into Confusion and Nonsense...
>
> I think in Justice, no Man has a Right to make any Abridgment of a Book, but the Proprietor of the Book; and I am sure no Man can be so well qualified for the doing it, as the Author, if alive, because no Man can be capable of knowing the true Sense of the Design, or of giving it a due Turn like him that compos'd it.
>
> (p. 25)

Two different types of problem associated with printing emerge from Defoe's writing.

First, unlicensed printing might seem unfair to authors (like Defoe). If others can print and sell an author's books, then consumers will buy those books from the unlicensed printer. The money that they pay to the unlicensed printer should really, in Defoe's view, go to the original author. After all, the original author is the one who put the hard work (or 'Industry') into the work's creation. Thus, unlicensed printing robs the author of their 'due Reward'.

Second, unlicensed printing is bad for society more generally. Unlicensed printers would be likely to print poor-quality copies of books containing errors. This would once again hamper the spread of learning (and thus such printing 'robs the Reader').

In later writing, Defoe extended this society-focused rationale further. He later wrote that giving authors copyright was needed to encourage authors to perform such intellectual labour in the first place. Why would anyone spend time and effort writing a book, Defoe asked, if unlicensed printers would then simply sell cheaper versions of the book and take all the profit? If such printing is restrained, however, consumers will buy the work directly from the author, giving the author a financial incentive to write the book in the first instance. Thus, some copyright was necessary 'for the encouraging of Learning, Arts and Industry'.[3]

Defoe's arguments were quickly picked up by the Stationers' Company. According to the historian Mark Rose, Defoe's advocacy for authorial rights provided the Stationers with a 'new strategy for pursuing their own interests'.[4] If the law granted the author exclusive privileges in their books, and if the authors assigned those privileges to the printers, then the printers could retain their monopoly over the selling of those books. To achieve this end, the Stationers lobbied Parliament to enact a new law protecting the author's exclusive ability to print their books.

The result was the enactment of the world's first copyright statute. In 1710 Parliament enacted 'An Act for the Encouragement of Learning, by Vesting the

Copies of Printed books in the Authors or Purchasers of such Copies, during the Times therein mentioned'. The legislation is more commonly known by its shorter title 'The Statute of Anne'. Key excerpts from the legislation are reproduced in Box 2.4 and see Figure 2.2.

BOX 2.4 THE STATUTE OF ANNE 1710

Whereas printers Booksellers and other persons have of late frequently taken the liberty of printing reprinting and publishing ...Books and other writings without the consent of the authors or proprietors of such books and writings to their very great detriment and too often to the Ruin of them and their families[.]

For preventing therefore such practices for the future and for the encouragement of learned men to compose and write useful books May it please Your Majestie that...the Author of any Book or Books already composed ... or that shall hereafter be composed and his assignee or assigns, shall have the sole liberty of printing and reprinting such Book and Books for the term of fourteen years[.]

Figure 2.2 Statute of Anne 1710.
Reproduced with permission from UK Parliamentary Archives

ACTIVITY 2.2

Can you spot the concerns that Defoe highlighted within the text of the statute?

Vincent van Gogh's *Starry Night* (Figure 1.1) is now in the public domain. So too are the writings of Locke and Defoe, and many other materials found in this book. Without the public domain, it would be very hard to produce a work such as this.

The Statute of Anne almost ended the debate surrounding press regulation. While the printing press was set free, the author – and, more importantly, their assignees – would enjoy a special 'liberty' (or privilege) not enjoyed by others: the liberty of exclusive printing. For fourteen years, only the author/assignee enjoyed the exclusive privilege of printing the book. After the initial fourteen-year period, the books fell into the **public domain**. The public domain is an important concept throughout this book. The term refers to all intellectual things that are not privately owned and which are free for the public to use without permission.[5]

However, this was not an uncontroversial solution. Perhaps predictably, the Stationers did not agree that books should fall into the public domain. Instead, they argued that after the period of statutory copyright expired, the common law continued to provide authors with an exclusive privilege to copy their books. Furthermore, unlike the protection conferred by the Statute of Anne, this common law privilege was supposedly perpetual. If courts agreed with the booksellers that the common law granted authors a perpetual copyright, then no books would ever fall into the public domain.

Much eighteenth-century litigation centred on the question of perpetual common law copyright. The booksellers scored an early victory in the case of *Millar v Taylor* (1769).[6] In that case, the King's Bench agreed with the booksellers and found the existence of a perpetual common law copyright. This victory was short-lived. In *Donaldson v Becket* (1774)[7] the House of Lords ultimately concluded that copyright in published works was not protected by the common law. Once an author published a book, the only protection offered by the law was the fourteen years of exclusivity conferred by the Statute of Anne. While historians continue to debate the reasoning and importance of *Donaldson*, the legal situation remains broadly the same today: following the expiry of statutory copyright protection, the work falls into the public domain.[8] Although, as discussed in Section 4.3, the period of copyright is now considerably longer than fourteen years.

2.2 ARGUMENTS FOR COPYRIGHT

Section 1.1.3 introduced the problem of monopoly. By granting property rights over creative works, copyright creates monopolies. Normally monopolies are bad things to be avoided. If someone has a monopoly over the production of this book, then prices for the book will be high and some consumers will not be able to use and enjoy it. The question, therefore, is whether there are any arguments in defence of copyright? Of course, Daniel Defoe and the Stationers' Company thought copyright could be defended. Yet, as a famous author and as sellers of books, Defoe and the Stationers financially benefited from copyright. What do we, as neutral and impartial parties, think about copyright?

Over the centuries, political philosophers have offered a range of arguments in defence of copyright. This section examines the three most historically influential types of argument: (1) the labour argument, (2) the utilitarian argument and (3) the personality argument. These arguments have enjoyed varying degrees of impact in different legal systems. British copyright law, for example, has been heavily influenced by the labour and utilitarian arguments in tandem. In continental Europe (such as France and Germany), the personality argument has often been viewed as the most important.

Are any of the arguments persuasive? The question is not easy because each of the arguments faces serious problems. Independent critical thinkers must accordingly evaluate the arguments, and the objections, and come to their own conclusions about copyright.

2.2.1 The Labour Argument

Section 2.1.1 introduced John Locke's criticism of the Licensing Order. Part of his criticism was directed at the monopoly the Stationers' Company enjoyed over the works of classical authors. Apart from this short extract, Locke did not produce any significant writing on copyright law. However, he did write extensively about property in general. Shortly before the enactment of the Statute of Anne, Locke published his famous '**labour theory**' of property. Lawyers subsequently used this theory as an argument in favour of copyright law. Defoe's argument that unlicensed printing robbed authors of the 'Reward of Industry' was an early attempt at justifying copyright using a labour argument.

Understanding Locke's labour theory of property requires some background information. John Locke's *Two Treatises of Government* (1690) is one of the most important works of political philosophy in the English-speaking world. The central question of this work was when, if ever, is a government legitimate? (Or, in other words, why should citizens do what the government tells them to do?) Prior to that point, the British monarchy had justified their power based on a theory known as the 'divine right of kings'. The monarch claimed to be God's representative on earth and that they had a divine right to rule. Locke was keen to show that this theory was wrong. Locke interpreted the Christian Bible as saying that all people were created as equals and that no person naturally could exercise political power over another. As a result, he argued that the British monarchy needed to find a better argument to support their power than their inherent superiority over regular citizens.

There was a potential flaw in Locke's argument. If all people are equal, is it right that some people are a lot wealthier than others? Some people amass great amounts of private property in their lifetime, while others live in poverty. Could this be reconciled with Locke's insistence that people are naturally equals?

In Box 2.5, Locke attempts to show how private property rights could be reconciled with the equality of individuals. To do so, Locke asks the reader to consider a **state of nature**. That is, imagine a world with no government, no laws and no organised society. Even in this 'natural' world, individuals would enjoy certain **natural rights**. Even in a state of nature, 'natural law' secures individuals rights to their life, their liberty and, more controversially, their property.

The fact that these arguments are derived from Western political philosophy might itself say something about copyright.

Many other cultures did not develop copyright, despite their long literary histories. Arguably the world's first novel (*Tale of Genji*, eleventh century) was written by Japanese author Murasaki Shikibu. Murasaki Shikibu composing the *Tale of Genji* at Ishiyamadera, by Yashima Gakutei (1786–1868). Digital version from Wikimedia Commons <https://commons.wikimedia.org/wiki/File:Murasaki_Shikibu_composing_the_Tale_of_Genji_at_Ishiyamadera,_by_Yashima_Gakutei.jpg>

Are there any natural rights? Locke's claims about 'natural rights' have long been disputed. An earlier political philosopher, Thomas Hobbes, famously claimed that there were no rights in a state of nature: only a life that was 'nasty, brutish, and short'.[9]

BOX 2.5 JOHN LOCKE, *TWO TREATISES OF GOVERNMENT* (1690) (REPRINTED IN *THE WORKS OF JOHN LOCKE* (1823))

Whether we consider natural reason, which tells us that men, being once born, have a right to their preservation, and consequently to meat and drink and such other things as Nature affords for their subsistence, or 'revelation', which gives us an account of those grants God made of the world to Adam, and to Noah and his sons, it is very clear that God, as King David says (Psalm 115. 16), 'has given the earth to the children of men', given it to mankind in common. But, this being supposed, it seems to some a very great difficulty how anyone should ever come to have a property in anything. . . But, this being supposed, it seems to some a very great difficulty how any one should ever come to have a property in anything. . . but I shall endeavour to show how men might come to have a property in several parts of that which God gave to mankind in common, and that without any express compact of all the commoners.

God, who hath given the world to men in common, hath also given them reason to make use of it to the best advantage of life and convenience. The earth and all that is therein is given to men for the support and comfort of their being. And though all the fruits it naturally produces, and beasts it feeds, belong to mankind in common, as they are produced by the spontaneous hand of Nature, and nobody has originally a private dominion exclusive of the rest of mankind in any of them, as they are thus in their natural state, yet being given for the use of men, there must of necessity be a means to appropriate them some way or other before they can be of any use, or at all beneficial, to any particular men. The fruit or venison which nourishes the wild Indian, who knows no enclosure, and is still a tenant in common, must be his, and so his – i.e., a part of him, that another can no longer have any right to it before it can do him any good for the support of his life.

Though the earth and all inferior creatures be common to all men, yet every man has a 'property' in his own 'person'. This nobody has any right to but himself. The 'labour' of his body and the 'work' of his hands, we may say, are properly his. Whatsoever, then, he removes out of the state that Nature hath provided and left it in, he hath mixed his labour with it, and joined to it something that is his own, and thereby makes it his property. It being by him removed from the common state Nature placed it in, it hath by this labour something annexed to it that excludes the common right of other men. For this 'labour' being the unquestionable property of the labourer, no man but he can have a right to what that is once joined to, at least where there is enough, and as good left in common for others.

(§§24–26)

> ### ACTIVITY 2.3
>
> Consider the following scenario. A lumberjack enters a forest. The forest is not currently owned by anyone. The lumberjack intends to cut down a tree and use the wood for building a house. She selects an appropriate tree. She then chops the tree down and drags it home. The whole process takes a few hours of work. Once she has left, thousands of trees remain in the forest for others to use. What do you think Locke would say about this scenario?

But why does labour make such a big difference? Why does the exertion of labour transform the tree (Activity 2.3) from something that is not owned, to something that is owned? Locke gives us his answer to this question in the third and final paragraph. Locke's argument goes like this:

Premise 1: Persons naturally own their labour.
Premise 2: Persons can join their labour to things in the world.
Conclusion: When a person joins their labour to a thing, the person then naturally owns that thing.

To Locke therefore, the lumberjack owns the tree because she has fused (or mixed) together something she owns (her labour) to something she does not initially own (the original tree in the forest). When this occurs, the property rights in her labour flow into the initially unowned thing, giving her a right of property over it.

Before moving on, note how Locke's view on the lumberjack case would change if the lumberjack decided to cut down every tree in the forest. In this alternative scenario, the lumberjack would not leave any trees standing for other people to use. In this case, Locke would argue that the lumberjack does not enjoy a natural right of property over all the trees she has cut down, because she has failed to leave behind 'enough, and as good' for others to use in the future.

Locke proceeded to argue that it is the responsibility of civil government to protect the natural rights of individuals. Kings and queens do not have a divine right to rule, Locke argued. But citizens do tacitly consent to be ruled by governments that protect their natural rights of life, liberty and property.[10] Government derives its legitimacy from this social contract. On the one hand, citizens agree to obey the law, and, on the other hand, governments must rule in a way consistent with the natural rights of the citizens. This means enacting laws that give labourers legal rights over the fruits of their labour.

Subsequently, IP lawyers have argued that it is the responsibility of governments to protect copyright as well. These writers have argued that, according to the law of nature, an author owns the works they create. Therefore, governments should enact copyright laws that enable authors to own their works. A modern version of this argument is presented in Box 2.6 by Robert Merges.

Professor Robert Merges (University of California, Berkeley) has written extensively on the philosophy and economics of IP law.

BOX 2.6 ROBERT MERGES, *JUSTIFYING INTELLECTUAL PROPERTY* (HARVARD UP 2011)

At a deep level, the logic of [Locke's] thinking applies to intellectual products at least as well as to the objects of physical property.[11] This is so for two basic reasons. First, the 'givenness' of the background materials out of which property is forged by labor is very apparent in the world of IP. What we call the public domain is an important, pervasive backdrop against which IP rights are defined. If some simple parallels are accepted... then the symmetry between Locke's state of nature and the public domain becomes quite apparent. The claiming of IP rights out of the public domain follows the same logic as the emergence of property rights from the state of nature.

Second, it is well understood that for Locke, labor plays a crucial role in both justifying and bounding property rights. Again, there are strong parallels to the world of IP rights. Although some well-known doctrines in IP law provide that 'mere' labor (or hard work) is not always enough to establish [IP], nontrivial creations presumably requiring significant effort are often said to be at the heart of IP law. Although labor is relevant in establishing some real property rights, it is a much larger, and much more prominent, part of the IP landscape. So Locke is more pertinent to IP.

(p. 33)

ACTIVITY 2.4

Let's use an example to illustrate Merges's argument.

William Shakespeare wrote the play *Hamlet* around 1600. The play is about a fictional Prince of Denmark called Hamlet (see Figure 2.3). In the play, Hamlet's uncle, Claudius, murders Hamlet's father, the King of Denmark, to seize the throne. After the murder, Hamlet sees the ghost of his father and flees to England. Later, Hamlet returns to Denmark seeking revenge for the murder of his father. The play was written before copyright law existed, and accordingly the story of Hamlet is in the public domain (everyone can use it however they wish).

Now consider a more modern story. In 1994, Walt Disney pictures released the film, the *Lion King*. Simba (a lion cub) is the prince of the Pride Lands. Simba's father, Mufasa, is the king of the Pride Lands. Simba's uncle, Scar, kills Mufasa and

seizes control of the Pride Lands. Simba flees into exile where he sees the ghost of his father. Simba finally returns to the Pride Lands, fights Scar, and takes his place as king of the Pride Lands. The story of the *Lion King* is acknowledged to be heavily influenced by the story of *Hamlet*.

What do you think Merges would say about the *Lion King*? Do you think he would say that Disney have a natural right to own the *Lion King*?

Figure 2.3 Sarah Bernhardt as Hamlet.
Credit: Bildagentur-online/Contributor (via Getty Images)

Why should society grant property rights over intellectual things? In Locke, we find one plausible answer: doing so is necessary to protect natural rights. Of course, no one likes the monopolies that property creates. But maybe we put up with them because it is the right thing to do.

2.2.1.1 PROBLEMS WITH THE LABOUR ARGUMENT

Does labour provide a good argument for copyright? Not everyone thinks so. This section introduces two important objections. The **mixing objection** disagrees with Locke's labour theory of property in general. The **use objection** agrees broadly with the labour theory of property but disagrees that the labour argument can be used to justify property in intangible phenomena.

The **mixing objection** was famously introduced by the political philosopher Robert Nozick. The previous section introduced Locke's view that when one mixes their labour (something owned) with something from the state of nature (something unowned), then natural law dictates that the labourer now owns the (previously unowned) thing. Nozick, however, was unconvinced.

An objection is a reason for rejecting an argument.

Robert Nozick (1938–2002) (Harvard University) was one of the most influential political philosophers of the twentieth century.

> ## BOX 2.7 ROBERT NOZICK, *ANARCHY, STATE, AND UTOPIA* (BASIC BOOKS 1974)
>
> Why does mixing one's labour with something make one the owner of it?[12] Perhaps because one owns one's labour, and so one comes to own a previously unowned thing that becomes permeated with what one owns. Ownership seeps into the rest. But why isn't mixing what I own with what I don't own a way of losing what I own rather than a way of gaining what I don't? If I own a can of tomato juice and spill it in the sea so that its molecules (made radioactive, so I can check this) mingle evenly throughout the sea, do I thereby come to own the sea, or have I foolishly dissipated my tomato juice?
>
> (p. 136)

Nozick therefore agrees that both premises in Locke's labour argument are true. He agrees that persons naturally own their own labour and that it is possible to join that labour to things in the world. But he questions the conclusion that Locke infers. Nozick is saying that Locke has made an invalid inference. The conclusion does not logically follow from the premises, as Peter Smith outlined in Section 1.2. Just because persons own their labour and can mix their labour with things, it does not automatically follow that the ownership of labour transfers over into ownership of the thing. Indeed, the opposite conclusion is just as possible: if someone spills tomato juice into the sea, they do not get to own the sea; instead, they have merely thrown away their juice!

Nozick's question is particularly salient in relation to copyright. To demonstrate, return to the example of the *Lion King*. Merges (following Locke) argues that when the people at Disney mixed their labour (something owned) with the story of *Hamlet* (something unowned), their ownership of their labour flowed into the original story of the *Lion King*. But is that the only conclusion which is compatible with the premises? One might say that, while it is jolly nice of the people at Disney to put their time and effort into writing the *Lion King*, doing so does not mean they get to own it. Instead, they have thrown away their time and effort just like someone who throws away their juice into the ocean.

Alternatively, some agree with Locke that the labour argument can justify property rights over tangible things like trees in the forest but disagree that the labour argument can justify ownership of intangible phenomena like the text of a book. Seana Shiffrin is an example of a scholar who takes this view. The next activity – and extract (Box 2.8) – introduce what we can call the '**use objection**'.

2.2 Arguments for Copyright   **31**

ACTIVITY 2.5

Take a moment and go back to the extract from Locke's *Two Treatises of Government* (Box 2.5). Pay close attention to the second paragraph.

Here we see Locke explain his view that God gives the world as a gift to people 'to make use of it'. For us to make use of God's gift, private property rights are sometimes necessary. For example, consider our lumberjack and the tree. The lumberjack wants to use the tree as building material for a new house. Once she cuts the tree down, private property rights allow her to say: 'this is mine now, keep your hands off'. If she does not have property in the felled tree, then she probably will not be able to build her house. As soon as she cuts the tree down, anyone else could simply take it away from her. So, without property rights, the lumberjack would not really be able to use the gift that God has given her. The tree would just stand there in the forest not being used by anyone.

Let's now think about copyright and the *Lion King*. Does there need to be an owner of the *Lion King* for that film to be used and enjoyed? Or, to put the question in another way, if no one owns the *Lion King*, could people still watch it and enjoy it?

To Shiffrin, this makes property in tangible and intangible phenomenon quite different. As she elaborates in the following extract, private ownership of tangible things might be necessary to ensure God's gift to humanity is fully used, but the same is not true of intangible things.

BOX 2.8 SEANA VALENTINE SHIFFRIN, 'LOCKEAN ARGUMENTS FOR PRIVATE INTELLECTUAL PROPERTY' IN STEPHEN R MUNZER (ED), *NEW ESSAYS IN THE LEGAL AND POLITICAL THEORY OF PROPERTY* (CUP 2001) 138–58

Professor Seana Shiffrin (University of California, Los Angeles) is a lawyer and philosopher who has worked in the fields of legal, moral and political philosophy.

Under an interpretation stressing the common property presumption, Lockean justifications for private property are more strained for intellectual property than for real property.[13] For real property, private appropriation proceeds because it is necessary for proper and full use to be made of the common. Failure to permit some private appropriation would be absurd, since it would frustrate the purpose for which common ownership of the resource was granted.

For most forms of intellectual property, the analogous argument falls flat ... The fully effective use of an idea, proposition, concept, expression, method, invention, melody, picture, or sculpture generally does not require, by its nature, prolonged exclusive use or control. Generally, one's use or consumption of an idea, proposition, concept, expression, method, and so forth, is fully compatible with others' use, even their simultaneous use...

> For the bulk of intellectual products, then, the basic Lockean justification for parceling them out to specific individuals for exclusive control is missing. The abilities to prevent the use of given intellectual works by others and to prevent the creation of derivative works run counter to the presumption of common ownership and the concomitant concern to make full use of resources.
>
> (pp. 156–57)

A potential third objection to the labour argument – the 'nature objection' – will also be discussed in Section 6.2.2 in the context of patent law.

It is up to students to decide if the labour argument for copyright is persuasive or not. Some might side with Merges and think that this provides a good justification for property in intellectual things. Alternatively, some might conclude that labour and natural rights justify some type of property in intangibles, but a type of property that falls short of 'exclusive control'. Some may disagree with the idea of natural rights altogether.

But labour is not the only argument for copyright. A second type of argument can be found in the political philosophy of utilitarianism.

Jeremy Bentham (1747–1832) made contributions to moral philosophy, political and legal philosophy. He was also a social reformer and an early advocate of animal rights. (Photo by Bildagentur/Universal Images Group via Getty Images)

2.2.2 The Utilitarian Argument

The second possible argument for copyright is derived from the political philosophy of another famous British thinker, Jeremy Bentham. Locke argued that legitimate governments must rule in accordance with the individual natural rights of citizens. But Bentham disagreed with Locke. Bentham famously thought that nature did not provide individuals with any rights at all. He called the whole notion of so-called 'natural rights' a lot of 'nonsense upon stilts'.[14] The only rights that persons have are the ones that governments give to them.

Instead, Bentham argued that governments are legitimate if they rule in accordance with something called the 'principle of utility'.[15] Bentham argued that the goal of all law should be to make people happy. Alas, no law can make everyone happy all the time. Every law will make some people happy, and some people unhappy. If a government passes a law that the speed limit on motorways is 50 mph, some will be happy that the probability of fatal accidents will reduce, while others will be unhappy that they can no longer drive above 50 mph. To be a legitimate source of political authority, a government must rule in a way that leads to the most happiness *overall*. Legitimate governments must enact laws that produce the 'greatest good for the greatest number'.[16]

Some IP lawyers argue that governments must enact copyright to satisfy the principle of utility. The essential idea is that copyright will encourage authors to write original works, and this will make society happier overall. This idea first appeared in the Statute of Anne, that called copyright an 'encouragement' to authors to 'compose and write useful books'. In the USA, the idea even appears in the Constitution, which gives the federal government a power to enact copyright laws because doing so might help 'promote the Progress of Science and the Useful Arts'.[17]

This argument is, however, deceptively simple. At first glance, the idea sounds so straightforward: copyright makes the world a better place by encouraging creativity. But, in reality, the argument is notoriously complex.[18] So complex, in fact, that even very good IP lawyers can get it wrong at times. To avoid making the same mistakes, we need to try to state the argument as precisely as possible.

To understand the utilitarian argument, we first need a clear grasp of why a copyright monopoly might be necessary to encourage the creation of original works. After all, we do not give monopolies to other businesses to encourage them to produce and sell new goods. Why would authors not engage in this activity without copyright? As Box 2.9 explains, the reason is related to the public goods nature of creative products and the economics of trading such goods.

> What is happiness? To Bentham, people will be happy if they enjoy more pleasurable experiences in life (such as enjoying good food or reading great books). This view is known as hedonism.

> Not all utilitarians are hedonists, however. Modern economists argue instead that laws should satisfy our preferences (also called 'welfare'). But this distinction is mostly sidestepped in this book.

BOX 2.9 OREN BRACHA AND TALHA SYED, 'BEYOND EFFICIENCY: CONSEQUENCES SENSITIVE THEORIES OF COPYRIGHT' (2014) 29 BERKELEY TECH LJ 229

From an economic perspective, the policy effects of copyright, like those of some other intellectual property rights, are analyzed against the backdrop of the public-goods character of informational goods.[19] Works of authorship – the sort of informational works protected by copyright law – exhibit the two defining features of public goods. One, they are nonexcludable, in the sense that once created and published it is very difficult to prevent others from using and consuming them. Two, they are also nonrivalrous, meaning that the use and consumption of the work by one person does not reduce the ability of others to use and consume it.

The source of the innovation policy problem is the nonexcludable character of the work, which allows others to reproduce and/or consume it for a fraction of the cost incurred by the creator. To the extent that such access by others does not allow the creator to appropriate enough of the social value of the work to cover its development cost, the work (or similar ones in the future) will not be created in the first place. The result: an insufficient or suboptimal level of compensation or incentives to produce and publish works of authorship.

> Oren Bracha (University of Texas, Austin) and Talha Syed (University of California, Berkeley) have made extensive contributions to the theory and history of IP law.

> Copyright solves this problem by conferring upon the creator a limited set of legal entitlements to exclude others from certain uses of the work. Copyright converts, in other words, a nonexcludable resource into a partially excludable one in order to allow the copyright owner to internalize a substantial part of the social value of the work, thereby boosting the financial resources or incentives for creation and publication.
>
> (pp. 237–38)

Bracha and Syed explain that the public goods nature of creative works causes a problem. In particular, the problem is the non-excludability of the goods. The next activity illustrates.

ACTIVITY 2.6

Imagine someone who has a business selling apples. Every day they pick 100 apples and take them to market to sell. Picking these apples takes a bit of time and effort every morning. The apple seller then goes to the market and puts the apples in a barrel. The seller keeps the people away from the apple barrel (i.e. excludes them). If anyone wants an apple, they need to buy one from the seller at a price the seller determines. At the end of the day, the seller has sold all the apples and made a decent profit. The amount of money they have earned is quite large and they are happy to start the process all over again tomorrow.

Now consider Disney's *Lion King*. How is selling the *Lion King* different from selling apples?

By creating property rights, copyright tries to solve this problem. The copyright given to Disney creates a monopoly over the production and sale of the *Lion King*. The law accordingly turns a non-excludable good into an excludable one. Now, Disney can exclude non-paying consumers from the good just like the apple seller does. Disney can therefore charge people a high price to use and enjoy the film. That high price means Disney earns profit (as explained by Ruth Towse in Box 1.3). It is this allure of profit that encourages Disney to create the films that make us consumers happy.

However, if that sounds good, do not forget the problem of monopoly. Because Disney has a monopoly, prices for the *Lion King* go up, and some people can no longer use and enjoy it. This is problematic for two reasons. First, there will be a lot of unhappy customers in the market who would love to watch the *Lion King*, but simply cannot afford the price Disney charges. And, second, the inability to use and enjoy the film might actually discourage future creativity. This happens because, as the next activity illustrates, creativity is often **cumulative**. Just as

Disney built on Shakespeare's *Hamlet* to create the *Lion King*, others might want to build on the *Lion King* in the future.

> ### ACTIVITY 2.7
>
> I am thinking about writing a novel. My novel will be a sequel to the *Lion King*. In my story, I will explore what happens to Simba after he reclaims the throne of Pride Rock. To write this story, however, I likely will require the permission of Disney. What might be the problem with this requirement?

Copyright accordingly has both good and bad effects on utility and society's happiness. This is known in IP law as the **incentive–access tradeoff.** Copyright can give some people – like Disney – the incentives to create original works (good!). But the problem of monopoly also means that some people can no longer 'access' the work, leading to some unhappy consumers and, in some instances, even discourage creativity (bad!).

The central point made by the utilitarian argument is that, when we calculate all the happiness and unhappiness caused, copyright is still a good idea *overall*. The thrust of the argument is that the good consequences of copyright outweigh the bad consequences, and thus enacting copyright satisfies the principle of utility.

Even better, society can design copyright law to limit some of the negative consequences while retaining the good consequences. We can, for example, decide that copyright only lasts for a short period and is not perpetual. That way, creators can still earn a profit for a time, but the restrictions on consumer access do not last any longer than necessary. Pro-copyright utilitarians therefore argue if society adopts appropriately **balanced** copyright systems (i.e. copyright that is not too weak nor too powerful), then society will be happier overall.

Finally, we can state precisely the utilitarian argument for copyright. Formally, the argument looks as follows:

Premise 1: An appropriately balanced copyright system encourages authors to create more original works.
Premise 2: If authors create more original works, society will be happier overall.
Conclusion: An appropriately balanced copyright system makes society a happier place overall.

2.2.2.1 PROBLEMS WITH THE UTILITARIAN ARGUMENT

Having stated the utilitarian argument precisely, the next question is: is the argument sound? Much like the labour argument, the utilitarian argument faces serious objections. This section considers two of the most common objections: the **empirical objection** and the **alternatives objection**.

In Boxes 1.4 and 1.5 Peter Smith summarised how a sound argument must have true premises. But are the premises in the utilitarian argument true? Is it true that an appropriately balanced copyright system encourages authors to create more original works? After all, Activity 2.7 demonstrates how copyright can also *discourage* creativity. And, even if an appropriately balanced copyright system does encourage creativity, is it true that the increased creativity will make society a happier place? After all, we have also seen how copyright can make some people unhappy by increasing the prices of goods.

The **empirical objection** states that surprisingly little evidence supports the premises. Particularly in the last thirty years, copyright lawyers have tested these premises: they have gathered data,[20] run experiments[21] and interviewed creators to learn what makes them tick.[22] One research centre at Glasgow University estimates that over 800 research papers studying the copyright system have been published since the year 2000.[23] The problem is, as one leading scholar puts it, the results are 'decidedly ambiguous'.[24] The evidence does not clearly show that the premises are obviously false, but nor do they provide much support for their truth.

Some scholars take the empirical objection even further. As we see in Box 2.10, Robert Merges doubts that it is even possible to gather the necessary evidence required to prove this claim.

> The concept of **empiricism** is central to contemporary IP law. While some knowledge can be acquired through reason alone (e.g. such as the sum of $2+2$) other knowledge can only be acquired by making observations about the world. Whether copyright increases or decreases happiness is what we call an 'empirical question'.

BOX 2.10 ROBERT MERGES, *JUSTIFYING INTELLECTUAL PROPERTY* (HARVARD UP 2011)

Current convention has it that IP law seeks to maximize the net social benefit of the practices it regulates. The traditional utilitarian formulation – the greatest good for the greatest number – is expressed here in terms of rewards. Society offers above-market rewards to creators of certain works that would not be created, or not created as soon or as well, in the absence of reward. The gains from this scheme, in the form of new works created, are weighed against social losses, typically in the form of the consumer welfare lost when embodiments of these works are sold at prices above the marginal cost of their production. IP policy, according to this model, is a matter of weighing these things out, of striking the right balance. At the conceptual level at least, the process involved is not particularly complex. It is easy to picture the toting up of costs and benefits, and to think of a good policy as one that equilibrates the scale at just the right point – the point that maximizes the number and quality of new creative works without costing society an arm and a leg.

The process is simple but, practically speaking, not at all easy. Impossibly complex, in fact. Estimating costs and benefits, modeling them over time, projecting what would happen under counterfactuals (such as how many novels or pop songs really would be written in the absence of copyright protection, and who would benefit from such a situation) – these are all overwhelmingly complicated tasks. And this complexity poses a major problem for utilitarian theory. The sheer practical difficulty of measuring or approximating all the variables involved means that the utilitarian program will always be at best aspirational. Like designing a perfect socialist economy, the computational complexities of this philosophical project cast grave doubt on its fitness as a workable foundation for the field.

In my research, I have become convinced that with our current tools we will never identify the 'optimal number' of patented, copyrighted, and trademarked works. Every time I play the archaeologist and go looking for the utilitarian footings of the field, I come up empty. Try as I might, I simply cannot justify our current IP system on the basis of verifiable data showing that people are better off with IP law than they would be without it.

(pp. 2–3)

ACTIVITY 2.8

Reconsider the formal utilitarian argument. Which premise does Merges disagree with?

The problems with the utilitarian argument are not merely empirical. In addition, some scholars raise a second objection, which we can call the **alternatives objection**. Consider premise 1 in Activity 2.8 (i.e. copyright encourages authors to produce more creative works). Even if that is true, it is not true that *only* copyright encourages authors to produce the right amount of creative works. There might be other ways of encouraging creativity. And these other ways of encouraging creativity may have fewer bad consequences than copyright.

In Box 2.11, Stephen Breyer explains that the government could use alternative mechanisms to encourage creativity. It might be that these mechanisms cause the same amount of happiness as copyright but cause even less unhappiness. In which case, these alternative mechanisms may better satisfy the principle of utility.

BOX 2.11 STEPHEN BREYER, 'THE UNEASY CASE FOR COPYRIGHT: A STUDY OF COPYRIGHT IN BOOKS, PHOTOCOPIES, AND COMPUTER PROGRAMS' (1970) 84 HARV L REV 281

In the absence of copyright protection, one might also consider using government subsidies to maintain publishers' and authors' revenues.[25]

Stephen Breyer was an associate justice of the Supreme Court of the United States. He was previously a professor of law at Harvard Law School and the extract comes from the first article he published.

> At present the government subsidizes scientific writing by paying for nearly two-thirds of all research and development work done in America and by paying a sizeable portion of the cost of disseminating the results. Insofar as the government pays for a book's creation and subsidizes its dissemination, a copyright fee is not needed to assure production and to charge such a fee will restrict the book's distribution. Moreover, government subsidies can, and do, take 'spillover' effects into account. The government may pay for a work containing a scientific theory, for example, that radiates benefits far beyond the circle of its readers. Because the sales revenue that such a book generates may not cover its costs, its subsidy by the government is necessary and desirable.
>
> In principle, substituting government funds for money raised through copyright may prove economically advantageous, for it can secure production without restricting a book's dissemination. But I doubt that one can devise an administratively practical government financing system that could be substituted on a wide scale for copyright protection without diluting much of this theoretical economic benefit.
>
> (pp. 306–07)

In this extract, Stephen Breyer considers whether the copyright system could be replaced with a **subsidy** scheme. The government could give tax money to creators (for example, those who work for public organisations like the BBC). In return, they would produce creative works for the public to consume but would not receive copyright in the work. This would have the benefit of encouraging creativity, but avoiding the major source of unhappiness with copyright (i.e. the restrictions on access). Potentially, therefore, this approach may cause more happiness overall.

Breyer is not entirely convinced about the alternatives. In this passage, he demonstrates that alternatives like subsidies cause their own special type of unhappiness. Breyer is concerned that such a subsidy scheme would not be 'administratively practical'. It would require a government body to oversee the system. This government body would need to be funded by public taxation. This means the government have less money to spend on other projects that make people happy (like healthcare). Nonetheless, one might conclude that when combined with the empirical objection, the utilitarian argument for copyright is far from obviously sound.

2.2.3   The Personality Argument

Locke and Bentham were both English philosophers. Traditionally the labour and utilitarian arguments for copyright have resonated most with the citizens of English-speaking countries like the UK and the USA. But the influence of these arguments outside of the English-speaking world has been more limited. In fact, lawyers in European countries (particularly France and Germany) have at times argued that the labour and utilitarian arguments fail to understand what is special about creativity. As the late French lawyer, Henri Desbois said, France 'repudiated the utilitarian' argument for copyright.[26] Instead, Desbois argued that French law protects an author's rights 'because a bond unites him to the object of his creation'. So, what is this special 'bond' that Desbois thought was so important?

> ### ACTIVITY 2.9
>
> The personality argument for copyright can be difficult to grasp. To help, let's start with an intuitive example. In my spare time, I (Patrick) am writing a book and I want to tell you about it.
>
> My book is going to be a fantasy novel. I decided to write a fantasy novel because this is the type of genre that I enjoy reading the most. It is also going to be quite a light-hearted fantasy novel and not involve much violence. I am not a big fan of fantasies, like the *Game of Thrones* series that involve a lot of violence; I prefer lighter and sillier comic fantasies such as those written by Terry Pratchett and Neil Gaiman. Also, I prefer fantasy novels that are set on earth rather than sci-fi novels which are set in outer space. I have decided to write a fantasy which is set in the wonderful city in which I live: London. Imagine that I publish the novel and you read it. We have never met and we may never meet in the future. But when you read the novel, do you think you start to get to know me in some way?

The special bond between author and work was a particular concern for the German Idealist philosophers. In Box 2.12, Georg Wilhelm Friedrich Hegel explains his understanding of this unique relationship.

> ### BOX 2.12 GEORG WILHELM FRIEDRICH HEGEL, *ELEMENTS OF PHILOSOPHY OF RIGHT* (1821) (PUBLISHED BY G BELL, LONDON, 1896; SW DYDE TR, 1896)
>
> It may be asked whether the artist, scholar, &c., is from the legal point of view in possession of his art, erudition, ability to preach a sermon, sing a mass, &c., that is, whether such attainments are 'things'. We may hesitate to call such abilities, attainments, aptitudes, &c., 'things', for while possession of these may be the subject of business dealings and contracts, as if they were things, there is also something inward and mental about it, and for this reason the Understanding may be in perplexity about how to describe such possession in legal terms, because its field of vision is as limited to the dilemma that this is 'either a thing or not a thing' as to the dilemma 'either finite or infinite'. Attainments, erudition, talents, and so forth, are, of course, owned by free mind and are some thing internal and not external to it,

Unlike Locke, Georg WF Hegel (1770–1831) was not seeking to defend the institution of the government, but instead explain its place in history. He argued that only the state is the 'rational end of man' and only the state is capable of providing the conditions for the fullest human autonomy and self-determination. (Photo by Fine Art Images/Heritage Images/Getty Images)

> but even so, by expressing them it may embody them in something external and alienate them (see below), and in this way they are put into the category of 'things'. Therefore, they are not immediate at the start but only acquire this character through the mediation of mind which reduces its inner possessions to immediacy and externality.
>
> (§43)

Hegel is a notoriously complicated philosopher with a unique style of writing. But he seems to split the world into two categories: 'things' and 'not things'. Hegel is particularly interested in knowing into which category our 'abilities, attainments, [and] aptitudes' fall. Is van Gogh's artistic talent a thing? No, says Hegel. This ability is something 'internal' or an 'inner possession' of the self; it is part of van Gogh rather than part of the world. We can however *externalise* these aspects of our selves. By creating *Starry Night*, van Gogh externalised himself onto the canvas. That externalised phenomenon is a thing that can, and should, be owned.

Some modern authors have subsequently argued that legitimate governments must protect this special personality bond by enacting copyright law. One such example is Justin Hughes. Hughes argues that the 'most powerful alternative to a Lockean model of property is a personality justification'.[27] Hughes argues that, like Locke's labour theory, 'the personality theory has an intuitive appeal when applied to intellectual property: an idea belongs to its creator because the idea is a manifestation of the creator's personality or self'.[28] If we have some right to control our personality, and if our creative works embody our personality, then surely we should control the works that embody our personality.

2.2.3.1 PROBLEMS WITH THE PERSONALITY ARGUMENT

But why, one might ask, is it necessary to give an author copyright to protect this 'bond'? Let's assume for the time being that the author does leave a little bit of their personality behind in their work. So what? Why does this mean the government should enact a system of copyright law that enables authors to control how people use those books?

ACTIVITY 2.10

Consider and compare the following two scenarios:
a. You read my fantasy novel (from activity 2.9) and decide that it is OK but needs some improvements. It needs a lot more violence in it to be really gripping. To improve the novel, you make some alterations to the text. Despite my desires to the contrary, you introduce some gory fight scenes and start distributing copies of this work.

> b. You read my fantasy novel and decide it is a fantastic novel and perfect in every way. You start making copies and selling them cheaply to everyone you can. You want to distribute the novel as far and wide as possible.
>
> In either case, has my personality been harmed in any meaningful way?

As Activity 2.10 highlights, there might be a difference between *altering* someone's work and merely *copying* someone's work. We might think the author deserves to prevent unlicensed alterations of their works to protect their personality. But it is not clear why empowering the author to control copying will protect their personality from harm. This might be understood as the **copying objection**. Yet, as illustrated particularly in Chapter 4, what copyright owners often want is a right to prevent copying.

Because of this objection, copyright in the English-speaking world and copyright in continental Europe have historically been quite different. In the English-speaking world, the most important part of copyright is the author's right to prevent unauthorised reproductions (justified by the labour and utilitarian arguments). But in mainland Europe, the situation is different. Some, like Desbois earlier, argue the central feature of these legal systems is that they protect the special bond between author and creation. By preventing the work from alterations (and other similar actions), these systems seek primarily to protect the author's personality rather than their financial interests. While this is a very broad and somewhat stereotypical division, and one that has become less important over time, we sometimes call these legal systems '**author rights** countries' (*droit d'auteur* in French or *Urheberrecht* in German) and distinguish them from the 'copyright countries' of the UK and USA.

Before moving on, a final mention ought to be made of another German philosopher, Immanuel Kant. In 1785, Kant wrote an essay called *On the Unlawfulness of Reprinting*. In this essay, Kant tried to justify copyright law using an argument that, while similar in some respects to the personality argument, also has some important differences. Kant was less concerned about the special bond that exists between *the author and the book*. Instead, Kant focused on the relationship of the *author and the reader*. Kant viewed writing a book as a form of speech. In the pages of my fantasy novel, I am in fact speaking directly to you the reader. The problem with unlicensed reprinting is that it is a form of 'compelled speech'. When someone reprints and sells a book to a third party, the reprinter has essentially forced the author to speak to the third party, even though the author has not freely chosen to do so. In recent years, some contemporary scholars have built on this theory and tried to justify the existence of copyright as a tool to prevent compelled speech.[29] One example is Abraham Drassinower, introduced in Box 1.1.

2.3 THE INTERNATIONALISATION OF COPYRIGHT

Section 2.2 demonstrated that copyright's legitimacy is contested. While there are arguments that support copyright, the arguments all suffer from their own unique flaws and weaknesses. As a result, different people come to different conclusions on the justifiability of copyright. You are encouraged to form your own view.

Despite its contested nature, copyright has spread around the world. The eighteenth century witnessed the birth of many national copyright systems. The newly formed United States enacted the Copyright Act of 1790 providing authors with a right to copy their works for a maximum of twenty-eight years. France likewise enacted the French Literary and Artistic Property Act of 1793 and Prussia enacted a general ban on unlawful printing in the Prussian Statute Book of 1794.

The next step in the evolution of copyright occurred in the nineteenth century with the genesis of the international copyright system. This occurred in response to the problems of purely national copyright. National copyright systems are **territorial** in nature. The UK copyright system was only effective in the UK and the French copyright system was only effective in France, and so on. This meant that a UK author could receive copyright protection in the UK under the Statute of Anne, but this did not entitle them to protection in any other countries. Likewise, French authors could not receive protection outside France, and so on. In the nineteenth century, the territorial nature of copyright became increasingly problematic.

> **Territoriality** is an important concept in public international law. The territoriality principle states that a sovereign state can only exercise legal authority over the individuals and legal persons within its territory. Thus the British Parliament could not enact copyright affecting peoples and activities in, say, France.

ACTIVITY 2.11

What do you think was problematic about the territorial nature of copyright during the nineteenth century? The cartoon (Figure 2.4), printed by a humorous magazine (*Puck*) in 1886, may give you a few clues.

Figure 2.4 'The Pirate Publisher', *Puck Magazine*. The Pirate Publisher – An International Burlesque that has the Longest Run on Record by Joseph Ferdinand Keppler, Puck (24 February 1886) 18(468).

Library of Congress, Washington, DC 20540 USA, reproduction number: LC-USZC4–6529.LC-DIG-ppmsca-28173. Restoration by Adam Cuerden (licensed under Creative Commons Attribution 3.0)

To combat this problem, countries in the nineteenth century started to enter into bilateral agreements with other states. For example, in 1851 the UK signed an agreement with France.[30] Under this bilateral agreement, the UK agreed to provide copyright protection to French authors, and France likewise provided protection for British authors (an arrangement known as **reciprocity**). However, making such bilateral agreements was a slow and laborious process. It often took several years to enact one single agreement between two countries. Clearly a more efficient solution was required.

In 1886 the Berne Convention for the Protection of Literary and Artistic Works was created. Unlike prior international copyright treaties, the Berne Convention was (and remains) a multilateral agreement among multiple parties. In 1886, the agreement was only between ten (mostly European) countries. But today the Berne Convention has 179 parties and remains the most important international copyright treaty.

The Berne Convention has two fundamental components. First, the treaty introduced the principle of '**national treatment**'. Under this principle, members of the convention must give authors from other member states the same protection that they currently offer their own authors. For example, under the national treatment principle, the UK must give French authors the same level of copyright protection as it provides to its own domestic British authors. Second, the treaty also requires that when a country provides protection to foreign authors, that protection must comply with a set of '**minimum standards**'. For example, the member state must protect the works of foreign nationals for the lifetime of the author plus an additional fifty years, and provide them with a set of exclusive rights (such as the right to make reproductions or adaptations of their works). This ensures that authors receive a reasonably strong ability to prevent the unauthorised reprinting of their works in other countries.

Today, the Berne Convention is administered by the World Intellectual Property Organization (WIPO) in Geneva, Switzerland. While the Berne Convention was the first multilateral international copyright treaty, it is now accompanied by a range of additional treaties, such as the World Trade Organization's Agreement on Trade Related Aspects of IP Rights (1994) (i.e. the TRIPS Agreement), and the World Intellectual Property Organization Copyright Treaty (1996).

> The term 'piracy' initially emerged to refer to criminal robbery and violence on the high seas. But the term has also been associated with copyright infringement for many centuries. The term is frequently used today to refer to intentional copyright infringement conducted for financial gain.

2.4 SUMMARY

Should society grant property in books? Should we, as Macaulay put it, accept this tax on readers?

This chapter has introduced a range of arguments in favour of such rights. The argument for the pre-copyright licensing regime – censorship and control of information – is clearly a bad argument in a modern liberal democracy. But do the other arguments fare any better? Should society grant property in creative works on the grounds that doing so protects labourers' natural rights, encourages creative work and/or respects personality? Are these reasons sufficiently compelling to make us accept the problem of monopoly discussed in Section 1.1.3? It is for students to decide.

While there are many possible answers to this normative question, it is worth highlighting two common ones. The first response can be called the **pluralist** response. That is, one might agree that each of the arguments in favour of copyright have problems. Nevertheless, one might argue that *together* they make a compelling case for copyright.

There remains a problem with this pluralist answer, however. Simply put, why do several *bad* arguments, when added together, make up one *good* argument. If one agrees that the labour argument is not compelling on its own, and the same too for the utilitarian and personality arguments, then how does the conclusion change when they are considered together as a group?

The second type of response is to say that some type of copyright system is justifiable. One might agree that authors should not have exclusive control over their works, but nor should they have no control at all. If this answer seems sensible, the next question is what rights should the author enjoy with respect to their work? What level of control can be justified on normative grounds? This answer will be considered in more depth in Chapters 4 and 5.

Despite these questions, copyright law has spread worldwide. Society has even created an additional layer of copyright protection through international copyright law. And, as discussed in Chapters 3–5, copyright has expanded in other important ways too.

2.5 SELF-ASSESSMENT

Before moving on, try to answer the following questions to consolidate your learning.

1. Which of the following statements best describes the concept of the public domain?
   a. The public domain refers to all intellectual things, including original works, that are not privately owned.
   b. The public domain refers to original works which were protected by copyright at one time, but are no longer.
   c. The public domain refers to the system of censorship that existed prior to copyright.
   d. The public domain refers to the period in which an original work is protected by copyright.
2. Select the *two* strongest objections to the labour argument for copyright protection.
   a. It is not clear why joining one's labour to a thing gives the labourer a right to own that thing.
   b. In Locke's theory, private property is incompatible with the equality of all individuals.
   c. It is not clear why private property over intangibles is needed to encourage use of those goods.
   d. There is no equivalent to the state of nature within copyright.
3. The utilitarian argument for copyright of IP is best summarised by which of the following statements?
   a. Copyright is necessary to protect natural property rights.
   b. Copyright is necessary to encourage authors to create original works.

c Copyright is necessary to satisfy the principle of utility.

d. Copyright is necessary to create a monopoly over original works.

4. Is there one good argument for copyright? No answer is provided for this question.

ACTIVITY DISCUSSION

Activity 2.1 Locke primarily expresses concern about the consequences of giving the Stationers a monopoly over the printing of books. He thought the monopoly allowed them to charge excessively high prices for such works. At the same time, he believed the lack of competition resulted in the Stationers producing poor-quality versions of these books (such as by printing texts which were inaccurate).

Nevertheless, Locke was not entirely against giving printers some rights in relation to their books. He wrote that no one should have rights in books that have been in print for fifty years already. But this suggests that printers potentially should be able to acquire some rights in relation to works which have been in print for fewer than fifty years. Later in the text, he also wrote that 'it may be reasonable to limit their property to a certain number of years after the death of the author or the first printing of the book, as, suppose, fifty or seventy years' (p. 387). Does this sound sensible to you?

Activity 2.2 The first paragraph highlights the feeling that unlicensed printing is in some way unfair or unjust to authors. The second paragraph (and the long title) highlights the more society-focused rationale that copyright law will encourage the production of 'useful' books.

Activity 2.3 Locke would say that the forest was originally given by God to all people 'in common'. In this 'state of nature' everyone owns the trees equally. However, something important happens when the lumberjack cuts the tree down. By cutting the tree down, the lumberjack has used her 'labour' to remove the tree from its natural state. Locke says that because the lumberjack has laboured to cut the tree down, and because enough trees remain in the forest for other people to use, natural law dictates that she now owns that felled tree.

Activity 2.4 Merges would say that Disney naturally owns the *Lion King*. *Hamlet* is in the public domain and Merges argues that the public domain is quite like the 'state of nature' that Locke was talking about. The things we find in the public domain (such as *Hamlet*) are, just like the things in the state of nature (such as trees), free for us all to use and enjoy. But Disney did not merely retell the story of Hamlet; instead, they transformed *Hamlet* into a fun story about lions. We could say that the people working for Disney joined their labour to the story of *Hamlet* and, in so doing, transformed it into something original. Merges would say it is the addition of their labour to the *Hamlet* story that makes Disney the natural owners of the *Lion King*. After all, everyone else is still able to use and enjoy *Hamlet* for free, even if Disney own the *Lion King*. Does this sound right to you?

Activity 2.5 Imagine the following: after Disney has turned the story of *Hamlet* into the *Lion King*, the new film falls immediately into the public domain and Disney receives no copyright. Because the film is in the public domain, everyone can use it. It seems therefore that if there is no copyright, then the film will still be used and enjoyed by people (maybe even more people will enjoy the film due to the absence of copyright protection!).

For Shiffrin, this means we ought to make a distinction between property in tangible and intangible phenomena.[31] When properly interpreted, Locke's labour theory might support property in tangibles because to do otherwise would frustrate God's gift to humanity. However, the labour theory does not support giving property rights in intangibles because intangibles will still be used even in the absence of ownership. Do you agree with her?

Activity 2.6 Selling a public good poses unique problems because of their non-excludability. Creating the *Lion King* cost Disney approximately US$45 million. Disney would like to go to market, just like the apple seller, and sell copies of this film and make a profit. However, the non-excludability of the film causes Disney a problem. Disney will sell one copy of the film to the first customer, but, then, that customer could simply put the film online for others to watch for free. Subsequent consumers will watch the film online for free rather than paying Disney for a copy. In the end, Disney will have spent US$45 million on the film, but have not made any profit in return. As a result, they will likely not continue making films in the future. Why would anyone waste their time and money on such unprofitable projects?

Activity 2.7 When I approach Disney to ask whether I can use the *Lion King* characters in a new sequel, they are likely to charge me a monetary fee to do so. Of course, some people will be able to afford that fee. But I cannot. I am just a poor IP lawyer, after all. The result is I cannot make my new story. Therefore, while copyright can encourage creativity it can, sadly, also make it harder in certain contexts..

Activity 2.8 Merges's argument is primarily with the truth of Premise 2. He notes in paragraph 1 that copyright will encourage creativity (what he calls the 'gains from the scheme') but also make some consumers less happy (the 'social losses...in the form of consumer welfare'). The utilitarian argument says the former good effects will outweigh the bad effects. In theory, Merges says, we can test this assertion. We can calculate all the good and bad parts of copyright and decide if it is overall a good idea. Sadly however, in practice, gathering this data is 'impossibly complex'. How would we calculate the unhappiness created by copyright? Would we go around asking everyone what they think?

Activity 2.9 Some would say that when you read my novel, you start to get a sense of what I am like as a person. It is almost as though I, the author, have left a bit of my *personality* on the paper. As you read the pages you start to see my personality coming through the words: I am a fantasy nerd who lives in London and is very silly at heart. Alternatively, if you read the works of William Shakespeare, like *Hamlet*, then you might start to understand what he was like (I imagine that he was a bit long-winded!). This is the special 'bond' that Desbois believed united the author and their creation: the creator puts part of themselves into the work.

Activity 2.10 Many readers have an intuitive response that scenario (a) seems wrong. Many (although certainly not everyone) have a sense that you have harmed the special bond that I have with my work. I have invested a bit of myself into this story and you have 'distorted' it. It is almost, therefore, like you have distorted a bit of me.

But it is not so clear whether the same sort of problem exists with scenario (b). Here, the special bond between me and my story seems to be intact. The story is still a pure expression of my personality. It has not been distorted in any way. It just so happens that there are more copies of my novel floating around the world.

Activity 2.11 The picture shows authors from various countries standing in a circle. On the left, you can see American authors such as Mark Twain, while on the right you can see European authors such as Thomas Hardy and Jules Verne. The authors are all pointing angrily at a man in the middle dressed like a sailor. The drawing calls the sailor the 'Pirate Publisher'. The Pirate Publisher takes works of European authors (like Hardy and Verne) and sells unauthorised copies of those works in America, and likewise sells American works (such as those of Mark Twain) in Europe. The authors are angry about what they see as this 'piracy' of their works. Meanwhile, the Pirate Publisher is pointing to a book on the ground called 'Law'. His gesture says that the law permits his activities.

The picture illustrates the problems of territorial copyright. In the absence of international copyright law, authors could not stop 'pirates' from selling their works in foreign countries. Authors (and their assignees) argued that the money the pirates made rightly belonged to them. But without any international copyright law, they could not stop this practice.

SELF-ASSESSMENT ANSWERS

1. **Correct answer: a.** Some may be tempted to select answer **b**. But this is only *part* of the public domain. The public domain contains things which previously were protected and which are no longer protected, but also materials which never received copyright in the first place (for example, *Hamlet* by Shakespeare, which was written prior to the enactment of copyright law).

2. **Correct answers: a.** and **c.** Answer **a.** corresponds to Nozick's mixing objection while option **c.** refers to Shiffrin's use objection. Answers **b.** and **d.** are less strong objections. Answer **b.** is false because Locke explicitly attempted to reconcile private property with the equality of individuals. Answer **d.** has some better prospects, but some, like Merges, would argue that the public domain is equivalent to the state of nature.

3. **Correct answer: c.** Some may be tempted to select answer **b**. This is only partially correct. Certainly, copyright is necessary to encourage authors to create original works. But the key to the utilitarian argument is that when we consider all the happiness created by these new works, and the unhappiness created by restrictions on access, copyright is necessary to satisfy the principle of utility.

Notes

1 John Locke, 'Memorandum on the Licensing Act 1662' reprinted in Lord King, *The Life of John Locke, with Extracts from his Correspondence, Journals and Common Place Books*, vol 1 (Henry Coldum & Richard Bently 1830) 376.

2 Ronan Deazley, *On the Origin of the Right to Copy: Charting the Movement of Copyright Law in Eighteenth Century Britain (1695–1775)* (Hart Publishing 2004) 1–29.

3 Daniel Defoe, 'A Review of the Affairs of France' (26 November 1709).

4 Mark Rose, *Authors and Owners: The Invention of Copyright* (Harvard UP 1993) 35.

5 Pamela Samuelson, 'Enriching Discourse on Public Domains' (2006) 55 Duke LJ 783.

6 (1769) 4 Burr 2303, 98 ER 201.

7 (1774) 2 Brown's Parl Cases (2d ed) 129, 1 ER 837; 4 Burr 2408, 98 ER 257; 17 Cobbett's Parl Hist 953.

8 Deazley (n 2); cf Tomas Gomez-Arostegui, 'Copyright at Common Law in 1774' (2014) 47 Conn L Rev 1.

9 Thomas Hobbes, *Leviathan* (1651) (McMaster University Archive of the History of Economic Thought) 78.

10 John Locke, *Two Treatises of Government* (1690) reprinted in *The Works of John Locke* (1823) para 119.

11 *Justifying Intellectual Property* (Harvard UP 2011) © Presidents and Fellows of Harvard College. Used by permission. All rights reserved.

12 Robert Nozick, *Anarchy, State, and Utopia* (Basic Books 1974) © 1974. Reprinted by permission of Basic Books, an imprint of Hachette Book Group, Inc.

13 Seana Valentine Shiffrin, 'Lockean Arguments for Private Intellectual Property' in Stephen R Munzer (ed), *New Essays in the Legal and Political Theory of Property* (CUP 2001) 138–58. Reproduced with permission.

14 Jeremy Bentham, 'A Critical Examination of the Declaration of Rights' in *The Works of Jeremy Bentham* (W Tait 1839) 500.

15 Jeremy Bentham, *An Introduction to Principles of Morals and Legislation* (1781).

16 Jeremy Bentham, *Fragments on Government* (1776).

17 US Constitution, art I, cl 8, s 8.

18 See Patrick R Goold and David A Simon, 'On Copyright Utilitarianism' (2024) Indiana L Rev (forthcoming).

19 Oren Bracha and Talha Syed, 'Beyond Efficiency: Consequences Sensitive Theories of Copyright' (2014) 29 Berkeley Tech LJ 229. Reproduced with permission of authors.

20 See Paul J Heald, *Copy This Book! What Data Tells Us about Copyright and the Public Good* (Stanford UP 2020).

21 See eg Christopher Buccafusco and Christopher Jon Sprigman, 'The Creativity Effect' (2011) U Chi L Rev 31.

22 Jessica Silbey, *The Eureka Myth: Creators, Innovators, and Everyday Intellectual Property* (Stanford UP 2015).

23 CREATe, Glasgow University, Copyright Evidence portal <https://www.copyrightevidence.org/> (accessed June 2023).

24 Mark A Lemley, 'Faith Based Intellectual Property' (2015) 62 UCLA L Rev 1328.

25 Stephen Breyer, 'The Uneasy Case for Copyright: A Study of Copyright in Books, Photocopies, and Computer Programs' (1970) 84 Harv L Rev 281. Permission conveyed through Copyright Clearance Center, Inc.

26 Henri Desbois *Le droit d'auteur en France* (Dalloz 1978) 438.

27 Justin Hughes, 'The Philosophy of Intellectual Property' (1988) 77 Georgetown LJ 330.

28 ibid.

29 Abraham Drassinower, *What's Wrong with Copying?* (Harvard UP 2015).

30 See Catherine Seville, *The Internationalisation of Copyright* (CUP 2006) 23.

31 Shiffrin (n 13) 138–67.

FIGURE ACKNOWLEDGEMENTS

2.1 Gutenberg printing the first page of the Bible, 1439. Johannes Gensfleisch zur Laden zum Gutenberg, *c.*1398–1468. German blacksmith, goldsmith, printer and publisher who introduced printing to Europe. After a nineteenth-century print. (Photo by: Universal History Archive/Universal Images Group via Getty Images)

2.2 HL/PO/PU/1/1709/8&9An32 – Public Act, 8 Anne, c 21. Reproduced with permission from the parchment copy in the UK Parliamentary Archives. Digital copy Statute of Anne, London (1710), *Primary Sources on Copyright (1450–1900)*, eds L Bently and M Kretschmer <www.copyrighthistory.org>

2.3 Actress Sarah Bernhardt portraying Hamlet. Credit: Bildagentur-online/Contributor (via Getty Images)

2.4 *The Pirate Publisher – An International Burlesque that Has the Longest Run on Record*, by Joseph Ferdinand Keppler, published as a centrefold in *Puck* (24 February 1886) 18(468). Library of Congress Prints and Photographs Division Washington, DC 20540 USA, reproduction number: LC-USZC4-6529.LC-DIG-ppmsca-28173 (digital file from original print). Restoration provided by Adam Cuerden (licensed under Creative Commons Attribution 3.0) <https://en.wikipedia.org/wiki/File:Joseph_Ferdinand_Keppler_-_The_Pirate_Publisher_-_Puck_Magazine_-_Restoration_by_Adam_Cuerden.jpg>

Marginal Fig. 2.1 Image reproduced with permission of the Stationers' Company

Marginal Fig. 2.2 John Locke, *c.*1680, English philosopher John Locke (1632–1704), known as the father of English empiricism. (Photo by Stock Montage/Getty Images)

Marginal Fig. 2.3 Portrait of Daniel Defoe. Engraving depicts a portrait of English novelist and journalist Daniel Defoe (1660–1731), late seventeenth/early eighteenth century. (Photo by Stock Montage/Getty Images)

Marginal Fig. 2.4 Murasaki Shikibu composing the *Tale of Genji* at Ishiyamadera, by Yashima Gakutei (1786–1868). Digital version from Wikimedia Commons <https://commons.wikimedia.org/wiki/File:Murasaki_Shikibu_composing_the_Tale_of_Genji_at_Ishiyamadera,_by_Yashima_Gakutei.jpg>

Marginal Fig. 2.5 Jeremy Bentham (1748–1832), an English philosopher, jurist and social reformer regarded as the founder of modern utilitarianism. (Photo by Bildagentur/Universal Images Group via Getty Images)

Marginal Fig. 2.6 Portrait of Georg Wilhelm Friedrich Hegel (1770–1831), 1831. Found in the Collection of Staatliche Museen, Berlin. (Photo by Fine Art Images/Heritage Images/Getty Images)

3

Copyright II: Subject Matter

Intellectual property (IP) scholars have long charted the evolution of copyright from a printer's privilege to an author's right. As historian Ronan Deazley puts it, the Statute of Anne 'was not concerned to secure rights of property to the author, but to regulate the marketplace of the bookseller and publisher'.[1] While the image of the author was used strategically by the Stationers to ensure the successful passage of the Statute of Anne, the modern idea of copyright as a property right in an author's work emerged more slowly. Together, Chapters 3–5 introduce the modern idea of copyright as a property in an author's original work.

The first aspect of copyright's historical transformation concerns subject matter. The Statute of Anne secured to printers the exclusive right to print books. It is probable that many lawyers at this time thought of books as tangible things; to those lawyers, a book was little more than ink on paper. But, by the nineteenth century, the subject matter of copyright began to change. Copyright became detached from the paper and ink, and instead protected something else entirely: the author's original **work**. You, for example, might own the paper copy of this book, but the publisher owns the words.

This evolution raises the metaphysical question introduced in Section 1.1.1. Are the words in a book 'things' that can be owned? If so, what other intangible things can be owned? Today, copyright protects a surprisingly long list of phenomena: from the street art of Banksy to the software of Microsoft. Moreover, that list is constantly expanding. Courts in the twenty-first century are besieged with requests by claimants who demand copyright in their flower arrangements, dance moves, the scent of their perfumes and even the taste of cheese. How far can that list possibly go?

The prevailing modern view is that original works are things that can be owned. But that has not always been the case. And, within that modern view, significant

This chapter contains public sector information licensed under the Open Government Licence v3.0.

disagreements remain. Anglo-American and continental European lawyers have not always agreed on what things should be owned. To explain, Section 3.1 first considers the twentieth century UK approach to copyrightable subject matter. The law in this period – which by and large remains good law – demonstrates the modern UK approach to copyrightable subject matter prior to significant European influence. Section 3.2 introduces European understandings of copyrightable subject matter, primarily as it exists today within the laws of the European Union. As part of the EU for many decades, UK law has had to evolve. That evolution continues despite the UK's departure from the EU in 2020.

3.1 TWENTIETH-CENTURY UK SUBJECT MATTER

Modern copyright law is no longer limited to books. Section 1 of the **Copyright, Designs and Patents Act 1988** (CDPA) states that:

> (1) Copyright is a property right which subsists in accordance with this Part in the following descriptions of work –
> (a) original literary, dramatic, musical or artistic works,
> (b) sound recordings, films or broadcasts, and
> (c) the typographical arrangement of published editions.

The section can be further subdivided into two parts. Subsection (a) lists what can be called 'original works'. Subsections (b) and (c) list what can be called 'non-original works' on the grounds that they do not require originality. The first part of this section considers the original works of subsection (a) before then briefly considering the non-original works of subsections (b) and (c).

3.1.1 Works

By labelling copyright a property right, section 1(1)(a) commits to a view that 'original, literary, dramatic, musical or artistic works' (LDMA) are things that can be owned. But what are 'original literary, dramatic, musical or artistic works'? This subsection unpacks the concept of a '**work**'. The next subsection considers what makes a work 'original'. The last subsection turns to the specific types of original works that enjoy protection in the UK (i.e. LDMA works).

The concept of a 'work' is enigmatic. While today UK courts think of works as a certain type of intangible thing, this was not always the case. Legal historians Lionel Bently and Brad Sherman argue that this feature of British IP law was an invention of the nineteenth century.[2] Copyright law of the eighteenth century, by contrast, understood the intangible phenomenon as an act, not a thing. An author's 'work' was not the resulting book, but the mental labour – the work – required to produce the book. This understanding has echoes today in the argument made by

Drassinower in Section 1.1. Importantly, that 'work' was not, prior to the nineteenth century, owned by anyone.

While the subject matter of the Statute of Anne was books, copyright gradually evolved. Over time, the subject matter of copyright became the work, and, simultaneously, the work became a thing – an object, a commodity – that could be owned. But what was the nature of that mysterious thing? Today, two possible answers to this question exist. The first answer – and, it is submitted, the better answer – is found in the next case. According to this view the 'work' is an intangible expressive form.

Case 3.1 *Donoghue v Allied Newspapers Limited* [1938] 1 Ch 106

Facts

Steven Donoghue (claimant) was a famous English jockey in the 1910s and 1920s. Allied Newspapers (defendants) published the *News of the World* newspaper. Mr Felstead was a reporter at *News of the World*. Felstead conducted a series of interviews with Donoghue about his life and racing career. With Donoghue's consent, Felstead then wrote articles about Donoghue's life which were published in the *News of the World*.

Subsequently, Felstead wanted to republish the articles in another newspaper called *Guide and Ideas*. Donoghue objected to the republication. Donoghue brought an action against Felstead's employer, Allied Newspapers for infringement of copyright.

Issue and Procedure

The question before Mr Justice Farwell in the Chancery Division was whether Donoghue had created something that could be owned. In the extract below, Mr Justice Farwell concludes that he had not. The only thing that Donoghue gave to Felstead, in Farwell's view, was a collection of anecdotes about his life and career. But no one can own mere 'ideas', Farwell concludes; one can only own the 'expression' of those ideas. While the case was decided under the Copyright Act 1911, the inapplicability of copyright to ideas lives on as a cornerstone of copyrightable subject matter.

FARWELL J

The first question that I have to determine is whether the plaintiff is or is not either the sole or the joint owner of the copyright in the original articles which appeared in the News of the World.

It is necessary, in considering whether the plaintiff is the owner or part owner of the copyright in this work, to see in what it is that

> copyright exists under the Copyright Act of 1911. This at any rate is clear beyond all question, that there is no copyright in an idea, or in ideas. A person may have a brilliant idea for a story, or for a picture, or for a play, and one which appears to him to be original; but if he communicates that idea to an author or an artist or a playwright, the production which is the result of the communication of the idea to the author or the artist or the playwright is the copyright of the person who has clothed the idea in form, whether by means of a picture, a play, or a book, and the owner of the idea has no rights in that product.
>
> The explanation of this is this, that in which copyright exists is the particular form of language by which the information which is to be conveyed is conveyed. If the idea, however original, is nothing more than an idea, and is not put into any form of words, or any form of expression such as a picture, then there is no such thing as copyright at all. It is not until it is (if I may put it in that way) reduced into writing or into some tangible form that there is any copyright, and the copyright exists in the particular form of language in which, or in the case of a picture the particular form of the picture by which, the information or the idea is conveyed to those who are intended to read it or to look at it.
>
> In the present case, the ideas of all these stories, apart altogether from what one may call merely the embellishments which were undoubtedly supplied wholly by Mr. Felstead – the ideas of all these stories, and in fact the stories themselves, were supplied by the plaintiff; but in my judgment, upon the evidence it is plain that the particular form of language by which those stories were conveyed was the language of Mr. Felstead and not of the plaintiff.
>
> (pp. 109–10)

A work, therefore, is not a mere idea. It is instead the expression of an idea. Mr Donoghue supplied Mr Felstead with ideas to use in the articles, but those ideas were not intellectual things, not works, that could be owned. The intellectual thing that copyright protects is the precise choice and sequence of words through which Mr Felstead expressed those ideas on the page. The thing that can be owned, therefore, is the intangible expressive form. This rule is now known as the **idea–expression distinction**.

One of the most difficult tasks in contemporary IP law is to divide unownable ideas from ownable expression. One American judge went as far as to say that wherever the line is drawn, it will almost certainly be arbitrary.[3] More recently, Lord Justice Lloyd in *Baigent v Random House* concluded that 'no clear principle' could separate the two phenomena;[4] although, in that particular case, he concluded that a book's 'central theme' was merely an idea. While some things are, by consensus, mere ideas – facts, plot lines, stock characters in fiction (like a gruff detective or a spy) – the tipping point between idea and expression remains elusive.

> ### ACTIVITY 3.1
>
> Think back to *Starry Night* (Figure 1.1) painted by Vincent van Gogh. This painting started with an idea: van Gogh wanted to paint the night sky. Copyright does not, however, allow van Gogh to own that mere idea; anyone is allowed to paint a night sky if they so wish. What copyright protects is the expression of that idea. What is the expression contained in *Starry Night*?

However, the answer that a work is the expression of an idea is not universally supported. The following extract comes from a Delhi High Court case in which Mr Justice Kirpal criticised the *Donoghue* decision.[5]

> Surely the intention of the Copyright Act cannot be to give the status of author only to the person in whose language the literary work is written while completely ignoring the person who contributed the underlying material which enabled that person to show his mastery over the language... A literary work consists of matter or material which is expressed in a language and is written down; both the subject matter and the language are important.

According to this alternative view, a 'work' is not merely expression. Instead, the 'work' is something behind the expression: an 'intangible essence' that is embodied within the expression.[6] It is submitted, however, that this view is intolerable. By permitting someone to own the 'underlying material' – the intangible essence – divorced from the expression, the law would merely allow ownership of ideas. By subjecting ideas – like the idea of painting a starry night – to private ownership, copyright risks severely limiting the creative freedom of future authors.

3.1.2 Original

Not all works enjoy the protection of copyright. The CDPA explains that only 'original' work can be owned. What then gives expression an 'original' nature? The House of Lords decision in *Walter v Lane* [1900] AC 539 sets the foundations for what is today known as the **originality** doctrine.

Copyright II: Subject Matter

Case 3.2 *Walter v Lane* [1900] AC 539

Facts

Between 1896 and 1898 Archibald Primrose, 5th Earl of Rosebery and former UK Prime Minister, delivered five public speeches. Reporters attended on behalf of *The Times* newspaper (claimants–appellants). The reporters for *The Times* made shorthand notes of the speeches, then subsequently wrote out their notes in fuller form complete with corrections, revisions and punctuation. The reports were subsequently published in *The Times*. Any copyright in the reporters' work was assigned to *The Times* under their employment contracts. In 1899, John Lane (defendant–respondent) copied the reports contained in *The Times* and published them in a book called *Appreciations and Addresses: Lord Rosebery*. Owner of *The Times*, Arthur Frasier Walter, sued Lane for copyright infringement.

Issue and Procedure

Were the reporters 'authors' of the news reports and thereby entitled to copyright under the Copyright Act 1842? At trial, Mr Justice North agreed with *The Times* and granted an injunction to restrain the publication of Lane's book.

The Court of Appeal agreed to rehear the case. At the trial, Lane was represented by two of the most famous copyright lawyers of the age: Augustine Birrell QC and Thomas Edward Scrutton. Together they argued that a reporter could not be an 'author' of the reports because, to be an author, there 'must be some originality' in their composition. The Court of Appeal was persuaded by their argument. In finding for Lane, Mr Justice Lindley MR decided that: 'No doubt it requires considerable education and ability to make a good report of any speech. But an accurate report is not an original composition, nor is the reporter of a speech the author of what he reports.'[7] The reporter's composition, they found, could not be original because the reporters had merely 'reproduced to the best of [their] ability not only the ideas expressed by the speaker, but the language in which the speaker expressed those ideas'.[8]

The Times appealed to the House of Lords. Each of the five justices wrote a separate judgment. Four of the five justices granted the appeal. The lone dissenter, Lord Robertson, agreed with the Court of Appeal. Because each judge wrote a separate opinion, the reasons provided by each judge are a bit different, but the extract below from Lord Davey's and Lord James of Hereford's judgments is representative of the reasoning. Subsequently, the Court of Appeal decision was reversed, and the House of Lords awarded *The Times* an injunction to restrain the publication of Lane's book.

Both Birrell and Scrutton spent time as professors at University College London where they published important books on copyright. These included Birrell, *The Law and History of Copyright in Books* (1899) and Scrutton, *The Law of Copyright* (1903).

DAVEY LJ

In my opinion the reporter is the author of his own report. He it was who brought into existence in the form of a writing the piece of letterpress which the respondent has copied. I think also that he and he alone composed his report. The materials for his composition were his notes, which were his own property, aided to some extent by his memory and trained judgment...

Copyright has nothing to do with the originality or literary merits of the author or composer. It may exist in the information given by a street directory: *Kelly v. Morris*; or by a list of deeds of arrangement: *Cate v. Devon and Exeter Constitutional Newspaper Co.*; or in a list of advertisements: *Lamb v. Evans*. I think those cases right, and the principle on which they proceed directly applicable to the present case. It was of course open to any other reporter to compose his own report of Lord Rosebery's speech, and to any other newspaper or book to publish that report; but it is a sound principle that a man shall not avail himself of another's skill, labour, and expense by copying the written product thereof.

(pp. 551–52)

JAMES OF HEREFORD LJ

A mere copyist of written matter is not an 'author' within the Act, but a translator from one language to another would be so. A person to whom words are dictated for the purpose of being written down is not an 'author.'

Now, what is it that a reporter does? Is he a mere scribe? Does he produce original matter or does he produce the something I have mentioned which entitles him to be regarded as an 'author' within the Act? I think that from a general point of view a reporter's art represents more than mere transcribing or writing from dictation.

(pp. 552–53)

The decision of *Walter v Lane* had a significant and somewhat unexpected effect on the originality doctrine. In one respect, it is not a case about originality at all. The case was litigated under the 1842 copyright law, wherein the word 'originality' did not appear. Lord Davey even went as far as to say 'copyright has nothing to do with originality'. And, yet, the case came retrospectively to embody the originality requirement. In the 1911 Copyright Act, Parliament stated that only 'original' work would be protected. In seeking to understand this new statutory term, courts sought answers in the *Walter v Lane* decision.

It came to be that a work was original if it displayed two cumulative factors. First, the work would be original if it were **not copied** from somewhere else. That is, the work had to 'originate from' the author. But, as both Lord Davey and Lord James of Hereford explain, something 'more' is also required. What is that something 'more'? In time, it came to be some combination of **skill, labour and/or judgement**. The following case illustrates.

The concept of 'origination' has not gone uncriticised. Some psychological literature claims that all creativity is a matter of copying from prior sources. To those who follow this view, the idea of origination is a 'meaningless concept'.[9]

Case 3.3 *Ladbroke (Football) Ltd v William Hill (Football) Ltd* [1964] 1 WLR 273

Facts

William Hill (Football) Ltd (claimants–respondents) were bookmakers (an agent who accepts and pays out on bets and wagers). Since 1951, William Hill had sent 'fixed odds football betting coupons' to their customers each week (an example of which is in Figure 3.1). A coupon was a sheet of paper on which were printed sixteen 'lists' of forthcoming matches. Beside each list were columns of squares on which the customer could indicate his prediction for the result of each match. The lists contained different types of bets. Sometimes the customer would win if they could predict the correct scores, sometimes they would win if they could predict correctly the total number of draws, etc. The odds (which determine the size of the customers' winnings) offered by the bookkeeper also differed across the lists (from as little as 5:2 up to 20,000:1).

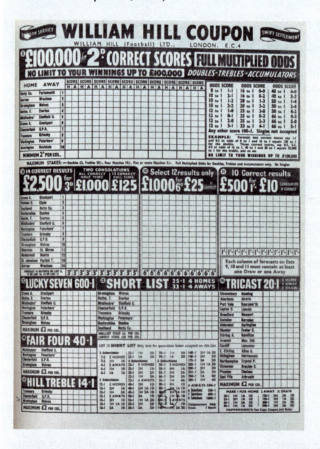

Figure 3.1 William Hill's betting coupon.
(Images reproduced with permission of the UK Parliamentary Archives)

Ladbrokes (Football) Ltd (defendants–appellants) were a rival bookmaker. In 1959, Ladbrokes started to send their customers similar fixed-odds betting coupons. These coupons closely resembled William Hill's coupons. Ladbrokes copied fifteen of the 16 lists from the William Hill coupon. The matches on which the customers could bet and the odds offered were different to those in the William Hill coupons, but the general arrangement of the lists and their headings was the same.

Issue and Procedure

Were the William Hill coupons 'original' literary works as required by the 1911 Copyright Act? The legislation had changed since the case of *Walter v Lane*. Section 2 of the 1911 Act stated for the first time that copyright existed only in 'original' works.

At first instance, Mr Justice Lloyd Jacob found that there was no copyright in the William Hills coupons because they were merely a 'commonplace arrangement of non-literary materials'. The Court of Appeal overturned the first instance judgment and Ladbrokes appealed. The case then proceeded to the House of Lords. The House of Lords found that the compilation of the lists qualified as a singular literary work. But the question remained: were they *original* literary works? Of course, it certainly was a lot of work for William Hill to decide which matches they would offer bets on, and at what odds, but these were merely uncopyrightable ideas. The question was whether the selection and arrangement of these bets was sufficiently 'original'. The House of Lords unanimously agreed they were. Appeal dismissed.

REID LJ

The appellants' main argument was based on quite a different ground. They deny that the respondents' coupon is an original compilation. There is no dispute about the meaning of the term 'original':

'The word "original" does not in this connexion mean that the work must be the expression of original or inventive thought. Copyright Acts are not concerned with the originality of ideas, but with the expression of thought, and, in the case of "literary work", with the expression of thought in print or writing. The originality which is required relates to the expression of the thought. But the Act does not require that the expression must be in an original or novel form, but that the work must not be copied from another work – that it should originate from the author.'

> *Per* Peterson J. in *University of London Press Ltd. v. University Tutorial Press Ltd.* And it is not disputed that, as regards compilation, originality is a matter of degree depending on the amount of skill, judgment or labour that has been involved in making the compilation.
>
> In the present case, if it is permissible to take into account all the skill, judgment and labour expended in producing the respondents' coupon, there can be no doubt that it is 'original'. But the appellants say that the coupon must be regarded as having been produced in two stages: first, the respondents had to decide what kind of business they would do – what kinds of bets they would offer to their clients – and then they had to write these out on paper. The appellants say that it is only the skill, judgment and labour involved in the latter stage that can be considered and that that part of their operation involved so little skill, judgment or labour that it cannot qualify as 'original'. In fact, the respondents did not proceed in that way. Their business was to devise a coupon which would appeal to the betting public, and its form and arrangement were not something dictated by previous decisions about the nature of the bets to be offered. The appellants likened the coupon to a trader's catalogue of his wares, and argued that in considering whether a catalogue is entitled to copyright you must disregard the trader's skill and work in deciding what wares he will stock for sale and only consider the skill and labour involved in the actual preparation of the catalogue. I do not think that that is a true analogy. And even in the case of a catalogue there may be a question whether the work, in deciding what to sell, and the work, in deciding how to sell it, are not so inter-connected as to be inseparable. Copyright in a catalogue in no way prevents honest competition – any other trader can decide to stock and sell any or all of the catalogued articles, and he can thereafter make a new catalogue of his own wares. What he must not do is simply to copy the other traders' catalogue.
>
> (pp. 277–78)

The skill, labour and/or judgement prong of the originality test was always somewhat imprecisely formulated. Sometimes courts referred to 'skill, labour *and* judgement', sometimes 'or' judgement, and sometimes omitting 'judgement' altogether.[10] Lord Davey in *Walter v Lane*, for example, refers to 'skill, labour, *and expense*'. Nevertheless, despite the linguistic vagaries, it was always clear that mere skill was insufficient to confer originality. As both Lord Davey and Lord James of Hereford explained, a mere copyist, like a clerk or transcriber, is not an 'author' of their composition although that copying may require significant skill.

ACTIVITY 3.2

In Activity 3.1, we separated the ideas and expression in *Starry Night*. But what, in the UK sense, made that expression 'original'?

Lastly, although the thing that is owned is an intangible expressive form, section 3(2) of the CDPA requires that those expressive forms be 'recorded, in writing or otherwise'. This is known as a **fixation** requirement. As a result, it was only when Mr Felstead committed his expression to paper, that he became a copyright owner. Had he, hypothetically, spoken the same words aloud without writing them down, he would own nothing at all. The result is a paradoxical one where the thing that is owned is the intangible expression, but that intangible thing is only owned once it has been locked down in some tangible medium.

> Curiously, the fixation requirement in UK law applies to literary, musical and dramatic works, but not artistic works.

In summary, what was 'traditional' UK copyright subject matter? It was a particular type of thing: the intangible expressive form produced by an author, not through copying, but through their skill, labour and/or judgement. As a practical matter, that thing only became protected, however, once it became fixed in a tangible form.

That understanding of copyrightable subject matter has in the twenty-first century evolved in large part due to external pressures. Section 3.2 introduces an alternative conception of copyrightable subject matter developed in continental Europe that forms the basis of EU copyright law. However, the fundamental metaphysical view of original work as a thing – capable of being owned, bought and sold just like any other property – remains.

3.1.3 A Closed List

Having concluded that original works are things, the next question is what original works can be owned through copyright? One of the unique features of twentieth-century UK copyright law is that it restricted copyright to only certain types of original work. The law granted property rights in original literary, dramatic, musical or artistic (LDMA) works, but not other types of work. While these categories remain significantly open-ended, section 1 provides what is known as a 'closed list'.[11] If, for example, a gardener creates a beautiful flower arrangement, it will only be protected if it can fall within the meaning of one of these statutorily identified phenomena. This, as we will see in Section 3.2 provides a major cleavage between traditional UK and contemporary EU copyright.

The question this leaves unresolved is what is special about LDMA work? If original works are things, then what make these particular things 'intellectual' in a way that warrants the label 'intellectual property'? As explained shortly, some things that arguably are 'original works' in the UK sense nevertheless do not enjoy copyright protection. After outlining the cases, this section provides some brief thoughts on this question.

3.1.3.1 LITERARY

Section 1(a) extends protection to all 'literary' works. But what is a literary work? The sonnets of Shakespeare clearly qualify, as do the *Harry Potter* novels. But what about more mundane things: bus timetables, shopping lists, Ikea flat-pack furniture instruction manuals? Are these latter things 'literary works'? Or are they insufficiently 'literary' in some important way?

In the following two foundational cases, UK courts adopted a principle of **aesthetic neutrality**. That is, courts do not consider the literary merit of the work. Together, these decisions paved the way for a modern approach in which nearly anything written down becomes IP.

Case 3.4 *University of London Press, Limited v University Tutorial Press, Limited* [1916] 2 Ch 601

Facts

Examiners at the University of London Press (claimant) wrote mathematics exam papers (Figure 3.2). The University Tutorial Press company (defendant) later published a book of mathematics exam questions. The University Tutorial Press company's book included questions originally contained in the University of London Press exam papers. The University of London Press asserted copyright in the examination papers and sued the University Tutorial Press for copyright infringement.

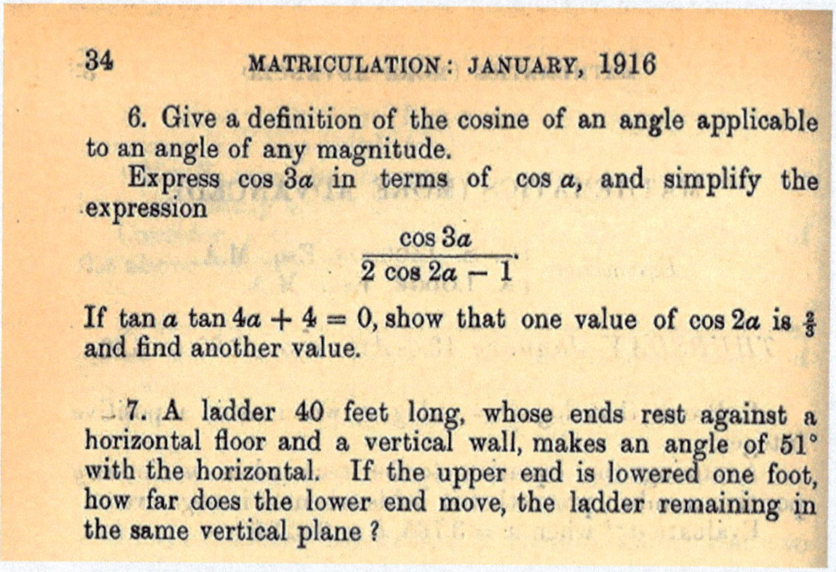

> 34   MATRICULATION: JANUARY, 1916
>
> 6. Give a definition of the cosine of an angle applicable to an angle of any magnitude.
>
> Express $\cos 3a$ in terms of $\cos a$, and simplify the expression
> $$\frac{\cos 3a}{2\cos 2a - 1}.$$
>
> If $\tan a \tan 4a + 4 = 0$, show that one value of $\cos 2a$ is $\frac{2}{3}$ and find another value.
>
> 7. A ladder 40 feet long, whose ends rest against a horizontal floor and a vertical wall, makes an angle of 51° with the horizontal. If the upper end is lowered one foot, how far does the lower end move, the ladder remaining in the same vertical plane?

Figure 3.2 An extract from University of London's exam papers.

(Image reproduced with permission of Senate House Library, University of London)

Issue and Procedure

Are mathematics examination papers 'literary' works? Or do they lack some necessary literary merit? The case was litigated under a predecessor to the CDPA 1988, the Copyright Act 1911. In the following extract, Mr Justice Peterson argues that examination papers are literary works.

PETERSON J

Although a literary work is not defined in the Act, s. 35 states what the phrase includes; the definition is not a completely comprehensive one, but the section is intended to show what, amongst other things, is included in the description 'literary work', and the words are '"Literary work" includes maps, charts, plans, tables, and compilations'. It may be difficult to define 'literary work' as used in this Act, but it seems to be plain that it is not confined to 'literary work' in the sense in which that phrase is applied, for instance, to Meredith's novels and the writings of Robert Louis Stevenson. In speaking of such writings as literary works, one thinks of the quality, the style, and the literary finish which they exhibit. Under the Act of 1842, which protected 'books', many things which had no pretensions to literary style acquired copyright; for example, a list of registered bills of sale, a list of foxhounds and hunting days, and trade catalogues; and I see no ground for coming to the conclusion that the present Act was intended to curtail the rights of authors. In my view the words 'literary work' cover work which is expressed in print or writing, irrespective of the question whether the quality or style is high. The word 'literary' seems to be used in a sense somewhat similar to the use of the word 'literature' in political or electioneering literature and refers to written or printed matter. Papers set by examiners are, in my opinion, 'literary work' within the meaning of the present Act.

(p. 608)

Case 3.5 *Exxon Corporation and others v Exxon Insurance Consultants International Ltd* [1982] Ch 119

Facts

The Exxon Corporation (claimants–appellants) sell oil and gas. Exxon claimed copyright in an invented word, 'Exxon', which formed part of their corporate name.

The claimants created this word after a long and expensive period of market research. They sought an injunction to restrain Exxon Insurance Consultants International (defendants–respondents) from using the name in connection with their business.

Issue and Procedure

Can a single word be a 'literary work'? The case was litigated under a predecessor to the CDPA 1988, the Copyright Act 1956. At first instance, Mr Justice Graham held that the word did not qualify for copyright protection. The decision was upheld on appeal, as Lord Justice Stephenson's judgment below explains. Appeal dismissed.

Although the claimant lost their copyright battle, they still received an injunction on the grounds of 'passing off'. We will cover this action in Chapter 15.

STEPHENSON LJ

The only help from the authorities which I have found is the judgment of Mr. Justice Peterson in the University of London Press case, which [Graham J] cited...

It is, however, certain that this is the first time, as far as the researches of counsel go, that any court has been asked to hold that there could be copyright in a single invented word or name... [Graham J] felt that this claim raised a matter which might affect the public interest adversely in other cases and, as he said, it might be far-reaching in its consequences if granted ...

I find rather more assistance in the last case to which Mr. Mummery referred us; in particular, the observations of Lord Justice Davey in that case of Hollinrake v. Truswell, (1894) 3 Chancery Division, 420. That case was concerned with copyright in a cardboard pattern sleeve with scales and figures and descriptive words upon it. In his judgment Lord Justice Davey said this: 'The preamble of the Act' – that was referring to the 1842 Act, of course – 'recites that it is expedient "to afford greater encouragement to the production of literary works of lasting benefit to the world"...Now, a literary work is intended to afford either information and instruction, or pleasure, in the form of literary enjoyment. The sleeve chart before us gives no information or instruction.'

Mr. Price [Counsel for Exxon Corporation] has not convinced me that this word 'Exxon' was intended to do, or does do, either of those things; nor has he convinced me that it is not of the essence of a literary work that it should do one of those things.

(pp. 140, 142–43)

You might think the word 'Exxon' does give some information. It informs the customer about where their oil is coming from (i.e. the Exxon Corporation). We will consider this argument in more detail in Part IV.

The principle of aesthetic neutrality as outlined in the two cases is significant. Together Peterson J and Stephenson LJ argue that nearly anything in print or writing will be a literary work and thus capable of ownership, providing they meet the minimal requirement of providing information, instruction or pleasure to a human audience. Under this broad approach, bus timetables, shopping lists, Ikea furniture instruction manuals are all clearly literary works.

The legacy of aesthetic neutrality continues today in the CDPA. The consequence of the two foundational cases is that a bewilderingly large list of phenomena can be understood as literary works. Section 3(1) of the CDPA elaborates:

> (1) In this Part –
> 'literary work' means any work, other than a dramatic or musical work, which is written, spoken or sung, and accordingly includes –
> (a) a table or compilation other than a database,
> (b) a computer program,
> (c) preparatory design material for a computer program and
> (d) a database;

Perhaps the most interesting additions within this clause are computer programs and databases. Databases include Excel spreadsheets filled with data. The term 'computer program' not only includes source code that humans write, but also object code – that is the strings of 1s and 0s of binary code.

3.1.3.2 DRAMATIC

The CDPA does not define the term 'dramatic' works, but it does say that it 'includes a work of dance or mime' (section 3(1)(d)). As a practical matter, this category applies to scripts for films or plays and choreographic works.

But why have a category of dramatic works at all? Surely scripts would qualify as literary works under the broad definition courts have given that category? The answer is to be found in history.[12] In the nineteenth century, literary works were protected by copyright and allowed the author to prevent others from reproducing the work. But what happened if a defendant did not reproduce a script, but instead *performed* it in a theatre without the playwright's permission? The script was not reproduced so presumably there was no copyright infringement, one might argue. The inadequacy of protection resulted in playwrights claiming that their works were different from literary works and that they needed a different type of protection. The result was the Dramatic Literary Copyright Act 1833.

The idea of a 'dramatic' work expanded during the twentieth century. As the Court of Appeal later explained, dramatic works are all 'works of action' that are 'capable of being performed'.[13] Although, as the next case demonstrates, there is arguably something more to dramatic work than merely being capable of performance.

Copyright II: Subject Matter

Case 3.6 *Green v Broadcasting Corp of New Zealand* [1989] RPC 700

Facts

The case concerned the TV game show *Opportunity Knocks*. In that case, Hughie Green, the show's creator and presenter, claimed the show had an original 'dramatic format'. As a live game show with contestants, the show was not entirely scripted. However, the show did have characteristic features that were repeated every episode, such as the use of the title ('Opportunity Knocks'), the presenter's catchphrases (e.g. 'for you [contestant's name], opportunity knocks') and the use of a device called a 'clapometer' to gauge the audience's reaction to a contestant's performance. When the Broadcasting Corporation of New Zealand aired a similar talent show, Hughie Green sued alleging he owned the 'dramatic format' of the show.

Issue and Procedure

The question was whether the dramatic format was a dramatic work. The Privy Council found that it was not.

BRIDGE OF HARWICH LJ

It is stretching the original use of the word 'format' a long way to use it metaphorically to describe the features of a television series such as a talent, quiz or game show which is presented in a particular way, with repeated but unconnected use of set phrases and with the aid of particular accessories. Alternative terms suggested in the course of argument were 'structure' or 'package'. This difficulty in finding an appropriate term to describe the nature of the 'work' in which the copyright subsists reflects the difficulty of the concept that a number of allegedly distinctive features of a television series can be isolated from the changing material presented in each separate performance (the acts of the performers in the talent show, the questions and answers in the quiz show etc.) and identified as an 'original dramatic work'. No case was cited to their Lordships in which copyright of the kind claimed had been established. The protection which copyright gives creates a monopoly and 'there must be certainty in the subject matter of such monopoly in order to avoid injustice to the rest of the world': Tare v. Fulbrook [1908] 1 K.B. 821, per Farwell 1. at page 832. The subject matter of the copyright claimed for the 'dramatic format' of 'Opportunity Knocks' is conspicuously lacking in certainty.

> Moreover, it seems to their Lordships that a dramatic work must have sufficient unity to be capable of performance and that the features claimed as constituting the 'format' of a television show, being unrelated to each other except as accessories to be used in the presentation of some other dramatic or musical performance, lack that essential characteristic.
>
> (p. 702)

3.1.3.3 MUSICAL

Eighteenth-century courts held that sheet music qualified as a type of written material, and thus enjoyed protection against copying under the Statute of Anne.[14] Since the 1911 Copyright Act, however, copyright has treated musical work as distinct from literary works. The modern CDPA understands music as a work 'consisting of music, exclusive of any words or actions intended to be sung, spoken or performed with the music' (section 3(1)(d)). But this definition does not tell us much about what 'music' is. One question often posed for copyright lawyers is whether 'silence' can be music. Cheng Lim Saw introduces that question in Box 3.1.

Contemporary pop songs typically involve three separate types of copyrightable work: the music (a musical work), the lyrics (a literary work) and the recording made of the previous works (a sound recording). Here we are only considering the musical work.

BOX 3.1 CHENG LIM SAW, 'PROTECTING THE SOUND OF SILENCE IN 4'33: A TIMELY REVISIT OF BASIC PRINCIPLES IN COPYRIGHT LAW' (2005) 27 EIPR 467–76

What does one understand by the word 'silence'?[15] Is it at all possible for one to personally experience absolute silence? Is there silence in music? Can a piece of music be wholly composed of silence? The American composer John Cage (1912–1992) purported to have the answers to these questions and in wanting to share his philosophical curiosity with the rest of the world, he left behind, what some claim to be an icon of twentieth century avant-garde music, the infamous '4 minutes, 33 seconds' (hereinafter 4'33).

John Cage is perhaps best known for his 'silent' composition entitled 4'33. Written in the year 1952 in three distinct movements, 4'33 requires the performer to remain absolutely silent at his instrument for, literally, 4 minutes and 33 seconds. The 'music', if any, will comprise the natural sounds of the environment and man-made sounds from the audience (in reacting to such a performance before them). This sort of 'music' is also known as experimental or

> indeterminate music, in which the composer and/or performer cannot foresee the greater part of the result of a performance, which essentially comprises unintended or unintentional sounds.
>
> In February 2002, an eight-member classical group, The Planets (formed by a British composer and songwriter named Mike Batt), released a music album entitled *Classical Graffiti* which, on track number 13, contained no music at all – instead, it comprised 'a one-minute silence' (which is, incidentally, the name of the track). Batt explained that this particular track, which is credited to 'Batt/ Cage', was not intended to be taken seriously but only as a space-filler.
>
> (p. 467)

At the time, it was reported that Cage's estate brought a copyright infringement action against Batt. Subsequently, it was revealed this was not true.[16] However, the question of whether silence is music is far from moot. Case 3.7 gestures towards some answers.

Case 3.7 *Sawkins v Hyperion Records Ltd* [2005] EWCA Civ 565

Facts

Michel Richard de Lalande (1657–1726) was a French Baroque composer. Some of his most famous musical compositions were his 'grand motets' – Latin hymns set to music. De Lalande's grand motets were called *Te Deum Laudamus*, *Sacris Solemniis*, *Venite Exultemus* and *La Grande Pièce Royale*. Because of their age, these musical compositions are no longer protected by copyright. Figure 3.3 demonstrates a section of *Te Deum Laudamus* written by de Lalande in approximately 1684. Modern musicians cannot easily perform this music today. De Lalande's original scores are written in an old form of musical notation that often omits important information (for example tempo) that contemporary musicians would expect.

Dr Lionel Sawkins (claimant–respondent) was an eminent musical scholar. He spent many years researching the work of de Lalande. In 2001, Sawkins published a collection of 'performing editions' of de Lalande's grand motets. These 'performing editions' were created to make de Lalande's original musical works performable by modern musicians. Sawkins spent about 300 hours on each of the four grand motets, in which he modernised the notation. During this time he also corrected wrong notes, recreated a missing viola part and added a figured bass line.

3.1 Twentieth Century UK Subject Matter

Figure 3.3 Original de Lalande *Te Deum Laudamus* score (1684). *(Reproduced with permission of Musiceano.com)*

Hyperion Records (defendant–appellant) was a small recording company that specialised in recording neglected works. In October 2002, Hyperion produced a CD featuring performances of the grand motets. The musicians used Sawkins's performing editions on the CD. While Hyperion paid Sawkins a flat fee to use his editions, they refused to pay him royalties. Sawkins sued for copyright infringement.

Issue and Procedure

Do 'performing editions' qualify as 'musical works' under the CDPA? The grand motets produced by de Lalande certainly would be 'musical works' but they were created long before the Statute of Anne and were therefore automatically in the public domain. In producing versions that could be performed by modern musicians, had Sawkins created some original musical work? At trial, Mr Justice Patten held that the performing editions were musical works and Hyperion had infringed Sawkins's copyright. Hyperion appealed to the Court of Appeal. Appeal dismissed.

A flat fee is a one-off payment. **Royalties** are ongoing payments for every use of the work.

MUMMERY LJ

The defendant's principal objection is that a performing edition does not amount to 'a new and substantive musical work in itself'. The edition does not, it submits, make an impact on the sound over and above that belonging to de Lalande's musical work. The critical question is whether the effort spent by the claimant resulted in a new musical work. On the 'sound test' approach the claimant's editing work on the texts had not made any significant relevant contribution to the musical content (i.e. sound) of de Lalande's original music. For example, transcription from one form of notation to another in the marked up scores was only a matter of the form of presentation of the original work. It did not result in the creation of a new musical work: all the notes and harmonies of the original work were retained. It was no different from the case of a person making a copy of another's work (such as the copy of a painting or the enlargement of a photograph): the process might call for effort, skill and judgment, but it did not transform a copy of a work into an original work attracting a fresh copyright...

In my judgment, the fallacies in the defendant's argument [is that]...they only treat the actual notes in the score as music...

In the absence of a special statutory definition of music, ordinary usage assists: as indicated in the dictionaries, the essence of music is combining sounds for listening to. Music is not the same as mere noise. The sound of music is intended to produce effects of some kind on the listener's emotions and intellect. The sounds may be produced by an organised performance on instruments played from a musical score, though that is not essential for the existence of the music or of copyright in it.

In principle, there is no reason for regarding the actual notes of music as the *only* matter covered by musical copyright, any more than, in the case of a dramatic work, only the words to be spoken by the actors are covered by dramatic copyright. Added stage directions may affect the performance of the play on the stage or on the screen and have an impact on the performance seen by the audience. Stage directions are as much part of a dramatic work as plot, character and dialogue.

It is wrong in principle to single out the notes as uniquely significant for copyright purposes and to proceed to deny copyright to the other elements that make some contribution to the sound of the music when performed, such as performing indications, tempo and performance practice indicators.

(paras 38, 49, 53, 55–56)

A 'fallacy' is either an untrue premise or an invalid inference (see Section 1.2). Here, Mumery LJ thinks the premise that only notes are musical works is false.

What this judgment means for Cage's 4'33 remains a matter of debate, depending on whether one views 4'33 as 'mere noise' as something 'intended to produce effects of some kind on the listener's emotions and intellect'.

3.1.3.4 ARTISTIC

Much like the category of dramatic works, artistic works became copyrightable subject matter in the UK in the nineteenth century. In 1862 Parliament passed the Fine Arts Copyright Act after lobbying efforts of the Society of Arts and thereby extended copyright to 'paintings, drawings, and photographs'. Today's CDPA defines artistic works in section 4 more broadly:

> (1) In this Part –
> 'artistic work' means –
> (a) a graphic work, photograph, sculpture or collage, irrespective of artistic quality,
> (b) a work of architecture being a building or a model for a building, or
> (c) a work of artistic craftsmanship.

As with literary works, there is broad consensus that some things are 'artistic works', e.g. Van Gogh's *Starry Night* or the sculptures of Picasso. But at the outer edges, problems emerge. What is the difference between, for example, a pile of bricks in a building site, and a pile of bricks in a gallery like the Tate Modern? Why is one 'art' and the other not? Why is the former 'intellectual' property, and the other only tangible property? Some possible answers are found in Case 3.8.

Case 3.8 *Creation Records Limited and others v News Group Newspapers Ltd* [1997] EMLR 444

Facts

In 1997, the Britpop group, Oasis, made the cover art for their forthcoming album, *Be Here Now*. The members of the band created a scene in front of a hotel. The scene consisted of a white Rolls-Royce car positioned in the swimming pool of the hotel together with various other objects scattered around (Figure 3.4). Reporters photographed the scene without the consent of the band members and published them in *The Sun* newspaper.

Noel Gallagher (lead guitarist and deviser of the scene) and Creation Records (licensed to distribute the album) (claimants) sued News Group Newspapers (owners of *The Sun*) (defendants) for copyright infringement.

Issue and Procedure

Was the 'scene' an 'artistic work'? The claimants tried many different arguments during the trial. They alleged that the scene was a 'sculpture' but this was rejected on the grounds that the band had not *sculpted* the work. They alleged that the scene was a work of 'artistic craftsmanship'. This too was rejected on the grounds that there was no element of 'craftsmanship' involved. Lastly, they alleged the scene was a 'collage'. But this too was rejected for the reasons given below by Mr Justice Lloyd. Ultimately, Mr Justice Lloyd did grant an injunction, but based on breach of confidence rather than copyright.

Figure 3.4 Oasis's *Be Here Now* cover art.
(© Michael Spencer Jones)

Works of 'artistic craftsmanship' are another one of copyright's enigmas. The category generally includes things such as handcrafted jewellery or pottery. In *Hensher v Restawile*, the House of Lords decided that a mass-market chair was a work of craftsmanship, but was insufficiently *artistic*. Only Simon L, cited here by Lloyd J, decided the chair was not a work of craftsmanship.

LLOYD J

Mr Merriman [counsel for the claimant] argued that it was an artistic work, as a sculpture or collage within section 4(1)(a) of the Copyright, Designs and Patents Act 1988 or a work of artistic craftsmanship within section 4(1)(c) of that Act.

I do not regard this as seriously arguable. I do not see how the process of assembling these disparate objects together with the members of the group can be regarded as having anything in common with sculpture or with artistic craftsmanship. No element in the composition has been carved, modelled or made in any of the other ways in which sculpture is made (see Breville (Europe) Plc v. Thorn EMI Domestic Appliances Ltd [1995] F.S.R. 77 at 94). Nor does it seem to me to be the subject or result of the exercise of any craftsmanship (see

3.1 *Twentieth Century UK Subject Matter* **71**

George Hensher Ltd v. Restawile Upholstery (Lancs) Ltd [1976] A.C. 64, especially Lord Simon at 91).

Mr Merriman submits that it is at least seriously arguable that the composition which Mr Gallagher put together as the subject of the photography is within the definition of collage in this sense, even though it did not involve the use of any adhesive. More generally, he submitted that this composition is the result of the exercise of artistic creativity and originality and that at a time when the creativity of visual artists is finding outlets in a great variety of novel forms the 1988 Act should not be construed so as to deny such novel works of art the possibility of copyright protection as artistic works within section 4. He asked forensically how it might be found that copyright subsisted in Carl Andre's bricks, in stone circles created by Richard Long, in Rachel Whiteread's house, in the living sculptures of Gilbert and George and in examples of installation art generally. I do not find it necessary or appropriate to answer that question. I would distinguish Mr Gallagher's composition from all of those examples as being put together solely to be the subject matter of a number of photographs and disassembled as soon as those were taken. This composition was intrinsically ephemeral, or indeed less than ephemeral, in the original sense of that word of living only for one day. This existed for a few hours on the ground. Its continued existence was to be in the form of a photographic image. Accordingly, it seems to me materially different from all the particular examples put to me in this context by Mr Merriman.

Even if it were otherwise, I would not accept that it is seriously arguable that this composition is a collage. In my view a collage does indeed involve as an essential element the sticking of two or more things together. It does not suffice to point to the collocation, whether or not with artistic intent, of such random, unrelated and unfixed elements as is seen in the photographs in question.

(pp. 448–50)

The judgment hints towards certain characteristics that might make a work artistic: the presence of an artistic intent, some sort of permanence or lack of 'ephemeralness', some sort of unity connecting the various elements. Some of these qualities are echoed in other cases too. For example, the earlier case of *Merchandising Corporation v Harpbond* denied copyright to face paints on the grounds that a painting must have a surface, and a human person is not a surface.[17]

Another possible characteristic of an artistic work is that art is non-functional. The difference between a pile of bricks in the building site, and the pile of bricks in the gallery, is that the former has some intended functional purpose: perhaps, for example, the builder is storing them ready to be used in construction. By contrast, the bricks in the gallery have no function other than to be art. Case 3.9 illustrates.

Case 3.9 *Lucasfilm Ltd and others v Ainsworth and another* [2011] UKSC 39

Facts

In 1977, Lucasfilm (claimant–appellant) published the science fiction film, *Star Wars* (later known as *Star Wars: Episode IV – A New Hope*). The film contains characters called 'stormtroopers'. In the film, stormtroopers are soldiers who wear helmets and armour. Under contract, Mr Ainsworth (defendant–respondent), working in England, created and made the helmets (see Figure 3.5) for use as part of the film.

Figure 3.5 Original stormtrooper helmet.
(Photo by Unique Nicole/Getty Images)

In 2004, Mr Ainsworth began selling stormtrooper helmets. Using his original equipment from the 1970s, Ainsworth produced exact replicas of the original stormtrooper helmets. Lucasfilm sued Ainsworth for copyright infringement arguing that the helmet was a 'sculpture' under the CDPA.

Issue and Procedure

We will return to the *Lucasfilm* case in Section 11.4.1. For, as we will see, another reason for denying copyright protection was to prevent Lucasfilm from enjoying both copyright and design rights in the helmet.

Does a stormtrooper helmet qualify as a sculpture – a type of artistic work – under the CDPA? Mr Ainsworth argued that the helmet was not artistic in nature and instead was merely a functional item. Mr Justice Mann, at first instance, agreed with Mr Ainsworth. Mr Justice Mann decided that the helmet's 'primary function' was 'to be worn as an item of costume in a film, to identify a character, [and] to portray something about the character'. This judgment was upheld by the Court of Appeal where Lord Justice Jacob held that the helmet had a function 'within the confines of the film'. In the following extract, Lord Walker and Lord Collins of the Supreme Court also upheld the first instance decision. Appeal dismissed.

WALKER AND COLLINS LJJ

[T]he appellants contend that the helmet had no practical function at all. Their case is that it is sculpture because its purpose is wholly artistic. Para 7 of their printed case puts it in these terms:

'In the present case, the question of functionality does not arise, because the articles in question have no functional purpose whatever. The Stormtroopers' helmets and armour did not exist in order to keep their wearers warm or decent or to protect them from injury in an inter-planetary war. Their sole purpose was to make a visual impression on the filmgoer. They are therefore artistic works.'

. . .

In this Court the appellants have challenged the reasoning of the judge and the Court of Appeal. Mr Sumption QC said that it was eccentric of the judge to describe the helmet's purpose as utilitarian, and that the Court of Appeal could find it to have a functional purpose only by treating it as having the same functional purpose as a real helmet 'within the confines of a film'.

This is quite a puzzling point. The Star Wars films are set in an imaginary, science-fiction world of the future. War films set in the past (Paths of Glory, for instance, depicting the French army in the first world war, or Atonement depicting the British Expeditionary Force at Dunkirk) are at least based on historical realities. The actors and extras in the trenches or on the beaches may be wearing real steel helmets, or (because real steel helmets of the correct style are unobtainable in sufficient numbers) they may be wearing plastic helmets painted khaki. In either case the helmets are there as (in the judge's words) 'a mixture of costume and prop' in order to contribute to the artistic effect of the film as a film. They are part of a production process, as Laddie J said in *Metix* at p 721, citing Whitford J in *Davis (J & S) (Holdings) Ltd v Wright Health Group Ltd* [1988] RPC 403, 410–412. In this case the production process was the making of a full-length feature film.

It would not accord with the normal use of language to apply the term 'sculpture' to a 20th century military helmet used in the making of a film, whether it was the real thing or a replica made in different material, however great its contribution to the artistic effect of the finished film. The argument for applying the term to an Imperial Stormtrooper helmet is stronger, because of the imagination that went into the concept of the sinister cloned soldiers dressed in uniform white armour. But it was the Star Wars film that was the

> work of art that Mr Lucas and his companies created. The helmet was utilitarian in the sense that it was an element in the process of production of the film.
>
> (paras 39, 42–44)

3.1.3.5 LDMA AS A GROUP

Armed with an overview of the cases, return to the question posed at the start of the section: what is special about LDMA work? Arguably other intangible things, like the Oasis *Be Here Now* scene, or the *Star Wars* helmet, qualify as 'original works' in the old British sense – they have some expressive form; that expressive form is **not copied** and requires some combination of **skill, labour and judgement**. And yet, they do not enjoy copyright protection. Meanwhile, things like Sawkins's performing editions and William Hill's betting coupons, do. Why should the latter, but not the former, become property?

There are many non-answers to this question. The answer certainly cannot be found in the phenomenon of all being of a certain quality or merit, as this runs against a clear principle of aesthetic neutrality. Instead, therefore, when applying the individual categories, courts appeal to other metaphysical qualities for guidance, such as their unity (*Green*), their functionality (*Lucasfilms*), the presence or absence of the relevant intention (*Creation Records*) etc. But none of these qualities connect the entire group. While functional artistic works do not enjoy protection, what are arguably functional literary works, like bus timetables or betting coupons, do enjoy protection. Meanwhile certain works, like the storm-trooper helmet were arguably created with artistic intention, and yet do not qualify for protection.

Nevertheless, there might be one metaphysical quality that connects them all. They are all non-excludable public goods (as explained in Section 1.1.3). As such they can all be easily copied. At different points in history, Parliament has been persuaded by various normative arguments (explained in Section 2.2) to grant property therein. If, however, this is what connects the category, it might suggest courts should interpret section 1(1)(a) with less reference to the metaphysical qualities of the phenomena beyond their non-excludability, and more reference to the normative values underlying the law. The chapter returns to this point in Activity 3.4.

3.1.4 Non-Original 'Works'

A final unique feature of UK copyrightable subject matter is that copyright is provided intangible things that are neither 'works' nor 'original' in the sense explained in the prior subsections. Subsections (b) and (c) creates property rights in:

- Sound recordings: for example, an MP3 file or some other tangible medium which captures sound.
- Films: for example, an MOV file or some other tangible medium which captures motion.
- Broadcasts: defined as the 'electronic transmission of visual images, sounds or information'.
- Typographical arrangements: including for example a newspaper composed of several articles.

In one sense, these phenomena share little in common with those listed in subsection (a). They are not works in the sense of an intangible expressive form. Indeed, some categories border into tangible property law as they protect not sound nor motion, but the recording thereof. Nor need they be 'original'. The legislation requires they be 'not copied' but their protection does not hinge on the skill, labour and judgement required to produce them.

On the other hand, they do share one important feature with the categories of original work. Much like the argument made in Section 3.1.3.5, they are all non-excludable public goods that, at times, Parliament has granted protection to in response to normative arguments.

3.2   EUROPEAN INFLUENCES

In 2001, the European Union enacted one of its central pieces of copyright legislation: the Information Society Directive.[18] Articles 2–4 of that Directive grants copyright protection to 'authors, for their works'. The preamble (recital 7) to the Directive labels IP as 'an integral part of property'.

Although contemporary EU law understands works as things that can be owned, continental European countries have not always agreed with that metaphysical theory. Laurent Pfister describes how the *Ancien Régime* of France from 1500 to the French Revolution predominantly understood the work as an act of speech, not a thing that could be owned.[19] Kant in Germany made the same argument, although it gained little traction.[20]

Despite these broad similarities with modern UK copyright subject matter, important differences remain. As this section explores, contemporary EU jurisprudence parts company from old UK law on the nature of an 'original' work, on which type of original works should receive protection and regarding whether non-original works should be protected by copyright.

As part of the EU for many decades, the Information Society Directive, as well as other copyright directives, and the associated case law of the Court of Justice of the European Union (CJEU), was binding law in the UK. The result is that over the past twenty years, the British conception of copyrightable subject matter has had to evolve. In many respects, that evolutionary process has not completed, despite the UK's withdrawal from the EU in 2020.

3.2.1 Original Works

What is an 'original work'? Section 3.1 highlighted the British idea that a work is an intangible expressive form produced not through copying, but through some combination of skill, labour and judgement. The section demonstrated how, in UK law, the ideas of 'work' and 'originality' come apart: there can be non-original works (like sound recordings and films), and there can also be original non-works (like *Star Wars* helmets).

While contemporary EU law also understands the work as an intangible expressive form, the 'work' and 'originality' concepts are inseparably fused together. To be a work, it must be original, among other things, as Case 3.10 demonstrates.

Case 3.10 *Levola Hengelo BV v Smilde Foods BV*, Case C-310/17, EU:C:2018:899

Facts

Heksenkaas is a spreadable dip containing cream cheese and fresh herbs created in 2007 by a Dutch retailer. The Dutch retailer assigned their IP rights in the cheese to Levola (claimant) in 2011. Smilde Foods (defendants) subsequently sold a product called Witte Wievenkaas in the Netherlands. Levola believed that the actions of Smilde Foods infringed the copyright in the taste of their Heksenkaas. By 'taste' Levola referred to the 'overall impression of the sense of taste caused by the consumption of a food product, including the sensation in the mouth perceived through the sense of touch'.

Issue and Procedure

Levola brought copyright proceedings against Smilde Foods in the Netherlands. Their initial case was unsuccessful and the Dutch trial court (Rechtbank Gelderland) rejected their claim on the ground that Levola had not indicated which elements, or combination of elements, of the taste gave Hekenkaas its unique, original character.

Levola appealed to the Dutch Regional Court of Appeal (Gerechtshof Arnheim-Leeuwarden). The Court of Appeal considered the key question to be whether 'taste' could be a copyrightable work. They stayed proceedings and sent a request for a preliminary ruling on the correct interpretation of EU law. Articles 2–4 of the Information Society Directive (Directive 2001/29) require EU member states to grant exclusive rights to authors for their 'works'. The first question asked of the CJEU was: does EU law preclude the taste of a food being granted copyright protection?

COURT OF JUSTICE, GRAND CHAMBER

It follows that the taste of a food product can be protected by copyright under Directive 2001/29 only if such a taste can be classified as a 'work' within the meaning of the directive (see, by analogy, judgment of 16 July 2009, *Infopaq International*, C-5/08, EU:C:2009:465, paragraph 29 and the case-law cited).

In that regard, two cumulative conditions must be satisfied for subject matter to be classified as a 'work' within the meaning of Directive 2001/29.

First, the subject matter concerned must be original in the sense that it is the author's own intellectual creation (judgment of 4 October 2011, *Football Association Premier League and Others*, C-403/08 and C-429/08, EU:C:2011:631, paragraph 97 and the case-law cited).

Secondly, only something which is the expression of the author's own intellectual creation may be classified as a 'work' within the meaning of Directive 2001/29 (see, to that effect, judgments of 16 July 2009, *Infopaq International*, C-5/08, EU:C:2009:465, paragraph 39, and of 4 October 2011, *Football Association Premier League and Others*, C-403/08 and C-429/08, EU:C:2011:631, paragraph 159).

Accordingly, for there to be a 'work' as referred to in Directive 2001/29, the subject matter protected by copyright must be expressed in a manner which makes it identifiable with sufficient precision and objectivity, even though that expression is not necessarily in permanent form.

That is because, first, the authorities responsible for ensuring that the exclusive rights inherent in copyright are protected must be able to identify, clearly and precisely, the subject matter so protected. The same is true for individuals, in particular economic operators, who must be able to identify, clearly and precisely, what is the subject matter of protection which third parties, especially competitors, enjoy. Secondly, the need to ensure that there is no element of subjectivity – given that it is detrimental to legal certainty – in the process of identifying the protected subject matter means that the latter must be capable of being expressed in a precise and objective manner.

The taste of a food product cannot, however, be pinned down with precision and objectivity. Unlike, for example, a literary, pictorial, cinematographic or musical work, which is a precise and objective form of expression, the taste of a food product will be identified essentially on the basis of taste sensations and experiences, which are subjective and variable since they depend, inter alia, on factors particular to the person tasting the product concerned, such as age, food preferences and consumption habits, as well as on the environment or context in which the product is consumed.

(paras 34–37, 40–42)

Although the court stated that there are two requirements for something to qualify as a work, it may be read as setting three requirements. According to that interpretation, only something that is (i) original, (ii) expressive and (iii) identifiable with sufficient precision and objectivity, can be a work. Note also what the court says is *not* required. In paragraph 40 it states that the expression need not necessarily be in 'permanent form'. Unlike the UK, that only protects a work once it is fixed in some tangible form, the same is not required in EU copyright.

What then makes expression original in the EU sense? The most significant impact came in the *Infopaq* case of 2009.[21] That case held that any authorial work eligible for copyright protection within the EU must be 'original in the sense that they are the **author's own intellectual creation**'.[22] In subsequent years, the CJEU has elaborated upon that standard, as Case 3.11 demonstrates.

Case 3.11 *Eva-Maria Painer v Standard Verlags GmbH*, Case C-145/10 [2012] ECDR (6) 89 (ECJ)

Facts

Ms Painer (claimant) worked as a freelance photographer. In the 1990s, she was employed to take photographs of an Austrian girl, Natascha Kampusch. Natascha was subsequently abducted in 1998 at age 10. The competent authorities began a search for Natascha and Painer's photographs were used as part of the rescue operation.

In 2006, Natascha escaped from her abductor. Several Austrian and German newspapers owned by Standard Verlags GmbH (defendant) covered the story. In their coverage, they reproduced some of the photographs previously taken by Ms Painer. Ms Painer sued the newspapers for copyright infringement in Austria.

Issue and Procedure

In the Austrian litigation, the newspapers argued that portrait photographs exhibit low levels of originality because the goal of the photographer is to create a 'realistic image'. As such, the newspapers claimed, the level of creative freedom or originality in such photographs is necessarily limited. The Austrian Oberster Gerichtshof (Supreme Court) referred the question to the CJEU for clarification of EU law. The CJEU subsequently decided that portrait photographs receive the same level of protection as other photographs, for reasons discussed in the extract. In doing so, it elaborated on the character of the 'author's own intellectual creation' standard introduced by *Infopaq*.

COURT OF JUSTICE, THIRD CHAMBER

As regards, first, the question whether realistic photographs, particularly portrait photographs, enjoy copyright protection under Article 6 of Directive 93/98, it is important to point out that the Court has already decided, in Case C-5/08 *Infopaq International* [2009] ECR I-6569, paragraph 35, that copyright is liable to apply only in relation to a subject-matter, such as a photograph, which is original in the sense that it is its author's own intellectual creation.

As stated in recital 17 in the preamble to Directive 93/98, an intellectual creation is an author's own if it reflects the author's personality.

That is the case if the author was able to express his creative abilities in the production of the work by making free and creative choices (see, *a contrario*, Joined Cases C-403/08 and C-429/08 *Football Association Premier League and Others* [2011] ECR I-0000, paragraph 98).

As regards a portrait photograph, the photographer can make free and creative choices in several ways and at various points in its production.

In the preparation phase, the photographer can choose the background, the subject's pose and the lighting. When taking a portrait photograph, he can choose the framing, the angle of view and the atmosphere created. Finally, when selecting the snapshot, the photographer may choose from a variety of developing techniques the one he wishes to adopt or, where appropriate, use computer software.

By making those various choices, the author of a portrait photograph can stamp the work created with his 'personal touch'.

(paras 87–92)

One notable feature of the *Infopaq* and *Painer* decisions is their theoretical coherence. If the underlying normative reason for granting protection is, as Desbois put it in Section 2.2.5, to protect the 'bond' that unites author to creation, then copyright should only be granted if such a bond exists. The requirement that the creation 'reflects the author's personality' neatly fits with the personality underpinnings of many copyright regimes in Europe.

However, despite the theoretical coherence, both cases run up against the copying objection, as outlined in Section 2.2.6. It is far from clear why a bond between author and creation should give the author control over the reproduction of the work in circumstances where reproduction does not harm the author's personality.

ACTIVITY 3.3

Think back to *Starry Night* (Figure 1.1) once more. What, in the EU sense, made that expression 'original'? How is your answer to this question, different to your answer to that in Activity 3.2?

Much academic writing has considered whether the traditional UK approach to originality is consistent with the EU approach.[23] Opinions on this matter vary. One

Just before publication of this book, in December 2023, the Court of Appeal in *THJ Systems v Sheridan* [2023] 1354 EWCA Civ held that the UK originality standard is now the personal intellectual creation standard.

current Court of Appeal justice, Lord Justice Arnold, has argued extrajudicially that *Walter v Lane* is no longer good law on the issue of originality, and that the UK approach today is that laid down by the CJEU.[24] At the same time, HHJ Birss QC (as he then was) indicated in *Temple Island Collections Ltd v New English Teas* that there is little difference in substance between the EU approach and the traditional UK approach.[25] If a photograph involves sufficient skill and labour, it is likely also to involve an intellectual creation, in the view of HHJ Birss QC.

Prior to the UK's departure from the EU on 30 January 2020, UK courts were bound to follow the CJEU law on originality, and the CJEU standard was adopted into UK copyright law.[26] Since the UK's departure from the EU, some have speculated as to whether UK courts will return to the traditional labour-focused approach.[27] However, at the time of publication, no UK courts have deviated from the CJEU standard.

3.2.2 An Open List

Unlike the CDPA, EU copyright law does not restrict the type of works that can enjoy protection. Following the *Levola Hengolo* case, the CJEU in *Cofemel* confirmed that if an intellectual phenomenon meets the requirements of being a 'work', then it 'must, as such, qualify for copyright protection'.[28] Unlike the UK, therefore, there is no need to debate what counts as a 'literary' work, or an 'artistic' work, etc. The CJEU in this sense operates an 'open list' in which any type of work can receive protection.

This difference between EU and UK law may have important consequences. Both *Levola Hengolo* and *Cofemel* are retained law. The result is that binding case law is inconsistent with the most natural interpretation of the CDPA. It has been suggested that, to avoid inconsistency, courts ought to read the categories of LDMA works expansively to, in practice, reach the same outcomes as required by EU law.

There remains, however, an alternative approach that courts may choose to take. The key advantage of the EU approach to subject matter is its theoretical coherence: the approach to subject matter is consistent with a personality argument for copyright protection. While we may have reasons to doubt the personality argument, UK courts could learn from the theoretical coherence of EU courts. If, for example, the most compelling argument for copyright protection in the UK is utilitarian, then whether any phenomenon should be recognised as copyrightable subject matter ought to be decided with reference to that set of normative values.

ACTIVITY 3.4

To illustrate the last point, reconsider two classic British cases: *University of London Press* and *Ladbrokes v William Hill*. Instead of appealing to metaphysical qualities (like being 'in print or in writing'), instead ask whether the normative arguments introduced in Section 2.2 support, or undercut, the case for granting mathematics papers copyright protection? The following discussion focuses on the utilitarian argument.

3.2.3 Non-Original Works

Unlike the UK, continental European countries do not protect sound recordings, films, broadcasts and typographical arrangements via copyright. With certain exceptions – such as Germany[29] – 'non-original' writings are protected, not as a form of 'author's rights', but in a separate category known as '**neighbouring**' (or '**related**') **rights**. While in practice the law comes to the same outcomes, the division further reinforces the European personality-based approach to 'author's rights'.

3.2.4 No Formalities

Copyright in the UK, the EU and continental European countries, all arises automatically. Providing the author creates an original work, there is no requirement that the author apply for protection or register their protection with any official government agency. There is also no requirement that the author attach copyright information to the work (such as attaching a © symbol or the date of creation). As a result, copyright is an '**unregistered right**' and distinguishable from '**registered rights**' such as patents and trademarks, discussed in Parts II and IV.

This was not always the case. The Statute of Anne only allowed authors (or their assignees) to recover remedies for copyright infringement if their books were registered with the Stationers' Company.[30] The USA required authors to register their works with the US Copyright Office and to attach notice to the work (i.e. attaching the famous © symbol to the work) up until the mid-twentieth century.[31]

The change in law was brought about by the Berne Convention of 1886, introduced in Section 2.3. As discussed in Chapter 2, this treaty requires countries to give foreign authors the same copyright protection it gives to its own authors. The treaty further states that the rights provided to foreign authors 'shall not be subject to any formality' (article 5(2)). This decision to ban formalities was both pragmatic and philosophical. On a pragmatic level, if an author wants to receive copyright protection in multiple different countries, and each country requires copyright registration, then the author will need to complete a lot of administrative work to receive international copyright coverage. On a philosophical level, if one believes that authors have a natural right to own their works, then it may be inconsistent to require authors to pass through administrative hoops in order to gain protection for their rights. The Berne Convention was heavily influenced by French author Victor Hugo and displays features of the personality argument underlying much continental European copyright.

Victor Hugo (1802–55) was the author of works such as *Les Misérables* and *The Hunchback of Notre Dame*. Hugo was president of the International Literary Association in Paris that drafted the initial text of the Berne Convention. (Photo c.1870s. Credit: Bettmann/Contributor via Getty Images)

3.3 SUMMARY

Today, copyright in the UK shares much in common with copyright in continental European countries. In the modern world, both systems broadly understand a 'work' as an intangible expressive form. Furthermore, while both systems have, at times shown reluctance to view intangible expressive forms as things, both have gradually come to understand them as objects of property.

There remain, however, significant differences. The principal difference is which intangible expressive forms can enjoy protection. European law shows a high degree of theoretical coherence. Based on the personality argument for copyright, it recognises copyright in all expressive forms that display the relevant personal bond. The UK, by contrast, becomes bogged down in metaphysical questions such as, what is a 'literary' work? Or what is an 'artistic' work?

From a British perspective, there is much to learn from the European approach to copyrightable subject matter. While the personality argument for copyright protection faces problems (identified in Section 2.2.6), the theoretical coherence of the European approach is admirable. Rather than appeal to whether, for example, a work is functional or not, it may be better for judges to foreground the normative question, and ask whether there is a compelling normative case for extending copyright protection to a given class of expressive forms, such as film costumes or photography scenes. This approach could help courts to determine if phenomena like the taste of cheese or silence should enjoy copyright protection.

3.4 SELF-ASSESSMENT

Before moving on, try to answer the following questions to consolidate your learning. Answers are provided in the section below.

1. Which of the following adjectives best describe the list of copyrightable works in CDPA, s 1? Pick one or more.
   a. exhaustive
   b. non-exhaustive
   c. open
   d. closed

2. In 2010, Author A wrote a historical book called *The Illuminati*. The book is a factual account of the Illuminati (a short-lived eighteenth-century secret society). The book discusses a theory that the Illuminati were responsible for causing the French Revolution (1789–99). In addition to the text, Author A illustrated the work with several hand-drawn images of individuals who were allegedly part of the Illuminati. Author A does not attach any form of copyright information to the book.

   Which of the following statements are true? Pick one or more.
   a. The book and its contents cannot be protected by copyright due to the lack of relevant copyright information.
   b. Author A does not own the idea of a book about the Illuminati's involvement in the French Revolution.
   c. Author A owns the text of the book.
   d. Author A owns the hand-drawn images.

3. The case of *Walter v Lane* (1900) AC 539 (and subsequent case law) sets the twentieth-century test for originality in the UK. Which of the following answers best summarise that test? Pick one or more.

   a. The work must be created through skill, labour and judgement.

   b. The work must be the author's own intellectual creation.

   c. The work must involve the author's personality.

   d. The work must originate from the author.

4. What is a 'work'?

ACTIVITY DISCUSSION

Activity 3.1 Van Gogh's idea was to paint the night sky. The expression is how he expressed that idea. The expression is, among other things, the choice of paints (dark blues, vibrant yellows), the long thick brushstrokes and the characteristic swirling pattern for the clouds and sky. Even more importantly, it is the combination of these individual ideas into a whole.

Activity 3.2 *Starry Night* originated from van Gogh in the sense that it was not copied from another source. It also is clearly the product of skill, labour and judgement. Despite the lack of recognition in his lifetime, van Gogh was clearly a skilful painter. He studied watercolours with his cousin Anton Mauve, he travelled to Antwerp and to Paris to help develop his skills. The process of creating *Starry Night* was painted after numerous preliminary sketches of the hillside of Saint-Rémy. His choices – about the paints, brushstrokes, etc. – were all based on his judgement about aesthetic value.

Activity 3.3 The painting is an original work in both the UK sense and the EU sense. What changes, however, is the reason for that conclusion. The choices he made (the paints, the brushstrokes, the swirling patterns) were not just the product of skill, labour or judgement, but were also reflective of his personality in some way. The turbulent nature of the painting comes from a mind that was also arguably highly turbulent. The painting seems to be the product of a man who was experiencing intense emotional and mental turmoil.

Therefore, one answer is the painting is original because we see some of van Gogh himself, his personality, 'shining through' the painting, giving it meaning and telling a unique story. It is the choices that van Gogh made when producing the painting that enabled him to express his personality in this original way.

Activity 3.4 From a utilitarian standpoint, whether the mathematics papers or betting coupons should be owned depends on an empirical assessment of the good and bad consequences of ownership.

Starting with mathematics papers, ownership has clearly bad consequences. Mathematics papers are valuable because they help students improve their knowledge. Ownership limits access to those works meaning that fewer students can benefit from them. Without copyright, the customers of University Tutorial Press would have enjoyed cheaper and easier access to mathematics papers.

But there is plausibly a good consequence to ownership. If producers of mathematics papers enjoy copyright, they will potentially be stimulated to create more of them. If the incentive effects result in the production of papers which otherwise would not exist, then society benefits from ownership.

The difficult question is which effect is 'stronger'? On this question, one might argue that the good effects are not sufficient to outweigh the bad ones. It is possible that the University of London would have created these mathematics examinations regardless of whether they were granted copyright or not. After all, they needed some way to assess their students. If that is true, it may suggest copyright produces the problem of monopoly without any offsetting benefits.

There may be even stronger reasons to be concerned about copyrighting football betting coupons, as in *Ladbrokes*. By granting copyright to William Hill, the UK legal system made it more difficult for Ladbrokes to offer a competing product. Was that insulation from competition a good idea? It seems highly likely that copyright was not required to incentivise this type of work. Once again, one might think that William Hill had sufficient incentive to create betting coupons, regardless of their copyright status. If that is true, then consumers enjoy less choice in the market with little redeeming benefit.

SELF-ASSESSMENT ANSWERS

1. **Correct answers: a**. and **d**. The UK list is a closed and exhaustive list meaning that only the eight types of work mentioned in the list are eligible for copyright protection. The contemporary European approach is open and non-exhaustive, meaning that other works not mentioned on the list are potentially eligible for copyright protection.
2. **Correct answers: b., c**. and **d**. Author A's mere idea to write a book on the Illuminati and the French Revolution is not protected by copyright. Accordingly, others are free to write their own books on this topic. However, the precise text and the hand-drawn images (which help Author A express his ideas) are protected by copyright. This copyright protection arises automatically once brought into a fixed existence. There is no requirement for Author A to attach any copyright information to the work(s).
3. **Correct answer:** the best answers are **a**. and **d**. The traditional test for originality is seen as requiring both that the work originate from the author (and not be copied from another source) and that it is created through the author's skill, labour and judgement. Answers **b**. and **c**. are more directly related to the EU originality standard. However, some may argue that the two approaches are not as dissimilar as first appearances suggest (see HHJ Birss QC in *Temple Island Collections*).

Notes

1 Ronan Deazley, *On the Origin of the Right to Copy: Charting the Movement of Copyright Law in Eighteenth Century Britain (1695–1775)* (Hart Publishing 2004) xix.
2 Brad Sherman and Lionel Bently, *The Making of Modern Intellectual Property: The British Experience, 1760–1911* (CUP 1999) 9–60.
3 *Nichols v Universal Pictures Corporation*, 45 F2d 119 at 122 (2d Cir 1930) (US) (per Hand J).
4 [2007] EWCA Civ 247, para 5.
5 *Heptulla v Orient Longman* [1989] 1 FSR 598 High Court (India) 609.
6 Yin Harn Lee, 'The Persistence of the Text: The Concept of the Work in Copyright Law – Part 2' (2018) 2 IPQ 107; Oren Bracha, *Owning Ideas: The Intellectual Origins of American Intellectual Property, 1790–1909* (CUP 2016) 124–87.
7 [1899] 2 Ch 749, 772.
8 ibid.
9 Christopher Buccafusco, 'There's No Such Thing as Independent Creation and It's a Good Thing Too' (2023) 64 Wm & Mary L Rev 1617.
10 *William Hill v Ladbrokes* [1964] 1 All ER 465, 469 ('or judgement') (per Reid L), and at 473f ('at judgement') (per Evershed L).

11 cf Poorna Mysoor, 'Does UK Really Have a "Closed" List of Works Protected by Copyright?' (2019) 41 EIPR 474–79.

12 R Deazley (2008) 'Commentary on Dramatic Literary Property Act 1833' in L Bently and M Kretschmer (eds), *Primary Sources on Copyright (1450–1900)* <www.copyrighthistory.org> (accessed 8 December 2023) (evidence before the Select Committee on Dramatic Literature was that 'as soon as a piece is published' other companies 'have a right to play it').

13 *Norowzian v Arks (No 2)* [2000] EMLR 67, 73.

14 *Bach v Longman* (1777) 2 Cowp. 623.

15 Cheng Lim Saw, 'Protecting the Sound of Silence in 4'33: A Timely Revisit of Basic Principles in Copyright Law' first published by Sweet & Maxwell in EIPR (2005) 27(12), 467–76 and reproduced by agreement with the publishers.

16 See 'Wombles Composer Mike Batt's Silence Legal Row "a Scam"', *BBC News* (9 December 2010) <https://www.bbc.co.uk/news/uk-england-hampshire-11964995> (accessed 8 December 2023).

17 [1971] 2 All ER 657.

18 Directive 2001/29/EC of the European Parliament and of the Council of 22 May 2001 on the harmonisation of certain aspects of copyright and related rights in the information society ('Information Society Directive').

19 Lauren Pfister, 'Author and Work in the French Print Privileges System: Some Milestones' in Ronan Deazley, Martin Kretschmer and Lionel Bently (eds), *Privilege and Property: Essays on the History of Copyright* (Open Book 2010).

20 Immanuel Kant, 'On the Unlawfulness of Reprinting' (1785). On the limited impact of the essay, see F Kawohl (2008) 'Commentary on Kant's Essay *On the Injustice of Reprinting Books* (1785)' in Bently and Kretschmer (n 12).

21 *Infopaq International v Danske Dagblades Forening*, Case C-5/08 [2009] ECR I–6569 (ECJ).

22 ibid para 37.

23 See eg Andreas Rahmatian, 'Originality in UK Copyright Law: The Old "Skill and Labour" Doctrine under Pressure' (2013) 44 IIC 4.

24 Richard Arnold, 'Walter v Lane Revisited (Again)' (2021) 2 IPQ 67.

25 [2012] EWPCC 1.

26 ibid.

27 Richard Arnold and others, 'The Legal Consequences of Brexit through the Lens of IP Law' (2017) 101(2) Judicature 9.

28 *Cofemel – Sociedade de Vestuário SA v G-Star Raw CV*, Case C-683/17, EU:C:2019:721.

29 Rehbinder, *Urheberrecht* (16th edn, Beck 2010) 69.

30 Statute of Anne (1710), s II. Stef van Gompel, *Formalities in Copyright Law: An Analysis of Their History, Rationales, and Possible Future* (Kluwer Law International 2011) 77.

31 Gompel (n 30) 78–79.

FIGURE ACKNOWLEDGEMENTS

3.1 HL/PO/JU/4/3/1121. Images reproduced with permission of the UK Parliamentary Archives

3.2 Image reproduced with permission of Senate House Library, University of London

3.3 Reproduced with permission of Musiceano.com

3.4 Photo: © Michael Spencer Jones – all rights reserved. Reproduced with permission of Michael Spencer Jones

3.5 An original stormtrooper helmet made for and used in *Star Wars: Episode IV – A New Hope* (Lucasfilm Ltd, 1977) on display at 'Julien's Auctions and TCM Present: Hollywood Legends', Press Preview, 11 July 2022, Beverly Hills, California. (Photo by Unique Nicole/Getty Images)

Marginal Fig. 3.1 Victor Hugo. Photo shows Victor Hugo (1902–1885), French poet and author of *Les Misérables*. Photo *c*.1870s. (Credit: Bettmann/Contributor via Getty Images)

4

Copyright III: Rights

Chapters 2 and 3 introduced copyright's historical evolution from printers' privilege into its modern incarnation as property in an author's original work. The last chapter presented the first part of the transformation: the change in copyright's subject matter from book to original work. Chapters 4 and 5 turn to the second part of the transformation: the evolution of copyright from a right to print into a right of property.

Copyright's transformation from printer regulation to property right raises the conceptual question introduced in Section 1.1.2. Is copyright really property? Even assuming that works are things, does anyone really own them? Does copyright law empower anyone to exclusively control all uses of the work? Or does the law merely create a bundle of rights in relation to the work: some of which are given to the creator, while others are given to the wider public? As discussed in this chapter and the next, sometimes copyright looks more like the latter; at other times, it looks more like the former.

The present chapter introduces the rights that contemporary copyright grants. This discussion can be split into four sections. Section 4.1 outlines the owner's economic rights. Section 4.2 outlines the author's moral rights. Section 4.3 considers the duration of the rights. Section 4.4 turns to ownership of the rights.

> What is a 'right' in law? One famous answer was provided by Yale Law School professor, Wesley Newcomb Hohfeld (1879–1918).

> In Hohfeld's view, rights are 'correlated' with duties. If X has a **legal right**, someone else must have a **legal duty** not to interfere with X's rights. The same is not true of '**liberties**' or '**privileges**'. If X has a liberty to do something, that does not necessarily impose duties on others.

> In copyright, a **liberty** or **privilege** of printing does not necessarily mean that others have a duty not to print. But a right to prevent copying does mean others have duties not to copy.

4.1 ECONOMIC RIGHTS

The Statute of Anne granted the copyright owner one narrow privilege: the exclusive liberty of printing books for fourteen years. This is not, however, the law today. The modern CDPA grants authors and their assignees something else entirely: **legal rights**. Indeed, contemporary copyright law creates an expansive set of **economic rights** (summarised in Table 4.1). These rights are, notionally, designed to protect the owner's financial interest in the work.

This chapter contains public sector information licensed under the Open Government Licence v3.0.

Table 4.1 The CDPA's economic rights

Name	CDPA sections	Statutory language
Reproduction right	16(a), 17	The exclusive right 'to copy the work'.
Distribution right	16(b), 18	The exclusive right 'to issue copies of the work to the public'.
Rental and lending right	16(ba), 18A	The exclusive right 'to rent or lend the work to the public'.
Performance right	16(c), 19	The exclusive right 'to perform, show or play the work in public'.
Communication right	16(d), 20	The exclusive right 'to communicate the work to the public'.
Adaptation right	16(e), 21	The exclusive right 'to make an adaptation of the work'.

In the terminology of the CDPA, these are called 'acts restricted by copyright' or the **'restricted acts'**, meaning that the owner alone can perform these acts.[1] If someone performs one of the restricted acts without the permission of the owner, they infringe the right and will be held liable. Furthermore, a person who aids someone to perform a restricted act – for example, by providing the means for the infringer to carry out the act – will also be liable under the doctrine of **secondary liability**, providing they knew, or ought to have known, the act was restricted.[2]

Other acts not listed in Table 4.1 – what can be called 'non-restricted acts' – cannot be controlled by the owner. For example, the owner does not have the exclusive right to read, smell or think about, a work. Everyone has the liberty to perform these non-restricted actions.

> The relevant remedies accompanying liability are discussed in Chapter 16.

ACTIVITY 4.1

What does the division between restricted and non-restricted acts say about copyright as a property right? Do the economic rights make copyright more like a right of exclusive control, or merely a bundle of rights?

This section provides a systematic overview of the economic rights. In doing so, the aim is not merely to understand the system of economic rights, but to assess what the historical expansion of the rights means for copyright as a property right.

4.1.1 Reproduction Right

While the **reproduction** right is, in some ways, the successor to the Statute of Anne's exclusive liberty of printing, it has become a vastly more powerful entitlement.

To illustrate, consider the case of *Gyles v Wilcox* (1740).[3] Mr Gyles owned the printing rights in Sir Matthew Hale's treatise, *The History of the Pleas of the Crown*. Gyles sued the publishers Wilcox and Barlow for printing a book called *The Treatise of Modern Crown Law*. *The Treatise* copied several chapters verbatim from *The History*, while also including some additional new chapters. When the case came before Lord Hardwicke in the Chancery, he decided there had been no infringement because *The Treatise* was not the 'same book' as *The History*. In Hardwicke's view, *The Treatise* was an entirely new book, or what he called, a 'fair abridgment'. But if this case were brought today, Gyles certainly could prevent the publication of *The Treatise*.

The CDPA's reproduction right has expanded in three ways compared to the original liberty of printing. First, the reproduction right is a right to prevent copying, not merely printing. Second, the reproduction right is a right to prevent copying the entire work or a 'substantial part' thereof. And, finally, the reproduction right is a right to prevent copying a substantial part of the work in 'any material form'. These points will be considered in turn.

4.1.1.1   COPYING

Today, the owner has the right to prevent all forms of copying. But what counts as 'copying'?

In thinking about copying, it is helpful to understand what copying is *not*. One does not copy a work, if one independently creates the same work. For example, consider a fictitious painter: Victor van Gone. Our fictitious van Gone has never seen the *Starry Night* before. Yet, through a miraculous coincidence, van Gone has recently produced a painting that looks identical to the *Starry Night*. In this instance, van Gone's painting is not a copy at all, but an independently created work that just so happens to look like *Starry Night*. The legal rule that **independent creation** is not copying is known as the independent creation doctrine.

The distinction between independent creation and copying became a foundation of modern copyright law during the nineteenth century. The rise of the independent creation doctrine was correlated with the evolution of copyright's subject matter.[4] As copyright became a right in expression, it followed that other authors should be free to use their own expression, even if it happened to be similar to prior expression. Vincent van Gogh should own his expression, but that should not stop Victor van Gone using his own, independently created, expression.

If the independent creation doctrine rose in the nineteenth century, it may well fall again in the twenty-first.[5] The decline of the independent creation doctrine is, in part, the result of a practical evidentiary problem: how can the owner prove the defendant's work was the product of copying rather than independent creation? Of course, the defendant might admit it. Or someone might have seen the defendant do it and be prepared to testify in court. These are both examples of **direct evidence of copying**. But, in many cases, there is no such direct evidence; no 'smoking gun'.

In response to this problem, courts permit owners to rely on **indirect evidence** of copying. In the absence of direct evidence, courts will infer copying from the surrounding circumstances. In practice, claimants try to prove copying by demonstrating that: (a) the defendant's work is sufficiently similar to the claimant's work to permit an inference of copying; and (b) the defendant had access to the protected work. This lessens the evidentiary burden facing owners, but at the expense of independent creators. If courts are too ready to infer copying from circumstances, the probability that an independent creator is held liable erroneously increases. This concern was clearly on display in the recent case of *Sheeran v Chokri*.

Case 4.1 *Sheeran v Chokri* [2022] EWHC 827 (Ch)

Facts

Ed Sheeran (claimant) wrote the 'Shape of You' ('Shape'). Shape, performed by Mr Sheeran, was released as a single on 6 January 2017. It became the bestselling digital song worldwide in 2017. The song included a 'hook' in which the phrase 'Oh I' is sung, three times, to the tune of the first four notes of the rising minor pentatonic scale commencing on C# (the 'OI phrase'). The musical notation for the hook is line (b) in Figure 4.1 (when the song is transposed into the key of A minor).

Sami Chokri (who performs under the name Sami Switch) wrote the song 'Oh Why'. The song was performed by Mr Chokri, released in mid-March 2015. The song included an eight-bar chorus in which the phrase 'Oh why' is repeated to the tune of the first four notes of the rising minor pentatonic scale, commencing on F# (the 'OW hook'). The musical notation for the chorus is line (a) in Figure 4.1 (when the song is transposed into the key of A minor). Although not identical, Chokri argued that Sheeran's OI phrase had been copied from the OW hook.

Figure 4.1 The chorus in 'Oh Why' ((a)); the hook in 'Shape' ((b)).
From Sheeran v Chokri *[2022] EWHC 827 (Ch)*

Issue and Procedure

In creating the OI phrase in 'Shape', did Sheeran copy the OW hook in 'Oh Why'? Sheeran brought a case seeking a declaratory judgment that he had not copied and therefore had not infringed Chokri's rights. Chokri disagreed. Chokri argued that the OI phrase was sufficiently similar to permit an inference of copying, and that Sheeran had access to 'Oh Why' and therefore the opportunity to copy.

Mr Justice Zacaroli ultimately decided that Sheeran had not copied the phrase from Oh Why. In this first extract, Mr Justice's Zacaroli decides that Sheeran's song was not sufficiently similar to permit an inference of copying.

ZACAROLI J

There are countless songs in the pop, rock, folk and blues genres where the melody is drawn exclusively from the minor pentatonic scale, and moves predominantly between the tonic and dominant (A and E). Given that there are limited ways of moving between them (with only two intervening notes) it is not surprising that Mr Ricigliano [counsel for Sheeran] was able to point to numerous examples where the melody follows the same contour as in Shape. Equally unsurprisingly, there are examples where the same pattern is found of repeating the first four notes of the minor pentatonic scale, such as (You Drive Me) Crazy by Britney Spears which contains precisely the same tune as the OI Phrase (albeit neither this, nor the other examples Mr Ricigliano found, was an example of the precise pattern *in a single bar phrase*). Others have a close approximation to it (for example Heartbreaker by Led Zeppelin, in which the guitar riff – A–A; C–C; D–D; E – follows the same pattern without the final E; and Praying by Tom Grennan, in which a vocal part set to 'mm, ah, mm, ah, mm, ah, yeah' does the same). The melody in No Diggity (to which I refer below, and which Mr Sheeran himself had performed and recorded) revolves almost exclusively around these four notes – sometimes rising up through the scale though more often descending it.

Mr Sheeran himself has written many songs in which a part of the tune has followed the pattern A–C–D–E, albeit without repeating each note as in the OI Phrase. Examples include Don't (2014), Give Me Love (2011); Grade 8 (2011), Afire Love (2014) and I See Fire (2013).

The defendants contend, nevertheless, that it is the fact that the OI Phrase shares multiple features in common with the OW Hook that indicates it was copied, rather than created organically on 12 October 2016. The other similarities relied on are: the rhythm of multiple quavers in a single bar; the instrumentation of a vocal chant with male lead and backing vocals pitched at low and high registers; and the use of alternating vowel sounds.

> In considering the likelihood of copying, it is important to note that all of these features are, however, commonplace and their use in Shape can be readily explained by other matters.
>
> (pp. 43–46)

Having considered the similarities between the two songs and whether they were sufficiently similar to permit an inference of copying, Mr Justice Zacaroli turned to the next question: did Sheeran have access to Chokri's song before he wrote 'Shape'? If Sheeran had never heard Chokri's song before because he had no ability to access it, then he simply could not have copied the OI phrase from the OW hook.

ZACAROLI J

[Sheeran and co-writers] said that to the best of their knowledge they had never heard Oh Why ... and had never heard of Mr Chokri before the defendants made their complaint about copyright infringement.

In this section, I consider the strength of the evidence that Oh Why may have been shared with, or discovered by, Mr Sheeran, so as (1) to test the credibility of Mr Sheeran's denial that he had deliberately copied the OW Hook, and (2) to determine the likelihood of him having heard it (despite his best recollection that he had not), in the context of the alternative case of subconscious copying.

Oh Why was played on the radio only twice, late at night on Radio 6 Music in July 2016. It was not suggested that Mr Sheeran or anyone associated with him heard it that way. There is no evidence that ... the track Oh Why or the video of it was ever played or shown by anyone to Mr Sheeran. In particular, although the defendants contend that they specifically wanted to get the song to Mr Sheeran's attention, it was never sent either to him, his manager or to anyone associated with Mr Sheeran with a request that it be passed on to him. Mr Chokri said that he would have been embarrassed to do so as it would have come across as needy.

The defendants instead rely on either (1) their efforts to publicise Oh Why and the Solace EP, including by getting it on the radar of people known to be associated with Mr Sheeran in the hopes that they may play it to him; or (2) the possibility that Mr Sheeran would himself have come across Mr Chokri and Oh Why in looking for new artists or inspiration for his own songs.

Mr Sutcliffe [counsel for Chokri] suggested that the evidence overall presented a picture of a successful and well-publicised campaign

Subconscious copying is a highly controversial concept. The idea presented in (2) is that Sheeran must have heard the OW hook before, committed it to his subconscious memory, and then copied the OW hook from his subconscious memory without conscious awareness of his act.

> involving renewing Mr Chokri's profile in the 'UK scene', bringing Mr Chokri to the attention of Mr Sheeran's associates and genuine exposure to the music industry more generally. I do not accept this. Mr Chokri is undoubtedly a serious and talented songwriter and while his management were unsurprisingly trying to create some hype around the release of [the Oh Why song], it had limited success. In my judgment, the possibility that these attempts might have led to it coming to Mr Sheeran's attention – either because someone he was associated with played it to him or because he found it himself – is at best speculative.
>
> (paras 72, 82–84, 146)

Having found insufficient similarity, and insufficient access to the original work, Sheeran won his case. Mr Justice Zacaroli concluded that Sheeran probably had not copied (either deliberately or subconsciously) but instead independently created a work that just happened to sound similar in some respects to Chokri's work.

However, Sheeran's victory may have been a pyrrhic one. While the case demonstrates that an owner only has a right to prevent actual copying, the case also demonstrates how easily any suspected copying can result in expensive court battles. Following the case, Sheeran released the following statement on Instagram.

Of course, it is not necessarily bad if copyright ditches the independent creation doctrine. Section 3.1.2 noted that some psychological literature claims all creativity is based on copying. If so, then no work is ever truly 'independently created'.[6]

> While we are obviously happy with the result, I feel like claims like this are way too common now and have become a culture where a claim is made with the idea that a settlement will be cheaper than taking it to court, even if there is no base for the claim.
>
> This is really damaging to the songwriting industry. There's only so many notes and very few chords used in pop music. Coincidence is bound to happen if 60,000 songs are being released every day on Spotify. That's 22 million songs a year and there are only 12 notes that are available.
>
> Lawsuits are not a pleasant experience and I hope with this ruling it means in the future baseless claims like this can be avoided. This really does have to end.[7]

On the other hand, reading the extracts from *Sheeran v Chokri* reveals how difficult the issue of copying is for judges and courts. The difficulty judges find themselves in is eased however by the burden of proof. The burden lies on the claimant to show, on the balance of probabilities, that the defendant has copied the work. Therefore, in a case like *Sheeran v Chokri*, Mr Justice Zacaroli does not need to decide what 'really' happened. All Mr Justice Zacaroli needed to do was look at the evidence before him and decide which account of events was more probable.

ACTIVITY 4.2

Having read the *Sheeran v Chokri* case, do you think a court would decide that van Gone probably copied his painting from van Gogh?

4.1.1.2 SUBSTANTIAL PART

The CDPA grants the owner the exclusive right to copy the entire work or a 'substantial part' thereof. But, once again, the malleable concept of 'substantial part' can be used to expand the control owners enjoy over the work. By modern standards, it would be undeniable that Wilcox had copied a 'substantial part' of *The History*. Consider the following House of Lords decision.

Case 4.2 *Designers Guild Ltd v Russell Williams (Textiles) Ltd* [2001] 1 WLR 2416

Facts

Designers Guild Ltd (claimant) designs and sells fabrics. In 1994, Designers Guild created a fabric called the 'Ixia' design (Figure 4.2) which consisted of vertical stripes and flowers. Russell Williams (Textiles) Ltd also designed and sold fabrics. In 1995, Russell Williams created a fabric called 'Marguerite' (Figure 4.2) which also consisted of vertical stripes and flowers. The claimant sued the defendants for infringing their reproduction right.

(a)

Figure 4.2 'Ixia' created by Helen Burke ((a)); 'Marguerite' created by Jane Ibbotson ((b)). *Reproduced with permission of the Library of Congress (Photo credit: Agata Tajchert)*

(b)

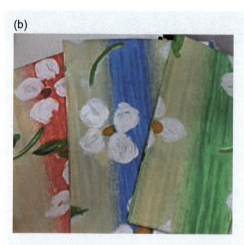

Figure 4.2 (*cont.*)

Issue and Procedure

At trial, it was held that the defendants had copied from the claimant's work (using indirect evidence). The trial judge also concluded that the defendants had copied a substantial part of the original expression. In coming to this conclusion, the judge identified several similarities and differences between the two works (see Table 4.2).

Table 4.2 The similarities and differences between 'Ixia' and 'Marguerite'

Similarities	Differences
Each fabric consists of vertical stripes, with spaces between the stripes equal to the width of the stripe, and in each fabric flowers and leaves are scattered over and between the stripes, so as to give the same general effect.	The 'Ixia' design is smaller and more delicate and the detail is different.
Each is painted in a similar neo-Impressionistic style. Each uses a brushstroke technique, i.e. the use of one brush to create a stripe, showing the brush marks against the texture.	In 'Marguerite' the effect of the stripes showing through the petals is not as marked as it is in 'Ixia'.
In each fabric the stripes are formed by vertical brush strokes, and have rough edges which merge into the background.	The leaves in 'Marguerite' are distinctly less impressionistic than those in 'Ixia'
In each fabric the petals are formed with dryish brushstrokes and are executed in a similar way (somewhat in the form of a comma).	
In each fabric parts of the colour of the stripes show through some of the petals.	
In each case the centres of the flower heads are represented by a strong blob, rather than by a realistic representation.	
In each fabric the leaves are painted in two distinct shades of green, with similar brush strokes, and are scattered over the design.	

The defendants appealed on the question of substantial part. The Court of Appeal overturned the trial judge finding that the two works 'just do not look sufficiently similar' to conclude that the defendants' work includes a 'substantial part' of the original expression. The case was further appealed to the House of Lords where the Court of Appeal decision was overturned, and the initial trial decision conclusions reinstated. The Lords each wrote their own opinion examining the issue of substantial part. Below is an extract from Lord Scott of Foscote's judgment that introduces different 'tests' for two different types of cases: **discrete** (also known as literal) copying and **altered copying** cases.

SCOTT OF FOSCOTE LJ

Section 16(3) of the Act of 1988 says that copying a copyright work is a copyright infringement if the copying is of 'the work as a whole or any substantial part of it'. Section 16(3) may come into play in two quite different types of case. One type of case is, obviously, where an identifiable part of the whole, but not the whole, has been copied. For example, only a section of a picture may have been copied, or only a sentence or two, or even only a phrase, from a poem or a book, or only a bar or two of a piece of music, may have been copied: see the examples given at pp. 88–89, para. 2–102 of *Laddie, Prescott & Vitoria, The Modern Law of Copyright and Designs*, 2nd ed. (1995), vol. 1 (which, for convenience, I will refer to as ' *Laddie*'). In cases of that sort, the question whether the copying of the part constitutes an infringement depends on the qualitative importance of the part that has been copied, assessed in relation to the copyright work as a whole. In *Ladbroke (Football) Ltd. v. William Hill (Football) Ltd. [1964] 1 W.L.R. 273* Lord Reid said, at p. 276, that: 'the question whether he has copied a substantial part depends much more on the quality than on the quantity of what he has taken'.

The present case is not a case of that type. The judge did not identify any particular part of *Ixia* and hold that that part had been copied. His finding of copying related to *Ixia* as a whole.

The other type of case in which a question of substantiality may become relevant is where the copying has not been an exact copying of the copyright work but a copying with modifications. This type of copying is referred to in *Laddie* as 'altered copying'. A paradigm of this type of case would be a translation of a literary work into some other language, or the dramatisation of a novel. The translation, or the play or film, might not have a single word in common with the original. But, assuming copyright existed in the original, the 'copy' might well, and in the case of a word-by-word translation certainly would, constitute an infringement of copyright.

The present case is an 'altered copying' case. [The claimants] put together a number of artistic ideas derived from various sources in order to produce her *Ixia* design, an original artistic design as it is accepted to be. Miss Ibbotson and Mrs. Williams, as the judge found, copied the *Ixia* design in order to produce their *Marguerite* design. But they did so with modifications. The *Marguerite* design is not an exact copy of *Ixia*. Nor is any specific part of the *Marguerite* design an exact copy of any corresponding part of the *Ixia* design. It is an altered copy.

The question, then, where an altered copy has been produced, is what the test should be in order to determine whether the production constitutes a copyright infringement. If the alterations are sufficiently extensive it may be that the copying does not constitute an infringement at all. The test proposed in *Laddie*, at pp. 92–93, para. 2–108, to determine whether an altered copy constitutes an infringement is: 'Has the infringer incorporated a substantial part of the independent skill, labour etc. contributed by the original author in creating the copyright work. . .'

My Lords, I think this is a useful test, based as it is on an underlying principle of copyright law, namely, that a copier is not at liberty to appropriate the benefit of another's skill and labour.

My noble and learned friend, Lord Millett, has made the point that once copying has been established, the question of substantiality depends on the relationship between what has been copied on the one hand and the original work on the other, similarity no longer being relevant. My Lords, I respectfully agree that that would be so in the first type of case. But in an altered copying case, particularly where the finding of copying is dependant, in the absence of direct evidence, upon the inferences to be drawn from the extent and nature of the similarities between the two works, the similarities will usually be determinative not only of the issue of copying but also of the issue of substantiality. And even where there is direct evidence of copying, as, for example, where it is admitted that the copier has produced his 'copy' with the original at his elbow, the differences between the original and the 'copy' may be so extensive as to bar a finding of infringement. It is not a breach of copyright to borrow an idea, whether of an artistic, literary or musical nature, and to translate that idea into a new work. In 'altered copying' cases, the difficulty is the drawing of the line between what is a permissible borrowing of an idea and what is an impermissible piracy of the artistic, literary or musical creation of another. In drawing this line, the extent and nature of the similarities between the altered copy and the original work

Lord Scott helpfully summarises the alternative decision of Lord Millett. Does Millett's alternative conclusion sound any better (or worse) than Lord Scott's?

must, it seems to me, play a critical and often determinative role. In particular, this must be so where there is no direct evidence of copying and the finding of copying is dependant on the inferences to be drawn from the similarities.

In the present case, the similarities between *Ixia* and *Marguerite*, as found by the judge, play, in my judgment a determinative role. If the similarities between *Ixia* and *Marguerite* were so extensive and of such a nature as to justify a finding that, in the absence of acceptable evidence of an independent provenance for *Marguerite*, *Marguerite* was copied from *Ixia*, it must, in my opinion, follow that the *Marguerite* design incorporated a substantial part of the *Ixia* design. It must follow also that, in designing the *Marguerite* design, the designers incorporated a substantial part of the skill and labour of [the claimants]. The judge's finding of copying made it, in my opinion, unnecessary for him to go on to ask whether the copying was of a substantial part. But both the judge and the Court of Appeal engaged in that inquiry.

(pp. 2430–32)

To appreciate the breadth of Lord Scott's decision, consider the two types of copying he identifies.

First, think about discrete copying. In such cases, Lord Scott makes a comparison between the copied part and the claimant's work as a whole. The question is whether the copied part is a qualitatively important of the claimant's work.

To illustrate discrete copying, consider **sampling** (i.e. the act of copying a small section from a prior sound recording to use in a second work). The American case of *Bridgeport Music v Dimension Films*[9] provides a good illustration. In that case, the claimant owned the sound recording called *Get Off Your Ass and Jam*. The defendants produced a new sound recording called *100 Miles and Runnin*. The *Get Off* recording opens with a three-note guitar riff lasting 4 seconds. The defendants copied 2 seconds of that riff, lowered the pitch, and 'looped' it so that it lasted sixteen beats. Because the part had been heavily edited, listeners to *100 Miles* would not appreciate that the sample was copied from *Get Off*. Yet, the American courts decided this amounted to a reproduction. And likewise, if one decides that the 4-second guitar riff was a 'qualitatively important' part of *Get Off*, then Lord Scott would agree.

> Recently the CJEU has indicated that a different test may be appropriate. In *Pelham v Hütter*, the court held that a 2-second sample from a prior sound recording would count as a reproduction unless it was modified such that it was now 'unrecognisable to the ear'. The case is discussed further in Section 5.1.1.2.[8]

Second, consider altered copying scenarios, like that in the *Designer Guild* case. In such cases, whether the defendant has copied a substantial part depends on a comparison between the claimant's and defendant's works. In such cases, the courts evaluate the similarities and differences between the works and draw a line between *de minimis* and substantial copying.

But something even more striking lies in the last paragraph of the extract. In altered copying cases, Lord Scott suggests that if the similarities between the works are sufficient to infer *copying*, then the similarities are also sufficient to qualify as a *substantial part*. This might be concerning, however, because it does not properly account for the distinction between ideas and expression, as the next activity illustrates.

ACTIVITY 4.3

One of the similarities between 'Marguerite' and 'Ixia' in the *Designer Guild* case was that both fabrics were painted in a 'neo-impressionistic style'. One might plausibly conclude that a style of painting is not expression but just an idea.

For the purpose of illustration, assume the court uses the similarity of styles as indirect evidence of copying. That is not itself objectionable. Of course, no one owns an idea like a style. But the similarity of styles might still be some evidence that copying, as a factual matter, occurred.

What then is the problem if the court then subsequently concludes that the similarities which prove copying are sufficient to establish that a substantial part has been taken?

The US Supreme Court famously once wrote that 'not all copying...is copyright infringement'.[10] According to that supposed view, a person does not reproduce a work if they merely copy a small (or *de minimis*) amount of expression, or if one merely copies ideas. Yet, one might wonder if that is true of UK law. If copying is very readily inferred from circumstances, and if such inference can be used as a basis for the substantial part analysis, then one might ask: what copying is not infringement?

4.1.1.3   ANY MATERIAL FORM

Lastly, unlike the Statute of Anne, the owner can prevent reproduction 'in any material form'.[11] For example, consider an artist who paints a bowl of fruit. The artist's exclusive right to make reproductions in all forms means that they alone would be allowed to take a photograph of the painting, or make a digital PDF copy of the painting, or recreate the painting as a sculpture.[12]

This expansion of copyright occurred alongside the evolution of copyright's subject matter. When copyright protected books, the scope of copyright was tied to that physical form.[13] A film, for example, is not physically the same thing as a book even if they both contain the same words: one is made of paper and ink, the other of photographic film reel. But as copyright came to attach to the original work, so the scope of copyright enlarged. Once the copyright attached not to the book, but the words in the book, then copyright owners could argue that they deserved the ability to stop people using their words regardless of the physical form of such use.

The 'any material form' language includes non-permanent digital versions of the work.[14] This is particularly important in the context of the Internet. Much of the material that exists online is protected by copyright (for example, films on YouTube, photos on Google Images, text written on blogs). To display this material, electronic devices make **temporary copies** of that material in their hard drives. These electronic copies only exist for a very short time – typically only fractions of a second – but they qualify as a form of copying nonetheless. As a result, simply browsing the Internet may breach the author's exclusive right to make reproductions.

Section 5.2 returns to the issue of temporary copies. To prevent copyright from 'breaking the Internet', society introduced a bespoke exception to the temporary copies rule.

> **ACTIVITY 4.4**
>
> Taking a step back, what does the modern reproduction right mean for copyright as a property right? Has copyright become a right of 'exclusive control'?

4.1.2 Distribution Right

Another right that can be traced back to the Statute of Anne is the **distribution** right. In its modern incarnation, the owner has the right to 'issue copies to the public'. This right enables the author to control the distribution of the tangible goods in which the intangible work – or substantial part thereof – appears. For example, an owner of a novel cannot only prevent others copying the words of their novel, but can also stop others selling tangible books in which the novel is contained. These tangible items are known as 'copies'.

The distribution right is subject to an important **limitation** known as the **exhaustion** doctrine. Under the exhaustion doctrine, the distribution right in a copy is said to 'exhaust' once the author puts the copy on the market.[15] For example, consider an author who writes a novel and fixes that work in a physical book. The author then sells the physical book to a reader. At this point, the distribution right 'exhausts' (or, more simply, ends). No one can stop the buyer from, for example, selling that book on to someone else. Of course, the author can still stop the buyer from making copies of the novel and selling those. But the author has no power to restrict onward sale of the tangible copy which they have consensually put on the market. In some jurisdictions, the exhaustion doctrine is called the 'first sale doctrine'.[16]

The exhaustion doctrine has a deep and significant connection with other areas of property law. In relation to land and chattels, the common law has historically disfavoured so-called restraints on alienation.[17] For example, if a person sells their home or their car, the seller cannot legally prevent the buyer from reselling the land or car. Lawyers have largely concluded that once the good becomes the property of the buyer, then the seller relinquishes all control over the good. And so too is the view taken in copyright. If, for example, you write a letter, you retain ownership of

Limitations and exceptions are important concepts in copyright. A limitation is a rule that helps to divide restricted acts from non-restricted acts. **Exceptions** are rules that permit someone to perform a restricted act. Chapter 5 considers exceptions.

The independent creation doctrine, introduced in Section 4.1.1 is relevant to all the economic rights. It is not an infringement of the distribution right, for example, to distribute independently created copies of works, or to communicate or perform such works in public.

the words of the letter, but the recipient owns the physical paper on which the words are written, and is free to dispose of it as they wish.[18]

The invention of the Internet has raised new questions about the **exhaustion** doctrine. Today, creative works are not packaged in tangible goods, but instead frequently distributed over the Internet. Novels are not only sold as physical paper books, but as eBooks – where a digital file containing the novel can be directly downloaded by a consumer onto a device, such as a Kindle. Similarly, software is also frequently purchased online as direct downloads. In times gone by, the buyer would be able to resell the tangible paper books and the CDs that contained the novel or software. But can someone who buys an eBook lawfully distribute that eBook when they are done reading it? Or, to put it another way, does the author's distribution right in the eBook exhaust after the eBook file is sold to the consumer? The following case says no.

Case 4.3 *Nederlands Uitgeversverbnd, Groep Algemene Uitgevers v Tom Kabinet Internet BV*, C-263/18 (2019) (CJEU)

Facts

Tom Kabinet (defendant) operated a website. From 8 June 2015 onwards, Tom Kabinet began the 'Tom's Leesclub' (i.e. 'Tom's Reading Club'). For a price of €1.75, members of the club could download used eBooks. The used eBooks had either been purchased by Tom Kabinet or donated to Tom Kabinet free of charge by members of the club. In the latter case, the members had to declare they did not retain a copy of the eBook. Membership of the reading club was subject to monthly payment by members of €3.99 (although the precise payment structure changed over time).

Nederlands Uitgeversverbond (NUV) and Groep Algemene Uitgevers (GAU) (claimants) were associations that defend the interest of Dutch publishers. NUV and GAU brought a copyright action against Tom Kabinet in the Netherlands. Tom Kabinet argued that when the publishers sold the eBooks, the distribution right in the digital files exhausted, and thus the eBooks could be redistributed by the buyers. In response, the publishers argued that selling the digital eBook files was not an act of distribution and, therefore, the distribution right had not exhausted in respect to those files.

Issue and Procedure

The Netherlands district court (the rechtbank Den Haag) referred a question to the CJEU on a matter of EU law. Article 4 of the Information Society Directive (EU Directive 2001/29) provides authors with a distribution right that is exhausted when the copyright owner puts a copy of a work on the market. The court asked whether the publisher's initial sale of the eBook files over the Internet was an act of distribution, and whether the distribution right in said files had therefore

---

We will see the exhaustion doctrine again in Parts II–IV. It is one of the few doctrines that is found in every area of IP.

exhausted. If the answer was 'yes' to both questions, then the buyers would be permitted to distribute the files to Tom Kabinet and beyond.

The CJEU decided that sale of the eBooks was not an act of distribution and the distribution right had not exhausted. But, in reaching the decision, the court also had to explain why they had previously held (in *Usedsoft* C-128/11) that sale of *software* files over the Internet was an act of distribution and therefore was subject to the exhaustion rule.

COURT OF JUSTICE, GRAND CHAMBER

In the first place, it must be noted that, as is apparent from recital 15 of Directive 2001/29, the directive serves, inter alia, to implement a number of the European Union's obligations under the WCT [WIPO Copyright Treaty]. . . .

Article 6(1) of the WCT defines the right of distribution as the exclusive right of authors to authorise the making available to the public of the original and copies of their works through sale or other transfer of ownership. It is apparent from the wording of the Agreed Statements concerning Articles 6 and 7 of the WCT that 'the expressions 'copies' and 'original and copies', being subject to the right of distribution and the right of rental under the said Articles, refer exclusively to fixed copies that can be put into circulation as tangible objects', and therefore that Article 6(1) cannot cover the distribution of intangible works such as e-books.

Admittedly, as the referring court notes, the Court of Justice has ruled, in relation to the exhaustion of the right of distribution of copies of computer programs mentioned in Article 4(2) of Directive 2009/24, that it does not appear from that provision that exhaustion is limited to copies of computer programs on a material medium, but that, on the contrary, that provision, by referring without further specification to the 'sale . . . of a copy of a program', makes no distinction according to the tangible or intangible form of the copy in question (judgment of 3 July 2012, *UsedSoft*, C-128/11, EU:C:2012:407, paragraph 55).

However, as the referring court correctly points out and as the Advocate General noted in point 67 of his Opinion, an e-book is not a computer program, and it is not appropriate therefore to apply the specific provisions of Directive 2009/24.

In that regard, first, as the Court expressly stated in paragraphs 51 and 56 of the judgment of 3 July 2012, *UsedSoft* (C-128/11, EU:C:2012:407), Directive 2009/24, which concerns specifically the protection of computer programs, constitutes a *lex specialis* in relation to

Directive 2001/29. The relevant provisions of Directive 2009/24 make abundantly clear the intention of the EU legislature to assimilate, for the purposes of the protection laid down by that directive, tangible and intangible copies of computer programs, so that the exhaustion of the distribution right under Article 4(2) of Directive 2009/24 concerns all such copies (see, to that effect, judgment of 3 July 2012, *UsedSoft*, C-128/11, EU:C:2012:407, paragraphs 58 and 59).

Such assimilation of tangible and intangible copies of works protected for the purposes of the relevant provisions of Directive 2001/29 was not, however, desired by the EU legislature when it adopted that directive. As has been recalled in paragraph 42 of the present judgment, it is apparent from the *travaux préparatoires* for that directive that a clear distinction was sought between the electronic and tangible distribution of protected material.

Second, the Court noted in paragraph 61 of the judgment of 3 July 2012, *UsedSoft* (C-128/11, EU:C:2012:407) that, from an economic point of view, the sale of a computer program on a material medium and the sale of a computer program by downloading from the internet are similar, since the online transmission method is the functional equivalent of the supply of a material medium. Accordingly, interpreting Article 4(2) of Directive 2009/24 in the light of the principle of equal treatment justifies the two methods of transmission being treated in a similar manner.

The supply of a book on a material medium and the supply of an e-book cannot, however, be considered equivalent from an economic and functional point of view. As the Advocate General noted in point 89 of his Opinion, dematerialised digital copies, unlike books on a material medium, do not deteriorate with use, and used copies are therefore perfect **substitutes** for new copies. In addition, exchanging such copies requires neither additional effort nor additional cost, so that a parallel second-hand market would be likely to affect the interests of the copyright holders in obtaining appropriate reward for their works much more than the market for second-hand tangible objects...

(paras 39–40, 53–58)

Pay close attention to the last two paragraphs. Why would reselling eBooks make it too hard for the owner to obtain an 'appropriate' reward? After all, we currently permit the reselling of software (whether sold initially as CD or online). Presumably, that does not make it too hard to obtain an 'appropriate' reward. Is the CJEU making the right comparisons here?

The conclusion that the transfer of an eBook online is not an act of distribution is a double-edged sword. On one side, the publisher's initial sale of the book was not a distribution, and therefore the distribution right was not exhausted. But, on the other side, Tom Kabinet's retransfer of the intangible eBook files could also be not conceptualised as an act of distribution either. That being the case, the owner's distribution right did not empower the owner to control the transfers made by Tom Kabinet.

Initially, this might seem like a good outcome for Tom Kabinet: they were doing something that the owner's distribution right did not prevent. This might suggest that the transfer was, like reading or smelling a work, a non-restricted activity. However, while the act of retransferring the eBook was not considered a distribution, the CJEU did consider it to qualify as something else: an act of 'communication to the public'. We will return to this right in Section 4.1.5.

4.1.3 Rental and Lending Right

In 1992, the EU adopted Directive 92/100 (the 'Rental and Lending' Directive). The directive required member states to give authors the exclusive right to 'rent' and to 'lend' their works or substantial part thereof. Both rental and lending involves making the work (the original or a copy) available to others for a period before it is returned. Rental is defined as making available 'for direct or indirect economic or commercial advantage' whereas lending is performed without such advantage.[19] The definition of lending excludes lending between private individuals, and only is implicated by lending through establishments that are 'accessible to the public' (such as libraries). The UK CDPA was subsequently updated to conform to the directive.

This right was adopted principally because of the home video rental market. In particular, the company Blockbuster LLC had achieved widespread geographic prominence and made a very profitable business from renting out VHS video tapes. Since the demise of the home video rental market, and Blockbuster LLC, the right has lost some significance. However, the right has taken on new relevance in relation to so-called e-lending. Will offering temporary access to works in electronic form over the Internet implicate the right? The CJEU in *Vereniging Openbare Bibliotheken (VOB) v Sichting Leenrecht* has so far concluded that the definition of lending includes e-lending, but the definition of rental does not include e-rentals.[20]

4.1.4 Performance Right

The public performance right was added in 1833 to protect the authors of dramatic works.[21] Typically plays are written for performance on the stage, and so playwrights desire legal rights to prevent unauthorised performances of their works. Today, the performance right applies not only to dramatic works, but also to literary works and musical works (but not artistic works).[22] The authors of such works enjoy the exclusive right to 'perform, show or play the work in public' (CDPA, section 16(c)). The owner can also prevent performance of a 'substantial part' of their work.

The difficult question posed by the performance right is what qualifies as a 'public' performance? Singing in the shower is surely a private performance, while performing a song in front of a packed crowd at Wembley Stadium is clearly a public performance. But what about performing a play for a private members club? In *Jennings v Stephens* the UK Chancery Court held that the performance of a play in front of sixty-two members of a branch of the Women's Institute qualified as a 'public' performance.[23] But courts have never settled on a precise test or method to distinguish between private and public performances.[24]

4.1.5 Communication Right

The communication right is one of the newer aspects of copyright law, but is fast becoming the most important right.

The right's origins can be found in the invention of radio broadcasting early in the twentieth century. Imagine, for example, a DJ plays a song on the radio. It might be disingenuous to say that DJ has *performed* the song; especially if all they have done is press the 'play' button. More appropriately, we might say the DJ has *communicated* that song to the public.

The communication right increased in importance during the twentieth century, with the invention of television and satellite broadcasting, and, more recently, the Internet. Uploading a file containing a copyrighted work to a peer-to-peer network, or to a platform like YouTube, both are examples of communication to the public in the digital era. Today, the owner enjoys the exclusive right to communicate the work, or substantial part thereof, to the public.

At the same time, the communication right has become increasingly controversial. To some, granting copyright owners broad powers to restrict *communication* threatens freedom of expression. At worst, the communication right may result in a form of censorship (see Figure 4.3).

> Section 2.1 explained the copyright's history as a form of censorship. To some, even modern copyright retains features of censorship.

Figure 4.3 Protests against the Directive on Copyright in the Digital Single Market (2019) took place in numerous European cities, including Berlin, as demonstrated here.
(Photo by Emmanuele Contini/NurPhoto via Getty Images)

The controversial nature of the communication right is echoed in case law. As the right has become a more powerful tool in the hands of copyright owners, more and more litigation surrounding the right has followed. In a mere fourteen years, the CJEU has delivered over twenty-five judgments relating to the right. In Case 4.4, Lord Justice Arnold provides a helpful summary of this case law, as well as illustrating how powerful the communication right can be.

In the Digital Single Market Directive, the EU legislated that when someone uploads copyrighted material to an online platform (e.g. YouTube, Google), both the uploader and platform are 'communicating' the work to the public.[25] Some argue that platforms will accordingly 'censor' the materials allowed on their platform.

Case 4.4 *TuneIn Inc v Warner Music UK Ltd* [2021] EWCA Civ 441

Facts

Warner Music UK and Sony Music Entertainment UK (claimants–respondents) own copyright in sound recordings of musical works. These sound recordings are played on radio stations around the world.

TuneIn Radio (defendants–appellants) operated a website and a series of apps that enabled Internet users to listen to over 100,000 Internet radio stations. For the most part, these Internet radio stations were owned and operated outside of the UK (for example, Capital FM Bangladesh). Internet users in the UK could log into the TuneIn system and select a radio station to which they wished to listen. At this point, a type of web framing occurred: through hyperlinks, the radio station broadcast was picked up and directed through TuneIn to the end user in the UK. Frequently, the radio stations broadcast the sound recordings owned by the claimants. Warner Music objected to TuneIn communicating the broadcasted works to UK-based listeners.

Issue and Procedure

The claimants brought a copyright infringement against TuneIn. But was TuneIn Radio communicating the work to the public in the UK against the claimants' exclusive rights? At first instance, Mr Justice Birss (as he then was) held that the defendants had infringed the communication to the public right. The defendants appealed to the UK Court of Appeals where Lord Justice Arnold began by summarising the rather voluminous case law on the subject.

ARNOLD LJ [INTERNAL CITATIONS OMITTED]

The judge quoted and applied a summary of the CJEU's case law down to *ITV* which I set out in *Paramount Home Entertainment International Ltd v British Sky Broadcasting Ltd [2013] EWHC 3479 (Ch), [2014] ECDR 7 ('Paramount')* at [12]. I would update that summary (so far as possible in the CJEU's own words) as follows:

(1) 'Communication to the public' must be interpreted broadly.

(2) 'Communication to the public' covers any transmission or retransmission of the work to the public not present at the place where the communication originates by wire or wireless means, including broadcasting. It does not include any communication of a work which is carried out directly in a place open to the public by means of public performance or direct presentation of the work.

(3) There is no 'communication to the public' where the viewers have no access to an essential element which characterises the work.

(4) 'Communication to the public' involves two cumulative criteria: first, an 'act of communication' of a work, and secondly, the communication of that work to a 'public'. Nevertheless, it is necessary to carry out an individualised assessment in the light of several factors which are complementary, interdependent and may be present in widely-varying degrees both individually and in their interaction with each other.

(5) 'Communication' refers to any transmission of the work, irrespective of the technical means or process used.

(6) Every transmission or retransmission of the work by a specific technical means must, as a rule, be individually authorised by the right holder.

(7) A mere technical means to ensure or improve reception of the original transmission in its catchment area does not constitute a 'communication'.

(8) A user makes an act of 'communication' when it intervenes, in full knowledge of the consequences of its action, to give its customers access to a protected work, particularly where, in the absence of that intervention, those customers would not be able to enjoy the work, or would be able to do so only with difficulty.

(9) It is sufficient for there to be 'communication' that the work is made available to the public in such a way that the persons forming that public may access it, whether or not those persons actually access the work.

(10) Mere provision of physical facilities does not as such amount to 'communication'. Nevertheless, the installation of physical facilities which distribute a signal and thus make public access to works technically possible constitutes 'communication'.

(11) 'The public' refers to an indeterminate number of potential recipients and implies a fairly large number of persons. 'Indeterminate' means not restricted to specific individuals belonging to a private group; and 'a fairly large number of people' indicates that the concept of 'public' encompasses a certain *de minimis* threshold, which excludes from the concept groups of persons which are too small, or insignificant.

> (12) For that purpose, the cumulative effect of making the works available to potential recipients should be taken into account, and it is particularly relevant to ascertain the number of persons who have access to the same work at the same time and successively.
>
> (13) Where there is a communication of works by the same technical means as a previous communication, it is necessary to show that the communication is to a new public, that is to say, a public which was not considered by the right holder when it authorised the original communication. Where there is a communication using a different technical means to that of the original communication, however, it is not necessary to consider whether the communication is to a new public.
>
> (14) In considering whether there is a communication to 'the public', it is not irrelevant that the communication is of a profit-making nature. A profit-making nature is not necessarily an essential condition for a communication to the public, however.
>
> (15) In order to establish whether the fact of posting, on a website, hyperlinks to protected works which are freely available on another website without the consent of the copyright holder, constitutes a 'communication to the public', it is to be determined whether those links are provided without the pursuit of financial gain by a person who did not know or could not reasonably have known the illegal nature of the publication of those works on that other website or whether, on the contrary, those links are provided for such a purpose, a situation in which that knowledge must be presumed.
>
> (para 70)

The extensive nature of Lord Justice Arnold's list reflects how quickly this area of law has developed in a relatively short length of time. But the foundational point in the list is number 4. The case law has repeatedly concluded that 'communication' and 'to the public' are two cumulative conditions. Nevertheless, courts have also stressed the need for an 'individualised assessment', meaning that a range of factors may need to be considered and some of these factors are interdependent; these factors are listed in points 5–15. Lord Justice Arnold then provided a helpful summary of what, so far, has qualified as communication to the public and what has not.

ARNOLD LJ

> Applying these principles, the following have been held by the CJEU to constitute 'communication to the public':

(1) The transmission of television and radio broadcasts, and sound recordings included therein, to the customers of hotels, public houses, spas, café-restaurants and rehabilitation centres by means of television and radio sets: *SGAE*; *Organismos*; *FAPL*; *PPIL*; *OSA*; *SPA*; *Reha*.

(2) Where a satellite package provider expands the circle of persons having access to the relevant works: *Airfield*.

(3) The retransmission of works included in a terrestrial television broadcast by an organisation other than the original broadcaster by means of an internet stream made available to the subscribers of that other organisation, even though those subscribers are within the area of reception of the terrestrial television broadcast and may lawfully receive the broadcast on a television: *ITV*.

(4) The provision by a website operator for profit of hyperlinks to files containing copyright photographs which had been posted on another website without the consent of the copyright owner and which the operator of the first website was aware had been posted without the consent of the copyright owner: *GS Media*.

(5) The sale of a multimedia player on which there are pre-installed add-ons containing hyperlinks to websites that are freely accessible to the public on which copyright-protected works have been made available without the consent of the right holders: *Filmspeler*.

(6) The making available and management on the internet of a sharing platform which, by means of indexation of metadata referring to protected works and the provision of a search engine, allows users of that platform to locate those works and to share them in the context of a peer-to-peer network: *Pirate Bay*.

(7) The provision of a cloud computing service for the remote video recording of copies of protected works: *VCAST*.

(8) The posting on one website of a copy of a photograph previously posted, without any restriction preventing it from being downloaded and with the consent of the copyright holder, on another website: *Renckhoff*.

(9) The supply to the public by downloading, for permanent use, of an e-book: *Tom Kabinet* (and see also *Soulier*).

By contrast, the following have been held by the CJEU not to constitute 'communication to the public':

(1) Television broadcasting of a graphic user interface of a computer program: *Bezpečností*.

(2) The communication of musical works to the public in the context of live circus and cabaret performances: *Circul*.

(3) The broadcast of sound recordings by way of background music to patients of a private dental practice: *SCF*.

Note here the reference to *Tom Kabinet*. As discussed in Section 4.1.1.2, Tom Kabinet's transfer of the eBooks was not a distribution of the work, but it was a communication to the public. Using the information here, can you see why?

(4) The provision on one website of a hyperlink to works which are freely available on another website with the consent of the right holder: *Svensson*; *BestWater*; *GS Media*; *Filmspeler*; *Renckhoff*; *VG Bild*. It makes no difference if clicking on the link results in 'framing' of the works on the first website: *Svensson*; *BestWater*; *VG Bild*. But it does make a difference if the link circumvents technical measures put in place on the second website to restrict access to the latter site's subscribers or to prevent framing: *Svensson*; *VG Bild*.

(5) The transmission by a broadcasting organisation of programme-carrying signals exclusively to signal distributors without those signals being accessible to the public, where those distributors then send those signals to their respective subscribers so that the latter may watch the programmes, unless the intervention of the distributors in question is just a technical means: *SBS*.

(6) The simultaneous, full and unaltered transmission within the national territory by the operator of a cable network of programmes broadcast by a national broadcaster: *AKM*.

(7) The supply of a radio receiver forming an integral part of a hired motor vehicle, which makes it possible to receive, without any additional intervention by the leasing company, the terrestrial radio broadcasts available in the area in which the vehicle is located: *Stim*.

(8)The transmission by electronic means of a protected work to a court as evidence in judicial proceedings between individuals: *BY*.

(paras 71–72)

Lord Justice Arnold found that TuneIn had communicated the work. This itself was relatively unsurprising. Several cases – the ones listed in paragraph 72(4) of Lord Justice Arnold's judgment – already concluded that hyperlinking to a page containing a work was a form of communication.

A more difficult question was whether TuneIn had communicated the work 'to the public'. The difficulty arose out of a tension between *Svensson* and another leading case, *Renckhoff*.[26]

In *Svensson*, the defendants hyperlinked to articles contained on newspapers' websites. The newspaper websites, and the articles thereon, were unrestricted and could be accessed by all Internet users (they were, as Lord Justice Arnold says in 72(4) 'freely available'). Under these conditions, it was held that while the act of hyperlinking was an act of communication, it was not a communication to the 'public' because the copyright holder had *already* communicated the work to the public. The defendant's act would only be within the scope of the communication right in these circumstances if the communication allowed a '**new public**' to access the work. A 'new public' was defined as a public that was not 'taken into account

Copyright III: Rights

by the copyright holders when they authorised the initial communication' of their work.

However, more recently in *Renckhoff*, the CJEU concluded that when a copyright holder uploads their work to a website, the only public they anticipate engaging with the work are the users of the website – and no one else. Accordingly, reposting a work to another website would qualify as communication to a new public.

The tension between the *Svensson* and *Renckhoff* cases was clear in *TuneIn*. Many of the foreign radio stations were playing the claimant's music lawfully (called 'Category 3 stations' in the extract below). Under the rules of their local jurisdictions, they were allowed to communicate the work providing they paid the copyright owners a statutory fee – which they had done. Mr Justice Birss concluded therefore that the claimants could be deemed to have consented to their work appearing on the Internet. Under *Svensson*, this might suggest that TuneIn's act of redirecting the music to a UK audience did not amount to a communication to a *new* public. However, Mr Justice Birss ultimately rejected that argument, as did Lord Justice Arnold on appeal.

> This is known as a '**compulsory licence**'. We will return to this idea in Section 4.1.4. A more significant consideration of the issue can also be found in Chapter 9.

ARNOLD LJ

The judge proceeded to consider whether TuneIn's communication was to a new public, and concluded that it was for the following reasons:

'The starting point in answer to this question must be the scope of the deemed consent. The most that this should be taken to be is a ratification of the work's appearance on the internet in the radio station stream in a manner which gives rise to the obligation to pay royalties under the local law. In other words it should be seen as deemed consent to the work appearing on the internet in a manner aimed either at users of the local website in question or, at most, at users in the locality in question as a whole. In neither case does this involve ratification of an act targeted to the UK, albeit that one has to recognise that the activity does in fact make the works freely available to internet users everywhere if they care to look for the relevant stream.

Accordingly, once the streams in the Category 3 stations are freely available on the internet, it is an inherent aspect of the function of the internet that they could be indexed by conventional search engines or linked to by publishers of conventional websites. The operation of conventional search engines and linking on conventional websites is something inherently taken into account when a work is placed on the internet.

Therefore it is appropriate to analyse the facts on the footing that the whole internet public, insofar as they encounter a link to a

> Although not the main feature of the case, Arnold LJ also believed that the foreign radio stations were 'communicating' the works to the UK listeners. This is a striking outcome. The radio stations had no knowledge of how their broadcasts were being used by TuneIn.

> Category 3 station which is provided either by a conventional search engine or some other conventional sort of website, has been taken into account. It is an inherent aspect of making this material available on the internet that that sort of linking is likely to happen.
>
> On the other hand, absent evidence to the contrary, there is no reason why the kind of public to whom TuneIn's system is addressed should have been taken into account. TuneIn's activity is a different kind of act of communication and is targeted at a particular public, i.e. users in the UK.
>
> Putting this together, I hold that the public to whom TuneIn's act of communication complained of is addressed cannot be said to have been taken into account in relation to the first act of communication. Accordingly TuneIn's act of communication in relation to Category 3 is to a new public . . .'
>
> TuneIn challenges this conclusion on no less than nine grounds (grounds 11–19), but most of them traverse points I have already addressed. TuneIn's core argument is that the judge was wrong to treat the right holders' authorisation of the original communication as territorially restricted because that is contrary to *Svensson*, but I disagree. As the judge correctly stated, TuneIn Radio is a different kind of communication (in the sense that it has the features of aggregation, categorisation, etc discussed above) targeted at a different public in a different territory. Even assuming that the operation of a statutory scheme in a foreign territory amounts to a form of deemed consent on the part of the rights holders to the original communication to the public, including persons who access the streams via simple hyperlinks or conventional search engines, there is no reason to conclude that that authorisation extended to the UK public targeted by TuneIn Radio's communication. On the contrary, counsel for TuneIn accepted that TuneIn had never sought to defend this claim on the basis that targeting UK users (let alone targeting them by TuneIn Radio's communication) was licensed by virtue of the payments made by foreign internet radio stations in their local territories.
>
> (paras 141–42)

The owner's ability to restrict communication necessarily implicates individuals' freedom of expression rights. TuneIn argued that holding them liable for communicating the protected works to the UK public failed to strike a fair balance between the claimant's copyright and their freedom of expression. But this argument was dismissed in relatively short order by Lord Justice Arnold. The principles that he summarised in paragraph 70 had already been judged by the CJEU as

Copyright III: Rights

striking the right balance between competing fundamental rights. This was in part the result of the previous *GS Media* case.

Case 4.5 *GS Media BV v Sanoma Media Netherlands BV and others*, C-160/15 (2016) (CJEU)

Facts

Britt Dekker is a Dutch celebrity. Nude photographs of Ms Dekker were due to appear in the November 2011 edition of the Dutch edition of *Playboy Magazine*. These photographs had been taken with her consent. The copyright in the photographs were owned by Sanoma Media (claimant). However, before the magazine was published, the photographs were leaked online. The leaked photographs were freely available on various third-party file-storing websites.

Geenstijl.nl is a Dutch blog owned by GS Media BV (defendants). The blog operators posted hyperlinks on their blog which, when clicked, directed Internet users to the third-party websites where the photographs could be accessed. Sanoma requested GS Media to remove the hyperlinks, but GS Media refused. Sanoma sued GS Media for infringing their right of communication to the public in the Netherlands.

Issue and Procedure

The Netherlands court stayed proceedings and referred various questions to the CJEU. The question for preliminary ruling was, in effect, whether and in what circumstances posting a hyperlink on a website to photographs on a freely available third-party website would qualify as a 'communication to the public'. GS Media responded, in part, that such a finding would have negative implications for the freedom of expression. The CJEU disagreed.

COURT OF JUSTICE, SECOND CHAMBER

GS Media, the German, Portuguese and Slovak Governments and the European Commission claim, however, that the fact of automatically categorising all posting of such links to works published on other websites as 'communication to the public', since the copyright holders of those works have not consented to that publication on the internet, would have highly restrictive consequences for freedom of expression and of information and would not be consistent with the right balance which Directive 2001/29 seeks to establish between that freedom and the public interest on the one hand, and the interests of copyright holders in an effective protection of their intellectual property, on the other.

Furthermore, it may be difficult, in particular for individuals who wish to post such links, to ascertain whether website to which those links are expected to lead, provides access to works which are protected and, if necessary, whether the copyright holders of those works have consented to their posting on the internet. Such ascertaining is all the more difficult where those rights have been the subject of sub-licenses. Moreover, the content of a website to which a hyperlink enables access may be changed after the creation of that link, including the protected works, without the person who created that link necessarily being aware of it.

In contrast, where it is established that such a person knew or ought to have known that the hyperlink he posted provides access to a work illegally placed on the internet, for example owing to the fact that he was notified thereof by the copyright holders, it is necessary to consider that the provision of that link constitutes a 'communication to the public' within the meaning of Article 3(1) of Directive 2001/29.

(paras 44–45. 49)

ACTIVITY 4.5

What does the historical evolution of the communication right mean for copyright as a property right?

4.1.6 Adaptation Right

Although less controversial than the communication right, the adaptation right also presents its own puzzles. Some countries, notably the USA, give authors a very broad right to 'prepare derivative works based upon the copyrighted work'; where the term 'derivative work' is defined broadly to include any 'work based upon one or more pre-existing works'.[27] By contrast, the UK's 'adaptation right' is narrower in two ways. First, only literary, dramatic and musical works (not artistic works) enjoy the right of adaptation. Second, the term 'adaptation' is defined specifically in relation to each type of work in section 21 CDPA.

> (3) In this Part 'adaptation' –
>   (a) in relation to a literary work, other than a computer program or a database, or in relation to a dramatic work, means –
>   (i) a translation of the work;

> (ii) a version of a dramatic work in which it is converted into a non-dramatic work or, as the case may be, of a non-dramatic work in which it is converted into a dramatic work;
>
> (iii) a version of the work in which the story or action is conveyed wholly or mainly by means of pictures in a form suitable for reproduction in a book, or in a newspaper, magazine or similar periodical;
>
> (ab) in relation to a computer program, means an arrangement or altered version of the program or a translation of it;
>
> (ac) in relation to a database, means an arrangement or altered version of the database or a translation of it;
>
> (b) in relation to a musical work, means an arrangement or transcription of the work.

4.2 MORAL RIGHTS

As a terminological matter, the word 'copyright' sometimes is used to refer to the economic rights only. The implication is that 'moral rights' are not 'copyright' at all, but instead something else entirely.

In addition to economic rights, contemporary copyright law also grants authors a set of **moral rights**. The moral rights provided by the CDPA are summarised in Table 4.3. The moral rights are notionally designed to protect the author's personality interest in the work.

Table 4.3 The CDPA's moral rights

Name	CDPA sections	Statutory language
Integrity right	80	The right 'in the circumstances mentioned in this section not to have his work subjected to derogatory treatment'.
Attribution right	77	The right to be 'identified as the author...of the work in the circumstances mentioned in this section'.
False attribution right	84	The right 'in the circumstances mentioned in this section not to have... work falsely attributed to him as author'.

Moral rights are a relatively modern addition to UK copyright law. The rights were gradually created in the civil law countries of central Europe during the late nineteenth century. It was not until the 1928 revision of the Berne Convention in Rome that the UK had to consider whether they too should adopt moral rights protection. Legal historian, Peter Baldwin, explains the 'strange birth' that moral rights enjoyed in the interwar years of 'Fascist Europe'.

> ## BOX 4.1 PETER BALDWIN, *THE COPYRIGHT WARS: THREE CENTURIES OF TRANS-ATLANTIC BATTLE* (PRINCETON UP 2014) 164–66
>
> Moral rights express legislative concern for the creative classes.[28] They have long been important in Europe but only belatedly and grudgingly so in the Anglophone world. Their supporters, both on the Continent and in the United States and Britain, have often assumed, in a vague and unarticulated sense, that moral rights arise from the Western tradition's most enlightened instincts. Their actual legislative pedigree, however, was less pristine. Moral rights first became part of the Berne Convention at the 1928 conference held in Fascist Rome. They did not just 'filter' onto the agenda. The Italian delegation placed them there to showcase the Mussolini regime's cultural credentials and register its ambitions for an honored and legitimate place in Europe's patrimony.
>
> Moral rights did not arrive unannounced in Mussolini's Rome. Though little had been codified, such ideas had worked their way through French and German case law for half a century. In 1886 the Berne Convention had foreshadowed the **attribution** right when it insisted that reprinted periodical articles name their source. Moral rights were legislated in Romania (1923), Poland (1926), Czechoslovakia (1926), Portugal (1927), and Italy itself (1925). The Italian act, which had been passed during the legislative session that approved the fundamental laws of the Fascist regime, served as the template of the Berne Rome conference's reforms in 1928.
>
> Still, moral rights faced obstacles in 1928. The Commonwealth nations considered such novelties irreconcilable with their copyright tradition. The distance between Anglo-Saxon and Latin mentalities was nowhere more evident, or so the New Zealand delegate reported back home. While the Continental delegates enthused, the English speaking nations 'coldly received' moral rights. The UK Board of Trade thought they fell outside the scope of copyright law. In any case, libel law sufficed to remedy violations.

Peter Baldwin is a professor of history at the University of California, Los Angeles.

Despite the early reservations expressed by the UK, the Berne Convention adopted a requirement that the moral rights of authors be protected under certain conditions. And, in the twentieth century, the UK adopted certain statutory provisions to comply with the requirement. Nonetheless, the divide between the common law countries and the civil law countries persists. Stark contrasts exist between the level of moral rights protection offered by the UK and, for example, France.

4.2.1 The Integrity Right

Section 80 of the CDPA grants authors the right to prevent derogatory treatment of their work in certain circumstances. Section 80(2)(b) states that treatment is derogatory if 'it amounts to distortion or mutilation of the work or is otherwise prejudicial to the honour or reputation of the author'. UK courts have held that a treatment can be derogatory only where there is evidence that such treatment affects the honour or reputation of the author. This contrast with French law, where the author can object to derogatory treatment without evidence that their honour or reputation has suffered.[29]

Case 4.6 *Confetti Records v Warner Music UK Ltd* [2003] EMLR 35

Facts

Andrew Alcee (claimant) was a musician and member of the UK garage band, Ant'ill Mob. In 1995, Alcee composed the track *'Burnin''*. The economic rights in the song were assigned to Confetti Records; Alcee retained the moral rights in the work.

The Heartless Crew was a UK garage band signed to a record label belonging to Warner Music UK (defendant). The Heartless Crew licensed the use of *'Burnin''* to use as a backing track, over which they rapped. The song appeared on their album, *Crisp Biscuit*. Warner Music UK distributed the album. The language used in the rap involved terms such as 'mish mish man', 'shizzle (or sizzle) my nizzle' and 'string dem up one by one', which Alcee and Confetti Records claimed were references to drug abuse and violence. Alcee and Confetti Records brought a copyright infringement action which included a claim that the Heartless Crew had violated Alcee's right of integrity.

Issue and Procedure

The issues presented included: must a claimant present evidence of harm to honour or reputation to demonstrate a violation of the right of integrity and, if so, had the claimants presented sufficient evidence of derogatory treatment? Mr Justice Lewison in the Chancery Division of the High Court found that such evidence is required in the UK and that the claimant had not presented such evidence.

LEWISON J

Under s. 80 of the Copyright Patents and Designs Act 1988 the author of a literary, dramatic, musical or artistic work has the right, in certain circumstances, not to have his work subjected to derogatory treatment. This is a claim that is separate from a claim for infringement of copyright.

Those circumstances include the issuing to the public of a sound recording including a derogatory treatment of the work.

The defendant accepts that it has issued to the public a sound recording including 'Burnin'', and also accepts that the addition of the rap line was a 'treatment' of it. The issue is whether the treatment is derogatory.

Under s.80(2)(b) of the 1988 Act a treatment is derogatory if: 'it amounts to distortion or mutilation of the work or is otherwise prejudicial to the honour or reputation of the author'.

Mr Howe submitted that there could be no derogatory treatment unless the treatment was prejudicial to the honour or reputation of the author. Mr Shipley, on the other hand, said that treatment was derogatory if it was a distortion or mutilation of the work, even if it did not prejudice the honour or reputation of the author. Both Laddie Prescott & Vitoria on The Modern Law of Copyrights and Designs (3rd ed.) para. 13.18, and Copinger & Skone James on Copyright (14th ed.) para. 11–42, disagree with this view. So do I. Section 80 is clearly intended to give effect to Art.6 bis of the Berne Convention. That article gives the author the right to object: 'to any distortion, mutilation or other modification of, or other derogatory action in relation to, the said work, which would be prejudicial to his honour or reputation'.

It is clear that in Art.6 bis the author can only object to distortion, mutilation or modification of his work if it is prejudicial to his honour or reputation. I do not believe that the framers of the 1988 Act meant to alter the scope of the author's moral rights in this respect. Moreover, in the compressed drafting style of the United Kingdom legislature, the word 'otherwise' itself suggests that the distortion or mutilation is only actionable if it is prejudicial to the author's honour or reputation. H.H. Judge Overend adopted this construction in *Pasterfield v Denham* [1999] F.S.R. 168, and in my judgment he was correct to do so. I hold that the mere fact that a work has been distorted or mutilated gives rise to no claim, unless the distortion or mutilation prejudices the author's honour or reputation.

The nub of the original complaint, principally advanced by Mr Pascal, is that the words of the rap (or at least that part contributed by Elephant Man) contained references to violence and drugs. This led to the faintly surreal experience of three gentlemen in horsehair wigs examining the meaning of such phrases as 'mish mish man' and 'shizzle (or sizzle) my nizzle'.

Mr Pascal did not himself claim to know what street meanings were to be attributed to the disputed phrases, but said that he had been told what they were by an unnamed informant conversant with the use of drugs. Mr Howe submitted, correctly in my opinion, that the meaning of words in a foreign language could only be explained by experts. He also submitted, again correctly in my opinion, that the words of the rap, although in a form of English, were for practical purposes a foreign language. Thus he submitted that Mr Pascal's evidence, not being the evidence of an expert, was inadmissible. I think that he is right, although the occasions on which an expert drug dealer might be called to give evidence in the Chancery Division are likely to be rare.

But even if I pay regard to Mr Pascal's evidence on this topic, I do not find that the meaning of the disputed words has been proved. Mr Pascal's evidence was hearsay, and the source of his information was not identified. Mr Hunter, one of the MCs with The Heartless Crew, (professionally known as MC Bushkin) had not heard of the meanings that Mr Pascal attributed to the disputed phrases. Nor had Mr Thomas. A search on the Internet discovered the Urban Dictionary which gave some definitions of 'shizzle my nizzle' (and variants) none of which referred to drugs. Some definitions carried sexual connotations. The most popular definitions were definitions of the phrase 'fo' shizzle my nizzle' and indicated that it meant 'for sure'. There were no entries for 'sizzle my nizzle' or for 'mish mish man', and Mr Hunter said that Elephant Man (the MC who uttered the disputed phrases) often made up words for their rhyming effect.

To be fair, Mr Shipley did not press this complaint in his closing submissions. Instead he sought to advance a new case. First he said that the treatment was derogatory because all coherence of the original work has been lost as a result of the superimposition of the rap. Secondly he said, whatever a 'mish mish man' was, the words of the rap 'string dem up one by one' was an invitation to lynching. It is by no means clear that the words on the rap are in fact 'string dem up'. Moreover, I am not at all sure that the meaning Mr Shipley attributes to the phrase 'string dem up' is the only possible meaning. A proponent of capital punishment who says that murderers should be 'strung up' would usually be taken to advocate the return of a hangman, rather than lynching.

However, it seems to me that the fundamental weakness in this part of the case is that I have no evidence about Mr Alcee's honour or reputation. I have no evidence of any prejudice to either of them. Mr Alcee himself made no complaint about the treatment of 'Burnin'' in his witness statement. Mr Shipley invites me to infer prejudice. Where the author himself makes no complaint, I do not consider that I should infer prejudice on his behalf.

(paras 145–51, 154–57)

4.2.2 The Attribution and False Attribution Rights

Sections 77 and 84 of the CDPA secure the right to be identified as an author, and to object to false attribution of authorship. But, once again, these rights are only applicable in certain circumstances. Such rights are therefore more limited than their corresponding equivalents in European civil law countries.

Case 4.7 *Sawkins v Hyperion Records Ltd* [2005] EWCA Civ 565

Facts

The facts of the case were introduced in Section 3.1.2.3. Dr Sawkins wrote to Hyperion Records on 6 February 2002, before the CD was made, asking that his authorship be acknowledged with the following attribution line: '© Copyright 2002 by Lionel Sawkins'. When published, the Hyperion CD included a booklet in which was printed the following: 'With thanks to Dr Lionel Sawkins for his preparation of performance materials for this recording'. Dr Sawkins claimed the line did not sufficiently recognise his role as an author.

Issue and Procedure

Once Mummery LJ decided that Dr Sawkins had created a musical work, and contributed sufficient original expression to said work, the next issue presented was: was recognising Dr Sawkins's 'preparation' of the performance editions sufficient attribution as required by section 77? Mummery LJ held that it was not.

MUMMERY LJ

Mr Norris [counsel for the Claimant] submits that this is inadequate. It does not identify the Claimant as the author of the musical work, as required by s. 77(1) of the 1988 Act. The reference to 'performance materials' is unclear and considerably understates what Dr Sawkins has in fact done. He also makes the point that where the author, in asserting his right to be identified under s. 78, specifies a particular form of identification, then s. 77(8) requires that form to be used. In this case the assertion of the right to be identified was made in the letter of 6th February 2002, in which Dr Sawkins said that the sleeve-notes must carry the legend: '© Copyright 2002 by Lionel Sawkins'. This has not been observed.

I agree with these submissions. Although Dr Sawkins is named, he is not identified as the author of the copyright work. The sleeve has to clearly convey Dr Sawkins' authorship to all possible readers and not simply to those who might have some inside or particular knowledge

> of what to infer from the words that have been used. The fact is that there was no intention of identifying Dr Sawkins as the author of the musical work and the sleeve-notes do not do so. This part of the claim also succeeds.
>
> (paras 84–85)

In the judgment above, Lord Justice Mummery refers to the requirement of 'assertion'. Section 78 of the CDPA states that the author's right of attribution cannot be infringed 'unless the right has been asserted'. The right of attribution can be asserted in an 'instrument in writing signed by the author' or in any written instrument assigning the economic rights. In addition, in relation to an artistic work for public exhibition, the author's signature appearing on the work will count as sufficient assertion. In the *Sawkins v Hyperion Records* case, it was decided that Dr Sawkins's letter was sufficient assertion. But there has been very little judicial consideration of the assertion requirement.

The opposite of the right of attribution is the right to object to false attribution. In contrast to the right of integrity and the right of attribution, the claimant does not need to be the author of a work in order to benefit from this right. Any 'person' can object when a work is wrongly attributed to him. For example, in *Clark v Associated Newspapers*, the former politician Alan Clark successfully sued the *Evening Standard* newspaper; the newspaper had printed a parody called 'Alan Clark's Secret Political Diary'.[30] Unlike the right of attribution, the right of false attribution does not need to be asserted.

4.3   DURATION

For how long should the economic and moral rights last? Fourteen years? A lifetime? Forever? The Statute of Anne provided authors with the exclusive right to print their work for the fourteen years following creation. Some have speculated that the initial fourteen years' term was chosen because it was twice the length of a bookbinder's apprenticeship.[31] If true, the fourteen-year term was a relatively arbitrary figure. Today both economic and moral rights last much longer.

Working out if the copyright in a work has expired is often a complicated task. For example, before 2010, it was generally believed that 'Happy Birthday to You' was still protected. This was proved to be wrong, at least in the USA, after Professor Robert Brauneis (George Washington University) performed extensive historical research into the song.[33]

In the UK, the economic rights, and the right of integrity and attribution, last for the lifetime of the author plus an additional seventy years in most jurisdictions. To illustrate, if author A created a work in 1999 and died in the year 2000, the economic rights in the work would expire on 1 January 2071 – that is, we wait until the end of the calendar year in which the author died, and then the seventy-year period starts to run. At which point, the works fall into the public domain. As a result, on 1 January every year, a selection of new works become freely available for everyone to use. 1 January is sometimes called 'Public Domain Day'.

4.3 Duration **121**

But although copyright lasts much longer today, the length of the copyright term remains arbitrary. From a utilitarian perspective, whether the current length of copyright aids or hinders the public good is a very important empirical question, as the next extract illustrates.[32] In the 1990s, both the USA and Europe increased the length of the copyright term from life of the author to life plus fifty years, to life of the author plus seventy years. This legislative extension for copyright was challenged in the USA as being unconstitutional, resulting in the US Supreme Court case of *Eldred v Ashcroft*. As part of the litigation, seventeen economists (including five Nobel Prize winners) submitted an argument to the court analysing the effects of the copyright extension.

Case 4.8 *Eldred v Ashcroft* 537 US 186 (2003), Brief of 17 Economists

Summary of the Argument

This brief provides an economic analysis of the main feature of the Copyright Term Extension Act of 1998 ('CTEA'), a twenty-year extension of the copyright term for existing and future works. An economist's perspective may be helpful to the Court as it considers Congress's reasons for passing the CTEA, particularly with respect to the extension for existing works.

One possibility is that Congress sought a policy that confers a net economic benefit, after subtracting the expected costs. The main economic benefit from copyright protection is to give an author an incentive to create new works. The size of this economic incentive depends upon the 'present value' of compensation, as anticipated by the author at the time of creation.

The two components of the CTEA differ markedly in their economic effect. The longer term for new works provides some increase in anticipated compensation for an author. Because the additional compensation occurs many decades in the future, its present value is small, very likely an improvement of less than 1% compared to the pre-CTEA term. This compensation offers at most a very small additional incentive for an economically minded author of a new work. The term extension for existing works makes no significant contribution to an author's economic incentive to create, since in this case the additional compensation was granted after the relevant investment had already been made.

The CTEA has two further effects on economic efficiency. First, the CTEA extends the period during which a copyright holder determines the quantity produced of a work, and thus increases the inefficiency from above-cost pricing by lengthening its duration. With respect to the term extension for new works, the present value of the additional

> cost is small, just as the present value of incremental benefits is small. By contrast, the cost of term extension in existing works is much larger in present value, especially for works whose copyrights would soon or already have expired but for the CTEA.
>
> Second, the CTEA extends the period during which a copyright holder determines the production of derivative works, which affects the creation of new works that are built in part out of materials from existing works. Where building-block materials are copyrighted, new creators must pay to use those materials, and may incur additional costs in locating and negotiating with copyright holders. Such transaction costs are especially large where the copyright holders whose permissions are required are numerous or difficult to locate. By reducing the set of building-block materials freely available for new works, the CTEA raises the cost of producing new works and reduces the number created.
>
> Taken as a whole, it is highly unlikely that the economic benefits from copyright extension under the CTEA outweigh the additional costs. Moreover, in the case of term extension for existing works, the sizable increase in cost is not balanced to any significant degree by an improvement in incentives for creating new works. Considering the criterion of consumer welfare instead of efficiency leads to the same conclusion, with the alteration that the CTEA's large transfer of resources from consumers to copyright holders is an additional factor that reduces consumer welfare.
>
> (pp. 1–3)

Steamboat Willie or, as we know him now, Mickey Mouse, fell into the public domain on 1 January 2024. But more modern versions of Mickey which contain original expression (e.g. Mickey with white gloves) might still be protected. (Photo by LMPC via Getty Images)

Given the rather negative assessment the economists provided of the copyright extension, one might ask why the US Congress passed it in the first place. One simple answer is the effect of lobbying. The copyright term extension quickly became known as the 'Mickey Mouse Protection Act'.[34] This was because the rights in the cartoon character, Mickey Mouse, were due to expire in 2004, and to avoid this fate, the Walt Disney Company backed the new law. As a result of the extension of copyright, Mickey Mouse only fell into the public domain on 1 January 2024.

Today, unlimited copyright is also not out of the question. In some European countries, moral rights protections are already unlimited and last forever.[35] Meanwhile, some academic authors in the Anglo-American world have proposed that copyright last forever, subject to periodic renewals.[36]

4.4 OWNERSHIP

Section 2.2.2 highlighted how the Stationers' Company used the figure of the author to justify copyright. Following that logic, one might expect that the author is the person who owns the property in their work. And while that is broadly true today, it is not universally true.

4.4.1 First Ownership

Both the economic and moral rights vest initially in the author of the work.[37] The CDPA defines an author as the person who 'creates' the work.[38] While no further guidance is given, courts have largely understood the author to be a person who supplies the original expression.[39]

When individuals collaborate to create the work, the work will be considered a 'joint work' and the authors are 'joint authors'.[40] To be a joint author, the authors must each make an original contribution to the making of the work, the work must have been produced in collaboration and the respective contributions must not be distinct or separate from one another. In such cases, the authors will own the economic and moral rights jointly (typically, although not exclusively, as tenants in common).[41]

However, there are two general deviations from the rule that the author is the first owner of the rights. The first case concerns works that have no clear author. This is particularly true of the entrepreneurial works, which do not require originality to enjoy protection. In respect to such works, the statute designates certain individuals as the author: the producer is taken to be the author of sound recordings, the producer and director are authors of films, and so on. Similarly, in cases of works generated by computer and with no human author, the author is deemed to be the person who made the necessary arrangements for the work's creation.[42] In these cases, the CDPA grants economic rights – and no moral rights – to the specified 'author'.

The second deviation concerns employees. Section 11(2) of the CDPA states that when a literary, dramatic, musical or artistic work is made by an employee in the course of employment, the employer will own the economic rights therein (unless there is an agreement to the contrary). This has naturally resulted in conceptual questions about who is an 'employee' and what is a work made in the 'course of employment'. Illustratively, in *Noah v Shuba*, a consultant epidemiologist at the Public Health Laboratory in London wrote a book entitled *A Guide to Hygienic Skin Piercing*. The author wrote the work in the evenings and on weekends, but used his employer's library and secretarial support. While his employment contract required him to produce articles as part of his work, it did not require him to write books. The UK Chancery Division held this did not qualify as a work produced 'in the course of employment'.[43]

4.4.2 Assignment, Licence, Waiver

As with other proprietary rights, ownership of the economic rights can be transferred by the owner. Section 91(1) of the CDPA says that copyright is

John Lennon and Paul McCartney (The Beatles) are joint authors of their musical works. To calculate the term of copyright in such cases, the seventy-year time clock starts to run after the death of the last joint author. (Photo by Sal Traina/Penske Media via Getty Images)

At the time of writing, the ownership of works generated by new AI tools such as ChatGPT remains unsettled. Perhaps an even more pressing question, however, is why such works should be owned at all.

Table 4.4 Licences

What	Exclusive	Non-Exclusive
Who	Voluntary	Compulsory
How	Express	Implied

'transmissible by assignment, by testamentary disposition or by the operation of law, as personal or moveable property'. Such transmissions must take place in writing to be effective. Furthermore, assignment can be 'partial': the owner can assign some economic rights while retaining others. The right of distribution, for example, might be assigned to a third party, while the owner retains the right of reproduction.

The exclusive nature of the rights means that if someone other than the owner wishes to perform one of the restricted acts, they will commonly need to receive a '**licence**'. A licence is permission to use the work. Licences come in many forms. Table 4.4 illustrates how licences differ along three dimensions.

The first dimension is what type of licence the user receives. Licences come in two major types: exclusive and non-exclusive. Under an '**exclusive licence**' the licensee is given permission to use the work and no other person is allowed to make the same use of the work (including the copyright owner). Alternatively, under a '**non-exclusive licence**', the licensee is given permission to use the work, but others in society may also be permitted use the work in the same way. An 'exclusive licence' therefore grants the licensee permission to use the work in exclusion of all others in society.

The second dimension is who grants the licence. In most circumstances, the copyright owner is the only agent with the power to grant a licence. These licences are known as '**voluntary licences**' and reflect the fact that the copyright owner voluntarily enters into the agreement. But in some limited circumstances, the state can grant a user a licence even if the copyright owner does not consent to the arrangement. Such licences are known as '**compulsory licences**' and reflect the fact that the copyright owner has been compelled to license the work.

Some of the works in this book are orphan works and have been reproduced under the UK orphan works scheme. For example, see the writings of Thomas Drescher in Chapter 12.

Why would the state force an owner to license the user of a work? There are many situations in which this may become relevant. One illustrative example concerns the problem of '**orphan works**'. Orphan works are works that are protected by copyright but where the owner cannot be located following a 'diligent search'. Section 116(A) of the CDPA permits the UK Intellectual Property Office to grant compulsory licences for up to seven years in such circumstances. In return, the user must pay a fee set by the office.

The final dimension of licences concerns how they arise. Licences can either be expressly granted (either in writing or orally) by the copyright holder or the state – so-called **express licences**. But licences can also be implied by courts – so-called **implied licences**. As with implied terms in a contract, a court may imply that the copyright owner has voluntarily given the user permission to use the work. For example, in *Robin v Classic FM* a musical expert was employed by a radio station to catalogue their musical recordings. Although the terms of employment were silent, the court implied that the radio station was granted a licence to use the resulting catalogues.[44]

Unlike the economic rights, moral rights cannot be assigned; they will remain with the author for their entire duration. However, in contrast to many European civil law systems, the author can waive their moral rights.[45] A waiver can be specific to a particular work, or general to future works. Such waivers must be made in writing. Lastly, the author cannot object to uses of their work on moral rights grounds to which they have already consented.

4.5 SUMMARY

What is copyright? Is copyright merely a bundle of rights, or is it the exclusive control of an intellectual thing? While we cannot answer that question fully before reading Chapter 5, we can draw some preliminary conclusions.

If one thinks property is the exclusive control over a thing, then there is an argument that copyright is not really property at all. Instead, one might see copyright as a system allocating a bundle of rights to various different people. Authors enjoy a set of economic and moral rights. While the moral rights stay with the author forever, the economic rights can be, and often are, assigned to another owner. The wider public also has certain entitlements in relation to the work. Copyright law frees non-owners to read, to smell or think about works, among other things. Furthermore, non-owners have the liberty to resell tangible copies, and to communicate the work providing they do not do so to a 'new' public. Far from exclusive control, copyright might be thought to fit the bundle of rights picture of property very well.

That view, however, might be naive. Historically, copyright has expanded dramatically. What started as an exclusive liberty to print, now amounts to a comprehensive system of broad and powerful rights. Meanwhile, old doctrines that limit the scope of that control – such as the independent creation and exhaustion doctrine – might be weakening in the Information Age. The question is whether these developments, when viewed holistically, reveal a picture of copyright in which owners control all economically valuable uses of the works. If so, then despite initial appearances, copyright may indeed be property of the exclusive control kind.

But this assessment necessarily must be preliminary. Chapter 5, and the topic of exceptions, may give us reason to think again.

4.6 SELF-ASSESSMENT

Before moving on, try to answer the following questions to consolidate your learning. Answers are provided in the section below.

1. Adam posts an URL link on his blog. If another Internet user clicks on the link, it will direct the user to a website called 'FreeMusic.com'. On FreeMusic.com is a song created by Beth that has been unlawfully uploaded. FreeMusic.com is freely accessible to all Internet users. Beth has previously asked Adam to remove the link from this blog and Adam has refused. Subsequently, Beth has sued Adam. What is the most likely outcome of Beth's lawsuit?
   a. Adam will not be liable because he has not communicated work to a new public.
   b. Adam will not be liable because he has not committed an act of communication.
   c. Adam will be liable because he has communicated a work to a new public.
   d. Adam will be liable because he has publicly performed the work.
2. In 1970, a group of friends – James, Petra, Rocky and Georgina – formed a band and started to write music. James passed away tragically in 1975 in a freak accident while on tour. Peter passed away in 1985 from a heart attack. Rocky and Georgina died of old age in 1990 and 1995, respectively. When will their musical work fall into the public domain in the UK?
   a. Upon the death of Georgina in 1995.
   b. On 1 January 2066.
   c. On 1 January 2065.
   d. On 1 January 2046.

3. A website called TheExchange.com buys and resells second-hand eBooks and second-hand software. The eBooks and software are supplied to TheExchange.com by consumers who initially buy the works lawfully from the copyright owner via direct download.

   Subsequently, TheExchange.com has been sued in two different copyright actions. In the first action, a group of eBook publishers claim the resale of their eBooks infringes their right of distribution. In the second action, a group of software publishers claim the resale of their software is an infringement of their distribution right. What is the most likely outcome of the litigation?

   a. TheExchange.com will not be liable in either case. The exhaustion doctrine allows them to resell eBook and software files.

   b. TheExchange.com will be liable in both cases. The exhaustion doctrine does not apply in either case.

   c. TheExhange.com will be liable in respect to the software but not the eBooks. The exhaustion doctrine applies in the case of eBooks but not software.

   d. TheExhange.com will be liable in respect to the eBooks but not the software. The exhaustion doctrine applies in the case of software but not eBooks.

4. Is all copying copyright infringement? Should it be?

ACTIVITY DISCUSSION

Activity 4.1 At first glance, the fact that only certain acts are restricted and controlled by the owner might suggest a bundle-of-rights picture of copyright. Some of those rights – reproduction, distribution, etc. – are given to the owner, while other rights – the right to read, smell or think about, a work – are given to the wider public.

However, is that view a bit naive? Consider smelling a work. Very few people want to smell books. If the owner charged people money to do so, very few people would pay. And what about reading, or thinking about, a book? How would an owner detect whether someone had read or thought about their book, in order to send them a bill? Trying to control such uses seems more trouble than it is worth.

The question, then, is whether the economic rights allow the author to control all *economically valuable* uses. Despite the initial bundle appearance, some might argue that contemporary copyright permits the owner to control any uses of the work for which consumers are able and likely to pay. So conceived, section 16 might start to appear more like a right of exclusive control.

Activity 4.2 It is highly likely that a court will infer that van Gone has copied *Starry Night*. He clearly had access to the original work: it is a famous work that can be found simply by searching Google. Furthermore, the two works are identical in both ideas and expression. This is certainly a similarity sufficient to infer copying.

Activity 4.3 The problem is that the similarity of styles has contributed to a finding of infringement. Therefore, although no one technically owns ideas, copying ideas might result in liability. If not careful, Lord Scott's inference allows ownership of ideas in a subtle way.

Activity 4.4 It is tempting to think of the modern reproduction right as just one right in the bundle. As such, it might point towards the existence of a bundle of rights. However, that view may be naive. Does it not depend on how broadly the right is interpreted? If, for example, a cake made from a recipe were deemed a reproduction, the breadth of the reproduction right would start to appear closer to exclusive control over all economically valuable uses of the work.

Activity 4.5 On one hand, the evolution of the communication right shows the exclusive control tendencies of copyright. Whenever society invents a new, economically valuable, way to exploit the work – e.g. by playing on the radio, or on YouTube – lawmakers grant owners new rights to control the new uses.

On the other hand, the communication of the public right also shows concern for the rights of others in society as well. In a case like *GS Media*, the CJEU did not permit the copyright owner's control to become so broad as to unduly limit the rights of others to exercise freedom of expression in relation to the work. At these points, we potentially see how lawmakers might try to limit copyright to a bundle of rights, or at least, something falling short of exclusive control.

SELF-ASSESSMENT ANSWERS

1. **Correct answer: c.** Posting a hyperlink is certainly an act of communication according to the CJEU. The more difficult question is whether in so doing Adam has communicated the work to a 'new public'. Following *GS Media*, it appears that he has communicated the work to a new public because, although the song was already freely available on FreeMusic.com, the song was uploaded to that website against Beth's wishes and Adam has been made aware of this fact.

2. **Correct answer: b.** The rule in such a case is that after the death of the last joint author – Georgina – we wait until the end of the calendar year (i.e. 31 December 1996), and then add on seventy years. The work therefore falls into the public domain on 1 January 2066.

3. **Correct answer: d.** TheExchange does not infringe any rights in respect of the software. The *Usedsoft* case decided that sale of software is an act of distribution (not communication to the public). The distribution right exhausts after the first distribution. Therefore, when the copyright owner initially distributed the software, they lost the ability to control further distributions, such as that performed by TheExchange.

   However, TheExchange does infringe the rights in relation to the eBooks. The *Tom Kabinet* case decided that the sale of eBooks is an act of communication (not distribution). The communication right does not exhaust after the first communication. Therefore, after the copyright owner's initial communication of the works to the consumers, they retain the right to control subsequent communications, like that performed by TheExchange.

Notes

1 CDPA ch 2.
2 ibid ss 22–26.
3 26 ER 489.
4 Oren Bracha, *Owning Ideas: The Intellectual Origins of American Intellectual Property, 1790–1909* (CUP 2016) 54–123; Isabella Alexander, *Copyright and the Public Interest in the Nineteenth Century* (Hart Publishing 2010) 155–232.
5 Christopher Buccafusco, 'There's No Such Thing as Independent Creation and It's a Good Thing Too' (2023) 64 Wm & Mary L Rev 1617, 1653–58.
6 ibid 1617.

7 Reported in Tristan Kirk, 'Ed Sheeran Hits out at "Baseless" Copyright Claims after Court Victory' *Evening Standard* (6 April 2022) <https://www.standard.co.uk/news/uk/ed-sheeran-baseless-copyright-claims-songwriting-industry-high-court-shape-of-you-instagram-b992764.html> (accessed June 2023).

8 *Pelham GmbH v Hunter* (C-476/17) EU:C:2019:624.

9 410 F3d 792 (US).

10 *Feist Publications, Inc v Rural Telephone Service Co, Inc*, 499 US 340 (1991) (US).

11 CDPA, s 17(2).

12 ibid s 17(3).

13 Yin Harn Lee, 'The Persistence of the Text: The Concept of the Work in Copyright Law – Part 2' (2018) 2 IPQ 107; Oren Bracha, *Owning Ideas: The Intellectual Origins of American Intellectual Property, 1790–1909* (CUP 2016) 124–87.

14 CDPA, s 17(6).

15 *Deutsche Grammophon GmbH v Metro GmbH*, Case C-78/70 [1971] ECR 487.

16 *Bobbs-Merrill Co v Straus* 210 US 339 (1908) (US).

17 Transfer of Property Act (1882) ss 10–18.

18 *Pope v Curll* (1741) 2 Atk 342.

19 Directive 92/100/EEC Council of 27 November 1992 on rental right and lending right and on certain rights related to copyright in the field of intellectual property No L 346/62, art 1, paras [2]–[3].

20 Case C-174/15 *Vereniging Openbare Bibliotheken* v *Stichting Leenrecht* (2016) ECLI:EU:C:2016:856, Opinion of AG Szpunar, paras [25] and [35]–[39].

21 Dramatic Literary Property Act (1833).

22 CDPA, s 3.

23 (1936) Ch 469, per Lord Wright MR 479.

24 cf *Jennings* with *Harms v Martans* [1927] 1 Ch 526.

25 Directive on Copyright in the Digital Single Market (2019) art 17.

26 *Svensson v Retriever Sverige AB*, Case C-466/12, EU:C:2014:76; *Land Nordrhein-Westfalen v Dirk Renckhoff*, Case C-161/17, EU:C:2018:634.

27 Copyright Act (1976) 17 USC, s 101 (US).

28 Peter Baldwin, *The Copyright Wars: Three Centuries of Trans-Atlantic Battle* (Princeton UP 2014) reprinted with permission of Princeton University Press.

29 Cass Ire civ, 5 December 2006: RIDA 1/2007, 359. Denis Flynn, 'A Comparative Analysis of the Moral Right of Integrity in the UK, Ireland and France' (2017) 7 King's L Rev 108.

30 (1998) 1 WLR 1558.

31 Paul K Saint-Amour, 'Introduction: Modernism and the Lives of Copyright' in *Modernism and Copyright* (OUP 2011) 24.

32 Rufus Pollock, 'Forever Minus a Day? Calculating Optimal Copyright Term' (2009) 6(1) Review of Economic Research on Copyright Issues, 35–60 <https://papers.ssrn.com/sol3/papers.cfm?abstract_id=1436186> (last accessed 29 June 2022).

33 Robert Brauneis, 'Copyright and the World's Most Popular Song' (2009) 56 J Copy Soc USA 335.

34 Sonny Bono Copyright Term Extension Act (1998) 17 USC §§302–04; Lawrence Lessig, 'Copyright's First Amendment' (2001) 48 UCLA L Rev 1057, 1065.

35 CDPA s 95(1)(a).

36 Richard A Posner and William M Landes, 'Indefinitely Renewable Copyright' (2003) 70(2) U Chi L Rev 471.

37 CDPA, s 16.

38 ibid s 9(1).

39 ibid s 10. cf works of co-authorship, ibid s 10A.

40 ibid s 10(1). See also *Martin v Kogan* [2019] EWCA Civ 1645.

41 CDPA, s 16.

42 ibid s 9(3).

43 (1991) FSR 14, per Mummery LJ.

44 (1998) ECC 488, per Lightman J.

45 CDPA, s 95(4).

FIGURE ACKNOWLEDGEMENTS

4.1 From *Sheeran v Chokri* [2022] EWHC 827 (Ch)

4.2 Betty Lupinacci, 'House of Lords Case Records Become (Micro) Film Stars' (23 June 2015). <https://blogs.loc.gov/law/2015/06/house-of-lords-case-records-become-microfilm-stars/>. Reproduced with permission of the Library of Congress. (Photo credit: Agata Tajchert)

4.3 People attend a demonstration against Article 13 of the planned EU reform of copyright and against censorship on the Internet, Berlin, Germany, 23 March 2019. (Photo by Emmanuele Contini/NurPhoto via Getty Images)

Marginal Fig. 4.1 Steamboat Willie lobbycard, Mickey Mouse, 1928. (Photo by LMPC via Getty Images)

Marginal Fig. 4.2 Musicians John Lennon and Paul McCartney introduce Apple Corps to the USA. Press conference, Americana Hotel, New York, 1968. (Photo by Sal Traina/Penske Media via Getty Images)

5

Copyright IV: Exceptions

The expansion of copyright's subject matter and rights is extraordinary. Never in human history have works been subject to such extensive private ownership. The situation is not, however, entirely without precedent. James Boyle argues that a similar event occurred with land from approximately 1450 to 1900.[1] During the 'enclosure movement', land owned in common increasingly became fenced off and subject to private ownership.[2] Today, Boyle argues, the world is witnessing a second enclosure movement: an 'enclosure of the intangible commons of the mind'.[3]

James Boyle is the William Neal Reynolds Professor of Law and co-founder of the Center for the Study of the Public Domain at Duke University School of Law, USA.

But there is another side to this story. As copyright expanded, lawyers developed a new concept: **exceptions**. An exception to copyright permits a person to perform one of the restricted acts. The person does not need permission from the owner to perform the '**permitted acts**'.[4] As an increasing number of acts have become restricted, copyright has threatened a range of other values: from the welfare of consumers, to access to knowledge and freedom of expression. Exceptions protect these other values from the threat copyright poses. They are sometimes thought of as '**user rights**'.[5]

Whether copyright grants the owner of the original work exclusive control or not depends, not only on the number and breadth of the owner's rights, but also on the exceptions to those rights. In other words, the **scope** of copyright can be understood as rights minus exceptions. Numerous exceptions to copyright exist. Table 5.1 lists all the CDPA's exceptions. This chapter focuses on five in particular: fair dealing (Section 5.1), temporary copying (Section 5.2), private use (Section 5.3), disclosure in the public interest (Section 5.4) and text and data analysis (Section 5.5).

Yet, paradoxically, these exceptions emerged at a point in history when copyright expanded rapidly. As a result, some historians emphasise their ideological purpose.[6] As more non-restricted activity has become restricted, some of that

This chapter contains public sector information licensed under the Open Government Licence v3.0.

Table 5.1 The CDPA's exceptions

Name	CDPA sections	Description
Temporary copying	28A	Permits users to create temporary electronic copies under certain conditions.
Fair dealing	29–30, 32	Permits users to perform the restricted acts for certain purposes when such use qualifies as 'fair dealing'.
Text and data analysis	29A	Permits users with lawful access to work to copy the work to perform non-commercial computational analysis under certain conditions. For example, if a developer of an artificial intelligence software copies millions of images in the process of training the software to generate new images.
Incidental use	31	Permits users to include a work incidentally in an artistic work, sound recording or film. For example, if a photographer takes a photograph and incidentally happens to capture a copyrighted sculpture in the background.
Access for people with disabilities	31A–31F	Permits users with disabilities to make accessible copies for personal use. For example, by reproducing a literary work in Braille.
Educational establishments	33–36A	Permits educational establishments to make copies for educational use. For example, it is not an infringement of copyright to include short extracts of copyrighted material in certain types of anthologies.
Libraries, archives and museums	37–44A	Permits libraries, archives and museums to perform the restricted acts for a variety of purposes. For example, it is not an infringement of copyright for a public library to lend a book.
Public administration	45–50	Permits individuals to perform the restricted acts within the context of parliamentary or judicial proceedings, or Royal Commission or statutory inquiry. For example, a witness statement taken by the police could be photocopied for purposes of a criminal trial.
Computer programs	50A–50C	Permits various acts in relation to computer programs, including making backup copies, decompilation and observation.
Databases	50D	Permits a user of an original database to perform restricted acts in order to access and use the database, provided the user has the right to make use of the database.
Works in electronic form	56	If a user of a work in electronic form has the right to make copies or adaptations thereof, so too is anyone to whom the electronic work is transferred unless express terms prohibit such use.

Table 5.1 (*cont.*)

Name	CDPA sections	Description
Miscellaneous exceptions for authorial works	57–66	Multiple exceptions in relation to literary, dramatic, musical and artistic works.
Miscellaneous exceptions for entrepreneurial works	66–75	Multiple exceptions in relation to films, sound recordings and broadcasts.

restricted activity will be permitted in certain circumstances. The question is whether exceptions are the 'user rights' in merely the bundle of rights that is copyright? Or whether they are a fig leaf that detracts attention from the underlying expansion of copyright's scope.

5.1 FAIR DEALING

The idea that some unauthorised use of work is 'fair' has a long history in copyright. In *Gyles v Wilcox* (1740), Lord Hardwicke decided that the *Treatise* was a 'fair abridgement' of Sir Matthew Hale's work.[7] In Hardwicke's opinion, abridgements like the *Treatise* were not only the product of skill and labour of the abridger, but also helped encourage learning in society. As the abridgements were sold at a lower cost than original books, they could be bought and enjoyed by a wider range of people. Abridgements therefore helped, rather than harmed, the 'encouragement of learning' that the Statute of Anne sought to promote.

Refer back to Section 4.1.1 for a summary of *Gyles v Wilcox*.

The 'fair abridgement' rule of *Gyles* evolved into what is today known as the doctrine of '**fair dealing**'.[8] Although, the difference between the two doctrines is significant. The fair abridgement rule provided a limitation on copyright: it helped to demarcate the restricted acts from the non-restricted acts. Today's fair dealing doctrine, by contrast, only provides an exception. What previously was non-restricted activity is today restricted activity, but potentially permitted under certain circumstances.[9]

Broadly, the CDPA fair dealing provisions permits people to perform a restricted act without the owner's permission providing that two conditions are met: (1) the act must be for one of the 'purposes' listed in the CDPA; and (2) the act must be 'fair'. Additionally, in many cases, the use must be accompanied by 'sufficient acknowledgement' of the claimant's work.

5.1.1 Statutory Purposes

The CDPA allows the defendant to perform a restricted act, so long as they are using the protected work for one of the purposes designated by the statute. Table 5.2 lists the protected purposes.

Table 5.2 Fair dealing statutory purposes

CDPA sections	Statutory purposes
29(1)	Non-commercial research or private study
30(1)	Criticism or review of works made available to the public
30(IZA)	Quotation of works made available to the public
30(2)	Reporting current events
30A(1)	Parody, caricature or pastiche
32	Non-commercial illustration for instruction

The concept of protected purposes distinguishes the UK fair dealing doctrine from a related American doctrine: **fair use**. American law – and increasingly other common law countries – permit people to perform restricted acts *regardless of the purpose* providing that the use is 'fair'.[10] By contrast, in the UK, the exception is restricted only to the *specified purposes* designated by Parliament in statute. In recent years, the UK government has considered replacing the fair dealing exception with a fair use exception.

The word 'growth' appears in the title of the report. But what is 'growth'? And why is it important to IP lawyers?

Recall the utilitarian argument from Section 2.2.3. According to that argument, an appropriately balanced copyright law will make society overall a better place: while copyright creates the problem of monopoly, society will be better off overall because authors have incentives to create original works. In 2010, the UK government started to question whether UK copyright really is appropriately balanced. Has copyright expanded to such an extent that the bad consequences now outweigh the good ones?

Creative works are goods (public goods). In the utilitarian view, they are valuable because they make us happy. If copyright encourages the creation of more creative works, the result is copyright is contributing to a country's economic growth, and its overall happiness.

To investigate this question, the UK government commissioned a report to consider the effects of copyright in the modern economy. If copyright harms society's overall utility, one possible solution would be to strengthen copyright exceptions. To that end, the reporters were asked to consider the possibility of replacing the UK fair dealing doctrine with a fair use doctrine. In Box 5.1, the final report explains how fair use may put the balance back into UK copyright why the UK ultimately decided not to adopt fair use.

Recall that Section 1.1.1 defined a 'good' as something that is valuable. Economic growth refers to an increase in the total goods (and services) produced by a country over time.

BOX 5.1 *DIGITAL OPPORTUNITY: A REVIEW OF INTELLECTUAL PROPERTY AND GROWTH* (DEPT FOR BUSINESS, INNOVATION & SKILLS 2011) ('HARGREAVES REPORT')

The US has a more flexible approach to copyright exceptions. It includes the concept of 'Fair Use', a defence in the US copyright framework which builds on certain general principles through case law to develop permitted uses of copyright works. Fair Use serves a number of purposes in the US, fixing what might otherwise be imbalances in the copyright system.

Under the European approach to exceptions, new kinds of copying which have become possible due to advancing digital technology are automatically unlawful. They require agreement of rights holders if they fall outside the pre-established and closed list of categories for permissible exceptions. Even copying which falls within one of the permissible areas at EU level can still require new action by national legislatures to create or develop the exception to meet new needs. The risk in this situation is twofold:

- Innovation may be blocked and growth hampered when unduly rigid applications of copyright law enables rights holders to block potentially important new technologies. We have experienced this when the interests of rights owners have put them in conflict with developers of video recorders and web search engines. Research scientists, including medical researchers, are today being hampered from using computerised search and analysis techniques on data and text because copyright law can forbid or restrict such usage. . .

- A second and also significant problem is that we have in recent years witnessed a growing mismatch between what is allowed under copyright exceptions, and the reasonable expectations and behaviour of most people. Digital technology has enabled use and reuse of material by private individuals in ways that they do not feel are wrong – such as sharing music tracks with immediate family members, or transferring a track from a CD to play in the car. It is difficult for anyone to understand why it is legal to lend a friend a book, but not a digital music file. . .

By contrast the US approach enables judges to take a view as to whether emerging activities in relation to copyright works should legitimately fall within the scope of copyright protection or not. Fair Use provides a legal mechanism that can rule a new technology or application of technology (like shifting music from a CD to a personal computer) as legitimate and not needing to be regulated, so opening the way to a market for products and services which use it. It has been suggested that this is one of the factors creating a positive environment in the US for innovation and investment in innovation.

It is equally true, however, that the economic benefits imputed to the availability of Fair Use in the US have sometimes been over stated. When the Review briefly visited Silicon Valley in February, providing the opportunity to meet companies such as Google, Facebook, Yahoo and Yelp, along with investors, bankers, lawyers and academics, a consistent story emerged, namely that Fair Use is (from the viewpoint of high technology companies and their investors) just one aspect of

The report finds that the benefits attributable to the fair use doctrine are sometimes overstated. This may be a good point to revisit the empirical objection in Section 2.2.4. What, if anything, is overstated: the case for copyright? Or the case for broader copyright exceptions?

> the distinctiveness of the American legal framework on copyright, albeit in the view of most an important part.
>
> The advice given to the Review by UK Government lawyers is that significant difficulties would arise in any attempt to transpose US style Fair Use into European law. It is against this background that the Review has stuck to its Terms of Reference and sought to isolate the particular benefits for economic growth that Fair Use exceptions provide in the US, with a view to understanding how these benefits can be most expeditiously obtained in the UK.
>
> (paras 5.9–5.10, 5.12, 5.16, 5.19)

As Box 5.1 notes, fair dealing was retained principally for two reasons. First, it was far from clear whether adopting a fair use doctrine would translate into concrete utilitarian benefits for the UK. Second, concerns existed about the compatibility of fair use with European law. The EU Information Society Directive, article 5(5) requires that exceptions be restricted to 'certain special cases which do not conflict with a normal exploitation of the work or other subject-matter and do not unreasonably prejudice the legitimate interests of the right-holder'. This rule is known as the **three-step test**. It is argued by some that the flexibility of the fair use doctrine makes it incompatible with this provision.

Post-Brexit, the UK no longer must comply with the Information Society Directive. However, the three-step test is also contained in the Berne Convention (art 9(2)) and the TRIPS agreement (art 13). The rule continues to be relevant not only to the ability to adopt a fair use doctrine, but is also relevant to the interpretation of non-fair use exceptions.

> As an introductory text, this book does not cover in much detail international IP treaties. However, increasingly in the twentieth century, expansion of copyright has taken place at the international level. Part of this expansion concerns the restrictions international IP law places on the ability of countries to enact exceptions.

Rather than abolish the fair dealing doctrine, the Hargreaves Report recommended more modest ways of rebalancing copyright. The result is that defendants who wish to benefit from the fair dealing exception must continue to fit their use within one of the designated purposes; a task which is often difficult, as the next subsections demonstrate.

5.1.1.1 PARODY, CARICATURE OR PASTICHE

While retaining the fair dealing doctrine, the Hargreaves Report recommended the UK adopt a new statutory purpose for 'parody, caricature or pastiche'. In 2014, the UK Parliament followed that recommendation and amended the CDPA to permit restricted acts for the purposes of 'parody, caricature or pastiche'. The principal reason was to protect freedom of expression values. However, there also was an economic reason: as the Hargreaves report concluded, 'comedy is big business'.[11] Case 5.1 demonstrates.

Case 5.1 *Shazam v Only Fools the Dining Experience* [2022] EWHC 1379 (IPEC)

Facts

Only Fools and Horses (OFAH) is a well-known television comedy. It was originally broadcast by the BBC in sixty-four episodes over seven series (1981–91) and a number of Christmas specials until 2003. OFAH has as its subject the ups and downs in the life of the Trotter family. It is set in South London during the 1980s and 1990s. The main characters are a market trader, Derek Trotter ('Del Boy'), and his younger brother, Rodney, who live together in a high-rise council flat in Peckham. The third occupant of the flat was originally Derek and Rodney's grandfather, but he was later replaced by an elderly uncle ('Uncle Albert').

Shazam (claimant) is a company owned and controlled by John Sullivan's family. Shazam was formed in 2003 to exploit the intellectual property rights held John Sullivan in connection with OFAH.

In May 2018, the third defendant (Ms Pollard-Mansergh) and the fourth defendant (Mr Mansergh) decided to develop an interactive dining show using the characters from OFAH. The show was produced and marketed under the name 'Only Fools The (Cushty) Dining Experience' (OFDE). The actors in the OFDE show used the appearance, mannerisms, voices and catchphrases of Del Boy, Rodney, Uncle Albert and others. The backstories of those characters and their relationship to each other as that had developed by Series 6 of OFAH was carried over into OFDE. The characters were presented, however, in a new context of an interactive pub quiz, which had not appeared in OFAH itself.

While the audience is being served a three-course meal, the actors in the OFDE show perform scenes based on a script produced collaboratively by a number of people over the course of a few weeks. The script was compiled by the Fifth Defendant. It gave flexibility for the actors to interact spontaneously with the diners and to improvise. OFDE was usually performed in hotel function rooms in front of an audience of no more than 120.

Issue and Procedure

The case presented a number of issues. Part of the litigation concerned whether the characters, separate from the text of the scripts, were 'original works'. Following the EU standard of *Levola* and *Cofemel*, John Kimbell QC (sitting as Deputy High Court Judge) found they were original works and thereby protected by copyright.

Having decided that copyright applied to the characters, the litigation turned to the question of whether the defendant's acts were for the purpose of 'parody, caricature or pastiche'. In this first extract, John Kimbell QC, interprets the meaning of 'parody' and 'pastiche'. In doing so, he summarises the recent

IPEC stands for the **Intellectual Property Enterprise Court**. The IPEC is a part of the High Court of Justice set up to hear 'small' IP cases where the damages sought are less than £500,000. Prior to reforms in 2013, the court was the Patents County Court.[12]

fundamental case of *Deckman v Vandersteen* Case C-201/13, EU:C:2014:2132 (see Figure 5.1).

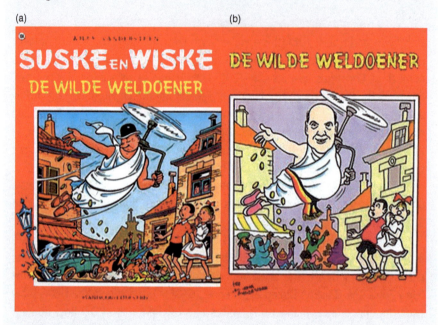

Figure 5.1 The Vandersteen comic ((a)); the Deckmyn comic ((b)).
Reproduced in Shazam v Only Fools the Dining Experience *[2022] EWHC 1379 (IPEC)*

KIMBELL QC

Parody

Parody as a legal concept in the context of Article 5(3)(k) of the Info Soc Directive has been considered by the CJEU in Deckmyn v Vandersteen C-201/13 [2014] Bus L.R. 1368. The case concerned the use made by a Mr Deckmyn of a drawing which closely resembled the title cover of a comic book from 1961. Mr Deckmyn was a member of a Belgian nationalist anti-immigration party. Mr Vandersteen's estate held the copyright in the image and objected to the use of the image for political purposes.

The title cover of the original comic book shows one of the main characters wearing a white tunic and throwing coins to people who are trying to pick them up under the title 'The Wild Benefactor'.

In the allegedly infringing work (the cover of a calendar), the flying main character was replaced by the Mayor of the City of Ghent and inserted into the background people wearing veils picking up the coins.

The Court of Appeal in Brussels referred the following questions to the CJEU:

'1. Is the concept of "parody" an autonomous concept of EU law?

2. If so, must a parody satisfy the following conditions or conform to the following characteristics: display an original character of its own (originality); display that character in such a manner that the parody cannot reasonably be ascribed to the author of the original work; seek to be humorous or to mock, regardless of whether any criticism thereby expressed applies to the original work or to something or someone else; mention the source of the parodied work?

3. Must a work satisfy any other conditions or conform to other characteristics in order to be capable of being labelled as a parody?'

The CJEU held in answer to those questions:

1. The concept of 'parody' appearing in that provision is an autonomous concept of EU law.

2. The essential characteristics of parody, are, first, to evoke an existing work, while being noticeably different from it, and secondly, to constitute an expression of humour or mockery.

3. The concept of 'parody', within the meaning of that provision, is not subject to any of the following conditions mentioned by the referring court: a. that the parody should display an original character of its own, other than that of displaying noticeable differences with respect to the original parodied work; b. that it could reasonably be attributed to a person other than the author of the original work itself; c. that it should relate to the original work itself or mention the source of the parodied work.

4. When applying the exception for parody, within the meaning of article 5(3)(k) of Directive 2001/29, a court must strike a fair balance between, on the one hand, the interests and rights of persons referred to in articles 2 and 3 of that Directive, and, on the other, the freedom of expression of the user of a protected work who is relying on the exception for parody, within the meaning of article 5(3)(k) 5. It is for the national court to determine, in the light of all the circumstances of the case in the main proceedings, whether the application of the exception for parody, within the meaning of article 5(3)(k) of Directive 2001/29, on the assumption that the drawing at issue fulfils the essential requirements of parody, preserves that fair balance.

There is no record of what happened to the case when it returned to the referring court.

Two Types of Parody

The Advocate General in his opinion at [61] distinguished between two types of parody, namely:

i. Parody directed at or concerned with the original work ('parody of')

ii. Parody or **target parody** where the original work parodied is merely the instrument of an intention aimed at a third-party individual or object ('parody with'). The second type of parody is sometimes called 'target parody'.

Pastiche

Pastiche is defined in the Shorter Oxford English Dictionary as: A n. A medley of various things: spec (a) a picture or a musical composition made up of pieces derived from or imitating various sources (b) a literary or other work of art composed in the style of a well-known author, artist etc. L19. B. v.t. & i. Copy or imitate the style of an artist or author'

In his opinion the AG in Pelham v Hutter said (in a footnote, n. 31):

'As for the concept of pastiche, it consists in the imitation of the style of a work or an author without necessarily taking any elements of that work. However, the present case concerns the reverse situation whereby a phonogram is taken to create a work in a completely different style.'

In the article relied upon by Mr St Quintin, Emily Hudson ['The pastiche exception in copyright law: a case of mashed-up drafting' IPQ 2017, 4, 346–368] notes that the term 'pastiche' is used less frequently in the English language than both parody and caricature. She notes that some musicologists draw a distinction between pastiche and pasticcio, with the former referring to works that deliberately imitate the style of another, and pasticcio to operas and other performances drawing from the works of different composers. She refers to Richard Dyer who has argued that the primary definition of pastiche is 'a kind of imitation that you are meant to know is an imitation'.

She comments that there appears to be a consensus that pastiche and parody can be contrasted owing to intention and impact. For instance, it has been said that while pastiche 'borrows closely, openly, appreciatively, and often playfully from the styles of previous works, frequently combining elements of different styles', the imitation present in parody is one 'in a spirit of mockery or ridicule'. That is consistent with the approach of the CJEU in Deckmyn set out above.

Emily Hudson is a professor of law at the University of Oxford.

Paragraphs 183–89 provide a superb example of how UK judges engage with arguments produced by academic lawyers.

She notes the suggested definition offered by the IPO for pastiche in the context of section 3A of CDPA was the use of 'small fragments from a range of films to compose a larger pastiche artwork'. Hudson concludes that: 'the ordinary meanings of pastiche suggest that it exhibits features that are distinct from, and operate well outside of, the genres of parody and caricature'. I agree.

She concludes that it is appropriate to start with the ordinary meaning of pastiche, which as discussed in the second section covers imitation of the style of pre-existing works, the incorporation of parts of earlier works into new works, and the production of medleys. She continues: 'Returning to s.30A, the copyright definition of pastiche should reflect the term's essential meaning, which covers two key activities: imitation of the style of pre-existing works, and the utilisation or assemblage of pre-existing works in new works.'

I agree. This approach seems to me to be consistent with the approach of the CJEU to parody in Deckmyn which involved starting with the meaning of the term in ordinary language and identifying its essential ingredients, the comments of the AG in Pelham v Hutter cited above and the Guidance published by the IPO in its Guidance.

It follows that the two essential ingredients for pastiche within the meaning of s30A are, in my judgment, that: a. The use imitates the style of another work; or b. It is an assemblage (medley) of a number of pre-existing works. c. In both cases, as with parody, the product must be noticeably different from the original work.

If this definition is adopted, pastiche in s. 30A could, according to Hudson, potentially apply to a broad spectrum of 'mash-ups', fan fiction, music sampling, collage, appropriation art, medleys, and many other forms of homage and compilation. This may be so. Each case will have to be assessed on its own merits. However, it is important to bear in mind that s.30A must be read in light of the first of the three-step tests. If pastiche is too widely interpreted, to cover any imitation or reproduction of subject matter it ceases to be a 'special case' of protected expression. It would encompass virtually any form of borrowing, imitation or reproduction. This was plainly not the intention of the European or UK legislature which created an exception for three limited specific types of use.

(paras 162–64, 166–69, 181–89)

Applying the provision as interpreted, Kimbell QC found that the OFDE was neither parody nor pastiche.

NO USE FOR THE PURPOSE OF PARODY

In my judgement, the use made of the characters, their backstories, jokes and catchphrases is not for the purpose of parody within the meaning of section 30A for the following reasons:

a. The September Script does not evoke OFAH in order to express humour about OFAH or anything else. In so far as the Script is humorous, the humour is already contained in the borrowed material. John Kimbell QC Shazam Productions v. Only Fools the Dining Experience sitting as Deputy High Court Judge [2022] EWHC 1379 IPEC 60

b. The September Script does not evoke OFAH in order to mock it or critically engage with either OFAH or situation comedy or anything else.

c. OFDE involves the wholesale transposition of the characters, language, jokes and backstories from OFAH into the setting of an imaginary pub quiz. It is closer in form to reproduction by adaptation than parody.

d. Although some of the characters may have appeared in OFDE in a slightly exaggerated fashion, this is not evident from the September Script and was not intended. The overall aim of the September Script was rather to represent the characters taken from OFAH in a pitch perfect familiar fashion.

e. Whilst the form of the September Script is noticeably different from the OFAH Script in that it is set in a live and interactive dining experience rather than being intended to be performed before a passive live audience, it is does not seek to target OFAH or use OFAH either to express humour about it or mock it (or anything else).

f. None of the marketing material or planning of the show or reviews of OFDE refers to any use of material from OFAH for the purpose of parody.

g. The overwhelming audience feedback was that it felt like being in another live episode of the OFAH. In that respect the September Script is not noticeably different from OFAH. It is a reproduction by adaptation to a live dining setting: i. As the show's website states 'it's a hoot . . . like being in the telly'. ii. 'Great night out. . . It was like being sat in the middle of an episode' iii. 'From start to finish it felt like we were in an episode of "Only Fools"'.

(para 194)

No Use for the Purpose of Pastiche

In my judgement, the use made of the characters, their backstories, jokes and catchphrases is not for the purpose of pastiche within the meaning of section 30A for the following reasons:

a. The September Script does not use elements from the Scripts to imitate the style of OFAH. Nor are the elements taken arranged in any sort of medley or assemblage. Rather it takes the characters, with their full back story and catch phrases and simply (re)presents them in a live dining format.

b. The use made of Del Boy and the other characters, their language, jokes and backstories from OFAH in the setting of an imaginary pub quiz involves a wholesale borrowing of content. It is closer to reproduction by adaptation than pastiche.

c. None of the marketing material or internal planning material refers to the OFDE Show as being intended as being a pastiche of OFAH.

d. None of the reviews of the OFDE Show refer to is as being perceived or understood to be a pastiche.

e. The September Script uses copyright material from OFAH to create an interactive adaptation of OFAH with the aim of giving the audience the feeling that they are meeting the characters from OFAH. The loose script built around the borrowed characters and backstories is a mere vehicle for facilitation this feeling of coming into contact with the characters from OFAH rather than being an attempt to use the style of OFAH. In that respect the September Script is not noticeably different from OFAH.

(para 195)

ACTIVITY 5.1

The consequence of the *Shazam* case does not mean that the OFDE cannot be performed. It only means that the OFDE will need to negotiate with the claimants and obtain permission to perform their work. Accordingly, one might ask: what's the problem? Copyright does not truly prevent reuse of the work. It only subjects it to a licensing requirement.

What might be the problem with subjecting parodies to a licensing requirement? What are the implications for this problem for copyright as a property right?

5.1.1.2 CRITICISM OR REVIEW

Given that the OFDE did not qualify as parody or pastiche, one might speculate about whether it could fit within any of the other statutory purposes. One plausible answer is that it is for the purposes of 'criticism or review'. This purpose has existed in the legislation since its enactment in 1988 and prior to 2014 and courts concluded that the provision should be construed 'liberally'.[13] This provision therefore allows individuals to copy passages of work, for example, for the purposes of writing a book or film review. Yet, it would seem likely that the OFDE would fail this test for the same reasons explained in the second extract from Kimbell QC: the defendants had not 'critically engaged' with the original work.

Similarly, a case like *Deckmyn* would also likely not fit within this purpose. Courts have held that a defendant is engaged in criticism or review only if they are criticising or reviewing another work or performance.[14] Deckmyn, however, did not criticise or review a work: his cartoon did not mock or make any comment on Vandersteen's original cartoon. Instead, Deckmyn was criticising the Mayor of Ghent.

5.1.1.3 QUOTATION

At first glance, the 'quotation' purpose would seem to be of little help to the OFDE. Some might think of quotation as applying to reuse of literary works only. However, as Case 5.2 illustrates, that is not necessarily the case.

Case 5.2 *Pelham GmbH v Ralf Hütter and Florian Schneider-Esleben*, Case C-476/17, EU:C:2019:624

Facts

Hütter and another (claimants) are members of the group Kraftwerk. In 1977, that group published a phonogram featuring the song 'Metall auf Metall'.

Mr Pelham and Mr Haas (defendants) composed the song 'Nur mir', which was released on phonograms recorded by Pelham GmbH in 1997.

Hütter and another submit that Pelham electronically copied ('sampled') approximately 2 seconds of a rhythm sequence from the song 'Metall auf Metall' and used that sample in a continuous loop in the song 'Nur mir', although it would have been possible for them to play the adopted rhythm sequence themselves.

Issue and Procedure

Hütter and another brought an action before the Landgericht Hamburg (Regional Court, Hamburg, Germany). That court upheld the action, and Pelham's appeal before the Oberlandesgericht Hamburg (Higher Regional Court, Hamburg, Germany) was dismissed. Subsequently, the Bundesgerichtshof (Federal Court of Justice, Germany)

As briefly mentioned in Section 4.1.1.2, the CJEU also decided that 2-second samples would count as a reproduction unless they have been modified by the defendant such that the sample is no longer recognisable.

referred questions to the Court of Justice of the European Union (CJEU), including the following: can it be said that a work or other subject matter is being used for quotation purposes within the meaning of Article 5(3)(d) of Directive 2001/29 if it is not evident that another person's work or another person's subject matter is being used?

COURT OF JUSTICE (GRAND CHAMBER)

As regards the usual meaning of the word 'quotation' in everyday language, it should be noted that the essential characteristics of a quotation are the use, by a user other than the copyright holder, of a work or, more generally, of an extract from a work for the purposes of illustrating an assertion, of defending an opinion or of allowing an intellectual comparison between that work and the assertions of that user, since the user of a protected work wishing to rely on the quotation exception must therefore have the intention of entering into 'dialogue' with that work, as the Advocate General stated in point 64 of his Opinion.

In particular, where the creator of a new musical work uses a sound sample taken from a phonogram which is recognisable to the ear in that new work, the use of that sample may, depending on the facts of the case, amount to a 'quotation', on the basis of Article 5(3)(d) of Directive 2001/29 read in the light of Article 13 of the Charter, provided that that use has the intention of entering into dialogue with the work from which the sample was taken, within the meaning referred to in paragraph 71 above, and that the conditions set out in Article 5(3)(d) are satisfied.

However, as the Advocate General stated in point 65 of his Opinion, there can be no such dialogue where it is not possible to identify the work concerned by the quotation at issue.

In the light of the foregoing considerations, the answer to the fourth question is that Article 5(3)(d) of Directive 2001/29 must be interpreted as meaning that the concept of 'quotations', referred to in that provision, does not extend to a situation in which it is not possible to identify the work concerned by the quotation in question.

(paras 71–74)

> Note the importance of 'dialogue' in the CJEU's decision. Does this have faint echoes of Drassinower's view that creative work is not a thing, but an act of communication (Section 1.1.1)?

What this means for a defendant like the OFDE is debatable. The quotation purpose is not limited to any particular type of work,[15] and it is certainly the case that the original OFAH is identifiable within the OFDE. But is the OFDE entering into a 'dialogue' with the original work?

Copyright IV: Exceptions

5.1.1.4 REPORTING CURRENT EVENTS

The characteristics of the fair dealing rule means that at times, as demonstrated by the parody provision, Parliament needs to introduce new statutory purposes. Nevertheless, the fair dealing doctrine is hardly without its own flexibility. Courts can stretch the existing purposes to cover new ways of exploiting the work. An example of this possibility can be found in Case 5.3.

Case 5.3 *England & Wales Cricket Board v Tixdaq & Fanatix* [2016] EWHC 575 (Ch)

Facts

The England & Wales Cricket Board together with British Sky Broadcasting (claimants) owned copyright in television broadcasts of cricket matches. The defendants operated websites, social media accounts and various mobile applications through which users had uploaded and viewed a considerable number of clips, lasting up to 8 seconds, of cricket match broadcasts. Typically, these clips were of the most important parts of the matches (e.g. wickets taken, centuries).

Issue and Procedure

The claimants sued for copyright infringement contending that each 8-second clip broadcast by the defendants constituted a substantial part of their copyrighted works, and that that infringement had been flagrant. The defendants relied on the defence of fair dealing for the purposes of reporting current events. In the following extract, Mr Justice Arnold (as he then was) finds that the clips were not for the purpose of reporting current events. While there was no dispute that the cricket matches were 'current events', the defendant's purpose was not the reporting of those events.

ARNOLD J

In considering these submissions, the starting point is that the verb 'reporting' is capable of bearing a broad or narrow meaning depending on context. It follows that it is necessary to construe it purposively. The purpose of section 30(2) of the 1988 Act ... is to provide an exception to, or limit upon, copyright protection in the public interest, namely freedom of expression. As discussed above, this favours a broad interpretation. ... In addition, the exception must be given a 'living' interpretation, at least in the sense that it must be interpreted in manner that takes into account recent developments in technology and the media.

> Accordingly, I consider that counsel for the Claimants was right to accept that section 30(2) and Article 5(3)(c) are not restricted to traditional media and that 'citizen journalism' can qualify as reporting current events. If a member of the public captures images and/or sound of a newsworthy event using their mobile phone and uploads it to a social media site like Twitter, then that may well qualify as reporting current events even if it is accompanied by relatively little in the way of commentary.
>
> Turning to the App, as discussed above, the question whether the use made of the Claimants' copyright works is for the purpose of reporting events is to be objectively assessed.
>
> In my judgment the use made of the copyright works in versions 8.2 and 8.3 of the App was not for the purpose of reporting current events. The clips were not used in order to inform the audience about a current event, but presented for consumption because of their intrinsic interest and value. Furthermore, although the fact that a news service is a commercial one funded by advertising revenue does not prevent its use from being for the purpose of reporting current events, I consider that the Defendants' objective was purely commercial rather than genuinely informatory.
>
> (paras 65–66, 115, 129)

5.1.1.5 NON-COMMERCIAL RESEARCH OR PRIVATE STUDY

Lastly, it is also permitted to perform a restricted act for purpose of research or private study. A law student who, for example, makes a photocopy of a journal article as part of their studies does not infringe the copyright therein. Nor does a scholar, provided that they are conducting non-commercial research. Disagreement may occur, however, over the boundary between commercial and non-commercial research.

5.1.2 Fairness

Assuming that a defendant's use does fall within one of the specified purposes, the second question arises: is the use 'fair dealing' for that purpose? Only if the defendant's use passes this second 'fairness' evaluation, will the restricted act be permitted.

Courts have long repeated that it is 'impossible to lay down any hard-and-fast definition of what is fair dealing, for it is a matter of fact, degree and impression'.[16] Nevertheless, courts are aided in their determination by a range of factors. Mr Justice Arnold considered these factors in the *England & Wales Cricket Board* case.

ARNOLD J

Was the use fair dealing?

At times, the 'normal exploitation' factor has been considered the most important factor in the fair dealing analysis.[17]

I shall assume for these purposes that, contrary to the conclusion I have reached above, the use was for the purpose of reporting current events.

Does the use conflict with normal exploitation of the works? The Claimants contend that the reproduction and communication to the public of the clips conflicts with their exploitation of the copyright works at a number of levels. The Defendants dispute this and contend that it does the Claimants no harm at all, but if anything whets fans' appetite for more.

I am not persuaded . . . [V]ersions 8.2 and 8.3 of the App provided users with potentially extensive highlights (there was no restriction on either the number of clips a user could upload or the amount a user could view) on a near-live basis. In those circumstances I accept [the claimant's] evidence that it would have reduced the attractiveness of Sky's cricket offering. For some subscribers at the margins, this might have an effect on their willingness to subscribe to Sky services which included cricket. On the other hand, it would not affect the vast bulk of subscribers.

Have the works been published? There is no dispute that this is the case.

The amount and importance of the works taken: is it justified by the informatory purpose? So far as versions 8.2 and 8.3 are concerned, the Defendants rely mainly on the fact that users were only able to upload 8 second clips. But even assuming that the use was for the purpose of reporting **currents**, the clips were mostly highlights of the matches and the extent of the use was potentially limitless. As discussed above, each user could upload an unlimited number of clips from each match and there was no restriction of the amounts of clips that each user could upload. In fact, the relatively small number of users of versions 8.2 and 8.3 while they were in use (most of whom were the Defendants' employees or contractors) means that the quantities of clips uploaded and viewed were not as extensive as they might have been. Even so, in the case of the first Ashes test at Cardiff, 44 clips were uploaded showing many of the highlights of the match. In any event, in my view the relatively small scale of the use does not affect the principle given that versions 8.2 and 8.3 were designed to be used by very large numbers of users and that the Defendants were seeking to attract as many users as possible. Accordingly, I do not consider that the extent of the use was justified by the informatory purpose.

> *Overall balance*. I have no hesitation in concluding that the use of the Claimants' copyright works by versions 8.2 and 8.3 of the App did not amount to fair dealing. The conflict with the Claimants' exploitation of their copyrights was not warranted by the nature and extent of the use, and thus the use was not proportionate.
>
> (136–37, 144, 148–49, 151)

Similarly, Kimbell QC also held in *Shazam* that, had he found the OFDE to be parody or pastiche, he would have held it to fail the fair dealing test.

KIMBELL QC

Assuming that I am wrong and the September Script does involve the use of copyright material for the purposes of pastiche or parody, in my judgment, that use does not qualify as fair dealing and fails the steps 2 and 3 of the three step test for the following reasons:

a. The taking from the Scripts is very extensive both in terms of the quantity of material and its quality: i. As to the extent of the taking, all the characters used in the September Script are lifted wholesale without any attempt to rework or rename them. ii. This taking includes the characters' full back stories, appearance, wants desires, frustrations, social context. It took the key moments, the key catchphrases, and most recognisable parts of OFAH and the characters were closely reproduced in what was intended to be pitch perfect manner. The effect is that the audience feels they have just lived an episode. iii. As the 'Break a Leggers' video review put it: 'It didn't try to add anything particularly new or inventive but why would you when you've got great source material with strong characters, with memorable lines and catchphrases, why would you feel the need.'

b. The use made of the Scripts is not a type of expression which attracts particular protection or engages fundamental rights. There is no expression of political view or any attempt to engage in an artistic dialogue or aesthetic criticism of OFAH specifically or through that show about comedy or television or popular culture generally.

c. The aim was of putting on the show was simply to entertain the audience by bringing them into contact with the copied characters.

d. OFDE plainly competes with Shazam's normal exploitation of OFAH: i. Whilst the most common exploitation of the works in issue is via television broadcast, that is not its only form of exploitation. Through its licensing agreement with the BBC, Shazam had a long established and on-going commercial interest in exploiting OFAH. It had been involved in a prequel and a sequel to OFAH and received licence fees for a wide range of OFAH themed promotional items. ii. Shazam had also invested large sums in a musical adaptation of OFAH. OFDE represented an adaption of OFAH in an interactive dining show. iii. ITI's aim was to extract value from the use of the OFAH characters in the form of a commercial enterprise of a live dining live show. I reject the submission that unless the OFDE can be shown to interfere with the sale of books containing the Scripts, there is no commercial interference with Shazam's normal exploit-ation of OFAH. Shazam's normal exploitation of the Works took many forms. It is irrelevant in this context that Shazam has not considered itself commis-sioning or presenting a dining show of the OFAH. iv. OFDE was launched and marketed at the same time as the fully authorized OFAH Musical was going through the same process. There was a significant risk that some people interested in seeing a live OFAH themed performance might go to see the OFDE rather than go to the Musical. It is not necessary for Shazam to show actual diversion of trade because of the existence of OFDE. A risk of diversion is sufficient to give rise to a potential conflict with Shazam's normal exploit-ation of the Works and Shazam's economic interest in the Works.

e. I accept Mr Hill's submission that OFDE amounted in substance to the creation of a new episode of OFAH adapted for a dining performance. It is obvious that what amounts to the writing of a new episode of an established and commercially successful work using the same principal characters, back story, catchphrases and social and temporal setting without permission unreasonably prejudices the legitimate interests of Shazam.

f. Shazam had a legitimate interest in controlling how the OFAH characters were portrayed and presented and commercially exploited. The conflict with Shaza's legitimate commercial interests in these circumstances was stark.

g. The presentation of the characters, catchphrases, backstories from OFAH (unchanged) in a live setting for the purpose of entertainment is a form of exploitation which a copyright holder would legitimately expect to be able to control (e.g. by licence).

(para 196)

ACTIVITY 5.2

In both cases, Arnold J and Kimberly QC say that the defendant's use of the copyrighted work would conflict with the 'normal exploitation' of the copy-righted work. The reason in both cases, is that allowing the use would make it harder for the copyright owners to make money from their work in certain ways. In *Shazam*, this included licensing adaptations like 'prequels and sequels' (point d (i)). Is there a problem with this argument?

5.1.3 Sufficient Acknowledgement

One last point of note is that in most cases, the fair dealing defence is only available if the defendant provides 'sufficient acknowledgement' of the author. In practice this means identifying the author and their work in some form. The sufficient acknowledgement requirement applies to all of the fair dealing purposes, except for cases of caricature, pastiche or parody. Once again, Mr Justice Arnold explained in relation to *England & Wales Cricket Board*.

ARNOLD J

Were the clips accompanied by a sufficient acknowledgement?

Version 8.2. As explained above, in version 8.2 of the App the Defendants relied upon users capturing the Sky logo which appears in the corner of the screen in Sky's broadcasts in order to acknowledge the source of the clips. There is no dispute that, as was held in Pro Sieben, the appearance of a broadcaster's logo can be a sufficient acknowledgement. The Claimants complain, however, that many of the clips did not show the Sky logo either because it had not been captured by the user who uploaded the clip or because it had been obscured by superimposition of the fanatix logo. The Defendants accept that, in the case of about half of the clips, this was so. The parties disagree as to the exact numbers, but this does not matter for present purposes.

In relation to all of the other days, however, the Defendants contend that any user paying a moderate amount of attention would have been likely to see the Sky logo in one or more of the clips and to have appreciated that all of the footage relating to a particular match (or at least a particular day of a test match) came from the same source. Relying on Fraser-Woodward, the Defendants argue that that amounted to a sufficient acknowledgement. I agree that, in principle, this argument is a sound one and that it may lead to the conclusion that many of the other clips which did not include the Sky logo were nevertheless sufficiently acknowledged.

(paras 130, 132)

5.2 TEMPORARY COPIES

Section 4.1.1.3 explained how temporary copies (that is, copies lasting only seconds or less) are understood as reproductions. Making such copies, therefore, is a restricted act. This poses problems in the context of the Internet. Even simply watching a video on YouTube may result in liability for copyright infringement, due to the temporary copies the user's computer makes in the hard drive.

Copyright IV: Exceptions

To prevent the reproduction right from breaking the Internet, UK law limits the right of reproduction through section 28A of the CDPA. Section 28A states that making temporary copies does not fall within the author's exclusive right of reproduction so long as the following conditions are met:

(i) The copy is transient or incidental; and

(ii) The copy is an integral and essential part of a technological process; and

(iii) The sole purpose of the temporary copy is to enable either: (a) a transmission of the work in a network between third parties by an intermediary; or (b) a lawful use of the work; and

(iv) The copy has no independent economic significance.

The meaning of this provision is, however, highly contentious. Courts have struggled to understand each of above conditions. Illustrative of this difficulty is the confusion surrounding what counts as a 'lawful' use, as the next two cases illustrate.

Case 5.4 *Public Relations Consultants Association Limited v The Newspaper Licensing Agency Limited and others* [2013] UKSC 18.

Facts

Public Relations Consultants Association (PRCA) (appellant–defendant) is a 'media-monitoring organisation'. Customers give the organisation search terms. PRCA then searches newspaper websites for their customers' terms. When a search term is found, PRCA sends an email to the customer. The email contains, among other things, the link to the website where the search term can be found. The customer can click on the link and then view the material online. If the material is behind a paywall, the user will need to pay the website owner for access to the material; if the material is publicly available, the customer will not need to pay for access.

The Newspaper Licensing Agency (NLA) (respondents–claimants) represents newspapers and licences their content. NLA sued PRCA for copyright infringement. When the customer clicks on the link provided by PRCA, and browses the copyright-protected material online, the reproductions made by their hard drive qualified as a reproduction and thus would infringe their exclusive right of reproduction. In response, PRCA argued that such reproductions were outside the scope of the reproduction right because of section 28A.

Issue and Procedure

The case presented the following issue: are copies made in the course of browsing publicly available material online was a 'lawful' use? At trial, Proudman J held that such copying did not constitute a 'lawful use' because the copies were not authorised by the copyright holder. This decision was upheld by the Court of Appeal. However, matters changed when the case reached the Supreme Court.

Lord Sumption, writing for a unanimous court, found that copies made while browsing the Internet did enable a 'lawful' use.

SUMPTION LJ

This appeal raises an important question about the application of copyright law to the technical processes involved in viewing copyright material on the internet. The owner of a copyright has the exclusive right to do or to authorise a number of acts defined in sections 16 to 26 of the Copyright, Designs and Patents Act 1988. Broadly speaking, it is an infringement to make or distribute copies or adaptations of a protected work. Merely viewing or reading it is not an infringement. A person who reads a pirated copy of a protected book or views a forgery of a protected painting commits no infringement although the person who sold him the book or forged the painting may do...

Lawful 'use' refers to the use of the work which is the subject of the copyright. It extends to use...whether or not authorised by the copyright owner, which is 'not restricted by the applicable legislation'. This necessarily includes the use of the work by an end-user browsing the internet.

(paras 1, 27)

The question of whether browsing constitutes a 'lawful use' was not the only issue in the case. Other issues included whether such copies were truly 'transient' and whether they had any 'independent economic significance'. But the court's discussion of 'lawful use' helpfully underscores the nature of copyright's economic rights. Not all acts are restricted. The economic rights create both restricted and non-restricted acts. And, in the UK Supreme Court's view, it is not a restricted act to merely *view* a protected work. But not every court agrees with that conclusion.

Case 5.5 *Stichting Brein v Jack Frederik Wullems (Filmspeler), Case C-527/15 (ECJ)*

Facts

Wullems (defendant), trading under the name Filmspeler, sold a multimedia player with hyperlinks installed. When a user of the multimedia player clicked on the hyperlinks, they were directed to websites which, without the authorisation of the copyright owner, offered unrestricted access to copyright-protected works such as films and TV series. Stichting Brein (claimant) is a Dutch organisation which protects the interests of copyright holders. Stichting Brein sued Wullems for copyright infringement in the Netherlands.

Issue and Procedure

The case presented the following issue: is browsing publicly available material online that was uploaded without the copyright holder's authorisation a 'lawful use'? European Union law contains the same temporary copies exception as UK law in article 5(1) of the Information Society Directive. The Dutch Court referred the question to the CJEU. The CJEU found that viewing this material was not a lawful use.

COURT OF JUSTICE OF THE EUROPEAN UNION (SECOND CHAMBER)

[I]n circumstances such as those at issue in the main proceedings, and having regard, in particular, to the content of the advertising of the multimedia player at issue mentioned in paragraph 18 above and the fact, noted in paragraph 51 above, that the main attraction of that player for potential purchasers is the pre-installation of the add-ons concerned, it must be held that it is, as a rule, deliberately and in full knowledge of the circumstances that the purchaser of such a player accesses a free and unauthorised offer of protected works.

It must also be held that, as a rule, temporary acts of reproduction, on a multimedia player such as that at issue in the main proceedings, of copyright-protected works obtained from streaming websites belonging to third parties offering those works without the consent of the copyright holders are such as to adversely affect the normal exploitation of those works and causes unreasonable prejudice to the legitimate interests of the right holder, because, as the Advocate General observed in points 78 and 79 of his opinion, that practice would usually result in a diminution of lawful transactions relating to the protected works, which would cause unreasonable prejudice to copyright holders (see, to that effect, judgment of 10 April 2014, *ACI Adam and Others*, C-435/12, EU:C:2014:254, paragraph 39).

(paras 69–70)

ACTIVITY 5.3

Compare the *Public Relations* and *Stichting Brein* cases. Which of these cases, if either, looks more like a bundle-of-rights picture of property, and which looks more like exclusive control?

5.3 PERSONAL COPYING FOR PRIVATE USE

Unlike some other European nations, the UK does not have a general exception permitting users to copy material for purely private use. This is not for want of trying. In 2014 the CDPA was updated to include a section 28B which would have permitted consumers to make purely private uses of copyrighted material. The term 'private use' was defined to include making backup copies of works, changing the format of works (e.g. from CD to MP3), and storing electronic copies of works (in, for example, a folder like Google Drive or Dropbox). However, section 28B was found to be unlawful in Case 5.6.

While there is no general personal copying exception, there are a few specific exceptions that permit some private use. For example, section 50A allows for backup copies of computer programs.

Case 5.6 *R (on the application of British Academy of Songwriters, Composers and Authors) v Secretary of State for Business, Innovation & Skills* [2015] EWHC 1723 (Admin)

Facts

Article 5(2)(b) of the EU Information Society Directive permits member states to enact a copyright exception permitting copying for private use. The Directive further states that if such an exception would cause more than *de minimis* harm to the copyright holder, then such right holders should receive 'fair compensation'. Many EU countries who adopted private use exceptions subsequently placed a 'levy' (or tax) on the sale of private copying equipment (e.g. on blank CDs and recording devices). The money raised via the levy was in turn distributed to the rights holders.

Following the 2010 Hargreaves Report (Digital Opportunity: A Review of Intellectual Property and Growth), the UK government introduced a private use exception in section 28B CDPA. While some EU member states enacted private use exceptions that allowed individuals to distribute copies among friends and family, section 28B did not go quite so far. The UK government wished to avoid a complicated levy-based compensation scheme. And so they enacted a narrow private use exception that permitted the user to copy for purely private purposes. The UK government argued that because the harm to the copyright owners was only *de minimis*, there was no requirement to pay compensation.

Issue and Procedure

The new provision was subject to a judicial review challenge brought by various copyright owner groups. The copyright owners argued that the harm caused by the private use exception was not merely *de minimis* and therefore the new law was unlawful without a fair compensation scheme. The UK government in turn relied principally upon a report issued by the UK Intellectual Property Office which suggested that copyright holders may already be 'pricing in' private use: that is, when copyright owners sell their works, they already take into account the fact that consumers make private copies, and to compensate for this, the copyright owners simply charge a higher price for their works in the first place. If such 'pricing in' already occurs, then the introduction of a private use exception would not result in any loss of revenue for rights holders. However, in the following extract, Mr Justice Green in the High Court Queen's Bench Division (Administrative Court) concluded that the government had insufficient evidence for that conclusion.

GREEN J

The IPO Research Report:

This brings me to the remaining, and principal, category of evidence relied upon, namely the independently commissioned IPO Research Report which I have summarised in Section E above. In this part of the judgment, I confine myself to setting out my conclusions only on this research.

First, it provides useful evidence in relation to the control (software) which supports the Defendant's intuitive conclusion that to some extent pricing-in occurs in copyright related industries. However, even in the software sector there is no analysis of whether pricing-in is complete or leaves *some* harm which is unaccounted for by pricing-in; and if so whether this residual harm is *de minimis*.

Second, a similar conclusion occurs in relation to books and in relation to films (see paragraphs [122]–[125] above). These provide some evidence supporting the proposition that pricing-in arises but it does not provide evidence that it is total and would leave only 'minimal or zero' harm.

Third, in relation to music (see paragraphs [118]–[121] above), there are three critical findings and points to be made: (i) the empirical research did not show evidence of pricing-in as between CDs and downloads but, on the contrary, it showed precisely the opposite effect; (ii) the researchers found this conclusion to be *'puzzling'* and the evidence, at best, *'ambiguous'* ; (iii) the researchers speculated about the reasons for these unexpected results and whether they were, for example, due to *'a lack of variability in the explanatory variables'* and/or the private copying was *'already largely fully priced-in in the UK market'* but this speculation served to highlight that the research was incomplete as an exercise designed to answer the *de minimis* question. Put another way it raised more questions than it answered.

> (iv) Conclusion
>
> Where does this lead to? In my judgment the inferences drawn in the Updated Impact Assessment about *de minimis* are not remotely supported by the evidence which the Defendant asserts and claims justify the conclusion drawn from it.
>
> (paras 264–67, 269)

Although the lack of a private use exception might be disappointing, the attention to evidence in the case was commendable. Recall the incentive–access tradeoff on which the utilitarian argument is based (Section 2.3.3). The central point of the utilitarian argument is that copyright has both good and bad consequences, but that a carefully balanced copyright system will have overall good consequences. But to make such a claim we need empirical evidence. Merges (Section 2.3.4) raises the point that we may never have sufficient empirical evidence to tell whether copyright is a net positive overall. Nevertheless, we can gather empirical evidence to help guide smaller questions, such as whether a private copying exception will cause harm to copyright holders. One of the recommendations of the Hargreaves Report was for IP law to be guided by objective evidence, as far as possible.

ACTIVITY 5.4

What would a private copying exception say in terms of exclusive control versus the bundle-of-rights conceptions of copyright?

5.4 DISCLOSURE IN THE PUBLIC INTEREST

Unlike fair dealing and the temporary copies exception, the disclosure in the public interest defence has no statutory basis and is entirely judge made. As a judge-made doctrine, courts have had to consider how broadly or narrowly the doctrine should be. As Case 5.7 makes clear, courts have been reluctant to use the defence.

Case 5.7 *Ashdown v Telegraph Group* [2002] Ch 149

Facts

Mr Paddy Ashdown (claimant) was leader of the Liberal Democrats political party in the UK from 1988 to 1999. In 1997, the Labour party won the general election and Tony Blair became prime minister. On 21 October 1997, Blair and Ashdown held a confidential meeting in 10 Downing Street. After the meeting, Ashdown dictated the events of the meeting to his secretary, who typed the events out in the form of a 'minute'.

In 1999, Ashdown stepped down from his position of leader of the Liberal Democrats and intended to publish his political diaries, including the minute of the meeting with Blair. In confidence, Ashdown showed some of the material, including the minute, to a number of newspapers and publishing houses.

On 28 November 1999, the *Sunday Telegraph* (defendant) published three articles which contained sections of the minute. In total, approximately 25 per cent of the minute appeared in the newspaper. It is unknown how the *Sunday Telegraph* came to obtain a copy of the minute.

Issue and Procedure

Two exceptions were raised in the litigation: fair dealing for purposes of reporting current events, and publication in the public interest. The former defence failed. While the use was for the purpose of news reporting, the use was not 'fair' in large part because the minute had not previously been published and would compete commercially with Ashdown's memoirs. And, as explained below, the public interest defence also failed. In the following extract, Lord Phillips of Worth Matravers explains the rare situations where such a defence might apply.

LORD PHILLIPS OF WORTH MATRAVERS MR

Public interest

In the rare case where it is in the public interest that the words in respect of which another has copyright should be published without any sanction, we have been concerned to consider why this should not be permitted under the 'public interest' exception, the possibility of which is recognised by section 171(3). Sir Andrew Morritt V-C considered that he was precluded from so holding by the decision of this court in *Hyde Park Residence Ltd v Yelland* [2001] Ch 143 . That case concerned an unusual breach of copyright – the publication by 'The Sun' of photographs of Princess Diana and Mr Dodi Fayed, with times recorded, taken by a security video camera owned by Mr Al Fayed. 'The Sun' claimed that it was in the public interest to publish these photographs as they gave the lie to claims being made by Mr Al Fayed that the two had enjoyed a lengthy tryst at his house in Paris.

In the leading judgment, Aldous LJ started his consideration of public interest with the following observation, at p 160:

'43. . . . The 1988 Act does not give a court general power to enable an infringer to use another's property, namely his copyright in the public interest. Thus a defence of public interest outside those set out in Chapter III of Part I of the 1988 Act, if such exists, must arise by some other route.

44. The courts have an inherent jurisdiction to refuse to allow their process to be used in certain circumstances. It has long been the law that the courts will not give effect to contracts which are, for example, illegal, immoral or prejudicial to family life because they offend against the policy of the law. In my view that inherent jurisdiction can be exercised in the case of an action in which copyright is sought to be enforced, as is made clear by section 171(3) of the 1988 Act: "Nothing in this Part affects any rule of law preventing or restricting the enforcement of copyright, on grounds of public interest or otherwise"'.

[W]e do not consider that Aldous LJ was justified in circumscribing the public interest defence to breach of copyright as tightly as he did. We prefer the conclusion of Mance LJ that the circumstances in which public interest may override copyright are not capable of precise categorisation or definition. Now that the Human Rights Act 1998 is in force, there is the clearest public interest in giving effect to the right of freedom of expression in those rare cases where this right trumps the rights conferred by the 1988 Act. In such circumstances, we consider that section 171(3) of the Act permits the defence of public interest to be raised.

(paras 47–48, 58)

> In 1984, the philosopher Ronald Dworkin argued that **rights are 'trumps'**. The idea is that if a person's rights and society's utility conflict, the person's rights always win. In other words, rights 'trump' other considerations.
>
> In Paragraph 58, Lord Phillips alludes to this idea. He writes that sometimes the right of freedom of expression might 'trump' (i.e. be more important than) copyright.
>
> One might ask why the right to freedom of expression should not always trump copyright?[18]

On the facts of the case, the Court of Appeal found that interest in freedom of expression did not 'trump' the interest of the copyright owner.

5.5 TEXT AND DATA ANALYSIS

Another exception introduced following the Hargreaves Report is the text and data analysis provisions. Section 29A of the CDPA permits copying of protected work for the purpose of text and data analysis conducted in the context of non-commercial research.

This provision has taken on significance in the context of machine learning. In brief, machine learning refers to computer programs that, in certain respects, learn to function like the human mind.[19] In particular, when those computer programs are exposed to significant quantities of data (whether that be text or images or something else entirely) the programs can identify patterns. In certain contexts, this permits the machine learning programs to generate new material. If 'trained' on a sufficiently large number of images, for example, the program can begin to generate its own images. In the USA under the fair use doctrine, some have argued that training a machine learning program in this way is a fair use.[20]

The UK Intellectual Property Office recently consulted on the copyright and patent regimes as they applied to machine learning and artificial intelligence more broadly. As explained in Box 5.2, the office proposes that the text and data analysis provisions of the CDPA be broadened to include text and data analysis for commercial purposes as well as non-commercial ones.

BOX 5.2 ARTIFICIAL INTELLIGENCE AND INTELLECTUAL PROPERTY: COPYRIGHT AND PATENTS: GOVERNMENT RESPONSE TO CONSULTATION (28 JUNE 2022)

Text and data mining (TDM) means using computational techniques to analyse large amounts of information to identify patterns, trends and other useful information. TDM is used for training AI systems, amongst other uses. It also has uses in research, journalism, marketing, business analytics and by cultural heritage organisations. The consultation outlined options in relation to text and data mining, which developers of AI and other copyright users had identified in the call for views.

Although factual data, trends and concepts are not protected by copyright, they are often embedded in copyright works. Data mining systems copy works to extract and analyse the data they contain. Unless permitted under licence or an exception, making such copies will constitute copyright infringement.

Some rights holders license their works to allow TDM, but others do not. This has financial costs for people using data mining software. To reduce these costs for researchers, an exception to copyright for TDM was introduced in 2014. This is set out in section 29A of the Copyright, Designs and Patents Act 1988. It is limited to non-commercial research, following EU rules which were in place at its creation.

Several other countries have introduced copyright exceptions for TDM. These encourage AI development and other services to locate there. Territories with exceptions include the EU, Japan and Singapore. TDM may also be fair use under US law, depending on the facts.

The consultation sought views on how to make it easier for people to data mine copyright materials. It did this with a view to supporting AI and wider innovation in the UK, in line with Government priorities on AI, data and innovation.

65 respondents expressed a preference, with a spread of views across the responses. Almost no quantitative evidence was provided on the licensing environment or other questions.

> Rights holders favoured no change or licensing solutions to help make more material available for TDM. Users of copyright and database material favoured a wider exception. They highlighted the costs of licensing and difficulties in obtaining licences, especially when many rights holders are involved.
>
> The Government has decided to introduce a new copyright and database exception which allows TDM for any purpose, along the lines of Option 4. This option is the most supportive of AI and wider innovation.
>
> (paras 31–38)

Whether such a broadened exception will be introduced remains to be seen. Copyright owners are likely to oppose such a move. At the time of writing, the first lawsuits concerning the use of copyrighted works for 'training' have only just started.[21]

5.6 SUMMARY

On one level, understanding exceptions as user rights fits the idea of copyright as a bundle of rights. Some of those rights – the right to reproduce and distribute the work etc. – are allocated to the owner; while other members of the public retain the right to parody the work, to quote from the work, or to disclose the work in the public interest. When the CDPA says that copyright is a property right, perhaps all that is meant is that copyright is this complex system of rights. The idea of copyright as property is simply the fact that different people have a different legal relationship to the works.

But a more critical understanding of exceptions remains. According to that more critical view, exceptions are deceptive. Rather than simply grant the owner a narrow set of rights, exceptions exist against a baseline assumption that the owner controls all economically valuable uses of the work unless there is a specific and compelling reason to the contrary (such as the presence of a market failure). What might initially seem like users' rights, simply masks how an increasing amount of activity has become restricted, and only occasionally permitted, over time. Is this what the CDPA means when it says that copyright is a property right?

Copyright has obviously come a long way since 1710. When faced with the fundamental questions, modern copyright law emphatically says that original works are things that can be, and indeed are, owned. The case for such ownership is, as Justice Stephen Breyer (Section 2.2.4) puts it, an 'uneasy' one.

And finally, this Part has only focused on copyright, and not on copyright's 'associated rights'. In the last three-hundred years, society has not only expanded copyright protection; it has also developed a range of new copyright-like rights. Some of the most significant of **copyright's associated rights** are summarised in Table 5.3.

Whether the expansion of copyright and associated rights is justifiable is a decision that any student of IP law will need to make themselves. Is expansion an inevitable feature of the modern world where intangible goods are more important to developed economies? Or does expansion merely represent the entrenchment of unjustifiable monopolies?

Table 5.3 Copyright's associated rights

Name	Key statutory provisions	Nature
Performers' rights	CDPA ss 180–212A	The right of a performer (e.g. actors, musicians) to control the exploitation and use of their performances.
Database rights	Copyright and Rights in Databases Regulations 1997 (SI 1997/3032)	The right to control information contained in non-original databases.
Technological protection measures	CDPA ss 297ZA(1), (6) and 296 ZD(1), (8)	The right to prevent the circumvention of technological measures designed to restrict copying.
Droit de suite	Artist's Resale Right Regulations 2006 (SI 2006/346)	The right of an artist to claim a royalty when their work is resold.
Press publishers' right	Directive on Copyright in the Digital Single Market 2019/790 (EU) art 15. Currently inapplicable to UK law.	The right for publishers of press publications to control the online reproduction and communication to the public of their publications by information society service providers.

5.7 SELF-ASSESSMENT

Before moving on, try to answer the following questions to consolidate your learning. Answers are provided in the section below.

1. Which of the following descriptions best summarise how courts in the UK assess whether a defendant qualifies for the fair dealing exception?
    a. A restricted act will be permitted if it is 'fair dealing'. It is for courts to decide what qualifies as fair dealing.
    b. A restricted act will be permitted if it is conducted for one of the fair dealing purposes.
    c. A restricted act will be permitted if it is conducted for one of the fair dealing purposes and the act is 'fair dealing'. There is no definition of what qualifies as 'fair' in such circumstances.
    d. A restricted act will be permitted if it is conducted for one of the fair dealing purposes and the act is 'fair dealing'. While there is no definition of what qualifies as 'fair', courts frequently consider a set of non-exhaustive factors.
2. Each of the following defendants have made temporary copies of copyrighted works in the hard drive of their computer while using the Internet. Which of the defendants is least likely to qualify for the temporary copies exception?
    a. Defendant 1 has browsed Google Images.
    b. Defendant 2 has watched an unauthorised stream of a Premier League football match.
    c. Defendant 3 has read an online newspaper article.
    d. Defendant 4 has watched an authorised stream of a Premier League football match.
3. Should the UK adopt a fair use doctrine?
4. Does every unpermitted use of a work conflict with the normal exploitation of the work by the copyright owner?

ACTIVITY DISCUSSION

Activity 5.1   Very few people enjoy being the object of criticism or parody. As a result, copyright owners may not license parodies even if the user is willing and able to pay. Thus, copyright may create a **'market failure'**.[22] By converting public goods into private goods, copyright law enables a market to exist in works (refer back to Activity 2.6 and Bracha and Syed in Section 2.2.3) in which valuable works will be produced, sold and bought. But, in this instance, copyright may result in valuable works – parodies – not being produced, bought and sold. According to this view, therefore, the purpose of copyright exceptions is merely to correct copyright-induced market failures.

This idea, however, is contentious. To some, the rationale reinforces the exclusive control nature of copyright. According to that view, all economically valuable uses of the work should and will be controlled by the owner, except in the relatively few situations of 'market failure'. The view rests on an unstated premise that the copyright owner already has exclusive control over the work and that any sort of deviation therefrom needs to be justified.

Activity 5.2   The problem is that the judges' arguments might be 'circular'.

Consider a friend who wants you to believe the following conclusion 'A is true'. You ask the person 'why is A true'? And they answer: 'because B is true'. You then ask, 'OK, but why is B true?' and this time, they answer 'because A is true'. Obviously, the reason the friend has given to support the conclusion is not persuasive. In fact, the reason seems to *assume* the truth of the conclusion. More formally, this is known as 'begging the question'.

Now consider Kimbell QC's argument in *Shazam*. That argument concludes that OFDE should not be permitted because it would harm the owner's 'normal exploitation' of the work (OFAH). Why would it harm the 'normal exploitation'? The answer is, in part, because Shazam have previously made money by licensing adaptations which are like the OFDE (including prequels and sequels). But this answer raises a question: how was Shazam previously *able* to license adaptations? The answer must be: because copyright made it unlawful to make adaptations without the owner's permission. If it were not for copyright, Shazam could not stop people from making adaptations, and could not make any money by licensing them.

Here we see the possible circularity. Why should uses like OFDE not be permitted? Answer: because uses like OFDE harm the owner's 'normal exploitation'. But why do uses like OFDE harm the owner's 'normal exploitation'? Answer: because uses like OFDE are not permitted. The reasons given seem to assume the truth of the conclusion.

Luckily, there might be a way to solve this problem and break the circle. One could bypass the concept of normal exploitation entirely. Instead, Shazam should be able to stop OFDE if there are good normative arguments (i.e. utilitarian, natural rights or personality arguments) for doing so. If there are no such arguments, then OFDE should be permitted.

Activity 5.3 Lord Justice Sumption's decision in *Stichting Brein* is consistent with a bundle-of-rights idea of copyright. In his judgment, the copyright owner's bundle did not contain the exclusive right to view the work.

By contrast, the CJEU decision in *Stichting Brein* seems to fit more naturally with an exclusive control model of copyright. This is in part the result, once again, of circular reasoning. Why is streaming not permitted? Answer: because it would affect the 'normal exploitation' of those works. But why would it affect the 'normal' exploitation of those works? Answer: because the law makes it unlawful thus giving the owner a monopoly. The circularity of the reasoning suggests that copyright is, in the CJEU's decision, something more akin to a right of exclusive control.

Activity 5.4 Some extend the market failure rationale for copyright exceptions (activity 5.1.) to personal copying. Assume, for example, that a consumer wishes to record a television broadcasted Premier League football match, to which they have lawful access. It is clearly unlikely that the consumer will contact the copyright owner – the Premier League – and ask for permission because contacting the copyright owner and negotiating permission will be a laborious and time-consuming task. The cost of the transaction (the '**transaction costs**') are just too high. Some may therefore ground the personal copying exception in the fact that the free market is unlikely to result in this type of transaction occurring. However, this once again rests on an unstated assumption that the copyright owner has the right to control such use of the work in the first place.

SELF-ASSESSMENT ANSWERS

1. **Correct answer: d.** Answer **a.** is more akin to the fair use doctrine adopted in the USA. Answer **b.** omits the necessary fair dealing analysis. Answer **c.** is not strictly incorrect, but answer **d.** is more accurate in capturing how contemporary courts actually decide fair dealing cases.
2. **Correct answer: b.** Following the *Stichting Brien v Wullems* case, it is likely that only activity **b.** would be an infringement of the copyright owner's right of reproduction.

Notes

1 James Boyle, 'The Second Enclosure Movement and the Construction of the Public Domain' (2003) 66 LCP 33–74.

2 'Enclosure' *Britannica* <https://www.britannica.com/topic/enclosure> (accessed June 2023).

3 Boyle (n 1) at 37.

4 CDPA, ch 3 ('Acts Permitted in relation to Copyrighted Works').

5 *Funke Medien v Bundesrepublik Deutschland*, Case C-469/17, EU:C:2019:623, [70].

6 Oren Bracha, *Owning Ideas: The Intellectual Origins of American Intellectual Property, 1790–1909* (CUP 2016) 54–123.

7 26 ER 489.

8 On the fair abridgement rule at common law, see Walter Arthur Copinger, *The Law of Copyright in Works of Literature and Art* (Stevens & Haynes 1870). The 'fair dealing' rule was first codified in the Copyright Act 1911, s 2(1)(i).

9 The public interest played, at best, an inconsistent role in this change. Isabella Alexander, *Copyright and the Public Interest in the Nineteenth Century* (Hart Publishing 2010) 155–232.

10 17 USC §107 (US). See also Copyright Act 2007, s 19 (Israel).

11 Hargreaves Report [5.35].

12 Crime and Courts Act 2013, s 61(3).

13 *Newspaper Licensing Agency v Marks & Spencer* [2000] 4 All ER 239.

14 *Ashdown v Telegraph Group* [2002] Ch 149, 171.

15 See generally Tanya Aplin and Lionel Bently *Global Mandatory Fair Use: The Right of Quotation in International Copyright Law* (CUP 2020).

16 The quote initially appeared in Hugh Laddie, Peter Prescott and Mary Vittoria, *The Modern Law of Copyright and Designs*, para 20.16. The quote was cited approvingly in *Ashdown v Telegraph Group* [2001] EWCA Civ 1142, para 70.

17 *Ashdown v Telegraph Group* [2001] EWCA Civ 1142, para 70 (on commercial competition).

18 Ronald Dworkin, 'Rights as Trumps' in J Waldron (ed), *Theories of Rights* (OUP 1984) 153–67.

19 See generally Ryan Abbott (ed), *Research Handbook on Intellectual Property and Artificial Intelligence* (Edward Elgar 2022).

20 Mark A Lemeley and Bryan Casey, 'Fair Learning' (2021) 99 Texas L Rev 743.

21 See Chris Vallance, 'AI Image Creator Faces UK and US Legal Challenges' *BBC News* (18 January 2022) <https://www.bbc.co.uk/news/technology-64285227> (accessed June 2023).

22 As first discussed in Wendy J Gordon, 'Fair Use as Market Failure: A Structure and Economic Analysis of the Betamax Case and its Predecessors' (1982) 82 Colum L Rev 1600.

FIGURE ACKNOWLEDGEMENT

5.1 Willy Vandersteen, Suske en Wiske: De Wilde Weldoener (1961) ((a)); John Deckmyn, De Wilde Weldoener (2011) ((b)). Reproduced in *Shazam v Only Fools the Dining Experience* [2022] EWHC 1379 (IPEC)

Part II

Patents

If we did not have a patent system, it would be irresponsible, on the basis of our present knowledge of its economic consequences, to recommend instituting one. But since we have had a patent system for a long time, it would be irresponsible, on the basis of our present knowledge, to recommend abolishing it.

—Fritz Machlup, An Economic Review of the Patent System
(1958) US Congress

6

Patents I: Foundations of Patent Law

Patents are property rights in inventions.[1] While there are many examples of invention, the story of the Lego brick provides a good starting point for newcomers to the patent system.

In 1947, a British inventor called Hillary Page invented a toy called the 'Self-Locking Brick'. The Self-Locking Bricks were small hollow plastic bricks with little 'studs' on top. The bricks could then be stacked on top of each other to make elaborate constructions. But there was a problem with the bricks: while they could be stacked on top of each other, they did not lock firmly together and lacked stability as a result.

In 1958, a Danish inventor called Godtfred Kirk Christiansen devised a solution to the problem. Christiansen invented something called the 'Toy Building Brick'. The Toy Building Brick was much like Page's Self-Locking Brick with one important modification. The Toy Building Brick incorporated something new: something called the 'stud-and-tube' coupling system (illustrated in Figure 6.1).[2] The new brick contained not only 'studs' on top of the brick, but crucially also 'tubes' inside the brick. When the bricks were stacked on top of each other, the tubes fitted neatly into the space left between the studs, creating something called 'clutch power'. The result was the bricks locked together securely. At the same time, the bricks could also be easily dissembled. The redesigned bricks have been sold by the Christiansen company – the Lego Company – ever since.

Upon inventing the coupling system, Christiansen applied for patents over the Toy Building Brick in a range of different countries. The patents were granted and enabled the Christiansens to prevent other toymakers from using the new stud-and-tube system in their own bricks for twenty years. Armed with patents on their invention, their business grew into one of the world's biggest toy companies.

While we celebrate his invention today, the idea that Christiansen ought to own it is more curious. How can someone own an abstract system of coupling toy

---

This chapter contains public sector information licensed under the Open Government Licence v3.0.

Figure 6.1 Christiansen's Toy Building Brick.

Figures from patent GB866557A

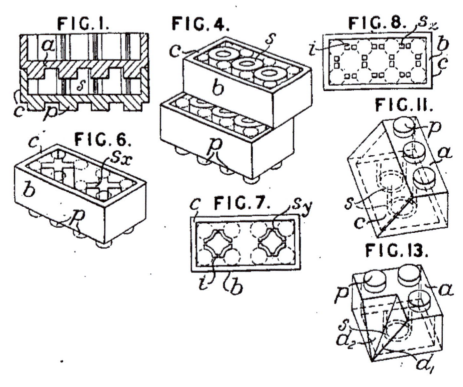

bricks? Why should the inventor have property in their inventions? After all, it was not always so. Much like copyright, patents present a story of how intangible inventions became property over time. Nor was this story a linear one. Support for patents has ebbed and flowed over the past 500 years. While one American President, Abraham Lincoln, once said that patents 'add the fuel of interest to the fire of genius in the discovery and production of new and useful things',[3] another American President, Thomas Jefferson, called patents an 'embarrassment'.[4] Patents have even been implicated in civil wars and the downfall of kings.

6.1 INVENTING PATENTS

The historian Christine MacLeod writes that the patent system is both 'older and younger' than we think.[5] It is older in the sense that patent law's prehistory can be found in the sixteenth and seventeenth centuries. But it is younger because the modern idea of patents as property in inventions emerged relatively recently.

The prehistory of patents begins with the **letters patent**. Far from a right of property, the letters patent is an instrument through which the monarch grants a person or organisation some special form of privilege (for example, an office or a title). The term 'letters patent' means 'open letter', so called because the letter is not sealed and is open to the public at large.[6] The English monarchy has issued letters patents since at least Edward III's reign (1312–77) and continues to do so today.[7]

6.1.1 Patents as Industrial Policy

In the sixteenth and seventeenth centuries, the letters patent system acquired a new role in **industrial policy**. Industrial policy is a country's official strategic effort to encourage economic development and growth. As Macleod explains, Elizabeth I and her Secretary of State, William Cecil, used the letters patent system to encourage foreign artisans to resettle in England and to introduce new trades to the realm (Box 6.1).

BOX 6.1 CHRISTINE MACLEOD, *INVENTING THE INDUSTRIAL REVOLUTION: THE ENGLISH PATENT SYSTEM, 1660–1800* (CUP 1988)

Christine MacLeod is a Professor Emeritus of Historical Studies at the University of Bristol, UK.

There are records since the reign of Edward III of 'letters of protection', given by the English crown to named foreign craftsmen, mainly weavers, saltmakers and glassmakers, with the intention of encouraging them to settle in England and transmit their skills to native apprentices.[8] These grants did not confer any exclusive privilege or monopoly. The practice was revived on a larger scale in the middle of the sixteenth century, again with the purpose of encouraging the introduction of Continental manufactures and skills. This time exclusivity was a major feature, through the influence of mainly Italian ideas.

Whether Venice granted property in inventions, rather than a privilege, is a point of debate.

The notion of creating property rights in technical achievements had arisen in the Italian city states. In the early fourteenth century the Venetian republic rewarded inventors of corn mills who submitted their designs to practical tests with long-term credits and free sites for their mills. Florence granted an exclusive monopoly patent in 1421 – to the architect Brunelleschi for a barge with hoisting gear, used to transport marble. But Venice was the first to regularize in law the award of monopoly patents, the Senate ruling in 1474 that inventions should be registered when perfected: the inventor thereby secured sole benefit for ten years, with a penalty of 100 ducats for infringement, while the government reserved the right to appropriate registered inventions. Emigrant Italian craftsmen, seeking protection against local competition and guild restrictions as a condition of imparting their skills, disseminated knowledge of their patent systems around Europe. Six of the first nine patents in the Archives of Brussels, for example, were issued to Italians. It is no coincidence that the first recorded patents in several countries at this time were for glassmaking, a skill in which the Venetians excelled. German merchants trading with Venice also returned with the idea, and the petty German states were among the first in Europe to grant patents. Indeed, 'one way or another, Italian influence shows like a thread in all incipient patent systems'.

England was no exception. Writing to Thomas Cromwell from Naples in 1537, Sir Antonio Guidotti proposed a scheme to bring Italian silk weavers to England... Then in 1552 a patent was granted for glass, apparently to an Englishman, Smyth, the next in 1561 to two immigrants for making Castile soap. The first Scottish patent was issued in 1565 to Francisco Berty, a Florentine, for saltmaking and the first Irish patent in 1586, again for glass.

Acquisition of superior Continental technology was the predominant motive for the issue of patents under the guidance of Elizabeth I's chief minister, William Cecil, later Lord Burghley. The shaping of patents to serve his policy of importing and improving technology left a lasting imprint, one which they bore for most of the period under review. Encouraging foreign artisans to settle in England remained the most apposite way of introducing new technology for so long as the English lagged behind their competitors.

(pp. 10–11)

As MacLeod highlights, the English use of letters patents as a tool to encourage domestic industry was, somewhat ironically, an idea copied from abroad. The idea of patents as an enticement to foreign artisans had been used to good effect in Venice, Italy, since the fifteenth century, culminating in the landmark 1474 Venice Senate Act (Figure 6.2). The Act encouraged 'men from different places' to resettle in Venice and thereby to bring to the dominion 'new ingenious contrivance' (see Box 6.2). This was particularly important in encouraging foreign artisans to work in the Venetian glass-blowing industry.

BOX 6.2 VENETIAN SENATE ACT 1474

There are in this city, and also there come temporarily by reason of its greatness and goodness, men from different places and most clever minds, capable of devising and inventing all manner of ingenious contrivances. ...Therefore, decision will be passed that, by authority of this Council, each person who will make in this city any new ingenious contrivance, not made heretofore in our dominion ... It being forbidden to any other in any territory and place of ours to make any other contrivance in the form and resemblance thereof, without the consent and license of the author up to ten years.

6.1 Inventing Patents   173

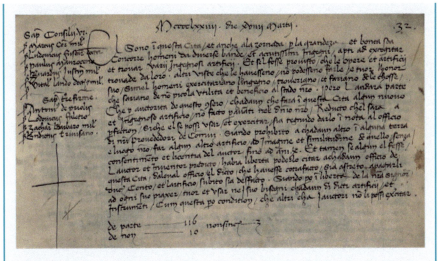

Figure 6.2 Venetian Senate Act 1474.
From Wikimedia Commons <https://commons.wikimedia.org/wiki/File:Venetian_Patent_Statute_1474.png>

Two features of the use of letters patents for industrial policy are noteworthy. First, the system was highly discretionary in nature. No one had any right to a letters patent.[9] They were instead handed out at the grace of the monarch. In return, the recipient performed an act of public service by helping a new industry to grow. Second, the idea of technological invention played a very minor role. While some patents were granted in relation to new inventions, the core purpose of the system was to encourage new industries to flourish.[10]

6.1.2 Hostility to Monopolies

The use of letters patents for industrial policy ran quickly into problems. As MacLeod explains in the next extract, not only were the new industries failing to flourish, but increasingly the system was open to abuse by the crown.

> **BOX 6.3 CHRISTINE MACLEOD, *INVENTING THE INDUSTRIAL REVOLUTION: THE ENGLISH PATENT SYSTEM, 1660–1800* (CUP 1988)**
>
> Burghley had worked hard to make his industrial policy a success, but most newly planted industries had not flourished as expected.[11] Even by 1569 he had gloomily, if irresolutely, decided 'not to move her h[ighness] any more to make grants whereof nothing did grow,

wherein her honour was touched'. Worse, without a committed, firm hand guiding the system to well-defined ends, malpractices began to creep in that were to bring it into disrepute and ultimately endanger its existence. Although no longer instruments of a deliberate policy of importing technology, patents could still be obtained for the introduction of foreign (and native) inventions; influence at Court was, to say the least, advantageous. More controversially, monopolies based on no new industry or invention were granted to courtiers and their clients who had a purely fiscal end in view. Since they interfered with established trades, protests were raised almost immediately by those whose interests, as producers or consumers, were in jeopardy.

Grievances concerning the crown's use of letters patent to regulate manufactures and trade were voiced in several of Elizabeth I's parliaments. They culminated in 1601 in a concerted attack on what was deemed an abuse of the royal prerogative.

(p. 14)

The concerted attack on the royal abuse in the early seventeenth century took place both in Parliament and in the courts. One illustrative example of this attack was the landmark *Darcy v Allein*. This case illustrates not only how the letters patent system was increasingly abused by the crown, but also how that abuse harmed the interests of producers and consumers.

Case 6.1 *Darcy v Allein* (1601) 77 ER 1260 ('The Case of Monopolies')

Facts

In 1571, Queen Elizabeth granted a letters patent to Ralph Bowes. The letters patent gave Bowes the sole authority to import and sell all playing cards in England. The motivation for the letters patent was in part the Queen's concern that playing cards was a problem among her subjects and ought to be tightly controlled. In 1598, after Ralph Bowes died, the patent was reissued to Edward Darcy (claimant) – a groom of the Privy Chamber. Allein (defendant) started to make and sell his own cards. Darcy brought a case against Allein for damages.

Issue and Procedure

Allein argued that the monopoly was invalid under the common law. In the next extract, Chief Justice Popham agreed.

POPHAM CJ

As to the first, it was argued to the contrary by the defendant's counsel, and resolved by Popham, Chief Justice ... that the said grant to the plaintiff of the sole making of cards within the realm was utterly void...

The sole trade of any mechanical artifice, or any other monopoly, is not only a damage and prejudice to those who exercise the same trade, but also to all other subjects, for the end of all these monopolies is for the private gain of the patentees ... and, therefore, there are three inseparable incidents to every monopoly against the commonwealth.

1. That the price of the same commodity will be raised, for he who has the sole selling of any commodity, may and will make the price as he pleases ...
2. [T]hat after the monopoly granted, the commodity is not so good and merchantable as it was before: for the patentee having the sole trade, regards only his private benefit, and not the common wealth...
3. It tends to the impoverishment of divers artificers and others, who before, by the labour of their hands in their art or trade, had maintained themselves and their families, who now will of necessity be constrained to live in idleness and beggary.

(pp. 1262–63)

The lawyer for Allein was Edward Coke (1552–1634). As discussed below, Coke later became instrumental in the attack on monopolies. After engraving by Davod Loggan. 1 February 1552, 3 September 1634 (photo by Culture Club/Getty Images)

ACTIVITY 6.1

Think back to the problem of monopoly introduced in Section 1.1.3. How does Popham CJ's decision compare to the analysis of monopolies provided by Ruth Towse?

6.1.3 The Statute of Monopolies

The attack on monopolies culminated in the 1624 Statute of Monopolies. As MacLeod explains in the following extract, the purpose of this law was to restrain the crown's ability to abuse the letters patent system. But by a 'quirk of history', the new law came to lay the foundation on which the modern patent system grew.

BOX 6.4 CHRISTINE MACLEOD, *INVENTING THE INDUSTRIAL REVOLUTION: THE ENGLISH PATENT SYSTEM, 1660–1800* (CUP 1988)

The dramatic story of this Act has often been told, usually in the context of the constitutional crisis of the early seventeenth century in which, according to whiggish interpretations, it marked a major blow struck by the Commons against the royal prerogative.[12] Intended to proscribe the crown's abuse of its dispensing powers, the Statute's role as the legal basis for the patent system was a curious side-effect, a quirk of history. It exempted letters patent for new invention from the general proscription. Its targets were rather the abuses of patents of registration (for example, of ale-houses), the various sharp practices that had grown up around industrial patents, and the licences issued to circumvent the restrictions of older corporations and companies, particularly in the export trades...

The new law was expounded and some of its immediate ramifications drawn out by Sir Edward Coke (1552–1634), who may be accredited as an expert on the Statute of Monopolies. Not only had he served as a law officer and Chief Justice, but he had appeared for the plaintiff in Darcy v. Allein (1602) – in which a monopoly of importing playing cards was set aside and the common law on patents hotly debated – and had investigated many patent and trade disputes since 1593. As an M.P., he had introduced (with William Noy) the 1621 bill against monopolies and served on the committee that considered the bill of 1624. The Statute, in Coke's view, permitted letters patent for the sole working of new manufactures, provided seven conditions were fulfilled. First, that the term was limited to fourteen years maximum. This limit was not chosen entirely at random: it was twice the statutorily prescribed, seven-year term of trade apprenticeship. Coke deliberated whether, as such, it was not still too long, for the first apprentices would be restricted by their master's patent for a further seven years and consequently discouraged. Secondly, 'it must be granted to the first and true inventor', and thirdly, 'it must be of such manufacture, which any other at the making of such letters patent did not use'.

(pp. 15, 18)

While outlawing monopolies generally, section 6 of the Statute of Monopolies provided an exception permitting patents on 'new manner of manufacture'. While hardly the animating force behind the Statute, this exception, and its focus on 'new' things, helped put the law on a path towards the modern patent system (see Figure 6.2).

BOX 6.5 STATUTE OF MONOPOLIES 1624, S 6

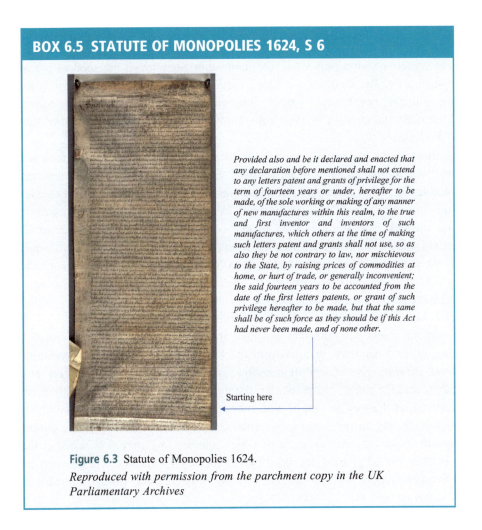

Provided also and be it declared and enacted that any declaration before mentioned shall not extend to any letters patent and grants of privilege for the term of fourteen years or under, hereafter to be made, of the sole working or making of any manner of new manufactures within this realm, to the true and first inventor and inventors of such manufactures, which others at the time of making such letters patent and grants shall not use, so as also they be not contrary to law, nor mischievous to the State, by raising prices of commodities at home, or hurt of trade, or generally inconvenient; the said fourteen years to be accounted from the date of the first letters patents, or grant of such privilege hereafter to be made, but that the same shall be of such force as they should be if this Act had never been made, and of none other.

Starting here

Figure 6.3 Statute of Monopolies 1624.
Reproduced with permission from the parchment copy in the UK Parliamentary Archives

If the primary purpose of the Statute was to limit royal abuse, then it had limited success. Subsequently, Charles I continued to grant monopolies for everyday products, such as soap and salt. Meanwhile, Parliamentarians continued to complain about the abuse. In 1640, the English Parliament submitted the 'Grand Remonstrance' (a list of grievances) to King Charles.[13] Monopolies were listed as one of the grievances. Today, the Grand Remonstrance is viewed as one of the chief events that precipitated the English Civil War. And, as Christine MacLeod says, the abuse of monopolies 'entered popular mythology as a major cause of the Civil War'.[14] When the monarchy was restored following the English Civil War and Interregnum, Charles II realised that the political risk of abusing the letters patent system was too great and largely desisted.[15]

6.1.4   The Patent Controversy in the Nineteenth Century

The Statute of Monopolies laid the foundation from which the modern patent system grew. The statutory provisions were interpreted and applied by courts for the following two hundred years.[16] But, while the Statute laid down the formal legal rules, the meaning of those rules evolved over time; new wine poured into old wineskins.

Illustrative is the case of Scottish Engineer, James Watt, who in 1776 invented the 'Watt Steam Engine'. Of course, steam engines had been invented quite some time earlier. What James Watt invented was a method for making steam engines run more efficiently, thus using less fuel. Watt subsequently received a patent on this method. But was a method of using an old machine a 'new manner of manufacture'? In one case pertaining to the patent, Judge Heath wrote: 'I asked in the argument for an instance of a patent for a method, and none such could be produced.'[17] Eventually, however, the patent was upheld.[18] And, increasingly, what the patentee owned was not a trade, nor physical contraptions, but something else: knowledge (a point discussed further in Chapter 7).

At the same time, the idea emerged that patents for inventions formed a unique legal category, distinct from the letters patent. Patents for inventions were increasingly subject to a unique set of bureaucratic procedures and administrative rules.[19] In particular, the patent came to be awarded only upon application. Part of the application process involved the applicant describing and disclosing an invention in a formal legal document known as the **patent specification**; an early example of which appears in Figure 6.4. Whether the patent would be granted depended on whether the applicant could satisfy a set of criteria, now known as the **patentability** criteria (and discussed in Chapters 7 and 8).

With change, however, came controversy. Two competing ideologies emerged to dominate the narrative around patents. On one hand, the view emerged that patents were not merely privileges, but were inventors' *rights*. As the practice of granting patents became more routine, the view flourished that if one satisfied the emerging patentability criteria, then one had a right to a patent. In America, when the 1790 Patent Act was passed (sometimes called the first modern patent law) one member of Congress argued that 'a citizen has a right in the inventions he may make' and that patent law was simply 'the mode by which he is to enjoy the fruits'.[20] To those in this camp, the hoops through which an applicant had to jump to secure a patent were simply too burdensome.

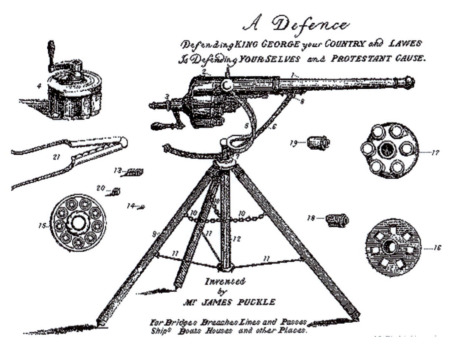

Figure 6.4 Patent specification for James Puckle's invention 'the autocannon' – or machine gun.

From patent number GB171800418A (with minor modifications by Patrick Goold)

There was, however, a counter-position emerging in the form of **laissez-faire capitalism**. The term 'laissez-faire' means 'allow to do'. As applied to the economy, the laissez-faire ideology opposes government taking an active role in the distribution of goods.[21] The government should not, for example, give subsidies to some industries, or to regulate the amount of goods imported from abroad. Instead, governments should stand back and let private citizens distribute goods by buying and selling them as they wish. Increasingly, those who advocated this view questioned the role of patents. Were these not monopolies through which the government interfered with the economy? If so, they should be decried like other forms of government meddling.

In Box 6.6, economists Fritz Machlup and Edith Penrose explain the rise of the antipatent movement.

'Laissez-faire' economics is heavily associated with Scottish liberal philosopher and economist, Adam Smith (1723–90). Smith's *The Wealth of Nations* (1176) argued, among other things, that free from government intervention, invisible market forces help society to distribute goods.

> ### BOX 6.6 FRITZ MACHLUP AND EDITH PENROSE, 'THE PATENT CONTROVERSY IN THE NINETEENTH CENTURY' (1950) 10 JOURNAL OF ECONOMIC HISTORY 1–29
>
> For two hundred years after the enactment of the Statute of Monopolies in England the patent law had not been brought up for consideration or amendment in the Parliament.[22] It was around 1827 that the subject of patent reform first began to claim the attention

Fritz Machlup (1902–83) was an Austrian-American economist at Johns Hopkins University (at the time of publication of the article in Box 6.6). Edith Penrose (1914–96) was an economist at the University of London.

In 1958, Fritz Machlup was commissioned by the US Congress to assess the effects of the patent system. His famously ambivalent conclusion provides the opening quote to this Part.

> of the legislature, chiefly because of complaints that the procedure for obtaining a patent was expensive, clumsy, and uncertain. Various groups were formed to obtain a law more favorable to inventors, and considerable agitation was carried on in Parliament and in the press. This provoked a counterattack, not from those who favored the existing law, but from those who wished to see the patent system abolished entirely. In the latter camp were the influential London Economist, the Vice-President of the Board of Trade, some outstanding inventors of the time, members of Parliament, and representatives of manufacturing districts such as Manchester and Liverpool.
>
> Select committees of Parliament and royal commissions investigated the operation of the patent system in 1851–1852, in 1862–1865, and again in 1869–1872. Some of the testimony before these commissions was so damaging to the repute of the patent system that leading statesmen in the two houses of Parliament proposed the complete abolition of patent protection. A patent-reform bill, drafted on the basis of the 1872 commission's report, provided for a reduction of patent protection years, strictest examination of patent applications, forfeit worked after two years, and compulsory licensing of all patents was passed by the House of Lords.
>
> (3–4)

In some countries – like the Netherlands – the patent abolitionists won, and the patent system was abolished for several decades. But the abolitionists lost their fight in the UK. The bill passed by the House of Lords was withdrawn from the House of Commons. Instead, the UK settled on a system of reforms designed to improve the patent system. Many of these reforms made the bureaucratic procedure of obtaining a patent easier and less burdensome on applicants.

The legislative changes that followed, such as the Patent Law Amendment Act of 1852, formed the basis of the modern patent system. Today, many of these reforms are incorporated in the controlling legislation, the **Patent Act 1977**. Far removed from its origins as a discretionary royal privilege, the modern patent system understands patents property rights in inventions.

6.2 ARGUMENTS FOR PATENTS

Why should society grant property in inventions? Much like copyright, property rights in inventions cause the problem of monopoly. And, much like copyright, one would expect a liberal democracy to put up with such monopolies only if there was a sufficiently compelling reason to do so.

But, unlike copyright, the personality and labour arguments provide somewhat weaker justifications for property in inventions. If there can be a defence of patents, therefore, it is most likely to be found in some version of the utilitarian argument – if such a defence can be found at all.

6.2.1 The Personality Argument Revisited

Section 2.2.5 introduced the personality argument for copyright. According to that argument, the original expression contained in the work is a part of the author's personality, and thus the author ought to control how it is used. This type of argument is less persuasive in relation to inventions, for reasons explored in Activity 6.2.

ACTIVITY 6.2

Take a moment and think back to the example of van Gogh's *Starry Night*. You will recall that van Gogh's painting started with an idea, i.e. to paint the night sky. Van Gogh then expressed that idea in an original and highly personal way. In painting the night sky, van Gogh made several choices, e.g. about what colours to use, what type of brush strokes to use and how to depict the moon and stars. It was through these creative choices that van Gogh imprinted his own personality onto the work.

Now compare the *Starry Night* to the toy brick invented by Christiansen. Christiansen also made choices when designing the brick. Crucially the new bricks were based on the 'stud-and-tube' coupling system. But how are those choices different from the choices made by van Gogh?

This is not to say that the figure of the inventor played no historical role in justifying patent law. While the Christiansen brick might not reveal something about the inventor's personality, might it reveal something else, namely his genius? When beholding the brick, one can surely appreciate the ingenuity of Christiansen's mind. And, at times, the image of an inventor as a genius has been deployed to justify patents, much like the romantic idea of the author has been in copyright.[23]

Whether the genius of inventors provides a good argument for patent rights is, however, debatable. While Christiansen's brick was arguably the product of genius, the premise that one should own the products of genius is not obviously true. Unlike copyright – where distorting a work might in some way harm the author's personality – there are very few ways of using an invention that detracts from the inventor's genius.

Patenting an invention without giving the inventor appropriate credit may provide an exceptional case. As will be demonstrated in Figure 6.5, patent specifications accordingly require identification of the inventor.

6.2.2 The Labour Argument Revisited

What then of labour? Does an inventor naturally own their invention because they labour to bring it into existence? Some think so. Section 2.2.1 introduced Robert Merges's application of Locke's theory of property to intellectual property. You will note that Merges is not only writing about copyright – he is also writing about patents, as Activity 6.3 illustrates.

> **ACTIVITY 6.3**
>
> Consider the Christiansen Brick once more. Can you see how the Lockean labour argument could be used to support Christiansen's natural ownership of the Lego brick?

Section 2.2.2 also introduced objections to the labour argument. These objections apply with equal force against the labour argument in relation to inventions. It was jolly nice of Christiansen to invent the stud-and-tube coupling system, but why does that mean he is allowed to own it? As Robert Nozick might ask, has Christiansen not just thrown away his labour much like someone who tips a can of tomato juice into the ocean? Likewise, Seanna Shiffrin would ask: why give Christiansen property rights over the products of his labour at all? People will still be able to use the system even if the stud-and-tube system is dedicated immediately to the public domain.

Furthermore, there is an even greater problem in applying the labour argument to patents. This argument was famously expressed by US President, Thomas Jefferson.

Thomas Jefferson (1743–1826) was not only the third president of the United States. He was also an inventor himself. One of his most famous inventions was the swivel chair. Before becoming president, Jefferson served as Secretary of State and had a leading role in developing the US Patent Office. Notoriously, he also was a slave owner. (Photo by GraphicaArtis/Getty Images)

> **BOX 6.7 THOMAS JEFFERSON, LETTER TO ISAAC MCPHERSON (13 AUGUST 1813) IN ANDREW A LIPSCOMB AND ALBERT ELLERY BERGH (EDS),** *THE WRITINGS OF THOMAS JEFFERSON*, **VOL 13 (THOMAS JEFFERSON MEMORIAL ASSOCIATION 1904) 333–34**
>
> It has been pretended by some (and in England especially) that inventors have a natural and exclusive right to their inventions, and not merely for their own lives, but inheritable to their heirs. But while it is a moot question whether the origin of any kind of property is derived from nature at all, it would be singular to admit a natural and even an hereditary right to inventors. . . .
>
> If nature has made any one thing less susceptible than all others of exclusive property, it is the action of the thinking power called an idea, which an individual may exclusively possess as long as he keeps it to himself; but the moment it is divulged, it forces itself into the possession of every one, and the receiver cannot dispossess himself of

it. Its peculiar character, too, is that no one possesses the less, because every other possesses the whole of it. He who receives an idea from me, receives instruction himself without lessening mine; as he who lights his taper at mine, receives light without darkening me. That ideas should freely spread from one to another over the globe, for the moral and mutual instruction of man, and improvement of his condition, seems to have been peculiarly and benevolently designed by nature, when she made them, like fire, expansible over all space, without lessening their density in any point, and like the air in which we breathe, move, and have our physical being, incapable of confinement or exclusive appropriation. Inventions then cannot, in nature, be a subject of property. Society may give an exclusive right to the profits arising from them, as an encouragement to men to pursue ideas which may produce utility, but this may or may not be done, according to the will and convenience of the society, without claim or complaint from anybody...

Accordingly it is a fact, as far as I am informed, that England was, until we copied her, the only country on earth which ever by a general law, gave a legal right to the exclusive use of an idea. In some other countries, it is sometimes done, in a great case, and by a special and personal act. But generally speaking, other nations have thought that these monopolies produce more embarrassment than advantage to society. And it may be observed that the nations which refuse monopolies of invention, are as fruitful as England in new and useful devices.

It is axiomatic that copyright does not protect ideas, and only protects original expression. But patent law does grant property in ideas. Patent law granted Christiansen property in the idea of stud-and-tube coupling bricks.

In Jefferson's mind, private ownership of ideas is simply not 'natural'. In fact, it is highly *unnatural*. Inventions are 'public goods' – that is, goods that are non-excludable and non-rivalrous (see Section 1.1.1). Their 'nature' is to be owned and enjoyed by the public. Like fire or air, ideas are not the kind of things that can naturally be owned by one person. It would be a strange world indeed if nature gave inventors private rights over phenomena which are inherently public.

The **nature objection** also is problematic for the labour argument as it applies to copyright and original works. After all, original works are also public goods. Nevertheless, original works are less 'pure' public goods than inventions. Ideas are extremely non-excludable: once the idea is made public, the idea spreads from person to person like fire or air. Original expression is similar, although maybe not identical. While original expression is still non-excludable, it does take some time

That natural rights arguments fared generally less well in patents than copyright is reflected in the fact that there was no historically significant argument for perpetual patent protection at common law (see Section 2.2.2).

Patents I: Foundations

and effort to duplicate it (e.g. to photocopy a book, or to copy a painting). While it is implausible, in Jefferson's view, that one can naturally own an idea, it may just be plausible that an author can naturally own their original expression of an idea.

6.2.3 The Utilitarian Arguments

Although he rejected the labour argument, Jefferson saw one possible argument for patents. In the extract, Jefferson writes that society might give patents to inventors as 'encouragement to men to pursue ideas which may produce utility' (Box 6.7). Of course, monopolies are bad things to be avoided, but perhaps patents provide an exception to this general rule. If patents make society a happier place overall, then perhaps society should just put up with them. Like copyright, maybe the good consequences of an appropriately balanced patent system outweigh the bad ones.

Since Jefferson's letter, scholars have proposed different theories to explain how patents might improve utility. These theories can be split into three groups: (a) invention theories; (b) disclosure theories; and (c) development theories. However, just like the utilitarian argument in copyright, each of these theories faces substantial objections. The question is whether any of the theories is sufficiently convincing to persuade us to put up with the problem of monopoly.

6.2.3.1 INVENTION

Section 2.2.3 outlined the utilitarian argument for copyright. A similar argument can be offered in favour of patents. Inventions are public goods that sometimes require significant costs to produce. In the case of the pharmaceutical industry, for example, billions of pounds are spent each year on researching and developing new medicines.[24] The patent monopoly enables the inventor to charge a high price to those who wish to use the invention. It is the expectation of increased profit that encourages inventors to invent in the first place. Indeed, the founder of classical utilitarianism, Jeremey Bentham, seemed to support this theory.

BOX 6.8 JEREMY BENTHAM, 'A MANUAL OF POLITICAL ECONOMY' IN JOHN BOWRING (ED), *THE WORKS OF JEREMY BENTHAM*, VOL 3 (1843)

With respect to a great number of inventions in the arts, an exclusive privilege is absolutely necessary, in order that what is sown may be reaped. In new inventions, protection against imitators is not less necessary than in established manufactures protection against thieves. He who has no hope that he shall reap, will not take the trouble to sow. But that which one man has invented, all the world can imitate. Without the assistance of the laws, the inventor would

> almost always be driven out of the market by his rival, who finding himself, without any expense, in possession of a discovery which has cost the inventor much time and expense, would be able to deprive him of all his deserved advantages, by selling at a lower price. An exclusive privilege is of all rewards the best proportioned, the most natural, and the least burthensome.
>
> (p. 71)

Of course, Bentham was no fool. Bentham also understood the problems caused by monopoly. Just like copyright, the bad consequences are twofold. First, some consumers will no longer be able to afford the invention. If Christiansen can charge a high price for his toy bricks, sadly, some children must go without. And, second, patents may even discourage invention because some invention is cumulative in nature. Christiansen did not invent his Toy Building Brick out of thin air, but instead modified a pre-existing invention, Page's Self-Locking Brick. Patents might slow down this cumulative (or 'follow-on') innovation. Activity 6.4 illustrates this point.

ACTIVITY 6.4

Imagine that Page had a patent in Denmark on his Self-Locking Brick. If so, then Christiansen would need to get permission from Page to start making and selling his Toy Building Brick in Denmark. To do so, Page is likely to ask Christiansen for a monetary fee. What might be the problem here?

The central claim Bentham is making in Box 6.8 is that if we calculate all the good and bad consequences, we will see that society is better off with a patent system than without. Just like copyright, supporters of the patent system argue that an appropriately balanced patent system is 'absolutely necessary' if we want society to be happier *overall*.

However, Section 2.2.4 introduced two objections to the utilitarian argument: the empirical objection and the alternatives objection. The former claims that society does not have sufficient empirical evidence to believe the utilitarian argument; the latter claims that alternative policy tools may be used to stimulate invention without the need for property rights and the monopolies they create. Both objections apply equally to patent rights.

The empirical counterargument with respect to patents is put forcefully by Boldrin and Levine (Box 6.9). There is surprisingly little evidence that an appropriately balanced patent regime does make society a better place overall.

The idea that scientific and technological progress is cumulative was made famous by Sir Isaac Newton. Newton (1642–1726) was an English polymath. His intellectual contributions include the formulation of the laws of motion and gravity. In a letter to fellow British scientist, Robert Hooke, in 1675, Newton humbly wrote that 'if I have seen further it is by standing on the shoulders of giants'.

Michele Boldrin and David Levine are both professors of economics at Washington University, USA.

BOX 6.9 MICHELE BOLDRIN AND DAVID K LEVINE, 'THE CASE AGAINST PATENTS' (2013) 27(1) JOURNAL OF ECONOMIC PERSPECTIVES 3

The case against patents can be summarized briefly: there is no empirical evidence that they serve to increase innovation and productivity, unless productivity is identified with the number of patents awarded – which, as evidence shows, has no correlation with measured productivity.[25] This disconnect is at the root of what is called the 'patent puzzle': in spite of the enormous increase in the number of patents and in the strength of their legal protection, the US economy has seen neither a dramatic acceleration in the rate of technological progress nor a major increase in the levels of research and development expenditure.

Unfortunately, the political economy of government-operated patent systems indicates that such systems are susceptible to pressures that cause the ill effects of patents to grow over time. The political economy pressures tend to benefit those who own patents and are in a good position to lobby for stronger patent protection, but disadvantage current and future innovators as well as ultimate consumers. This explains why the political demand for stronger patent protection comes from old and stagnant industries, not from new and innovative ones.

(3–4)

'**Political economy**' refers to the interaction between politics and economics. Here Boldrin and Levin highlight how current industries lobby (a political matter) lawmakers for patent monopolies (an economic matter) out of self-interest.

Indeed, some empirical evidence supports the opposite theory: that the *absence* of patents can at times encourage invention. In fact, Jefferson himself acknowledged this in his letter to McPherson. In the very last paragraph in Box 6.7, Jefferson writes that other countries without patent systems were 'as fruitful as England' when it came to producing 'new and useful devices'. This is because, without a patent system, it might become easier for inventors to build on prior inventions, just like Christiansen did.

In Box 6.10, Petra Moser considers this idea in more detail through an analysis of inventions exhibited at nineteenth-century world fairs. World fairs were international exhibitions which showcased the achievements of nations. Among other things, such fairs provided countries a chance to show off their newest inventions. Moser analyses data from world fairs to assess whether countries with patent systems produced more inventions for exhibition than countries without patent systems. If countries without patent systems produced more inventions than countries with patent systems, then arguably the existence of patents causes the problem of monopoly without any redeeming benefit.

BOX 6.10 PETRA MOSER, 'PATENTS AND INNOVATION: EVIDENCE FROM ECONOMIC HISTORY' (2013) 27 JOURNAL OF ECONOMIC PERSPECTIVES 23–44

Petra Moser is Professor of Economics at New York University, USA.

Historical variation in patent laws in the nineteenth century – when some countries had not yet adopted patent laws while other abolished them for political reasons – offers unique opportunities to investigate the effects of patent laws on innovation.[26] Switzerland, for example, had no patents until the country adopted a rudimentary patent system in 1888 and switched towards a full-fledged system in 1907. Denmark provided limited patent protection for up to five years in 1874, but waited until 1894 to enact an official patent law. The Netherlands abolished its patent system in 1869 after a political victory of the free trade movement, which reflected a common view of patents as a form of protectionism and rejected them as a restriction on trade. Even for countries with patent laws, the strength of patents was far from uniform. In 1876, for example, patents in Denmark and Greece expired after five years, while patents in other countries lasted for a minimum of twelve years. . .

Analyses of technologies that were exhibited at nineteenth-century world's fairs exploit such variation to examine differences in innovation for countries with and without patent laws. . . Exhibition data are available for the Crystal Palace Exhibition in London in 1851, the American Centennial Exhibition in Philadelphia in 1876, the World's Columbian Exhibition in Chicago in 1893, and the Panama-Pacific International Exposition in San Francisco in 1915. . .

Analyses of the 1851 and 1876 exhibits reveal a perhaps surprising amount of high-quality innovations in countries without patent laws. In 1851, Switzerland and Denmark contributed 110 exhibits per million people, compared with a mean of 55 and a median of 36 per million people for all countries. Swiss exhibits were also more likely to win prizes for exceptional novelty and usefulness. In 1851, 43 percent of Swiss exhibits won a prize, compared with a mean of 35 percent and a median of 33 percent for all countries. In 1876, Switzerland contributed 168 exhibits per million in population, compared with a mean of 87 and a median of 61 for all countries. The Netherlands – which had abolished patents in 1869 – won more prizes per exhibit than any other country, with 86 percent, compared with a mean of 46 and a median of 45 percent for all countries.

Another notable contribution to this debate is found in work by Josh Lerner.[27] Lerner analysed the impact of changes in patent policy across sixty countries and 150 years, only to come to the 'puzzling' conclusion that strengthening patent rights did not have a meaningful impact on invention.

(25–27)

ACTIVITY 6.5

If countries like the Netherlands did not grant patents, why do you think inventors from those countries produced so many inventions at the world fairs? Petra Moser hints towards a possible reason in her extract (Box 6.10).

6.2.3.2 DISCLOSURE

However, there may be more benefits to patents than simply creating incentives to invent. An alternative version of the utilitarian argument claims that the real benefit of patents lies in providing incentives to disclose new knowledge to the world.

Consider, for example, Coca-Cola. The Coca-Cola drink was invented in Georgia (USA) by John Pemberton in the nineteenth century. When Pemberton died, only four people knew the secret recipe.[28] Since then, the Coca-Cola Company has tried to keep the recipe secret. As long as the recipe remains secret, then it cannot be copied, and the Coca-Cola Company can maintain their monopoly over the drink. This is known as a **trade secret**.

The purpose of patents, therefore, is not simply to encourage inventors to invent, but also to disclose the technical knowledge that lies behind their invention. Society offers the inventor a twenty-year property right, and in return, the inventor teaches the world how to make the new invention. Section 6.3 examines how the inventor uses the patent application document to complete this task.

Does this provide a better version of the utilitarian argument? In Box 6.11, two economists explain the argument, and its problems, in further depth.

BOX 6.11 FRTIZ MACHLUP AND EDITH PENROSE, 'THE PATENT CONTROVERSY IN THE NINETEENTH CENTURY' (1950) 10 JOURNAL OF ECONOMIC HISTORY 1–29

Whether or not it is necessary for society to provide special pecuniary incentives to induce people to engage in an adequate amount of inventive activity was controversial. A supplementary or substitute argument in support of patents for inventions was advanced proposing that patents were necessary as incentives to induce inventors to disclose their new inventions instead of keeping them secret. Perhaps there would be enough inventive activity without patents, but could one count on disclosure of inventions so that they would become part of society's general fund of technological knowledge?

The 'incentive-to-disclose' theory of patent protection was often formulated as a social-contract theory. This use of the Rousseau conception was another part of the strategy of the French politicians to avoid interpretation of patents as privileges. The patent was represented not as a privilege granted by society but as the result of a bargain between an inventor, a contract in which the inventor agreed to disclose his secret and the state agreed, in exchange, to protect the inventor for a number of years against imitation of his idea. Why should anybody object to such a fair bargain with such a reasonable *quid pro quo*?

But there were objections and rather serious ones. They were based on the following lines of reasoning: (1) If inventors should prefer to keep their ideas secret and if they should succeed in doing so, society would not lose much, if anything, because usually the same or similar ideas are developed simultaneously and independently in several quarters. (2) It is practically impossible to keep inventions secret for any length of time; new products, new tools, and new processes are soon found out by eager competitors. (3) Where an inventor thinks he can succeed in guarding his secret, he will not take out a patent; hence, patent protection does not cause disclosure of concealable inventions but serves only to restrict the use of inventions that could not have been kept secret anyway. (4) Since patents are granted only on inventions developed to a stage at which they can be reduced to practical use, the patent system encourages secrecy in the developmental stage of inventions; without patents, inventors would hurry the publication of their ideas at earlier stages in order to secure recognition and fame, and this would hasten technological progress on all fronts.

(25–26)

ACTIVITY 6.6

Machlup and Penrose provide four objections to the disclosure version of the utilitarian argument. These reasons together suggest that we may not need patents to encourage disclosure of technical information. Thinking back to the Coca-Cola example (Section 6.2.3.2), are any of their points illustrated by Coca-Cola's attempt to keep their recipe secret?

The example of Coca-Cola demonstrates how even with a patent system, some companies may wish to keep their inventions secret. To a certain extent, UK law also helps companies like Coca-Cola maintain secrecy. If secret information, such as Coca-Cola's secret recipe is divulged, the secret holder may potentially bring a **breach of confidence** action against the individual who has disclosed that information.[29]

Patents I: Foundations

6.2.3.3 DEVELOPMENT

There is potentially a third version of the utilitarian argument. According to the **'prospect theory'**, patents are not needed to encourage invention, or to encourage disclosure, but are needed to encourage firms to efficiently develop new inventions.

The prospect theory of patents was developed by Edmund Kitch in his famous article 'The Nature and Function of the Patent System' in 1977.[30] Activity 6.7 illustrates the main claim Kitch makes.

Edmund W Kitch is the Mary and Daniel Loughran Professor of Law at the University of Virginia, USA.

ACTIVITY 6.7

Think back to the story of Page's Self-Locking Brick and Christiansen's Toy Building Brick.

According to Kitch and the prospect theory, Christiansen should have left Page's Self-Locking Bricks alone. Society does not need two inventors – Page and Christiansen – working on the same project. It would be far more efficient if just one inventor was tasked with developing the idea further. That way, the two inventors would not duplicate their efforts. The person to be tasked with developing the invention further should be the original inventor, Page. Christiansen, meanwhile, should have spent his time working on something else.

Overall, although patent rights have bad consequences, they are necessary to prevent wasteful duplication of research and development activities. Are you convinced? There is no discussion for this activity.

---

*The concept of **efficiency** has a long and complex history within utilitarianism and its modern successor, welfare economics. Efficiency in this context means achieving the best possible good consequences, while minimising the bad consequences.*

Not everyone is convinced by Kitch's prospect theory. Some argue that competition (or 'rivalry') from other researchers is a better way to incentivise the development of inventions. We can call this the **competition objection**. In Box 6.12, Robert Merges and Richard Nelson take this view. In so doing, they introduce another fascinating example from patent history: the invention of the lightbulb.

We encountered Robert Merges in Part I. This article was co-authored by Merges and Richard Nelson, a professor of economics at Columbia University.

BOX 6.12 ROBERT P MERGES AND RICHARD R NELSON, 'ON THE COMPLEX ECONOMICS OF PATENT SCOPE' (1990) 90 COLUM L REV 839

We have trouble with the view that coordinated development is better than rivalrous.[31] In principle it could be, but in practice it generally is not. Much of our case is empirical. But there are sound theoretical reasons for doubting the advantages of centralization.

For one thing, under rivalrous competition in invention and innovation there is a stick as well as a carrot. Block rivalry and one blocks or greatly diminishes the threatened costs of inaction. Kitch assumes a model of individual or firm behavior where if an action is profitable it will be taken, regardless of whether inaction would still allow the firm to meet its desired (but suboptimal) performance goals. Different models of behavior... predict otherwise. As we shall see, there are many instances when a firm that thought it had control over a broad technology rested on its laurels until jogged to action by an outside threat. . . .

1. Electrical Lighting Industry – The chain of reasoning in our critique of the prospect theory, and our view of the patent system, is consistent with most of the historical evidence on cumulative technologies. The early electrical illumination industry illustrates this most clearly.

No single patent better illustrates this than [Thomas] Edison's U.S. Patent 223,898, issued in 1880. This was 'the basic patent in the early American incandescent-lamp industry,' covering the use of a carbon filament as the source of light; it proved to have a profound effect on the industry until it expired.

Although the Edison General Electric Company had some difficulty establishing the validity of its basic patent, once it did the industry changed drastically. In 1891, U.S. Patent No. 223,898 was held valid and infringed by a competing design. General Electric officials then quickly obtained a series of injunctions that shut down a number of competitors. As the aptly-named industry historian Arthur Bright stated, 'For twelve years [after the issuance of the 223,898 patent] competition had been possible; it suddenly became impossible'. The company's market share grew from 40 to 75 percent; entry into the industry slowed from 26 new firms in 1892 to 8 in 1894, the last year of the patent's life; and the steady downward trend of lamp prices slowed until the patent expired.

More importantly for our purposes, the validation of Edison's broad patent slowed the pace of improvements considerably...

This was especially true in Great Britain, where the Edison Company's patent position was even more commanding, due to its control of a basic patent on a process for producing carbon filaments. A series of court victories over its largest competitors gave the British 'Ediswan' company 'a practical monopoly of incandescent-lamp production'.

Given the lack of competition, it is perhaps not surprising that the pace of technical advance slowed. According to the historian Bright:

After the introduction of the incandescent lamp and its first rapid changes . . . . the Edison Electric Light Company did not introduce many important new developments. Edison himself turned to other problems, and the company's technical leadership in incandescent

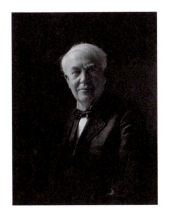

Thomas Edison (1947–31) is one of history's most prolific inventors. He held over 1,000 patents in his lifetime. One of his most influential inventions was his version of the lightbulb invented in 1879 and called the 'incandescent lamp'. (Photo credit: Bettmann/Contributor)

This was also one of the key reasons that led Machlup to his ambivalent conclusion expressed in this Part's opening quote.

> lighting was not revived until after the merger [that formed General Electric in 1896].
>
> Prior to the enforcement of the patent, Edison's competitors were quickening the pace of technical advance:
>
> Despite the improvements in the Edison lamp, a number of its competitors had improved their lamps even more rapidly . . . . Efficiency advantages permitted many of the other American concerns to compete very successfully with the Edison lamp after 1885 . . . until the corporate reorganizations and the establishment of patent supremacy regained for the Edison lamp commercial supremacy as well.
>
> The same was true overseas: 'In England, filament improvement was almost entirely halted during the period of Edison patent monopoly from 1886 to 1893.' Bright concludes:
>
> The lengthy and expensive patent struggle in the lamp industry from 1885 to 1894 was a serious damper on progress in lamp design, although process improvement continued. The Edison interests concentrated on eliminating competition rather than outstripping it. . . . After 1894, when it was no longer protected by a basic lamp patent, General Electric devoted more attention to lamp improvement to maintain its market superiority.
>
> Thus the broad Edison patent slowed down progress in the incandescent lighting field. The lesson, however, is not that this patent should not have been granted. It is rather a cautionary lesson: broad patents do have a significant impact on the development of a technology and hence on industry structure, and this should be reflected in those doctrines that collectively determine patent scope.
>
> (872, 885–87)

To further illustrate their argument, consider what Merges and Nelson would think about the Christiansen Brick. It seems highly likely that Merges and Nelson would argue that Page should not be able to 'block' Christiansen's development of the brick. Theory and historical anecdotes suggest that giving broad patents to the first inventor does not result in efficient development of the technology thereafter; instead, it simply encourages the inventor to 'rest on their laurels'. The way to encourage development of technology is to create a competitive market in which inventors race to produce even better ideas and inventions; as Christiansen did.

Having canvassed the arguments for patents, and the objections to those arguments, it is for students to draw their own conclusions. The question is whether there is any sufficiently good reason for granting property rights in inventions when doing so inevitably causes the problem of monopoly. The personality argument provides little support. The labour argument, while not completely implausible, faces substantial objections, particularly in the form of the nature objection. As a result, most advocates of the patent system appeal to the utilitarian benefits it produces in terms of more inventions, more disclosure, and more efficient development of ideas. The problem, however, is that all these claimed benefits are somewhat speculative. How well does the empirical evidence support these claims? To some, the answer is: not enough.

6.3   REGISTRATION

One of the core differences between copyright and patent is that the latter is a registered right. This is in large part the legacy of the nineteenth century. In response to international developments like the Berne Convention, copyright increasingly became understood as an automatic right to protect the author's natural property. At the same time, in response to the controversy discussed in Section 6.1.4, the patent system became increasingly bureaucratic. The registration system which was introduced remains foundational to the modern patent system.

6.3.1   Patent Specification

Section 6.1.4 briefly introduced the patent specification. The specification forms the core of modern patent law and practice. As discussed in Chapters 8 and 9, whether an inventor will receive a patent depends on the content of the specification, and the specification in turn defines the scope of the patent owner's property. As a result, it is important to understand the main features of this document.

Figure 6.5 provides a modern patent specification for another famous invention: Christiansen's minifigure. After the success of the brick, Christiansen invented small yellow figurines that could be attached to the bricks. The 'minifigures' had recesses in their legs and feet allowing them to connect to the bricks. Christiansen then patented the invention in Denmark in 1977, and thereafter in a range of other countries. The specification in Figure 6.5 is Christiansen's application in the UK filed in 1978.

ACTIVITY 6.8

Take some time to look over the minifigure specification. Do not try to understand the content in detail. You will find some of the language highly scientific and technical. Simply try to identify the main features of the document. There is no discussion for this activity.

UK Patent Application (19)GB (11) 2 006 028 A

(21) Application No 7833681
(22) Date of filing
17 Aug 1978
(23) Claims filed
17 Aug 1978
(30) Priority data
(31) 3818/77
1902/78
(32) 29 Aug 1977
2 May 1978
(33) Denmark (DK)
(43) Application published
2 May 1979
(51) INT CL² A63H 33/06
(52) Domestic classification
A6S 6A1 6EX
(56) Documents cited
None
(58) Field of search
A6S
(71) Applicant
Interlego AG
3 Sihlbruggstrasse
CH 6340 Baar
Switzerland
(72) Inventors
Godtfred Kirk Christiansen
Jens Nygard Knudsen
Erik Peter Tapdrup
(74) Agents
Gill Jennings & Every

(54) **Toy figure**

(57) A toy figure for detachably mounting on a base plate pertaining to a toy building set and provided with coupling studs, has a leg assembly comprising a pair of identical leg elements 20 having substantially plane rear faces (calves) formed with recesses comprising lengthwise extending channels or pairs of holes 22. The width of these recesses is substantially equal to the width of the studs of the base plate. The recesses are symmetrical with respect to the lengthwise extending median plane of the leg elements and, in the position of the leg elements wherein their rear faces coincide, the distance between the axes of symmetry of the recesses is equal to the module m of the building set. The soles of the foot of the by elements are also adapted to engage the studs on a base plate.

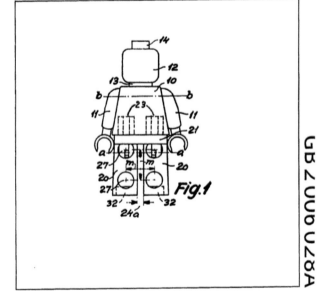

Figure 6.5 Christiansen minifigures patent.
Patent GB2006028A

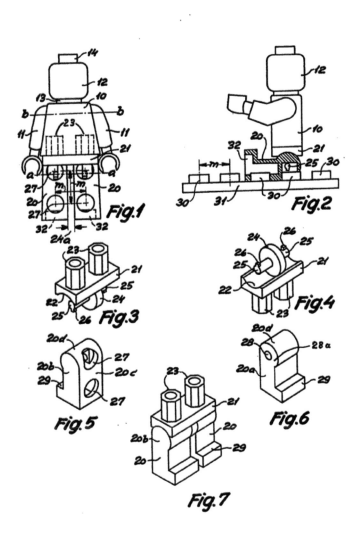

Pay attention to the shape of the figures. This shape is not only interesting in the context of patent law, but as we will see in Section 13.1.3.2, in the context of trade mark law as well.

Figure 6.5 (*cont.*)

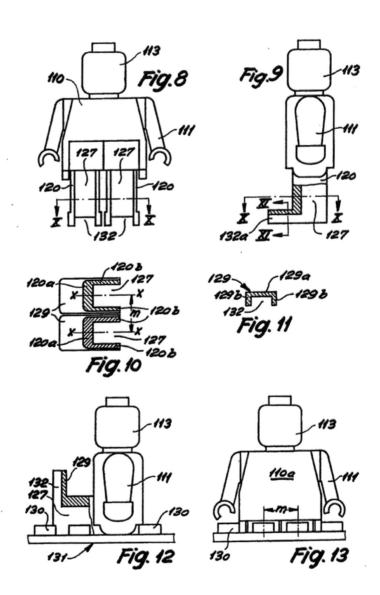

Figure 6.5 (cont.)

SPECIFICATION

Toy figure

5 This invention generally relates to toy figures and, more particularly, to a toy figure for use as a component in a toy building set composed of building blocks and other elements provided with coupling means for detachably
10 inter-connecting adjacent blocks or other components. Such toy building sets are well-known and a typical example is described in British patent no: 866,557. A characteristic of such building sets is that base plates forming
15 part of such sets have a series of coupling studs uniformly spaced apart in both longitudinal and transverse directions, so that two pairs of adjacent studs define a square in which the distance between the axes of adja-
20 cent studs is equal to the module m of the building set.

More recently, it has been suggested to supplement the known building sets with dolls and similar toy figures provided with movable
25 limbs and coupling means for detachably connecting them to other components of the building set.

According to the invention, a toy figure for this purpose comprises a body having a head,
30 a pair of arms, and a leg assembly comprising a connecting piece removably mounted on the body and including a pair of sidewardly extending pivots, carrying a pair of identical, removable leg members, the leg members
35 having substantially flat rear faces (calves) formed with respective recesses and foot parts having plane bottom faces (soles) also formed with respective recesses, each of the recesses having a width substantially equal to the
40 width of the coupling studs of the base plate and being disposed symmetrically with respect to an axis extending in the lengthwise direction of the leg member and foot part respectively, the distance between the said
45 axes of symmetry, in the position of the leg members wherein the planes of their flat rear faces (calves) coincide, being equal to the module m of the building set. This improvement enables the figure to be mounted in
50 many different positions relatively to the base plate and, in particular, in both upright and seated positions.

Two examples of toy figure in accordance with the invention will now be described with
55 reference to the accompanying drawings, in which:—

Figure 1 is a rear elevation of one form of figure showing the back and the rear face of the leg members in an upright position;
60 Figure 2 is a side view showing the same figure in a seated position;

Figure 3 is a perspective view of a connecting plate for detachably mounting the leg members in the body member of the figure;
65 Figure 4 is a similar perspective view show-

ing the lower face of the connecting plate;
Figure 5 is a perspective view of a leg member showing the rear face and one side face thereof;
70 Figure 6 is a similar perspective view showing the front face and the other side face of the leg member;

Figure 7 is a perspective view showing the leg assembly comprising a pair of identical leg
75 members mounted on the connecting plate of Figs. 3 and 4;

Figure 8 is a rear elevation similar to Fig. 1 showing a second form of figure with a modified form of the rear face of the leg mem-
80 bers;

Figure 9 is a side elevation of the same figure, partly in vertical section;

Figure 10 is a sectional view taken on the line X–X of Fig. 8;
85 Figure 11 is a sectional view taken on the line XI–XI of Fig. 9;

Figure 12 is a side elevation, partly in vertical section, showing the figure of Figs. 8 and 9 in a seated position on a base plate;
90 and

Figure 13 is a rear elevation of the figure shown in Fig. 12.

The toy figure illustrated in Figs. 1 to 7 comprises a body member 10 having a pair or
95 arms 11 pivotally mounted on the body member around a horizontal axis b–b. The upper portion of the body member 10 is provided with a neck portion 13 and a head 12 mounted thereon and comprising a coupling
100 stud 14 for detachable inter-connection with elements pertaining to a toy building set.

The body member 10 comprises a cavity receiving a pair of coupling studs 23 on the top face of a connecting plate 21, the bottom
105 face of which is formed with a cylindrical cavity 22 providing a concave bearing face for a corresponding convex upper face 20d of a pair of identical leg members 20 each having side faces 20a and 20b and a substantially
110 flat rear face (calf) 20c. In the middle of the bottom face 22 of the connecting plate 21 there is provided a substantially disc-shaped holder 24 having a pair of laterally extending pivots 25 for pivotally mounting the leg mem-
115 bers 20 on the connecting plate 21. A bore 28 is provided in one side face 28a of the upper cylindrical portion of each leg member co-axially with the cylindrical face 20d and 22 for pivotally mounting the leg member 20 on
120 the pivot 25. Projections 26 adjacent the ends of the pivots 25 provide for a snap locking effect when mounting the leg members on the pivots.

In this construction, recesses in the flat rear
125 face (calf) of the leg members comprise two identical circular bores 27 in each leg member, and the distance between the centres of these bores is equal to the module m of the building set, i.e. to the distance between the
130 axes of a pair of adjacent coupling studs 30

Figure 6.5 *(cont.)*

on a base plate 31 pertaining to the building set. Moreover, the width of the disc 24 between the leg members 20 is such that, in the position shown in Fig. 1 where the planes of
5 the rear faces 20c coincide, the lateral distance between the centres of the bores 27 is also equal to the module m of the building set. In this position, therefore, the four bores 27 define a square, the side of which is equal
10 to the module m, which enables the figure to be mounted in a seated position on two adjacent pairs of the studs 30 of the base plate 31, as shown in Fig 2.

In order that this figure may also be
15 mounted in an upright position on the base plate 31, the leg members comprise foot parts 29, the bottom face (sole) of each of which is provided with a recess 32 for detachably connecting to the studs 30 of the base plate
20 31.

Referring next to Figs. 8 to 13, the illustrated construction will generally be preferred because it enables the toy figure to be moved relatively to the base plate instead of being
25 locked to the studs, as explained with reference to the figure illustrated in Figs. 1 to 7. Whether or not it is of particular importance to provide for a slideable or rocking interconnection between a toy figure and its base
30 plate is chiefly a matter of choice, but it is generally considered that most children will prefer the toy figure to be movable relatively to the base plate and, therefore, the figure shown in Figs. 8 and 13 will be referred to as
35 the preferred form.

In this construction the reference numbers correspond to those of Figs. 1 to 7, but are preceded by the digit "1". Thus, the body 10 to Figs. 1 and 2 is designated at 110 in Figs.
40 8, 9, 12 and 13, the leg members 20 of Figs. 1 to 7 are designated as 120 in Figs. 8 to 13, and so on.

The characteristic feature of the preferred form of construction shown in Figs. 8 to 13,
45 is that the recesses in the calves of the leg members 120 and in the sole of the foot parts 129 are channels or grooves 127 and 132 respectively. As shown in Fig. 10, the channels 127 are symmetrical with respect to
50 lengthwise extending median planes X–X which are inter-spaced at a distance which is equal to the module m of the building set, and the width of these channels is substantially equal to the width of the coupling studs
55 130 of the base plate 131, shown in Figs. 12 and 13. Likewise, the recesses in the foot parts 129 are formed as channels 132 which extend in the lengthwise direction of the foot parts and hence at right angles to the recesses
60 127 of the leg members 120, the width of the channels 132 being also equal to the width of the studs 130.

As shown in Fig. 9, the channels 132 in the foot parts 129 may be open at the front
65 end 132a, so as to enable the figure in the

upright position to slide along two rows of studs 130 of the base plate. In the seated position of Figs. 12 and 13, the figure is slideably mounted on the base plate along an
70 adjacent pair of rows of studs 130 which engage the channels 127.

As shown in Figs. 10 and 11, the leg members 120 comprise a front face 120a and two side faces 120b, and the foot members
75 129 comprise a top face 129a and two side faces 129b.

CLAIMS

1. A toy figure for detachably mounting
80 on a base plate pertaining to a building set and having a series of coupling studs uniformly spaced apart in both longitudinal and transverse directions, so that two pairs of adjacent studs define a square in which the
85 distance between the axes of adjacent studs is equal to the module m of the building set, the toy figure comprising a body having a head, a pair of arms, and a leg assembly comprising a connecting piece removably mounted on the
90 body and including a pair of sidewardly extending pivots, carrying a pair of identical, removable leg members, the leg members having substantially flat rear faces (calves) formed with respective recesses and foot parts
95 having plane bottom faces (soles) also formed with respective recesses, each of the recesses having a width substantially equal to the width of the coupling studs of the base plate and being disposed symmetrically with re-
100 spect to an axis extending in the lengthwise direction of the leg member and foot part respectively, the distance between the said axes of symmetry, in the position of the leg members wherein the planes of their flat rear
105 faces (calves) coincide, being equal to the module m of the building set.

2. A toy figure according to claim 1, wherein the recesses in the flat rear faces (calves) of the leg members are channels
110 extending in the lengthwise direction of the leg members.

3. A toy figure according to claim 2, wherein the recesses in the bottom face (sole) of the foot parts are channels debouching into
115 the channels in the flat rear faces (calves) of the leg members.

4. A toy figure according to claim 1, wherein the recesses in the flat rear faces (calves) of the leg members comprise a pair of
120 cylindrical bores, the distance between the axes of which is equal to the module m of the building set.

5. A toy figure according to claim 4, in which the recess in the bottom face (sole) of
125 each foot part is a cylindrical bore having substantially the same diameter as that of the coupling studs of the base plate.

6. A toy figure according to any one of the preceding claims, in which the body is
130 formed with a cavity receiving a pair of con-

> **3**
>
> GB 2 006 028A   **3**
>
> necting studs extending upwardly from the top face of a connecting plate forming part of the leg assembly which also includes a sub-stantially disc-shaped pivot holder extending
> 5 downwardly from the middle of the bottom face of the connecting plate and on which the transversely extending pivots are provided at either side, the width of the pivot holder being such that the leg members mounted
> 10 thereon are inter-spaced, so as to provide for a distance between the axes of symmetry of the recesses in the leg members equal to the module *m* of the building set.
>   7. A toy figure substantially as described
> 15 and as illustrated with reference to Figs. 1 to 7 or 8 to 13 of the accompanying drawings.
>
> Printed for Her Majesty's Stationery Office by Burgess & Son (Abingdon) Ltd.—1979. Published at The Patent Office, 25 Southampton Buildings, London, WC2A 1AY, from which copies may be obtained.

Figure 6.5 (*cont.*)

The minifigures specification can be helpfully broken down into four sections. These sections are to be found in any modern patent specification.

   i. *Cover page.* The first page, or the **cover page**, contains identifying information about the patent. Among other things, it says who the inventor is, the date of filing, and any 'priority' information (a concept to which we return in Section 6.3.2). It also provides a short abstract of the invention.

   ii. *Technical drawings.* Following the cover page, the inventor will typically provide a series of technical drawings to represent the invention.

   iii. *Description.* Now we are coming to the core of the specification. The purpose of the **description** (starting on page 4 in this specification) is to explain the invention and how it works. As a result, this section fulfils the disclosure rationale explained in Section 6.2.3.2. Here, the inventor describes the nature of the invention, why it has been invented (what problem it seeks to solve), and why it is different from prior inventions. As a result, it reads much like a scientific or technical article.

   iv. *Claims.* The document then ends with a section of '**claims**'. The purpose of the claims is not to describe the invention and explain how it works, but is to demarcate the scope of legal protection. In non-legal language, this section is where the inventor says 'this is what I *claim*' or, to put it another way, 'this is what is mine'. In this example, there are seven 'claims' listed.

Claims also come in three different types:

   1. *Product claims.* All of the claims listed above related to *a product*, that is, the Lego Minifigure (or, as claim 1 explains 'a toy figure for detachably mounting on a base plate').

   2. *Process claims.* Inventors can also claim inventive processes. For example, Christiansen might have tried to patent *the process* of creating the minifigures.

Patents I: Foundations

3. *Product-by-process claims*. Lastly, sometimes inventors claim products are produced in a particular way. For example, Christiansen might have tried to patent the minifigures produced in a particular way.

Any of the above claims can either be 'independent' or 'dependent'. Claim 1 in the above example is an independent claim. Claims 2–7 are all 'dependent' claims because they refer back to previous claims. Typically, dependent claims are narrower and more specific than dependent claims. If a court later strikes down an independent claim, the narrower and more specific dependent claims may be left standing.

6.3.2   Registration Process

Armed with an understanding of the specification, let's turn to how the registration process works in practice. We can split the application process into various steps (see Figure 6.6). For now, we will consider the application process for a UK patent.

1. Application Filed
- To apply for a UK patent, the application is filed at the UK Intellectual Property Office (UK IPO). The filing date is important because it establishes the **priority date**. This is relevant to step 4.

2. Preliminary Examination
- The office then makes a preliminary examination to check whether the formal requirements have been satisfied. The application must be in the correct language and the applicant must have paid the relevant filing fees. The office also conducts a preliminary search for any relevant 'prior art' (a concept explained further in chapter 8).

3. Publication of Patent Application
- The office publishes the application within 18 months of the filing date (in the UK IPO's Patent Journal). Third parties can then make 'observations' as to whether the application ought to be granted or not.

4. Substantive Examination
- Within 24 months from filing, the office performs a substantive examination to decide whether to grant a patent. Only if the application meets a set of patentability requirements will a patent be granted. These requirements are discussed in Chapters 7 and 8. The priority date of the invention determines how the office applies the patentability criteria.

5. Grant / Rejection
- If the office finds the application to satisfy the substantive examination, the patent will be granted. The patent specification is then entered on the UK IPO Official Journal. The patent owner enjoys 20 years of protection from the filing date. Alternatively, the patent application may be rejected.

6. Revocation
- Mistakes, however, are made and sometimes patents are granted to inventions which fail to meet the patentability requirements. Accordingly, a UK patent can be revoked either by a UK court or by the Comptroller of the IPO.

Figure 6.6 UK patent registration

As discussed in Section 6.4, these steps change slightly when international patent law is considered.

While we have represented the application process as a series of linear steps, the reality is frequently a messier affair. The substantive examination is more like a conversation between the applicant and the office. The examiners will alert the applicant to any concerns they have, and the applicant will respond to those concerns or even amend the patent. Even after the patent has been granted, the applicant may under certain circumstances amend the patent document.

6.3.3   Entitlement

The historical evolution of patents from industrial policy to rights in inventions had consequences for who was entitled to own patents. Today while almost anyone is entitled to apply regarding a patent, patents can only be granted to certain individuals. Under section 7(2) of the Patents Act, the invention ought to be granted 'primarily to the inventor or joint inventors' and their successors in title. Although, much like copyright, there is an important exception for employees. Under section 39, inventions made in the 'course of the normal duties' of an employee will be granted to the employer.

Contrary to early patent law the modern Patents Act 1977 (s 7(1)) makes clear that there is a *right to apply for and obtain a patent*.

In cases where the patent office receives multiple patent applications for the same invention, the UK and EPC systems operate on a 'first-to-file' basis. In a first-to-file system, the patent should be granted to the first person to file an acceptable application. This contrasts with a small number of countries operating a 'first-to-invent' system, under which the patent should be granted to the first person to invent the invention.[32]

But enough of history; what of the future? In the twenty-first century, advancements in machine learning technology mean that inventions can now be produced by artificial intelligence (AI) systems. This raises the question of whether machines should be a recognised as inventors by patent law? The case in Box 6.13 discusses.

BOX 6.13 *THALER V COMPTROLLER-GENERAL OF PATENTS, DESIGNS AND TRADEMARKS* [2021] EWCA CIV 1374

Facts

In 2018, Dr Stephen Thaler (claimant–appellant) filed two patent applications: one for a new type of food container and one for a flashing light. The patent specification listed 'DABUS' as the inventor. While Thaler claimed that he should own the patent, he argued that the machine was the real inventor.

DABUS is a computer program composed of two 'artificial neural networks'. Artificial neural networks are sub-elements of a computer system which loosely models how neurons interact in the human biological brain. Each network underwent a 'training' process. This process involved, in simple terms, showing the networks vast amounts of information about how humans had solved technical problems in the past. In addition, the first network showed how to identify links between topics, while the second showed what qualified as new and useful inventions. When fully trained, the first network identified links between different topics, while the second network assessed those links to identify whether any qualified as new and useful inventions.

Thaler's application for a patent was rejected by the UK IPO on the grounds of section 13 of the Patents Act. This section requires that the 'inventor' be identified on the patent specification. In the view of the UK IPO (defendant–respondent), a machine could not be an 'inventor'. Thaler appealed the UK IPO decision to the High Court.

Issue and Procedure

The case presented the following issue: can an AI system be an 'inventor' for the purposes of patent law (including both section 13 and section 7 of the Patents Act)? The High Court rejected Thaler's appeal and the Court of Appeal affirmed, as discussed in the following extract from Lord Justice Arnold.

ARNOLD LJ

The applications are part of a project involving parallel applications to patent offices around the world in which Dr Thaler and his collaborators, . . . seek to establish that artificial intelligence systems can make inventions and that the owners of such systems can obtain patents in respect of those inventions: see www.artificialinventor .com. It is therefore a test case. Although similar test cases are pending in other jurisdictions, we must apply the law of the United Kingdom. Furthermore, at the risk of stating the obvious, we must apply the law as it presently stands: this is not an occasion for debating what the law ought to be.

In my judgment it is clear that, upon a systematic interpretation of the 1977 Act, only a person can be an 'inventor'. The starting point is section 130(1) which provides that '"*inventor*" has the meaning assigned to it by section 7 above'. Section 7(3) provides that '"*inventor*" in relation to an invention means the actual deviser of the invention'. A dictionary definition of 'deviser' is 'a person who devises; a contriver, a planner, an inventor' (*Shorter Oxford English Dictionary*, 5th edition, Oxford University Press, 2002). Section 7(2) provides that a patent may be granted (a) 'primarily to the inventor or joint inventors', (b) 'to any person or persons who . . .', (c) 'the successor or successors in title of any person or persons mentioned in

> paragraph (a) or (b) above', but 'to no other person'. . . . It is clear from this code that category (a) must consist of a person or persons, just as much as categories (b) and (c) do. Section 7(4) creates a presumption that 'a person who makes an application for a patent shall be taken to be the person who is entitled under subsection (2) above to be granted a patent'. Again, it is plain that only a person can be entitled under section 7(2), and thus only a person can fall within paragraph (a).
>
> (pp. 114, 116)

As noted in Lord Justice Arnold's judgment, similar litigation has taken place in several other jurisdictions as well. One noticeable example comes from Australia where Thaler also sought to patent the inventions. At first instance, Mr Justice Beach concluded in *Thaler v Commissioner of Patents* that an AI could qualify as an inventor under the Australian Patents Act 1990.[33] The decision was, however, subsequently overturned on appeal.[34]

If patent law evolved historically from artisan privilege to inventor's property rights, then the rise of AI inventors prompts us to look to the future: what is the next step in patent law's evolution?

In December 2023, in *Thaler v Comptroller-General of Patents, Designs, and Trademarks* [2023] UKSC 49, the UK Supreme Court unanimously upheld the Court of Appeal decision.

6.4 THE INTERNATIONALISATION OF PATENTS

Today UK patents are granted under the Patents Act 1977. Patents, like copyrights, are territorial rights. As a result, a patent granted by the UK government only applies in the UK, and a patent granted in France only applies in France, etc. If an inventor receives a patent in the UK, they can stop others using their patented invention in the UK, but they cannot stop people using the invention outside the UK.

In the modern globalised world, this causes practical problems. Consider the Christiansen brick. As the family business grew, the Christiansens began to sell toys in multiple different countries. To stop imitators using their invention around the world, Christiansen had to apply for patent protections in a range of different countries (not only the UK and Denmark, but the USA, France, Japan, among others). This is obviously a very time-consuming and costly process.

International patent law developed, in part, to solve the practical problems associated with the territorial nature of patent rights within the context of a globalised world. This process took place across several different phases.

6.4.1 Paris Convention

The first phase of internationalisation occurred in the nineteenth century with the signing of the **Paris Convention** for the Protection of Industrial Property 1883. Like the Berne Convention in copyright, the Paris Convention established the

The term 'industrial property' is an out-of-date label for patents, trade marks, and designs.

principle of 'national treatment'. Under this principle, signatories to the convention must give inventors from other countries the same protection that they offer to their own inventors.[35]

In addition to the principle of national treatment, the Convention also set rules relating to priority. As Figure 6.6 notes, the priority date in the UK is normally the date of filing. This changes, however, if the inventor has filed a patent application in another Paris Convention member within the preceding twelve months. In that case, the priority date will be the filing date of the foreign application.[36]

ACTIVITY 6.9

Look back to the minifigures specification (Figure 6.5). On page 1 you will see both a 'filing date' – 17 August 1978 – and a section called 'Priority Data'. Using the information provided, what is the priority date for this invention?

While making significant strides forward, the Paris Convention did not entirely solve the challenges facing inventors who required protection in multiple jurisdictions. Inventors still needed to apply for patents in multiple different countries.

6.4.2   European Patent Convention and Patent Cooperation Treaty

The challenges facing inventors in a globalised world was addressed in the second stage of internationalisation. In the 1970s, two international treaties sought to address this issue: the **European Patent Convention 1973** (subsequently updated in 2000) (EPC) and the **Patent Cooperation Treaty 1970** (PCT).

The EPC is an intergovernmental treaty. The EPC was designed to give inventors an alternative method of achieving protection in multiple different jurisdictions. Despite the word 'European' in the treaty title, it is entirely separate from the European Union. As the treaty is not connected with the European Union, the system is unaffected by Brexit. When the UK adopted the Patents Act 1977, one of the key purposes was to ensure consistency between the provisions of UK patent law and the provisions of the EPC. The treaty currently has sixteen signatories and thirty-nine parties.

The EPC creates and regulates the '**European patent**' system. Under this system, an inventor can apply to the **European Patent Office** in Munich, Germany for a European patent. In their application, the applicant designates several different member countries in which they wish to receive patent protection. For example, the applicant may designate the UK, France and Germany. The EPO Examining Division conducts a substantive examination of the application and decides whether to grant the European patent (equivalent to stage 4 of Figure 6.6) If the EPO grants the patent, then the applicant receives national patents in each of the designated states (the UK, France and Germany in the example). The national courts then are responsible for interpreting the patent document in any potential infringement actions.

Alternatively, the EPO Examining Division may reject the application. In this case, the applicant may appeal to the EPO's **Technical Board of Appeals** (TBA) or **Legal Board of Appeal** (LBA), or in rare cases, the **Enlarged Board of Appeal** (EBA). If the patent is granted, it may also be subject to opposition proceedings before the EPO Opposition Division (analogous to stage 6 of Figure 6.6). If the opposition is successful, then all the national patents will be revoked.

The PCT operates in a broadly similar manner to the EPC. The PCT currently has 157 contracting states. Under the PCT system, an inventor from one of these states can apply to any of the international offices, including the most famous of all, the World Intellectual Property Organization (WIPO). The international patent office will conduct a search to determine whether the invention has been patented anywhere within the member states. But unlike the EPO, the international patent office will not decide whether to grant a patent. Instead, it will send on the patent application to the national patent offices (including the EPO) designated in the inventor's application. It is then up to the national patent office to decide whether to grant a national patent.

6.4.3 TRIPS

Like the Berne Convention, the Paris Convention introduced some minimum standards including, for example, the right of inventors to be named as inventors on the patent specification.[37] But a far more significant harmonisation of national patent laws was accomplished by the TRIPS Agreement. Under this agreement, all WTO members must conform to certain substantive patent rules. Those include the requirement that patents be available for all fields of technology[38] and must last for twenty years from the date of filing.[39] As a result, the TRIPS agreement represents another distinct stage of the internationalisation of patent law.

6.4.4 European Union Influence

Although the EPC is distinct from the European Union, the European Union has played a significant role in the internationalisation of patents. In some instances, the European Union has issued directives which member states must follow. The Biotechnology Directive 1998, for instance, sets important rules for patents in relation to biotechnical inventions.[40]

But the most important intervention is just now beginning. For fifty years, the European Union has considered adopting a unitary patent system (also known as the 'European patent with unitary effect').[41] The **unitary patent** is different from the existing European patent system. Unlike the European patent, which is a bundle of national patents, the unitary patent is a singular patent that covers the entire European Union. Nevertheless, inventors continue to submit applications for unitary patents to the EPO. Litigation relating to the unitary patent will be adjudicated by a centralised Unified Patent Court. The unitary patent came into force in June 2023.

6.5 SUMMARY

Why should Christiansen's brick be property? Given the objections facing the personality and labour arguments, it is common for lawyers to answer this question in utilitarian terms. Patents create monopolies. This has the unfortunate effect that Christiansen's toy bricks will be sold at a high price, and may restrict future cumulative innovation. Nevertheless, defenders of the patent system claim that the bad consequences are outweighed by the good consequences. After all, it is patents that encourage invention, disclosure of technical information, and the efficient development of ideas. Society, it is argued, will be a happier place with an appropriately balanced patent system than without one.

This utilitarian argument for patents is sometimes called the '**patent bargain**'. According to this metaphor, society strikes a bargain (or a quid pro quo) with inventors: society gives inventors property in their inventions, and in return inventors invent, disclose and develop new ideas. This bargain is modelled diagrammatically in Figure 6.7. As Machlup and Penrose rhetorically ask in Box 6.11: 'Why should anybody object to such a fair bargain?'.

However, not everyone is convinced the bargain is a particularly good one. The fundamental problem is that, as Boldrin and Levine argue, we have little empirical evidence to back up the utilitarian argument. Furthermore, as argued by the likes of Thomas Jefferson, Petra Moser, Robert Merges and Richard Nelson some evidence points in the opposite direction: that the *absence* of patents may result in more inventions, more disclosure and more development of ideas. Of course, none of this evidence shows that the utilitarian argument is clearly wrong. But nor does it clearly support it. The question, then, is whether the public gives lucrative monopolies to inventors, and receives too little in return.

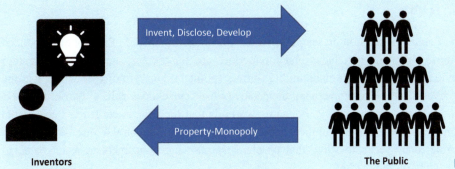

Figure 6.7 The patent bargain

6.6 SELF-ASSESSMENT

Before moving on, try to answer the following questions to consolidate your learning. Answers are provided in the section below.

1. Jeremey Bentham, the founder of classical utilitarianism, argued that patents are 'absolutely necessary'. While patents have bad consequences (i.e. higher prices and some restrictions on future inventions), patents also give inventors the incentive to invent in the first place. Overall, Bentham claims, society is a better place with an appropriately balanced patent system than without one. However, not all agree. Which of the

following objections can be made against Bentham's arguments concerning incentives to invent? Select one or more answers.

  a. Insufficient empirical evidence supports the conclusion that patents make society a better place overall.

  b. Mechanisms other than patents, including prizes, can be used to encourage invention.

  c. Inventors will struggle to keep their inventions secret for an extended period of time.

  d. The best way to encourage development of an invention is through competition, not monopoly.

2. Section 6.4 summarises six phases of the internationalisation of patents. At which stage did a system for international patent applications emerge?

  a. The first phase.

  b. The second phase.

  c. The third phase.

  d. The fourth phase.

3. An inventor has invented a new form of mousetrap. The inventor files for a French patent on 1 January 2024. She applies for a German patent on 1 February 2024. She applies for a UK patent on 1 March 2024. All three countries are members of the Paris Convention. What is the priority date of the UK patent?

  a. 1 January 2024

  b. 1 February 2024

  c. 1 March 2024

  d. None of the above.

4. Is there one good argument for patents?

ACTIVITY DISCUSSION

Activity 6.1 Chief Justice Popham's decision presciently predicts the economic model of monopoly produced in later centuries. Popham concludes that monopolies are for the 'private gain' of patentees because they enable the seller to maintain high prices (point 1). Furthermore, he writes that the monopoly prevents others from practising their trade (what Towse today calls a 'barrier to entry' (Section 1.1.3)) (point 3). In point 2, Popham also finds that the consumers suffer because the goods become less 'merchantable' in the presence of a monopoly. Section 9.4. discusses how the exhaustion rule today seeks to solve that problem by allowing consumers to resell patented products put freely on the market.

Activity 6.2 Although both van Gogh and Christiansen made choices in the creation of their good, the type of choices they made, and the reasons behind those choices, were quite different. Van Gogh's choices, according to the personality argument, reflected something *internal* to him: his character, his lived experiences, his emotional state. By contrast, Christiansen's choices were made in response to *external* demands. Christiansen simply wanted to improve the functionality of the bricks by making them more stable. As a result, it is hard – although perhaps not impossible – to see Christiansen's personality 'shining through' the brick.

Activity 6.3 Merges would argue that it is natural for Christiansen to own his invented brick. The concept of interlocking toy bricks had been around for some time (we will see some examples of earlier bricks in Chapter 8). This concept was accordingly part of the public domain. Christiansen modified that basic idea by incorporating the stud-and-tube system. Merges would argue that by mixing his labour with the public domain (the concept of interlocking toy bricks), Christiansen created something new. Because that new thing contains something he naturally owns – his labour – Christiansen naturally owns the resulting new thing.

Activity 6.4 Much like copyright (see Activity 2.7), the problem is the patent can potentially stop inventive activity. Perhaps Christiansen can pay the fee demanded by Page. But if he does not have the money to pay, then he cannot develop his new toy. Thus patents, like copyright, have this dual effect: they both encourage, and discourage, invention at the same time. As explained in Section 2.2.3, this is known as the incentive–access tradeoff.

Activity 6.5 Ultimately, we do not know why countries without patent rights seemed to successfully produce lots of inventions. However, Petra Moser's extract (Box 6.10) indicates that inventors may have faced non-patent incentives to invent. In particular, those who invented new and useful inventions won **prizes** at the world fairs. The potential to win prizes (including money and fame) may have stimulated invention.

At various times, governments have sought to stimulate innovation through awarding prizes. In the eighteenth century, the British government gave prizes to inventors who developed new ways of determining a ship's location at sea.[42] And today, Prince William has launched the 'Earthshot Prize': a yearly competition where inventors can earn prizes for inventions that can help solve climate change.

Activity 6.6 Perhaps the most obvious point illustrated by the Coca-Cola example is point (3), that is, that patents may still fail to provide incentives to disclose. The Coca-Cola corporation decided not to patent the invention. If they had done so, they would have been required to disclose their recipe to the world through the patent application document. The company preferred to keep their invention secret, and maintain a perpetual monopoly, rather than make the invention public in return for a twenty-year monopoly. It is accordingly not clear whether the incentive-to-disclose argument provides a sufficiently strong justification for granting property and monopolies.

Activity 6.9 Lines 31–33 explain that two patents have already been filed in relation to this invention. Patent Application 3818/77 was filed in Denmark on 29 August 1977 and Patent Application 1902/78 was filed also in Denmark on 2 May 1978. Because Denmark is a Paris Convention member state, and because 29 August 1977 is within twelve months of the UK filing date (17 August 1978), the priority date is 29 August 1977. This will be important when evaluating the patentability criteria discussed in Chapter 8.

SELF-ASSESSMENT ANSWERS

1. **Correct answers: a.** and **b.** Answer **c.** is more related to the claim that patents will encourage disclosure of inventions. Answer **d.** could potentially work as an objection to Bentham's claims, but it is slighty more related to the argument that patents encourage coordinated development of an invention.
2. **Correct answer: b.** Only when the EPC and PCT emerged in the 1970s did a mechanism for international patent filing emerge.
3. **Correct answer: a.** The French patent has been filed within twelve months of the UK application. This is the priority date. It is unaffected by the fact that there has been a filing in Germany in the intervening period.

Notes

1 Patents Act 1977, s 30(1).

2 Henry Wiencek, *The World of Lego Toys* (Abrams 1987) 35–57.

3 Abraham Lincoln, Lecture on Discoveries and Inventions, 6 April 1958, Bloomington, Illinois.

4 Thomas Jefferson, Letter to Isaac McPherson (13 August 1813) in Andrew A Lipscomb and Albert Ellery Bergh (eds), *The Writings of Thomas Jefferson*, vol 13 (Thomas Jefferson Memorial Association 1904) 333 ('generally speaking, other nations have thought that these monopolies produce more embarrassment than advantage to society').

5 Christine MacLeod, *Inventing the Industrial Revolution: The English Patent System, 1660–1800* (CUP 1988) 1.

6 William Blackstone, *Commentaries on the laws of England*, 4 vols (OUP 1765–79) 2: 346; Edward Chamberlayne, *Angliae notitiae; or the Present State of England* (18th edn, 1694) 81; Ephraim Chambers, *Cyclopaedia: or, an universal dictionary of arts and sciences*, 2 vols (5th edn, 1741), sub 'Letters Patent', 'Patent'.

7 For an example, see 'Letters Patent of Edward III dated 14 April 1341' Royal Collection Trust <https://www.rct.uk/collection/71317/letters-patent-of-edward-iii-dated-14-april-1341> (accessed July 2022).

8 MacLeod (n 5). Reproduced with permission of the Licensor through PLSclear.

9 This remained the case for many hundreds of years. WA Hindmarch, *Treatise Relating to the Law of Patent Privileges for the Sole Use of Inventions* (V & R Stevens and GS Norton and W Benning 1847) 3–4. See also *Ex parte O'Reily*, 30 ER 256 (Ch 1790).

10 Oren Bracha, *Owning Ideas: The Intellectual Origins of American Intellectual Property, 1790–1909* (CUP 2016) 15–25.

11 MacLeod (n 5). Reproduced with permission of the Licensor through PLSclear.

12 ibid. Reproduced with permission of the Licensor through PLSclear.

13 'The Grand Remonstrance' in Samuel Rawson Gardiner (ed), *The Constitutional Documents of the Puritan Revolution, 1625–1660* (Clarendon Press 1906) 202.

14 MacLeod (n 5) 16.

15 ibid 20.

16 See eg *Liardet v Johnson* (1780) (1778) 62 ER 1000 (KB).

17 *Boulton and Watt v Bull* (1795) 126 ER 651.

18 *Hornblower & Maberly v Boulton* (1799) 101 ER 1285 (KB).

19 E Wyndham Hulme, 'On the Consideration of the Patent Grant Past and Present' (1897) 13 LQR 313.

20 Comments of Congressman William Vans Murray, 3 Annals of Cong 855 (1793); Bracha (n 10).

21 See generally Sidney Fine, *Laissez Faire and the General-Welfare State* (University of Michigan Press 1964).

22 Reproduced with permission of Cambridge University Press.

23 Bracha (n 10); Alain Pottage and Brad Sherman, *Figures of Invention: A History of Modern Patent Law* (OUP 2010) 45–64.

24 See generally Walter Garcia-Fontes, *Incentives for Research, Development, and Innovation in Pharmaceuticals* (Springer 2011).

25 Michele Boldrin and David K Levine, 'The Case against Patents' (2013) 27(1) Journal of Economic Perspectives 3–22.

26 Copyright American Economic Association; reproduced with permission of the *Journal of Economic Perspectives*.

27 Josh Lerner, '150 Years of Patent Protection' (2002) 92(2) American Economic Review 221.

28 Frederick Allen, *Secret Formula: The Inside Story of How Coca-Cola Became the Best-Known Brand in the World* (Open Road Integrated Media 2015).

29 See eg *Racing Partnership Ltd v Sports Information Services Ltd* [2020] EWCA Civ 1300; Lionel Bently, 'Trade Secrets: Intellectual Property But Not Property?' in Helena Howe and Jonathan Griffiths (eds), *Concepts of Property in Intellectual Property* (CUP 2013) 60–94.

30 Edmund W Kitch, 'The Nature and Function of the Patent System' (1977) 20 Journal of Law and Economics 265–90; John F Duffy 'Rethinking the Prospect Theory of Patents' (2004) 71 (2) U Chi L Rev 439.

31 Reproduced with permission through Copyright Clearance Center.

32 The most notable first-to-invent system was the US one prior to the America Invents Act 2011.

33 [2021] FCA 879.

34 *Thaler v Commissioner of Patents* [2022] HCATrans 199.

35 Paris Convention for the Protection of Industrial Property (as amended 28 September 1979) art 2.

36 ibid art 4.

37 ibid art 4*ter*.

38 Agreement on Trade Related Aspects of Intellectual Property Rights 1994, art 27.

39 ibid art 33.

40 Directive 98/44/EC of the European Parliament and of the Council of 6 July 1998 on the legal protection of biotechnological inventions.

41 Regulation (EU) No 1257/2912 of the European Parliament and of the Council of 17 December 2012 implementing enhanced cooperation in the area of the creation of unitary patent protection.

42 *The Quest for Longitude: The Proceedings of the Longitude Symposium, Harvard University* (Collection of Historical Scientific Instruments, Harvard University 1996).

FIGURE ACKNOWLEDGEMENTS

6.1 Figures from patent GB866557A

6.2 Venetian Patent Statute 1474, the Senate of Venice, held in the Archivio di Stato (ASV, Senato Terra, reg 7, c 32r). From Wikimedia Commons <https://commons.wikimedia.org/wiki/File:Venetian_Patent_Statute_1474.png>

6.3 HL/PO/PU/1/1623/21j1n3. Reproduced with permission from the parchment copy in the UK Parliamentary Archives. Digital copy Statute of Monopolies, Westminster (1624) in L Bently and M Kretschmer (eds), *Primary Sources on Copyright (1450–1900)* <https://www.copyrighthistory.org/cam/tools/request/showRecord.php?id=record_uk_1624>

6.4 Patent specification for James Puckle's invention 'the autocannon' – or machine gun. From patent number GB171800418A. With minor modifications by Patrick Goold

6.5 Patent GB2006028A

Marginal Fig. 6.1 Sir Edward Coke, English barrister, judge, opposition politician. Key jurist of the Elizabethan and Jacobean eras. After engraving by Davod Loggan. 1 February 1552, 3 September 1634 (photo by Culture Club/Getty Images)

Marginal Fig. 6.2 Portrait of Thomas Jefferson by Rembrandt Peale (1778–1860) (oil on canvas from the White House collection, Washington, DC), 1853. (Photo by GraphicaArtis/Getty Images)

Marginal Fig. 6.3 American inventor Thomas Edison. Thomas Edison invented or developed a great many of the twentieth-century's essential electronic devices, such as the phonograph, the incandescent lightbulb and the motion picture camera. (Photo credit: Bettmann/Contributor)

7

Patents II: Patentability

Chapter 6 outlined the evolution of patents from discretionary artisan privileges to a system of rights in inventions. Particularly from the nineteenth century onwards, the notion emerged that if one could satisfy the patentability requirements, one had a right to a patent. Today, the patentability requirements are a core feature of the patent registration process. One who satisfies the patentability criteria has a 'right to apply for and obtain a patent' in the language of the Patents Act 1977.[1]

Chapters 7 and 8 consider the patentability requirements. This chapter starts with the fundamental requirement: the **invention**. Section 1(1) of the Patents Act 1977 and article 52(1) EPC state that a patent 'may be granted only for an invention'. Accordingly, the invention forms the core of **patentable subject matter**. Chapter 8 then turns to the requirements that the invention also be new, involve an inventive step, be capable of industrial application and be sufficiently disclosed by the patent specification.

What is an 'invention'? Much like Chapter 3, a metaphysical question looms large over this chapter. For some the idea of an invention conjures up images of machines and moving parts. Yet, today a far broader and more abstract set of phenomena are considered inventions: from human genes to computer programs, to methods of doing business. Much like Chapter 3, the question is whether these are things that can be owned.

The chapter explores patentable subject matter in three sections. Section 7.1 considers the 'invention'. Section 7.2 considers some phenomena that are statutorily defined as 'not inventions'. Section 7.3 considers some phenomena that are inventions, but that are nevertheless excluded from patent protection.

7.1 INVENTIONS

Much like the work in copyright, the idea of the invention in patent law is enigmatic. For patent lawyers sitting at the cusp of modernity in the nineteenth

---

This chapter contains public sector information licensed under the Open Government Licence v3.0.

century, the invention was often a physical thing. As Robert Merges explains, for patent lawyers of this epoch, if one put an invention in a bag and shook it, 'it would make some noise'.[2]

But as Talha Syed explains in Box 7.1, it is important to guard against such 'physicalist' misconceptions. The patentable invention is not a physical thing, but knowledge. The question, then, is whether such knowledge is a thing that can be owned?

BOX 7.1 TALHA SYED, 'RECONSTRUCTING PATENT ELIGIBILITY' (2021) 70 AM U L REV 1937

[C]ourts and commentators often speak as if what is being claimed is the *thing* itself, a persistent 'physicalist' misconstrual of the object of patent rights.[3]

The object of patent rights is always and only 'knowledge of' something and never some*thing* itself. Patent rights obtain, that is, always in some intangible space of knowledge, and never in some tangible 'thing'. Why? Because to think otherwise would be to fail to internalize what it means to understand patents as a regime of intellectual property, obtaining in intangible objects... To think otherwise would be to miss the distinguishing characteristics of patent law as a distinct field of property law and social policy: namely, that it deals with intangible as opposed to tangible objects, or informational goods as opposed to other kinds of resources.

(pp. 1944, 1949–50)

Much like Thomas Jefferson before him, Syed is keen to stress that patent law grants ownership over knowledge and ideas. But this in turn raises another question: what kind of knowledge can be owned? There is a lot of knowledge in this world and not all is owned: no one owns Pythagoras's theorem and no one owns $E=MC^2$.

Syed argues that patents do not protect 'basic' knowledge, and only protect 'applied' knowledge. While the former is better produced through publicly funded research (such as giving universities money to conduct research) and should remain free as a 'foundation' on which other researchers can build, the latter *might* be better encouraged through monopolies:

Because the former spaces of knowledge are platforms of basic understanding, the domain of science, while the latter are tools of applied interventions, the domain of technology. And while the latter spaces of knowledge, being functional, are apt candidates for patent protection, the former are not: their generation is better suited to the alternative innovation policy of publicly funded, open science.

(p. 1945)

Of course, it remains an empirical question whether even applied knowledge is better produced through patents or through some alternative mechanism, as discussed in Section 6.2.3.

ACTIVITY 7.1

Think back to Christiansen's 1958 toy brick complete with the stud-and-tube coupling system. Almost certainly this is an invention. But what makes it so according to Syed? And what is the 'physicalist' mistake we should avoid?

The basic–applied knowledge distinction does not appear in the UK Patents Act nor the EPC. But, then again, neither of these statutes provide any definition for the 'invention' term. Courts have shouldered the burden of interpreting this term.

While they do not use the same terminology as Syed, UK and EPO courts broadly agree with the essential point that inventions are 'applied interventions' and the 'domain of technology'. This, in the UK and EPC systems, has a unique legal term: **technical character**. But what gives knowledge a 'technical character'? The EPO and the UK courts provide different answers. These different approaches are summarised in Box 7.2 by one of the leading authorities on the subject, Justine Pila.

BOX 7.2 JUSTINE PILA, *THE SUBJECT MATTER OF INTELLECTUAL PROPERTY* (OUP 2017)

Justine Pila is a Professor of Law at Oxford University.

In conclusion, the inventions for which a patent may validly be granted are defined under European law as technical teachings, namely, subject matter involving technical character, in the sense of depending for their existence on some human intervention in the material world utilizing the forces of nature to produce a causal, perceivable, and repeatable result.[4] In the jurisprudence of the EPO, this definition is both supported by the EPC and the starting point for reading its provisions on inherent patentability, including its definition of 'invention' (via a list of non-inventions) in Article 52(2) and (3). Its premise is a view of the requirement for an invention as legally and analytically separate from the further patentability requirements of novelty, inventive step, and susceptibility of industrial application respectively, such that a subject matter need not be new, inventive, or industrially applicable to be an invention within the meaning of European law. . .

[T]he real difference between UK and European law in this area derives not from the wording of the legislation, but from the interpretation of that wording by the relevant judicial authorities. To date the UK courts have refused to accept the EPO's understanding of 'inventions' as technical subject matter on the basis of its stated inconsistency with Article 52(2) and (3) and established UK precedent. This is despite their obligation under section 130(7) of the Patents Act to interpret section 1 and other key Patents Act provisions … so far as practicable to be consistent with the interpretation of the corresponding European provisions, and despite the alternative conception supported by UK precedent having itself been derived from the EPO's 1985 Guidelines for Examiners. According to that alternative conception, first articulated by the Principal Examiner of the UK Patent Office in Merrill Lynch Inc's Application, an invention within the meaning of section 1(2) of the Patents Act is any subject matter that contributes something technical to what had been known previously. Being technical is therefore not a sufficient – although almost certainly still a necessary – property of an invention in UK law. Strictly speaking, however, the courts do not ask of a subject matter 'is it technical?', but rather, 'does it make a contribution to the art that is technical?'.

(pp. 115–17)

> The divergence between the EPO and UK approaches only emerged in the year 2000 with the case of *Pension Benefits Systems Partnership*, T931/95 OJ EPO 441. Prior to that point, the EPO largely followed the same approach as that of the UK.

ACTIVITY 7.2

Return now to the Christiansen Toy Building Brick example. Why, according to UK courts or the EPO, does this brick have a technical character?

There are pros and cons to both the UK and EPO approaches. On one hand, the EPO standard seems quite easy to pass. What things do not involve some human intervention in the material world? Conceivably Einstein's formula $E=MC^2$ required some human intervention. Plausibly climate change would pass this test too.

On the other hand, the UK approach arguably confuses distinct elements of patentability. In asking whether an invention makes a 'technical contribution' to the art, are UK courts really asking whether the invention is new or useful in some way? If so, then the approach seems to muddle the patentability requirements. Chapter 8 considers the requirements that an invention be new, involve an inventive step and be capable of application in industry. In defining an invention as something that makes a technical contribution to the art, are UK courts merely saying that an invention must be new, inventive and useful in some way?

7.2 NOT INVENTIONS

The Statute of Monopolies defined an invention as a 'manner of new manufacture'. On some level, it was necessary to demonstrate how the applicant's invention fit

Patents II: Patentability

within that definition. Some countries continue this tradition today. The USA and Canada both define 'invention' as a 'manufacture or composition of matter'.[5] Australia also continues to retain the old Statute of Monopolies definition.[6]

The Patents Act 1977, however, departs from that approach. Section 1(1) neither provides a definition of the term 'invention' nor requires an applicant to prove their invention fits within that definition. Instead, section 1(2) of the Patents Act simply provides a list of things that are 'not inventions'. Section 1(2) of the Patents Act states the following:

> An analogous provision is found in article 52(2) of the EPC.

> (2) It is hereby declared that the following (among other things) are not inventions for the purposes of this Act, that is to say, anything which consists of –
>
> (a) a discovery, scientific theory or mathematical method;
> (b) a literary, dramatic, musical or artistic work or any other aesthetic creation whatsoever;
> (c) a scheme, rule or method for performing a mental act, playing a game or doing business, or a program for a computer;
> (d) the presentation of information;
>
> but the foregoing provision shall prevent anything from being treated as an invention for the purposes of this Act only to the extent that a patent or application for a patent relates to that thing **as such**.

What connects this apparently disparate collection of things and makes them all 'not inventions'? Perhaps the answer is simply: nothing. In *Aerotel*, Lord Justice Jacob found that there was 'no common, overarching concept' connecting the subsections.[7] Instead, each of these items found its way onto the list of 'not inventions' because of an idiosyncratic mix of policy objectives, pragmatic concerns and historical contingency. But there is another possible answer. What might be said to connect these subsections is that the list is broadly composed of things lacking a technical character.[8]

The concept of technical character has taken on paramount importance in the interpretation of the statutory exclusions. In part, this is the result of the rather ambiguous proviso at the end stating that a thing will only fail to qualify as an invention if it relates to one of the excluded categories 'as such'. To illustrate, consider a scientist who finds a new plant with medicinal properties. The new plant would almost certainly qualify as a 'discovery' under section (2)(a). *As such*, it would be unpatentable. Nevertheless, if the scientist were to use the plant to make a new medicine, they would be able to patent the medicine. The difference is that the medicine, unlike the plant, arguably has a technical character.

> Sometimes this idea is expressed as a requirement that the invention be 'reduced to practice'.

As a result, courts in the EPO and the UK use the technical character concept as a guide to the interpretation and application of the exclusions. In making this determination, EPO courts ask whether the claimed invention has a technical character in the sense outlined in Section 7.1. The UK courts have, by contrast, adopted a multistage analysis to help determine whether an invention falls within the scope of the section 1(2) exclusion. In *Aerotel*, the Court of Appeal not only rejected the broad EPO approach to technical character, but also recommended courts consider the following steps when applying section 1(2):

(1) construe the claim (that is, ask what is being claimed);
(2) identify the contribution (that is, ask what contribution the invention makes to the art);
(3) identify whether that contribution falls within one of the excluded categories; and
(4) check whether the invention is technical.

Subsequently in *Symbian* the Court of Appeal has said that steps (3) and (4) can be read together.[9] The practical consequence being that whether something falls within the scope of the section 1(2) exception or not depends foremost on whether the contribution claimed is 'technical' or not. *Symbian* also stressed that while the four steps can provide assistance, they ought not to be 'followed blindly in every case'.[10]

The remainder of this section examines how courts have put these general principles into practice. To do so, the section skips over the first two steps in the *Aerotel* analysis. These steps are unpacked in the following chapters: Chapter 9 considers the process of **claim construction**, Chapter 8 considers how courts identify the contribution made by the invention. Instead, this section focuses on how courts use the concept of technical character to help determine what is, and what is not, an invention. While this chapter cannot possibly cover all the categories, it can illustrate the key concepts by surveying some of the most important things listed in section 1(2): discoveries, computer programs, business methods, presentations of information and mental acts. The approach to determining what is an 'aesthetic creation' is broadly similar to the rules outlined in Part I.

7.2.1 Discoveries

Some phenomena are discovered rather than invented: the moon, dinosaur fossils, previously unknown species of insect, etc. However, the advancement of modern biotechnological science has presented patent lawyers with new challenges. Are substances found in, and extracted from, the human body inventions with a technical character? Or are such substances discoveries as such?

This question is particularly relevant to human genetics. The human genome is sometimes understood as the human blueprint. Inside almost every human cell is a set of chromosomes inherited from our parents. Chromosomes are composed of DNA (deoxyribonucleic acid) that coils around itself in a familiar 'double helix' shape (Figure 7.1). Genes are sections of DNA. Each gene contains information which instructs the body how to perform basic functions – most commonly on how to produce proteins. These proteins control the operation of the human body and determine such features as eye colour or blood type. One of the greatest scientific

Some countries, like the USA, have an analogous provision that prevents patenting 'products of nature'.

Figure 7.1 DNA function.
File licensed under the Creative Commons Attribution 4.0 International licence (Wikipedia <https://en.wikipedia.org/wiki/File:Chromosome_DNA_Gene.svg>)

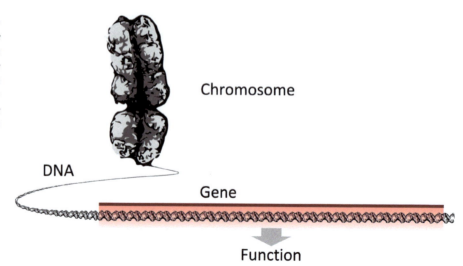

projects of the late twentieth century was the attempt to identify all human genes and their functions.

But are genes and the proteins they produce 'discovered' or 'invented' by scientists? The following two cases – one from the EPO and one from the US Supreme Court – suggest different approaches to this question.

Case 7.1 *Howard Florey/Relaxin* [1995] EPOR 541, 548–49

Facts

Relaxin is a hormone first discovered in 1926 that aids childbirth in humans and other animals. Relaxin is composed of three different peptides (that is, short chains of amino acids): H1, H2 and H3. The human genome also contains three genes, each of which encodes (that is, contain the genetic instructions on how to produce) one of the peptides.

In the 1980s, the Howard Florey Institute of Experimental Physiology and Medicine (now known as the Florey Institute of Neuroscience and Mental Health) identified human H2-relaxin. They developed a process for obtaining the relaxin and the DNA encoding it. The Institute applied for a European patent on the process for obtaining these substances, and more importantly, the substances themselves.

Issue and Procedure

The patent was opposed before the EPO Opposition Division by the Green Party within the European Parliament on various grounds. The issue explored in Box 7.3 is whether the claims as to the substances failed on the grounds that they related to discoveries as such. The EPO decided they did not.

BOX 7.3 EPO OPPOSITION DIVISION

The opponents further assert that the subject-matter of the patent represents a discovery and is hence not patentable under Article 52(2)(a) EPC. This argument ignores the long-standing practice of the European Patent Office concerning the patentability of natural substances. As explained in the Guidelines, C-IV, 2.3, to find a substance freely occurring in nature is mere discovery and therefore unpatentable. However, if a substance found in nature has first to be isolated from its surroundings and a process for obtaining it is developed, that process is patentable. Moreover, if this substance can be properly characterised by its structure and it is new in the absolute sense of having no previously recognised existence, then the substance *per se* may be patentable.

The above guideline is highly appropriate in the present case. Human H2-relaxin had no previously recognised existence. The proprietor has developed a process for obtaining H2-relaxin and the DNA encoding it, has characterised these products by their chemical structure and has found a use for the protein. The products are therefore patentable under Article 52(2) EPC.

The opponents complained that equating discoveries with inventions led to unduly broad patents which prevented anyone else from making, in the case at issue, a selection invention on H2-relaxin. However, the Opposition Division finds it perfectly justified to grant broad protection in view of the fact that H2-relaxin has been made available to the public for the first time. This does not exclude the possibility of further inventions, for example improved derivatives of the protein, better processes for its preparation, and so on. The situation is comparable to that existing for inventions relating to air pumps, to use the example repeatedly mentioned by the opponents, where the original inventor of an air pump would certainly have been entitled to a broad patent.

The opponents also contended that the above reasoning would mean that discoveries such as the moon (after the Americans landed on it in 1969), 'Ötzi' (a mummified, around 5,000-year-old man found in ice in the Italian/Austrian Alps) or a new animal found in some remote area would also be patentable. However, this is not the case. As already pointed out, the mere finding of something freely occurring in nature is not an invention. An invention must have a technical character, that is, should constitute an industrially applicable technical solution to a technical problem, and must be reproducibly obtainable without undue burden. A product must furthermore be novel in the

---

Remember: beware the 'physicalist' misconceptions identified by Talha Syed. Howard Florey did not have any rights in the actual, physical, hormone produced by the body, nor its associated DNA. Instead, Howard Florey had rights over the *knowledge of* that hormone, including knowledge about what the hormone is, what it does and how it can be used.

> sense of having had no previously recognised existence and must in addition be inventive. None of the discoveries cited by the opponents fulfil these criteria.
>
> In conclusion, the subject-matter of the disputed patent does not represent a discovery and is hence not excluded from patentability under Article 52(2) EPC.
>
> (paras 5.1–5.5)

The long-standing EPO practice of granting patents on substances that result from some technical process was subsequently adopted by the European Union in the Biotechnology Directive.[11] Article 3(2) of that Directive states that 'biological material that is isolated from its natural environment or produced by means of a technical process may be the subject of an invention even if it previously occurred in nature'. Article 5(2) confirms that this rule applies to genes. This rule was also adopted in updates to the EPC and the Patents Act 1977.

As the *Howard Florey/Relaxin* case and subsequent statutory provisions suggest, one key argument in favour of treating some biological substances as inventions is that they must be 'isolated' from their natural environment. It is the process of isolating the material that is said to supply the necessary technical character. In relation to genes, the **isolation** process involves breaking the chemical bonds that connect the gene to the rest of the DNA. But is isolating the gene enough of a human intervention to make that gene a human invention rather than a mere discovery? In the next famous case (Case 7.2), the US Supreme Court said no.

Case 7.2 *Association for Molecular Pathology et al v Myriad Genetics Inc et al* 596 US 576 (2013) (US)

Facts

The gene is sometimes called the 'Jolie gene' by news outlets on the grounds that American actor and humanitarian, Angelina Jolie, has the gene.

Myriad Genetics (defendant–respondent), Inc (Myriad), discovered the precise location and sequence of two human genes: BRCA1 and BRCA2. Mutations of these genes can substantially increase the risks of breast and ovarian cancer. Myriad obtained several patents relating to the genes. Myriad subsequently developed medical tests for detecting mutations in a patient's BRCA1 and BRCA2 genes and evaluating their risk of developing cancer. The existence of the patent prevented other institutions from freely testing individuals for BRCA1 and BRCA2 genetic mutations.

The Association for Molecular Pathology (claimant–appellant) is an American non-profit professional society in the field of molecular diagnostics. The Association brought a lawsuit seeking a declaration that Myriad's patents were invalid.

Issue and Procedure

Was the act of isolating the DNA – separating a specific gene from the rest of the chromosome – an inventive act? The trial court held it was not and that the genes were discovered 'products of nature' rather than inventions. The issue was appealed to the Court of Appeals for the Federal Circuit that rejected the trial court decision and found isolated DNA to be an invention. The case was further appealed to the US Supreme Court who unanimously agreed that genes were discovered products of nature rather than inventions.

THOMAS J

We have 'long held that this provision contains an important implicit exception[:] Laws of nature, natural phenomena, and abstract ideas are not patentable'. Rather, 'they are the basic tools of scientific and technological work' that lie beyond the domain of patent protection. As the Court has explained, without this exception, there would be considerable danger that the grant of patents would 'tie up' the use of such tools and thereby 'inhibit future innovation premised upon them'. This would be at odds with the very point of patents, which exist to promote creation. . . .

The rule against patents on naturally occurring things is not without limits, however, for 'all inventions at some level embody, use, reflect, rest upon, or apply laws of nature, natural phenomena, or abstract ideas', and 'too broad an interpretation of this exclusionary principle could eviscerate patent law'. As we have recognized before, patent protection strikes a delicate balance between creating 'incentives that lead to creation, invention, and discovery' and 'imped[ing] the flow of information that might permit, indeed spur, invention'.

It is undisputed that Myriad did not create or alter any of the genetic information encoded in the BRCA1 and BRCA2 genes. The location and order of the nucleotides existed in nature before Myriad found them. Nor did Myriad create or alter the genetic structure of DNA. In stead, Myriad's principal contribution was uncovering the precise location and genetic sequence of the BRCA1 and BRCA2 genes within chromosomes 17 and 13. The question is whether this renders the genes patentable.

Myriad recognizes that our decision in *Chakrabarty* [447 US 303 (1980)] is central to this inquiry. In *Chakrabarty*, scientists added four plasmids to a bacterium, which enabled it to break down various components of crude oil. The Court held that the modified bacterium was patentable. It explained that the patent claim was 'not to a hitherto unknown natural phenomenon, but to a nonnaturally occurring manufacture or composition of matter – a product of human ingenuity 'having a distinctive name, character [and] use'. . . . In this case, by contrast, Myriad did not create anything. To be sure, it found an important and useful gene, but separating that gene from its surrounding genetic material is not an act of invention.

(pp. 589–90 [internal citations omitted])

ACTIVITY 7.3

Think back to the three different utilitarian arguments offered for patent rights in Chapter 6 (i.e. invention, disclosure and development). Can you see any of the rationales appearing in the decisions of the EPO and the US Supreme Court above? Do you find those reasons helpful or persuasive?

Although the US Supreme Court decided that naturally occurring DNA cannot be patented, it also held that *synthetic* DNA created in the laboratory was a patentable invention. Each gene contains genetic information – nucleotides known as 'exons' – that tells the body how to complete a given function. However, the gene also contains information – nucleotides known as 'introns' – that does not tell the body how to complete the function. Scientists can use naturally occurring DNA in the laboratory to produce DNA that only includes exons and omits introns – called cDNA (or complementary DNA). In all jurisdictions, cDNA remains an invention rather than a discovery.

Ada Lovelace (1815–52) was the first to invent an algorithm intended to be carried out by a computer. (Photo Interim Archives/Getty Images)

7.2.2 Computer Programs

A computer program is a series of instructions for a computer to perform. As programs are written in programming languages, it was initially believed in the 1970s that copyright, not patents, provided the appropriate legal tool for protecting them. As a result, and as highlighted in Chapter 3, computer programs are protected by copyright as a type of literary work. Hence, programs as such were excluded from patent protection.[12]

It might be puzzling to learn, therefore, that computer programs are today frequently protected by patents, as Case 7.3 illustrates. These cases also illustrate some of the practical consequences of the diverging approaches to technical character adopted by the UK and EPO.

Case 7.3 *Pension Benefits Systems Partnership/Controlling Pension Benefits Systems*, T931/95 [2002] EPOR 52

Facts

The Pension Benefits System Partnership (applicant–appellant) applied for a European patent in which they claimed a method for operating a pension benefits programme. This method involved using a range of data (e.g. average age of employees enrolled in the pension, the cost of life insurance), to make important calculations (e.g. the amount of benefits to be received by each employee upon retirement). In the patent, the partnership also claimed an apparatus that would execute the above method. The apparatus involved, in essence, programming a computer to carry out the relevant calculations.

Issue and Procedure

The application was denied by the EPO Examining Division on the grounds that the claimed method was a business method and thus excluded from patentability (Section 7.2.3 turns to business methods). The partnership appealed to the EPO Technical Board of Appeals (TBA). One of the issues raised was whether a computer programmed to carry out a method of pension calculations qualified as an unpatentable computer program as such. In a pithy section of their decision, the TBA held that the computer system was an invention.

> As we will see in the following sections, the nature of modern inventive activity means that many different types of inventions involve computers in some way. Business methods and presentations of information frequently are conducted on computers. These inventions are sometimes known broadly as 'computer-related inventions'.

> Again, remember to bear in mind the 'physicalist' misconceptions identified by Talha Syed. What is owned is the *knowledge* of how to program a computer to perform pension benefit calculations.

TBA

In the board's view a computer system suitably programmed for use in a particular field, even if that is the field of business and economy, has the character of a concrete apparatus in the sense of a physical entity, man-made for a utilitarian purpose and is thus an invention within the meaning of Article 52(1) EPC.

This means that, if a claim is directed to such an entity, the formal category of such a claim does in fact imply physical features of the claimed subject-matter which may qualify as technical features of the invention concerned and thus be relevant for its patentability.

(para 5)

Although the extract is short, the outcome is profound. The approach adopted by the EPO is sometimes called the '**any hardware**' approach. In essence, the TBA decided that if the computer system involved 'physical features', such as being operated by some form of hardware, then it would be an invention and not excluded under article 52. The practical result is that, despite the

Patents II: Patentability

Given the broad understanding of invention adopted by the EPO, some propose to reform article 52 EPC, potentially by removing computer programs from the list of 'not inventions'.[13]

statutory language, almost any computer program will be considered an invention by the EPO.

But as noted above, the UK does not adopt such a broad approach to technical character and accordingly did not adopt the 'any hardware' approach to computer programs. Case 7.4 illustrates how the UK courts' approach turns on whether the computer program makes a technical contribution to the field.

Case 7.4 *Symbian Limited v Comptroller General of Patents* [2008] EWCA Civ 1066

Facts

Symbian (respondent–claimant) created an invention called 'Mapping dynamic link libraries in a computing device'. A dynamic link library (DLL) is a library within a computer system that stores code. The code in the library tells the computer how to perform certain basic functions (e.g. email sending). Therefore, when a programmer writes a new app, they do not need to tell that app how to perform those basic functions. Instead, they can simply link the app to the DLL. This process essentially involves telling the app where in the DLL it will find the necessary code (a process called 'linking by ordinal'). This means the app can run faster and use less memory.

Unfortunately, problems can arise if the DLL is updated (e.g. through an operating system update). In that case, the location of the functions within the DLL can change. The result is that apps that previously linked to the functions may find those functions no longer working. In such cases, the app would likely crash and not function.

Symbian fixed this problem by splitting the DLL into two parts: a fixed part that could never change; and an extension part that could be updated. The fixed part contained functions that could be linked directly to the apps. The extension part could only be linked to the app via a secondary library which would update when the DLL was updated. The result was that the DLL could be updated without the links becoming broken.

Issue and Procedure

Was the invention a computer program as such? Or did it have a technical character? The UK IPO thought it fell within the computer program exclusion and rejected the application. Symbian appealed to the High Court where Mr Justice Patten agreed with Symbian that it was not a computer program as such. The UK IPO (appellant–defendant) appealed to the Court of Appeal. Among their arguments, the UK IPO claimed that for a computer program to have a technical character, it must have some novel effect *outside of the computer*. Another way of saying this is that a computer program that simply makes the computer work better is a computer program 'as such' and thus not patentable. As explained in the extract below, the Court of Appeal denied the appeal.

LORD NEUBERGER OF ABBOTSBURY

We turn to address the issue whether the Application in this case was excluded from registration on the ground that it was a 'program for a computer as such'. The mere fact that what is sought to be registered is a computer program is plainly not determinative. Given that the Application seeks to register a computer program, the issue has to be resolved by answering the question whether it reveals a 'technical' contribution to the state of the art. Despite Mr Prescott's [counsel for the appellant] sustained and elegant, and not unjustified, attack on the vagueness and arbitrariness of the term 'technical', that question embodies the consistent jurisprudence of the Board (even though the precise meaning given to the term has not been consistent), and it has been applied by this court in *Merrill Lynch*, *Gale*, and (arguably with an inconsistent result) *Fujitsu*; indeed, it was accepted, through stage 4, in *Aerotel*.

Based on these principles, we consider that Patten J was right and that the claimed invention does make a technical contribution, and is not therefore precluded from registration by art 52(2)(c)...

More positively, not only will a computer containing the instructions in question 'be a better computer', as in *Gale*, but, unlike in that case, it can also be said that the instructions 'solve a "technical" problem lying with the computer itself'. Indeed, the effect of the instant alleged invention is not merely within the computer programmed with the relevant instructions. The beneficial consequences of those instructions will feed into the cameras and other devices and products, which, as mentioned at [3] above, include such computer systems. Further, the fact that the improvement may be to software programmed into the computer rather than hardware forming part of the computer cannot make a difference see *Vicom*; indeed the point was also made by Fox LJ in *Merrill Lynch*.

Putting it another way, a computer with this program operates better than a similar prior art computer. To say 'oh but that is only because it is a better program the computer itself is unchanged' gives no credit to the practical reality of what is achieved by the program. As a matter of such reality there is more than just a 'better program', there is a faster and more reliable computer.

(paras 48, 53–54, 56)

Although the Court of Appeal found that the invention in question had effects *outside* the computer (i.e. by making 'cameras and other devices and products' work better), it was sympathetic to the idea that an invention that simply makes the computer itself work better supplied a technical effect. Subsequently, the UK IPO

Patents II: Patentability

issued a Practice Notice stating that computer programs which solve technical problems either external or internal to the computer (such as the tendency to crash) would be regarded as having the necessary technical effect.[14]

Does the acceptance of effects within the computer itself make the UK position the same as the EPO's position on computer programs? After all, computer programs are necessary for computers to work at all. It could be argued that the mere fact that the program allows a computer to work is a technical effect. However, that argument was dismissed by the UK Chancery Division in *Gemstar*.[15] In that case, Mr Justice Mann found that for a program to make a technical contribution within the computer, it must have some effect such as making the computer work more efficiently or effectively.

The result is that a more restrictive approach to the patentability of computer programs lives on in the UK, while the EPO has adopted a more permissive approach. Nevertheless, even within the UK, the scope of computer program patentability has widened significantly beyond that imagined when the Patents Act and EPC were drafted.

7.2.3   Business Methods

In the twenty-first century, one of the most contentious exclusions relates to methods of doing business. Businesses frequently 'invent' new ways of selling goods and services: the McDonald brothers invented the modern drive-through restaurant in the 1940s,[16] the Singer Company invented the idea of franchising to distribute their sewing machines.[17]

The idea that business methods are not inventions with a technical character has, however, faced challenges since the advent of modern computing. Today many new ways of doing business involve computers in some way. This raises a question: if a business method is performed using a computer, does that method now have the necessary technical quality that means it can be patented? In the EPO jurisprudence, the answer appears to be yes.

Case 7.5 *Hitachi/Auction method* (T258/03) [2004] EPOR 55

Facts

A 'Dutch auction' is an auction for goods where the starting price is initially set high, and then gradually reduced until a buyer is found. This form of auction is centuries old. Hitachi (applicant–appellant) applied for a European patent on their system of conducting Dutch auctions. Claim 1 of the application claimed 'an automatic auction method executed in a server'. Claim 1 involved conducting a Dutch auction over a computer network. Their application was denied by the EPO Examining Division on various grounds. The case was appealed to the EPO's TBA.

Issue and Procedure

Among the issues presented was: whether performing a Dutch auction over a computer network was a business method 'as such' or whether it involved a technical character? The TBA found that it was an invention with a technical character and, in so doing, extended the 'any hardware' conception of technical character to business methods.

TBA

4.5 Finally, the Board in its present composition is not convinced that the wording of Art. 52(2)(c) EPC, according to which 'schemes, rules and methods for performing mental acts, playing games or doing business' shall not be regarded as inventions within the meaning of Art. 52(1) EPC, imposes a different treatment of claims directed to activities and claims directed to entities for carrying out these activities. What matters having regard to the concept of 'invention' within the meaning of Art. 52(1) EPC is the presence of technical character which may be implied by the physical features of an entity or the nature of an activity, or may be conferred to a non-technical activity by the use of technical means. In particular, the Board holds that the latter cannot be considered to be a non-invention 'as such' within the meaning of Arts 52(2) and (3) EPC. Hence, in the Board's view, activities falling within the notion of a non-invention 'as such' would typically represent purely abstract concepts devoid of any technical implications.

4.6 The Board is aware that its comparatively broad interpretation of the term 'invention' in Art. 52(1) EPC will include activities which are so familiar that their technical character tends to be overlooked, such as the act of writing using pen and paper. Needless to say, however, this does not imply that all methods involving the use of technical means are patentable. They still have to be new, represent a non-obvious technical solution to a technical problem, and be susceptible of industrial application.

(paras 33–34)

Once again, some might find the short extract rather startling. Despite the exclusion for business method patents in the legislation, the TBA has embraced the view that merely writing a business method down on paper using a pen is sufficient to give it a technical character.

As with computer programs, the UK's approach does not go so far. The requirement that the alleged invention make some technical contribution to the

Patents II: Patentability

art, and not merely be operated through a physical means, has resulted in several rejected applications. To illustrate, in *Merrill Lynch's Application*, the Court of Appeal agreed that an automatic share-trading system operated by a computer program was an unpatentable business method.[18]

7.2.4 Presentation of Information

The fissure between the EPO and UK approach is also to be found in presentations of information. This category excludes claims which relate merely to ways of presenting information to humans. As Case 7.6 demonstrates, the UK adopts an approach similar to that used when assessing computer programs.

Case 7.6 *Gemstar-TV Guide International Inc v Virgin Media Ltd* [2009] EWHC 3068 (Ch)

Facts

In recent decades, the number of television channels has increased significantly. Programming guides are timetables that tell the viewer what will be broadcast on the channels at any given time. In the pre-digital age, programming guides were printed on paper. Gemstar (claimant) owned patents on electronic programming guides (or EPGs). EPGs presented the timetables on the television screen.

Virgin (defendant) provided its subscribers with a set-top box which enabled them to receive and record its programmes. It broadcast programme information on the television as an EPG.

Issue and Procedure

Gemstar sued Virgin for patent infringement. Virgin claimed in response that the patent was related to excluded subject matter because the invention consisted merely of the presentation of information. Mann J adopted the same analysis for presentations of information as is today adopted for computer programs. The key question is therefore whether some technical contribution is made outside of the information itself. Mr Justice Mann held that, in this instance, that test was not met.

MANN J

I do not consider that the single channel element of the Single Channel patent achieves this. One starts with the provision of TV programme information in a grid. This seems plainly to be the presentation of information. The raw information is the detailing of the programmes. This has to be given over somehow (otherwise it exists only in some abstract ether). If it were spoken, that would be a presentation. If it were a written list, that would be presentation. In fact it starts (in this patent) in a grid. That, equally, is presentation of that information. Then, as a result of cursor movement and marking, the information is then presented in a different format – a list. That end result is, equally, a presentation of information. All that has happened is that information is presented in a different way (and perhaps in a different quantity). So the starting point and the end point are, in my view, plainly presentation of information. The middle factor is the movement of a cursor, the marking of the chosen programme which (unstated in the claims) causes the display to change. That seems to me to be accurately described as part of the selection mechanism. No-one suggested that it involved a new technical step – selecting material on screen and clicking on it so as to cause a change in its appearance on screen was part of the common general knowledge by 1990.

I reach the same conclusion by standing back and looking at the thing overall. It is still the presentation of information with no, or no new, technical effect. Mr Birss [for the claimant] sought to say that there was a technical effect, and it lay in a better user interface (his mantra in this part of the case). I think that that is a form of words which disguises the reality. Providing a better (or new) user interface is not a technical description. What matters is technical effects, and that description does not shed any light on that. He frankly admitted that if that is not a technical effect, then he loses. It is not, and he does.

(paras 58–59)

Although the Gemstar patent failed, other patents have successfully met the requirement of technical effect outside of the information. To illustrate, *HTC Europe v Apple* concerned the 'slide to unlock' feature of older Apple iPhones.[19] iPhone users unlocked the screen by sliding their finger horizontally across the touch screen. Apple owned a patent on this feature. It was upheld in part because the feature did not merely tell users some information (i.e. how to unlock the screen). Instead, the feature made some technical contribution beyond the information in the sense that it made for an improved unlocking mechanism.

The EPO courts have also adopted the same analysis as used in respect of computer programs (i.e. the any hardware approach). Presumably therefore, the Gemstar patent would be upheld under the EPO approach because the programming information was delivered by some technical means.

ACTIVITY 7.4

We have now examined a range of phenomena which, according to statute, are 'not inventions': discoveries, computer programs, business methods, presentations of information, mental acts. Yet, the reality is that genes are patentable, and in the EPO system, nearly all inventions implemented on computers are patentable. Using the utilitarian arguments for and against patents, covered in Section 6.2.3, do you think the expansion of patentable subject matter is justifiable?

7.2.5   Mental Acts

Again, bear in mind 'physicalist' misconceptions. No one can own the physical process of a brain performing mental acts. But one might be able to own the knowledge associated with such mental acts.

Despite the growing divide between the UK and EPO, one area where the two approaches might converge is the exclusion for methods of performing mental acts. Mental acts, such as performing arithmetic calculations (e.g. finding the square root of a number), are excluded from patentability. But questions arise, once again, when those acts are carried out on a computer. The EPO's any hardware approach often results in the patentability of such inventions. In Case 7.7, the UK arrived at much the same result albeit through distinct reasoning.

Case 7.7 *Halliburton Energy Service's Patent Application* [2011] EWCH 2508 (Pat)

Facts

Roller cone drill bits are used to drill oil wells. As the drilling continues, the drill bit eventually wears out. In this case, the invention concerned a computer simulation that enabled drill bit designers to calculate how quickly a drill bit would wear out. With that information, designers could design drill bits which would last longer before wearing out. Halliburton Energy Service's (claimant–appellant) patent application was denied by the Comptroller-General of Patents of the UK IPO (defendant–respondent) on the grounds that it was related to a method of performing a mental act.

Issue and Procedure

In the High Court Chancery Division, Mr Justice Birss (as he then was) summarised two ways of interpreting the exclusion on mental act methods: a wide and a narrow interpretation. According to the wide interpretation, an application should be rejected if it relates to something which is *capable* of being performed mentally. Accordingly, a computer program that finds the square root of numbers would be rejected because it relates to something that the human mind could perform (i.e.

finding the square root). Alternatively, under the narrow interpretation, the exclusion should apply only to acts that are *actually* carried out mentally. Thus, while one could not claim the process of calculating a square root, one could claim a computer program that has been programmed to perform the calculation. In the following extract, Birss explains why the narrow interpretation is appropriate. Consequently, the implementation of the calculation by a computer was sufficient to avoid the exclusion.

BIRSS J

This narrow interpretation is the one favoured by Jacob LJ in Aerotel, doubting the views of Aldous LJ on this point in Fujitsu [favouring the wide interpretation]. As Jacob LJ said (in paragraph 98 of Aerotel):

we are by no means convinced that Aldous L.J.'s provisional view is correct. There is no particular reason to suppose that 'mental act' was intended to exclude things wider than, for instance, methods of doing mental arithmetic (every now and then someone comes up with a trick for this, for instance Trachtenberg's system) or remembering things (e.g. in its day, Pelmanism).

The mental act exclusion came up again in Kapur [2008] EWHC 649 (Pat) before Floyd J. In this judgment Floyd J again reviewed the same line of authorities (now up to and including Cappellini) and held that the narrow view of the mental act exclusion was the right one. Floyd J said:

In Cappellini and Bloomberg [2007] EWHC 476 (Pat) Pumfrey J held that, as the reasoning about the mental act exclusion was not necessary for the decision in either Fujitsu or Aerotel, he was free to choose between them as authority, while acknowledging that Aerotel, the more recent, comes with a clearly expressed doubt as to the correctness of Fujitsu. He considered that the exclusion will apply if it is possible to infringe the claim simply by doing mental acts, such as calculations. Although Mr Cappellini's application had been rejected on this amongst other grounds, it is not clear to me that Pumfrey J in fact came to a conclusion on this exclusion in the appeal. Be that as it may, the weight of authority favours a rather narrow view of this exclusion, namely whether the claim actually covers a purely mental implementation of the claimed invention.

In my judgment the narrow view of the exclusion is the correct one. More specifically I think the correct view is that, provided the claim cannot be infringed by mental acts as such, its subject matter is not caught by the exclusion. It seems to me that if this were not so the scope of the exclusion would be unacceptably broad, as well as being

> uncertain in scope. It follows that the exclusion will not apply if there are appropriate non-mental limitations in the claim. In those circumstances it will not be possible to infringe the claim by mental acts alone, and the invention will not comprise a method for performing a mental act.
>
> So the balance of authority in England is in favour of the narrow approach to the mental act exclusion. I will only add that, if the matter were free from authority, I would favour the narrow interpretation on its own merits. The wide construction seems to me to be uncertain in scope and I am not aware of any good reason why the exclusion needs to be interpreted widely. On the other hand I can see a logic behind the narrow interpretation, preventing patents being granted which could be infringed by a purely mental process. Allowing for the possibility of patent infringement by thought alone seems to me to be undesirable.
>
> (paras 43, 53, 57)

The UK approach to mental acts has some similarities to the EPO any hardware approach. Under both approaches, the introduction of a computer is sufficient to transform an otherwise unpatentable mental act into an invention with a technical character.

ACTIVITY 7.5

Can you see any 'good reason why the exclusion needs to be interpreted widely' *contra* the findings of Mr Justice Birss?

7.3 EXCLUDED INVENTIONS

An application may be rejected because its subject matter is not an invention. But there is also a group of inventions (i.e. things that might have a technical character) that are nevertheless not patentable subject matter. This group includes: inventions that are immoral or whose patenting would contravene public policy; varieties of plants and animals and biological processes for production of plants and animals; and methods of veterinary and medical treatment.

7.3.1 Public Policy and Morality

Section 1(3) of the Patents Act says that a patent 'shall not be granted for an invention the commercial exploitation of which would be contrary to public policy or morality'. Article 53(a) EPC has an analogous provision for inventions, the commercial exploitation of which would be contrary to '*ordre public*' or morality'. For simplicity, we will treat 'public policy' and '*ordre public*' as synonyms in this subsection.

This provision is somewhat puzzling. After all, some inventions – for example firearms and other weapons – are routinely patented despite a compelling argument that their commercial exploitation is profoundly immoral. Furthermore, many jurisdictions outside of the UK/EPC systems do not have such a rule.[20]

> As illustrated in Figure 6.4, the first patent specification disclosed James Puckle's machine gun!

Within the UK and EPC systems, this provision was used only infrequently before breakthroughs in modern biotechnology in the late twentieth century. These breakthroughs prompted the European Union to pass the Directive on the Legal Protection of Biotechnological Inventions 1998. The rules contained therein were then subsequently imported into the UK Patents Act. Schedule A2 paragraph 3 now clarifies that the following are not to be considered inventions:

> 3. The following are not patentable inventions –
>   (a) the human body, at the various stages of its formation and development, and the simple discovery of one of its elements, including the sequence or partial sequence of a gene;
>   (b) processes for cloning human beings;
>   (c) processes for modifying the germ line genetic identity of human beings;
>   (d) uses of human embryos for industrial or commercial purposes;
>   (e) processes for modifying the genetic identity of animals which are likely to cause them suffering without any substantial medical benefit to man or animal, and also animals resulting from such processes;
>   (f) any variety of animal or plant or any essentially biological process for the production of animals or plants, not being a micro-biological or other technical process or the product of such a process.

An analogous provision appears in rule 28 of the Implementing Regulations to the Convention on the Grant of European Patents.

Subsequently, courts have considered the inventions listed in paragraph 3 to be *ipso facto* (i.e. by that fact) inventions which would breach section 1(3). But even if a biotechnological invention does not fall into this list, it may still nevertheless be denied a patent on the more general section 1(3) grounds. This relationship is demonstrated in Case 7.8: the long-running battle over the OncoMouse.

Case 7.8 *Harvard/Transgenic Animals*, T315/03 (2006) OJ EPO 15

Facts

In the 1980s, scientists at Harvard University (applicant–respondent) developed the OncoMouse. The OncoMouse is a type of mouse that had been genetically modified to carry a specific gene: an 'activated oncogene'. The presence of the activated oncogene significantly increased the probability that the mice would develop cancer. Scientists could then use the mice in cancer research.

Issue and Procedure

In 1985, Harvard University applied for a European patent on the OncoMouse. Their initial patent claimed a 'transgenic non-human eucaryotic animal whose germ cells and somatic cells contain an activated oncogene'. And so began a legal battle that would last approximately two decades.

The EPO Examining Division initially rejected the patent but refused to engage with article 53(a) on the grounds that it was not the place of patent law to resolve ethical questions. Harvard appealed to the TBA who remitted the case back to the Examining Division with an instruction to consider the article 53(a) issue. The TBA found that applying this provision would require 'a careful weighing up of the suffering of animals and possible risks to the environment on the one hand, and the invention's usefulness to mankind on the other' (known below as the 'T 19/90 test' in the following extract). This approach was framed as a 'utilitarian balancing' test.

The Examining Division subsequently granted the patent, finding the benefit to mankind in cancer treatment outweighed the suffering of the mice. After which, the patent was opposed by several parties. The opposition proceedings before the Opposition Division continued throughout the 1990s until 2003. This eventually resulted in an amended version of the patent being upheld. The amended patent claimed 'a transgenic *rodent* whose germ cells and somatic cells contain an activated oncogene. . .'.

The decision of the Opposition Division was then appealed to the Technical Board of Appeal. At which time, Harvard University made an 'auxiliary request' to the TBA wherein it asked the court to consider, not only the patentability of a 'transgenic rodent' but also to consider the patentability of a 'transgenic *mouse*'. The extract below concerns that auxiliary request. The issue presented is: does it contravene the rules on *ordre public* to commercially exploit a transgenic mouse? The TBA thought not.

Before beginning, the TBA refers to 'Rule 23(d)'. This rule is now contained in Rule 28(d) and is analogous to the UK Patents Act Schedule A2 paragraph 3(e).

TBA

13.2 Article 53(a) EPC

The Rule 23d(d) test

Under Article 53(a) EPC the first auxiliary request must first be assessed according to the 'balancing test' in Rule 23d(d) EPC. As regards the likelihood of animal suffering, there is evidence in the patent itself showing that the specific oncomice produced by the method of the opposed patent develop specific neoplasms and that they have been used for testing compounds suspected of being carcinogens or else suspected of conferring protection against the development of these neoplasms. There is thus not just a likelihood but a certainty of animal suffering. Moreover, as already observed in respect of the main request, the parties agreed that any animals resulting from the method of the patent would suffer and this must include mice.

As regards the likelihood of substantial medical benefit, this can at the very least be inferred from the patent itself: the purpose of both the claimed method and the oncomice thereby produced and used for test purposes is to further cancer research. Additionally there is evidence on file, in the form of declarations and post-published documents, demonstrating actual medical benefits achieved using mice such as those obtained by the claimed process. For example, it is stated in document (81) that 'the oncomouse may be the closest we can get to a human situation' and that 'key genetic pathways controlling mammary gland development (and as an extension cancer) are conserved between mouse and man, and thus the mouse serves as the best approximation'. . . .

Accordingly, the Board considers that the subject-matter of claims 1 and 19 of the first auxiliary request 'passes' the test in Rule 23d(d) EPC and thus does not fall within the category of inventions for which patents shall not be granted under that Rule. The request must therefore be assessed under Article 53(a) EPC without reference to that Rule: in other words, a 'real' Article 53(a) EPC objection arises.

The T 19/90 test

The limitation of the auxiliary request to 'mouse' also produces a different result in the application of the test in T 19/90 test (OJ EPO 1990, 476, Reasons, paragraph 5). Applying this test, on one side of the balance it is again agreed between the parties that the patented method causes actual suffering to the mice used. On the other side of the balance, actual medical benefit has been demonstrated and this benefit is clearly of use to mankind. Unlike the main request, no suffering is envisaged to any animals without a corresponding prospect of benefit. Thus far, assessment under the T 19/90 test leads to the same result as under the Rule 23d(d) EPC test. However, the T 19/90 test permits other considerations to be taken into account as mentioned above. In the present case two such other considerations were raised in argument by the appellants and opponent the degree of animal suffering and the possibility of using non-animal alternatives to achieve the same aims as the patent in suit.

No evidence of the degree (as opposed to the existence) of animal suffering, an argument advanced by appellant 1 and opponent 3, was produced, which the Board finds wholly unsurprising. To suggest that the degree of suffering could be material is to suggest the possibility of a distinction between 'acceptable suffering' and 'unacceptable suffering'. In the Board's opinion this is not a distinction which the parties in question really wished to evoke and it is certainly not a distinction which would assist in deciding this or similar cases. ... Accordingly, the degree of animal suffering argument is of no assistance in making the T 19/90 test and, if anything, the unhappy distinction it suggests detracts from the case of those making the argument.

As regards non-animal alternatives, appellants 1 and 3 to 6 and opponent 3 all argued that these should be taken into account. The most pertinent of the alternatives mentioned was cell cultures but no evidence was filed showing any advantage over, or even equality of benefit with, the method of the patent. The respondent rebutted these arguments by observing that only an animal offers the opportunity to use an entire organism including for example the immune system. The respondent also filed a declaration explaining why oncomice provided advantages over cell cultures (document (81), paragraphs 3 and 4). Thus, if this alternative is added to the matters to be weighed up in the T 19/90 test, the result will be, on the available evidence, to tilt the balance away from the appellants and in favour of the respondent.

The same result is reached when applying the T 19/90 test to balance environmental risks against usefulness to mankind. In this case, the same factors are considered except that the agreed suffering to animals is replaced by possible threats to the environment if oncomice were to escape (or to be released, deliberately or accidentally) into the wild. As is only to be expected of a danger yet to materialise, there was no evidence to support such environmental arguments which played very little part in the appeal proceedings. The environmental arguments are thus if anything weaker in this case than in [*Plant Genetic Systems/Glutamine Synthetase Inhibitors*] T 356/

93 (OJ EPO 1995, 545, Reasons, paragraphs 18 to 19) in which, as regards similar arguments relating to the alleged risks of 'escape' of genetically modified plants, Board 3.3.4 considered a threat to the environment could be grounds for an Article 53(a) EPC objection but that, on the evidence before it, such a threat had not been established. . .

The Board considers the environmental issues are at the utmost of neutral effect on the case. While a risk of release or escape exists, just as there is such a risk with zoo or circus animals, the risk can only be regarded as minimally more than hypothetical when one considers the secure conditions under which laboratory mice are kept and the level of regulation of the use and keeping of animals for experimental purposes in most countries. Further, in the event of release or escape, it must be questionable whether oncomice would cause any damage, let alone any lasting damage, to the environment. The only perceivable threat is that, by mating with mice already in the wild, the oncogene would be spread. Against that, there must be the possibility that, because of their manipulated state, oncomice would not survive as long in the wild as non-manipulated mice.

(paras 13.2.1–13.2.2, 13.2.4–13.2.9 [internal cross referencing omitted])

By contrast, the TBA rejected the patent claim on a 'transgenic *rodent*'. The term 'rodent' included not just mice, but other animals such as squirrels and beavers. Yet, no evidence had been provided that genetically modifying the latter type of rodent would be helpful for cancer research. As a result, the TBA found that claim related to unpatentable subject matter as contained in the old Rule 23(d) (now Rule 28(d)).

There are, however, competing approaches to public policy and morality, and the TBA in *Harvard/Transgenic Animals* was careful to limit their analysis to cases concerning genetic manipulation of animals. Case 7.9 is conventionally understood to depart from the 'utilitarian balancing' test employed by the TBA in *Harvard/Transgenic Animals*.

Case 7.9 *Plant Genetic Systems* [1995] OJ EPO 545

Facts

Herbicides are often applied to agricultural plants to kill weeds and fungal diseases. Unfortunately, the application of the herbicides can also damage the plants.

In 1990, a European patent was granted to Plant Genetic Systems (applicant–respondent) for genetically engineered plants and seeds. This involved modifying the DNA of the plants. The genetic modification in question made the plants and seeds resistant to a particular class of herbicides. The result was that herbicides could be applied to the plants without doing lasting damage to them.

The patent was opposed by the environmental organisation, Greenpeace (opponent–appellant) on the grounds that exploitation of the patent was contrary to *ordre public* or morality.

Issue and Procedure

The Opposition Division dismissed the opposition and upheld the patent. In doing so, it departed from the T 19/90 utilitarian balancing approach.

Greenpeace appealed to the TBA. In making their appeal, Greenpeace argued that surveys conducted in Sweden demonstrated a negative public opinion about genetically modified crops, and that if the T19/90 balancing test had been adopted, the patents would have been denied. On the latter point, Greenpeace argued that the exploitation of genetically modified plants risked serious environmental damage by altering the ecosystem.

This left the TBA to decide: what was the correct approach to *ordre public* and morality in a case such as this? And what is the role of survey evidence in making that decision? They answer these questions in the following extract and upheld the patent. The case took place before the Biotechnology Directive. There is accordingly no discussion of Rule 28 EPC.

> The approach to morality adopted here was broadly followed as well in the *Howard Florey Institute Relaxin* case discussed in Section 7.2.1.

TBA

It is generally accepted that the concept of 'ordre public' covers the protection of public security and the physical integrity of individuals as part of society. This concept encompasses also the protection of the environment. Accordingly, under Article 53(a) EPC, inventions the exploitation of which is likely to breach public peace or social order (for example, through acts of terrorism) or to seriously prejudice the environment are to be excluded from patentability as being contrary to 'ordre public'.

The concept of morality is related to the belief that some behaviour is right and acceptable whereas other behaviour is wrong, this belief being founded on the totality of the accepted norms which are deeply rooted in a particular culture. For the purposes of the EPC, the culture in question is the culture inherent in European society and civilisation. Accordingly, under Article 53(a) EPC, inventions the exploitation of which is not in conformity with the conventionally-accepted standards of conduct pertaining to this culture are to be excluded from patentability as being contrary to morality.

In order to establish that the subject-matter claimed in the patent in suit is objectionable under Article 53(a) EPC, the Appellants rely inter alia on:

(i) a survey conducted among Swedish farmers on questions relating to genetic engineering and 'super crops', according to which the large majority (82%) is against genetic engineering, and, in particular, against 'super crops' (e.g. herbicide-resistant plants); and

(ii) an opinion poll carried out in Switzerland on the patentability of animals and plants, according to which the majority (69%) is opposed thereto.

They submit that both survey and opinion poll are probative of public opinion to the effect that patents should not be granted for these kinds of inventions. The Board does not agree with this conclusion. The results of surveys or opinion polls can scarcely be considered decisive per se when assessing patentability of a given subject-matter with regard to the requirements of Article 53(a) EPC, for the following reasons:

- Surveys and opinion polls do not necessarily reflect 'ordre public' concerns or moral norms that are deeply rooted in European culture.

- The results of surveys and opinion polls can fluctuate in an unforeseeable manner within short time periods and can be very easily influenced and controlled, depending on a number of factors, including the type of questions posed, the choice and the size of the representative sample, etc.

- Surveys of particular groups of people (e.g. farmers) tend to reflect their specific interests and/or their biased beliefs.

- As stated above, the question whether Article 53(a) EPC constitutes a bar to patentability is to be considered in each particular case on its merits.

- Consequently, if surveys and opinion polls were to be relied upon, they would have to be made ad hoc on the basis of specific questions in relation to the particular subject-matter claimed. For obvious reasons, such a procedure is scarcely feasible.

- Like national law(s) and regulation(s) approving or disapproving the exploitation of an invention (cf. point 7 supra), a survey or an opinion poll showing that a particular group of people or the majority of the population of some or all of the Contracting States opposes the granting of a patent for a specified subject-matter, cannot serve as a sufficient criterion for establishing that the said subject-matter is contrary to 'ordre public' or morality.

In the present case, no conclusive evidence has been presented by the Appellants showing that the exploitation of the claimed subject-matter is likely to seriously prejudice the environment. In fact, most of the Appellants' arguments are based on the possibility that some undesired, destructive events (e.g. the transformation of crops into weeds, spreading of the herbicide-resistance gene to other plants, damage to the ecosystem) might occur. Of course, such events may occur to some extent. This fact has even been admitted by the Respondents. However, in the Board's judgement, the documentary evidence submitted on this subject is not sufficient to substantiate the existence of a threat to the environment such as to represent a bar to patentability under Article 53(a) EPC.

However, in the Board's view, the quoted documents do not lead to the definite conclusion that the exploitation of any of the claimed subject-matter would seriously prejudice the environment and is, therefore, contrary to 'ordre public'. It would be unjustified to deny a patent under Article 53(a) EPC merely on the basis of possible, not yet conclusively-documented hazards.

In the present case, since no sufficient evidence of actual disadvantages has been adduced, the assessment of patentability with regard to Article 53(a) EPC may not be based on the so-called 'balancing exercise' of benefits and disadvantages, as submitted by the Appellants. The Board observes that such a 'balancing exercise' is not the only way of assessing patentability with regard to Article 53(a) EPC, but just one possible way, perhaps useful in situations in which an actual damage and/or disadvantage (e.g. suffering of animals as in the case of decision T 19/90 supra) exists.

(paras 5–6, 15, 18.6–18.8)

Despite the potential differences between the TBA's approaches, the TBA in *Harvard/Transgenic Animals* wrote that they were in 'full agreement' with the position from *Plant Genetic Systems* that opinion poll and survey evidence provide little probative evidence as to morality.

7.3.2 Plants and Animals

But there might potentially be another reason why the OncoMouse should not qualify as patentable subject matter. Schedule A2, paragraph 3(f) says that 'any variety of animal or plant' or any 'essentially biological process for the production of animals or plants' should not be protected by patents. The same rule is found in article 53(b) EPC 2000.

The origin of this provision is slightly mysterious. In 1961, the International Convention for the protection of New Varieties of Plants (UPOV) created a **sui generis** regime for the protection of plant varieties. Given that plant varieties could be protected by other non-patent means, it was agreed by the EPC contracting states that plant varieties should not be subject to patents as well.[21] But it is not entirely clear why animal varieties have been excluded too.

In any event, in the OncoMouse litigation, the TBA also confronted the claim that the OncoMouse could not be patented because it amounted to patenting a variety of animal. This resulted in a particularly difficult interpretive problem: the French, English and German versions of the EPC all used slightly different language. The English version refers to animal 'varieties', the French version refers to animal 'races' and the German version uses animal 'species'. Problematically, these terms do not have precisely the same meaning.

Within biology, taxonomy is the science of naming and classifying different organisms based on shared characteristics. The organisms are typically categorised according to their taxonomic rank. To illustrate, consider the species *Mus musculus*, commonly known as the house mouse. The taxonomic rank of the house mouse is illustrated in Figure 7.2. Reading Figure 7.2 from the top to bottom illustrates the house mouse taxonomy.

Starting from the top, one finds that the house mouse is a eukaryotic organism (they are not, for example, bacteria) and falls into the domain of 'eukarya'. They are not a fungus or plant life, but are a type of animal so they fall into the

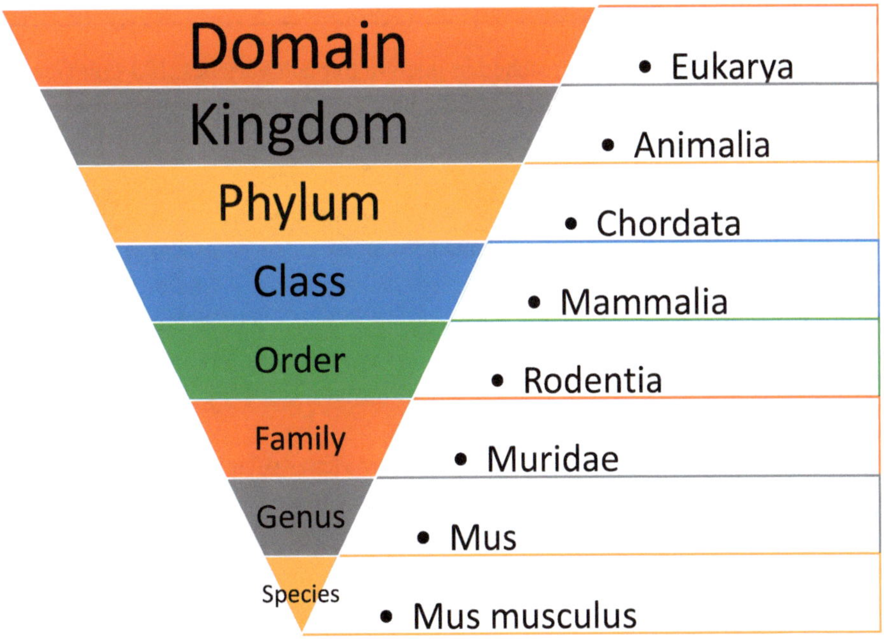

The term **'sui generis'** appears quite a lot in IP law. The term is Latin for 'of its own kind'. In IP, the term is used to refer to some type of rights which are distinct from the standard IP rights.

Domain	• Eukarya
Kingdom	• Animalia
Phylum	• Chordata
Class	• Mammalia
Order	• Rodentia
Family	• Muridae
Genus	• Mus
Species	• Mus musculus

Figure 7.2 *Mus musculus* taxonomy

'animalia' kingdom. Jumping to class, one finds that house mice are mammals (not reptiles or birds, for example). They are part of the order of 'rodentia' or rodent. And their genus is mouse. The term 'variety' does not appear in Figure 7.2 but is considered a subpart of 'species'. The term 'race' also does not appear because it is not typically considered a 'formal' taxonomic rank. It is, however, informally used to mean a subpart of species, much like variety.

In the OncoMouse case, the TBA decided that the claim to a transgenic 'rodent' did not fall within the scope of article 53(b). By claiming a 'rodent', Harvard University were claiming a type of *order* in taxonomic terms (i.e. 'rodentia'). This aided Harvard University's case. To see why, consider the German version of the EPC. It says that *species* cannot be patented. But Harvard were not trying to patent a *species*, they were trying to patent an *order*. Similarly, Harvard did not attempt to patent a *variety* or a *race*, as specified in the English and French versions of the EPC. Thus, regardless of which version of the EPC was adopted, Harvard avoided the article 53(b) exclusion on the grounds that their claim was to a *higher taxonomic rank* than that prohibited in the treaty. The very same conclusion was reached in relation to their auxiliary claim to a transgenic *mouse*. The term *mouse* was understood to refer to the genus *mus*, not to a particular species.

ACTIVITY 7.6

Having considered the *Harvard/Transgenic Mouse* case, take some time to reflect. Why is it impermissible to patent a species, but it would be permissible to patent an even higher classification of organism, such as a genus or order? There is no discussion for this activity.

A similar result has been reached in relation to plant varieties. In *Plant Genetic Systems*, the Opposition Division initially held that the genetically modified plants were not a plant variety; instead, the claim related to a much 'broader group' (or higher taxonomic rank) than a variety. The TBA subsequently agreed that the claim was not directed to a plant variety. Nevertheless, the TBA held the claim *included* plant varieties and thus related to an excluded invention. This position however has largely been overturned subsequently. Article 4(2) of the Biotechnology Directive, incorporated into the Patents Act 1977 and EPC, makes clear that an invention will be patentable if the claim is 'not confined' to plant varieties. The result is that while a plant variety cannot be claimed, broader taxonomic ranks can be.

The last part of the exclusion relates not to varieties of animals or plants, but to 'essentially biological processes' for the production of animals or plants. One cannot, for example, patent a process of selectively breeding racehorses for a certain type of characteristic (e.g. speed) or a process of crossbreeding dogs to create designer breeds (e.g. labradoodles or cockapoos). However, one might be able to patent a process which has a sufficiently technical character to mean the process is no longer 'essentially biological'. While the existence of some technical step is not generally sufficient, it may be possible to patent a process in which the technical step introduces a new trait to the genome. For example, the process of introducing a specific type of characteristic into the genome of racehorses (e.g. increased fast-twitch muscle fibres) may have the sufficient type of technical character to make it patentable.

7.3.3 Methods of Veterinary and Medical Treatment

A last point to note is alongside immoral inventions and plant and animal varieties, methods of treatment (including surgery or therapy) and methods of diagnosis are also not patentable subject matter, according to article 4A of the Patents Act 1977 (and article 53(c) of the EPC 2000). Crucially, this exception only relates to *methods* and not to *products*. The result is that new drugs, new vaccines (such as the Covid-19 vaccines), or surgical tools are patentable subject matter.

7.4 SUMMARY

In 1597, the famous English scientist, Sir Francis Bacon wrote that 'knowledge … is power'.[22] And through patents, society tries to grant ownership over a certain type of knowledge: knowledge with a technical character. Yet, whether knowledge is metaphysically the kind of thing that can be owned is contentious. To some, like Jefferson, the very nature of knowledge is to be uncontrollable like fire or air.

Nevertheless, there might be a utilitarian case for granting some rights in relation to knowledge. While society is better off with some types of foundational knowledge remaining in the public domain (such as $E=MC^2$), granting patents to inventors like Christiansen might encourage invention, disclosure and technological development. Whether that utilitarian case is persuasive in cases of computer programs, genes, business methods, genetically modified mice, is another matter. Although these phenomena as such are exempted from patentability, the reality is that they are frequently subject to patent rights.

How does this affect the 'patent bargain' introduced in Section 6.5? It depends significantly on whether expanding the scope of patentable subject matter will result in greater amounts of invention, disclosure, and development in the future. The public grants inventors monopolies over a far greater range of intangible phenomena today than it ever has before. If the effect of this expansion is that inventors will invent and disclose more knowledge, then the public is the ultimate winner. However, if those benefits do not transpire, then the public only loses.

7.5 SELF-ASSESSMENT

Before moving on, try to answer the following questions to consolidate your learning. Answers are provided in the section below.

1. A scientist working at the University of London has identified an important new gene: the LGI3 gene. Individuals with the gene have a higher chance of suffering from epilepsy. The scientist has successfully isolated the gene in the laboratory. Which of the following statements best describe the patentability of the gene in the UK or European patent systems?
   a. The gene is patentable because it has been successfully isolated.
   b. The gene is patentable because new genes are always patentable.
   c. The gene is not patentable because it is a discovery, not an invention.
   d. The gene is not patentable because genes are never patentable.
2. A computer program (and more broadly, computer-related inventions) will qualify as patentable subject matter under EPO jurisprudence in which of the following scenarios?
   a. The computer program can never qualify as patentable subject matter due to article 52(2)(c) of the EPC 2000.
   b. The computer program can qualify as patentable subject matter if it makes a technical contribution outside of the computer.
   c. The computer program has the character of a concrete apparatus in the sense of a physical entity (known as the 'any hardware' approach).
   d. The computer program can qualify as patentable subject matter under all circumstances.

3. A biotechnology corporation has produced a new type of genetically modified mouse. The mice are likely to develop Alzheimer's disease and are used in Alzheimer's research. Which of the following items are EPO courts least likely to consider (or take into account) when applying the *ordre public* and morality provision?

a. A report issued by the International Union for Conservation of Nature highlighting the important ecological role fulfilled by mice and the wider risks to the ecosystem associated with biological changes in the mouse population.

b. A peer-reviewed article appearing in a medical journal arguing that, due to substantial differences between mice and human biology, effective treatments of Alzheimer's in mice is very unlikely to have a similar efficaciousness in humans,

c. A recently issued patent which discloses a computer programmed with artificial intelligence software that can be used to identify potential Alzheimer's treatments without the need for animal testing.

d. Opinion poll evidence from the UK public demonstrating overwhelming support for genetic modification of mice for purposes of dementia research.

4. After considering the EPO and UK understandings of 'technical character', how would you define an 'invention'? What are the implications of your definition for things such as computer programs, business methods and mental acts?

ACTIVITY DISCUSSION

Activity 7.1 The invention that Christiansen produced in 1958 was the *knowledge* of the stud-and-tube coupling system. After a period of research, Christiansen learned that this system of coupling offered practical advantages. This knowledge is what the patent allows him to own. During the lifetime of the patent, Christiansen alone could use that knowledge to build toy bricks. It would be inaccurate to say what he owned was the bricks themselves: that is the 'physicalist' error.

Activity 7.2 The brick fits within Pila's summary of the EPO approach. The brick exists because a human (Christiansen) intervened in the material world (material in the sense of relating to matter). The result is a toy brick which can be perceived and which can be produced repeatedly by humans.

For different reasons, the brick also fits within Pila's summary of the UK approach. The brick 'contributes something technical to what had been known previously'. The brick introduced toy makers to the idea of the stud-and-tube coupling system and the idea of 'clutch power'. The knowledge that such a coupling system could improve the stability of the bricks was not known to the 'art' of toy making prior to Christiansen's intervention.

Activity 7.3 The EPO focuses slightly more explicitly on the disclosure rationale. In paragraph 5.3, the opposition division judges say that the patent is 'justified' on the grounds that Howard/Florey was the first to make the invention of H2-relaxin and its associated DNA available for the first time.

There is a different tenor to the US Supreme Court decision. Instead, they highlight that awarding a patent on the 'basic tools' of science and technology will 'tie up' those tools resulting in less invention in the future. They conclude that genetic information is one of those basic tools that should not be so tied up by patents. The EPO, by contrast, concludes that even 'broad' patent protection would not unduly harm follow-on creation.

Whether either of these reasons is persuasive is debatable. Someone who agrees with the EPO may worry that the US Supreme Court has undercut scientists' incentive to disclose new inventions. However, some, like Machlup and Penrose, might reasonably ask the EPO whether the information about H2 relaxin would come out at some point anyway. In which case, granting the patent does not seem particularly necessary.[23]

Who is right? It is very difficult to say with any certainty. As Merges warned, quite quickly we find ourselves trying to make 'impossibly complex' judgements about the consequences of patent protection.[24]

Activity 7.4 One might start out answering this question by considering the utilitarian arguments for expanding patentable subject matter. Broadly, one might take the position that allowing genes, computer programs, business methods, etc., to enjoy patent protection will result in good consequences overall. While the additional patents granted will result in additional monopolies and correspondingly higher prices, society may enjoy more inventions, more disclosure and efficiently coordinated development of those inventions in the future. If so, the expansion would seem justifiable.

On the other hand, one may take the view that the claimed benefits are all rather speculative. Will the additional patent monopolies really result in more invention, disclosure and development? In the absence of patent protection, would the Howard Florey Institute reduce its genetic research? Or would it rely on other sources of funding to continue its research? In the absence of patent protection, would claimants like Hitachi or Gemstar try to keep their inventions secret? Or would they be disclosed to the public in any case? One might take the view that given the benefits of expanding patents are speculative, yet the costs of expanding patents are very real, the overall expansion of patents is unjustifiable.

Activity 7.5 One possibly good reason is the problem of monopolies. In a case such as this, allowing the computer program to enjoy patent protection increases the price of the program and restricts its use. This might be justifiable if there is some corresponding benefit conferred by the patent. Yet, once again, we are confronted with the utilitarian counterpoint that such programs would be invented and the technical knowledge disclosed even in the absence of patents.

SELF-ASSESSMENT ANSWERS

1. **Correct answer: a.** is the best answer. Contrary to the position taken in the USA, isolation is generally sufficient to confer a technical character upon a gene. Students may wish to consider for themselves whether that is a particularly good rule.

2. **Correct answer: c.** is the best answer. Answer **a**. gives insufficient weight to the 'as such' provision of article 52(2). Answer **b**. is a better description of the UK courts' approach, rather than that adopted at the EPO. Answer **d**. is too broad and insufficiently considers the role of article 52(2).

3. **Correct answer: d.** Following the TBA's firm stance against survey evidence and opinion polls in *Plant Genetic Systems* and *Harvard/Transgenic Animals*, it is very unlikely that EPO courts would consider opinion poll evidence, regardless of which side they support.

Notes

1 Patents Act 1977 (right to apply for and obtain a patent and be mentioned as inventor).

2 Robert P Merges 'As Many as Six Impossible Patents before Breakfast: Property Rights for Business Concepts and Patent System Reform' (1999) 14(2) Berkeley Technology Law Journal 577, at 585.

3 Reproduced with permission of author.

4 Reproduced with permission of the Licensor through PLSclear.

5 35 USC §101 (US). Patent Act (RSC 1985 c P-4) s 27(3) (Can).

6 Patent Act 1990, s 18 (Aus).

7 *Aerotel Ltd (a Company Incorporated under the Laws of Israel) v Telco Holdings Ltd, Telco Global Distribution Ltd, Telco Global Ltd* [2006] EWCA Civ 1371 [9].

8 Justine Pila, 'Dispute over the Meaning of "Invention" in Art. 52(2) EPC: The Patentability of Computer-Implemented Inventions in Europe' (2005) 36(2) IIC 173 (questioning the continued role of technical character due to its extreme opacity).

9 *Symbian Limited v Comptroller General of Patents* [2008] EWCA Civ 1066.

10 ibid [16].

11 Directive 98/44/EC of the European Parliament and of the Council of 6 July 1998 on the legal protection of biotechnological inventions.

12 Justine Pila, 'Article 52(2) of the Convention on the Grant of European Patents: What Did the Framers Intend? A Study of the *travaux préparatoires*' (2005) 26(7) IIC 768–70.

13 President's Reference/Patentability of programs for computers, G 3/08 [2011] OJ EPO 10, [7.2.7].

14 IPO Practice Notice, *Patents Act 1977: Claims to Programs for Computers* (5 May 1999) 1.

15 *Gemstar v Virgin* [2011] EWCA Civ 302 (upholding decision of Mann J).

16 Gregory A Stobbs, *Business Method Patents* (Wolters Kluwer Law & Business 2021) §1.01.

17 Thomas S Dicke, *Franchising in America: The Development of a Business Method, 1840–1980* (University of North Carolina Press 1992) 34.

18 [1989] 4 WLUK 219.

19 [2012] EWHC 1789 (Pat).

20 David O Taylor, 'Immoral Patents' (2021) 90 Miss LJ 271.

21 Margaret Llewelyn and Mick Adcock, *European Plant Intellectual Property* (Bloomsbury 2006).

22 Francis Bacon, *Meditationes Sacrae* (1597).

23 Boxes 6.6 and Boxes 6.11.

24 Boxes 2.6 and Boxes 2.10.

FIGURE ACKNOWLEDGEMENTS

7.1 Author: Thomas Shafee. A gene is a region of DNA that encodes function. A chromosome consists of a long strand of DNA containing many genes. A human chromosome can be up to 250 mega base pairs of DNA and contain thousands of genes. File licensed under the Creative Commons Attribution 4.0 International license. (*Wikipedia* <https://en.wikipedia.org/wiki/File:Chromosome_DNA_Gene.svg>)

Marginal Fig. 7.1 Portrait of English author and mathematician Ada Byron (later Lovelace, 1815–52), *c*.1835. New York Public Library. (Photo Interim Archives/Getty Images)

8

Patents III: Patentability (Continued)

Chapters 6 and 7 introduced the argument that patents are granted for utilitarian reasons. Patents, it is claimed, will lead to more inventions, more disclosure, and better coordination between inventors. Of course, patents also lead to bad consequences as well in the form of less competitive markets. But the heart of the utilitarian argument is that the good consequences of an appropriately balanced patent system will outweigh the bad consequences.

Nevertheless, even the most ardent supporter of the patent system will agree that in some cases the bad consequences of patents outweigh the good consequences. One person who was keenly aware of this fact was Thomas Jefferson. Before serving as President of the United States, Thomas Jefferson headed the US Patent Review Board where he reviewed patent applications. As he later recounted: 'I know well the difficulty of drawing a line between the things which are worth to the public the embarrassment of an exclusive patent, and those which are not.'[1]

This chapter explores how that line is drawn by turning to the remaining patentability requirements. Those patentability requirements are found in sections 1 and 14 of the Patents Act (see Box 8.1).

Terminology is somewhat mixed in this area. The Patents Act 1977 limits the term 'patentability' to the section 1 requirements. That notwithstanding, some authors refer to the section 1 requirements as the 'external requirements of patentability' and section 14 requirements as the 'internal requirements of patentability'.

> **Section 1**
> (1) A patent may be granted only for an invention in respect of which the following conditions are satisfied, that is to say —
>   (a) the invention is new;
>   (b) it involves an inventive step;
>   (c) it is capable of industrial application;

This chapter contains public sector information licensed under the Open Government Licence v3.0.

> **Section 14**
>
> (3) The specification of an application shall disclose the invention in a manner which is clear enough and complete enough for the invention to be performed by a person skilled in the art.
>
> (5) The claim or claims shall –
>
>   (b) be clear and concise;
>
>   (c) be supported by the description; and
>
>   (d) relate to one invention or to a group of inventions which are so linked as to form a single inventive concept.

Analogous provisions relating to European patents are found in article 52(1), and articles 82–84, of the EPC.

This chapter takes these requirements of novelty, inventive step, industrial application and the specification, in turn.

8.1 NOVELTY

Section 1(1)(a) of the Patents Act states that patents shall be granted only to inventions that are 'new'. Section 2 further states that an invention is new if it does not form part of the **state of the art**' (or '**prior art**'). Patent lawyers assess newness – or as it is more commonly known, **novelty** – by first identifying the 'state of the art' (also known as 'prior art'). Once the state of the art is identified, whether the inventor's contribution is novel or not is determined through the '**enabling disclosure**' test. This section explains how the novelty analysis is applied before finishing with a discussion of a special type of novelty problem: novelty-of-purpose patents.

8.1.1 State of the Art

In the UK and European patent systems, the state of the art is defined in very broad terms. The state of the art, according to section 2(2), comprises:

Article 54 EPC contains analogous rules to section 2 of the Patents Act.

> all matter (whether a product, a process, information about either, or anything else) which has at any time before the priority date of that invention been made available to the public (whether in the United Kingdom or elsewhere) by written or oral description, by use or in any other way.

This is known as a rule of '**absolute novelty**'. It marks a departure from the old rule in the Patents Act 1949 under which the state of the art included only information 'known or used' in the United Kingdom at the time of the priority date.[2]

How the novelty rule applies can be illustrated once again by thinking about the Christiansen brick, as Activity 8.1 shows.

> ## ACTIVITY 8.1
>
> Figure 8.1 demonstrates how toy bricks evolved during the twentieth century.
>
>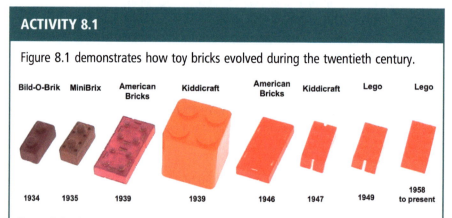
>
> **Figure 8.1** The evolution of toy bricks.
> *(Photograph authorship unknown. Permission issued under UK orphan licensing scheme)*
>
> Starting at the far left, we find three bricks built from 1934 to 1939: the Bild-O-Brik, the MiniBrix and the American Brick. We also find a later version of the American Brick slightly further to the right in 1946. The American Bricks were sold only in America.
>
> In the middle we find two bricks called Kiddicraft Bricks: one from 1939 and one from 1947. Both bricks were invented by Hillary Page. Kiddicraft was the name of Page's company. The 1947 brick is the Self-Locking Brick' first introduced in Chapter 6.
>
> On the far right-hand side, we find two Lego bricks. Both of these were bricks sold by Christiansen's Lego company. You will note that the 1949 brick was an exact copy of Page's 1947 Self-Locking Brick. The 1958 Lego brick is the Toy Building Brick that Christiansen later invented complete with the famous stud-and-tube coupling system.
>
> In 1958 Christiansen applied to the UK IPO for a patent on the 1958 Lego Brick. Which bricks would form the state of the art under the old 1949 rule? And which bricks would form the state of the art under the absolute novelty rule?

Some patent systems (not the UK or EPC) provide a 'grace period', i.e. a short period of time before the priority date in which an inventor can disclose their invention without destroying the novelty of the invention.

Note also that the state of the art includes material that the inventor has disclosed themselves. For example, in Activity 8.1, when Christiansen applied for a patent on the 1958 Toy Building Brick, the state of the art would include the 1949 brick the Lego company sold. This rule has the important consequence that an inventor can sabotage the novelty of their own invention. Hypothetically, if Christiansen had disclosed the 1958 brick to the public before the priority date of the patent application, then that would also have been included in the state of the art. If that prior disclosure amounted to an enabling disclosure (to shortly be discussed), then Christiansen's Toy Building Brick would no longer be novel at the time of the priority date.

Furthermore, the state of the art in Activity 8.1 would include not only these bricks. In addition to the bricks themselves (all 'products'), the state of the art would also include information about those products. Any documents that explain what the bricks are or how to make them, any public speeches delivered orally about the bricks, and, in the present day, any information on the Internet about the bricks (providing the public has 'direct and unambiguous access' to that information through, for example, an URL).[3] As the information only need be 'available' to the public, it is immaterial whether anyone has accessed the information or not.

And if that was not already broad enough, the state of the art is made even broader still by section 2(3) of the Patents Act. That rule states that information included in other patents will form part of the state of the art, even if, at the time of the applicant's priority date, those other patents have not been disclosed to the public. This rule only holds, however, if those other patents have an earlier priority date than that of the applicant's patent.

However, there is some information which is excluded from the state of the art under the modern rule. First, any information which is obtained unlawfully or through breach of confidence and which has been made available to the public within six months of the applicant's priority date is excluded.[4] Second, any information presented at an 'international exhibition' within six months of the applicant's priority date is also excluded.[5]

8.1.2 PSITA

Once the state of the art has been identified, the next step is to ask whether the applicant's invention forms part of the state of the art through application of the enabling disclosure test. However, before discussing that test, it is helpful to first introduce a foundational concept within the test: the **person having skill in the art**, or **PSITA**, for short.

The PSITA is a legal fiction. Much like the reasonable person in tort law, the term does not refer to a real person.[6] Instead, courts must imagine who the PSITA is, how that person would think, and how that person would act. However, courts can consult real people (real scientists, real engineers, etc.) to help determine what the fictional PSITA would think. This is often referred to as 'primary evidence'.

The PSITA is an expert in a technical field. To use a helpful example from the EPO Technical Board of Appeals: if the invention concerns 'a computer implementation of a business, actuarial or accountancy system, the skilled person will be someone in data processing, and not merely a businessman, actuary or accountant'.[7] Likewise, if the application is for a new type of medical substance, the PSITA will likely be someone with the average skills of a biochemist. In the case of a toy brick, the PSITA would likely be someone with the average skills of a

Patents III: Patentability (Continued)

mechanical engineer. What skills and knowledge that person will have depends on the nature of the field.

The PSITA has a variety of functions in patent law. When it comes to novelty, the state of the art is interpreted through their eyes. As a result, what information the prior art reveals to the public is assessed from the perspective of the fictional PSITA. Thereafter, the PSITA is used as the notional addressee for purposes of assessing enabling disclosure.

8.1.3   Enabling Disclosure

We will return to the enabling disclosure test again in Section 8.4.

Once the state of the art is identified, the final step is to assess whether the applicant's invention 'forms part' thereof. To that end, courts ask: has there been an '**enabling disclosure**' in the state of the art? If there has been an enabling disclosure, the applicant's invention has been '**anticipated**' and is therefore not new.

The idea of 'practising' an invention can sound a little unusual at first. In simple terms, one practises an invention if one makes or uses the invention in some way.

In turn, the enabling disclosure test can be split into two sub-questions. First, does the state of the art *disclose* the invention? That is, if one examines the state of the art, will one find the applicant's invention already contained therein? Second, has there been an *enablement*? That is, does the state of the art contain sufficient information which would enable the PSITA to 'practise' the invention. Only if there has been both disclosure and enablement, will the applicant's patent be anticipated and therefore lack novelty. This relationship is illustrated by Case 8.1.

Case 8.1 *Synthon BV v SmithKline Beecham plc* [2005] UKHL 59

Facts

Paroxetine methanesulfonate (PMS) is a salt that can be used in the treatment of depression and related health conditions. On 10 June 1997, Synthon BV (claimant–appellant) applied for a patent over a broad class of substances, including PMS. The specification described how to make PMS in crystalline form. That description directed the reader to make PMS by dissolving paroxetine in ethanol. This, however, was a mistake. Dissolving paroxetine in ethanol would not produce PMS in crystalline form because ethanol inhibits the crystallisation process. In slightly metaphoric language: the patent contained a recipe explaining how to make the invention, but the recipe was wrong.

On 6 October 1998, SmithKline Beecham (defendant–respondent) filed for a patent on a particular form of crystallised PMS. The patent was granted.

Issue and Procedure

Synthon commenced proceedings to have the SmithKline patent revoked. Synthon argued that the SmithKline invention was not new because it had been anticipated by the information in their prior patent. The issue presented was: had the state of the art both disclosed and enabled the invention? At first instance, the High Court and Mr Justice Jacob (as he then was) said there had been both disclosure and enablement and therefore the SmithKline invention was anticipated. This decision was reversed by the Court of Appeal but reinstated by the House of Lords.

LORD HOFFMANN

a. Disclosure

There seems to me no doubt that the application disclosed the existence of PMS crystals of 98% purity and claimed that they could be made. Whether in fact they could be made is the question of enablement which I shall come to in a moment. But their existence and their advantages for pharmaceutical use were clearly disclosed in the application.

b. Enablement

Once one has decided that the disclosure in the application was crystalline PMS ..., the question of enablement is whether the skilled person would have been able to make crystalline PMS. If he did, he would necessarily have made the product claimed in the patent. There is no dispute that the disclosure enabled him to make PMS. The issue is whether he would have been able to get it to crystallise. That is a question of fact, involving the application of the standards laid down in cases like *Mentor Corporation v Hollister Incorporated* [1993] RPC 7 to the evidence of the nature of the problem, the assistance provided by the disclosure itself and the extent of common general knowledge. Synthon, as I have said, got off to a bad start by specifying, in their main example, a solvent which proved unsuitable for crystallisation. Nevertheless, the [High Court] judge found that the skilled man would have tried some other solvent from the range mentioned in the application or forming part of his common general knowledge and would have been able to make PMS crystals within a reasonable time. This is a finding of fact by a very experienced judge with which an appellate court should be reluctant to interfere: compare *Biogen Inc v Medeva Plc* [1997] RPC 1, 45.

(paras 35, 38)

The test for disclosure is sometimes known as the **'reverse infringement' test**, under which disclosure occurs where the prior art discloses something which, if practised, would infringe the applicant's patent.

Patents III: Patentability (Continued)

To anticipate an invention, the prior art must disclose the invention completely. When assessing disclosure, courts do not assume that the PSITA will undertake further experiments. However, as Lord Hoffmann outlines above, the standard changes when considering enablement. Even if the disclosure does not accurately tell the PSITA how to practise the invention, enablement will occur so long as the PSITA can practise the invention without undue difficulty and experimentation. In reinstating Mr Justice Jacob's decision, Lord Hoffmann found the Court of Appeal had erroneously confused and conflated disclosure and enablement.

ACTIVITY 8.2

Refer back to the toy bricks in Figure 8.1. Look first at the Lego Brick produced by Christiansen in 1949. Hypothetically, imagine Christiansen applied for a UK or European patent on this brick first with a priority date of 1 January 1949. Thereafter, consider the 1958 brick. Has either brick been anticipated? If so, that brick forms part of the state of the art and is not new.

Recall that in *Darcy v Allein*, Popham CJ argued that patents not only hurt consumers, but also prevent other traders from practising their trade. The right to work doctrine sought to provide some protection for other traders by barring patents that would stop them from doing what they had been doing before.

Applying the concepts of enablement and disclosure is particularly troublesome in cases of '**secret**' or '**inherent**' **use**. What happens if someone practises the invention prior to the applicant's priority date, but in a way that is not obvious to the public? Does such use disclose and enable the invention such that the applicant's patent will be denied for lack of novelty? Under the old 1949 Patents Act, the answer was 'yes'.[8] The rationale was that if such secret use did not anticipate the invention, then the invention could be patented; in turn, that patent could be used to stop anyone from using the invention, including those who were using it (albeit without conscious awareness) prior to the patent. This was known as the 'right to work' doctrine. But the right to work doctrine has become more nuanced under the 1977 law, as Case 8.2 illustrates.

This situation has come to be known as '**evergreening**'. Evergreening is the use of various strategies to prolong the effective life of the patent.

Case 8.2 *Merrell Dow v Norton* [1996] RPC 76 (HL)

Facts

In 1972, the pharmaceutical company Merrell Dow (claimant–appellant) received a patent on the drug terfenadine – a type of antihistamine (allergy relief) which does not make the patient drowsy. The patent expired in 1992.

In 1980, Merrell Dow discovered how the terfenadine worked. When ingested, the terfenadine passed through the stomach and was absorbed in the small intestine where it was metabolised in the liver. As part of the metabolism process, the liver produced an acid metabolite (the chemical name for which was the pithy: 4-[4-(4-hydroxydiphenylmethyl-I-piperidinyl)-I-hydroxybutyl]-a,a-dimethylbenzeneacetic).

Merrell Dow subsequently applied for a patent on the acid metabolite. This patent expired in 1997.

In 1992, after the expiry of the first patent, the pharmaceutical company Norton (defendant–respondent) began making terfenadine. Merrell Dow sued them for patent infringement on the ground that they were making the acid metabolite and thus infringing the second patent.

Issue and Procedure

The defendants Norton responded that the second patent lacked novelty for two reasons and was accordingly invalid. First, they argued the second patent was anticipated 'by use'. Essentially, they argued that in the period between 1972 and 1980, people were already making and using the acid metabolite: although no one was consciously aware of it, they were making the acid metabolite in their livers every time they ingested the terfenadine. As a result, they argued that the second patent was anticipated. Second, they argued that the second patent was anticipated by the first patent's specification (referred to below as anticipation 'by disclosure'). Although that specification did not mention the acid metabolite, it did outline broadly how terfenadine worked as an antihistamine without inducing drowsiness.

Merrell Dow acknowledged that under the old 1949 law, their second patent would have been anticipated. However, they argued that the Patents Act 1977 changed the rule such that anticipation could only occur if the public were aware of the prior use.

At the trial Mr Justice Aldous revoked the patent for lack of novelty. This was then upheld by the Court of Appeal. In the next extract, Lord Hoffmann finds that the secret use was not enough to anticipate the patent. Nevertheless, the patent specification was anticipatory.

LORD HOFFMANN

8. Anticipation by Use

(a) The Old Law

I think that there can be no doubt that under the Patents Act 1949, uninformative use of the kind I have described would have invalidated the patent. One of the grounds for revocation in section 32(1) was (e): 'the invention . . . is not new having regard to what was known or used, before the priority date of the claim, in the United Kingdom'. Ground 32(1)(i) was that before the priority date the invention was 'secretly used' in the United Kingdom. In Bristol-Myers Co. (Johnson's) Application [1975] R.P.C. 127 this House decided that use included secret or otherwise uninformative use.

(b) The New Law

Mr. Floyd submitted that Bristol-Myers Co. (Johnsons) Application was still good law.

I think that this argument, which in any event depends upon a rather refined inclusio unius construction of the parenthetical expansion of the words 'all matter', dissolves completely when one looks, as one must, at Article 54. This provision makes it clear that to be part of the state of the art, the invention must have been made available to the public. An invention is a piece of information. Making matter available to the public within the meaning of section 2(2) therefore requires the communication of information. The use of a product makes the invention part of the state of the art only so far as that use makes available the necessary information.

The 1977 Act therefore introduced a substantial qualification into the old principle that a patent cannot be used to stop someone doing what he has done before. If the previous use was secret or uninformative, then subject to section 64, it can. Likewise, a gap has opened between the tests for infringement and anticipation. Acts done secretly or without knowledge of the relevant facts, which would amount to infringements after the grant of the patent, will not count as anticipations before.

9. Anticipation by disclosure

I turn therefore to the ground upon which the respondents succeeded before Aldous J. and the Court of Appeal, namely that the disclosure in the terfenadine specification had made the invention part of the state of the art. This is different from the argument on anticipation by use because it relies not upon the mere use of the product by members of the public but upon the communication of information. The question is whether the specification conveyed sufficient information to enable the skilled reader to work the invention.

Mr. Thorley [counsel for Merrell Dow] says that no one can know about something which he does not know exists. It follows that if he does not know that the product exists, he cannot know how to work an invention for making that product in any form. The prior art contained in the terfenadine specification gave no indication that it would have the effect of creating the acid metabolite in the human body. Therefore it did not contain sufficient information to enable the skilled reader to make the substance in that or any other form. It did not make the acid metabolite available to the public.

What does Mr. Thorley mean when he says that no one knew that the acid metabolite existed? What Merrell Dow's research revealed was that something was created in the liver which could be given a chemical description. But the same thing may be known under one description and not known under another.

For example, the inhabitants of a village may know the elderly gentleman of military bearing as a prize-winning rose grower without knowing that he had won the VC in the war. In answer to the question: 'Do you know the holder of the VC in your village?' they would truthfully answer 'I did not know that such a person existed'.

My Lords, I think that on this point the Patents Act 1977 is perfectly clear. Section 2(2) does not purport to confine the state of the art about products to knowledge of their chemical composition. It is the invention which must be new and which must therefore not be part of the state of the art. It is therefore part of the state of the art if the information which has been disclosed enables the public to know the product under a description sufficient to work the invention.

In this case, knowledge of the acid metabolite was in my view made available to the public by the terfenadine specification under the description 'a part of the chemical reaction in the human body produced by the ingestion of terfenadine and having an anti-histamine effect'. Was this description sufficient to make the product part of the state of the art? For many purposes, obviously not. It would not enable anyone to work the invention in the form of isolating or synthesising the acid metabolite. But for the purpose of working the invention by making the acid metabolite in the body by ingesting terfenadine, I think it plainly was. It enabled the public to work the invention by making the acid metabolite in their livers. The fact that they would not have been able to describe the chemical reaction in these terms does mean that they were not working the invention. Whether or not a person is working a product invention is an objective fact independent of what he knows or thinks about what he is doing.

(pp. 85–87, 89–90)

The change brought in by the Patents Act 1977 makes it easier for the patent applicant to establish novelty. On the facts of the case, Merrell Dow's second patent was anticipated by the first patent's specification. But, in other cases, where the only possible anticipation is the secret/inherent use, the patent will no longer be anticipated, contra the position under the 1949 law.

8.1.4 Novelty of Purpose

Not only are new products patentable, but so too are new uses of old products. Particularly in the medical and chemical fields, researchers often find new ways of using old substances. For example, aspirin, when rubbed on the skin, might work as an insect repellent. Patents on new uses of old products are frequently granted. More controversial is the question of whether patents ought to be granted to those who use an *old product* in an *old way* but for a *new purpose* – so-called novelty-of-purpose patents. Answering this question brings us back to our old friend, technical character.

Case 8.3 *Mobil/Friction Reducing Additive*, G2/88 [1990] OJ EPO 114

Facts

Mobil (applicant–appellant) applied for a patent on a substance which could be added to lubricating oils (used in engines and other similar machines). Mobil claimed that this could be used to help reduce friction. Their application was opposed by Chevron (opponent–respondent), who argued that the substance in question was already known and was already added to lubricating oils to prevent the formation of rust. And so Chevron argued that this was an old substance, used in an old way (e.g. addition to lubricating oil and then poured into engines), merely being used for a new purpose.

Issue and Procedure

The question for the Enlarged Board of Appeal was: is the use of an old substance in an old way, but for a new purpose, sufficient to make an invention 'new'? As we will see below, the EBA initially seems to say 'no'. However, it then qualifies that statement to, in effect, permit the patentability of novelty-of-purpose claims.

ENLARGED BOARD OF APPEALS

In the Enlarged Board's view, the distinction drawn by the respondent is a fundamental one, and can be developed as follows. In relation to a claim to a use of a known entity for a new purpose, the question initially arises: what are the technical features of the claim? If the claim includes as a technical feature a 'new means of realisation' by which the new purpose is achieved, in the form of steps of a physical activity, which are not disclosed in the state of the art in association with the known entity, then the claim is clearly novel because of the presence of that technical feature.

In relation to a claim to a use of a known entity for a new purpose, the initial question is again: what are the technical features of the

> claimed invention? If the new purpose is achieved by a 'means of realisation' which is already within the state of the art in association with the known entity, and if the only technical features in the claim are the (known) entity in association with the (old) means of realisation, then the claim includes no novel technical feature. In such a case, the only 'novelty' in the claimed invention lies in the mind of the person carrying out the claimed invention, and is therefore subjective rather than objective, and not relevant to the considerations that are required when determining novelty under Article 54(1) and (2) EPC.
>
> (para 7,1)

Understanding inventions as knowledge may perhaps strengthen the conclusion reached in *Mobil*. If inventions are knowledge, then granting a patent to one who discloses new knowledge about a product is not surprising, even if that knowledge relates to merely a new purpose.

So far, this seems to make some sense: using an old substance in a new way to achieve a new purpose involves a technical effect and should be patented, but simply using an old substance in an old way does not add any 'technical feature' which can be patented. After reading this, one might conclude that Mobil's patent was denied. After all, they used the old substance in an old way (adding it to lubricating oils) just with a new purpose, right? But this did *not* happen. The next paragraph is key in this regard. The most significant wording in the paragraph is in italics.

> In other words, when following the method of interpretation of claims set out in the Protocol, what is required in the context of a claim to the 'use of a compound A for purpose B' is that such a claim should not be interpreted literally, as only including by way of technical features 'the compound' and 'the means of realisation of purpose B'; it should be interpreted (in appropriate cases) as also including as a *technical feature the function of achieving purpose B*, (because this is the technical result). Such a method of interpretation, in the view of the Enlarged Board, is in accordance with the object and intention of the Protocol to Article 69 EPC.
>
> (para 9.1. [emphasis added])

Therefore, the EBA finds that while a new purpose is not a technical feature, actually *achieving* that purpose is a technical feature. Thus, while the new purpose (reducing friction) is not sufficient to produce novelty, *bringing about* that new purpose is new. The result is that an invention is new when it merely relates to an old substance used in an old way to achieve a new purpose.

ACTIVITY 8.3

Think back to Thomas Jefferson, who tried to draw a line between those inventions which 'are worth to the public the embarrassment of an exclusive patent, and those which are not'. Do you think the benefits of granting patents to inventions like the one in *Mobil* produce more benefits than costs?

The *Mobil* case concerned non-medical uses of old substances. But before the *Mobil* case, it had already been decided that new purposes of old medicines used in old ways could be patented.[9] As discussed briefly in Chapter 7, methods of treatment are not patentable subject matter – although substances and devices used in medical treatment are. To make this rule more palatable to the aggrieved pharmaceutical industry, section 4A(3) of the Patents Act allows one to claim the use of an old substance (e.g. a chemical compound), used in an old way (e.g. ingested) for a new purpose. And courts have subsequently decided that subsequent new purposes can also be patented.

8.2 INVENTIVE STEP

Assuming the invention is new, the next question is whether it involved an '**inventive step**'. Another way of stating the question is to ask whether the invention was merely **obvious**? Even if an invention is new, a PSITA may nevertheless find the invention to be rather obvious. If so, the patent will be denied.

It is generally assumed that there is no need to use the patent system to encourage the production of obvious inventions. The more obvious the invention, then the more likely that inventors will invent it even in the absence of patent rights. As a result, the costs of awarding patents on obvious inventions are substantial, while the benefits are minimal. By limiting patents to non-obvious inventions, society gives incentives to inventors to undertake more ambitious research and development activities.

Yet, distinguishing between an obvious invention, and an invention that involves a sufficient inventive step, presents a notoriously difficult question of fact. So difficult is the task that the famous American judge, Judge Learned Hand, wrote that the doctrine is 'as fugitive, impalpable, wayward, and vague a phantom as exists in the whole paraphernalia of legal concepts'.[10]

> Judge Learned Hand (1872–1961) was particularly influential in crafting American copyright and patents. He also developed the famous 'Learned Hand' test in negligence law.

The novelty and inventive step analyses share some important features. Once again, the state of the art and the PSITA are involved. When it comes to assessing the obviousness of the invention, courts do so through the eyes of the PSITA. The PSITA is deemed to know the state of the art at the priority date of the invention. There is one exception, however. When it comes to assessing inventive step, the PSITA is not deemed to know the content of patent applications that have not yet been published at the priority date.[11] This marks a departure from the rules found in the novelty assessment.

Despite the similarities, the character of the two doctrines is quite different. Novelty is a quantitative analysis. The enabling disclosure test seeks to uncover whether there is any quantitative difference between the invention and the state of the art. Inventive step, by contrast, is a qualitative analysis. The key question is whether the invention is inventive *enough* to be worthy of a patent.

Another difference concerns 'mosaicking'. When asking whether an invention is obvious, it is assumed the PSITA will combine different pieces of knowledge from different pieces of prior art. The PSITA is assumed not to perform such mosaicking when it comes to assessing novelty.

8.2.1 The Inventive Step Standard

How UK courts assess inventive step is helpfully illustrated by Case 8.4.

Case 8.4 *Windsurfing International v Tabor Marine* [1985] RPC 59 (CA)

Facts

The case involved the invention of the windsurfing board. To understand the invention, a short background on sailing is required. For centuries, sail boats have adopted different types of sail. Two types of sails are square-rigged sails (also known as kite-rigged sails) and Bermuda-rigged sails (see Figure 8.2). The sails in a square-rigged boat are square, while the sails in a Bermuda-rigged sailboat are triangular. One advantage of Bermuda-rigged sails is they can be more easily manoeuvred by sailors to catch the wind.

Figure 8.2 Bermuda-rigged sail ((a)); square-rigged sails ((b)).
Licensed under Creative Commons Attribution 2.5 Generic license.

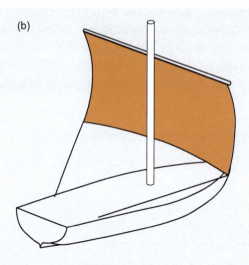

Figure 8.2 (cont.)

Windsurfing International (claimant–appellant) owned a British patent on a 'wind-propelled vehicle'. Figure 8.3 shows a drawing from their patent application that depicts the invention. The core of their invention was the 'free-sail concept'. That is, the board's mast to which the sail was attached was not fixed rigid in place, but instead employed a 'universal joint' mechanism that allowed it greater manoeuvrability. In technical language, this was known as an 'unstayed spar'. The defendant's patent also described the invention as using a Bermuda sail.

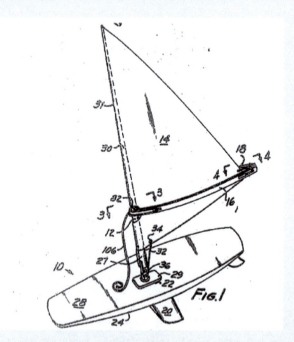

Figure 8.3 Wind-propelled vehicle, technical drawing.
(From patent GB1258317A)

Windsurfing International sued Tabor Marine (defendant–respondent) for allegedly infringing the patent. Tabor Marine responded by claiming that the patent should be revoked because the invention lacked an inventive step. To make this argument, they pointed to a publication written by Newman Darby – 'Sailboarding: Exciting New Water Sport' – which had appeared in an American publication – *Popular Science Monthly* – in 1965. In the article, Darby described how to make a 'sailboard' with an unstayed spar. The principal difference, however, was Darby's sailboard used a *square-rigged* sail, not a Bermuda-rigged sale.

Issue and Procedure

Did the claimant's 'free-sail' concept involve an inventive step? The Darby sailboard already disclosed how to make a sailboard with an unstayed spar. The only difference between the two inventions was the choice of sail. The difference in sail meant that the claimant's invention had not been anticipated by the Darby article. But the question remained: were the differences merely obvious? The High Court said they were obvious and so the invention did not involve an inventive step. This was upheld by the Court of Appeal.

OLIVER LJ

There are, we think, four steps which require to be taken in answering the jury question. The first is to identify the inventive concept embodied in the patent in suit. Thereafter, the court has to assume the mantle of the normally skilled but unimaginative addressee in the art at the priority date and to impute to him what was, at that date, common general knowledge in the art in question. The third step is to identify what, if any, differences exist between the matter cited as being 'known or used' and the alleged invention. Finally, the court has to ask itself whether, viewed without any knowledge of the alleged invention, those differences constitute steps which would have been obvious to the skilled man or whether they require any degree of invention.

As regards the first step, we respectfully agree with the learned judge that the inventive concept of the patent is the free-sail concept. It is that which constitutes the essential difference between the patent in suit and other conventional vehicles propelled by sail. Going back, then, to the priority date, anyone familiar with sailing and sailing craft would then have known, as part of his general knowledge, the difference between square sail and Bermuda rigs and the disadvantages as regards manoeuvrability presented by the former. . . .

To make the passage easier to read, the text has been broken up into smaller paragraphs.

The extract focuses on whether the invention was obvious in light of the Darby article. But there was also another important piece of prior art. In 1958, a 12-year-old boy named Peter Chilvers made a similar sailboat to sail around Hayling Island on the south coast of the UK. Oliver LJ found this also would have rendered the claimant's invention obvious.

> We agree, of course, that one must not assume that the skilled man, casting his experienced eye over [the Darby article], would at once be fired with the knowledge that here was something which had a great commercial future which he must bend every effort to develop and improve, but he must at least be assumed to appreciate and understand the free-sail concept taught by Darby and to consider, in the light of his knowledge and experience, whether it will work and how it will work. In the light of the evidence, it seems to us inescapable that anyone skilled in the art and contemplating Darby's article in 1966 would immediately recognise, as the witnesses did, that the kite rig suggested for this very simple and elementary device would suffer from the disadvantages that it would perform poorly upwind and would require to be manipulated from the lee side of the sail. It does not, in our judgment, require the attribution to the skilled addressee of any inventive faculty to say that, if he applied his mind to it at all, it would be immediately obvious to him that these disadvantages would disappear if the rig were changed to Bermuda, a change which, as would also be obvious to him, required the sail to be stretched by means of a wishbone boom. . . . All the evidence suggests that such a person would immediately see, by application of his own general knowledge, the adoption of a Bermuda rig as an obvious way of improving the performance of the Darby vehicle.
>
> (pp. 73–74, minor modifications by Patrick Goold)

Subsequently, in the case of *Pozzoli*, the 'steps' outlined by Lord Justice Oliver in *Windsurfing* were modified slightly. Following the *Pozzoli* decision, courts: (1) identify the PSITA and their common general knowledge; (2) identify the inventive concept in the patent application; (3) identify the difference between the state of the art and inventive concept in the patent; and (4) ask whether the differences would have been obvious to the PSITA.[12] But the central question – are the differences between the state of the art and the invention obvious? – remains the same.

The European patent system assesses obviousness in a slightly different way to British courts. The EPO primarily follows a 'problem-and-solution' approach in which it asks what technical problem is being solved by the invention, and would the applicant's solution to that problem have been obvious to a PSITA?[13] But once again, the crucial question – obviousness – remains the same. Despite that basic similarity, UK courts have not adopted the problem-and-solution approach. Not all inventive activity neatly fits a problem-and-solution model. This is particularly the case of inventions wherein the key inventive concept is the realisation that a particular problem can actually be solved.

Given the complexity in assessing obviousness, courts have at times created a variety of sub-tests and principles to aid their determinations. One consideration is how much inventive choice was available to the inventor. If there was, for example, only one or two ways of producing the invention, then the chances are greater that the invention would be deemed obvious. A related question is whether the research avenue was 'obvious to try'? If so, the greater the chances are that the invention will be deemed to lack an inventive step. How this principle is applied is summarised in Case 8.5.

Case 8.5 *Hospira v Genentech* [2016] EWCA Civ 780

Facts

Genetech Inc. (appellant–defendant) owned patents on the breast cancer drug, Herceptin. The active ingredient in Herceptin was trastuzumab. Hospira (respondent–claimant) brought proceedings for revocation of the patent on the ground that it lacked an inventive step. Hospira argued that Herceptin was obvious in light of a pair of documents which disclosed that at the time of the priority date trastuzumab was in phase II clinical trials for breast cancer.

Issue and Procedure

At first instance, Mr Justice Birss (as he then was) held that the patent was invalid for lack of inventive step. After comparing the prior art and the patented Herceptin, he found that the only material difference was the prior art disclosed a liquid formation, while the claims related to a freeze-dried (or 'lyophilised') formation. In his view, it would not take any inventive effort from a PSITA to invent the freeze-dried version. Genentech appealed and Mr Justice Birss's decision was upheld by the Court of Appeal. In doing so, Lord Justice Floyd explained how principles such as 'obvious to try' fit within the broader obviousness analysis.

FLOYD LJ

I start with the well-known passage from the judgment of Kitchin J. (as he then was) in Generics (UK) Ltd v H. Lundbeck A/S [2007] EWHC 1040 (Pat), [2007] R.P.C. 32, at [72], which has been approved at the highest level:

> 'The question of obviousness must be considered on the facts of each case. The court must consider the weight to be attached to any particular factor in the light of all the relevant circumstances. These may include such matters as the motive to find a solution to the problem the patent addresses, the number and extent of the possible avenues of research, the effort involved in pursuing them and the expectation of success.'

It follows that the court is required to embark on a multi-factorial assessment. The approach of the appellate court to such questions is well-known:

the decision is not open to independent evaluation in this court unless the judge has made an error of principle: see Biogen Inc v Medeva Plc [1997] R.P.C. 1 at [45] per Lord Hoffmann.

It is also well-settled that 'obvious to try' is not a substitute test for obviousness: see e.g. per Lewison L.J. in MedImmune Ltd v Novartis Pharmaceuticals UK Ltd [2012] EWCA Civ 1234, [2013] R.P.C. 27 at [181]. There is only one statutory question, namely whether the invention was obvious at the priority date. In the same case at [90] to [95] Kitchin L.J. explained that whether the invention was obvious to try was merely one of many considerations which it may be appropriate for the court to take into account in addressing the statutory question. It must in any case be coupled with a reasonable or fair prospect of success. At [91] Kitchin L.J. emphasised:

'Whether a route has a reasonable or fair prospect of success will depend upon all the circumstances including an ability rationally to predict a successful outcome, how long the project may take, the extent to which the field is unexplored, the complexity or otherwise of any necessary experiments, whether such experiments can be performed by routine means and whether the skilled person will have to make a series of correct decisions along the way.'

Thus a judge's assessment whether an approach has a reasonable or fair prospect of success is itself another multi-factorial assessment, where this court should again pay proper respect to the evaluation of a trial judge.

There is also no single standard of what amounts to a fair expectation of success. Thus Jacob L.J.'s statement in Saint Gobain PAM SA v Fusion-Provida Ltd [2005] EWCA Civ 177 at [35] that it must be 'more-or-less self-evident that what is being tested ought to work' is far from being a test of universal application. In Novartis AG v Generics (UK) Ltd (trading as Mylan) [2012] EWCA Civ 1623 Kitchin L.J. (with whom Lewison and Munby L.JJ. agreed) warned against imposing a straitjacket on the law by adopting any form of words as a standard. He said at [55]:

'What is a reasonable or fair expectation of success will again depend upon all the circumstances and will vary from case to case. Sometimes, as in Saint Gobain, it may be appropriate to consider whether it is more or less self-evident that what is being tested ought to work. So, as this court explained in that case, simply including something in a research project in the hope that something might turn up is unlikely to be enough. But I reject the submission that the court can only make a finding of obviousness where it is manifest that the test ought to work. That would be to impose a straitjacket on the assessment of obviousness which is not

> warranted by the statutory test and would, for example, preclude a finding of obviousness in the case where the results of an entirely routine test are unpredictable.'
>
> Indeed, so much was confirmed by Lord Hoffmann in Conor Medsystems Inc v Angiotech Pharmaceuticals Inc [2008] UKHL 49, [2008] R.P.C. 28 at [42], approving Jacob L.J.'s comprehensive review of the authorities in this area in the Court of Appeal in that case, including his view that 'how much of an expectation depended upon the particular facts of the case'.
>
> (paras 9–14)

8.2.2 Secondary Evidence

The question of obviousness potentially creates a problem for judges. Judges are typically trained in law and are unlikely to have worked in scientific or engineering professions. So how can judges predict what a PSITA would think? One answer is they can rely on the testimony of real scientists and engineers. In *Windsurfing International*, Lord Justice Oliver relied upon the evidence of experts produced by the parties. But this so-called **primary evidence** is not the only evidence a judge can rely upon when deciding whether an invention is obvious or not. Judges frequently rely on a range of '**secondary evidence**' as well.

Case 8.6 *Haberman v Jackel International* [1999] FSR 683

Facts

In 1992, Mandy Nicola Haberman (claimant) successfully applied for a patent on a 'drinking vessel suitable for us as a trainer cup'. The cup contained a valve which prevented liquid from leaving the container unless a certain level of lip pressure or suction was applied. This meant that the liquid would not drip out of the cup accidentally. The invention became a large commercial success and was marketed as the 'Anywayup Cup'.

Issue and Procedure

Haberman sued Jackel International (defendant) for infringing the patent. Jackel introduced evidence of prior inventions that functioned similarly and argued that Haberman's cup did not involve an inventive step. In response, Haberman argued that the cup's commercial success was evidence of the cup's inventive step. This raised the question: to what extent can 'secondary evidence' be used to establish inventive step?

MR JUSTICE LADDIE

If skilled workers in the art had looked at the priority date both at the prior art relied on and had turned their minds to solving a known problem their reactions would come closer to showing what would have been the approach of the hypothetical skilled man. Unfortunately evidence in that form rarely exists. However some insight into the thinking of those in the art at the priority date can be provided by evidence of commercial success. To this end patentees sometimes prove schedules of sales to support their claims to inventiveness. In most cases this type of evidence is of little or no value because it does no more than show that a particular item or process which employs the patented development has sold well. The mere existence of large sales says nothing about what problems were being tackled by those in the art nor, without more, does it demonstrate that success in the market place has anything to do with the patented development nor whether it was or was not the obvious thing to do. After all, it is sometimes possible to make large profits by selling well an obvious product. But in some circumstances commercial success can throw light on the approach and thought processes which pervade the industry as a whole. The plaintiffs rely on commercial success here. To be of value in helping to determine whether a development is obvious or not it seems to me that the following matters are relevant:

(a) What was the problem which the patented development addressed. Although sometimes a development may be the obvious solution to another problem, that is not frequently the case.

(b) How long had that problem existed.

(c) How significant was the problem seen to be. A problem which was viewed in the trade as trivial might not have generated much in the way of efforts to find a solution. So an extended period during which no solution was proposed (or proposed as a commercial proposition) would throw little light on whether, technically, it was obvious. Such an extended period of inactivity may demonstrate no more than that those in the trade did not believe that finding a solution was commercially worth the effort. The fact, if it be one, that they had miscalculated the commercial benefits to be achieved by the solution says little about its technical obviousness and it is only the latter which counts. On the other hand evidence which suggests that those in the art were aware of the problem and had been trying to find a solution will assist the patentee.

(d) How widely known was the problem and how many were likely to be seeking a solution. Where the problem was widely known to many in the relevant art, the greater the prospect of it being solved quickly.

(e) What prior art would have been likely to be known to all or most of those who would have been expected to be involved in finding a solution. A development may be obvious over a piece of esoteric prior art of which most in the trade would have been ignorant. If that is so, commercial success over other, less relevant, prior art will have much reduced significance.

(f) What other solutions were put forward in the period leading up to the publication of the patentee's development. This overlaps with other factors. For example it illustrates that others in the art were aware of the problem and were seeking a solution. But it also is of relevance in that it may indicate that the patentee's development was not what would have occurred to the relevant workers. This factor must be treated with care. As has been said on more than one occasion, there may be more than one obvious route round a technical problem. The existence of alternatives does not prevent each of them from being obvious. On the other hand where the patentee's development would have been expected to be at the forefront of solutions to be found yet it was not and other, more expensive or complex or less satisfactory, solutions were employed instead, then this may suggest that the ex post facto assessment that the solution was at the forefront of possibilities is wrong.

(g) To what extent were there factors which would have held back the exploitation of the solution even if it was technically obvious. For example it may be that the materials or equipment necessary to exploit the solution were only available belatedly or their cost was so high as to act as a commercial deterrent. On the other hand if the necessary materials and apparatus were readily available at reasonable cost, a lengthy period during which the solution was not proposed is a factor which is consistent with lack of obviousness.

(h) How well has the patentee's development been received. Once the product or process was put into commercial operation, to what extent was it a commercial success. In looking at this, it is legitimate to have regard not only to the success indicated by exploitation by the patentee and his licensees but also to the commercial success achieved by infringers. Furthermore the number of infringers may reflect on some of the other factors set out above. For example if there are a large number of infringers it may be some indication of the number of members of the trade who were likely to be looking for alternative or improved products (see (iv) above).

> (i) To what extent can it be shown that the whole or much of the commercial success is due to the technical merits of the development, i.e. because it solves the problem. Success which is largely attributable to other factors, such as the commercial power of the patentee or his licensee, extensive advertising focusing on features which have nothing to do with the development, branding or other technical features of the product or process, says nothing about the value of the invention.
>
> 4. I do not suggest that this list is exhaustive. But it does represent factors which taken together may point towards or away from inventiveness. Most of them have been addressed in this case.
>
> [Mr Justice Laddie then proceeded to analyse the secondary evidence presented.]
>
> I have come to the conclusion that had it really been obvious to those in the art it would have been found by others earlier, and probably much earlier. It was there under their very noses. As it was it fell to a comparative outsider to see it. It is not obvious.
>
> (paras 32, 45)

ACTIVITY 8.4

Let's return to Christiansen Toy Building Brick. We saw that the 1949 brick was not novel. And so we do not need to ask whether it involved an inventive step. But we decided that the 1958 brick probably was novel. The next question, therefore, is whether it was sufficiently inventive to enjoy a patent? Of course, we know that Christiansen did in fact receive a patent on this brick in the UK. But that itself does not tell us the answer to the question: the UK IPO could have been wrong in its assessment of the application.

Historian Henry Weincek explains the circumstances surrounding the brick's 1958 development.[14] On a long ferry crossing to England, the owner of a Copenhagen department store lamented that there was no really good toy system on the market. After considering this problem, Christiansen and associates decided to create a toy system that would 'give children the opportunity to create complicated and interesting constructions'.

The first brick they produced – the 1949 brick – was a straightforward copy of the Page Self-Locking Brick. However, Christiansen found that this brick did not sell particularly well. In the face of sluggish sales, they redesigned the bricks to include the stud-and-tube system. This provided the bricks with not only stability, but also versatility. Children could stack two bricks, each with eight studs, in twenty-four different ways. Subsequently, the Lego brick was a 'solid hit' with children in Denmark. Very soon, Lego was exporting the bricks to Sweden, Norway, the Netherlands, France, Italy and Germany. Today, reflecting on the invention, Wiencek calls it an 'ingenious' design.

On the basis of this short summary, do you think the 1958 brick passes the inventive step test as explained in the case law in this section?

8.3 INDUSTRIAL APPLICATION

The last of the section 1(1) requirements is that the invention be 'capable of **industrial application**'. Section 4 further elaborates that an invention is capable of industrial application if it can be 'made or used in any kind of industry'. The same definition can be found in article 57 EPC 2000. Subsequently, courts have clarified that to have such application, the invention must serve a 'useful purpose'.[15] Inventions that contravene laws of physics (for example, perpetual motion machines) fail this standard.[16] But there are borderline cases, particularly in the field of biotechnology, where courts need to decide whether an invention has a sufficiently useful purpose to enjoy a patent. One illustrative case is that of *Human Genome Sciences v Eli Lilly*.

> Some jurisdictions, such as the USA, call this the 'utility' doctrine.

Case 8.7 *Human Genome Sciences v Eli Lilly* [2011] USKC 51

Facts

Human Genome Sciences (HGS) (applicant–appellant) was a biopharmaceutical corporation. In 1996, they filed a European patent for a new invention: a human protein called Neutrokine-α. Neutrokine-α was part of a 'superfamily' of proteins called the TNF ligand superfamily. The proteins in this family regulate several different cell functions, including those relating to immune response and inflammation. Knowledge of the proteins is helpful because it enables scientists to produce new treatments for individuals who suffer from immune-related diseases (such as leukaemia).

HGS's patent specification argued that understanding the properties of Neutrokine-α would be helpful in the diagnoses, prevention and treatment of a number of immune system disorders. However, the patent provided no data or experimental evidence to support that claim. Instead, the patent pointed to the properties of other proteins in the TNF ligand superfamily and inferred that Neutrokine-α would be similarly beneficial.

Issue and Procedure

Eli Lilly (opponent–respondent) opposed the patent before the EPO Opposition Division and simultaneously brought a revocation action in the UK High Court. The question presented was whether Neutrokine-α was capable of industrial application. In 2008 the EPO Opposition Division agreed with Eli Lilly and revoked the patent. But this was overturned by the EPO Technical Board of Appeals. Meanwhile, in the parallel litigation in the UK High Court, Mr Justice Kitchin (as he then was) revoked the patent finding that the functions of Neutrokine-α were 'at best, a matter of expectation and then at far too high a level of generality to constitute a sound or concrete basis for anything except a research project'.

HGS appealed the UK High Court decision to the Court of Appeal on the basis that it was inconsistent with the EPO's interpretation of the EPC. The Court of Appeal upheld Mr Justice Kitchen's decision. HGS appealed to the UK Supreme Court where, as discussed below, their appeal was successful.

During the litigation, an important intervention was made by the BioIndustry Association (BIA). The BIA is a trade association for the UK bioscience sector. While not supporting HGS's case directly, the BIA argued that upholding the Court of Appeal's judgment would cause UK bioscience companies great difficulty in attracting investment at an early stage in the research and development process. BIA explained that bioscience firms first isolate a new protein and apply for a patent. Once their protein is protected by a patent, that attracts investors to give them funds to explore the protein further in the hope of finding concrete medical treatments.

NEUBERGER LJ

The essence of the Board's approach in relation to the requirements of Article 57 in relation to biological material may, I think, be summarised in the following points:
The general principles are:
(i) The patent must disclose 'a practical application' and 'some profitable use' for the claimed substance, so that the ensuing monopoly 'can be expected [to lead to] some ... commercial benefit' (T 0870/04, para 4, T 0898/05, paras 2 and 4);
(ii) A 'concrete benefit', namely the invention's 'use ... in industrial practice' must be 'derivable directly from the description', coupled with common general knowledge (T 0898/05, para 6, T 0604/04, para 15);

(iii) A merely 'speculative' use will not suffice, so 'a vague and speculative indication of possible objectives that might or might not be achievable' will not do (T 0870/04, para 21 and T 0898/05, paras 6 and 21);

(iv) The patent and common general knowledge must enable the skilled person 'to reproduce' or 'exploit' the claimed invention without 'undue burden', or having to carry out 'a research programme' (T 0604/04, para 22, T 0898/05, para 6);

Where a patent discloses a new protein and its encoding gene:

(viii) A 'plausible' or 'reasonably credible' claimed use, or an 'educated guess', can suffice (T 1329/04, paras 6 and 11, T0640/04, para 6, T 0898/05, paras 8, 21, 27 and 31, T 1452/06, para 6, T 1165/06 para 25);

[An argument against the High Court's decision is] that the disclosure in the Patent as to the uses of Neutrokine-α, even when taken together with common general knowledge, was no more than 'speculative' and did not give rise to an 'immediate concrete benefit' – i.e. invoking on points (ii) and (iii). This argument (which was also relied on by the Court of Appeal – see at [2010] RPC 14, para 132) proceeds on the implicit assumption that the disclosure of the Patent . . . is not sufficient in itself to satisfy the requirements of Article 57.

However, if, as I consider, the effect of the Board's jurisprudence is that the sort of disclosure [in the patent] does justify patentability, then the fact that the 'plausible' predictions for the use of the invention could also be said to involve speculation takes matters no further. If the known activities of the TNF ligand superfamily were enough to justify patentability for the disclosure of a novel molecule (and its encoding gene) which was plausibly identified as a member of that family, the fact that further work was required to see whether the disclosure actually had therapeutic benefits does not, at least without more, undermine the validity of a patent. In other words, in agreement with Lord Hope, I think that the approach of the Board in this case, in particular at T 0018/09, paras 22–30, appears more in line with the previous EPO jurisprudence than the approach of Kitchin J and the Court of Appeal.

The Court of Appeal made much of the Board's statement that a patent should yield an 'immediate concrete benefit' (see at [2010] RPC 14, paras 146, 149, 155 and 156). I certainly accept that, in some cases, different tribunals can and will legitimately come to different views as to whether a particular claimed invention can satisfy the requirement of providing an 'immediate concrete benefit'. However, I am not persuaded that such an argument is open to Eli Lilly in this case. . . .

I appreciate that the dividing line between 'plausibility' and 'educated guess', as against 'speculation', just like the contrast between 'a real as opposed to a purely theoretical possibility of exploitation', can be difficult to discern in terms of language and application, and is a point on which tribunals could often differ. (I might add that the notion that the dividing line is not very satisfactory is illustrated by the fact that, at one point in his evidence, Professor Saklatvala effectively equiparated speculation with an educated guess.) However, as a result of the decisions discussed above, the Board's approach to patents such as that in this case is, I believe, tolerably clear.

Just as it would be undesirable to let someone have a monopoly over a particular biological molecule too early, because it risks closing down competition, so it would be wrong to set the hurdle for patentability too high, essentially for the reasons advanced by the BIA and discussed in paras 97–100 above. Quite where the line should be drawn in the light of commercial reality and the public interest can no doubt be a matter of different opinions and debate. However, in this case, apart from the fairly general submissions of the parties and of the BIA, we have not had any submissions on such wider policy considerations.

(paras 119–21, 123, 130)

ACTIVITY 8.5

Chapter 6 introduced one type of utilitarian argument that says patents are necessary to help efficiently coordinate research and development activities (also known as the 'prospect theory'). How does this idea relate to the issue of industrial application and the *Human Genome Sciences* case? And how can the objections to that theory be used to evaluate the UK Supreme Court's decision?

8.4 INTERNAL REQUIREMENTS

We now turn to the last set of patentability requirements: the internal requirements. Unlike the rules discussed in the prior sections, these rules do not relate to the invention itself. Assuming the invention is new, involves an inventive step and is capable of industrial application, the focus then switches to how the patent specification is drafted. Section 14(3) of the Patents Act states that the patent specification must 'disclose the invention in a manner which is clear enough and complete enough for the invention to be performed by a person skilled in the art'. Section 14(5) requires the claims to be 'clear and concise', 'supported by the description' and relate to one 'inventive concept'.

8.4.1 Sufficiency of Disclosure

A patent application that provides an 'insufficient' disclosure – that is, a disclosure which is not clear and complete enough – will be rejected by the UK IPO. Alternatively, if the patent is granted, then it may be revoked later by the UK IPO or courts. This rule is justified by the disclosure version of the utilitarian argument discussed in Chapter 6. If patents are meant to encourage disclosure, then such rights should only be granted to applicants who disclose their inventions sufficiently clearly and completely. Unlike the other patentability requirements, the date for assessing the sufficiency of disclosure is not the priority date, but instead the date of filing.[17]

When assessing sufficiency of disclosure, courts once again use the 'enabling disclosure' test. Section 8.1.3 demonstrated how courts use this test to assess whether an invention is new. When it comes to sufficiency of disclosure, courts also use this test. Importantly, however, they use that test in a slightly different way.

To illustrate, think back to the case of *Synthon BV*. Recall that Synthon BV (SBV) first received a patent on a broad class of substances, including PMS in crystallised form. Later, SmithKline Beecham (SKB) applied for a patent on a particular form of crystallised PMS. SBV argued that the SKB patent should be revoked because their patent already disclosed and enabled PMS. At this point, SKB could have offered two possible lines of defence:

- The first line of defence was to deny that the SBV patent was anticipatory. This is the line of defence that SKB actually pursued. They ultimately lost this argument when it was held that the SBV patent both disclosed and enabled the PMS in crystallised form.
- A second line of defence – not actually pursued in the case – would be to argue that the SBV patent was invalid for lack of sufficient disclosure. SKB might have argued that the SBV patent did not both disclose and enable PMS in crystallised form. If that argument was sound, then SBV's claim to PMS in crystallised form would be invalid.

Thus, the enabling disclosure test does double work: it provides a standard to assess novelty, and a standard to assess sufficiency of disclosure.

Insufficiency takes many forms. So-called classical insufficiency occurs when the patent specification does not enable the PSITA to perform the invention at all.[18] Hypothetically, in the *Synthon BV* case, if the SBV patent was so unclear that a PSITA would need to use some 'inventive skill' to make the PMS, or doing so would cause the PSITA 'undue burden', then the patent would have been insufficient. Classical insufficiency can be contrasted with insufficiency due to ambiguity.[19] The latter case arises when the disclosure is so ambiguous that the PSITA cannot know whether they have practised the invention or not.

But perhaps the most challenging of all types of insufficiency is insufficiency due to 'excessive breadth'. To understand this idea, consider the following famous example relating to the invention of the lightbulb.

ACTIVITY 8.6

American inventors Sawyer and Man applied successfully for a patent on an 'incandescent light bulb' in 1880. Figure 8.4 illustrates their invention. Just like a modern lightbulb, it has a glass outer case (A on the diagram). Electricity is then passed through a 'filament' (B on the diagram). The filament heats up and gives out light. The problem is that the filament might burn up too quickly. Sawyer and Man solved this problem. They found that carbonised paper would serve as a good filament and would not disintegrate quickly.

Sawyer and Man applied for a patent. In their patent, they explained how a lightbulb could be made using a carbonised *paper* filament. However, their patent did not merely claim a lightbulb using a carbonised paper filament. Instead, they claimed a lightbulb that used a filament made of 'carbonized fibrous or textile material'. This claim language covered not only carbonised paper, but a group of approximately 6,000 vegetable materials.

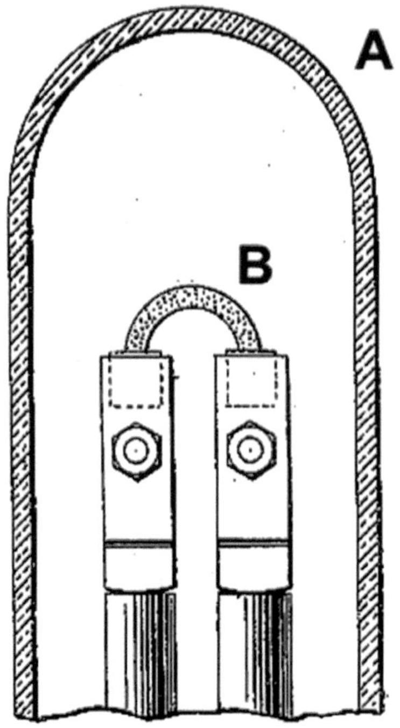

Thomas Edison subsequently invented a lightbulb with a *bamboo* filament. After inspecting the Sawyer and Man lightbulb, Edison carried out extensive experiments to determine what material would work best as a filament. In this process, Edison tested tens of different materials. He finally realised that bamboo had unique qualities that would allow it to burn for a very long time before disintegrating. Sawyer and Man sued Edison for infringing their patent. Edison responded by asking the court to revoke the patent on the grounds that the specification did not clearly and completely tell a PSITA how to make lightbulbs using filaments of 'carbonized fibrous or textile material'.

Using the disclosure version of the utilitarian argument, what might be the problem with allowing Sawyer and Man to claim lightbulbs using filaments of 'carbonized fibrous or textile material'?

Figure 8.4 The Sawyer and Mann incandescent light.
(From patent US317676A)

You will recall we came across the Edison lightbulb in Section 6.2.3.3 as well.

8.4 Internal Requirements 277

Famously, the US Supreme Court revoked the Sawyer and Man patent because it failed to sufficiently disclose the claimed invention.[20] Of course, the Sawyer and Man patent disclosed how to make and use a lightbulb with a carbonised *paper* filament. If they had only claimed a lightbulb using a carbonised paper filament, then their disclosure would have been sufficient. It was the fact that their claimed invention was much broader than merely 'carbonized paper' which resulted in the insufficient disclosure problem. In patent terminology, we say that their patent only disclosed one '**embodiment**' of the claimed invention. They did not, however, disclose how to make all the other potential embodiments of their invention.

This rule might prove problematic in modern patent law. In many cases, inventors attempt to patent an invention that has a broad range of embodiments. This is often the case in the biotechnological fields. An inventor might invent a method of producing a broad range of new compounds or substances. Does the inventor need to disclose how to make and use every single compound or substance in the range? This question was taken up recently by the UK Supreme Court.

> In the UK, this type of insufficiency is sometimes called *Biogen* sufficiency, following the case of *Biogen v Medeva* [1997] RPC 1.

Case 8.8 *Regeneron Pharmaceuticals Inc v Kymab Ltd* [2020] UKSC 27

Facts

'Antibodies' are proteins created by the human body to fight bacterial and virus infections. People with immune system diseases often cannot produce their own antibodies. But scientists can produce antibodies in the lab and insert them into immunocompromised individuals to help them fight infections. Antibodies are composed of both a variable part and a constant part.

Regeneron Pharmaceuticals (applicant–respondent) invented a type of transgenic mouse that would produce human antibodies. This involved editing the genetic sequence of mice. In particular, the process involved putting human antibody-producing genes into the genetic structure of mice. This is a complicated process. Scientists cannot simply replace mouse genes with human genes without the mice becoming 'immunologically sick'. So, instead, Regeneron only replaced *part* of the mice's antibody-producing genes. They replaced the part of the genes that produced the *variable* part of the antibody (see Figure 8.5). The result was the mice would produce antibodies with human variable parts and mouse constant parts. The constant part could then be switched later in the lab, and the resulting antibodies used then in humans. This genetic editing was known as the 'reverse chimeric locus'.

In 2001, Regeneron applied for European patents on the mice. Their patents claimed 'a transgenic mouse that produces hybrid antibodies containing human variable regions and mouse constant regions' (known as 'Claim 1'). But problematically, it was still not technically feasible in 2001 to implant *all* of the human variable regions into the genetic structure of mice. It was only possible to implant *some* of the human variable regions into the structure. A PSITA reading the patent

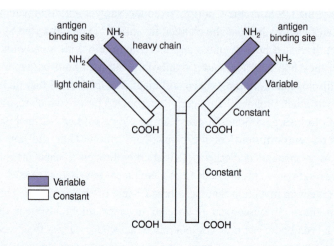

Figure 8.5 Antibody structure displaying variable part.
From Regeneron Pharmaceuticals Inc v Kymab Ltd [2018] EWCA Civ 671

in 2001 would know how to produce mice with *some* of the variable regions replaced, but not be enabled to replace the entire variable section. It was only some years later, after further scientific investigation, that scientists successfully inserted the entire human variable region producing part into mice.

Issue and Procedure

Regeneron sued Kymab (defendant–appellant) for infringement in 2013. Kymab countered with a claim of invalidity due to insufficient disclosure. The issue was: did the patent sufficiently disclose how to make transgenic mice complete with reverse chimeric locus? Kymab argued it did not.

The High Court initially agreed with Kymab that the disclosure was insufficient. But the Court of Appeal reversed this decision. The Court of Appeal stressed that Regeneron's reverse chimeric locus idea was a ground-breaking 'general principle'. This general principle was sufficiently disclosed in the patent specification even if the PSITA could not make all embodiments thereof. Writing for the majority of the Supreme Court, Lord Briggs vigorously disagreed with the Court of Appeal on this point and reinstated the High Court decision.

LORD BRIGGS

Reflection upon those European and UK authorities yields the following principles:
...
(iv) The disclosure required of the patentee is such as will, coupled with the common general knowledge existing as at the priority date, be sufficient to

> enable the skilled person to make substantially all the types or embodiments of products within the scope of the claim. That is what, in the context of a product claim, enablement means.

Application of those principles to the facts of the present case shows clearly that Claim 1 fails for insufficiency. At the priority date the disclosure of the two patents, coupled with the common general knowledge, did not enable transgenic mice to be 'made' with a Reverse Chimeric Locus containing more than a very small part of the human variable region gene locus. . . .Thus the claim to a monopoly over the whole of that range went far beyond the contribution which the product made to the art at the priority date, precisely because mice at the more valuable end of the range could not be made, using the disclosure in the patents.

. . . I do not accept [the Court of Appeal's] conclusion that an invention may be 'enabled' in relation to a particular type of product falling within the scope of the claim even if it does not permit the skilled person to make it. They thought it was enough that the benefits which the invention unlocked (in terms of preventing murine immunological sickness) would in due course be realised over the whole range, if and when all embodiments within the range could be made. In practical terms they upheld a monopoly over that part of the range of products answering the broad description in Claim 1 which was likely to be of most benefit to medical genetic engineering, at a time when the disclosure in the patent only enabled the skilled person to make products over a very small part of the range. . .

Nor is the Court of Appeal's analysis to be regarded as a legitimate development of the law. The sufficiency requirement, namely that the disclosure in the patent should enable substantially all products within the scope of a product claim to be made by the skilled person as at the priority date, is part of the bedrock of the law, worked out over time both in the UK and by the EPO, which is essential to prevent patentees obtaining a monopoly which exceeds their contribution to the art. To water down that requirement would tilt the careful balance thereby established in favour of patentees and against the public in a way which is not warranted by the EPC, and which would exceed by a wide margin the scope for the development of the law by judicial decision-making in a particular Convention state.

It may well be, as the Court of Appeal clearly thought, that the consequence of confining the patentee with a ground-breaking invention to protection only over a range of products which the invention currently enables to be made at the priority date will give the patentee scant and short-lived reward for their efforts and ingenuity, viewed in particular with the benefit of hindsight. The Court of Appeal put this point forcefully to counsel for Kymab at the hearing in October 2017, and the transcript discloses that little was said in response by way of mitigation. A little more was attempted in this court in the appellant's reply, but it would not be a useful exercise to engage with it. What matters is that it is settled law, in relation to a product claim, that sufficiency requires substantially the whole of the range of

> products within the scope of the claim to be enabled to be made by means of the disclosure in the patent, and this both reflects and applies the principle that the contribution to the art is to be measured by the products which can thereby be made as at the priority date, not by the contribution which the invention may make to the value and utility of products, the ability to make which, if at all, lies in the future.
>
> (paras 56–60)

While inventors need not spell out how to make and use every embodiment of their invention, they do need to provide such information that would enable a PSITA coupled with common general knowledge to make and use substantially all the embodiments of the invention. How many embodiments are necessary to achieve that end depends on the facts of the case. There will be instances where the patent specification simply explains how to make one embodiment of the invention, but that is nevertheless enough information to enable the PSITA to make substantially all the other embodiments. In other cases – including both the lightbulb case and the *Regeneron* case – more embodiments would be necessary to render the disclosure sufficient. This, as both the US Supreme Court in the lightbulb case, and the UK Supreme Court in *Regeneron* explain, is necessary to prevent the applicant from enjoying an undeservedly broad monopoly.

8.4.2 Claims

The final question concerns whether the patent claims are adequate. As section 14 (5) says, the claims must be 'clear and concise', 'supported by the description' and 'relate to one invention'. Failure to meet these criteria will result in rejection of the patent application. Unlike the other criteria, however, failure in this respect is not grounds for revocation of the patent post-grant.[21] Inadequately drafted claims might, however, result in the UK IPO denying the patent in the first instance.

Nevertheless, there is one way in which the claim language may be important post-grant. The requirement that the claim language be 'supported by the description' overlaps substantially with the issue of sufficiency of disclosure. In a case like the Edison lightbulb, one could say that the specification did not sufficiently disclose how to make a lightbulb with a filament made from 'carbonized fibrous or textile material'. Or one could say that this claim language was not supported by the description (which merely described how to make a carbonised paper filament). As a result, although the requirement that the patent be supported by the description is not strictly grounds for revocation, in practice, it will go hand in hand with a finding of insufficiency, which is grounds for revocation.[22]

A similar result may occur with respect to the 'clarity and conciseness' requirement. The clarity and conciseness of the claims is assessed through the eyes of the

PSITA. If a PSITA has difficulty understanding the claim language, that may provide evidence that the disclosure provided is insufficiently ambiguous. The requirement that claims be clear and concise does not, however, mean they need to be simple. Reading through the claims for the minifigures patent (Section 6.3.1) will demonstrate that frequently claims are highly complex.

Lastly, the claims must relate to only one invention. Two separate inventions should be claimed in two separate patents. In cases where the invention has multiple embodiments – like the Edison lightbulb case or *Regeneron* – the embodiments must all relate to one single inventive concept.

8.5 SUMMARY

One of the striking features of patents is the extent of the patentability requirements. Whereas an author receives copyright in original work automatically, an inventor must demonstrate that their invention is new, non-obvious, capable of industrial application, and that their patent specification is appropriately drafted. The path to patent protection is paved with many more hazards than the path to copyright.

Another interesting feature of the patentability requirements is how they have evolved in recent years. Part I suggested that copyright has expanded over time in all dimensions. Chapter 7 likewise suggested that patentable subject matter has also expanded. But the direction of travel is different when one considers the remaining patentability requirements. In some respects, the patentability requirements have relaxed. For example, it is now possible to patent novel purposes. One might potentially also argue that allowing a merely 'plausible' use to satisfy the industrial application requirement is a further relaxation. But in other respects the patentability requirements have become more demanding. The adoption of the rule of absolute novelty has made it more difficult for inventors to establish novelty. Equally, as demonstrated in *Regeneron*, courts have tried to preserve rules that prevent relaxation of the patentability requirements.

How the patent bargain has been affected by these developments is an empirical question. The introduction of novelty-of-purpose claims and the lower threshold for industrial application might be said to expand the size of the monopoly arrow (see Figure 6.7). On the other hand, the introduction of the absolute novelty rule might be said to counteract that expansion. The overall result, maybe, is that the patent bargain has been broadly preserved.

8.6 SELF-ASSESSMENT

Before moving on, try to answer the following questions to consolidate your learning. Answers are provided in the section below.

1. In January 2020, an inventor applied for a patent on a new type of lightbulb. The Intellectual Property Office must determine whether the lightbulb is novel. Which of the following would be *excluded* from the state of the art in the UK Intellectual Property Office's novelty inquiry?
   a. A similar type of lightbulb made by a Japanese inventor in 2010. The lightbulb was sold solely in Japan and only for six months.
   b. A blog post written by an American inventor in 2015 describing how to make the lightbulb. The blog post can be accessed through all major search engines, such as www.google.com.
   c. A presentation of the lightbulb made by the inventor in October 2019 at an international exhibition. In the patent application, the inventor states the invention was displayed at the exhibition.
   d. A book written in 1990 by an unknown author, found in a UK library, describing how to make the lightbulb.
2. In January 2020, an inventor applies for a patent on a new type of lightbulb. The Intellectual Property Office must determine whether the lightbulb involves an inventive step. Which of the following things may be used as evidence to establish the lightbulb's non-obviousness.
   a. Testimony from electrical engineers with familiarity of electrical lighting.
   b. Survey evidence that the invention is likely to be commercially successful.

c. Evidence that prior lightbulbs suffered from a well-known and long-standing limitation or defect.

d. All of the above.

3. In order to receive a patent, an invention must have an industrial application. According to *Human Genome Sciences v Eli Lilly & Co* [2011] UKSC 51, which of the following answers will establish industrial application?

a. A 'vague…indication of possible objectives that might or might not be achievable'.

b. A 'plausible' or 'reasonably creditable' claimed use.

c. A 'purely theoretical possibility of exploitation'.

d. A 'merely speculative' use.

4. Do UK and EPO courts do a good job at 'drawing a line between the things which are worth to the public the embarrassment of an exclusive patent, and those which are not'?

ACTIVITY DISCUSSION

Activity 8.1 Applying the old 1949 rule, only those bricks which had been 'known' in the United Kingdom before Christiansen's 1958 priority date would form part of the state of the art. This would very likely exclude the American Bricks sold in America but not in the UK. All of the other bricks would likely be in the state of the art.

Applying the new rule of absolute novelty would lead to a different conclusion. If that rule is applied, then all the bricks prior to the priority date, regardless of where they were made available to the public, would form part of the state of the art.

Activity 8.2 The 1949 brick certainly has been anticipated. The Kiddicraft 1947 brick seems to disclose the exact same invention. Furthermore, the brick discloses sufficient information that would enable a PSITA to make that invention. A mechanical engineer will likely be able to recreate that brick without much difficulty. Hence the information contained in the 1947 Kiddicraft brick is sufficient to both disclose and enable the invention (i.e. the 1949 brick).

The 1958 brick, however, does not seem to be anticipated. The stud-and-tube element of the invention does not appear to be disclosed by anything which forms the state of the art. Therefore, the 1958 brick is novel.

Activity 8.3 In my mind, the costs of novelty-of-purpose patents probably outweigh the benefits. It does seem that the public only gains something relatively modest: knowledge of the new purpose. Yet the costs are quite substantial: monopolisation of the substance for that particular purpose for the term of the patent. Given the problem of monopoly, there may be merit in permitting such claims only if some reasonably robust empirical evidence supports the conclusion that novelty-of-purpose patents have significant utilitarian benefits in terms of more innovation, disclosure or development.

Activity 8.4 If we use the *Pozzoli* test, it seems quite likely that the Christiansen brick involved an inventive step. As this is a mechanical invention (as opposed to say a chemical or biological invention), the PSITA is likely to be a mechanical engineer with the common general knowledge of toy making. The inventive concept in Christiansen's patent application is the stud-and-tube system. The patent specification says that the 'main characterising feature of the invention' is how the studs and tubes are spaced on the brick. It was this feature of the invention which distinguished it from the state of the art. And there is at least some evidence that this difference was not obvious. Historians view it as 'ingenious'. And, if we consider the secondary evidence, the brick solved problems associated with the previous bricks and enjoyed high commercial success.

Activity 8.5   The BIA's intervention in *Human Genome Sciences* was largely based on the prospect theory (although, perhaps without conscious awareness of this fact).

The idea is that if we grant patents to scientists who make an early-stage discovery of some new substance, then those scientists will be able to attract monetary investment with which to turn the discovery into some concrete medical treatment. Without an early-stage patent, then anyone would be able to work on the discovery. The investment money would then be distributed across lots of different teams of scientists who all are merely duplicating their efforts. As a result, the prospect theory supports giving patents to scientists who make an early stage scientific break-through. From this perspective, the UK Supreme Court decision was entirely right.

However, as discussed in Merges and Nelson (Box 6.12), the quickest way to turn an early-stage discovery into something really useful might be through *rivalry* rather than monopoly. Rather than grant a patent, society might instead allow lots of scientists to develop the idea simultaneously. The first one to successfully develop the discovery wins the prize of the market rewards.

Activity 8.6   The problem is that Sawyer and Man had not disclosed how to make lightbulbs with all 6,000 vegetable materials included in the phrase 'carbonized fibrous or textile material'. In essence, Sawyer and Man were attempting to own something – lightbulbs made with carbonised fibrous or textile filaments – but had failed to disclose to the public how to make and use that invention. We know that their disclosure was insufficient, because Edison had to exercise a lot of 'inventive skill' – through a highly burdensome experimentation process – to invent his version of the lightbulb. The patent therefore granted Sawyer and Man a broad monopoly – with all the costs associated with monopoly – and the public received very little benefit in return.

SELF-ASSESSMENT ANSWERS

1. **Correct answer: c.** Remember that state of the art is defined broadly under the rule of absolute novelty. The lack of geographical restriction means that **a.** is included (although it would have been excluded under the 1949 law). The blog post (**b.**) is also easily accessible to all in the UK. The lack of authorship in **d.** is also immaterial.

2. **Correct answer: d.** The question demonstrates the broad range of evidence that can be taken into account by courts when assessing obviousness. Note that answer **a.** refers to primary evidence while **b.** and **c.** are both forms of secondary evidence.

3. **Correct answer: b.** The UK Supreme Court in *Human Genome Sciences v Eli Lilly* rejected answers **a.**, **c.** and **d.** as acceptable satisfaction of the industrial application doctrine. Students might want to reflect on what, if any, is the meaningful differences between them.

Notes

1 Thomas Jefferson, Letter to Isaac McPherson (13 August 1813) in Andrew A Lipscomb and Albert Ellery Bergh (eds), *The Writings of Thomas Jefferson*, 13 vols (Thomas Jefferson Memorial Association 1904) 333.

2 Patents Act 1949, s 32(e).

3 *Philips/Public Availability of Documents on the World Wide Web*, T 1553/06 [2012] EPOR 383.

4 Patents Act 1977, s 2(4)(a)–(b).

5 ibid s 2(4)(c).

6 *Positec Power Tools v Husqvarna* [2016] EWHC 1061 (Pat), [2016] FSR (29) 798, [8].

7 *Two Identities/COMVIK*, T 0641/00 [8].

8 Patents Act 1949, s 32(i).

9 *Boulton and Watt v Bull* (1795) 126 ER 651.

10 *Harries v Air King Prod. Co*, 183 F.2d 158, 162 (2d Cir 1950) (US).

11 *BASF/Metal Refining*, T 24/81 [1979–85] B EPOR 354.

12 *Pozzoli SpA v BDMO SA* [2007] EWCA Civ 588.

13 *ICI/Containers*, T 26/81 [1982] *OJ EPO* 211.

14 Henry Wiencek, *The World of Lego Toys* (Abrams 1987) 35–57.

15 *Chiron v Murex (No 12)* [1996] *RPC* 535, 607.

16 Christopher Wadlow, 'Patents for Perpetual Motion Machines' (2007) 2 JIPLP 136.

17 *Biogen v Medeva* [1997] RPC 1.

18 See eg *Genentech/t-PA*, T 923/92 [1996] EPOR 275, 302.

19 *Kirin-Amgen v Transkaryotic Therapies* [2002] EWCA Civ 1096 [31].

20 *Incandescent Lamp Patent*, 159 US 465 (1895).

21 Patents Act 1977 s 14(3).

22 *Biogen* (n 17) 47.

FIGURE ACKNOWLEDGEMENTS

8.1 Photograph authorship unknown. Permission issued under UK orphan licensing scheme. Licence number: OWLS000351. Licensee: Patrick R Goold. Date of issue 28/04/2023. Text added by Patrick Goold

8.2 Tomasz Rojek, Bermuda catboat sail-plan, Creative Commons Attribution 2.5/GNU Free Documentation License, from Wikimedia Commons <https://commons.wikimedia.org/wiki/File:Rigging-catboat-berm.svg>. Tomasz Rojek, Square rig, Creative Commons Attribution 2.5/GNU Free Documentation License, grom Wikimedia Commons <https://commons.wikimedia.org/wiki/File:Rigging-square-sail.svg>

8.3 From patent GB1258317A

8.4 From patent US317676A

8.5 From *Regeneron Pharmaceuticals Inc v Kymab Ltd* [2018] EWCA Civ 671

Patents IV: Scope

The Patents Act states that patents are property rights.[1] But is that label a good one? To those who think property is exclusive control over a thing, the question is: does patent law grant anyone exclusive control over inventions? Or does patent law merely grant inventors a bundle of rights falling short of exclusive control?

Consider, for example, another toy brick: the 'Wonder Block' sold by the Asahi Toy Company (ATC) in Japan in the 1970s, shown in Figure 9.1. In some respects, the Wonder Block is similar to Christiansen's Toy Building Brick. Both inventions are toy bricks with studs on the top and some sort of coupling mechanism inside. Indeed, the ATC bricks were inspired by the Christiansen bricks. The ATC bricks are even 'interoperable' with the Christiansen bricks: both the ATC and Christiansen bricks lock together neatly allowing children to build structures.

Does Christiansen's patent prevent ATC from selling these bricks? Today patents are far more powerful rights than they were in the past. When James Watt invented the Watt Steam Engine, he could only prevent others from fraudulently imitating his product.[2] But today, patent rights are much broader in scope. To explain, Section 9.1 introduces the patent right. Section 9.2 then considers how broadly the patent right is construed. Section 9.3 turns to exceptions. Section 9.4 finishes with compulsory licensing.

9.1 THE PATENT RIGHT

> There is no analogous European Patent Convention (EPC) 2000 provision. Once the European patent is granted, it takes effect as a bundle of national patents. Therefore national patent law alone defines the rights the patentee enjoys.

Chapter 4 discussed how copyright provides authors with two sets of rights: economic rights and moral rights. In contrast, the Patents Act does not provide a list of patent 'rights'. Instead, the Patents Act labels the patent as a property right and thereafter, lists the type of actions that will infringe that property right. The infringing acts are listed in section 60 and summarised in Table 9.1.

This chapter contains public sector information licensed under the Open Government Licence v3.0.

Table 9.1 Patent infringing acts

A person infringes the patent in a product if they…	A person infringes the patent in a process if they…
… *make* the product	… *use* the process
… *dispose of* the product	… *offer to use* the process
… *offer to dispose of* the product	
… *use* the product	
… *import* the product	
… *keep* the product	

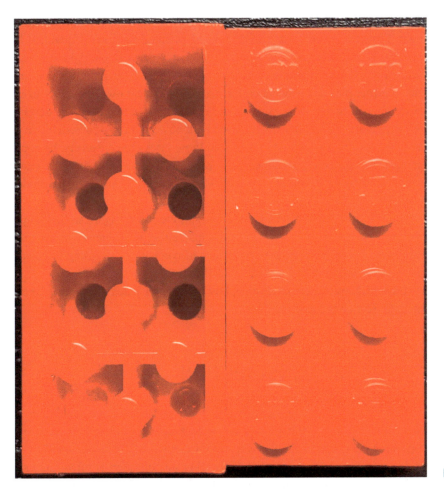

Figure 9.1 ATC brick

ACTIVITY 9.1

Does section 60 fit the 'exclusive control' or 'bundle of rights' model of property? Pay close attention to provisions relating to use of a product or process.

Patents IV: Scope

The patent right is distinguishable from copyright in three further respects. First, the owner's rights only last for twenty years from the date of filing the patent application.[3] Noticeably, the rights are significantly shorter in duration than in copyright.

Second, there is no analogous provision for moral rights. This broadly reflects the utilitarian, and non-personal, normative foundation to patent law. Although the inventor does have a right to be named on the patent specification.[4]

Finally, on its face the patent right is broader than copyright. In copyright, the author's rights are qualified by an important set of exceptions. By contrast, in patent law, any 'use' of the invention will result in infringement, and there are fewer exceptions that qualify the right (explored further in Section 9.3).

Nevertheless, like copyright, there are limitations on the scope of the patent right. First, the owner's right to dispose of patented products is qualified by the doctrine of exhaustion (just like the copyright distribution right discussed in Section 4.1.2). When the invention is embodied in a tangible product, and the patent owner puts that product on the market, the patent owner's ability to control distribution of that product exhausts and cannot be used to prevent the onward sale of the product. Thus, after Christiansen built physical bricks embodying his stud-and-tube coupling system, and then sold those bricks to consumers, he could not prevent the consumers reselling those physical bricks. Second, while making a patented product is an infringement of the patent right, *repairing* those products is not an infringement.[5]

> Recall the limitation–exception distinction introduced in Section 4.1.2.

As with the economic rights in copyright, the patent right can be assigned in writing, and can be licensed.[6] Licences may either be voluntary or compulsory, express or implied. Given the importance of compulsory licensing in patent law, this concept is elaborated further in Section 9.4.

> For a refresher on these concepts, return to Section 4.4.2.

What perhaps is more interesting, however, is how patents have broadened over time, as Section 9.2 discusses.

9.2 CLAIM CONSTRUCTION

The patent owner has the exclusive ability to make, use, and sell the invention (among other things). But what counts as making, using, or selling the invention? Or, to put the question another way, what exactly does the owner own?

In other areas of property law, answering this question is often quite simple. Imagine that you own a plot of land called Blackacre. What you own is a physical thing: land. Of course, you do not own all the land in the world, you only own a certain parcel of land: Blackacre. And you can put up fences around the outside of Blackacre to help distinguish your land from that of other people.

Patent law creates property in inventions. As discussed in Chapter 7, an invention is not a physical thing, but a type of technical knowledge. But clearly the patent owner does not own all technical knowledge in the world. And, so, society

9.2 Claim Construction 289

needs some way to distinguish the bit of knowledge that the patent owner owns, from knowledge that is unowned and remains in the public domain.

Without physical fences to perform this demarcation, courts instead rely on the patent claims to define the boundaries of the patented invention. The problem, however, is that patent claims are written in informal languages (like English), and informal languages often pose problems of vagueness, ambiguity, and generality. The following activity demonstrates the problem.

You might want to flick back to Section 6.3. to refresh your memory regarding patent claims.

ACTIVITY 9.2

The following language is a claim from Christiansen's Toy Building Brick patent:

> In a toy building set, a hollow building block of rectangular parallelopiped shape comprising a bottom and four side walls, at least four cylindrical projections extending normally outwardly from said bottom and arranged in two rows of opposed projections to define a square, a tubular projection extending normally from the inner face of said bottom.[7]

The language will seem complicated at first, but the important parts can be clarified relatively easily. The claim states that Christiansen's patented invention is a 'hollow building block' with 'at least four cylindrical projections extending normally outwardly'. These cylindrical projections are the *studs* in the 'stud-and-tube' coupling system. The claim further states that the invention comprises 'a tubular projection extending normally from the inner face' of the brick. This refers to the *tubes* in the 'stud-and-tube' coupling system.

When reading the claim language pay close attention to the word 'tubular'. If we look up the word 'tubular' in the *Oxford English Dictionary* it says 'constituting or consisting of a tube; cylindrical, hollow, and open at one or both ends'.[8] Furthermore, the *Oxford Dictionary of Mechanical Engineering* defines a tube as a 'long hollow cylinder'.[9]

Now consider the ATC brick shown in Figure 9.1. You will note that the ATC brick has solid (not hollow) 'tubes' inside. The question is, does the Christiansen patent mean that Christiansen owns only toy bricks with hollow tubes inside? Or does the patent allow him to own toy bricks with either hollow tubes or solid 'tubes' inside? In the latter case, then ATC has potentially infringed the Christiansen patent by practising the patented invention.

There is no discussion for this activity; we will instead continue with the example through the chapter.

This claim is taken from the US patent. The UK patent also claims a hollow brick with 'tubular' internal projections, although through a complex series of independent and dependent claims.

This is an entirely hypothetical example. In reality, Christiansen did not bring any form of patent infringement action against ATC. Whether he could have done so would have depended on the content of Japanese patent law as it stood in the 1970s. Here we focus on how contemporary UK law would apply in such a scenario purely for illustration purposes.

Answering questions like the one posed in Activity 9.2 requires some knowledge of **claim construction**. Claim construction refers to the process by which courts and other legal actors 'construct' language in the claims. Claim construction is accordingly the process through which the owner's property is defined.

But, first, what does the word 'construction' mean? Law students are perhaps more familiar with the idea of 'interpretation'. Lawyers interpret documents and statutes all the time. So how do **interpretation** and **construction** differ? Here is one common way of understanding the distinction:

- Interpretation is the process of deciding what is the *meaning* of words.
- Construction is the process of deciding what is the *legal effect* of words.[10]

The **interpretation–construction distinction** is important because courts might decide to give words a broader legal effect than their meaning. For example, consider the Christiansen and ATC bricks once more. A court might reasonably conclude that the word 'tubular' in the claim means a 'hollow cylinder'. After all, this is how some major dictionaries define the term.

Nevertheless, the court may, as a legal matter, give the words a different legal effect. It may, for example, decide that the legal effect of the word 'tubular' is broader than the dictionary definition, and covers both hollow and solid cylinders. If the claim language is construed broadly, then Christiansen might own not only bricks with hollow tubes, but also bricks with solid tubes. In the latter case, they can use the patent to stop the manufacture and sale of the ATC bricks.

> Or, more accurately, what he owns would be knowledge of how to produce these bricks, what they do, and how they can be used.

Understanding how UK courts construct claim language is not easy. The rules on claim construction have changed considerably over time. It is therefore helpful to break the topic down into three parts. This section first introduces the old British approach: the principle of purposive construction. The section then introduces an idea that largely comes from jurisdictions outside the UK: the doctrine of equivalents. Finally, the section turns to how UK courts have recently tried to bring these approaches together in the *Actavis* standard. This historical exploration reveals how the patent right today has become broader over time.

9.2.1   Purposive Construction

Different countries have, at different times, adopted different approaches to claim construction. Some patent historians argue that British courts traditionally adopted a strict approach to claim construction.[11] Under this strict approach, courts interpreted the claim language literally and give it a very narrow legal effect. This approach was summarised in the pithy aphorism 'what is not claimed is disclaimed'.[12] By contrast, Germany is often given as an example of a jurisdiction that adopted a more flexible approach to claim construction.[13] Under the more flexible approach, claims were merely guidelines, and not to be taken too literally.

There are pros and cons to both approaches. The literalistic approach is good for third parties. If courts always construct claims using a strict literal approach, third parties should be able to read the patent specification and know precisely what the patent owner owns and what remains free to use. However, as discussed in the following case, an overly literal reading of patent claims might be detrimental to the patent owner. For this reason, courts in the UK no longer adopt a literal approach to claim construction.

Case 9.1 *Catnic Components Ltd v Hill & Smith Ltd* [1982] RPC 183 (HL)

Facts

If you look just above a door in a wall, you might find something called a 'lintel'. A lintel is a type of beam that builders put at the top of a door to support the heavy material above. Without such support, there is a risk that the heavy building materials above the door frame will collapse.

Catnic (claimant–appellant) successfully applied for patent in 1969 on a type of lintel. Figure 9.2 ((a)) displays a drawing of the lintel taken from the patent specification. The patent specification claimed a lintel including: 'a second rigid support member *extending vertically* from or near the rear edge of the first horizontal plate or part to join with the second plate or part adjacent its rear edge'. This rigid support member is marked with 9 A on Figure 9.2 ((a)).

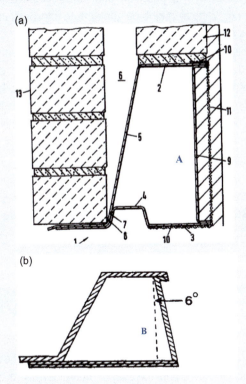

Figure 9.2 Catnic lintel ((a)); Hill & Smith lintel ((b)).
Catnic lintel from patent GB 1503491. Hill & Smith lintel from Catnic Components Ltd v Hill & Smith Ltd *[1982] RPC 183, 241 (HL)*

The Catnic lintel was commercially successful and attracted would-be competitors. Hill & Smith (defendants–respondents) began to sell their own lintels in the 1970s based on the Catnic one. Like the Catnic one, their lintel initially also had a 'vertical' rigid support member.

Patents IV: Scope

This process of designing a product in a way to avoid infringing an existing patent is often known as 'designing around' the patent.

In 1975, Catnic informed Hill & Smith of their patent. Hill and Smith therefore deliberately redesigned their lintel to avoid potential patent infringement. To do this, they changed the angle of the rigid support member. Instead of being perfectly vertical, the new Hill & Smith lintel was angled between 6 and 8 degrees (as illustrated at point B in Figure 9.2 ((b)). Importantly, this slight angling of the member had no significant effect on how well the lintel worked: it was still highly able to provide structural support.

Issue and Procedure

Catnic sued Hill & Smith, alleging their new lintel still infringed the patent. Hill & Smith denied infringement on the grounds that their lintel, although the same in all other respects, did not include a *vertical* support member. The issue was: how should the term 'vertical' in the patent claim be construed? If one adopts a very literal approach to claim interpretation and construction, then one might be tempted to say no. Vertical might be thought to mean straight up and that anything which is angled is not vertical.

At first instance, Mr Justice Whitford upheld the claim for patent infringement. This was reversed, however, by the Court of Appeal. Lord Justice Waller thought that the word 'vertical' must be a 'word of precision'. That is, he thought that a PSITA would understand the word vertical would be used in a highly precise way to mean only things which are straight up. Accordingly, he concluded that, by making a lintel with an angled support member, Hill & Smith were not making the patented invention.

The House of Lords disagreed. Below is an extract from Lord Diplock which introduced a new approach to claim construction in the UK – the so-called **purposive construction** approach. Applying this purposive approach, Lord Diplock upheld the appeal.

DIPLOCK L

My Lords, a patent specification is a unilateral statement by the patentee, in words of his own choosing, addressed to those likely to have a practical interest in the subject matter of his invention (i.e. 'skilled in the art'), by which he informs them what he claims to be the essential features of the new product or process for he claims to be essential that constitute the so-called 'pith and marrow' of the claim. A patent specification should be given a purposive construction rather than a purely literal one derived from applying to it the kind of meticulous verbal analysis in which lawyers are too often tempted by their training to indulge. The question in each case is: whether persons with practical knowledge and experience of the kind of work in which the invention was intended to be used, would understand that strict compliance with a particular descriptive word or phrase appearing in a claim was intended by the patentee to be an essential requirement of the invention so that any variant would fall outside the monopoly claimed, even though it could have no material effect upon the way the invention worked.

The question, of course, does not arise where the variant would in fact have a material effect upon the way the invention worked. Nor does it arise unless at the date of publication of the specification it would be obvious to the informed reader that this was so. Where it is not obvious, in the light of then-existing knowledge, the reader is entitled to assume that the patentee thought at the time of the specification that he had good reason for limiting his monopoly so strictly and had intended to do so, even though subsequent work by him or others in the field of the invention might show the limitation to have been unnecessary. It is to be answered in the negative only when it would be apparent to any reader skilled in the art that a particular descriptive word or phrase used in a claim cannot have been intended by a patentee, who was also skilled in the art, to exclude minor variants which, to the knowledge of both him and the readers to whom the patent was addressed, could have no material effect upon the way in which the invention worked.

The essential features of the invention that is the subject of claim 1 of the patent in suit in the instant appeal are much easier to understand than those of any of the three patents to which I have just referred; and this makes the question of its construction simpler. Put in a nutshell the question to be answered is: Would the specification make it obvious to a builder familiar with ordinary building operations that the description of a lintel in the form of a weight-bearing box girder of which the back plate was referred to as 'extending vertically' from one of the two horizontal plates to join the other, could not have been intended to exclude lintels in which the back plate although not positioned at precisely $90°$ to both horizontal plates was close enough to $90°$ to make no material difference to the way the lintel worked when used in building operations? No plausible reason has been advanced why any rational patentee should want to place so narrow a limitation on his invention. On the contrary, to do so would render his monopoly for practical purposes worthless, since any imitator could avoid it and take all the benefit of the invention by the simple expedient of positioning the back plate a degree or two from the exact vertical.

(pp. 242–44)

294   *Patents IV: Scope*

ACTIVITY 9.3

Lord Diplock's judgment is not easy to read. To start off, just focus on the first and third paragraphs. In the Court of Appeal, Lord Justice Waller concluded that the legal effect of the term 'vertical' should depend on how a PSITA would interpret that word. Put another way, the term 'vertical' means whatever a PSITA would understand it to mean. How is Lord Diplock's test different? Hint: focus on the distinction he draws between a 'purposive construction' and a 'meticulous verbal analysis'.

As discussed in Section 9.2.3, Lord Neuberger in *Actavis v Eli Lilly* criticised this 'conflation' of interpretation and construction.

Lord Diplock's approach is interesting for two reasons. First, he equated (or perhaps conflated) claim interpretation with claim construction. In a nutshell, when confronted with a word like 'vertical', Diplock asked: what would a PSITA understand the patent owner to have intended the word to mean? Would the PSITA understand the owner to have intended that 'strict compliance' with the literal meaning of the word was an 'essential' part of the invention? That is fundamentally a question of interpretation. In this particular case, Lord Diplock could see 'no plausible reason' why the owner would want to limit the scope of their patent to only perfectly vertical lintels, and presumably a PSITA would also see the case that way. Hence, the claim language was interpreted to mean vertical and slightly angled lintels.

Thereafter, Diplock decided to use the interpretation of the claim to guide its construction. That is, he decided that the meaning of the word 'vertical', and its legal effect, should be exactly the same. Because the claim's legal effect was to include both vertical and slightly angled lintels, then Catnic owned both types of lintel. Hill & Smith had accordingly infringed the patent right.

The second interesting point appears in the second paragraph. Lord Diplock explains here that courts do not always need to use the purposive construction test. There are two situations where this is the case:

- First, the purposive construction principle is not applied when the '**variant**' (i.e. the defendant's product) works differently to the patented invention (i.e. has a 'material effect' on how the invention works). If the variant works differently, then it must be outside the scope of the claims.
- Second, imagine that the defendant's variant does work in much the same way as the owner's invention. When the patent specification was published, would it have been *obvious* to a PSITA that the defendant's variant would work much the same way? If the answer is 'no, that would not have been obvious' then the defendant's variant is once again outside the scope of claims.

Neither of these situations arose in the *Catnic* case. In the *Catnic* case, the defendant's angled lintel worked much the same as the owner's claimed invention. Furthermore, in 1969 when the Catnic patent was published, it would have been obvious to a PSITA that a lintel with a slightly angled rigid support member would work much like one with a vertical rigid support member. Because neither of these two exceptions applied, Lord Diplock had to apply the principle of purposive construction.

The *Catnic* decision was decided under the old Patents Act 1949. In 1977, the new Patents Act was enacted. One of the goals of the Patents Act 1977 was to align domestic patent law with the European Patent Convention (EPC) 1973.[14] One of the questions for the British courts following the 1977 Act was whether the purposive interpretation approach to claim construction was consistent with the new EPC and therefore continued to be good law under the 1977 Act.

When it was enacted, one of the aims of the EPC was to find a compromise between the UK and German approaches to claim construction.[15] It was thought that the English preference for literalism and the German understanding of the claims as merely guidelines were incompatible. The EPC sought a middle ground between these two approaches in article 69, which states that the extent of protection granted to the patent 'shall be determined by the claims'. When the EPC was signed, member states also agreed to a separate protocol that explained further how article 69 should be interpreted. Article 1 of the Protocol on the Interpretation of Article 69 states the following:

> Article 69 should not be interpreted as meaning that the extent of the protection conferred by a European patent is to be understood as that defined by the strict, literal meaning of the wording used in the claims ... Nor should it be taken to mean that the claims serve only as a guideline ... On the contrary, it is to be interpreted as defining a position between these extremes which combines a fair protection for the patent proprietor with a reasonable degree of legal certainty for third parties.

This issue was resolved in 1990 in the case of *Improver Corp v Remington Consumer Products*.[16] The Improver Corporation manufactured the 'Epilady'. The Epilady was a hand-held electrical device for removing body hair. A technical drawing of the Epilady appears in Figure 9.3 ((a)). At the top of the device was a coil made from metal (A in Figure 9.3). This coil was composed of metal in a 'helical spring' shape. Figure 9.3 ((b)) also provides a closer view of that helical spring shape. When the device was turned on, the coil would rotate, catching hair in the spring, and then ripping it from the body. Improver owned the relevant patent which claimed a hair removal device employing a 'helical spring'.

Remington also produced a hair removal device called the Lady Remington Smooth and Silky. It was also a handheld electrical device. However, rather than use a coil to remove hair, it used a rubber rod with little notches (or 'radial slits') cut into it. This is depicted in Figure 9.3 ((c)). Once again, the idea was that the

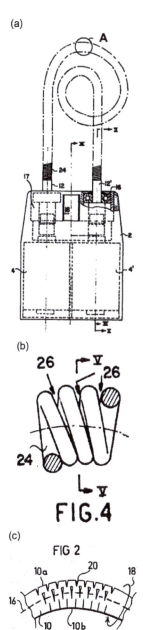

Figure 9.3 Epilady ((a)); Epilady helical spring ((b)); Lady Remington rubber rod ((c)).

Epilady technical drawings from EP0101656A1. Lady Remington technical drawings from US4726375

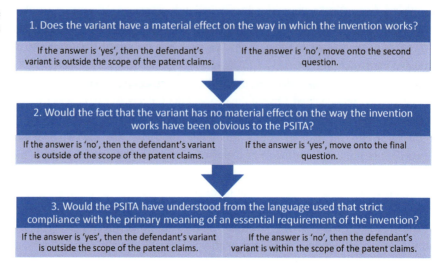

Figure 9.4 The *Improver* questions

hair would get caught in the notches, the rubber disk would then rotate, and the hair would be ripped from the body.

The case is important for three reasons. First, Mr Justice Hoffmann decided that the purposive construction approach was consistent with the EPC and continued to apply under the Patents Act 1977. Second, Mr Justice Hoffmann 'reformulated' the purposive construction approach into a three-question analysis. In his view, courts should ask three questions, stated in Figure 9.4. Only if the answers to these questions are 'no, yes, no' is the defendant practising the patented invention.

This test – called the *Improver* questions – has had a mixed history. It had considerable importance in patent litigation between 1990 and 2004.[17] But in 2004, the test started to lose its importance after *Kirin-Amgen v Hoechst*.[18] In that case, Lord Hoffmann (then sitting in the House of Lords) emphasised that the principle of purposive construction was the 'bedrock' of claim construction.[19] By contrast, the *Improver* questions were labelled as 'only guidelines' – helpful in some cases, but not all.[20] However, more recently in the 2017 decision of *Actavis*, the Supreme Court gave the test, albeit in a modified form, new importance. Section 9.2.3 discusses that new standard.

The third reason the *Improver* case was important was the outcome. Mr Justice Hoffmann decided that Remington had not practised the patented invention. Their rubber rod variant worked much the same way as Improver's helical spring (both rotated and plucked hair from the body), and the fact that the two products worked similarly would have been obvious to a PSITA at the time the specification was published. And, so, the question came down to the purposive construction standard. On that question, Mr Justice Hoffmann held that upon reading the term 'helical spring', a PSITA would think that the owner must have intended their patent only to cover helical springs, and that anything else would be outside the scope of the patent. In his view, a rubber rod with notches was a 'different thing' to a spring.[21] A defendant could only practise the patented invention, therefore, if they made a hair removal device with a helical spring coil. It was, in other words, an essential requirement of the invention.

This outcome was markedly different to the outcome arrived at by other European courts. Improver and Remington litigated this case not only in the UK, but in a range of European countries, including Germany. In contrast to Mr Justice Hoffmann, the German courts held that the term 'helical spring' could be construed to include things like rubber rods.[22] And, so, Remington was held to infringe the patent in Germany, but not in the UK. This suggested that, despite the EPC's attempt to reach a compromise, a difference in approach to claim construction still existed among EPC countries.

ACTIVITY 9.4

Now is a good time to return to the Christiansen brick. As we will see in Section 9.2.3, the *Improver* questions have been modified by the *Actavis* standard. Nevertheless, it is helpful to try to apply these questions now. This will make the later *Actavis* standard more intelligible. With that in mind, how do the *Improver* questions apply to the ATC bricks? Has ATC made something that falls within the scope of Christiansen's claims?

To answer that question, some additional information is helpful. In 1957, Christiansen was actively considering various types of coupling system. At this point, he produced some prototypes of bricks that used solid tubes in the inside of the brick. Ultimately, Christiansen decided not to use those solid tubes. This was because they found the hollow tubes had greater 'clutch power' – that is, they locked more tightly with the studs than the solid tubes.

9.2.2 Doctrine of Equivalents

The post-*Catnic* British approach focused on the words contained in the claims. As Diplock and Hoffmann explained, those words should be given a purposive interpretation. Moreover, the claims should be construed consistently with that purposive interpretation. The overall result was that a defendant could only infringe the patent rights if they made something that fell *within* a purposive construction of the claims. If the defendant made something that was *outside* the claims, there could be no infringement of the patentee's rights.

But not all countries agreed with that approach. Some countries developed a legal rule called the '**doctrine of equivalents**'. Under this rule, a defendant could be liable for infringing a patent even if they made something which fell *outside* the scope of the claims, in limited circumstances. The following American case demonstrates.

Patents IV: Scope

Case 9.2 *Graver Tank & MFG Co, Inc v Linde Air Products Co, 339 US 605 (1950) (USA)*

Facts

Welding is the process of joining metals together. The welding process involves heating two or more pieces of metal to very high temperatures, such that they melt and can be fused together. A 'flux' is a chemical agent used in this process. Adding flux to the melting metals helps the fusion process in various ways, in particular by preventing oxidation of the metals.

Linde Air Products (claimant–respondent) owned patents on a certain type of flux. Their patent claimed a flux composed of silicates of calcium and magnesium. Graver Tank (defendants–appellants) made their own flux out of silicates of calcium and manganese. Despite the similar name, manganese and magnesium are distinct elements and occupy different positions in the periodic table.

Issue and Procedure

Linde Air Products sued Graver Tank for patent infringement. It was agreed by the parties that the defendant's flux was outside the claim language: the patent owner claimed a flux made of magnesium and the defendants had not made a flux made of magnesium. Nevertheless, it was also agreed that the two elements worked in a similar way. Thus the trial judge concluded that 'for all practical purposes, manganese silicate can be efficiently and effectively substituted for calcium and magnesium silicates as the major constituent of the welding composition'. The issue for the US Supreme Court was: should a defendant who makes something not within the claim language nevertheless be liable for patent infringement? The court answered that with a resounding 'yes'.

JUSTICE JACKSON

In determining whether an accused device or composition infringes a valid patent, resort must be had in the first instance to the words of the claim. If accused matter falls clearly within the claim, infringement is made out, and that is the end of it.

But courts have also recognized that to permit imitation of a patented invention which does not copy every literal detail would be to convert the protection of the patent grant into a hollow and useless thing. Such a limitation would leave room for – indeed, encourage – the unscrupulous copyist to make unimportant and insubstantial changes and substitutions in the patent which, though adding nothing, would be enough to take the copied matter outside the claim, and hence outside the reach of law. One who seeks to pirate an invention, like one who seeks to pirate a copyrighted book or play, may be expected to introduce minor variations to conceal and shelter the piracy. Outright and forthright duplication is a dull and very rare type of infringement. To prohibit no other would place the inventor at the mercy of verbalism, and would be subordinating substance to form. It would deprive him of the benefit of his invention, and would foster concealment, rather than disclosure, of inventions, which is one of the primary purposes of the patent system.

The doctrine of equivalents evolved in response to this experience. The essence of the doctrine is that one may not practice a fraud on a patent. Originating almost a century ago in the case of *Winans v. Denmead*, 15 How. 330, it has been consistently applied by this Court and the lower federal courts, and continues today ready and available for utilization when the proper circumstances for its application arise. 'To temper unsparing logic and prevent an infringer from stealing the benefit of the invention', a patentee may invoke this doctrine to proceed against the producer of a device 'if it performs substantially the same function in substantially the same way to obtain the same result'.

(pp. 607–08)

The court agreed that the defendant's flux infringed the patent. Because manganese performed the same function as magnesium, and worked in substantially the same way as magnesium, and achieved overall the same result as magnesium, manganese was deemed to be an 'equivalent' of magnesium. While the defendant did not make something that fell within the claim language, they made something which was substantially equivalent thereto. Following this decision, American patent owners own not simply the invention as demarcated by the claims, but also other inventions that are substantially equivalent to that invention.

Historically, the UK did not adopt a doctrine of equivalents. Although the *Catnic* case moved away from literalism, the principle of purposive construction still limited the scope of the patent protection to the claim language. Applying that principle to the *Graver Tank* case would require the court to decide what the word 'magnesium' meant by appealing to the PSITA's understanding of the patentee's intentions. That would be a very different test to the one adopted by the US Supreme Court. The US Supreme Court did not spend any time deciding what the word 'magnesium' meant or was intended to mean. Instead, their analysis was an objective inquiry into whether the two things – magnesium and manganese – were functionally equivalent.

Germany, much like the USA, has long adopted a doctrine of equivalents.[23] And this once again posed a difficulty for the EPC. How could the EPC

Patents IV: Scope

accommodate both the UK and Germany when one did not adopt a doctrine of equivalents and the other did? Answers to this question started to emerge in the year 2000 when the EPC was updated. In that year, a new article (article 2) was added to the Protocol on the Interpretation of Article 69 EPC. The new article 2 concerns 'equivalents' and says the following:

> For the purpose of determining the extent of protection conferred by a European patent, due account shall be taken of any element which is equivalent to an element specified in the claims.

The natural question to ask is whether EPC countries must adopt a doctrine of equivalents following this update? At least initially, the UK courts thought this was not necessary. In the 2003 House of Lords case of *Kirin-Amgen v Hoechst Marion*, Lord Hoffmann decided that article 69 EPC 'firmly shuts the door on any doctrine which extends protection outside the claims'.[24] After all, article 69 says clearly that the claims determine the scope of protection. At the same time, article 2 of the protocol only says that 'due account' needs to be taken of equivalents. It does not, for example, say that equivalents are clearly to be treated as infringements of the patent.

9.2.3   The New British Approach: *Actavis*

Everything changed in 2017. Until that point, the patentee's property was still demarcated by the scope of the claims (albeit those claims were to be interpreted and construed purposively, not literally). Meanwhile other countries allowed the patent owner to own inventions not described in the claims, if those inventions were nevertheless 'equivalent' to the invention. In *Actavis v Eli Lilly*, the UK Supreme Court brought the UK closer into alignment with the USA and Germany. This modern approach is now the controlling law.

Case 9.3 *Actavis v Eli Lilly* [2017] UKSC 48

Facts

Pemetrexed is a chemical which can help treat cancerous tumours. But it can also have damaging side effects for the patient. Eli Lilly (claimants–respondents) helpfully found that if a compound called pemetrexed disodium was administered in combination with vitamin B12, then the patient would suffer fewer side effects. To that end, they claimed the 'use of pemetrexed disodium...in combination with vitamin B12' for the use in cancer therapy.

Actavis (defendant–appellant) made their own cancer treatment. Actavis also used vitamin B12 in their treatment. But rather than use pemetrexed *disodium*, they used pemetrexed *diacid*, pemetrexed *ditromethamine* and pemetrexed *dipotassium*.

Issue and Procedure

Eli Lilly sued Actavis for infringement of the patent. At first instance, Mr Justice Arnold (as he then was) held that there was no infringement of the patent. Applying the purposive construction standard of *Catnic* and *Improver*, he concluded that the term 'pemetrexed disodium' could not include drugs that used pemetrexed diacid, etc. This was upheld by the Court of Appeal. Eli Lilly then appealed to the Supreme Court. The issue the court had to answer was: what is the correct approach to claim construction?

LORD NEUBERGER

In my view, notwithstanding what Lord Diplock said in *Catnic* [1982] RPC 183, 242, a problem of infringement is best approached by addressing two issues, each of which is to be considered through the eyes of the notional addressee of the patent in suit, ie the person skilled in the relevant art. Those issues are: (i) does the variant infringe any of the claims as a matter of normal interpretation; and, if not, (ii) does the variant nonetheless infringe because it varies from the invention in a way or ways which is or are immaterial? If the answer to either issue is 'yes', there is an infringement; otherwise, there is not. Such an approach complies with article 2 of the Protocol, as issue (ii) squarely raises the principle of equivalents, but limits its ambit to those variants which contain immaterial variations from the invention. It is also apparent that the two issues comply with article 1 of the Protocol in that they involve balancing the competing interests of the patentee and of clarity, just as much as they seek to balance the encouragement of inventions and their disclosure with the need for a competitive market. In my view, issue (i) self-evidently raises a question of interpretation, whereas issue (ii) raises a question which would normally have to be answered by reference to the facts and expert evidence.

In *Kirin-Amgen* [2005] RPC 9, Lord Hoffmann, following his approach in *Improver* [1990] FSR 181 (which itself had followed Lord Diplock's analysis in *Catnic* [1982] RPC 183) effectively conflated the two issues, and indicated that the conflated issue involved a question of interpretation. I have considerable difficulties with the notion that there is a single conflated, or compound, issue, and, even

> if that notion is correct, that that issue raises a question of interpretation. Indeed, in my view, to characterise the issue as a single question of interpretation is wrong in principle, and unsurprisingly, therefore, can lead to error.
>
> I had wondered whether the question whether issue (ii) truly involves a question of interpretation raised what was merely an arid issue of categorisation. However, I have concluded that that nettle needs to be grasped, because, so long as the issue is treated as one of interpretation, it will lead to a risk of wrong results in patent infringement cases and it will also lead to a risk of confusing the law relating to the interpretation of documents. In my opinion, issue (ii) involves not merely identifying what the words of a claim would mean in their context to the notional addressee, but also considering the extent if any to which the scope of protection afforded by the claim should extend beyond that meaning.
>
> (paras 54–56)

Whereas Lord Diplock conflated the issues of interpretation and construction, Lord Neuberger introduced a new two-stage analysis which separates them more clearly. That new test is shown in Figure 9.5.

The first step in the analysis is, according to Lord Neuberger, a question of interpretation. Elsewhere in the judgment he explains that this should follow the same principles that lawyers would follow when interpreting language in a contract. To illustrate his point, Neuberger cites a recent Supreme Court case on contract law which summarises those principles.[25] That case explains that the court's task is to interpret language to ascertain it's 'objective meaning'.[26] That interpretation does not need to be literalistic, but must be read according to the wider context. When it came to the facts of the case, Neuberger held that 'disodium' could not be interpreted in a way that would include the diacid, ditromethamine or dipotassium.

While the first question is a question of interpretation, the second question is not. The point of the second question is to introduce into UK law a doctrine of equivalents that allows courts to give the claims a broader construction than would be arrived at through a process of interpretation. When this new doctrine was applied to the facts, the court found that Actavis's product did infringe the patent: the use of pemetrexed diacid, ditromethamine or dipotassium was merely an 'immaterial' variation.

How then is the new doctrine of equivalents to be applied? Lord Neuberger answered this by appealing to the *Improver*

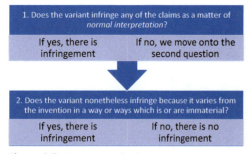

Figure 9.5 *Actavis* standard

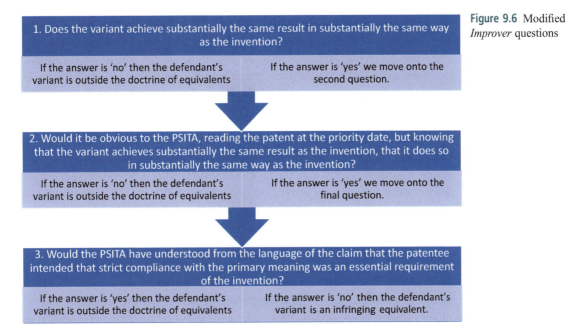

Figure 9.6 Modified *Improver* questions

questions. In Lord Neuberger's view, the idea of purposive interpretation and the following *Improver* questions was never about interpretation at all, and it was wrong to say they were. Instead, such rules were always really about constructing the claims' legal effect beyond their interpretation. And so he adopted them, albeit with some clarifications and modifications, to guide the second step of the new *Actavis* analysis. The modified questions appear in Figure 9.6.

The changes to the *Improver* questions are both subtle and important. Let's break them down a bit further:

- Question 1 was clarified but not changed dramatically. Previously courts asked whether the defendant's variant had a 'material effect' on the way the invention worked. Now courts ask whether the defendant's variant achieves the same result and works in the same way.
- Question 2 was changed in a slightly more significant way. Now, the question is whether the PSITA, *having been told* that the variant achieves the same result, would conclude that it does so in the same way. The consequence is that the answer is more likely to be 'yes'.
- Question 3 was changed in the most subtle and most important way of all. Here courts are using the same question as before, but for a different purpose. Remember that the *Catnic–Improver* approach was superficially about claim *interpretation*. The point of the old question 3 was to determine what the word in the claim *meant*. To that end, courts used a purposive test. Under the new

question 3, courts still use the purposive test. But they are no longer suggesting that this will help us understand what the claim *means*. Courts are in other words not doing interpretation. Instead, they are using the test to do construction and ask how far beyond the interpretation the legal effect of the claims can go.

This last point about question 3 is important because it can change case outcomes, as illustrated by the *Improver* case. Recall that Hoffmann decided that under a purposive interpretation, the rubber rod was not within the scope of the claims. In essence, Hoffmann decided that the patentee could not have meant the claim words – 'helical spring' – to mean anything other than a helical spring; ergo no infringement. However, a PSITA today might plausibly say 'I know the patentee did not intend the specific term "helical spring" to *mean* rubber rods, but they did intend for *legal effect* of the claims to extend to an equivalent like a rubber rod'. This approach inevitably widens the scope of claim construction.

It is important to grasp the last point to make subsequent post-*Actavis* case law intelligible. Some judges have recently, when considering step 1 of the *Actavis* analysis concluded that 'normal interpretation is purposive interpretation'. This has prompted some to ask: does that not mean step 1 and step 2 have become confused and duplicative? To which the answer is 'no'. At step 1, courts use a purposive test to *interpret* what the claims mean. At step 2, question 3, we use a purposive test to decide how far beyond the claim meaning the legal effect can go (i.e. to *construct* the claim).

To round off the discussion, let us return to the ATC example.

> ### ACTIVITY 9.5
>
> Using the new *Actavis* standard, do you think that ATC can be said to have practised the patented invention? And what does the new standard mean for the conceptual question about whether patents are property?

And this is where the story of claim construction ends, for now at least. Today the patent owner's property right is not only a right to exclusively use the invention as claimed in the patent, but also any substantially equivalent inventions as well. The consequence is patent rights are, quite probably, broader than ever before in British history.

9.3   EXCEPTIONS

Section 9.1 characterised the owner's rights as broader in scope than the author's rights in copyright. In part, this is because the author's copyright is qualified by a range of important exceptions. By contrast, fewer exceptions exist to patent rights. But that does not mean exceptions to patent rights do not exist nor that they are

9.3 Exceptions **305**

unimportant. The Patents Act lists several exceptions to the patentee's rights. Three defences are particularly noteworthy: experimental use, private use and prior use.

9.3.1 Experimental Use

As summarised in Chapter 6, innovation is often cumulative. It was only through building on Page's Self-Locking Brick that Christiansen was able to develop his Toy Building Brick. This idea is summed up in Sir Isaac Newton's memorable claim that 'if I have seen further it is by standing on the shoulders of giants'. The problem this presents – explored in Activity 6.4 – is that in some contexts, patents may discourage invention, rather than encourage it.

Nevertheless, utilitarians argue that an appropriately balanced patent system will still make society a happier place. One important way such balance is achieved is the **experimental use** defence. Section 60(5)(b) of the Patents Act states that it is not an infringement to use the patented invention providing that the use is 'for experimental purposes relating to the subject-matter of the invention'. To claim this defence, the defendant must (a) have an experimental purpose, and (b) their experiments must relate to the subject matter of the invention. That second requirement means that using the OncoMouse (see section 7.3.1.) to perform cancer research would not fall within the scope of the defence: while the research arguably has an experimental purpose, the experimental purpose is being carried out in relation to cancer, rather than in relation to the patented subject matter, that is, the OncoMouse.

Whether a defendant will be able to benefit from the defence depends significantly on whether they have an experimental purpose. In some cases, this will be relatively easy to establish. A scientist carrying out non-commercial research in a university setting who merely aims to understand how the invention works will be seen to have an experimental purpose. But the issue becomes more complicated when the defendant is a commercial actor, as Case 9.4 discusses.

Case 9.4 *CoreValve Inc v Edwards Lifesciences* [2009] EWHC 6 (Pat)

Facts

Edwards Lifesciences (defendant) owned a patent on a type of artificial heart valve. CoreValve (claimant) was a competitor of Edwards and also produced artificial heart valves. CoreValve ran a clinical programme with selected hospitals in Europe. Under this programme, CoreValve supplied the hospitals with their artificial valve and trained their cardiologists in the use of the valves. CoreValve stated that this clinical programme had a number of purposes, including to investigate the efficiency of safety of the valve on a long-term basis over a large number of patients.

However, CoreValve did not give the hospitals the valves for free; instead, they charged the hospitals a rather substantial amount for them.

Issue and Procedure

CoreValve claimed that the Edwards patent was invalid. Edwards responded that the patent was valid and infringed by CoreValve. CoreValve claimed that if the patent was valid and infringed, their use was merely experimental use. This presented the following issue: was their use for an 'experimental purpose'? Ultimately, Mr Justice Prescott QC in the High Court Chancery Division Patents Court found that the patent was not infringed. This finding was significant because he also held that this was not merely an experimental use.

MR JUSTICE PRESCOTT QC

It is well settled (*Monsanto v. Stauffer* [1985] RPC 515, C.A.) that mere field trials which are intended to demonstrate the efficacy of the product for the purposes of regulatory approval do not qualify for the exception set for in s. 60(5)(b) of the Act. In general, the purpose of this defence is to encourage scientific research while protecting the legitimate interests of the patentee. This involves a balance.

Section 60(5)(b) is based on Article 27(b) of the Community Patent Convention. The Federal Supreme Court of Germany considered the equivalent provision in Klinische Versuche (Clinical Trials) I [1997] RPC 623. The only part of the court's official headnote that is relevant for present purposes is as follows (English translation):

> An act for experimental purposes which is related to the subject-matter of the invention and therefore legitimate can exist if a patented pharmaceutically active substance is used in clinical trials with the aim of finding whether and, where appropriate, in what form the active substance is suitable for curing or alleviating certain other human diseases.

In that case the substance in question (an interferon) was known for use in the treatment of rheumatoid arthritis and the defendants were conducting clinical trials to see if that substance could be used for treating other diseases such as cancer, AIDS and hepatitis. The invention – the thing that was claimed in the patent – was the substance as such. I can see that those clinical trials were squarely within the purpose of the exception, for their immediate purpose was to generate scientific information by experimenting with the substance that was the subject of the patent claim.

However, there must surely be an outward limit to that principle. Suppose the defendants in the German case had been selling a pharmaceutical that was fairly new to the market and their defence had been that, by so doing, they were gaining valuable information that was not otherwise available – contraindications, for instance, which could be stated in the product literature. Would that be acts done for 'experimental' purposes?

A defendant could always say, and with some truth, that by putting his product on the market (general or special) he was gaining valuable information that might even prompt him to modify his device in future. I have referred to Henry Ford's Model T car. I dare say that vehicle went through various modifications in the light of experience on the roads of early twentieth century America, and that is usually the case with any engineering product.

I acknowledge that the mere fact that the purpose of the defendant is commercial is no rebuttal of the statutory defence. After all, most pharmaceutical research organisations are commercial. They do research because they hope to make money one day. However, in the present case it cannot be denied that an immediate and present purpose of CoreValve is to generate revenue – which was not so in the German case.

I therefore think that a more complete statement of the principle – it did not arise in the German case – should involve the consideration whether the immediate purpose of the transaction in question is to generate revenue.

The relevant statutory phrase is 'acts done for experimental purposes'. The difficulty arises where the defendant has mixed purposes. I would reject the extreme proposition that, so long as one of the defendant's purposes is to generate information of scientific or technical value, it is irrelevant that another of his purposes is to generate ready cash. There may be no help for it but to consider the defendant's preponderant purposes.

On the evidence in this case I would hold that CoreValve's purposes are threefold: (1) to establish confidence in their product within the relevant market; (2) to generate immediate revenue of a substantial character; and (3) to gain information about clinical indications and, possibly, future modifications to be made to the physical structure of the device in the light of experience. I do not find that purpose (3) was their preponderant purpose.

I have not found this point easy, but on the whole I would hold that, on the assumption that the CoreValve device falls within Claim 1 of the patent in suit, section 60(5)(b) of the Patents Act 1977 is not a valid defence on the facts of this case.

(paras 72–81)

While establishing the importance of the defendant's 'preponderant purpose', one point has remained unexamined by the courts. Consider a defendant who experiments on a patented invention to learn more about how it works. The defendant intends to use this information to later manufacture and sell a competing product. Is that use still experimental?

9.3.2 Private Use and Prior Use

In addition to experimental use, defendants are permitted to engage in private non-commercial use of the patented invention under section 60(5)(a) of the Patents Act. While private does not necessarily mean the defendant's use must be secret, it does mean that the use must primarily be for the defendant's own personal use.

A somewhat related idea is the defence of prior use in section 64(1) of the Patents Act. When determining the state of the art for purposes of novelty, as discussed in Section 8.1, we include all matter which is available to the public at the priority date. But what happens if someone had made and used the invention prior to that priority date, and kept that use secret? Because that use would not form part of the state of the art, the applicant may well receive a patent on the invention. That patent could theoretically then be later used to restrain use of the invention by the prior user. To avoid this result, section 64(1) permits the prior user to continue their use within the UK providing they do so in 'good faith'. The defence can also apply when the prior user has not entirely used the invention prior to the priority date, but nevertheless made 'serious and effective preparations' to do so.

9.4 COMPULSORY LICENSING

Section 4.1.2 initially introduced the idea of compulsory licences within the discussion of copyright. That section briefly explained why the state might choose to compel the copyright owner to license their work against their wishes (for example in cases of orphan works).

Compulsory licensing is arguably even more important in patent law due to its subject matter. Granting inventors property rights and thereby enabling them to restrict supply may have life-changing consequences particularly in cases of pharmaceuticals. As a result, compulsory licensing provisions both in international and domestic UK law play an important role in alleviating the problem of monopoly.

9.4.1 International Provision

One of the few substantive provisions contained in the Paris Convention relates to compulsory licensing. Article 5A(2) of that Convention states that:

> (2) Each country of the Union shall have the right to take legislative measures providing for the grant of compulsory licenses to prevent the abuses which might result from the exercise of the exclusive rights conferred by the patent, for example, failure to work.

Failure to work means failure to make, use, sell, etc. the patented invention in the state. Such compulsory licences cannot however be issued within the first three years of the patent's term, or within four years from the date of filing.[27] The compulsory licence should also not be granted if the patent owner can justify their failure to work with 'legitimate reasons'. If such licences are granted, then they take the form of a non-exclusive and non-transferable licence.

The ability of states to issue compulsory licences was further restricted by article 31 of the TRIPS Agreement, subsection (b) of which states:

> such use may only be permitted if, prior to such use, the proposed user has made efforts to obtain authorization from the right holder on reasonable commercial terms and conditions and that such efforts have not been successful within a reasonable period of time. This requirement may be waived by a Member in the case of a national emergency or other circumstances of extreme urgency or in cases of public non-commercial use. In situations of national emergency or other circumstances of extreme urgency, the right holder shall, nevertheless, be notified as soon as reasonably practicable.

In addition, subsection (f) states that the right holder is to be 'paid adequate remuneration in the circumstances of each case, taking into account the economic value of the authorization'. What is lost, it is sometimes claimed, is not money but the patentee's ability to control the invention's use.

ACTIVITY 9.6

When the Paris Convention was debated, a famous French lawyer, M. Charles Lyon-Caen, argued that compulsory licensing was a derogation of the right of property and compared the inventor subject to such licensing to 'a man who owned his house but was required to allow all who requested it, to live with him on the payment of a rental'. This is certainly a provocative argument. I am not allowed to live in your home without your permission even if

> I promise to pay you rent. So why might I be allowed to use your patented invention for a fee but without your permission?!
>
> What do you think Lyon-Caen means when he says 'property'? Does he mean exclusive control or a bundle of rights?

As a practical matter, however, the patent owner might well lose money if a compulsory licence is issued. Recall that the problem of monopoly is that market power enables the owner to raise prices and restrict output. This enables the owner to earn competitive profits above that achieved under conditions of perfect competition. Even if someone pays 'adequate remuneration' under a compulsory licence, it is far from certain that such remuneration will be as high as the supra-competitive profit the owner can earn through voluntary licensing within a monopolistic marketplace.

States that are party to the Paris Convention and TRIPS Agreement interpret and apply these requirements in unique ways. Section 9.4.2 examines the UK's national implementation of the compulsory licensing provisions. But before turning to the UK, it is instructive to look first to India, where compulsory licences have been issued more frequently. The following case concerns the first compulsory licence issued in India.

Case 9.5 *Bayer v Natco*, Indian Intellectual Property Appellate Board OA/35/2012/PT/MUM (4 March 2013) (India)

Facts

Sorafenib is a pharmaceutical compound used for the treatment of liver and kidney cancer and was patented by Bayer Corporation (patentee–appellant), Germany, in India. Sorafenib is marketed worldwide under the brand name 'Nexavar'.

The Indian manufacturer CIPLA started producing and marketing Sorafenib in 2008 under a brand name 'Soranib'. Bayer filed a suit for infringement against CIPLA before the Indian courts. At the time of the suit, Bayer charged 280,438 INR (~ US$5,280) per month compared to CIPLA's version marketed at 27,960 INR (~ US$525) for the same number of tablets.

During the ongoing dispute between CIPLA and Bayer, another manufacturer, Natco (applicant–respondent) Pharma Limited, filed a request for compulsory licence against Bayer's patent on Sorafenib before the Indian Controller of Patents. Natco requested the compulsory licence based on section 84(1) of the Indian Patents Act of 1970, as amended in 2005. Section 84(1) of the Act as amended provides for compulsory licence after the expiration of three years from the date of the grant of a patent on any of the following grounds: (a) the reasonable requirements of the public with respect to the patented invention have not been satisfied, or (b) the patented invention is not available to the public at a reasonably affordable price, or (c) the patented invention is not worked in the territory of India.

On 6 December 2010, before the request for a compulsory licence was made, Natco sent a letter to Bayer requesting a voluntary licence. In that letter, Natco wrote that the cost charged by Bayer was too high and that most Indian patients 'can seldom afford such expensive drug'. They further wrote that they would be willing to make the product available to the public in India at a cost of less than 10,000 INR (~ US$120) per month. But in addition to requesting a voluntary licence, they wrote that their request was 'without prejudice' to their right to bring an invalidity claim later.

Bayer responded on 27 December denying the request for a voluntary licence. They stated that Natco must appreciate the very significant investment they make in researching and developing new drugs. They accordingly denied that Nexavar was not available to the patients in India at an affordable price. They also stated they may begin an infringement action against Natco.

Subsequently, the Controller found that Natco Pharma was deserving of a compulsory licence as Bayer had failed to meet the requirements of section 84 of the Patents Act 1970. The Controller drafted the terms and conditions of the compulsory licence and awarded a 6 per cent royalty from profits to Bayer.

Issue and Procedure

Bayer appealed the Controller's decision before the Indian Intellectual Property Appellate Board (IPAB). In their appeal, Bayer made a number of arguments.

First, Bayer claimed that Natco had not made a proper request in compliance with the Indian Patents Act, section 84(6)(iv). Section 84(6)(iv), consistent with Article 31 TRIPS, requires the applicant for a compulsory licence to first seek out a voluntary licence from the patentee. Bayer alleged that the letter sent on 6 December 2010 did not amount to a genuine attempt to license the drug, but instead was a 'veiled threat'. This argument was dismissed by the IPAB.

HON'BLE SMT. PRABHA SRIDEVAN, CHAIRMAN

'Compulsory licence' is not an unmentionable word. It is found in our Patents Act. Under a different name, it was there in the TRIPS (Trade-related Aspects of Intellectual Property Rights) too where it is called, 'Other use without authorization of the right holder'. It has been there even in the Paris Convention of 1883 'to prevent abuse which might result from the exercise of exclusive rights'. The TRIPS Agreement did not give a carte blanche to the Members in the grant of compulsory licence but it hedged this 'other use with sufficient conditions and authorization of this use would be considered only on a case to case basis of individualness'. This appeal challenges the compulsory licence ordered by the Controller-General.

. . .

We find from a reading of the two documents, viz., the letter and the response that the 3rd respondent who is the compulsory licence applicant had stated what according to it was a reasonable cost. The letter stated that Rs.2,80,000/- was not accessible to a large number of patients for whom the drug is meant and that they were willing to make available the drug at less than Rs.10,000/- per month if the appellant would grant licence. The appellant calls this letter more in the nature of a threat than a real request. We find that the third respondent had stated that the price at which it would offer the drug was less than Rs.10,000/-. On these terms, NATCO applied for voluntary license.

It is true that the letter spells out three conditions for the grant of licence in paragraph-6 and states that because of the prohibitory high cost, these three conditions are not satisfied, but yet, the offer had been made. The appellant on its part had understood the tenor of the letter. According to the appellant it had satisfied all the requirements of law. If there was a veiled threat, it was met equally by a veiled answer.

If the appellant thought that less than Rs.10,000/- was not a bargaining point, all that it should have stated was that there was some room for negotiation. But, the response did not indicate that, instead it clearly indicated that the appellant did not consider it appropriate to grant voluntary licence. Therefore, the offer was made and it was rejected. The 3rd respondent is not required to make another request when its efforts had failed. The law does not require that. On a consideration of these two documents, the Controller was of the view that the 3rd respondent had made an effort but it could have been 'more humble in writing and not hurting the sensibility' of the patented persons. They are after all rivals in business and we do not think there would be room for such sensibilities. The requirement of law was fully met and we reject this ground.

(paras 1, 14–16)

Second, Bayer claimed, somewhat audaciously, that the invention was not eligible for a compulsory licence because it was, contrary to TRIPS and the Indian Patents Act, being 'worked' in India for a reasonably affordable price. To prove this point, Bayer pointed to the activities of CIPLA. While suing

CIPLA for patent infringement, Bayer simultaneously argued that CIPLA's manufacture and sale of the drug in India meant that the invention was being 'worked' in the country and that the drug was available to the public at a reasonable cost.

Our Act is clear and we must decide according to this law. It is self-contained and the grant of approval to CIPLA is based on a different statute and is not related to this issue. CIPLA's presence is irrelevant for deciding whether the reasonable requirement of the public has been met or whether the patented invention has been made available to the public at a reasonably affordable price or whether the patented invention has been worked in the territory of India. . ..

For the grant of compulsory licence, the applicant should show and satisfy the Controller that the reasonable requirements of the public with respect to the patented invention have not been satisfied or that the patented invention is not available to the public at a reasonably affordable price or that the invention has not been worked in India. The reasonable requirements of the public would not be deemed to have been satisfied, if the patented invention was not being worked in the territory of India on a commercial scale to an adequate extent or on reasonable terms and was not being so worked to the fullest extent that is reasonably practicable [vide: Section 84(7)(d)]. The failure to meet the demand on reasonable terms must logically mean both quantity and price. The Controller has considered the Form-27 filed by the appellant. We have already extracted the crucial paragraphs from the affidavits of Dr. Manish Garg and others. All of them have deposed that this price is reasonably affordable one for the inventor. In none of the affidavits the deponents had considered the perspective of reasonable affordability from the public eye i.e. the patients' view. All that they would say is that the process of drug invention is long drawn and expensive, and that several trials and experiments must be made at the laboratory for hours together before the drugs are successfully launched and many of the experiments would end up in failure and loss. Therefore, they had spent huge amounts in Research and Development for invention and considering this, they fixed the price which accordingly, is reasonably affordable. . ..

The reasonably affordable price necessarily has to be fixed from the view point of the public and the word, 'afford' itself indicates whether the public can afford to buy the drug and therefore, we must consider this question from the view point of whether Rs.280,000/- per month is reasonably affordable price to the public. All the evidence filed by the appellant; the affidavits, the reports, etc. relating to the cost are not relevant to decide what the public can reasonably afford. The

> Controller was satisfied that the 'reasonably affordable price' has to be construed with reference to the public. The appellant has taken the stand that the statistics given by the respondent regarding the number of patients and the requirements cannot be accepted in full. Even if we take the appellant's own number, we find that the supply made by it cannot be said to be adequate and the price definitely is the factor that will determine whether the public will reach out for a particular invention. The Act also refers to the working of invention on a commercial scale and if the invention is not worked in the territory of India on a commercial scale to an adequate extent, then, the deeming provision of Section 84(7) will come into play.
>
> (paras 31, 38, 40)

It should be noted that Bayer also imported a small quantity of the drug into India. Bayer argued that, even if the CIPLA activities were put to one side, the importation of drugs amounted to a 'working' of the patent in India. This argument was dismissed however on the grounds that the importation was at a low level and not on a commercial scale.

9.4.2 UK Provision

The Patents Act 1977 permits actors to apply to the UK IPO for compulsory licence. Section 48 of the Act provides some 'general' provisions which must be considered in all cases of compulsory licensing. In addition, sections 55–59 provide for a specific type of compulsory licence known as 'crown use'. But, in contrast to India, these provisions are rarely, if ever, put into use.

9.4.2.1 GENERAL

Section 48 provides a set of criteria under which the UK IPO can issue a compulsory licence. The section is split into two parts 48A and 48B. The A section lists criteria which must be complied with when the patent is owned by an organisation from another WTO member state; the B section lists criteria relevant when the patent is owned by an organisation from a non-WTO member state. As there are currently 164 WTO members, the section 48B provisions are highly unlikely to ever be applied.

Section 48A states that the UK IPO can grant a compulsory licence in the following circumstances:

> (a) where the patented invention is a product, that a demand in the United Kingdom for that product is not being met on reasonable terms;

> (b) that by reason of the refusal of the proprietor of the patent concerned to grant a licence or licences on reasonable terms –
>   (i) the exploitation in the United Kingdom of any other patented invention which involves an important technical advance of considerable economic significance in relation to the invention for which the patent concerned was granted is prevented or hindered, or
>   (ii) the establishment or development of commercial or industrial activities in the United Kingdom is unfairly prejudiced;
> (c) that by reason of conditions imposed by the proprietor of the patent concerned on the grant of licences under the patent, or on the disposal or use of the patented product or on the use of the patented process, the manufacture, use or disposal of materials not protected by the patent, or the establishment or development of commercial or industrial activities in the United Kingdom, is unfairly prejudiced.

Since the year 2000, only four applications for compulsory licences have been made. Two of the applications were later withdrawn, and two were later dismissed by the Comptroller when challenged.

Is it concerning that the UK IPO does not frequently issue compulsory licenses? On one account, we ought not to be overly concerned about this lack of use. It has been argued that the mere existence of the provision in the statute will stimulate the patentee into either working the invention in the UK or licensing it on reasonable terms. Even if the provision is not used frequently, the 'threat' remains. One might ask, however, when does a 'threat' become a bluff? While a legitimate threat may stimulate an actor into behaving a certain way, this might not happen if the actor perceives the threat as a mere bluff.

See Swansea Imports v Carver Technology, 10 June 2004, O/ 170/04.

9.4.2.2 CROWN USE

Although section 48A lays out general conditions under which a compulsory licence can be issued, further provisions in the Act state additional situations wherein such licences can operate. The most important of which is the 'crown use' provisions contained in sections 55–59. Section 55 allows the UK government, or any person authorised in writing by the government, to practise the patented invention without the permission of the patent holder. The government need not apply to the UK IPO before using the compulsory licence. But in cases where the government has a commercial purpose, there must be some form of negotiation between the government and the patentee (in order to satisfy the TRIPS article 31(b) requirement).

Once again, however, this provision is rarely used. The UK government's policy is to voluntarily license inventions wherever possible. This has not always been the case, however. One illustrative case from patent history is *Pfizer v Ministry of Health*.[28] Pfizer owned patents on the antibiotic tetracycline. In 1961, the Ministry of Health announced that they would use the crown use provision with respect to tetracycline in order to 'reduce expenditure' in the NHS. When Pfizer sued, the Ministry's crown use was upheld by the House of Lords. Despite the win for the NHS, this pattern is not commonplace today, even when there may be a case for employing the crown use provisions. To illustrate, Orkambi is a drug for the treatment of cystic fibrosis. The patent owner is Vertex. The price of a year's supply of Orkambi is typically above £100,000. For some time, the NHS was unwilling (or unable) to reach a voluntary licence agreement with Vertex. For a time, this left the 10,000 cystic fibrosis sufferers in the UK without access to life-saving medicine. The crown use provision was not however put into use. Eventually the UK government and Vertex reached a voluntary licence agreement.[29]

9.5 SUMMARY

Having completed the analysis of patent law, it is now instructive to step back and reconsider the patent bargain introduced in Chapter 6 and modelled in Figure 6.7. Recall that the 'property–monopoly' arrow represents the property rights, and the consequent monopolies, the public grants inventors in return for invention, disclosure and development. Over time, one might argue, that the monopoly arrow has grown. This growth is illustrated in Figure 9.7.

The growth in size of the property–monopoly arrow is attributable to two major factors. First, as the subject matter of patents have changed, a greater number of things are now subject to patent rights (discussed in Chapter 7). Patents do not merely grant exclusivity over a certain area of economic activity, nor do they apply only the 'new manner of manufactures'. Instead, patents enable ownership of a certain type of technical knowledge, in all its forms. Today, things as diverse as knowledge of human genes, instructions for computer programs, and the use of old things in old ways to achieve new purposes, are all potentially patentable.

Second, as explored primarily in this chapter, patents have moved closer to the ideal of exclusive control. While eighteenth-century patent law gave relatively narrow rights against fraudulent imitation of the invention, today the patent owner has the exclusive ability to practise not only the invention as claimed in the specification, but also equivalents to that invention under the *Actavis* standard. This broadened patent right is subject to narrow exceptions such as those for experimental use. Where flexibilities do exist in the system, such as in the case of compulsory licensing, they are rarely used.

Of course, the law's path is not unidirectional. Some developments such as the rule of absolute novelty push in the opposite direction. Nevertheless, one might conclude that the expansionary forces outstrip those forces that seek to constrain and limit the domain of patents.

The question that this prompts is whether the public wins or loses from this expansion of the patent monopoly. That answer depends on whether the broader and more powerful patent monopolies translate into more invention, more disclosure and better development of inventions, as discussed in Chapter 6. If this does occur, then the invent–disclosure–develop arrow on the model will expand in size as well (to the size of the lightly shaded blue arrow). If so, the public 'loses' in the sense that it must put up with more monopolies, but it is adequately compensated for that loss.

However, we also have reasons to be sceptical that greater monopoly power will simply translate into more inventive disclosure. Section 6.2 provided several reasons to believe that patents either do not automatically translate into more inventive disclosure, or that there are less costly ways of achieving this result. If one is persuaded by those

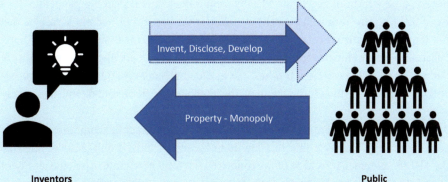

Figure 9.7 A sceptical view of the patent bargain

objections, then one might conclude that while the monopoly arrow has grown and expanded in size, the invent–disclosure–develop arrow has remained static. If so, this bargain is a good one for inventors, but not for the public.

Finally, as with copyright, there are also a range of rights that are not part of patent law but are 'associated' with patent law. Not only have patents expanded in several dimensions, but inventors also enjoy a range of new patent-like rights. The two most significant patent-associated rights are **supplementary protection certificates** (SPCs) and **plant variety protections**.

SPCs enable a patent owner to prolong their monopoly over the invention beyond the patent term for up to an additional five years.[30] This *sui generis* right came into being because of the troubles pharmaceutical companies face in receiving regulatory approval for new drugs.[31] Often it takes many years for a country to examine new pharmaceuticals and grant permission for a drug to be used among the public. There is a danger that the time it takes for a pharmaceutical company to gain regulatory approval will cut into the owner's monopoly. SPCs alleviate this potential problem. They are issued upon a successful application to the UK IPO.

As explained in Section 7.3.2, plant varieties are not patentable subject matter. Instead, they enjoy a *sui generis* form of protection that was established after the 1961 International Convention for the Protection of New Varieties of Plants. The relevant provisions are now contained in the Plant Varieties Act 1997.

9.6 SELF-ASSESSMENT

Before moving on, try to answer the following questions to consolidate your learning. Answers are provided in the section below.

1. Which of the following is not a right conferred by the grant of a patent for a product?
   a. The exclusive right to repair the patented product.
   b. The exclusive right to make the patented product.
   c. The exclusive right to offer to dispose of the product.
   d. The exclusive right to keep the patented product.
2. Which of the following statements best summarises the principle of purposive construction first introduced by Lord Diplock in *Catnic v Hill & Smith*?
   a. Claim language means what it is intended to mean by the patentee.
   b. Claim language means what a PSITA would understand it to mean.
   c. Claim language means what a PSITA would understand the patentee to have intended the claim language to mean.
   d. Claim language should be interpreted using normal methods of interpretation.
3. The year is 2030. In January, a new form of potentially deadly viral influenza is declared a pandemic. X, a pharmaceutical company in the UK, already owns a patent in India for the process of making a vaccine that prevents infection of this form of influenza. So far, however, the vaccine is not made in, or imported into, India. In February, Y, a pharmaceutical company in India, applies to the Indian Patent Office for a compulsory licence. They have so far not asked X for permission to use the patented technology. But if the compulsory licence is granted, they will write to X to inform them of the compulsory licence and will adequately remunerate them.

   Assume that domestic Indian patent law permits the Indian Patent Office to grant the compulsory licence under such circumstances. However, X objects that this law is in breach of India's obligations under the Paris Convention and the TRIPS agreements. Which of the following answers best summarises the ability of India to grant compulsory licences in such circumstances? Both the UK and India are WTO members.

a. The Indian Patent Office cannot grant the licence because Y has not made efforts to obtain authorisation from the rights holder on reasonable commercial terms.

b. The Indian Patent Office cannot grant the licence because the patent has been worked in India.

c. The Indian Patent Office can grant the licence because the pandemic represents an emergency.

d. The Indian Patent Office can grant the licence because there has been a failure to work the invention by X in India and, due to emergency nature of the pandemic, Y is not required to make efforts to obtain authorisation before a compulsory licence is granted.

4. When, in your opinion, should a defendant who makes something that falls outside the literal meaning of a patent's claims be liable for patent infringement, if ever?

ACTIVITY DISCUSSION

Activity 9.1 The patent right seems to fit the exclusive control model. The Patents Act does not obviously create a bundle of rights (held by different people). Instead, it says that the invention is property and that property means the owner alone can control how the invention is used. Although, contra copyright, the property lasts for only a short time: twenty years.

Activity 9.3 The key point of difference is how Lord Diplock focuses on *purpose*. The question we should ask, according to Diplock, is not what the PSITA thinks the word 'vertical' means. Instead, the question is what does the PSITA think the patent owner *intended* the word vertical to mean. Would the PSITA think, by using the word vertical, the patent owner *intended* the patent only to cover perfectly vertical rigid support members? Or would a PSITA think that the patent owner intended the patent to cover vertical and slightly angled support members? In other words, the legal effect of the word 'vertical' should be defined by a purposive interpretation carried out by the PSITA.

Activity 9.4 Here is my attempt to apply the *Improver* questions.

1. The answer to the first *Improver* question is debatable. In my view, they work in materially the same way. Both the Toy Building Brick 'tubular projections' and the ATC ones fit into the central area left between the studs, allowing the bricks to lock together; the difference is only how well the variant performs at that task. As my answer is 'no', we move onto the next question. But, if you disagree and answer 'yes', then we can stop here: ATC have not practised the patented invention.

2. I think the answer to question 2 would be 'yes'. Christiansen seems to have been aware of this variant when he applied for a patent on the brick. My understanding is that it was obvious that the variant worked similarly, but did not adopt it because it worked less well. As my answer is 'yes', we move onto the final question. But, if you disagree and answer 'no', then we can stop here: ATC have not practised the patented invention.

3. Again, the answer to question 3 is highly debatable without further evidence – particularly primary evidence that is usually used to guide a PSITA analysis (see Section 8.1.2). But my initial sense is that when the patentee used the words 'tubular projections', they used them to mean hollow tubes. Although not impossible, it would be a bit strange if they used the word 'tubular' to mean things which, according to their ordinary meaning, were not tubular.

   And so my tentative conclusion is that under the *Improver* questions, ATC would not be considered to have practised the patented invention.

320 *Patents IV: Scope*

Activity 9.5 I think it is more likely now that ATC could be said to have practised the invention. I'll explain why.

In the first step, we subject the claim language to a 'normal interpretation'. Although not certain, my conclusion is that under a normal interpretation, a 'tubular' projection must be a hollow cylinder. That is consistent with the dictionary definitions. Furthermore, even if we approach this interpretive exercise purposively, we arguably arrive at the same result (see my tentative conclusion to Activity 9.4).

Nevertheless, the analysis changes when we come to the second step of the analysis and the new doctrine of equivalents. If we conclude, as I did in Activity 9.4, that the ATC variant has the same effect as the patented invention and works in the same way, and that this would have been obvious to the PSITA, then we answer the first two questions in the affirmative (i.e. 'yes, yes').

Therefore, the conclusion depends once more on the final question. And here it strikes me that the answer might be 'no'. Of course, it seems unlikely to me that the patentee intended the word 'tubular' to *mean* things like solid internal projections. But remember, at this point, we are no longer doing interpretation, but construction. And it strikes me as possible at least that the patentee intended the claim language to have a broader legal effect than the strict meaning. It is plausible, in other words, that the patentee intended the legal effect of the claim wording to cover solid, as well as hollow, internal projections.

This starts to push patents further in the direction of 'exclusive control'.

Activity 9.6 While not necessarily the case, Lyon-Caen's argument more naturally fits an 'exclusive control' understanding of property. Compulsory licensing is, in his view, an affront to the patentee's rights of exclusive control.

SELF-ASSESSMENT ANSWERS

1. **Correct answer: a.** Although the rights of a patentee are broad, they do not extend as far as a right of repair. The dividing line between repair and make was considered in *Schütz v Werit* [2013] UKSC 16.

2. **Correct answer: c.** Answer **a**. is not entirely incorrect, but is not the best answer because it gives insufficient weight to the role of the PSITA. On the other hand, answer **b**. is also not the best answer because it fails to appreciate the purposive nature of the inquiry. Answer **d**. starts to mix up the purposive construction approach with the new approach outlined in *Actavis v Eli Lilly*.

3. **Correct answer: d.** Answer **a**. is not the best answer because the pandemic likely makes the situation an emergency, meaning that Indian law can waive the requirement that efforts be made to reach a voluntary licence. Answer **b**. is not the best answer because on the facts presented it does not appear that the patented technology has been worked in India. Answer **c**. is partially correct but, unlike **d**., does not reference the nature of the pandemic as an emergency.

Notes

1 Patents Act 1977, s 30(1).

2 WA Hindmarch, *Treatise Relating to the Law of Patent Privileges for the Sole Use of Inventions* (V & R Stevens & GS Norton and W Benning 1847) 258 ('[t]o be an infringement of a patent privilege, the defendant's act must be either a use of the art invented by the patentee, or a fraudulent imitation of it, made for the purpose of evading the privilege').

3 Patents Act 1977, s 25.

4 ibid s 13.

5 *Schütz v Werit* [2013] UKSC 16.

6 Patents Act 1977, s 30.

7 United States Patent 3,005,282, claim 1.

8 'tubular *adj*' (*OED Online*, OUP June 2023) <https://www.oed.com/view/Entry/207206?redirectedFrom=tubular#eid> (accessed June 2023).

9 'tube' (*Dictionary of Mechanical Engineering*, online, OUP 2013) <https://www.oxfordreference.com/display/10.1093/acref/9780199587438.001.0001/acref-9780199587438-e-6899?rskey=mm7WxG&result=6861> (accessed June 2023).

10 Tun-Jen Chiang and Lawrence B Solum, 'The Interpretation–Construction Distinction in Patent Law' (2013) 123 Yale LJ 530.

11 But see Hugh Laddie, '*Kirin-Amgen*: The End of Equivalents in England?' (2009) 40 IIC 3.

12 *Electric and Musical Industries Ltd v Lissen Ltd* (1938) 56 RPC 23, 39.

13 Donald Chisum, 'Common Law and Civil Law Approaches to Patent Claim Interpretation' in David Vaver and Lionel Bently (eds), *Intellectual Property in the New Millennium* (CUP 2004) 97.

14 Phillip Johnson, 'Mr Skemp's Preposterous Provision: The Drafting of the Patents Act 1977 and Harmonization in the 1970s' (2015) 5 QMJIP 367.

15 *Actavis v Eli Lilly* [2017] UKSC 48, [32] (per Lord Neuberger) (the Protocol on the Interpretation of Article 69 'bears all the hallmarks of the product of a compromise agreement').

16 [1990] FSR 181.

17 See eg *PLG Research Limited and another v Ardon International Limited* [1995] FSR 116; *AssiDoman Multipack (formerly Multipack Wraparound Systems) v Mead Corp* [1995] FSR 225.

18 [2004] UKHL 46.

19 ibid [52].

20 ibid.

21 *Improver* (n 16) 197.

22 ibid 197–99.

23 German Patent Ac 1981, s 14; Schneidmesser I BGH, (2002) 33 IIC 873.

24 *Kirin-Amgen* (n 18) [44].

25 *Wood v Capita Insurance Services Ltd* [2017] 2 WLR 1095, paras 8–15.

26 ibid para 10.

27 Article 5A(4).

28 [1964] Ch 614.

29 Nick Triggle, 'Cystic Fibrosis Drug Given Green Light in England' *BBC News* (24 October 2019) <https://www.bbc.co.uk/news/health-50144742> (accessed 19 December 2023).

30 The Patents (Amendment) (EU Exit) Regulations 2019. Supplementary Protection Certificates (Amendment) (EU Exit) Regulations 2020.

31 See generally Peter L Koker, 'The Supplementary Protection Certificate: The European Solution to Patent Term Restoration' [1997] IPQ 249.

FIGURE ACKNOWLEDGEMENTS

9.1 Photograph credit Patrick Goold

9.2 Catnic Lintel from patent GB 1503491. Hill & Smith lintel from *Catnic Components Ltd v Hill & Smith Ltd* [1982] RPC 183, 241 (HL) with minor modifications by Patrick Goold

9.3 Epilady technical drawings from EP0101656A1. Lady Remington technical drawings from US4726375

Part III

Designs

An absurd maze.
—William R Cornish, in WR Cornish, D Llewelyn and T Aplin,
Intellectual Property (7th edn Thomson 2010) 632

10

Designs I: Foundations of Design Law

Dragon's Den is a British reality television show. In the show, budding entrepreneurs are given three minutes to pitch their business idea to a group of multimillionaire investors known as 'the dragons'. The goal is to entice the dragons into investing in the proposed business.[1]

In 2006, British entrepreneur, Robert Law appeared on *Dragon's Den*. Law had produced a product that he called the Trunki. The Trunki (Figure 10.1) is a 'ride-on suitcase' for children. A child sits on the suitcase while their parents pull them along behind them. Law was seeking investment from the dragons to enable him to produce and sell more Trunkis.[2]

Unfortunately for Law, the dragons chose not to invest in his business. In part, the reason for the decision was IP rights – or rather, the lack thereof. Robert Law had the idea for ride-on suitcases in the 1990s and made the idea public without first obtaining a patent. By 2006, it was too late because the suitcase was no longer a new invention. And, without a patent, the dragons worried the Trunki would be copied by competitors.

But Law had the last laugh. Although he did not have a patent, Law had something else: design rights. Design rights are property rights in the **design** of the product. Thus, while Law could not stop competitors producing their own ride-on suitcases, he could stop them producing ride-on suitcases that looked like the Trunki. Armed with that property right, Law's company flourished. By 2016, over three million Trunkis had been sold in over one hundred countries.[3]

Much like copyrights and patents, design rights are a frequent source of controversy. This controversy can be attributed to three reasons. First, design rights rest on questionable normative foundations. As demonstrated in this Part, today's law is more a product of industry lobbying than reasoned argument.

Second, the design right system is almost comically complicated. Unlike copyright and patent, there is no one single design right. Instead, there are

William Cornish was Professor of Intellectual Property (Herchel Smith) at the University of Cambridge from 1995 to 2004.

This chapter contains public sector information licensed under the Open Government Licence v3.0.

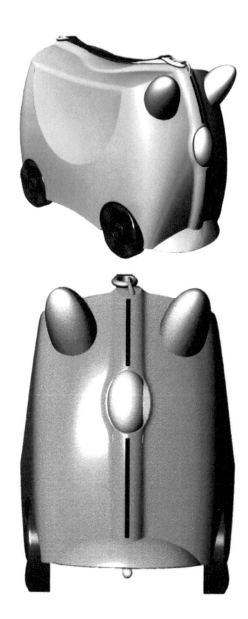

Figure 10.1 The Trunki. Community design right representation No 43427-0001

currently *four* different ways of owning designs in the UK. The result is, as William Cornish once put it, an 'absurd maze'. The UK's post-Brexit relationship with the EU makes matters even worse.

Third, design rights frequently **overlap** with other IP rights. So far, this book has presented IP rights as falling into neatly divided categories: copyright for works, patents for inventions, and design rights for designs. But reality is often a messier affair. For example, in addition to owning a design right, could Law also claim that the Trunki was an 'artistic work' (perhaps as a sculpture) and thus protected by copyright? Or what about the sketches Law made when initially designing the Trunki? If someone copies the Trunki, would they infringe copyright in those drawings? And, although Law did not have a patent on the ride-on suitcase, he could have had one. If Law had applied for a patent in the 1990s when the idea was still new, then he could potentially have enjoyed both patent and design rights relating to the Trunki. But what could possibly justify granting multiple property rights in the same phenomenon?

This chapter begins with the normative question: why should designs be property? As with Chapter 2 and 6, this question is introduced in its historical context. Perhaps even more than copyright and patent, a firm grasp of history is required to appreciate and evaluate the 'absurd maze' that is design protection in the UK.

10.1 DESIGNING DESIGNS

Ironically, the history of design law is not pretty. For two hundred years, lawmakers have tried to manage the boundaries between design rights and other IP rights. As legal historian Lionel Bently explains, this task was complicated by corporate interests who had 'much to gain from dismantling barriers between [the] categories' of IP protection.[4] This section sets the foundations for the rest of Part III by outlining how the 'barriers' between the rights have shifted over time.

10.1.1 Inauspicious Beginnings

UK design law began with an insult. As Bently explains, the initial argument for design rights was the sense that the British were simply not good enough at designing products.

> ### BOX 10.1 LIONEL BENTLY, 'THE DESIGN/COPYRIGHT CONFLICT IN THE UNITED KINGDOM: A HISTORY' IN ESTELLE DERCLAYE, *THE COPYRIGHT/DESIGN INTERFACE* (CUP 2018)
>
> #### 6.2.1 The Beginnings
> The regulation of the making, sale and consumption of designed goods by the grant of exclusive rights has normally been dated to the eighteenth century.[5] Not long after the abolition of legislative restrictions on the sale and wearing of calicoes in 1774, Parliament passed laws granting a right lasting two months to the 'inventor and designer' of patterns applied to calicoes, cottons, muslins and linens, thereby enabling the designer to control the copying of such patterns.
>
> The argument for protection of designs across the whole field of industrial production was made forcefully before William Ewart's Select

Lionel Bently is Professor of Intellectual Property (Herchel Smith) at the University of Cambridge.

Calico is a type of cotton fabric. It has a long history with Britain's colonial and imperial past. It originated in India (Kerala). Importation and manufacture of the cloth was restricted in 1700 to protect the British textile industry from competition. Repeal of the restrictions led to investment in the British cotton spinning industry, and the Industrial Revolution.

Committee on Arts and Manufactures, which sat between 1835 and 1836, hearing witnesses from a range of sectors, including manufacturers of iron stoves and fenders, silk manufacturers, lace making and japanning, as well as retailers, painters, sculptors and architects. The task of the Ewart Committee was to determine 'the best means of extending a knowledge of the arts and of the principles of design among the people (especially the manufacturing people) of this country'. The Report found that design in British manufacturing was inferior to that of competitor nations, particularly France. The Committee attributed this inferiority to a lack of taste amongst the public, as well as the failure to invest in improved designs caused by the absence of effective legal protection. The Report proposed the establishment of galleries and museums that would display good design, design schools that would teach design, as well as protection for designs similar to that which already was recognised in France. Given the overwhelming evidence of 'piracy', and the problems of enforcement of any existing rights, the Report favoured a new system with protection.

The idea of a registration system was taken forward by the president of the Board of Trade, Charles Poullett Thomson. As initially envisaged, however, a system of protection premised on registration was not attractive to many of the Manchester calico printers. Given their experience of systematic copying of designs as soon as they were displayed in London shops, the Manchester printers feared that a central register would inevitably facilitate copying rather than protect against it. They therefore sought exclusion from the new regime, and instead achieved only extension of protection to other fabrics (silk and wool, and mixtures) as well as to Ireland. The legislature did, however, adopt a registration system for all other designs, both three and two dimensional, protection being awarded for a limited term of one year from registration (though it further provided that for designs applied to articles of metal this was to be three years). The link to the Calico Printers Acts was maintained at least in the standard for protection, namely that the designs were 'new and original'.

(pp. 177, 180–81)

Note the short term: initially designs were only protected for one year from registration.

In 1842, the Designs Registration Act was passed creating a register of protected 'ornamental designs'. The newly established designs register was welcomed by the textile industry. The register enabled textile designers to clearly establish ownership over their designs in a clearly visible and public way. Quickly, however, the new law became caught up in the patent controversy of the nineteenth century (see Section 6.1.4). To avoid the expensive and cumbersome process of obtaining patent rights, inventors often sought to register their *inventions* as designs.

BOX 10.2 LIONEL BENTLY, 'THE DESIGN/COPYRIGHT CONFLICT IN THE UNITED KINGDOM: A HISTORY' IN ESTELLE DERCLAYE, *THE COPYRIGHT/DESIGN INTERFACE* (CUP 2018)

6.2.2 Overlap: 1839–1911

Looking back, one might have expected the question of the relationship with copyright law to arise immediately following the introduction of a design registration system. . .However, the question of overlap hardly seems to have arisen.

In practice, the real issue of boundary drawing in the mid- to late nineteenth century lay between the design registration system and the archaic and expensive patent system. The 1839 Registration Act allowed for the registration of designs 'for the shape or configuration of any article of manufacture', a mysterious formula that was soon recognised as offering the possibility of protection through registration to any article, including those whose functioning could be linked to its form. In today's terms, the 1839 Act was thought to offer both design protection and protection of 'utility models'. As is explained in detail elsewhere, faced with a spate of such registrations, the Registry sought to devise a mechanism to differentiate between different types of application. Consequently, from 1843 through to 1883, the Office operated two registers, one for designs for the purpose or ornament and the other for designs for the purpose of utility.

(pp. 183, 190)

A '**utility model**' is a sometimes described as a 'petty patent'. These rights are shorter and often weaker than patent rights, but easier and cheaper to obtain. UK law offers no such protection, unlike some other jurisdictions.[6]

10.1.2 Demarcation

It was not until the twentieth century that overlap between designs and copyright became a source of concern. In the next extract, Lionel Bently explains how that overlap came about in large part due to expansion of UK copyright caused by the Berne Convention.

BOX 10.3 LIONEL BENTLY, 'THE DESIGN/COPYRIGHT CONFLICT IN THE UNITED KINGDOM: A HISTORY' IN ESTELLE DERCLAYE, *THE COPYRIGHT/DESIGN INTERFACE* (CUP 2018)

6.2.3 The End of the Nineteenth Century

It was at this point, with the registered design system at its zenith, that internal and external pressures started to emerge to expand the copyright regime in various ways that could affect the registration regime.

Although the desire to replace concrete, particular, subject-matter categories with ones which were abstract and open-ended (such as

French law has long taken a **'unity of art'** approach to designs. The idea is that there is no difference between artistic works – like the *Starry Night* – and an artistic design – like the Trunki. Therefore, they ought to be treated in the same way by the law.

> 'artistic work') raised the question of the copyright-design border, a more significant impetus was the external pressure associated with the growing internationalisation of copyright. As is well known, the Berne Convention was agreed in 1886, with Great Britain as a signatory. The 1908 Revision at Berlin radically extended the significance of the Treaty, requiring the abandonment of national regimes of formalities. At the behest of the French, the Berlin Revision saw the addition of a requirement that 'works of art applied to industry are protected'. However, on the basis of the objections of the British delegation, which had received instructions that inclusion of designs within the Convention was 'inadvisable', the extension of the subject-matter was qualified, so that the obligation was only to offer protection 'to the extent permitted by the internal legislation of each country'. As the delegates explained, the effect was that countries were left free to choose whether to protect works of applied art as 'artistic works' or 'industrial designs'.
>
> (pp. 191, 192, 194)

As it expanded to cover works of 'applied art', increasingly copyright could protect subject matter previously protected only by design rights. This was ultimately to the benefit of emerging British industries, such as the jewellery, fashion, and furniture industries, who could achieve a longer term of protection using copyright instead of registered design rights.[7] Illustrative is the case of *Britain and others v Hank Brothers* in 1902, that held that toy soldiers were copyrighted sculptures.[8]

At this point, British policy makers adopted a policy of '**demarcation**'. Under this policy, Parliament tried to prevent design rights and copyright from overlapping. Something like a toy soldier, they decided, should be protected by either copyright or design rights, but not both.

BOX 10.4 LIONEL BENTLY, 'THE DESIGN/COPYRIGHT CONFLICT IN THE UNITED KINGDOM: A HISTORY' IN ESTELLE DERCLAYE, *THE COPYRIGHT/DESIGN INTERFACE* (CUP 2018)

6.3 The Period of Demarcation
6.3.1 The Policy of Demarcation: 1911–1940
With growing pressures to generalise the field of application of 'copyright', and concern to take advantage of the Berne Convention, the British Government decided on a policy of 'demarcation'. It would

confer copyright protection on any work of applied art as long as it was not intended to be mass-produced, in which case the appropriate form of protection was by way of design registration. To have done otherwise, it was believed, would be to undermine the functioning of the registration system for designs. Copyright would be permitted to expand, but not at the cost of the design registration system.

Given the breadth of the definition of artistic work to include sculptures and works of artistic craftsmanship, as well as the broadening of the circumstances in which a work might be infringed, the [Copyright Act 1911] sought to 'demarcate' the two systems so as to prevent overlap. This was done by section 22, which excluded from protection by copyright any work that was capable of registration as a design and which was intended to be applied by an industrial process. The intention was that the subject matter of designs would not be protected by copyright. Rules followed defining the concept of an 'industrial process' as multiplication of more than fifty articles, or the application of the design to certain specified types of article.

(pp. 196, 198)

The policy of demarcation continued through the middle of the twentieth century. However, the doctrinal tools used to achieve demarcation changed with time.

The **Registered Designs Act 1949 (RDA 1949)** granted designers ownership over features of designs that 'appeal to and are judged solely by the eye' and that were non-functional.[9] For example, one could not own the shape of a car exhaust pipe, because that shape is not usually designed for aesthetic attractiveness; instead the shape is designed merely to achieve a utilitarian function (expelling exhaust fumes efficiently). The right lasted for five years and could be renewed twice, providing a maximum term of protection of fifteen years.[10]

However, there was an exception built into the RDA. One could not register a feature of a design that was of 'primarily literary or artistic character'.[11] For example, van Gogh's *Starry Night* or Pablo Picasso's sculptures, could not be owned as a registered design on the grounds that they are 'primarily' artistic in character. But one could still register phenomena that had a more mixed character – like a toy soldier – on the grounds that those things are not *primarily* artistic in nature.

Meanwhile, the Copyright Act 1956 (which replaced the Copyright Act 1911) applied to original works.[12] 'Works' included phenomena with a primarily literary and artistic character (e.g. Picasso sculptures), and phenomena with a more mixed nature (e.g. a toy soldier). This lead to overlap wherein some phenomena (like toy soldiers), were protected by *both* registered design rights and copyright.

Designs I: Foundations

However, to avoid the worst effects of the overlap, the Copyright Act 1956 contained an important exception. Section 10 ruled that if the design was capable of registration, and either had been registered or had been used in mass production, then copying the design became a permitted act. Of course, such copying still could infringe any design right therein, but such copying would not infringe copyright. Therefore, copyright became practically irrelevant in these cases.

10.1.3 Cumulation

Today, however, the policy of demarcation is dead. While the present position is complex and still changing, the policy is one of **cumulation**. Under a policy of cumulation, overlapping IP rights in the same phenomenon are accepted. Thus, a design might be protected by both design rights and copyright. In the next extract, Bently explains how the fall of demarcation, and the rise of cumulation, began.

BOX 10.5 LIONEL BENTLY, 'THE DESIGN/COPYRIGHT CONFLICT IN THE UNITED KINGDOM: A HISTORY' IN ESTELLE DERCLAYE, *THE COPYRIGHT/DESIGN INTERFACE* (CUP 2018)

6.3.3 Questioning Demarcation: The Road to 1968

The first signs of a change in resolve (to support demarcation) appeared in the 1961 Report of the Johnston Committee. The Committee had been established in 1959 to investigate the law of designs. While it acknowledged that there remained strong support for the retention of the registered design regime, for the first time, the Johnston Committee recognised that there were design sectors for whom the existing system was not offering the sort of protection that was wanted. As a result, the Committee was no longer prepared to prop up the registered design system on behalf of the textile industry, by making it the sole form of protection in the field. Instead the Report proposed cumulation of traditional registered designs, which it dubbed a 'design monopoly' regime, with a new less bureaucratic system, which it called 'design copyright'.

6.4 The Era of Cumulation

6.4.1 Partial Cumulation and the Era of 'Industrial Copyright': 1968–1989

In 1968, the political economy of intellectual property had so altered that Parliament abandoned the policy of demarcation to which it had adhered at least since 1911, instead adopting a policy of 'partial cumulation'. The move was made in response to a Private Member's Bill, brought by Jill Knight, MP for Edgbaston, motivated by the goal of ensuring copyright protection for jewellery.

Similar political economy pressures were identified by Boldrin and Levine in Box 6.9.

Knight's Bill sailed through Parliament unopposed and received Royal Assent on 25 October 1968. The 1968 [Design Copyright] Act amended section 10 of the 1956 Copyright Act so as to allow copyright to be recognised for fifteen years (a term equivalent to the period of design registration) even where the design had been industrially applied to articles, but leaving the rest of defence introduced in the 1956 Act to operate thereafter as it had before. The effect was that for fifteen years the designer had a choice between using the registration regime, or relying on copyright, or using both. The policy of demarcation was dead. Partial cumulation had become a reality.

At this juncture, other problems with the Copyright Act 1956 started to become increasingly apparent. Section 10 had made non-cumulation dependent on *registrability* and the 1968 Act now offered the possibility of dual protection for *registrable* designs, but with a limited fifteen-year term. However, because registered design protection was *not* available for functional shapes, copyright *could* protect functional designs embodied in **design drawings** (as 'artistic works') precisely because those designs were so functional and unappealing that they were *unregistrable*. This became clear in *Dorling v. Honnor*, where functional parts of a dinghy were recognised as falling outside the section 10 defence, and thus were fully protected by copyright. The issue became a more urgent concern following a decision of the House of Lords in October 1971 [*Amp v Utilux* [1971] FSR 572] which gave a broad reading to the exclusion of functional designs from the registration system. Thereafter, for example, drawings of a rivet, bolt or screw, washers, pulley wheels, spare parts for vacuum cleaners and exhaust pipes all came to be regarded as protected by copyright. Widely known as '**industrial copyright**', the resulting situation was described as 'bizarre', 'logically odd' or simply 'daft'. Apart from rendering the design/copyright interface illogical, many commentators objected that conferring copyright protection on such 'works' might have deeply anti-competitive implications. Chief amongst such critics were the makers of spare parts for automobiles who quickly found themselves as defendants in litigation.

(pp. 204–06, 210–12)

The idea of industrial copyright sounds odd to most students at first. The key is to remember that copyright's reproduction right prevents copying in all material forms (Section 4.1.1.3). Therefore, if copyright protects the *drawings* of an exhaust pipe, then *making an exhaust pipe* corresponding to those drawings infringes the copyright in the drawings.

This exact situation came before the House of Lords in *British Leyland v Armstrong*.[13] British Leyland sold cars complete with exhaust pipes. Armstrong copied the design of the exhaust pipe and sold them as spare parts. British Leyland sued Armstrong. But, due to its functional nature, the British Leyland exhaust could not be protected as a registered design. Instead, British Leyland argued that Armstrong was indirectly copying the design drawings for the exhaust pipes. As Lord Scarman put it, British Leyland claimed that 'the tentacles of copyright' were used to monopolize a secondary market.[14]

The House of Lords in British Leyland adopted a creative solution to prevent such monopolization. But it was clear that Parliament needed to intervene. And, so, to remedy the 'daft' situation, Parliament introduced the Copyright, Designs and Patents Act 1988. In the CDPA, Parliament introduced a new tripartite system of rights. The three rights in this system were as follows:

- The RDA 1949 continued to protect features of products which appealed to the eye (and were non-functional), providing they did not have a primarily literary or artistic character.[15] Once again, the term of protection was five years. But the RDA was amended so that the right could be renewed five times, providing a maximum term of protection of twenty-five years.[16]
- Artistic works received copyright as normal under the CDPA.[17] Some overlap was accepted because some phenomena – like toy soldiers and design drawings – could be protected by both copyright and design rights. However, in such cases, section 52 CDPA created an exception. If the copyrighted work had been used by the owner in an 'industrial process' (e.g. by manufacturing exhaust pipes corresponding to exhaust pipe design drawings), then copying the work would be a permitted act. The exception only applied after the first twenty-five years of protection. Thus, even if copyright and design rights both applied, the copyright became practically irrelevant after twenty-five years.
- Finally, the CDPA introduced a new right: the **unregistered design right**, which granted protection to the shape and configuration of *functional* products proving they were original.[18] This right was intended as a replacement for industrial copyright. Rather than protect functional designs (e.g. the shape of an exhaust pipe) indirectly through copyright, these designs were protected by the new unregistered design right. This was an automatic right that lasted for fifteen years.[19]

Thus, the CDPA followed a policy of partial cumulation. While accepting there could be an overlap, particularly between registered design rights and copyright, the extent of overlap was mitigated through specific provisions, like section 52.

Alas, the system did not last very long. While the foundations of modern UK design law remain broadly the same today, the content of the law has evolved over time. As we will see in Chapter 11, designs continue to be owned through a complex mix of registered design rights, unregistered design rights, and copyright. But membership of the EU led to even greater overlap between the rights.

In response to EU law, the UK policy has moved from a position of partial cumulation to a position of full cumulation. Today, as we will see, designs can be protected by both design rights and copyright, and the copyright will last for life of the author plus seventy years.

10.2 ARGUMENTS FOR DESIGN RIGHTS

Why should designs be property? An attractive product appearance or shape is, just like an original work or invention, an intangible public good. Furthermore, just like copyright and patents, property rights over those public goods create monopolies. Indeed, in the extract in Section 1.1.3, Ruth Towse uses an example from design law – a monopoly over designer pots – to illustrate how property rights create the problem of monopoly.

Because of the similarities between copyright, patents, and designs, one might expect lawyers to have extensively considered the merits, or demerits, of design rights. Yet, strangely, that is not the case. While political philosophers have spent significant energy arguing about copyrights and patents, they have devoted comparatively little time discussing design rights. Society has quietly acquiesced to design rights.

To the extent that anyone has sought to defend design rights it has, typically, been on utilitarian grounds. The utilitarian strand to design protection can be traced back to the law's earliest beginnings, as the next activity illustrates.

ACTIVITY 10.1

Flip back to the first extract from Bently in Box 10.1 Bently summarises the Ewart Committee's argument that design rights would encourage designers to invest in 'improved designs'. What is different about this argument to the other utilitarian arguments encountered in Chapter 2 and 6? And why is it still utilitarian?

The utilitarian strand of thinking remains clear in contemporary design law, although the argument has become more quantitative in nature. While the desire to see encouragement for improved designs still exists on some level, it is often coupled alongside a desire to simply encourage more designs. Consider, for example, contemporary EU law, that states:

> (7) Enhanced protection for industrial design not only promotes the contribution of individual designers to the sum of Community excellence in the field, but also encourages innovation and development of new products and investment in their production.[20]

Designs I: Foundations

Or alternatively, consider the US Supreme Court's briefly articulated justification for design rights:

> Note that the court refers to 'patents for designs'. Somewhat strangely to European ears, the US offers a legal right called the 'design patent' for designs.

Case 10.1 *Gorham Mfg Co v White* 81 US 511 (1872) (US)

The acts of Congress which authorize the granting of patents for designs were plainly intended to give encouragement to the decorative arts... And the thing invented or produced, for which a patent is given, is that which gives a peculiar or distinctive appearance to the manufacture, or article to which it may be applied, or to which it gives form. The law manifestly contemplated that giving certain new and original appearances to a manufactured article may enhance its saleable value, may enlarge the demand for it, and may be a meritorious service to the public.

(pp. 525–26)

However, Chapter 2 and 6 also demonstrated the objections to the utilitarian argument as it applied to copyright and patents. These objections apply with just as much force in design law as they do in copyright and patents. This is particularly true of the empirical objection. For there is not only a lack of evidence that design rights do lead to better consequences overall, but once again, some evidence points in the opposite direction. An example can be found in the next extract.

In Box 10.6, Kal Raustiala and Christopher Sprigman look to the American fashion industry and find a puzzling result. Although American law gives fashion designers little design protection, it remains a highly innovative and creative industry. They call this, the 'piracy paradox'.

BOX 10.6 KAL RAUSTIALA AND CHRISTOPHER SPRIGMAN, 'THE PIRACY PARADOX: INNOVATION AND INTELLECTUAL PROPERTY IN FASHION DESIGN' (2006) 92 VIRGINIA L REV 1687

> Kal Raustiala is the Promise Institute Distinguished Professor of Comparative and International Law at the University of California, LA.
>
> Christopher Sprigman is the Murray and Kathleen Bring Professor of Law at New York University.

This argument about the effects of copying is logically straightforward, intuitively appealing, and well reflected in American law.[21] Yet, few seem to have noticed a significant empirical anomaly: the existence of a global industry that produces a huge variety of creative goods in markets larger than those for movies, books, music, and most scientific innovations, and does so without strong IP protection. Copying is rampant, as the standard account would predict. Competition, innovation, and investment, however, remain vibrant.

That industry is fashion. Like the music, film, video game, and book publishing industries, the fashion industry profits by repeatedly originating creative content. But unlike these industries, the fashion industry's principal creative element – its apparel designs – is outside the domain of IP law. And as a brief tour through any fashion magazine or department store will demonstrate, while trademarks are well protected against piracy, design copying is ubiquitous. Nonetheless, the industry develops a tremendous variety of clothing and accessory designs at a rapid pace. This is a puzzling outcome. The standard theory of IP rights predicts that extensive copying will destroy the incentive for new innovation. Yet, fashion firms continue to innovate at a rapid clip, precisely the opposite behavior of that predicted by the standard theory.

Why is copying in the fashion industry treated so differently from copying in other creative industries? Why, when other major content industries have obtained and made use of increasingly powerful IP protections for their products, does fashion design remain mostly unprotected? That the fashion industry produces high levels of innovation, and attracts the investment necessary to continue in this vein, is a puzzle for the orthodox justification for IP rights. This Article will explore this puzzle and offer an explanation for it. We will argue that copying fails to deter innovation in the fashion industry because, counter-intuitively, copying is not very harmful to originators. Indeed, copying may actually promote innovation and benefit originators. We call this the 'piracy paradox'. In this Article, we will explain how copying functions as an important element of – and perhaps even a necessary predicate to – the apparel industry's swift cycle of innovation.

(pp. 1689, 1691)

We will later see that UK law offers fashion designers more protection than American law, due to the presence of unregistered design rights (see Section 10.4).

ACTIVITY 10.2

How might copying contribute to the fashion industry's 'swift cycle of innovation'?

Another curiosity of design rights is that hardly anyone has offered labour or personality arguments for designs. Does that mean there cannot be such an argument? The next activity considers.

ACTIVITY 10.3

With your knowledge from Chapters 2 and 6, is there any labour or personality argument for design rights?

10.3 SUMMARY

Design rights were born out of a desire to improve the quality of British designs. The registered design system introduced in 1839 granted a short one-year monopoly to British designers. While monopolies are generally harmful to consumers, such protection was justified with the speculative argument that monopoly profits would encourage designers to supply the public with new and better designs.

Since then, the system has grown and expanded. The system of design rights has been influenced by both international pressures (such as the expansion of copyrightable subject matter and the Berne Convention) and domestic lobbying efforts. While the UK initially adopted a policy of demarcation and tried to clearly separate copyright, patents and design rights, that demarcation policy eventually gave way to one of cumulation. By 1988, the UK adopted a complex tripartite structure, whereby designs could be owned through a mix of registered design rights, unregistered design rights, and copyright. That system has continued to evolve, particularly in response to influences from the European Union. That evolution is picked up in the next chapter.

Despite the march towards more and stronger design rights, the utilitarian claim that society is a better place overall with design rights remains objectionable. Some evidence, illustrated by the piracy paradox, suggests that competition, not monopoly, provides the best incentive for innovation in design. If so, design rights not only result in consumers paying higher prices for their ride-on suitcases and the like, but also that they have fewer designs to enjoy than they would under a free market.

10.4 SELF-ASSESSMENT

Before moving on, try to answer the following questions to consolidate your learning. Answers are provided in the section below.

1. This chapter has discussed the difference between demarcation and cumulation. Which of the following legal systems most clearly follows a policy of cumulation?
   a. **Japan.** Japanese law grants a registered design right. It does not grant an unregistered design right. The national copyright legislation excludes works of applied art from protection via copyright.
   b. **Australia.** Australian law grants a registered design right. It does not grant an unregistered design right. Australian law permits both registered design rights and copyright to apply to two-dimensional works (e.g. design drawings). Three dimensional designs (e.g. models) lose copyright if the design is registered.
   c. **United Kingdom**. As explained in this chapter, the UK grants a registered design right, an unregistered design right, a supplementary design right and copyright.
   d. **France (1957–2001)**. French law previously granted a registered design right and copyright for designs (and no unregistered design right). The novelty requirement for obtaining a registered design, and the originality requirement for obtaining copyright, were defined identically. Thus, if one right applied to a design, the second right would automatically also apply. The law changed in 2001 in response to the Design Directive 1998.
2. Is there any good argument for design rights?

ACTIVITY DISCUSSION

10.1 The argument remains utilitarian because it concludes that society will be a happier place overall with design rights. But despite that similarity, an important difference remains.

In copyright and patents, the utilitarian argument is *quantitative* in nature. Although there are variations, the core argument is that copyright and patents will encourage the production of *more* original works and inventions, and thereby, society will be happier overall. This fits neatly with the utilitarianism of Jeremy Bentham, who (as discussed in Section 2.2.2) argued that a person who has more pleasurable experiences in life (such as reading more books, listening to more music, etc.) will be a happier person.

While the Ewart Committee argument remains utilitarian, it was *qualitative* in nature. Design rights, it was claimed, would encourage the production of *better* (not necessarily more) designs. Of course, monopolies have negative consequences as well. But, implicitly, the Ewart Committee argued that the production of better designs would make society a better place overall.

This qualitative utilitarianism fits neatly with the thinking of another utilitarian philosopher, John Stuart Mill.[22] Unlike Bentham, Mill argued that simply having more pleasurable experiences in life does not necessarily make us happier people. Instead, we become happier if we have

> The philosopher John Stuart Mill (1806–1873) not only made contributions to utilitarianism, but also to liberalism and feminism.

better pleasurable experiences. We might be happier overall, therefore, with the same number of new designs being produced each year, if those designs are of a higher, more artistic, quality. To many modern thinkers, Mill's views are a bit snobbish and elitist. One might criticise the Ewart Committee along similar lines.

10.2 Raustiala and Sprigman's answer is similar to the competition objection offered by Merges and Nelson in relation to the prospect theory in Section 6.2.2.3. That is, competition, not monopoly, is the best incentive to develop ideas.

When a fashion designer launches their latest design, they will enjoy a short window of time before that design is copied by competitors. During that window, the designer enjoys a monopoly over the design. Of course, the designer has no legal property rights giving them a monopoly. Instead, their monopoly results from the simple fact that the designer faces no competition from copyists. This is often known as the **first mover advantage**. Free from competition, the designer can keep prices high.

Soon, however, the competitors will catch up. Copies will appear on the market and the original designer will lose their monopoly and prices will come down. The only thing the designer can do to retain their profits is to create a *new design* and start the process over again. Thus, copying actually stimulates innovation and creativity in design.

10.3 There is no obvious reason why a labour argument cannot be offered. A designer such as Robert Law took something from the public domain – the idea of a ride-on suitcase – and through mixing his labour with that idea, created something new: the Trunki design. If one is persuaded by the labour argument in copyright and patents, it is not entirely clear why labour would not apply equally well to designs. However, to the extent a labour argument can be put forward for designs, it continues to face the mixing, use, and nature objections (discussed in Sections 2.2.2 and 6.2.2).

The personality argument may be trickier. Recall that Activity 6.2. drew a distinction between van Gogh's *Starry Night* and Christiansen's Toy Building Brick. While van Gogh's choices were an expression of something internal to him, his personality, the same could not be said of the Toy Building Brick, whose features were chosen in response to functional and external demands. To which is Law's Trunki more similar?

SELF-ASSESSMENT ANSWERS

1. **Correct answer: d.** Japanese law follows a clear policy of demarcation. Australian law allows cumulation only in respect to two-dimensional designs. The UK law is close to full cumulation. However, French law prior to the 2001 amendments demonstrates the most obvious policy of cumulation.

Notes

1 'Dragons' Den', BBC <https://www.bbc.co.uk/programmes/b006vq92> (accessed June 2023).

2 'Rob Law', Roblaw.com <https://www.roblaw.com/> (accessed June 2023).

3 Temie Laleye '"Worthless" Dragons' Den Reject Left with Nothing – Business Now Worth over £9million' *Daily Express* (28 April 2022) <https://www.express.co.uk/finance/personalfinance/1602598/dragons-den-reject-success-millionaire-trunki> (accessed June 2023).

4 Lionel Bently, 'The Design/Copyright Conflict in the United Kingdom: A History' in Estelle Derclaye, *The Copyright/Design Interface* (CUP 2018) 225.

5 Reproduced with permission of author.

6 Lionel Bently and Brad Sherman, 'The United Kingdom's Forgotten Utility Model: The Utility Designs Act 1843 (1997) 3 IPQ 265.

7 Bently (n 4) 176.

8 (1902) 86 LT 765.

9 Registered Designs Act 1949 (Ch 88, 12, 12 & 14 Geo 6, Original: King's Printer Version) s 1(3).

10 ibid s 8(2).

11 ibid s 1(4).

12 Copyright Act 1956, s 2(1).

13 [1986] AC 577.

14 ibid 628.

15 Registered Designs Act 1949 (as amended by the CDPA 1988), s 1(3).

16 ibid s 8(2).

17 Copyright, Designs and Patents Act 1988, s 1(1).

18 ibid s 213.

19 ibid s 216.

20 Council Regulation (EC) No 6/2002 of 12 December 2001 on Community designs, Preamble; SI, *Brompton Bicycle v Chedech/Get2Get*, Case C-833/18, EU:C:2020:79, [AG37]–[AG40] (AG Sánchez-Bordona).

21 Reproduced with permission through Copyright Clearance Center.

22 John Stuart Mill, *Utilitarianism* (1861); Patrick R Goold and David A Simon, 'On Copyright Utilitarianism' (2024) Indiana LJ.

FIGURE ACKNOWLEDGEMENT

10.1 From Community Registered Design No 43427-0001. Reproduced in *Magmatic ('Trunki') v PMS International Group* [2013] EWHC 1925 (Pat)

11

Designs II: Contemporary Design Rights

Chapter 10 introduced the tangled history of UK design law up to 1988. Section 10.1.3 ended with Parliament's adoption of a tripartite system of design ownership, composed of registered design rights, unregistered design rights and copyright. The tripartite system was built on the largely untested claim that society is better off with, rather than without, design rights. But the worst effects of overlap were mitigated through a series of creative legal provisions.

Chapter 11 continues the story. As briefly noted in Section 10.1.2, European nations have long taken different approaches to ownership of designs. Most notably France adopted a unity of art theory, under which ownership of a design right automatically resulted in the designer owning copyright as well.[1] As such differences may affect the movement of goods within Europe, European Union law was developed to harmonise the laws of member states. As explained in this chapter, harmonisation placed UK law on a path to full cumulation, wherein many designs are not only protected by design rights, but also are protected by copyright for the designer's life plus seventy years. Once again, the question this presents is whether such extensive ownership is warranted.

This chapter is split into four sections, each discussing one of the four ways that designs can be owned in the UK today. In section order, those rights are: the registered design right, the unregistered design right, the supplementary unregistered design right and copyright for designs.

This chapter contains public sector information licensed under the Open Government Licence v3.0.

11.1 REGISTERED DESIGN RIGHT

The **registered design right** is governed by the RDA 1949 (as amended). This section outlines this right. In turn, it considers the registration process, subject matter, grounds for invalidity, rights and exceptions.

The registered design right has been influenced by European Union law in two ways. First, the **Design Directive 1998** sought to harmonise member state registered design rights.[2] The RDA was amended to comply with the Directive. Second, the **Design Regulation 2001** introduced another EU-wide registered design right, known as the community design right.[3] Following Brexit, that right no longer applies within the UK territory. Nevertheless, the substance of the community design right and UK registered design right are highly similar. Cases relating to the community design right are likely to remain important when interpreting similar provisions contained in the RDA.

> The UK is also part of the Hague Agreement concerning International Registration of Industrial Designs 1925. Under this system, a designer can apply to WIPO to obtain protection in several different countries.

11.1.1 Registration

The registered design right is obtained through application to the Designs Registry at the UK IPO. The application for protection must include: (i) 'representations' of the design[4] and (ii) a statement identifying the product to which the design is applied.[5] Typically, representations will be drawings or photographs, but may also include verbal descriptions. Figure 10.1 is one of the representations that Robert Law submitted in an application for a community registered design (CRD) in 2003.

The application may also include written disclaimers. Disclaimers allow the designer to identify features in the represented design that they do not wish to own. For example, when applying for rights in the Trunki design, Law could submit the image in Figure 10.1, but also explain that certain features – e.g. the shape of the wheels – are not part of the protected design. If there are no disclaimers, it will be assumed that the design is composed of everything in the representation.

The application will be examined by the Registrar. The Registrar will refuse the application if it does not relate to appropriate registered design subject matter (explored in Section 11.2.2).[6] If the application is successful, the designer will receive five years of protection over the design. The right can be renewed a maximum of five times, providing a maximum term of protection of twenty-five years.[7]

11.1.2 Subject Matter

Designs are defined according to section 1(2) of the RDA 1949 as:

> Recall that when initially passed, the RDA protected features which 'appeal to . . . the eye'. That definition was deleted and replaced with the current s 1(2) so that the RDA would comply with the Design Directive 1998.

> the appearance of the whole or a part of a product resulting from the features of, in particular, the lines, contours, colours, shape, texture or materials of the product or its ornamentation.

11.1.2.1 APPEARANCE

'Appearance' is not defined by the RDA. Courts have, however, understood it broadly to mean some aspect of the product that is 'discernible or recognisable'.[8] There is no requirement that the design be aesthetically attractive. What exactly a product's appearance is, however, is often a matter of disagreement. To illustrate, consider the Trunki.

Case 11.1 *Magmatic ('Trunki') v PMS International Group* [2013] EWHC 1925 (Pat) revd in *PMS International Group v Magmatic ('Trunki')* [2014] EWCA Civ 181, affd in [2016] UKSC 12

Facts

Robert Law founded Magmatic Ltd (claimant–respondent) to sell Trunkis. In 2003, the company obtained a CRD. Figure 10.1 is a computer-generated representation of the design that was submitted as part of the application. While the body of the suitcase in the image is grey, the wheels, the strap and the strip above and below the nose are all in a contrasting black colour (or shade).

PMS International Group (defendants–appellants) began importing and selling competing ride-on suitcases called the 'Kiddee case'. Two examples of the Kiddee Case appear in Figure 11.1.

Like the Trunki, the Kiddee Cases were designed to look like animals. The example (a) was coloured red and black; the example (b) was coloured orange and black. But note that the colour of the straps and wheels do not contrast with the colour of the body. This is especially noticeable on image (b) in Figure 11.1 where both the strap and body are orange.

Issue and Procedure

Magmatic sued PMS International Group for infringement of the CRD right. The case presented a question of interpretation: what precisely was the appearance that was protected by the design right?

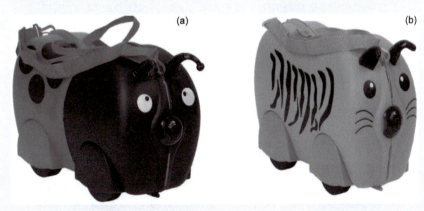

Figure 11.1 Two versions of the Kiddee Case

We will later see some parts of Mr Justice Arnold's decision.

In the High Court, Mr Justice Arnold (as he then was) considered the appearance to be the *shape* of the ride-on suitcase. He concluded that the design right in that shape was valid. He then proceeded to compare the shape to the shape of the Kiddee Case and found the latter infringed the rights in the former. PMS appealed to the Court of Appeal.

In the Court of Appeal, Lord Justice Kitchin overturned Mr Justice Arnold's decision in part. Like Arnold, he agreed that the design right was valid. But he disagreed about what precisely was the 'appearance' of the product, and what exactly Magmatic owned. Crucially, in Lord Justice Kitchin's view, the appearance was not just the shape. Instead, it was a shape that was designed to *look like a horned animal* and which used *contrasting colours for the body and wheels/strap*.

KITCHIN LJ

I believe that in interpreting the CRD as he did the judge fell into error in two respects. The CRD consists of six monochrome representations of a suitcase. These representations are not simple line drawings, however. Rather, they are computer generated three dimensional images which show the suitcase from different perspectives and angles and show the effect of light upon its surfaces. Further and importantly, the suitcase looks like a horned animal with a nose and a tail, and it does so both because of its shape and because its flanks and front are not adorned with any other imagery which counteracts or interferes with the impression the shape creates. As Mr Vanhegan submits, the CRD is, in that sense, relatively uncluttered and it conveys a distinct visual message. Here then the first of the judge's errors can be seen: he failed to appreciate that this is a design for a suitcase which, considered as a whole, looks like a horned animal.

Second, I entirely agree with the judge that it is striking that the various representations are shown in monochrome, and so it must be concluded that this design is not limited to particular colours. Just as in the Procter & Gamble case, PMS cannot point to the colour of the Kiddee Case as being a point of distinction. That is not the end of the analysis, however, because each of the representations shows a distinct contrast in colour between the wheels and the strap, on the one hand, and the rest of the suitcase, on the other. I have given anxious consideration to whether this is simply an artefact of the computer generation process or a visual cue to indicate that the wheels and the strap are each separate components. However, I do not find either of these alternative explanations convincing. The clasps are also separately functioning

> components and they are not shown in a contrasting colour and it seems to me that the wheels could perfectly well have been shown and depicted as separate components in the same colour as the rest of the body. Moreover, depicted as they are and standing as they do at the four corners of the animal, the wheels are, to my eye, a rather striking aspect of the design as a whole.
>
> (paras 41–42)

Having identified what exactly was protected by the right, Lord Justice Kitchin then proceeded to compare the appearance to the appearance of the Kiddee Case. As discussed later (Section 11.2.4), Kitchin concluded that while the shapes might be similar, the overall appearance of the two products was quite different. Crucially, the Kiddee Case did not look like a horned animal. Accordingly, PMS had not infringed Magmatic's rights. Kitchin's decision was then upheld upon appeal to the Supreme Court.

11.1.2.2 PRODUCT

Section 1(2) states that the appearance of a product can be owned as a registered design. Section 1(3) defines a product as:

> any industrial or handicraft item other than a computer program; and, in particular, includes packaging, get-up, graphic symbols, typographic type-faces and parts intended to be assembled into a complex product.

Because the definition of 'product' is broad, it covers everything from machinery parts to high-end fashion. Nevertheless, some items have failed to qualify as 'industrial or handicraft' in nature. For example, the EU IPO rejected an application for the heart-like shape of tomatoes (which was their natural shape) on the grounds that the shape was not the result of a manual or industrial process.[9]

A **complex product** is defined by section 1(3) as a product 'which is composed of at least two replaceable component parts permitting disassembly and reassembly of the product'.

11.1.3 Excluded Subject Matter

Section 1C excludes from protection 'designs dictated by their technical function'. The section describes two situations where the exclusion is applicable:

> (1) A right in a registered design shall not subsist in features of appearance of a product which are solely dictated by the product's technical function.

It will be recalled that the RDA 1949 in 1988 also excluded designs that were 'primarily' artistic or literary in character. This exclusion was abolished to comply with the Design Directive.

> (2) A right in a registered design shall not subsist in features of appearance of a product which must necessarily be reproduced in their exact form and dimensions so as to permit the product in which the design is incorporated or to which it is applied to be mechanically connected to, or placed in, around or against, another product so that either product may perform its function.

To understand subsection (1), consider the shape of the wheels on the Trunki. The wheels have a round shape. This round shape is solely functional in purpose: they are round for no aesthetic reasons; they are round only because that enables the suitcase to roll along the ground. As such, Robert Law could not own that particular feature of the Trunki, even if he wanted to. All competitors are, accordingly, allowed to create ride-on suitcases with round wheels.

By contrast, the shape of the horns is not *solely* functional. While they do enable the rider to hang on to the suitcase while it is being pulled, there is some aesthetic purpose to those horns (i.e. to make the suitcase look like a horned animal). Therefore, the appearance of the horns is a feature that Law can own.

This exclusion helps to minimise the overlap between registered design rights and patents. Features that have a technical function are excluded from ownership under the registered design law, but can be owned – providing they pass the patentability requirements – under patent law.[10]

Meanwhile, subsection (2) operates to prevent the designer obtaining a de facto monopoly in a secondary market. Consider, for example, someone who designs a razor blade handle. They could design the handle in such a way that only razor blades which reproduce certain features of the handle will connect properly. In that case, the designer of the handle could prevent competition in the market for razor blades. Subsection (2) prevents this outcome.

This provision is similar to the 'must fit' exclusion discussed in more detail in Section 11.3.2.2.

Finally, section 1D also prevents registration of designs that are contrary to public policy or morality. While infrequently used, this section might prevent registration of designs that are discriminatory.[11]

11.1.4   Grounds for Invalidity

Section 1B(1) of the RDA states that only designs that are 'new' and have an 'individual character' can be owned. Importantly, however, the Registrar has no power to reject an application on these grounds.[12] A design can only be declared invalid for lack of novelty or lack of individual character by a court post grant.

11.1.4.1 NOVELTY

Section 1B(2) of the RDA 1949 states that a design is new:

> if no identical design or no design whose features differ only in immaterial details has been made available to the public before the relevant date.

Much like novelty in patent law, the novelty analysis involves: (i) establishing the prior art, and (ii) comparing the design to the prior art.

But what counts as prior art? Initially, the language of section 1B would suggest a rule of absolute novelty, like patent law (Section 8.1.1). That is, everything 'made available to the public' (regardless of geographic location) is to be included in the prior art. But despite this broad language, some material will nevertheless be excluded from the prior art.

The most important exclusion is the '**obscure disclosures**' exclusion. This provision was discussed by Mr Justice Arnold in the *Trunki* case trial. In 1998, when he was a university student, Law invented the ride-on suitcase and designed a version of it called the 'Rodeo' (Figure 11.2). The Rodeo even won an award for its novel design. At trial, PMS argued that the Rodeo was part of the prior art and anticipated the Trunki design.

The 'relevant date' is different if claiming priority. The Paris Convention 1883 establishes six months' priority for prior designs.

Although he chose not to, Law could have tried to obtain patent protection for ride-on suitcases at this point.

Figure 11.2 The Rodeo. Robert Law

Designs II: Contemporary Design Rights

This part of the judgment, and the following extract on individual character, were not appealed and were regarded as correct by the parties.

> ## ARNOLD J
>
> ### Legal principles
>
> In short, any disclosure which makes the design public in any part of the world will suffice. This is subject to two exceptions, however. These may conveniently be labelled 'obscure disclosures' and 'confidential disclosures'. Only the first of these is relevant for present purposes. This applies where 'these events could not reasonably have become known in the normal course of business to the circles specialised in the sector concerned, operating within the Community'.
>
> ### Assessment
>
> The Rodeo. As I have said, there is no dispute that the design of the Rodeo was disclosed to the public at the Award ceremony in 1998. Magmatic contends that that disclosure falls within the exception for obscure disclosures, however. It is common ground that the relevant sector is the suitcase sector. Accordingly, the question is whether the design of the Rodeo could not reasonably have become known in the normal course of business to circles specialising in suitcases within the Community as a result of the Award ceremony.
>
> Magmatic relies on two main points as showing that it could not have become known: first, the Award was for plastics design; and secondly, as discussed above, there is no evidence that the design of the Rodeo was publicised more widely following the Award and prior to the filing date of the CRD. In my judgment neither of these points suffices to establish that the design of the Rodeo could not reasonably have become known in the normal course of business to those specialising in suitcases. So far as the first point is concerned, while the Award was for plastics design, it seems clear that it was a well-known award in the field of product design in the UK at that time. Furthermore, the theme of the competition in 1998 was luggage. In those circumstances, it is possible that people connected with the luggage trade will have attended the Award ceremony and thus seen the design of the Rodeo. Accordingly, I conclude that the obscure designs exception does not apply.
>
> (paras 33, 53–54)

Therefore, in Mr Justice Arnold's view, the Rodeo did form part of the prior art. Nevertheless, upon comparing the Rodeo and the Trunki, it was clear that the latter was not identical nor only immaterially different from the former. While there is little precedent to help courts make such determinations of fact, it was relatively clear that the Rodeo did not anticipate the Trunki and that the Trunki was a new design.

Mr Justice Arnold's decision also mentions the second type of material that will be excluded from the prior art. Disclosures that are made in confidence, as well as disclosures made in breach of confidence, will be excluded.[13] There is also a 'grace period' that allows the disclosure of their designs to the public within twelve months of the priority date.[14] These disclosures will also be excluded from the prior art.

11.1.4.2 INDIVIDUAL CHARACTER

Section 1B(3) of the RDA 1949 states that a design will have an **individual character**:

> if the overall impression it produces on the informed user differs from the overall impression produced on such a user by any design which has been made available to the public before the relevant date.

In addition, complex products can only be new and have individual character to the extent that they remain visible in use.[15]

Once again, this involves comparing the design to the prior art. The prior art is the same for the purposes of novelty and individual character. When assessing individual character, the statute directs courts to consider the 'degree of freedom of the author in creating the design'.

The idea of individual character can again be illustrated by the Trunki. Mr Justice Arnold considered the Trunki to be new and not anticipated by the Rodeo. But did the Trunki have an 'individual character'? Or would the informed perceive the Rodeo and Trunki as having the same 'character'?

ARNOLD J

The informed user. The Rodeo, the CRD and the Kiddee Case are all ride-on suitcases for a child aged 3–6. Accordingly, it is common ground between the parties that the informed users in the present case are (i) a 3–6 year old child and (ii) a parent, carer or relative of such a child. I have to say that I am dubious about (i), since the child will not be a purchaser (unlike Grupo Promer/PepsiCo, this is not a case about toys which might be purchased by a child with his or her pocket money), but since this is agreed I shall proceed on that basis. I doubt that it makes any difference either way.

Although the Rodeo has similarities to the CRD, there are quite a number of differences. The basic shapes are different. The Rodeo has a relatively simple shape with straight sides, a curved top surface and curved front and rear. The curved surfaces are curved essentially in one direction, although the corners between the surfaces are rounded. The ridge where the clamshells meet is unobtrusive. The

CRD has a rather more complex shape. The case has a prominent ridge round the top and sides which flares out in the middle of the top. The sides have semi-circular indentations. The front and rear surfaces are curved both up-and-down and side-to-side. The CRD has projecting lips at the bottom of the front and rear which have no equivalent in the Rodeo. The proportions are different: the Rodeo appears to be shorter, wider and not quite as long as the CRD. This gives it a squatter appearance than the CRD. The clasps are of different appearance: the clasps on the Rodeo are approximately rectangular, whereas the clasps on the CRD are both ovals with a slice removed. The clasps are also lower down on the CRD than on the Rodeo, particularly in the case of the front clasp which is on the top surface of the Rodeo. The CRD has two horns on the front and a strap attached to two eyelets on the top, whereas the Rodeo has a handle shaped like an elongated dumb-bell attached to a pull-out strap and a circular indented winder for the strap. The CRD also includes a luggage tag attached to the rear eyelet which has no counterpart in the Rodeo, but I think the informed user would regard that as a removable feature of little significance.

In my judgment the informed user would notice both similarities and differences between the CRD and the Rodeo when comparing them in detail. What matters is how those similarities and differences would affect the informed user's overall impression. The Rodeo is rather squat and chunky, and the handle forms an important part of its appearance. Despite the novelty of the concept, the appearance of the Rodeo is somewhat crude and old-fashioned. By comparison, the CRD is slimmer and more sculpted, and the ridge and the horns form important parts of its appearance. The CRD appears to be considerably more sophisticated and modern than the Rodeo. Furthermore, the clasps have a rather different visual impact, looking much more like the nose and tail of an animal than the winder and the rear clasp on the Rodeo. Thus the overall impression created by the CRD is different to that created by the Rodeo.

(paras 55, 63–64)

11.1.5 Scope

The registered design right is a property right that, according to section 7(1) of the RDA 1949 gives:

the registered proprietor the exclusive right to use the design and any design which does not produce on the informed user a different overall impression.

Unlike copyright, the registered design right is not an exclusive right to copy the design, but an exclusive right to use the design. Thus, like patent law, one infringes the right by using the design even if that use was not the product of copying. Someone who independently creates a design that is protected by a registered design right will infringe the right. Furthermore, although the applicant must identify a product in the registration process, their right is not confined to that product. Someone will infringe the right if they use the design on a different product. For example, if someone were to recreate the Trunki as a miniature toy sculpture, doing so would infringe Law's registered design right.

The more difficult question is whether a defendant's design produces the same overall impression on the informed user as the owner's design. Mr Justice Arnold in the High Court *Trunki* trial concluded that PMS had done so, as the next extract demonstrates.

ARNOLD J

The CRD is evidently for the shape of the suitcase, and the proper comparison is with the shape of the Kiddee Case.

In my judgment the informed user would notice both similarities and differences between the CRD and the Kiddee Case when comparing them in detail. What matters is how those similarities and differences would affect the informed user's overall impression. In my view the most noticeable differences between the Kiddee Case and the CRD are (i) the more rounded contours of the Kiddee Case around the seating area compared to the more angular contours and semi-circular indentation of the CRD in that area and (ii) the covered wheels of the Kiddee Case. Also noticeable are (iii) the more flared areas of the ridge around the clasps and (iv) the absence of the lip. Nevertheless, there is an overall resemblance between the designs.

If it were not for the Rodeo, I would have little hesitation in saying that the Kiddee Case produced the same overall impression on the informed user having regard to the broad scope of protection to which the CRD would otherwise be entitled. I am rather more doubtful as to whether it can be said the overall impression produced by the Kiddee Case is the same as the CRD and yet the overall impression produced by the Rodeo is different. Nevertheless, I have come to the conclusion that that is the correct assessment. Despite the differences between the Kiddee Case and the CRD, the overall impression the Kiddee Case creates shares the slimmer, sculpted, sophisticated, modern appearance, prominent ridge and horn-like handles and clasps looking like the nose and tail of an animal which are present in the CRD, but which are absent from the Rodeo. Moreover, neither the Kiddee Case

> nor the CRD have anything like the handle which is a prominent feature of the Rodeo.
>
> Conclusion. PMS has infringed the CRD.
>
> (paras 69, 76–78)

However, this decision was overturned by Lord Justice Kitchin in the Court of Appeal. Recall, he interpreted the design as protecting not just the shape, but a shape that gave the overall impression of a *horned animal* complete with *contrasting colours for the body and the wheels/strap/strip*. And in Kitchin's view, the Kiddee Case simply did not look like a horned animal!

KITCHIN LJ

First and most importantly, it seems to me the judge failed to carry out a global comparison having regard to the nature of the CRD and the fact that it is clearly intended to create the impression of a horned animal. This is plainly one of its essential features. Necessarily, therefore, a global assessment of the CRD and the accused designs requires a consideration of the visual impression they each create and in so far as that impression is affected by the features appearing on their front and sides, it seems to me those other features must be taken into account. Thus taking the insect version of the Kiddee Case, I believe that the impression its shape creates is clearly influenced by the two tone colouring of the body and the spots on its flanks. As a result it looks like a ladybird and the handles on its forehead look like antennae. Overall the shape conveys a completely different impression from that of the CRD. It was, in my judgment, wrong for the judge to eliminate the decoration on the accused design from his consideration entirely because it significantly affects how the shape itself strikes the eye, and the overall impression it gives. At least in the case of this particular registered design, the global comparison necessarily requires account to be taken of the context in which the accused shape appears. Precisely the same considerations apply to the other version of the Kiddee Case. The stripes on its flanks and the whiskers on either side of its nose immediately convey to the informed user that this is a tiger with ears. It is plainly not a horned animal. Once again the accused design produces a very different impression from that of the CRD.

The second error concerns the colour contrast between the wheels and the body of the CRD. This is, as I have said, a fairly striking feature

> of the CRD and it is simply not present in the accused designs. In my view it was another matter which the judge ought to have taken into account in carrying out the global comparison.
>
> Further, the overall impression created by the two designs is very different. The impression created by the CRD is that of a horned animal. It is a sleek and stylised design and, from the side, has a generally symmetrical appearance with a significant cut away semi-circle below the ridge. By contrast the design of the Kiddee Case is softer and more rounded and evocative of an insect with antennae or an animal with floppy ears. At both a general and a detailed level the Kiddee Case conveys a very different impression.
>
> I would therefore allow the appeal. I believe the judge ought to have found that the Kiddee Case does not infringe the CRD.
>
> (paras 47–48, 53, 55)

The Supreme Court, when it upheld Lord Justice Kitchin's decision, was sympathetic to Robert Law. Lord Neuberger described the design as 'original and clever' and also accepted that PMS was inspired by the Trunki design.[16] However, as they concluded: 'this appeal is not concerned with an idea or invention, but with a design'.[17]

The scope of the registered design right is similar to patents in another way: there exist relatively few exceptions to the right. Like patent law, there are exceptions that permit use of the design for private and non-commercial purposes, and for experimental purposes.[18] In addition, the RDA provides an exception permitting use of the design for purposes of citation or teaching, providing that such acts are compatible with 'fair trade practices' that do not 'unduly prejudice the normal exploitation of the design'.[19]

Finally, the design rights in a particular product will exhaust when that product is placed on the market in the UK or European Economic Area by the owner or with their consent.[20]

11.2   UNREGISTERED DESIGN RIGHT

Section 10.1.3 introduced the 'daft' idea of industrial copyright. The CDPA attempted to replace industrial copyright with a new **unregistered design right** that would protect functional designs (e.g. the shape of an exhaust pipe). Section 213 of the CDPA states that the unregistered design right 'is a property right which subsists ... in an original design'. The right is automatic and exists for fifteen years from the date of creation.[21] The right initially vests in the designer or their employer and can be assigned and licensed.[22]

Confusingly, the CDPA refers to this right as simply the 'design right'. We will call it the 'unregistered design right' for the sake of clarity.

11.2.1 Subject Matter

Section 213(2) of the CDPA states that a design for the purposes of the unregistered design right is:

> the shape or configuration (whether internal or external) of the whole or part of an article.

What is 'shape or configuration'? While 'shape' is reasonably clear, the term 'configuration' is a bit more opaque. But the concept can be illustrated by returning to the Trunki.

After Magmatic registered their design, it proceeded to sell Trunkis in the UK. The commercially sold Trunkis were different in some ways to the design represented in Figure 10.1. For example, the commercially sold Trunkis were far more colourful and ornate. When it came to trial, Magmatic argued that, in addition to their CRD, they had several *unregistered* design rights as well. The first unregistered design right related to the configuration of the Trunki Mark I. The Trunki Mark I, and Magmatic's description of its 'configuration', appear in Figure 11.3.

Figure 11.3 Trunki Mark I

Design C(1): External appearance – Mark I
The design comprising (that is to say consisting of) the aspect of the external appearance of the Mark I Trunki case consisting of the combination of the following aspects of shape and configuration of that case:

(i) a clamshell case, with a saddle shaped top, and a substantially rectangular base with 4 wheels in the corner;

(ii) the case having the general appearance of an animal, with two horns on the upper front portion of the case, and a nose and a tail each comprising a generally rounded plastic locking cover with a cut out to one side;

(iii) [not used]

(iv) a ridge where the two clamshell portions meet, running up the front, along the top and down the back of the case; the ridge expanding to form an oval shape in the portion of the ridge in the centre of the saddle of the case and around the clasp at the front and rear;

(v) two eyelets in the top front and top back of the case;

(vi) a strip located between the two clamshell portions, which protrudes from the case so that it is approximately level with the top of the ridge;

(vii) a hinge comprising multiple interleaved protrusions from each side of the clamshell case;

(viii) the wheels having a diameter which is of a particular proportion to the size of the rest of the case; the proportion being a ratio of 1:5 of wheel diameter to total length of case.

At trial, Magmatic argued that the combination of points (i)–(vii) was a 'configuration' and therefore protected by the unregistered design right. PMS, however, disagreed arguing that the 'configuration' was of a far too 'general' nature. Nevertheless, in the next extract, Mr Justice Arnold concludes that this was a configuration.

ARNOLD J

Are designs C–F designs? PMS accepts that designs A and B are 'designs' within the meaning of section 213(2), but disputes that designs C–F are. This depends on whether the designs consist of the design of 'any aspect' of the 'configuration' of the Trunki. ('Shape' can be ignored for present purposes, since counsel for Magmatic did not contend that designs C–F consisted of aspects of shape.)

Counsel for PMS submitted first that a 'design' could only consist of a single 'aspect' of configuration, not multiple aspects. I do not accept that submission. Construing section 213(2) purposively, I see no reason to exclude designs that consist of multiple aspects of configuration.

Counsel for PMS submitted secondly that the aspects selected by Magmatic did not consist of aspects of 'configuration' at all. The argument can be illustrated by reference to design C(1) (the external appearance of the Trunki Mark I). As counsel for Magmatic accepted, design C(1) consists of a verbalised description of certain features of the external appearance of the Trunki which are also to be found in the Kiddee Case. Not only that, but as counsel for Magmatic also accepted, the features are not described at the level of specificity to be found in the Trunki, but at a more generalised, abstract level.

The consequence is that, as counsel for PMS pointed out:

(i) The clamshell case may be of any shape provided it has a saddle-shaped top and a substantially rectangular base.

(ii) The general appearance can be of any animal. The horns can be of any size and shape. The nose and tail can be of any size and any shape which be described as 'generally rounded . . . with a cut out to one side'.

(iii) [omitted]

(iv) The ridge can be of any size and shape provided it expands to oval shape in two stated places.

(v) The eyelets can be of any size and shape.

(vi) The strip may be of any size and shape provided it is approximately level with the top of the ridge.

(vii) The hinge can be of any size and shape provided it has the interleaved portions.

(viii) The wheels can be of any shape, provided they have the stated proportion of diameter to the length of the case.

Neither party appealed Mr Justice Arnold's conclusions in relation to the unregistered design right.

> Counsel for PMS argued that, even on the basis that 'configuration' extended to the relative arrangement of elements of the article, it did not extend to abstracted generalisations of this kind. I see considerable force in this argument. Nevertheless, I do not feel able to accept it, because much the same could be said about a circuit diagram of the kind in issue in Mackie, which is essentially an abstract description using conventional symbols of the selection of components and their interconnections.
>
> (paras 89–93)

The term 'article' is not defined by the legislation. In some way, it presumably is to be contrasted with the term 'product' that is found in the RDA 1949.

11.2.2 Excluded Subject Matter

Section 213(3) states that certain designs will be excluded from protection, namely:

> (a) a method or principle of construction,
> (b) features of shape or configuration of an article which – (i) enable the article to be connected to, or placed in, around or against, another article so that either article may perform its function, or (ii) are dependent upon the appearance of another article of which the article is intended by the designer to form an integral part, or
> (c) surface decoration.

11.2.2.1 METHOD OR PRINCIPLE OF CONSTRUCTION

Subsection 3(a) functions much like the idea–expression dichotomy in copyright. The section excludes from protection principles or ideas underlying a shape, or the method of making the shape. Therefore, although Mr Justice Arnold agreed that the C(1) design was a configuration, he subsequently decided that it was nevertheless excluded from protection.

> **ARNOLD J**
>
> Are designs C–F methods or principles of construction? PMS contends that, even if designs C–F are 'designs' at all, no design right subsists in them because they are methods or principles of construction. In my judgment, this is the real objection to design C(1). As can be seen from paragraph 92 above, design C(1) covers a multitude of different specific appearances. It is more like a patent claim than an identification of particular aspects of configuration of the Trunki.
>
> (para 94)

As Mr Justice Arnold acknowledges, ideas can only be owned through patent rights, providing they pass the patentability criteria.

11.2.2.2 MUST FIT AND MUST MATCH

Subsection 3(b)(i) is somewhat colloquially known as the 'must fit' exclusion. It can be illustrated by considering another part of the Trunki. On the front and the back of the Trunki are clasps designed to close the suitcase. The orange clasp is visible in Figure 11.3. On later versions of the Trunki – the Trunki Mark II – the clasps were designed with a key slot in the centre. Box 11.1 presents Magmatic's description of the newly designed clasp. Pay close attention to point (3).

Magmatic could not own the shape or configuration of the 'slot in the central locking mechanism' because of the 'must fit' exception. The shape of this slot enables the clasp to be connected to a key. Only if the two shapes – the shape of the key and slot – fit together can either perform their function. The two items 'must fit' together to work. Ergo, subsection 3(b)(i) applies.

BOX 11.1 TRUNKI CLASP DESIGN

(A) The metal parts of the clasps (Trunki Mark I)

(1) The design comprising (that is to say consisting of) the aspects of shape and configuration (as a whole) of the metal clasps on the front and rear of the Mark I Trunki case that is to say the C shaped bar and the U shaped base to which the C shaped bar is attached.

(B) The clasp as a whole (Trunki Mark II)

(1) The design comprising (that is to say consisting of) the combination of the aspects of shape and configuration of the metal clasps identified in paragraph 1 above, and the aspect of shape and configuration consisting of generally rounded locking covers with a cut out to one side and a central rotating portion.

(2) The aspects of the locking covers relied upon are . . . the following aspects of shape and configuration: An outer portion being shaped like an inverted bowl which has (on the side located away from the hinge) two protruding ribs. The inverted bowl has a cut away portion located close to the hinge. The inverted bowl has a circular central locking mechanism.

(3) The claimant does not rely upon the aspects of shape and configuration of the slot in the central locking mechanism to take a key. The claimant does, however, rely upon (a) the existence of a slot in the end of the central locking mechanism and (b) the aspects of shape and configuration of the inside of the circular central locking mechanism facing the case.

By contrast, subsection 3(b)(ii) is concerned with appearance, rather than functionality, and is known colloquially as the 'must match' exclusion. Imagine, for example, that you own a Trunki and one day the clasp becomes damaged and falls off. You go to a local mechanic and ask them to make a spare part for you. You ask the mechanic not to make just any old clasp, but make one exactly like the Trunki clasp (as described in point (2) in Box 11.1). Under certain circumstances, the mechanic will be allowed to make you a spare part without infringing any unregistered design rights in that article.

Whether the mechanic can make the spare clasp for you depends on whether the overall appearance of the Trunki is 'dependent' on the appearance of the clasp. You, for example, might argue that your Trunki will simply no longer be a Trunki if it does not have a clasp that looks like the one in Box 11.1. To be a Trunki, you claim, the clasp 'must match' the rest of the suitcase. If so, then the appearance of the Trunki is 'dependent' on the appearance of the clasp, and therefore, the clasp cannot be owned. Alternatively, if the clasp could be replaced with a different looking clasp, without 'radically altering' the appearance of the Trunki overall, then the appearance of the Trunki is independent of the appearance of the clasp. In that case, the clasp can be owned and is not excluded from protection.

> The 'must match' exception was introduced to prevent car companies monopolising the market for spare parts. As the Trunki example demonstrates, the provision allows other people to supply spare parts under certain circumstances.

ACTIVITY 11.1

Do you think the Trunki clasp is excluded under the must match exclusion?

11.2.2.3 SURFACE DECORATIONS

Finally, surface decorations on the article will not be protected by the unregistered design right. For example, the Trunki Mark II was decorated with ornamental spots and stripes. Figure 11.4 displays the Trunki Mark II as well as the description provided by Magmatic. As you read, you will note that Magmatic did not try to own the spots and stripes. The reason is likely that, as surface decorations, the spots and stripes cannot be owned through the unregistered design right. Such decoration might potentially be protected by copyright, however.

> This helps minimise the overlap between unregistered design rights and copyright.

Figure 11.4 Trunki Mark II

(C2) External appearance design 2 – Mark IIA Trunki

7. The design consisting of the aspect of the external appearance of the Mark IIA Trunki case (also referred to as the Mark IB Trunki case) consisting of the combination of the following aspects of the case:

   (1) the aspects of shape and configuration of that case listed in paragraphs 6(i), 6(ii) and 6(iv) to 6(viii) above, and

(2) the following aspects of the cloth handles on the top of the case, namely (a) the particular length (about 15 cm); (b) the handles being folded in half and sewn in their middle third to form a narrower centre portion;

(c) the handles being spaced around the expanded portion of the central ridge in the top of the case;

(d) the handles being mounted in slots cut between the inner and outer portion of the clamshell halves, and terminated with a (metal) C shaped grip folded over the ends;

(The fact that the handles are made of cloth and the grip is made of metal is not relied upon as an aspect of shape or configuration).

Figure 11.4 (*cont.*)

ACTIVITY 11.2

Using your knowledge of Chapter 3, could the surface decorations be considered a copyrightable artistic work?

11.2.3 Originality

Only original designs will be protected. Section 213(4) states that a design is not original if:

> it is commonplace in a qualifying country in the design field in question at the time of its creation and 'qualifying country' has the meaning given in section 217(3).

Courts have interpreted the originality requirement as involving two steps. First, the design must be original in the sense found in copyright law.[23] To illustrate, consider design C2 of Trunki Mark II in Figure 11.4. Ultimately, Mr Justice Arnold held that this design, like C1 was excluded from protection as a principle or method of construction. However, in the following extract, he explains that if they were protected designs, he would have held C2 to be original in the copyright sense.

ARNOLD J

Are designs C(2) and C(3) original? PMS contends that, even if designs C(2) and C(3) are not excluded from protection as being methods or

360 *Designs II: Contemporary Design Rights*

Note the reference to 'skill' and 'effort'. It remains an open question whether the originality standard for unregistered designs should be skill, labour and/or judgement, or the personal intellectual creation standard (see Section 3.2.1).

> principles of construction, they are not original over designs C(1) and C(2) respectively. Given my conclusion that these designs are excluded from protection because they consist of methods or principles of construction, this issue does not arise. Accordingly, I shall deal with it very briefly. In my judgment the combinations of features in C(2) and C(3) are both original compared to the combinations in C(1) and C(2) respectively. While the differences are relatively small, they are discernible and they were the product of Mr Law's skill, effort and aesthetic judgement.
>
> (para 96)

Assuming the feature of the design is original in the copyright sense, then the next question is whether it is 'commonplace'. A good illustration concerns design D submitted by Magmatic. Design D related to the straps and pouch inside the suitcase, and is explained in Box 11.2.

BOX 11.2 INSIDE OF THE TRUNKI

(D) The inside of the case – straps and pouch

12. The design consisting of the aspect of the internal part of one of the shells of the Mark II Trunki case (also included in the Mark III Trunki cases) consisting of the combination of the following aspects:

    (i) the following aspects of the shape and configuration of X shaped retaining straps and their associated fixings and mountings: (1) they are X shaped retaining straps affixed to the 4 internal corners of the case; (2) they are sewn at their inner ends around the loop of a clasp (the clasp forming the centre of the X shaped straps); (3) they are fixed by (inverted) L shaped grips clamping the straps at the top of the case, which are held in place by a screw fastened to the inside top of the case (excluding any aspect of the L shaped grip extending beyond the outer part of the inner wall of the shell); (4) they are fixed by generally L shaped grips clamping the straps at the bottom of the case which cover the top and run down the side of a wedge shaped portion of the case which fills the lower corners of the case and which are held by a screw into that wedge shaped portion.

    (ii) the shape and configuration and position of the pocket made of cloth; the pocket being approximately 38 cm in length and 8cm in depth and attached to where the X-shaped cross-straps are secured to the case; and further including a folded hem, containing a flat elastic cord; elastic cord being flat and running the length of the pocket.

At trial, PMS argued that design D was commonplace because lots of suitcases have cross-straps and pockets inside. However, Mr Justice Arnold disagreed. The design was not merely for cross-straps and pockets (that certainly would have been commonplace). But instead, the design was for the 'specific shape and configuration' of those cross-straps and pockets.[24] Hence this design was original and thus protected.

In addition, designs A and B for the clasp (Box 11.1) were also held to be original as was a final design, design F, for the shape and configuration of the tow strap.

11.2.4 Scope

Under section 226(1) of the CDPA, the owner of the unregistered design right has:

the exclusive right to reproduce the design for commercial purposes –

(a) by making articles to that design, or
(b) by making a design document recording the design for the purpose of enabling such articles to be made.

Much like copyright, reproduction 'means copying the design so as to produce articles exactly or substantially to that design'.[25] In a case like the Trunki, PMS admitted that their design was 'derived from' the Trunki design. Accordingly, there was no question about whether the design was 'copied' or not. In other cases, however, defendants will deny copying. In such cases, courts try to infer copying from circumstantial evidence.[26] This process is similar to copyright (explained in Section 4.1.1.1) and requires an assessment of the defendant's access to the claimant's design, as well as the degree of similarity.

Having agreed that their designs were copied from the Trunki designs, the question remained: were the PMS designs 'substantially' the same as the protected designs? While PMS agreed that their clasps and straps were substantially the same as the protected designs A, B and F, they disagreed that the internal part of their Kiddee Case was substantially the same as design D.

ARNOLD J

In the case of designs A (the metal parts of the clasps), B (the clasps as a whole less the must-fit features) and F (the strap), counsel for PMS did not seriously argue to the contrary. In the case of design D (the internal cross-straps and pocket), counsel for PMS relied upon a

> number of detailed differences between the design of the Trunki and that of the Kiddee Case as showing that there was no relevant copying alternatively that the Kiddee Case was not substantially to design D. I do not accept that there was no relevant copying for the reasons given above. Furthermore, while I acknowledge that there are a number of detailed differences, I have concluded after some hesitation that the cross-straps and pocket are substantially to design D.
>
> Conclusion. I conclude that PMS has infringed Magmatic's design right in designs A, B, D and F.
>
> (paras 99, 110)

Much like the registered design right, exceptions exist to permit acts done privately for purposes which are not commercial, for acts which are done for experimental purposes, and for teaching and citation purposes.[27]

In addition, section 236 of the CDPA regulates the interaction of the unregistered design right and copyright. That section states that if an article is protected by a design right, and is also a work protected by copyright, then it is not an infringement of the design right to do something that infringes the copyright. This overlap will be considered in more depth in Section 11.4.

11.3 SUPPLEMENTARY UNREGISTERED DESIGN RIGHT

Section 10.2 introduced Kal Raustiala and Christopher Sprigman's 'piracy paradox'. Raustiala and Sprigman argue that American law grants fashion designers relatively little IP protection. Unlike UK and EU law, American law only grants designers one right: a registered design right (known in American law as a design patent). That registered design right is difficult and expensive to acquire. Surprisingly, the authors claim, the industry is still a highly creative and innovative one with new designs being produced every year.

Unlike American law, EU law offers designers a higher level of protection. In addition to introducing the registered community design right, the Community Design Regulation of 2001 introduced an additional unregistered design right. The unregistered community design right grants designers an automatic three-year property right over their designs within the EU territory. The argument for such protection was that some industries – like the fashion industry – have short 'product life cycles'.[28] New fashion designs are produced, sold and quickly go out of style. Therefore, the argument goes, these industries needed short-term protection to stimulate creativity and innovation.

> ### ACTIVITY 11.3
>
> What is wrong with the argument that fashion designers need a short automatic property right to encourage creativity and innovation?

Following the UK's withdrawal from the EU, the unregistered community design right no longer applies in the UK. However, the UK has replaced the right with another right: the '**supplementary unregistered design right**'.[29]

The UK supplementary design right grants three years of protection automatically to those who produce a design that is new and has an individual character, so long as that design was first made available to the public within the United Kingdom.[30] If the design is first published outside the UK, then it is ineligible for protection via this right. The terms 'design', 'new' and 'individual character' are defined in the same way as they are in the registered design right (see Section 11.2.4).

The scope of the right is like the scope of the existing UK unregistered design right. The owner only has a right of reproduction.[31] Thus, infringement of the right requires copying. Once again, exceptions exist for non-commercial, experimental, citation or teaching purposes.[32]

> Designs that were protected prior to Brexit under the unregistered community design right were, in the immediate years following Brexit, protected under another UK right: the continuing unregistered design right. Mercifully, this no longer exists.

11.4 COPYRIGHT FOR DESIGNS

As outlined in Section 10.1.3, the CDPA 1998 created a tripartite system of protection. This tripartite system recognised that at times, copyright could also apply to designs. Nevertheless, Parliament tried to coordinate the relationship between copyright and design rights to minimise the problems of overlap.

However, as Lionel Bently writes, how copyright applies to designs has been 'completely refigured' in recent years.[33] The impact of EU law has radically changed what designs can be protected by copyright, and the scope of that protection.

11.4.1 Subject Matter

Chapter 3 introduced copyrightable subject matter. Section 3.1 examined how copyrightable subject matter was understood in the UK primarily in the twentieth century. Section 3.2 then considered briefly how UK law has changed in the twenty-first century in response to European influences. It is helpful to break down this section in the same way.

11.4.1.1 TWENTIETH-CENTURY UK SUBJECT MATTER

It will be recalled that under section 1(1)(a) of the CDPA, copyright exists in 'original literary, dramatic, musical or artistic works'. If a design can fit within

Designs II: Contemporary Design Rights

that definition, then it will be eligible for copyright protection. On the other hand, if a design cannot fit within that definition, it will not enjoy copyright protection. The following two cases demonstrate how a design may fail to acquire copyright.

The first case is the *Lucasfilm v Ainsworth* case (discussed in Section 3.1.3.4). In that case, the UK Supreme Court held that the *Star Wars* helmet was not an artistic work because it was functional in nature. But the Supreme Court also gave a second reason for their conclusion. As the next extract demonstrates, the Supreme Court also thought that the helmet was something to be protected by design rights, not copyright.

WALKER LJ AND COLLINS LJ

There is one other matter to which the Court of Appeal attached no weight, but which seems to us to support the judge's conclusion. It is a general point as to the policy considerations underlying Parliament's development of the law in order to protect the designers and makers of three-dimensional artefacts from unfair competition. After reviewing the legislative history the Court of Appeal took the view (para [40]) that there was no assistance to be obtained from the relationship between copyright and registered design right. We respectfully disagree, especially if the relatively new unregistered design right is also taken into account. It is possible to recognise an emerging legislative purpose (though the process has been slow and laborious) of protecting three-dimensional objects in a graduated way, quite unlike the protection afforded by the indiscriminate protection of literary copyright. Different periods of protection are accorded to different classes of work. Artistic works of art (sculpture and works of artistic craftsmanship) have the fullest protection; then come works with 'eye appeal' (AMP Inc v Utilux Pty Ltd [1971] FSR 572); and under Part III of the 1988 Act a modest level of protection has been extended to purely functional objects (the exhaust system of a motor car being the familiar example). Although the periods of protection accorded to the less privileged types have been progressively extended, copyright protection has always been much more generous. There are good policy reasons for the differences in the periods of protection, and the Court should not, in our view, encourage the boundaries of full copyright protection to creep outwards.

(para 48)

Following the *Lucasfilm* case, it seems unlikely that the Trunki could be protected by copyright as a sculpture.

The second case concerns design drawings. This time, we return to the story of the Christiansen brick.

Case 11.2 *Interlego AG v Tyco Industries* [1989] AC 217

Facts

Chapter 6 introduced the story of Christiansen's stud-and-tube coupling system for toy bricks. Christiansen and Interlego AG (claimants–respondents) enjoyed both patent protection and registered design right protection in that invention.

In the 1980s, an American company called Tyco Industries (defendants–cross appellants) operated in Hong Kong. When the patents and registered design rights in the bricks expired, Tyco made their own version of the bricks.

Interlego sued Tyco arguing that they owned copyright in the design drawings for the bricks (see Figure 11.5 for example). By copying the brick, Interlego argued, Tyco infringed that copyright. The case was appealed to the Privy Council.

> At this time, Hong Kong was a British dependent territory and subject to British rule. Previously, Hong Kong was a British colony, having been acquired by the British Empire in 1841. Sovereignty was transferred to China in 1997.

Issue and Procedure

There was a problem, however, for Interlego. The Copyright Act 1956 was only extended to cover Hong Kong in 1973. The legislation that extended the Copyright Act to Hong Kong stated that any artistic works made *before* 1973 would not be protected by copyright, if they were capable of registration under the RDA 1949 and had been used in an industrial process. The Privy Council decided, therefore, that the design drawings made by Interlego before 1973 were excluded from copyright protection.

But Interlego had another argument waiting. They argued that copyright still protected drawings they made *after* 1973. After 1973, they had made very minor alterations to their pre-1973 drawings. For example, in the post-1973 drawings, the tubes on the bricks had sharper edges, and the radii of the studs had been increased from 0.2mm to 0.33m. Interlego argued that these post-1973 drawings

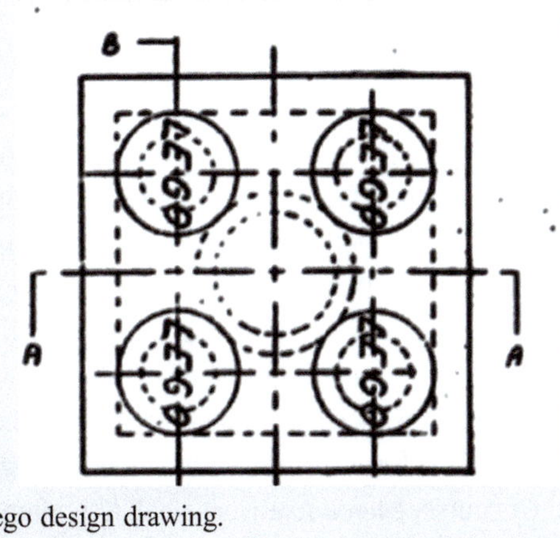

Figure 11.5 Interlego design drawing.
Photos by UCL photo dept. Made available by Centre for Intellectual Property and Information Law Virtual Museum

Designs II: Contemporary Design Rights

were original artistic works, eligible for copyright. That copyright had then been infringed by the defendants.

However, in the next extract, Lord Oliver of Aylmerton concluded that the post-1973 drawings were not original artistic works and thus not eligible for copyright protection.

OLIVER L

Section 8.1.3 introduced the concept of 'evergreening'. This provides another example of evergreening, albeit in copyright rather than patents.

In these proceedings Lego base their monopoly on copyright asserted not for the bricks but for the uninspired and uninspiring engineering drawings of bricks. By attributing new periods of copyright protection to every minor alteration in the form of a brick which is recorded in such a drawing they seek to obtain, effectively, a perpetual monopoly. In In re A Coca-Cola Co. [1986] 1 W.L.R. 695, 697, the House of Lords drew attention to the undesirable practice of seeking to expand the boundaries of intellectual property rights beyond the purposes for which they were created in order to obtain an unintended and undeserving monopoly. These proceedings are a further illustration of that undesirable practice.

... To accord an independent artistic copyright to every such reproduction would be to enable the period of artistic copyright in what is, essentially, the same work to be extended indefinitely. Thus the primary question on Tyco's appeal can be expressed in this way: can Lego, having enjoyed a monopoly for the full permitted period of patent and design protection in reliance upon drawings in which no copyright any longer subsists, continue their monopoly for yet a further, more extensive period by re-drawing the same designs with a number of minor alterations and claiming a fresh copyright in the re-drawn designs?

Tyco Industries was represented by the barrister Sir Robin Jacob. Sir Robin later became Lord Justice Robin Jacob and today is the Hugh Laddie Chair of Intellectual Property at UCL, in the UK.

The significant thing about all these changes is that they involve no substantial alteration to the drawing as such ... What is important about a drawing is what is visually significant and the re-drawing of an existing drawing with a few minimal visual alterations does not make it an original *artistic* work, however much labour and skill may have gone into the process of reproduction or however important the technical significance of the verbal information that may be included in the same document by way of information or instruction.

There must in addition be some element of material alteration or embellishment which suffices to make the totality of the work an original work. Of course, even a relatively small alteration or addition quantitatively may, if material, suffice to convert that which is substantially copied from an earlier work into an original work. Whether it does so or not is a question of degree having regard to the quality rather than the quantity of the addition. But copying, per se, however much skill or labour may be devoted to the process, cannot make an. original work. A well executed tracing is the result of much labour and skill but remains what it is, a tracing. Moreover it must be borne in mind that the Copyright Act 1956 confers protection on an original work for a generous period. The prolongation of the period of statutory protection by periodic reproduction of the original work with minor alterations is an operation which requires to be scrutinised with some caution to ensure that that for which protection is claimed really is an original artistic work.

(pp. 255–56, 258, 263)

11.4.1.2 EUROPEAN INFLUENCES

When the Design Directive 1998 and Design Regulation were adopted, both included the following requirement (in articles 17 and 96(2) respectively):

A design protected by a design right registered in or in respect of a Member State in accordance with this Directive shall also be eligible for protection under the law of copyright of that State as from the date on which the design was created or fixed in any form. The extent to which, and the conditions under which, such a protection is conferred, including the level of originality required, shall be determined by each Member State.

At first glance, this requirement may not seem problematic. The CDPA might seem to comply with the rule on the grounds that it grants copyright to designs when they fit within the definition of section 1(1)(a). However, recent CJEU case law has complicated matters.

The first problem concerns the CDPA's 'closed list' approach to subject matter (see Section 3.1.3). The retained cases of *Levola Hengolo* and *Cofemel* conclude that a work is anything that is original, expressive and identifiable with sufficient precision and objectivity.[34] The implication is that anything that satisfies the definition of a work must be protected by copyright – and that a closed-list approach to subject matter is not to be followed (see Section 3.2.3). This may have consequences in cases like *Lucasfilm*. If the helmet is original, expressive and identifiable with sufficient precision and objectivity, then the helmet should – under the *Levola Hengolo/Cofemel* approach – receive copyright regardless of whether it can be squeezed into the category of 'artistic work' or not.

The second problem concerns 'originality'. The retained cases of *Infopaq* and *Painer* conclude that expression is original when it is the 'personal intellectual creation' of the author.[35] Although articles 17 and 96(2) say that member states can determine the level of originality, the *Cofemel* case (which concerned copyright in the design of jeans) concluded that only if a design met the 'personal intellectual creation' standard would copyright apply. This has implications for cases like *Interlego*. Whether the post-1973 alterations should be protected by copyright or not, should – under the *Infopaq/Painer* approach – depend on whether they were original in the sense of being the author's personal intellectual creation, and not on the level or type of skill, labour and judgment required.

Of course, these problems only exist if Parliament, the Supreme Court and the Court of Appeal, choose not to diverge from the retained case law in the future.

11.4.2   Scope

But perhaps the most troublesome aspect of the CJEU's intervention in design law concerns scope and, in particular, copyright exceptions.

11.4.2.1   SECTION 52

As summarised in Section 11.1.3, the CDPA originally included an exception in section 52. According to section 52, if the work had been used in an 'industrial process', then copying the work would be a permitted act. The exception only applied after the first twenty-five years of protection.

ACTIVITY 11.4

To illustrate the defence, imagine, for example, that the Interlego company produced design drawings for toy bricks in 1990 and (unlike the ones discussed above) those drawings are protected by copyright. Assume also that in 1990, Interlego started to sell toy bricks corresponding to the design drawings. These bricks are protected by a registered design right which expired in 2015. In 2016, Tyco copy the Interlego bricks and sell the copies. Under section 52, have Interlego infringed the copyright in the design drawings?

The purpose of this provision was to limit the effective term of copyright to twenty-five years and thereby prevent designs being protected by copyright for the life of the designer plus seventy years.

However, this section has now been repealed. In the retained case of *Flos v Semararo*,[36] the CJEU pointed out that the EU Term Directive mandates that copyright be for life of the author plus seventy years. As a result, the CJEU concluded that EU member states must provide copyright in designs and that copyright must last the same length of time as all other copyrights (i.e. life plus seventy years). At the time, the UK was a member state and, as Bently explains in Box 11.3, repealed section 52 without consultation and in response to lobbying.

> ## BOX 11.3 LIONEL BENTLY, 'THE DESIGN/COPYRIGHT CONFLICT IN THE UNITED KINGDOM: A HISTORY' IN ESTELLE DERCLAYE (ED), *THE COPYRIGHT/DESIGN INTERFACE* (CUP 2018)
>
> Lobbyists working for companies that held rights in classic mid-century designs jumped on the Court's dictum, calling on the United Kingdom Government to remove the restriction in section 52 on the availability of copyright for mass-produced articles after twenty-five years of production.[37] Fearing Francovich liability, and without conducting any formal consultation, the Government announced it intended to repeal section 52 of the 1988 Act. This was done by section 74 of the Enterprise and Regulatory Reform Act 2013. The Government met criticisms of its failure to consult, and concerns about the implications of what was in substance (if not form) a 'revival' of long-lapsed rights, with a promise of lengthy transitional provisions.
>
> (pp. 223–24)

Revival occurs where a work has fallen into the public domain, and then later becomes protected by copyright again.

Although the UK has left the EU and could reinstate section 52, there are currently no plans to do so. The result is the effective term for copyright in designs is, like other works, life of the author plus seventy years.

11.4.2.2 SECTION 51

Although section 52 was repealed, a similar section – section 51 – remains. That section states that:

> It is not an infringement of any copyright in a design document or model recording or embodying a design for anything other than an artistic work or a typeface to make an article to the design or to copy an article made to the design.

The crucial language is the 'other than an artistic work' clause. To illustrate, consider a sculptor who is designing their next artistic sculpture to display in a museum. They may start this process by drawing the sculpture on paper. Because this design is *for an artistic work*, section 52 does not apply. If someone makes the sculpture, they will infringe the copyright in the design drawing.

However, if the design is for something *other than an artistic work*, then section 51 will permit people to copy the design. When the *Lucasfilm* case went to trial, Mr Justice Mann decided that if the helmets were *not* artistic works, then Ainsworth would be permitted to copy the helmets (a 'model') under this section.

> ## MR JUSTICE MANN
>
> The section is therefore capable of barring a copyright claim in relation to the design document if it is for 'anything other than an artistic work'. If the items were not artistic works, the section works in Mr Ainsworth's favour and prevents his acts being infringements. The designs could only be for artistic works in this case if they were for a sculpture or a work of artistic craftsmanship. I have held that they were not artistic works in either of the two candidate senses. Therefore the designs were for something other than an artistic work and section 51 operates in Mr Ainsworth's favour to prevent his copying of the work being an infringement of copyright. Arguments of some sophistication were advanced before me as to what Mr McQuarrie might have had to have intended in terms of creating sculptures or works of artistic craftsmanship. I do not think the link is that difficult. He was designing what he was designing. The part that intention plays in determining whether something is a sculpture or work of artistic craftsmanship has already been dealt with in relation to those concepts. I do not consider that any further refinement is required here.
>
> (para 141)

Prior to Brexit, there was some concern that section 51 may also be challenged by lobbyists and, like section 51, repealed.[38] The section ultimately was not repealed. However, that does not mean the controversy is over. As *Flos* is retained case law, then there still may be an inconsistency between the CDPA and case law. This may cause courts problems in the future.

11.5 SUMMARY

This chapter has explored the four different ways that designs can be owned in contemporary UK law. As demonstrated by the *Trunki* case, often multiple design rights can exist in the same product: such as the registered design right for the appearance of a horned animal, and unregistered design rights for the configuration. And while copyright was not asserted in that particular case, there remains the possibility that copyright might attach to certain features associated with the Trunki, such as the design drawings or surface decorations.

The existence of multiple different design rights in one product has consequences for the conceptual question. It is unlikely that any one right gives the owner exclusive control over the entirety of the Trunki. However, the ability to own different features of the Trunki through a series of different rights amounts to a very high level of control over all intangible features of the Trunki. It is questionable to what extent that level of propertisation is desirable.

11.6 SELF-ASSESSMENT

Before moving on, try to answer the following questions to consolidate your learning. Answers are provided in the section below.

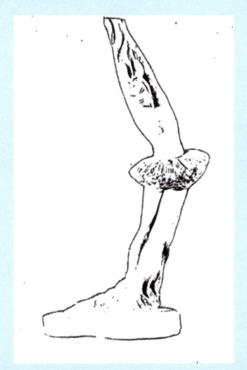

Figure 11.6 Stein lamp base

1. The Stein family business produced and sold electric lamps. One of the family members – Rena Stein – designed lamps with a base that looked like a person dancing (Figure 11.6). The appearance of the lamp base is new and possesses individual character, and the shape is original. The design was first made available in the USA. The base is compatible with a wide range of bulbs and lampshades.

    What rights, if any, could Rena Stein obtain in the lamps today under British law? (No options are provided, but a discussion appears later.)

2. A UK designer has designed a clock. The designer has been granted a registered design. A court is considering whether the design is invalid for lack of novelty. Which of the following things is most likely to be excluded from the state of the art for purposes of this assessment?
    a. 'Big Ben' (officially known as the Great Westminster Clock).
    b. A clock sold by Ikea in all European countries.
    c. A design drawing for a clock by a Swedish clockmaker, shown only to friends and family.
    d. A cuckoo clock popular in Germany.
3. Is it fair to call the contemporary law of designs an 'absurd maze'? If so, what makes it 'absurd'?

ACTIVITY DISCUSSION

Activity 11.1 The clasp is not excluded subject matter under the must match exclusion. One probably could replace the clasp with a clasp that looks different, and yet the overall appearance of the Trunki would not radically change.

Activity 11.2 Section 4(1) of the CDPA states that an artistic work includes 'graphic works ... irrespective of artistic quality'. Furthermore, section 4(2) states that graphic works include drawings and diagrams. In addition, the drawings are not obviously performing a useful function. There is at least a plausible case that they amount to a work. There is, however, also a reasonable likelihood that they would not pass the originality threshold.

Activity 11.3 There is potentially quite a lot wrong with the argument. But the most obvious problem is that it does not take into account the empirical objection. Not only is there little evidence to suggest that protection is needed to encourage such creativity, but the piracy paradox (Section 10.2) seems to provide evidence that it is not.

Activity 11.4 No, under section 52, they have not infringed the copyright in the drawings. Normally, by copying the bricks, Tyco would indirectly copy the protected design drawings. This would usually infringe the copyright therein. However, after 2015 (twenty-five years post 1990), the section 52 exception became applicable. Thus, after 2015, it would not be an infringement of copyright in the drawings to copy the brick.

SELF-ASSESSMENT ANSWERS

1. It seems likely that Stein would be able to obtain a registered design right covering the appearance of the lamp base. It is not likely to be excluded on functionality grounds because although a lamp base has a function (i.e. to hold a lamp bulb), the design of the base is not solely dictated by that function. It also seems likely that Stein would enjoy an automatic unregistered design right covering the shape of the lamp base.

   Stein would not, however, enjoy a supplementary unregistered design right on the grounds that the design has first been made available in the USA. It is also unlikely to be protected by copyright because a lamp is (much like the *Star Wars* helmet in *Lucasfilm*) a functional item.

   (This example comes from a famous American US Supreme Court decision – *Mazer v Stein* 347 US 201 (1954).)

2. **Correct answer: c.** It is debatable whether the design drawing has been 'made public'. In the case that a UK court considers this to be a public disclosure, it is likely to be excluded from the prior art under the obscure disclosures doctrine.

Notes

1 Anne-Emmanuelle Kahn, 'The Copyright/Design Interface in France' in Estelle Derclaye (ed), *The Copyright/Design Interface* (CUP 2018) 7.

2 Directive of 13 October 1998 on the legal protection of designs 98/71/EC.

3 Council Regulation of 12 December 2001 on Community designs (Community Design Regulation (CDR)) 6/2002/EC.

4 Registered Designs Rules 2006 (SI 2006/1975) r 4.

5 ibid r 5.

6 RDA 1949, s 3(A)(4).

7 ibid s 8.

8 *A Fulton v Totes Isotoner (UK)* [2003] EWCA Civ 1514, [2004] RPC (16) 301, [31].

9 *Groente en fruit*, R 595/2012–3 (18 February 2013); EUIPO, *Guidelines for Examination: Invalidity Applications* (1 October 2017) [5.1.1].

10 *Doceram v CeramTec*, Case C-395/16, EU:C:2018:172 [30].

11 For one of the few cases on the provision, see *Masterman's Design Application* [1991] RPC 89.

12 Regulation Reform (Registered Designs) Order 2006.

13 RDA 1949, s 1B(6).

14 ibid.

15 ibid s 1B(8).

16 [2016] UKSC 12 [57].

17 ibid.

18 RDA 1949, s 7A(2)(a)–(c), (3).

19 ibid.

20 ibid s 7A(4).

21 CDPA, s 216.

22 ibid s 212.

23 *Farmers Build v Carier Bulk Materials Handling* [1999] RPC 461, 481.

24 *Magmatic ('Trunki') v PMS International Group* [2013] EWHC 1925 (Pat) [97].

25 CDPA, s 226(2).

26 *Farmers Build* (n 23) 481.

27 CDPA, s 244A.

28 CDR, recital 16.

29 Designs and International Trade Marks (Amendment etc) (EU Exit) Regulations 2019 (SI 2019/638).

30 Retained CDR, art 11.

31 ibid art 19(2).

32 ibid art 20(1).

33 Lionel Bently, 'The Design/Copyright Conflict in the United Kingdom: A History' in Derclaye (n 1) 222.

34 *Levola Hengelo BV v Smilde Foods BV*, Case C-310/17, EU:C:2018:899; *Cofemel – Sociedade de Vestuário SA v G-Star Raw CV*, Case C-683/17, EU:C:2019:721.

35 *Infopaq Int v Danske Dagblades Forening*, Case C-5/08, [2009] ECR I–6569; *Eva-Maria Painer v Standard VerlagsGmbH*, Case C-145/10, EU:C:2011:798 [2011] ECDR (13) 297.

36 *Flos SpA v Semararo Case e Famiglia SpA*, Case C-168/09, [2011] ECR I–181.

37 Reproduced with permission of author.

38 Bently (n 33) 224–25.

FIGURE ACKNOWLEDGEMENTS

11.1 From *PMS International Group v Magmatic ('Trunki')* [2014] EWCA Civ 181, and *PMS International Group v Magmatic ('Trunki')* [2016] UKSC 12. Photograph authorship unknown

11.2 From *Magmatic ('Trunki') v PMS International Group* [2013] EWHC 1925 (Pat). Concept board produced by Robert Law included in 1998 BASF/Institute of Materials Design Awards

11.3 From *Magmatic ('Trunki') v PMS International Group* [2013] EWHC 1925 (Pat). Photograph authorship unknown

11.4 From *PMS International Group v Magmatic ('Trunki')* [2014] EWCA Civ 181, and *PMS International Group v Magmatic ('Trunki')* [2016] UKSC 12. Photograph authorship unknown

11.5 Institute of Advanced Legal Studies (Microfilm). Photos by UCL Photo dept. Made available by Centre for Intellectual Property and Information Law Virtual Museum <https://www.cipil.law.cam.ac.uk/virtual-museum/interlego-v-tyco-1989-ac-217>

11.6 From *Emmanuel L Mazer and William Endicter, Doing Business as June Lamp Manufacturing Company v Benjamin Stein and Rena Stein, Doing Business as Reglor of California*, Brief for Respondents, Supreme Court of the United States, October term AD 1953, No 228, Exhibit 8

Part IV

Trade Marks and Passing Off

A proper trademark is not a public good; it has social value only when used to designate a single brand.

—William M Landes and Richard A Posner, 'Trademark Law: An Economic Perspective' (1987) Journal of Law and Economics 265

12

Trade Marks I: Foundations of Trade Marks and Passing Off

Signs are ubiquitous in modern market economies. So ubiquitous that we hardly notice them much of the time. But take time to look and they pop out from the scenery. On the back of my MacBook appears a little Apple icon. My spectacles bear the word OAKLEY. My shoes proudly display the word NIKE and the famous Nike 'Swoosh'. If you look around you now, what signs do you see?

Part IV discusses the legal rights relating to signs used in commerce. In doing so, this Part marks a major turning point in the book. One might even say that Parts I–III are about intellectual property law, but Part IV is not. To see why, consider the simple definition of intellectual property provided in Chapter 1: intellectual property is property in intellectual things.

Are signs 'intellectual things'? They certainly are very different from the other intellectual things examined in this book. Unlike original works, inventions and designs, signs are not public goods. While signs are intangible phenomena, they are not public goods because they are not *goods* at all. Works, inventions and designs are all goods because they are, in some way, valuable. The *Starry Night* is valuable because it is beautiful to admire. The Trunki is valuable because it is fun for children to ride on. Christiansen's new brick coupling system was valuable because it made toy bricks work better. By contrast, there is nothing particularly valuable about a little Apple icon: it is not beautiful, fun, nor solves any technical problems. No one would pay to own a copy of the little Apple logo.

> Recall the definition of 'goods' from Section 1.1: phenomena that are valuable. Unless otherwise stated, this Part uses the term good to refer to both goods and services produced by a business.

What then of property? Is the legal protection of signs a type of property? Once again, the statutes and cases say they are.[1] But this is debatable. As discussed in this Part, the legal protection of signs is the least property-like of all IP rights.

This chapter contains public sector information licensed under the Open Government Licence v3.0.

If one thinks of property as exclusive control over something, then for much of human history, signs were not property. Although, in the face of twenty-first-century capitalism, this might be slowly changing. One of the curious themes explored in this Part is how businesses today increasingly argue they exclusively control the use of their signs.

Finally, why should signs be property? Once again, ownership of signs creates the problem of monopoly, albeit in a slightly different form. And, once again, critical IP thinkers must question why traders should have market power. But, because signs are not public goods, gone are arguments based on incentives, labour and personality. Instead, they are replaced with arguments about the importance of signs as informational tools that consumers use when making purchasing decisions. As with previous parts, this chapter starts with this normative question.

12.1 SIGN FUNCTIONS

The introduction claimed that no one would pay to own a copy of the Apple icon. That is, signs have no **inherent value**. The little Apple icon *itself* is remarkably uninteresting. Nevertheless, signs can still have **instrumental value**. While signs are not fun or beautiful, they can be *used* in valuable ways. In the modern economy, signs can be important tools used by businesses. Activity 12.1 illustrates.

ACTIVITY 12.1

Imagine that you walk into the supermarket one hot summer day looking for something to quench your thirst. You see a row of glass bottles all filled with a dark brown liquid. On the bottles, you see the following sign (Figure 12.1). What comes to mind when you see this sign?

Figure 12.1 A figurative sign used by the Coca-Cola Company

As the activity demonstrates, the Coca-Cola Company uses their sign to achieve certain ends. The Coca-Cola Company uses the sign to give you, the consumer, important information about where the bottle was produced and that its contents is safe to drink (among other things). These things that signs do are called their '**functions**'.

This section explores how sign functions have evolved historically. Starting from their earliest uses in trade, the section briefly outlines how signs have acquired new functionality as the economic system has evolved.

12.1.1 Signs as Badges of Origin

The story of sign functions begins in the Neolithic period, when signs were used as a mark of possession, or to indicate ownership.

BOX 12.1 THOMAS DRESCHER, 'THE TRANSFORMATION AND EVOLUTION OF TRADEMARKS: FROM SIGNALS TO SYMBOLS TO MYTH' (1992) 82 TM REP 301

Trademark history probably dates as far back as the advent of personal property, which puts us in the Neolithic period.[2] Many commentators date trademarks back to the use of brands on livestock as evidenced by biblical references, Egyptian wall paintings, or even cave-paintings of bison. It has also been frequently noted that the modern English 'brand', as in 'brand name', is derived from the Anglo-Saxon verb for 'to burn' and that, modern brand marks, therefore, have descended directly from the practice of branding. This is a seductively straightforward etymological assumption which might lead us to overlook the radical differences between modern 'brands' and Neolithic brands, but it provides a good starting point.

Marks were used from as early as 4000 B.C. and flourished in the days of the Roman Empire. Ancient marks were of various types. Many were personal marks or maker's marks. Stonecutter's marks allowed Egyptian workers to prove their claim for wages; the mark of personal seals served as a legal signature in Babylon, while seals bearing unique inscriptions were used as early as 2500 B.C. by the merchants of Harappan to label their goods. Thus, personal marks used by merchants to indicate ownership, and by makers to indicate origin appear to have been known in various forms during the period 4000–1000 B.C.

(pp. 309–10)

The term **'brand'** is a difficult word to define. At times, the word 'brand' is used synonymously with the word 'sign'. If not otherwise stated, the word 'brand' is used in this part in this way.

But the most important function of signs was yet to come. The fundamental sign function is the ability of the sign to inform consumers where the good to which it is attached was produced. This is known as the '**origin function**' of signs. Signs that perform this function are often known as '**badges of origin**'.

BOX 12.2 THOMAS DRESCHER, 'THE TRANSFORMATION AND EVOLUTION OF TRADEMARKS: FROM SIGNALS TO SYMBOLS TO MYTH' (1992) 82 TM REP 301

By the second century, the Roman Empire encompassed most of Europe and surrounded the Mediterranean. Trade between Rome and its far flung provinces was extensive. Silk from China, paper and jewels from the East ... all flowed to Rome. Manufactured goods, exports from Rome, were shipped to distant purchasers. These included oil lamps bearing the names of their makers, such as Fortis, and Faustis, and marked with devices, signs such as circles, half-moons, and the vine leaf. Bronze instruments, knives, and iron articles bore their maker's marks. Wine and cheese for export were marked to indicate geographic origin, and popular patent medicines carried the physician's name. The application of maker's marks and marks of geographic origin to goods traded over great distances represents trademark use in the modern sense; that is, these marks became symbols of good will identified with a single source. They indicated the source of origin of the goods to remote customers who might wish to place repeat orders.

(p. 310)

The word 'trademark' (rather than 'trade mark') is the American spelling.

ACTIVITY 12.2

There is a lot packed into this little extract. As you read, consider two questions:
1. What were the signs ('circles, half-moons' etc.) doing? There are at least two possibilities here.
2. What does the author mean by 'good will' (more commonly known as **goodwill**)?

12.1.2 Signs as Adverts

While still used today as badges of origin, signs have acquired new functions with the passage of time. During the Middle Ages, signs were adopted by trade associations, called guilds, to identify their members. Only members of the guild could attach the sign to their goods.

The Stationers' Company was one such guild, and their sign can be found in Section 2.1.

But something even more significant was to come: the advent of modern capitalism. In this new world of markets and private profit, businesses began to use signs to advertise their goods.

BOX 12.3 THOMAS DRESCHER, 'THE TRANSFORMATION AND EVOLUTION OF TRADEMARKS: FROM SIGNALS TO SYMBOLS TO MYTH' (1992) 82 TM REP 301

The next major step in the evolution of trademarks comes in the later nineteenth century. Any qualms about the godliness of the individual pursuit of wealth had long since been swept away along with the hierarchic order of feudalism. . . . As for regulation of trade and industry, laissez faire and market forces could surely perform that task more efficiently than the officers of the guild. An environment of global markets, free competition, and mechanized production might be expected to have had an effect on the function and nature of the trademark, and it did, the most notable of which was the advent of the 'brand'.

Up until roughly the post-Civil War period in the United States, grocers offered their goods for sale in the form of commodities. Oats, coffee, and crackers, for instance, were sold in bulk form. The shopper might bring a bag with him and the grocer would fill it with the desired amount of oats, flour, or beans. Pickles were sold from the pickle jar and crackers were indeed sold from a cracker barrel. What we find, then, is that many consumer products were interchangeable. Soap, for instance, was pretty much a generic combination of fat and lye just as it always had been.

Suppose, however, that certain oats are taken out of the grocer's bulk bin and packaged neatly into a canister upon which appear symbols of purity and praise for their health-giving properties. Somehow, the attributes of that symbol, and the promises of that praise attach themselves to these particular oats as distinct from those sold by the barrel. These oats now have a distinct identity conjured up by a sign which embodies all those healthy properties proclaimed by the packaging . . .

A further distinction between modern and historic marks is the brand mark's advertising function. Early Quaker Oats packaging and advertising copy exploited the Quaker symbol with its connotations of moral and physical strength in order to lend those attributes to the oats themselves: 'Women who exercise, men who walk are the Quaker Oats enthusiasts'. The advertising copy creates a context which informs and begins to obsess the mark. Thus, the trademark becomes an integral part of the advertising function because of its inherent power and range of meaning as a symbol, and because the advertisement itself creates a context which informs the mark.

It is remarkable how many early brand name advertisements go to great lengths to educate the consumer. Many full page magazine advertisements might take up as much as half the page with two or three columns of tightly packed print . . .

Laissez-faire was also discussed in Section 6.1.4 in relation to the patent controversy of the nineteenth century.

Thankfully businesses are no longer allowed to make such outlandishly false claims under modern false advertising laws.

> These educational advertisements explain the 'reason-why' consumers should purchase a particular brand. WRIGLEY'S chewing gum, we are told, is good for you for five reasons: it steadies nerves, allays thirst, aids appetite, helps digestion, keeps teeth clean ... COCA-COLA is 'the ideal brain tonic for headache and exhaustion' as knowledgeable pharmacists can testify. Such reasoned persuasion is of a different character than the primarily visual, sensual appeals of today, and its effectiveness was challenged early on by those who favored suggestion over logic as a motivating force.
>
> (pp. 321–22, 324–25)

ACTIVITY 12.3

What does Drescher mean when he says goods, like oats and soap, were 'interchangeable'? How is the interchangeability of goods affected by the 'advertising function' of signs?

12.1.3 Signs as Quality Indicators

The advertising function was not the only sign function to emerge from the Industrial Revolution and the beginning of modern market economies. Signs also developed an important function as indicators of quality. This is described below as the 'warranty function' of signs. It can also be called the **quality function**.

BOX 12.4 THOMAS DRESCHER, 'THE TRANSFORMATION AND EVOLUTION OF TRADEMARKS: FROM SIGNALS TO SYMBOLS TO MYTH' (1992) 82 TM REP 301

It was the warranty function which provided the economic incentive to the creation and promotion of brands. By setting and maintaining a consistent quality for his product the manufacturer or packager could also set a consistent and uniform price. The buyer could be certain that the oats, coffee, chocolate, or soap sold under the trademarked name would be of the same quality from one day, one package, or one store to the next. For this assurance the consumer was willing to pay and the producer was able to charge a premium price.

The soap industry provides an outstanding early example of the entire branding process from the creation of a distinct product to the promotional exploitation of trademarks as symbols. As late as the 1880s, soap was either made at home or purchased in bulk. Bars of soap were cut by the grocer from large slabs at the customer's request, and were sold by weight. Not only were soaps interchangeable, their quality was inconsistent from one batch to the next. The inconsistency was inherent in the process of making soap because the actual chemical conversion of fats into soap was erratic and little understood.

By the turn of the century, William Procter and James Gamble in the United States, and William Hesketh Lever in Great Britain had changed all this. With the help of a newly discovered chemical formula, both were able to create soap products of a consistent quality. IVORY was registered as a trademark in 1879; SUNLIGHT in 1884. The themes of purity and quality suggested by the trademarks were immediately exploited in full-fledged promotional campaigns, informative handbooks, packaging that projected the symbolic themes, and highly visible advertising. Lever promoted SUNLIGHT as a soap to meet the needs of the working woman. After the success of SUNLIGHT was established, Lever followed through in 1894 with another brand, LIFEBUOY, which was promoted as a disinfectant soap. Thus, a once generic product of inconsistent quality was branded with highly suggestive marks embodying themes which were exploited and reinforced by aggressive advertising campaigns targeted at a specific market.

(pp. 326–27)

> Procter & Gamble and Unilever (founded by Lever) are today among the world's largest corporations, each employing hundreds of thousands of people and earning billions of pounds in revenue.

An analogous or related function is the **investment function**. Because the sign is an indicator of quality, businesses have an incentive to invest money into their products. Not only do they invest money to ensure their goods are of a certain quality, but they are also encouraged to invest in innovative products and services.

> Terminology concerning sign functions is notoriously disputed. What some might call the investment functions, others might call the **communication function**, discussed below.

12.1.4 Signs as Identity

The origin function, quality function and advertising functions might be seen as the core signs functions. But there are more. One important development during the twentieth century was the development of signs as a way of building an identity. Drescher calls this the 'mythical' or 'symbolic' function of signs (Box 12.5).

BOX 12.5 THOMAS DRESCHER, 'THE TRANSFORMATION AND EVOLUTION OF TRADEMARKS: FROM SIGNALS TO SYMBOLS TO MYTH' (1992) 82 TM REP 301

Once the trademark becomes a symbol, it becomes capable of different levels of meaning. On one level, the mark symbolizes a bundle of themes, values, and associations which, taken together, we will call a 'myth'. Numerous such bundles or mythical cells combine, like a deck of cards, to form our culture as a whole.

PEPSI-COLA, for instance, denotes the objective features of a product; PEPSI-COLA is a soft drink with a particular appearance and taste. At the same time, we might say that PEPSI-COLA, itself a meaningless term, 'means' or connotes youth-culture. PEPSI-COLA has achieved this meaning on the symbolic level through a variety of advertising devices. PEPSI-COLA is endorsed by a culture-hero, such as Michael Jackson; it is something to which he imparts his identity. Through the use of such obsessing techniques, advertising creates the 'drawing power' of the trademark symbol. The symbol becomes 'congenial' precisely because advertising informs it with a set of values and beliefs congenial to the targeted consumers and does so by placing the mark within the context of whatever mythical unit has been chosen for it.

This process of transference and fusion explains why consumers will so often prefer one product over another despite the fact that the preferred product may be indistinguishable from a less expensive rival. In order to make identical products attractive to different consumer groups, advertisers distinguished the products on the basis not of substance but of mythic appeal; the bundle of values represented by the brand name was matched with the bundle of values belonging to segmented market groups.

It becomes possible then, for the consumer to step into 'the BMW experience'. Presumably, when the consumer wears a BMW jacket, carries a BMW briefcase, and drives his BMW car, he has entered a BMW branded experience and purchased a BMW engineered identity. Jaguar Cars Limited has also extended its mark to a wide range of products evocative of the lifestyle conjured up by its famous automobile, including, among others, fragrances and leather goods. The trademark no longer merely identifies the product, it also identifies the consumer; it brings him into the myth; it touches an entire range of experience which can be packaged as an identity. The consumer no longer buys a product; he buys, consumes and seeks to assume an identity.

(pp. 328–30, 333)

ACTIVITY 12.4

Drescher gives an example of PEPSI-COLA. We can illustrate his point by thinking about a recent PEPSI-COLA advert.

In the mid-2010s, American police forces were heavily criticised for the deaths of several unarmed Black men. This resulted in widespread protests against police brutality. The protests were met with hostility from some elements of American society, who pointed to the difficult and often dangerous role that police officers perform.

In 2017, the Pepsi Company released a TV advert called 'Live for Now' featuring fashion model Kendall Jenner. The advert starts by depicting a large group of youthful protesters with a row of American police officers looking on. Kendall Jenner then emerges from the protesting crowd, picks up a can of Pepsi, strides over to the police officers and hands the can to one of them. The police officer then takes the can of Pepsi from Jenner, drinks it and smiles. The protestors then erupt in joy.

What identity is Pepsi trying to create in this advert? And how does the PEPSI-COLA sign help that identity-building process?

This function is sometimes also known as the **communication function**. By this it is meant that the sign communicates some non-origin information about the goods, for example, the businesses' values.

12.2 MANUFACTURING TRADE MARKS

A **trade mark** is a legal right in a sign. The purpose of trade marks is to enable businesses to achieve the sign functions. Trade marks were initially granted to help businesses indicate the origin of their goods. But as signs have acquired new functions with time, trade marks have expanded. Parliament and the courts now give businesses much more control over their signs than ever before. Indeed, society now grants businesses property in their signs.[3] This section starts to explain how this came to be.

In reading this section, one must be very careful not to mix up the historical with the normative: or what *is* and what *ought to* be. The fact that businesses can use signs to achieve a range of functions does not mean that they should or that the law should assist in any way. That normative question is discussed in Section 12.3.

Some people will occasionally use the word 'trade mark' to refer, not to the legal rights, but to the sign itself. This should be avoided to prevent confusion.

12.2.1 The Action of Deceit

Although the earliest reported cases date to the sixteenth century,[4] modern trade mark law began in the nineteenth century. At this point, businesses brought actions in the Court of Chancery to prevent deceitful uses of their signs by competitors. One exemplary case involved the Day and Martin boot polish business.

This is a lesson to remember in all areas of law, and not simply trade mark law. The Scottish philosopher, David Hume (1712–76) is often credited with highlighting that we cannot logically infer anything about 'ought' from premises about what merely 'is'.

Case 12.1 *Croft v Day* (1843) 7 Beavan 84

Facts

'Blacking' is a nineteenth-century term for boot polish. The company Day and Martin, established in 1802 by Charles Day and Benjamin Martin, was a highly successful seller of blacking. The Day and Martin blacking was produced by a factory located at 97 High Holborn Street, London. When Charles Day died in 1836, the business continued to operate with John Weston as general manager.

After Charles Day's death in 1836, his nephew, Charles William Day started to sell blacking, also under the name of 'Day and Martin'. To do so, he gained the permission from someone named 'Martin'. This blacking was produced at a factory at 90 ½ Holborn Hill, London. The blacking was then sold in bottles that resembled that of the original Day and Martin blacking with some minor alterations, namely: the address read 90 ½ Holborn Hill, and the factory in the centre was substituted for the royal coat of arms.

Issue and Procedure

Croft (claimant), one of the executors of Charles Day's will, brought an action against Charles William Day (defendant) to prevent him from using the 'Day and Martin' sign. In the next extract, Master of the Rolls Lord Langdale granted an injunction to restrain Charles William Day from selling blacking under the same name and in similar bottles.

LORD LANGDALE MR

The accusation which is made against this Defendant is this: – that he is selling goods, under forms and symbols of such a nature and character, as will induce the public to believe, that he is selling the goods which are manufactured at the manufactory which belonged to the testator in this cause. It has been very correctly said, that the principle, in these cases, is this: – that no man has a right to sell his own goods as the goods of another. You may express the same principle in a different form, and say that no man has a right to dress himself in colours, or adopt and bear symbols, to which he has no peculiar or exclusive right, and thereby personate another person, for the purpose of inducing the public to suppose, either that he is that other person, or that he is connected with and selling the manufacture of such other person, while he is really selling his own. It is perfectly manifest, that to do these things is to commit a fraud, and a very gross fraud. I stated, upon a former occasion, that, in my opinion, the right which any person may have to the protection of this Court, does not depend upon any exclusive right which he may be supposed to have to

12.2 Manufacturing Trade Marks — 387

a particular name, or to a particular form of words. His right to be protected against fraud, and fraud may be practised against him by means of a name, though the person practising it may have a perfect right to use that name, provided he does not accompany the use of it with such other circumstances as to effect a fraud upon others.

My decision does not depend on any peculiar or exclusive right the Plaintiffs have to use the names Day & Martin, but upon the fact of the Defendant using those names in connection with certain circumstances, and in a manner calculated to mislead the public, and to enable the Defendant to obtain, at the expense of Day's estate, a benefit for himself, to which he is not, in fair and honest dealing, entitled. Such being my opinion, I must grant the injunction restraining the Defendant from carrying on that deception. He has a right to carry on the business of a blacking manufacturer honestly and fairly; he has a right to the use of his own name; I will not do anything to debar him from the use of that, or any other name calculated to benefit himself in an honest way; but I must prevent him from using it in such a way as to deceive and defraud the public, and obtain for himself, at the expense of the Plaintiffs, an undue and improper advantage.

(pp. 88–90)

> The remedy granted by the common law courts prior to the nineteenth century was typically monetary damages. What makes this case, and others in the Chancery important, is the grant of injunctive relief. As Langdale concludes, he must 'prevent' this type of fraud.

In today's language, Lord Langdale sought to 'protect' the sign's origin function. Croft wanted the sign 'DAY AND MARTIN' to perform an origin function: he wanted consumers to see the sign and know that the bottle came from the 97 High Holborn Street manufacturer. The defendant's use of the sign made it much harder for Croft to achieve this end. If there are other businesses selling blacking on which the DAY AND MARTIN sign appears, then consumers will be confused: they will not know whether the blacking comes from 97 High Holborn Street or not. Thus, the defendant's use of the sign made it more difficult for Croft to realise the sign's origin function. The court injunction was granted to restrain the defendant's use, and to assist Croft in achieving the origin function.

However, Langdale also makes clear that Croft had no exclusive right to the sign. What Croft owned was instead the *goodwill* in the business. As a result, there was no problem, necessarily, in the defendant's use of the sign. The problem was the way in which the sign was being used: as a deliberate attempt to 'steal' Croft's consumers. Theoretically, if the defendant had used the sign 'honestly and fairly', there would be no reason to grant an injunction.

ACTIVITY 12.5

What does this judgment say about trade marks as 'property'?

Cases like *Croft v Day* gradually came to be known as the tort of '**passing off**'. The idea is that one should not 'pass off' one's goods as those of another's. The tort of passing off is still in use today and is explored further in Chapter 15.

While the action against deceit was helpful to businesses, it was limited in important respects. First, to win a case, the claimant had to show there was some goodwill in the business. They had to prove that their customers already recognised their goods and their signs. Second, the line between legally permissible and impermissible use of the sign depended on the defendant's intentions: did the defendant intend to defraud the public in using the sign? Both of these problems were overcome with the invention of the trade mark right and the **trade mark register**.

12.2.2   The Trade Mark as Property

As legal historian, Lionel Bently, argues, judges such as Lord Langdale MR did not see themselves as protecting a business's property, but rather preventing deceitful and fraudulent communication. This began to change in the 1860s. Increasingly judges and Parliament came to understand the protection of the origin function as a type of property. One of the most significant steps towards a property right of trade marks was the Trade Mark Registration Act 1875.

BOX 12.6 LIONEL BENTLY, 'FROM COMMUNICATION TO THING: HISTORICAL ASPECTS OF THE CONCEPTUALISATION OF TRADE MARKS AS PROPERTY' IN GRAEME DINWOODIE AND MARK JANIS (EDS), *TRADEMARK LAW AND THEORY: A HANDBOOK OF CONTEMPORARY RESEARCH* (EDWARD ELGAR 2008)

Understood as being based in the law of deceit, the rationale for the protection of signs used in trade derived from their communicative significance: were the signs intended to, and likely to, deceive?[5] Would their continued use be likely to deceive the 'ordinary run of persons', so that a court of Equity should step in and prevent such frauds? However, in the 1860s, this communication-based model started to be challenged by a model of protection based upon ideas of property. That is, trade mark law started to be reconceptualised as protecting a trade mark as an asset, rather than fixing on particular qualities of communicative act. The transformation occurred in the context of calls for legislative protection of traders, in developing case law, and in the increasing number of commentaries. . . .

C. Judicial Activity

While the attempt to obtain legislative recognition for trade marks as property had (temporarily) failed, Richard Bethell, who from 1861 was Lord Chancellor Westbury (1861–65), elaborated a theory of trade marks

---

The idea that the sign was not a thing, but an act of communication echoes with the history of original works (Section 3.1) and the views today of Drassinower (Section 1.1.1). It should be noted, however, that Box 12.6 is only a small part of a more complex story.

as property in a series of cases beginning with Edelsten v Edelsten. In so doing, he expressly rejected the analysis of Lord Langdale MR and Page-Wood V-C, and provided an explanation for Millington v. Fox.

[In Edelsten v Edelsten] Lord Westbury LC took the opportunity provided to state the law of trade marks in proprietary terms: 'The questions are whether the Plaintiff had property in the trade mark . . . and, if so, whether the mark of the Defendants is substantially the same as the trade mark of the Plaintiff, and therefore an invasion of his property'. He continued by observing that while '[a]t law the proper remedy is by action on the case for deceit: and proof of fraud on the part of the Defendant is of the essence of the action' but that the Court of Equity 'will act on the principle of protecting property alone, and it is not necessary for the injunction to prove fraud in the Defendant'. Having stated these principles, Lord Westbury LC found that the defendant knew of the claimant's mark and had deliberately adopted an essential part of it for use in relation to the defendant's wire, and this was 'piracy' of the plaintiff's trade mark.

E. Legislative Activity: The 1875 Act

The property analysis seemed to have come to be accepted by the late 1860s, and was reinforced by the passage of the 1875 Act which established a registration system for trade marks, and made the existence of such registration equivalent to public use. It is important to note that, in contrast with later trade marks Acts, this one did not purport to establish a self-contained or exhaustive scheme. Rather, the 1875 Act built upon the existing common law system – the Act led to a presumption of public use, but the consequences of such public use for other traders remained governed wholly by the judicially-developed law of trade marks. . . .

While the 1875 Act did not declare trade marks to be property, it did introduce proprietary language: the registrant became the registered proprietor of the trade mark, the relationship being described in the language of 'title'. Consequently, it was widely understood as reinforcing the reconceptualisation (developed particularly by Lord Westbury) of trade marks as property. Moreover, the effect of the introduction of the bureaucratic structure was to cement the previously-recognised status of trade marks as property (as well as to alter certain of the dynamics of that property). Indeed, the use of the registration system gave a sense of closure and certainty to the subject matter of protection: being defined through the representations required by the Registry, trade marks appeared as visualized forms, capable of allocation as 'objects' to particular owners. Trade marks evolved from communications to things.

(pp. 15–16, 20–22, 28)

From this point on, the legal protection offered to businesses split in two directions. On one hand, if a business had not registered their sign, they could continue to bring actions of passing off against competitors who used the sign. To be successful in those actions, the businesses needed to prove goodwill. On the other hand, a business with a registered trade mark could also bring actions against competitors using the sign, but they did not need to prove goodwill to be successful. Over time, *both* actions would come to be seen as protecting a distinct type of property: the sign in the case of trade marks, and goodwill in the case of passing off.

12.2.3 Protecting Functions beyond Origin

Although trade marks had formally become property, they were clearly not property in the sense of exclusive control over a sign. At the end of the nineteenth century, a business with a trade mark could only prevent others from using their signs in a narrow range of circumstances. Namely, the trade mark only gave businesses the right to prevent uses of their sign that would impair the sign's ability to indicate origin. Activity 12.6 illustrates.

ACTIVITY 12.6

The Coca-Cola Company owns a trade mark on the word 'COKE' and sells cola. Currently, this sign achieves the origin function: consumers who see bottles of cola with the word COKE on them know something about where the bottle was produced – particularly, that it was produced by the Coca-Cola company.

But what will happen to the sign's ability to indicate origin, in the following scenarios?

1. Pepsi, who also sells cola, want to put the word 'COKE' on their cola.
2. The Newcastle Coal company sells coal. The company wants to put the words 'COKE-A-COAL-A' on their coal. 'Coke' is the name for a type of coal with a high carbon content, and COKE-A-COAL-A is a play on words.

In the late nineteenth and early twentieth centuries, trade mark owners could prevent scenario 1-type uses of their signs, but not scenario 2-type uses.

At the same time, a key 'test' emerged to distinguish between these different types of use: **consumer confusion**. How could courts determine whether a defendant's use was likely to impair a sign's origin function or not? The answer was to determine whether the use would confuse consumers as to the origin of their goods. Pepsi's planned use is likely to confuse some consumers: some people will buy cola from Pepsi, incorrectly thinking it is from the Coca-Cola Company. Therefore, Pepsi's use is the type that will impair a sign's origin function. But it is less likely that consumers will be confused in scenario 2: it seems doubtful that

12.2 Manufacturing Trade Marks   **391**

many consumers when buying coal would think to themselves: 'this must come from the Coca-Cola Company!'. After all, the Coca-Cola Company is very well known for selling soft drinks, not coal. The absence of such confusion is a good indicator that the sign's origin function is not impaired.

However, the law's focus on the origin function relaxed during the twentieth century. As summarised in Section 12.1, sign functions were in a state of evolution at this time. Increasingly, signs could be used as advertising tools or quality indicators. At the same time, businesses wanted trade marks to 'protect' these other functions. That is, they wanted legal rights to prevent uses of their signs which, while not impairing the sign's origin function, might impair the ability of the sign to achieve the other functions. While the Newcastle Coal Company's use does not impair the COKE sign's origin function, plausibly it will impair the sign's other functions, such as the ability to communicate a brand identity.

This idea was popularised in a famous article by Frank Schechter. His article began by attacking what he saw was the received wisdom of the day: that the core function of signs is to indicate origin.

Frank Isaac Schechter (1890–1937) was a New York trade mark lawyer and one of the first historians of the trade mark system.[6]

BOX 12.7 FRANK SCHECHTER, 'THE RATIONAL BASIS OF TRADE MARK PROTECTION' (1927) 40 HARV L REV 813

Four hundred years ago a trademark indicated either the origin or ownership of the goods to which it was affixed. To what extent does the trademark of today really function as either? Actually, not in the least. It has been repeatedly pointed out by the very courts that insist on defining trademarks in terms of ownership or origin that, owing to the ramifications of modern trade and the national and international distribution of goods from the manufacturer through the jobber or importer and the retailer to the consumer, the source or origin of the goods bearing a well known trademark is seldom known to the consumer. Over twenty years ago it was pointed out by the Circuit Court of Appeals for the Seventh Circuit that 'we may safely take it for granted that not one in a thousand knowing of or desiring to purchase "Baker's Cocoa" or "Baker's Chocolate" know of Walter Baker & Co., Limited'. The same fact has been noted concerning 'Coca-Cola' and 'Yorkshire Relish'.

A trademark may be affixed to goods by a manufacturer thousands of miles away from the consumer, or by an importer or jobber who has not manufactured but merely selected the goods and put them on the local market, or by a commission merchant who has not even selected the goods or rendered any service relating to them except to sell such as may have been sent to him by the owner.

(pp. 814–16)

Note that Schechter uses 'trademark' to refer to the *sign*, not the legal protection thereof.

The term 'jobber' means 'wholesaler', i.e. a business that buys products from a manufacturer in bulk and resells to smaller businesses or the public.

This is a rather startling claim. Up until this point, trade mark lawyers had assumed that the core function of a sign was to indicate the origin of the goods. Schechter, however, forces us to reconsider that idea. How much do we really know about where our goods come from? Think back to the bottle of Coca-Cola introduced in Activity 12.1. How much origin information is conveyed by the words COCA-COLA? How many consumers, for example, know where the product is manufactured? Or who puts the cola into the bottles? And what does the average consumer know of the Coca-Cola Company? How many know of the Coca-Cola Company, as a corporate entity, in the first place?

What do signs do if they do not indicate origin? The answer, in Schechter's view, is that the sign 'actually sells the goods'.

> ### BOX 12.8 FRANK SCHECHTER, 'THE RATIONAL BASIS OF TRADE MARK PROTECTION' (1927) 40 HARV L REV 813
>
> Discarding then the idea that a trademark or tradename informs the consumer as to the actual source or origin of goods, what does it indicate and with what result? It indicates, not that the article in question comes from a definite or particular source, the characteristics of which or the personalities connected with which are specifically known to the consumer, but merely that the goods in connection with which it is used emanate from the same – possibly anonymous – source or have reached the consumer through the same channels as certain other goods that have already given the consumer satisfaction, and that bore the same trademark.
>
> The true functions of the trademark are, then, to identify a product as satisfactory and thereby to stimulate further purchases by the consuming public ... [T]oday the trademark is not merely the symbol of good will but often the most effective agent for the creation of good will, imprinting upon the public mind an anonymous and impersonal guaranty of satisfaction, creating a desire for further satisfactions. The mark actually sells the goods. And, self-evidently, the more distinctive the mark, the more effective is its selling power.
>
> (pp. 816, 818)

The real function of signs is, therefore, twofold. First, signs perform a quality function. Even if most consumers have no idea where their cola is made, they probably have consumed cola with the words COCA-COLA on it. Even more importantly, they probably enjoyed that cola when they drank it. As a result, when those consumers go to the supermarket in the future, they probably will reach for the cola with COCA-COLA on it. They will see the sign and remember the satisfaction they previously had when drinking the cola. The sign, therefore, is not telling the consumer something about the *producer*, but something about the *product*: that it is probably quite tasty.

But, even more important, in Schechter's view, is the second function: the sign helps sell the goods. If the sign performs the quality function, then businesses will be able to sell their goods more easily. If consumers begin to 'identify a product as satisfactory' then the sign will 'stimulate further purchases'.

And there is one last piece of Schechter's argument. According to Schechter, if a sign is more *unique*, then the better it will be able to sell the goods. Trade mark rights, therefore, should prevent uses of the sign – like that of the Newcastle Coal Company – that make the sign less unique.

BOX 12.9 FRANK SCHECHTER, 'THE RATIONAL BASIS OF TRADE MARK PROTECTION' (1927) 40 HARV L REV 813

We have seen that the proper expansion of trademark law has been hampered by obsolete conceptions both as to the function of a trademark and as to the need for its protection. Commencing with the assumption that a trademark designates either origin or ownership – in other words, source – the law, even in its most liberal interpretation at the present time, will prevent the misuse of that mark only where there is an actual confusion created by such misuse, resulting in either diversion of trade or other concrete financial liability or injury to trade repute. However, we have intimated the possibility that the use of trademarks on entirely non-related goods may of itself concretely injure the owner of the mark even in the absence of those elements of damage noted above. If so, what is the injury, and to what extent, if any, should the law take cognizance of such injury?

The history of important trademark litigation within recent years shows that the use of similar marks on non-competing goods is perhaps the normal rather than the exceptional case of infringement. In the famous English Kodak case, cameras and bicycles were the articles in question; in the Aunt Jemima's case, pancake flour and syrup; in the Vogue case, fashion magazines and hats; in the Rolls-Royce case, automobiles and radio parts; in the Beech-Nut case, food products and cigarettes. In each instance the defendant was not actually diverting custom from the plaintiff, and where the courts conceded the absence of diversion of custom they were obliged to resort to an exceedingly laborious spelling out of other injury to the plaintiff in order to support their decrees. The real injury in all such cases can only be gauged in the light of what has been said concerning the function of a trademark. It is the gradual whittling away or

In property law, an 'appurtenance' is some right that flows from ownership, such as a right of way. In this context, 'appurtenant to' means that a sign is only valuable to the extent it indicates goodwill in the business.

> dispersion of the identity and hold upon the public mind of the mark or name by its use upon non-competing goods. The more distinctive or unique the mark, the deeper is its impress upon the public consciousness, and the greater its need for protection against vitiation or dissociation from the particular product in connection with which it has been used. At the present time the courts, misconstruing, as we have pointed out above, the rule that a trademark can only be used as appurtenant to a going business, are unwilling to base their protection of trademarks squarely upon this principle that 'the value of the plaintiff's symbol depended in large part upon its uniqueness'.
>
> (pp. 824–26)

Schechter's argument was highly influential. From a logical standpoint, it is also highly objectionable. As Activity 12.7 demonstrates.

ACTIVITY 12.7

Schechter's argument runs as follows:

Premise 1: Trade marks should help businesses to sell their goods.
Premise 2: A more unique sign makes it easier for a business to sell their goods
Conclusion: Therefore, trade marks should help businesses preserve the uniqueness of the sign.

What do you make of this argument? Do all the premises strike you as true? Start particularly with premise 1.

Despite the problems with premise 1, the trade mark right expanded under the influence of Schechter's argument. Increasingly, trade mark lawyers accepted that signs could achieve functions beyond indicating origin, and that trade mark rights should help businesses achieve those functions. Legislators and courts began granting businesses the ability to prevent uses of their signs, like that of the Newcastle Coal Company, that did not confuse consumers as to origin. These uses were said to make the sign less unique; an idea known as **dilution**. This idea is explored further in Chapter 14.

Putting aside problems with premise 1, one might also question premise 2. Do more unique marks help sell goods, as Schechter claimed? Since Schechter's article, social scientists have conducted empirical research to assess whether this is true. In Box 12.10, Rebecca Tushnet summarises and critiques some empirical research that supports that claim.

BOX 12.10 REBECCA TUSHNET, 'GONE IN 60 MILLISECONDS: TRADEMARK LAW AND COGNITIVE SCIENCE' (2008) 86 TEX L REV 507

Rebecca Tushnet is the Frank Stanton Professor of the First Amendment at Harvard Law School.

In 2000, Maureen Morrin and Jacob Jacoby conducted an experiment... The study had participants view diluting ads for Dogiva dog biscuits, Heineken popcorn, and Hyatt legal services.[7] The ads were 'tombstone' ads – print only and highly informational. The Heineken and Hyatt ads contained prominent disclaimers of affiliation with Heineken beer and Hyatt hotels, respectively. Computers measured how long it took for participants to identify the senior marks after exposure to the junior marks. Morrin and Jacoby found that exposure to dilutive ads slowed participants' accuracy and response time in associating some brands with product categories and attributes, such as linking Godiva to chocolate and rich taste. Heineken beer was similarly affected by ads for Heineken popcorn, though Hyatt hotels were not affected by ads for Hyatt legal services.

Senior mark refers to the business that first used the sign. A **junior mark** refers to a later business also using the sign.

Exposure to dilutive ads led to an average response time of 770 milliseconds before respondents recognized the senior brand as fitting in its category, versus 675 milliseconds after exposure to an ad for the senior brand (reinforcement) and 748 milliseconds after exposure to unrelated ads (control).

Dilution proponents maintain that delayed responses . . . are likely to affect purchasing decisions, given that advertisers often only have a few seconds – or even milliseconds – to catch consumers' attention. If a dilutive use defamiliarizes consumers with a mark, their positive emotional associations based on familiarity may be lost, giving them less reason to choose the underlying product. In the lab, dilution-generated delayed response times have been correlated with later decreases in the likelihood that subjects will choose a diluted brand from among competing alternatives.

The initial question is whether we can reliably extrapolate from lab to store . . .

Consider: Have you ever put your suitcases into a cab in a major U.S. city, asked for 'American' or 'United,' and received the response 'Which one?' No rational cab driver would take a person who said 'American' to the local American Apparel or a person who said 'United' to the local United Van Lines. This is so even though American and United are conceptually weak, diluted marks.

Anecdotal evidence from the market further indicates that marks can be strong without being unique. Steve Hartman examined twenty-one trademarks that were the leading brands in their product

> categories in 1925, nineteen of which were also leading in 1985 (the other two were in second place). All but four had nontrademark meanings, including Swift, Life Savers, Ivory, and a variety of personal names. In the abstract, these marks 'are bound to be associated with or call to mind things other than the products they identify'. Context has been enough to keep them strong as marks.
>
> Why, then, did laboratory studies reveal an apparent dilutive effect from a single exposure to Dogiva biscuits and Heineken popcorn? One possibility is that the test environment was itself decontextualizing, depriving subjects of the cues they would ordinarily use to distinguish a dilutive use from a senior mark.
>
> (pp. 521–22, 527, 529, 531)

12.2.4 The Functionalist Metaphysics of Trade Marks

The last historical theme to highlight relates to the metaphysics of signs. So far, we have assumed that signs are things like words and logos. But, increasingly, courts accept a range of other things – like colours, smells and shapes – as signs. Activity 12.8 helps to introduce this concept.

> **ACTIVITY 12.8**
>
> Imagine you see this bottle with cola inside (Figure 12.2). Do you know the origin of this bottle of cola?

Figure 12.2 A 3D sign used by the Coca-Cola Company

This can be understood as the 'functionalist metaphysics of signs'. The idea is that some things in life are understood by reference to their functions. To illustrate, a bicycle break is something that slows down a moving bicycle. Of course, there are lots of different types of bicycle brakes (rim brakes, disc brakes, etc.), and they all look quite different. But they are all connected by the common function of slowing down a moving bicycle. And, similarly, a sign might be anything that performs the sign functions, particularly the origin function.

The result is that the modern trade mark law is radically different from that at the end of the nineteenth century. Today, businesses can own a staggeringly long list of 'signs'. At the same time, the scope of the trade mark has expanded drastically. No longer does a trade mark only empower a business to prevent uses of their sign that might impair the sign's origin function. Instead, businesses are empowered to prevent uses of their sign that might dilute the sign's uniqueness.

Perhaps, then, trade marks have become property in the sense of the exclusive control of a thing.

12.3 ARGUMENTS FOR TRADE MARKS

Section 12.2 explained how trade marks became property. But a question remains: why should signs be property? The last section was historical, and explained how trade mark law evolved to protect a variety of sign functions. But whether trade mark law should protect these functions – whether it should assist businesses who want to use their signs to achieve these ends – is a normative matter.

In many ways, rights in signs are less controversial than rights in creative works, inventions or designs. There is a strong utilitarian argument for giving businesses some control over how their signs are used. Businesses should be able to prevent uses that would impair the origin function. What is controversial, however, is the question of how much protection businesses should be granted. Should businesses be able to prevent uses that do not impair a sign's origin function? The case in favour of this type of trade mark protection is far more contested.

12.3.1 Utilitarian Argument

As with other IP subjects, our analysis begins with the problem of monopolies. But that problem takes a slightly different form in trade mark law.

12.3.1.1 MONOPOLIES AND MONOPOLISTIC COMPETITION

Copyrights and patents both create monopolies in the sense that they give someone (typically the creator) market exclusivity over a good. This in turn insulates the producer of the good from competition, and results in market power, that is, the ability to charge a higher price for the goods. The result is higher prices for goods, and fewer goods enjoyed by consumers. Do trade marks also create monopolies? The answer is 'yes and no' as Box 12.11 indicates.

BOX 12.11 NICHOLAS ECONOMIDES, 'THE ECONOMICS OF TRADEMARKS' (1988) 78 TM REP 523

Trademarks have been criticized as creators of monopolies which are legally protected indefinitely, and thus limit competition.[8] This thesis was proposed by Chamberlin [Theory of Monopolistic Competition (1933)] who finds no useful purpose for trademarks. On the face of it, it is true that a trademarked product x is a monopoly, since no other firm is allowed to sell an identical product, where identity includes the trademark. But, a competitor can produce a product y, identical in all

Elasticity of demand refers to the change in quantity of a good consumers will buy when the price changes. 'Perfectly elastic demand' means that any change in price for good x will result in consumers buying less of x and more of good y.

observable and unobservable respects with x except for the symbol, name or design used as its trademark. Whether the consumer derives utility from the symbol, name or design of the trademark by itself, i.e., divorced from its significance in identifying the product, is debatable. But if there is no direct pleasure afforded by the symbol, products x and y will be of equal value to a consumer, and therefore the producer of good x, although a monopolist, will have no market (monopoly) power. Otherwise put, product x will have a perfect substitute, y, and therefore its producer will have no ability to increase its price over the price of y without losing all his customers. Product x (and y) will be facing a perfectly elastic demand, and will have to be sold at marginal cost and zero profits. Obviously, this very competitive situation is not desirable for either firm, and both firms will take steps to avoid it by differentiating their products in the variety and quality dimensions.

A trademarked product can be varied in many different ways, one of which is through advertising. Advertising can change the perceived image of the product; it can add attributes to the product as seen by the consumer. This kind of advertising has sometimes been called persuasive advertising to distinguish it from informative advertising which disseminates information about prices, location of stores, dates of sales, and the like. More appropriately, it should be called perception advertising. In perception advertising a desired mental image is added to the physical commodity. The consumer buys the advertised mental image together with the physical commodity, and in his mind the commodity bought contains both. The perceived features are consumed like all other features of the commodity. The fact that some attributes are only perceived, and are not represented by hard physical evidence, does not diminish their significance in the mind of the consumer. Now, advertising of a brand is useless without a trademark – anyone can imitate the product and profit from the advertising of the first maker. Thus, the existence of a trademark makes advertising of perceived images possible. Instead of limiting competition, trademarks allow firms to compete in one more dimension.

(pp. 532–33)

In the first paragraph, Economides explains that trade mark law does not create monopolies in the strict sense. If the Coca-Cola Company owns a trade mark on the sign COCA-COLA, that does not prevent other sellers from selling cola; it simply prevents other sellers from using the COCA-COLA sign on their cola. If Coca-Cola try to raise the price of their cola, strictly rational consumers will simply switch to one of the cheaper alternatives in the market, e.g. the cola produced by Pepsi or Dr Pepper. Thus, in a sense, the trade mark owner is not in the same position as the author of a novel or the inventor of a new drug. In those latter cases, consumers cannot simply switch their purchasing habits. If a consumer wants to see the new Marvel film, they will not be happy watching the new DC movie. The result is that copyright and patent, on their face, seem to give owners a market power that a trade mark owner does not enjoy.

However, Economides also says at the end of the first paragraph that this situation is 'not desirable' for firms. So instead, they will try to 'differentiate' their products (a process known as **product differentiation**) through 'persuasive advertising'.[9]

To understand product differentiation, consider Coca-Cola once more. If Coca-Cola decides to increase the price of their cola an extra £1 a bottle, would everyone switch to drinking Pepsi? Clearly the answer is no. Some consumers will always prefer to buy Coca-Cola rather than Pepsi, even if it is more expensive. In part, the reason for this outcome is advertising. Through persuasive advertising, Coca-Cola tries to make consumers perceive their product as different from, and better than, its competitors. If the adverts are successful, some consumers will always be willing to pay a higher price for the good. Thus, the trader does have some market power – the ability to raise prices above a perfectly competitive level.

The result is that trade marks do not create monopolies, but they do facilitate something similar: **monopolistic competition**. While Coca-Cola does not have a monopoly over cola, they still have some market power to keep prices above a competitive level. The market is therefore neither monopolistic, nor perfectly competitive, but somewhere in between. Sadly, some consumers will not be able to afford the higher prices and the problem of monopoly lives on, albeit in a weaker form. It is the use of signs in advertising that helps differentiate the products leading to monopolistic competition.

If you have time, go to a supermarket website and compare the price of supermarket own-brand toothpaste with the price of name-brand toothpaste. You will see the prices of name-brand products are much higher.

Furthermore, in some cases, the ability of trade marks to create monopolistic competition can possibly stray into the territory of creating real monopolies. As indicated in Section 12.2.4, trade marks are increasingly applied to things like shapes, sounds or smells. To take an extreme example for illustrative purposes, imagine that the Coca-Cola company is granted a trade mark over the particular brown colour of their cola. In turn, they could use this trade mark to prevent other cola companies from selling cola with a similar brown colour. Clearly, this would result in Coca-Cola enjoying a monopoly in the cola market, because it is nearly impossible to sell non-brown cola. While trade mark law has rules to prevent such monopolisation, it is important to note that whether trade marks create monopolies or not depends on what things we consider as appropriate trade mark subject matter.

12.3.1.2 THE PRO-COMPETITIVE EFFECTS OF TRADE MARKS

Trade marks, like copyrights and patents, have some anti-competitive effects which, in utilitarian terms, is a problem because it reduces consumers' happiness. What argument could justify such an outcome?

The central arguments offered for copyright and patents no longer apply. Recall that those arguments focused on the dynamic benefits of protection: copyright and patents may result in more creative works and inventions in the future. But signs are not public goods because they are not inherently valuable. The idea that we ought to incentivise future creation of new signs is very hollow because such signs are not themselves valuable. Remember, no one would ever pay just to own a copy of a little Apple logo.

Nevertheless there is an even stronger reason for trade mark protection than copyright and patent protection. Unlike copyrights and patents, there are also *pro-competitive* features of trade marks too. Whereas copyrights and patents only have anti-competitive effects today, trade marks have some immediately good characteristics. As Economides hints at in Box 12.11, trade marks limit competition in one sense, but they also promote competition between traders in another sense. To see why, consider the argument from William Landes and Richard Posner (Box 12.12). To understand their opening example, know that 'Sanka' was a type of decaffeinated coffee sold by the General Foods company in America in the 1980s.

BOX 12.12 WILLIAM M LANDES AND RICHARD A POSNER, 'TRADE MARK LAW: AN ECONOMIC PERSPECTIVE' (1987) JOURNAL OF LAW AND ECONOMICS 265

Suppose you like decaffeinated coffee made by General Foods.[10] If General Foods's brand had no name, then to order it in a restaurant or grocery store you would have to ask for 'the decaffeinated coffee made by General Foods'. This takes longer to say, requires you to remember more, and requires the waiter or clerk to read and remember more than if you can just ask for 'Sanka'. The problem would be even more serious if General Foods made more than one brand of decaffeinated coffee, as in fact it does. . . .

To perform its economizing function a trademark or brand name (these are rough synonyms) must not be duplicated. To allow another maker of decaffeinated coffee to sell its coffee under the name 'Sanka' would destroy the benefit of the name in identifying a brand of decaffeinated coffee made by General Foods (whether there might be offsetting benefits is considered later). . . .

The Market for Trademarked Goods. The benefits of trademarks in reducing consumer **search costs** require that the producer of a trademarked good maintain a consistent quality over time and across consumers. Hence trademark protection encourages expenditures on quality. To see this, suppose a consumer has a favorable experience with brand X and wants to buy it again. Or suppose he wants to buy brand X because it has been recommended by a reliable source or because he has had a favorable experience with brand Y, another brand produced by the same producer. Rather than investigating the attributes of all goods to determine which one is brand X or is equivalent to X, the consumer may find it less costly to search by identifying the relevant trademark and purchasing the corresponding brand. For this strategy to be efficient, however, not only must it be cheaper to search for the right trademark than for the desired attributes of the good, but also past experience must be a good predictor of the likely outcome of current consumption choices – that is, the brand must exhibit consistent quality. In short, a trademark conveys information that allows the consumer to say to himself, 'I need not investigate the attributes of the brand I am about to purchase because the trademark is a shorthand way of telling me that the attributes are the same as that of the brand I enjoyed earlier'.

We may seem to be ignoring the possibility that, by fostering product differentiation, trademarks may create deadweight costs, whether of monopoly or (excessive) competition. We have assumed that a trademark induces its owner to invest in maintaining uniform product quality, but another interpretation is that it induces the owner to spend money on creating, through advertising and promotion, a spurious image of high quality that enables monopoly rents to be obtained by deflecting consumers from lower-price substitutes of equal or even higher quality. In the case of products that are produced according to an identical formula, such as aspirin or household liquid bleach, the ability of name-brand goods (Bayer aspirin, Clorox bleach) to command higher prices than generic (nonbranded) goods has seemed to some economists and more lawyers an example of the power of brand advertising to bamboozle the public and thereby promote monopoly; and brand advertising presupposes trademarks – they are what enable a producer readily to identify his brand to the consumer. Besides the possibility of creating monopoly rents, trademarks may transform rents into costs, as one firm's expenditure on promoting its mark cancels out that of another firm. Although no monopoly profits are created, consumers may pay higher prices, and resources may be wasted in a sterile competition.

The short answer to these arguments is that they have gained no foothold hold at all in trademark law, as distinct from antitrust law. The implicit economic model of trademarks that is used in that law is our model, in which trademarks lower search costs and foster quality control rather than create social waste and consumer deception. A longer answer, which we shall merely sketch, is that the hostile view of brand advertising has been largely and we think correctly rejected by economists. The fact that two goods have the same chemical formula does not make them of equal quality to even the

> most coolly rational consumer. That consumer will be interested not in the formula but in the manufactured product and may therefore be willing to pay a premium for greater assurance that the good will actually be manufactured to the specifications of the formula. Trademarks enable the consumer to economize on a real cost because he spends less time searching to get the quality he wants. If this analysis is correct, the rejection by trademark law of a monopoly theory of trademarks is actually a mark in favor of the economic rationality of that law.
>
> (pp. 268–69, 274–75)

While trade marks harm consumers in one way, consumers also benefit from the existence of trade mark rights. Such rights not only lower the 'search costs' consumers face, but also increase competition between producers. Now when a consumer goes to the supermarket, they can directly compare Pepsi and Coca-Cola. As a result, trade marks bring Pepsi and Coca-Cola into more direct competition with one another. Greater competition then translates into lower prices.

The heart of Landes and Posner's argument, as with all other utilitarian arguments, is that the good consequences of trade mark rights outweigh the bad ones. This argument is on stronger footing than in other areas of IP, however, because trade marks clearly do have some good utilitarian consequences. Whereas the good consequences of copyright and patents are somewhat speculative, and maybe even beyond empirical proof altogether, the benefits of trade marks are revealed every time one enters the supermarket.

The real problem is not whether trade marks should exist, but how broad they ought to be. In particular, should the trade mark owner be able to restrain non-confusing uses of the sign. Landes and Posner's argument that trade marks reduce search costs does not obviously apply in these cases, as illustrated in Activity 12.6 with the Newcastle Coal Company. In that example, very few consumers would have been confused as to the origin of the goods in the first place. In which case, allowing Coca-Cola to prevent the Newcastle Coal Company from using the sign seems unnecessary. The rationale that Landes and Posner provide, therefore, gives reasons to support the trade mark owner's ability to prevent confusing uses of the sign, but it does not provide a good reason to prevent non-confusing uses of the signs.

12.3.2   Free Riding

Why should trade mark owners be able to prevent non-confusing uses of their signs? Schechter in Section 12.2 argued that preserving the uniqueness is necessary to preserve the selling power of the sign. That argument faces significant problems, as already discussed. But there is another, simpler, argument often used by courts today to justify protection against dilution. Courts often describe dilution protection as protection against '**free riding**'. The idea being that there is something ethically wrong about such behaviour.

The 'free rider problem' is one that is discussed in both philosophy and economics. Imagine, for example, that you are on a bus one day. You paid £2 for the bus ticket. You then see someone else hop onto the bus without paying. You might feel that the individual has done something wrong. You and your fellow passengers have paid the price of entry. Your ticket price in turn helps to pay the bus driver and keep the bus running, ensuring future transport services. Yet this person has not contributed to the collective good, and instead is enjoying simply a 'free ride' at your expense.

The problem, some might argue, with the Newcastle Coal Company in Activity 12.5 is that the Company is free riding on Coca-Cola's reputation. Coca-Cola have put effort into creating a famous sign: the COKE sign. By using the COKE sign, the Newcastle Coal Company enjoys the benefit of Coca-Cola's effort, while shouldering none of the burden for creating that sign in the first place.

The problem, however, is that it is not clear to everyone whether free riding is ethically wrong. Robert Nozick illustrates this point in Box 12.13.

BOX 12.13 ROBERT NOZICK, *ANARCHY, STATE AND UTOPIA* (BASIC BOOKS [1974] 2013)

Suppose some of the people in your neighbourhood (there are 364 other adults) have found a public address system and decide to institute a system of public entertainment.[11] They post a list of names, one for each day, yours among them. On his assigned day (one can easily switch days) a person is to run the public address system, play records over it, give news bulletins, tell amusing stories he has heard, and so on. After 138 days on which each person has done his part, your day arrives. Are you obligated to take your turn? You have benefited from it, occasionally opening your window to listen, enjoying some music or chuckling at someone's funny story. The other people have put themselves out. But must you answer the call when it is your turn to do so? As it stands, surely not. Though you benefit from the arrangement, you may know all along that 364 days of entertainment supplied by others will not be worth your giving up one day. You would rather not have any of it and not give up a day than have it all and spend one of your days at it. Given these preferences, how can it be that you are required to participate when your scheduled time comes? It would be nice to have philosophy readings on the radio to which one could tune in at any time, perhaps late at night when tired. But it may not be nice enough

> for you to want to give up one whole day of your own as a reader on the program. Whatever you want, can others create an obligation for you to do so by going ahead and starting the program themselves? In this case you can choose to forgo the benefit by not turning on the radio; in other cases the benefits might be unavoidable. If each day a different person on your street sweeps the entire street, must you do so when your time comes? Even if you don't care that much about a clean street? Must you imagine dirt as you traverse the street, so as not to benefit as a free rider? Must you refrain from turning on the radio to hear the philosophy readings? Must you mow your front lawn as often as your neighbours mow theirs?
>
> (pp. 82–83)

Some might say that taking your turn running the public address system is supererogatory. That is: a good thing to do, but not ethically required.

The point Nozick is making is that there is some philosophical question over whether the mere receipt of benefits from someone else, generates ethical obligations. Of course, it might be jolly nice of you to take your turn running the public address system. But it is not clear whether refusing to do so is wrong.

In some ways, protecting a trade mark owner against dilution is even more controversial than the above examples. In the case of someone who jumps on the bus without paying, the problem is that person is free riding on a public good. A good transport network is a valuable thing for a society to have. If that transport network can only operate when everyone pays their fair share, then free riding may result in no future transport services. But, once again, signs are not public goods. It would certainly be unfortunate if endemic free riding today resulted in no bus services in the future. But that argument is hollow when it comes to signs which, as established, are not inherently valuable. If there were no future little apple icons on laptops, that would not itself seem to be a great loss for society. Even if one thinks free riding is bad in some cases, it is not clear why it is bad in the case of diluting a sign.

On the other hand, there are some reasons to view trade mark dilution as more akin to the bus riding example than Nozick's public address system example. In the case of the bus rider, the person has actively sought out the benefits – they jumped on the bus on purpose. The person in Nozick's public address system example, on the other hand, has not sought out the benefit: it has just been thrust upon them. One might argue that the Newcastle Coal Company has, like the bus rider, sought out the benefit, and this active pursuit of the benefit translates into some ethical obligations.

But if the latter point seems persuasive, remember to keep a sense of perspective. Recall the problem of monopolistic competition. The more powerful trade marks are, the more unique the sign becomes. According to some, like Schechter, that makes consumers more likely to buy the products to which they are attached.

The result is market power and the ability to raise prices. Against this backdrop, the question is not simply: is it wrong to free ride on a sign? The question is instead: is free riding so wrong that it justifies giving traders protection which can necessarily be used to increase prices? That is a harder question of judgement.

Lastly, before concluding this section, it is helpful to consider why we have skipped the other arguments introduced first in Chapter 2. One might, for example, be tempted to argue that a business labours to create a new and attractive sign and thus should enjoy property therein, and that should allow them exclusive control over the sign, regardless of whether it appears on similar or dissimilar products. The problem, however, is that it is very difficult to use Locke's state of nature analysis to argue for the existence of trade marks. Recall that Locke argued that individuals living in a pre-political state of nature already have rights to life, liberty and property. It is extremely hard, however, to argue that in the state of nature one has exclusive rights over signs used in trade because the very idea of trade is preconditioned upon the existence of society. As seen in Sections 12.1 and 2, signs are only helpful within modern market economies. In a true state of nature, where there is no society and no markets, signs used in trade would simply not exist.

Similarly, one might want to turn back to Activity 6.1. to see why there is little personality interest in signs. Once again, as illustrated in this chapter, signs are created for their functions, not as an expression of internal personality.

12.4 REGISTRATION

The Trade Mark Registration Act 1875 created the trade mark registration system. This system is now regulated by the controlling legislation, the **Trade Mark Act 1994**. Under this Act, the UK IPO can register trade marks that take effect in the United Kingdom. Figure 12.3 sets out the main features of the registration process.

ACTIVITY 12.9

A practical knowledge of the trade mark registry is helpful for new IP students. Using a search engine, navigate to the UK IPO website. Once there, use the 'Search for a Trade Mark' section of the website to search for registered trade marks in the UK. Can you find, for example, who owns the trade mark on the sign 'COKE'?

While on the UK IPO website, you may also wish to examine the 'Register a Trade Mark' section to acquire a first-person view of the application process. There is no discussion for this activity.

Figure 12.3 UK trade mark registration

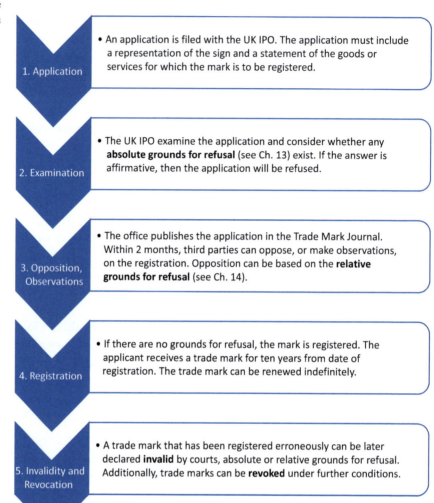

Chapters 13 and 14 introduce the absolute and relative grounds for refusal, alluded to briefly in Figure 12.3. If such grounds for refusal exist, the application ought to be refused. If the trade mark is erroneously granted, it could be later declared invalid. Additionally, the registration could be revoked in four situations: (1) where the sign has not been put to genuine use within five years of the registration without proper reason;[12] (2) where the sign has been suspended for an uninterrupted period of five years;[13] (3) where the sign has become generic;[14] and (4) the sign has been used in a deceptive way.[15] We will explain the key concepts – 'use', 'generic', 'deceptive', etc. – in Chapters 13 and 14.

12.5 THE INTERNATIONALISATION OF TRADE MARKS

Much like copyrights and patents, the international trade mark system was a response to the challenges of territoriality.

The first step towards internationalisation was the Paris Convention of 1883. The Convention not only requires national treatment in respect of patents, but also trade marks.[16] As a result, members of the Convention must grant to foreign nationals the same trade mark rights as are granted to home nationals. The Paris Convention also grants trade mark owners six months of priority.[17]

The principle of national treatment ensured that traders could receive trade marks in all Paris Convention member states. But receiving adequate international protection still required traders to file multiple different applications in multiple different jurisdictions. The challenges this posed to traders was simplified by two developments. The first was the Madrid Agreement on the International Registration of Marks (1891) and the Madrid Protocol (1989). The second was the establishment of the **European Union Trade Mark** (EUTM) system.

The Madrid Agreement on the International Registration of Marks (1891) and the Madrid Protocol (1989) simplify the process of obtaining trade mark protection in multiple jurisdictions. After filing a registration in the trader's home jurisdiction, they may apply international registration. To do so, the trader files the application in their 'office of origin' – typically the national IPO.[18] The office of origin certifies the application and sends it to WIPO. WIPO will check it meets the formal requirements; if it does not, it will be denied. If it meets the formal requirements, the sign is published in the *WIPO Gazette of International Marks* and the applicant receives a certificate of registration. After which, the application is sent back to the office of origin, and any other states in which the applicant seeks protection. The receiving offices then conduct a substantive examination and decide whether to grant or deny protection in their territory. If the office does not refuse the application within eighteen months, the sign will be treated as having been registered.[19]

The EUTM system was established by the Trade Mark Directive 1998 and Trade Mark Regulation 1994.[20] Under this system, as amended in the Trade Mark Directive 2015 and Trade Mark Regulation 2017,[21] a trader can apply to the European Union Intellectual Property Office (Alicante, Spain) for an EUTM. The application process is similar to that described in Figure 12.3. If successful, the trader will receive a trade mark that takes effect across the entire European Union. Prior to Brexit, an EUTM would take effect within UK. This is no longer the case. However, British traders are still able to apply for an EUTM (indeed, any trader in the world is, regardless of country of origin).

A quick note on terminology: previously the EU Trade Mark was known as the Community Trade Mark (CTM), and previously the EU IPO was known as the Office for Harmonization of the Internal Market (OHIM); both of these terms will be referenced in the following case law. Furthermore, over time, the numbering of the relevant provisions in the Directive and Regulation have altered; this will be pointed out throughout this Part.

The UK decision to withdraw from the EU has had consequences for trade marks in the UK. As part of the EU for decades, UK trade mark law (primarily contained in the Trade Mark Act 1994) was shaped by EU trade mark law. The most recent EU trade mark legislation, the Trade Mark Directive 2015, was incorporated into the UK Trade Mark Act 1994 prior to Brexit, and remains retained law after Brexit.

Finally, as with copyrights and patents, the WTO TRIPS Agreement introduced a range of minimum standards for trade mark protection. The minimum standards include: the requirement that trade marks be available for all signs that are 'capable of distinguishing the goods or services of one undertaking from those of other undertakings, shall be capable of constituting a trademark';[22] the requirement that the owner of a registered trademark shall have the 'exclusive right to prevent all third parties not having the owner's consent from using in the course of trade identical or similar signs for goods or services which are identical or similar to those in respect of which the trademark is registered where such use would result in a likelihood of confusion'.[23]

12.6   SUMMARY

This chapter began by highlighting the differences between trade marks, and other forms of IP. We conclude with one final difference.

Trade marks are less politically and philosophically contentious than copyrights, patents and designs. Some readers might reasonably conclude that no good argument exists for these latter rights. But it is harder to reach the same conclusion with respect to trade marks. There is a reasonably solid utilitarian argument for granting traders some control over their signs. To be sure, trade marks help traders differentiate their products, and thereby facilitate monopolistic competition. But they also have good consequences: lower search costs, facilitating competition and preventing confusion. These are real, and not merely speculative, benefits. For the most part, the good consequences of trade marks very likely outweigh the bad ones. It is almost universally accepted, therefore, that trade mark rights should protect the origin function of signs.

That does not mean, however, trade marks are free from controversy. While there is broad support for the trade mark system, two questions remain. First, what things should be protected by trade marks? As indicated in Section 12.3.1, if trade marks are granted on some things – like the colour brown for cola – then trade marks may create monopolies, not merely monopolistic competition. If trade marks are granted on these signs, the bad consequences of protection may well outweigh the good. Chapter 13 therefore considers what signs should be protected by trade marks.

Second, how much control should the owner have over their sign? Should trade marks protect non-origin functions of signs? If so, what other functions should be protected? Should we, for example, agree with Schechter that businesses should be able to prevent non-confusing uses of their signs, on the ground that such uses might impair the sign's selling power? Or are such non-confusing uses a form of unethical free riding? If you think of property as exclusive control over a thing, then should there be property rights in signs? This question is considered in Chapter 14.

12.7   SELF-ASSESSMENT

Before moving on, try to answer the following questions to consolidate your learning. Answers are provided in the section below.

1. Which of the following statements best describes the origin function of signs?
   a. The sign's ability to indicate the quality of the goods.
   b. The sign's ability to indicate the producer of the goods.
   c. The sign's ability to indicate the brand's values.
   d. The sign's ability to indicate the owner of the goods.
2. Which of the following statements best describes how trade marks create monopolistic competition?
   a. Trade marks prevent other firms from producing similar goods.
   b. Trade marks encourage firms to produce identical products.
   c. Trade marks enable firms to differentiate their products from those of competitors.
   d. Trade marks lead to a decrease in product prices.
3. Which of the following are reasons that have been offered for granting traders the ability to prevent non-confusing uses of their signs? Choose one or more answers.
   a. Non-confusing uses of signs dilute the sign's uniqueness.

410 *Trade Marks I: Foundations*

b. Non-confusing uses of signs impede the ability of traders to use signs for functions beyond indicating origin.

c. Non-confusing uses of signs deceive consumers about the origin of goods.

d. Non-confusing uses of signs may involve unethical free riding.

4. Is free riding on a sign ever ethically wrong?

ACTIVITY DISCUSSION

Activity 12.1 I suspect that the first thing which comes to mind is the Coca-Cola Company. You quite probably assume that bottles bearing this sign have all been produced by that particular company. Of course, you could check to see if this is actually true. You could track down a sales assistant and ask whether the bottles actually come from that company. But I expect that you probably would not bother doing so.

Something else which might come to mind is quality. Upon seeing the sign, you might reasonably assume that the contents of the bottle are safe to drink; indeed, it probably is quite enjoyable to drink. The sign, in other words, indicates something about the quality of the product.

But keep thinking about the sign. Where else have you seen it? What other connections does it conjure up? To some, it might represent globalism and the international community. The sign is very prominently displayed at some of the world's most iconic global sporting events, such as FIFA World Cup and the Olympic Games. To some, the sign might even conjure up cosy and comforting images of jolly Father Christmas.

Activity 12.2 1. The signs indicated two different types of 'origin'.

First, the signs indicated *geographic* origin, that is, where in the world the goods were produced. Today, businesses who want to indicate the geographic origin of their goods can apply for a *sui generis* right known as a **geographic indication**.[24] These rights will not be discussed much in this Part.

Second, the signs also indicated the *producer* origin. That is, they indicated what an individual, company or guild produced the product. When lawyers speak of the origin function today, it is largely used in this second sense of who produced the goods.

2. Goodwill is a trader's ability to retain customers. Or, as Lord Macnaghten put it *IRC v Muller and Co's Margarine Ltd*: 'It is a thing very easy to describe, very difficult to define. It is the benefit and advantage of the good name, reputation, and connection of a business. It is the attractive force which brings in custom.'[25] One function of signs is their ability to help a business develop goodwill. A more extensive discussion of this concept appears in Chapter 15.

Activity 12.3 In claiming that oats and soap are 'interchangeable', Drescher means that they are all basically the same from a consumer's point of view. One producer's soap is just like another producer's soap. From an economic perspective, they are **substitutes**: if a consumer cannot find one producer's soap, they can easily switch to that of another producer. Importantly, if one producer starts unilaterally selling soap at a higher price, then consumers will probably switch to one of the producer's cheaper competitors in the market.

But the advertising changes the interchangeability of goods, at least in consumers' minds. If producer A convinces you, through persuasive advertising, that their soap is better than that of producer B, then they might be able to increase prices without losing all their customers.

Advertising therefore creates a certain amount of market power. Signs have an 'advertising function' in the sense that they make it easier to advertise goods.

Activity 12.4 You will need to interpret the advert for yourself and come to your own conclusions. But, in my mind, the advert is trying to indicate that Pepsi drinkers have certain qualities. Pepsi drinkers are youthful idealists who embody the spirit of change. When they see problems in society, they do not sit back and wait for solutions to appear; instead they become the change they want to see. Pepsi drinkers are also inclusive, and bring together people who may be at odds with one another. Pepsi drinkers – people like Kendall Jenner – are also simply, cool.

As it so happens, the advert was a complete flop. The advert was heavily criticised for trivialising police brutality and Pepsi decided to withdraw it. It seems that the advert, and their sign, was not creating the identity that they had initially hoped it would.

Activity 12.5 If one thinks of property as exclusive control over a thing, then Day and Martin clearly did not have property in their sign. Indeed, they did not have any rights in the sign at all. At most, they had a right to prevent the defendants engaging in deliberate fraud that would harm their goodwill or reputation. This right seems more at home in a subject like tort law, than property law.

What then of goodwill? Even if the business did not own their *sign*, did they own the *goodwill*? This question will be taken up further when we return to passing off in Chapter 15.

Activity 12.6 The sign's ability to achieve the origin function will likely be impaired if Pepsi begin putting the word COKE on their cola too (scenario 1). If that happens, consumers who see the word COKE on a bottle of cola, will no longer know where the cola comes from. It might come from the Coca-Cola Company, but it might not. The COKE sign, therefore, is no longer capable of performing an origin function, much to the Coca-Cola Company's annoyance.

But the same is not so obviously true in scenario 2. Even if the Newcastle Coal Company uses the words COKE-A-COAL-A, it seems likely that consumers who see the word COKE on a bottle of cola will know that the bottle comes from the Coca-Cola company. If so, then the Newcastle Coal Company's use of the sign does *not* impair the sign's origin function.

Activity 12.7 At no point, does Schechter defend the premise that trade marks should help traders sell their products. Why should trade marks help sellers to sell goods? It's not obvious why they should. Why should we care whether Coca-Cola makes more, or fewer, sales? It seems that Schechter has made the mistake forewarned against at the start of the section: he mixes up the historical with the normative. The fact that signs *can* help businesses sell goods, does not mean that trade mark law *ought to* help them to do so. Whether society ought to grant trade marks at all, and how powerful they ought to be, is a normative question explored in Section 12.3.

Activity 12.8 Many readers will instantly recognise this as a bottle of Coca-Cola. The shape therefore is performing an origin function. And, so, the shape of the bottle can be understood as a sign.

SELF-ASSESSMENT ANSWERS

1. **Correct answer: b. a**. describes the warranty function or quality function; **c**. describes the identity or communication function; **d**. describes the possession function.

2. **Correct answer: c.** Signs can be used in advertising (see Section 12.1.2). Advertising can encourage consumers to pay higher prices for goods than would occur in a perfectly competitive market. This is a form of market power.

3. **Correct answer: a., b.** and **d.** Non-confusing uses are uses where, by definition, consumers are not confused about the origin of goods. However, Schechter argues that even non-confusing uses may dilute the sign's uniqueness and this will make it harder for traders to make sales. A more modern take on this argument says that if dilution occurs, then it will eventually make it harder for the sign to perform the origin function. Some, as we will see in later chapters, argue that it is simply unfair.

Notes

1 Trade Mark Act 1994, s 2(1); *AG Spalding & Bros v AW Gamage Ltd* (1915) 32 RPC 273, 284.

2 Reproduced under UK orphan licensing scheme. License number OWLS000351.

3 Trade Mark Act 1994, s 2(1).

4 *JG v Samford* (1584).

5 Reproduced with permission of author and editors.

6 Frank Schechter, *The Historical Foundations of the Law Relating to Trade-Marks* (Columbia UP 1925).

7 Reproduced with permission of author.

8 Reproduced with permission of author.

9 The classic exposition is found in Edward Chamberlin, *The Theory of Monopolistic Competition* (1933) Appendix E. See also Michael Spence, 'Product Differentiation and Welfare' (1976) 66(2) American Economic Review 407; Glynn S Lunney Jr, 'Trademark Monopolies' (1999) 48 Emory LJ 367. On persuasive advertising as a source of product differentiation, see Ralph S Brown Jr 'Advertising and the Public Interest: Legal Protection of Trade Symbols' (1948) 57 Yale LJ 1265.

10 © University of Chicago Press. Reproduced with permission through Copyright Clearance Center.

11 © 1974. Reprinted by permission of Basic Books, an imprint of Hachette Book Group, Inc.

12 Trade Mark Act 1994, s 46(1)(a).

13 ibid s 46(1)(b).

14 ibid s 46(1)(c).

15 ibid s 46(1)(d).

16 Paris Convention for Industrial Property as amended (1883) art 2.

17 ibid art 4C.

18 Protocol Relating to the Madrid Agreement Concerning the International Registration of Marks (as amended 12 November 2007) art 2(2).

19 ibid art 5(2).

20 First Council Directive 89/104/EEC of 21 December 1988 to approximate the laws of the Member States relating to trade marks. Council Regulation (EC) No 40/94 of 20 December 1993 on the Community trade mark.

21 Directive (EU) 2015/2436 of the European Parliament and of the Council of 16 December 2015 to approximate the laws of the Member States relating to trade marks. Regulation (EU) 2017/1001 of the European Parliament and of the Council of 14 June 2017 on the European Union trade mark.

22 TRIPS (1994) art 15.

23 ibid art 16.

24 ibid art 22.1.

25 [1901] AC 217, 223–24.

FIGURE ACKNOWLEDGEMENTS

12.1 UK Trade mark number UK00000427817. Owner: the Coca-Cola Company. Date of entry in register 11 July 1922. Renewed 12 January 2017

12.2 UK Trade mark number UK00002000548. Owner: the Coca-Cola Company. Date of entry in register 1 September 1995

13

Trade Marks II: Absolute Grounds for Refusal

What signs should businesses be allowed to own? If the Coca-Cola Company should own the word 'COKE' and Apple should own the little apple icon, what else should be subject to trade mark protection? Should Coca-Cola be allowed to own the shape of their famous glass bottle? What about the colour red? As we will see, a recurring theme in all these issues is the role of competition. While there is a strong utilitarian case for trade marks on certain types of signs, there are some instances where the public would be better served by leaving signs in the public domain.

Broadly the rules regarding what can and cannot be registered as a trade mark are found in section 3 of the Trade Mark Act (TMA) 1994. This section contains the absolute grounds for refusal. When a business applies to the UK IPO for trade mark protection, their application will be denied if any of the absolute grounds for refusal apply. If the application is erroneously granted, it may be later declared invalid.[1]

It is helpful to split the absolute grounds for refusal into three parts. This chapter first examines phenomena that fail to qualify as 'signs'. The second part considers signs that can only be registered if they satisfy a condition: the acquisition of a distinctive character. The third part examines signs that can never be registered, even if they acquire a distinctive character.

> The same rules that apply to EU Trade Marks can be found in TMD 2015 article 4. Under the old Trade Mark Directive 2008 the relevant provision was article 3.

13.1 SIGNS

Section 1(1) of the TMA 1994 defines trade mark subject matter:

This chapter contains public sector information licensed under the Open Government Licence v3.0.

> (1) In this Act 'trade mark' means any sign which is capable –
>   (a) of being represented in the register in a manner which enables the registrar and other competent authorities and the public to determine the clear and precise subject matter of the protection afforded to the proprietor, and
>   (b) of distinguishing goods or services of one undertaking from those of other undertakings.
>
> A trade mark may, in particular, consist of words (including personal names), designs, letters, numerals, colours, sounds or the shape of goods or their packaging.

Furthermore, section 3(1) of the TMA 1994 states that failure to satisfy the requirements of section 1(1) will result in the application's refusal. Those requirements can be broken down into three necessary conditions: the application must relate to (1) a sign, that is (2) capable of being represented on the register and (3) capable of distinguishing goods and services in the market. This section considers these conditions in turn.

13.1.1 Signs

What is a '**sign**'? The answer is: almost anything. Recall the functionalist metaphysics of trade mark law introduced in Section 11.2.4. Much like bicycle brakes, trade mark lawyers understand signs as anything capable of performing the sign functions – the most important being the origin function.

The result is that signs can be 'words (including personal names), designs, letters, numerals, colours, sounds or the shape of goods or their packaging'. Furthermore, this list is only illustrative. It is possible for scents, textures and tastes to be signs, even though they are not specifically mentioned in section 1.

However, there are some minimal limits on what a sign can be, as Case 13.1 illustrates.

Case 13.1 *Dyson Ltd v Registrar of Trade Marks*, Case C-321/03 [2007] ECR I–687

Facts

Since 1993 Dyson (applicant–appellant) has manufactured and marketed vacuum cleaners. The Dyson vacuum cleaners are bagless cleaners in which the dirt and dust is collected in a transparent plastic container forming part of the machine. The company is owned by James Dyson – the British inventor of the Dyson vacuum cleaner.

In 2002, Dyson (respondent) applied for a trade mark. The claimed sign was a 'transparent bin or collection chamber forming part of the external surface of a vacuum cleaner' and was to be used in relation to vacuum cleaners. Importantly, Dyson did not apply for a trade mark in relation to a certain shape of the bin. Instead, the application was for a transparent bin regardless of shape.

Issue and Procedure

Dyson's application was rejected by the UK IPO. The decision was appealed to the High Court of Justice of England and Wales. Although the High Court found that consumers recognised the bin, they referred questions to the CJEU for preliminary ruling. The question in the next extract is whether a 'transparent bin' can be a sign? According to the CJEU the answer is no. The idea of a transparent bin was not sufficiently specific to be a sign. Instead, the bin was merely a 'mere property' of the vacuum cleaner, and to allow it to be owned would have deleterious effects on competition.

COURT OF JUSTICE (THIRD CHAMBER)

According to the Commission, the application lodged by Dyson does not fulfil the first of those conditions because it relates to a concept, in this case, the concept of a transparent collecting bin for a vacuum cleaner, irrespective of shape. Since a concept is not capable of being perceived by one of the five senses and appeals only to the imagination, it is not a 'sign' within the meaning of Article 2 of the Directive. If a concept were able to constitute a trade mark, the logic behind Article 3(1)(e) of the Directive, namely to prevent trade mark protection from granting its proprietor a monopoly on technical solutions or functional characteristics of a product, would be frustrated. Accordingly, it should not be possible to achieve that advantage by registering all the shapes which a particular functional feature might have, which would be the result of allowing the registration of a concept which can cover many physical manifestations.

By contrast, Dyson, supported on this point by the United Kingdom Government, takes the view that, even if it is true, as it stated at the hearing, that a concept is not a sign capable of being registered as a trade mark, its application does relate to a 'sign' within the meaning of Article 2 of the Directive. The concept of a 'sign', which is defined broadly by the case-law, in fact covers any message which may be perceived by one of the five senses. It is apparent from the main proceedings that consumers associate the transparent collecting bin which is the subject-matter of the application with Dyson. Moreover, consumers are able, first, to see that collecting bin, which is a physical

Article 2 TMD 1988 mentioned here corresponds to article 3 TMD 2015.

component of the vacuum cleaner, and, second, to see that it is transparent. The transparent collecting bin is thus perceptible by sight and therefore cannot be considered to be a product of consumers' imagination.

It follows that, unlike the applications which gave rise to the judgments in Sieckmann and Shield Mark, the subject-matter of the application in the main proceedings is capable of taking on a multitude of different appearances and is thus not specific. As pointed out by the Advocate General in point 51 of his Opinion, the shape, the dimensions, the presentation and composition of that subject-matter depend both on the vacuum cleaner models developed by Dyson and on technological innovations. Likewise, transparency allows for the use of various colours.

Given the exclusivity inherent in trade mark right, the holder of a trade mark relating to such a non-specific subject-matter would obtain an unfair competitive advantage, contrary to the purpose pursued by Article 2 of the Directive, since it would be entitled to prevent its competitors from marketing vacuum cleaners having any kind of transparent collecting bin on their external surface, irrespective of its shape.

It follows that the subject-matter of the application at issue in the main proceedings is, in actual fact, a mere property of the product concerned and does not therefore constitute a 'sign' within the meaning of Article 2 of the Directive (see, to that effect, *Libertel*, paragraph 27).

(paras 29–30, 37–39)

13.1.2   Capable of Representation

Although almost anything can be a sign, the sign can only be owned if it is capable of being represented on the register.

Prior to the TMD 2015, the TMD 1988 and the old text of the TMA 1994 required that the sign be capable of 'graphic' representation.[2] While the graphic representation requirement was easily satisfied in cases of word or figurative signs (like logos), it was more difficult in cases of non-traditional signs, such as scents, which are not naturally easy to represent graphically.

The TMD 2015 removed the graphic representation requirement and replaced it with the requirement that the presentation must be sufficiently to enable 'competent authorities and the public to determine the clear and precise subject matter'. The TMA 1994 was amended to bring it into line with EU law. While the graphic representation requirement was changed, the case law interpreting that clause remains relevant for assessing whether the sign is sufficiently represented on the register.

Case 13.2 *Ralf Sieckmann v Deutsches Patent-und Markenamt, Case C-273/00 [2002] ECR I–11737*

Facts

Ralph Sieckmann (applicant–appellant) applied to the German Patent and Trade Mark Office (respondent) for a trade mark for the scent of 'methyl cinnamate'. In the application, Sieckmann described the scent as 'balsamically fruity with a hint of cinnamon' and provided the following chemical formula for the scent: $C6H5-CH = CHCOOCH3$. The application also contained a sample of the scent. Sieckmann wished to register the scent in relation to, among other things, perfumes.

Issue and Procedure

The German Patent and Trade Mark Office refused to register the mark. One ground provided for the refusal was inability to represent the sign graphically, as then required under the TMD 1988. The decision was appealed and the appellate court sent questions for preliminary ruling to the CJEU. While not deciding whether or not the scent in question could be registered, the CJEU elaborated on the graphic representation requirement.

COURT OF JUSTICE

First, the function of the graphic representability requirement is, in particular, to define the mark itself in order to determine the precise subject of the protection afforded by the registered mark to its proprietor.

Next, the entry of the mark in a public register has the aim of making it accessible to the competent authorities and the public, particularly to economic operators.

On the one hand, the competent authorities must know with clarity and precision the nature of the signs of which a mark consists in order to be able to fulfil their obligations in relation to the prior examination of registration applications and to the publication and maintenance of an appropriate and precise register of trade marks.

On the other hand, economic operators must, with clarity and precision, be able to find out about registrations or applications for registration made by their current or potential competitors and thus to receive relevant information about the rights of third parties.

If the users of that register are to be able to determine the precise nature of a mark on the basis of its registration, its graphic representation in the register must be self-contained, easily accessible and intelligible.

Furthermore, in order to fulfil its role as a registered trade mark a sign must always be perceived unambiguously and in the same way so

> that the mark is guaranteed as an indication of origin. In the light of the duration of a mark's registration and the fact that, as the Directive provides, it can be renewed for varying periods, the representation must be durable.
>
> Finally, the object of the representation is specifically to avoid any element of subjectivity in the process of identifying and perceiving the sign. Consequently, the means of graphic representation must be unequivocal and objective.
>
> In the light of the foregoing observations, the answer to the first question must be that Article 2 of the Directive must be interpreted as meaning that a trade mark may consist of a sign which is not in itself capable of being perceived visually, provided that it can be represented graphically, particularly by means of images, lines or characters, and that the representation is clear, precise, self-contained, easily accessible, intelligible, durable and objective.
>
> (paras 48–55)

In the coming years, the requirement that the representation be 'clear, precise, self-contained, easily accessible, intelligible, durable and objective' was frequently repeated, and became known as the *Sieckmann* criteria. The use of the *Sieckmann* criteria can be seen in Cases 13.3 and 13.4 regarding colours.

The Benelux Union is composed of Belgium, Netherlands and Luxembourg.

Case 13.3 *Libertel Groep BV v Benelux-Merkenbureau*, Case C-104/01 [2003] ECR I–3793

Facts

Libertel (applicant–appellant) was a company established in the Netherlands whose principal activity is the supply of mobile telecommunications services. On 27 August 1996 Libertel filed with the Benelux Trade Mark Office (respondent) an orange colour as a trade mark for certain telecommunications goods and services. The application form contained an orange rectangle and, in the space for describing the trade mark, the word Orange without reference to any colour code. Various colour coding systems exist. These coding systems categorise different colours and provide each colour with a unique code. One commonly used categorisation system is provided by Pantone.[3]

Issue and Procedure

The Benelux Trade Mark Office refused the registration on various grounds. Libertel appealed and the appellate court referred questions to the CJEU for preliminary ruling. In the following section of the judgment, the CJEU concluded that a single colour might be capable of being represented graphically and meeting the *Sieckmann* criteria.

COURT OF JUSTICE

Furthermore, as the Court has held, a graphic representation within the meaning of Article 2 of the Directive must enable the sign to be represented visually, particularly by means of images, lines or characters, so that it can be precisely identified (Case C-273/00 Sieckmann [2002] ECR I-11737, paragraph 46).

In order to fulfil its function, the graphic representation within the meaning of Article 2 of the Directive must be clear, precise, self-contained, easily accessible, intelligible, durable and objective (Sieckmann, paragraphs 47 to 55).

In this case the query referred to the Court relates to an application to register a colour per se, represented by a sample of the colour on a flat surface, a description in words of the colour and/or an internationally recognised colour identification code.

A mere sample of a colour does not, however, satisfy the requirements set out in paragraphs 28 and 29 of this judgment.

In particular a sample of a colour may deteriorate with time. There may be certain media on which it is possible to reproduce a colour in permanent form. However with other media, including paper, the exact shade of the colour cannot be protected from the effects of the passage of time. In these cases, the filing of a sample of a colour does not possess the durability required by Article 2 of the Directive (see Sieckmann, paragraph 53).

It follows that filing a sample of a colour does not per se constitute a graphic representation within the meaning of Article 2 of the Directive. On the other hand, a verbal description of a colour, in so far as it is composed of words which themselves are made up of letters, does constitute a graphic representation of the colour (see Sieckmann, paragraph 70).

A description in words of the colour will not necessarily satisfy the conditions set out in paragraphs 28 and 29 of this judgment in every instance. That is a question which must be evaluated in the light of the circumstances of each individual case.

A sample of a colour, combined with a description in words of that colour, may therefore constitute a graphic representation within the meaning of Article 2 of the Directive, provided that the description is clear, precise, self-contained, easily accessible, intelligible, and objective. For the same reasons as those set out at paragraph 34 of this judgment, the designation of a colour using an internationally recognised identification code may be considered to constitute a graphic representation. Such codes are deemed to be precise and stable.

Where a sample of a colour, together with a description in words, does not satisfy the conditions laid down in Article 2 of the Directive in order for it to constitute a graphic representation because, inter alia, it lacks precision or durability, that deficiency may, depending on the facts, be remedied by adding a colour designation from an internationally recognised identification code.

(paras 28–38)

Case 13.4 *Société des Produits Nestlé SA v Cadbury UK Ltd* [2013] EWCA Civ 1174

Facts

Cadbury UK Limited (applicant–respondent) sought to register the shade of the colour purple as a trade mark in relation to chocolate. The sign was described in the application as: 'The colour purple (Pantone 2685C), as shown on the form of application, applied to the whole visible surface, or being the predominant colour applied to the whole visible surface, of the packaging of the goods'.

The trade mark was unsuccessfully opposed by Nestlé before the UK IPO and the trade mark was granted.

Cadbury have had some more luck recently. In *Cadbury UK Ltd v Société des Produits Nestlé SA (Comptroller-General of Patents, Designs and Trade Marks intervening)*, Mr Justice Meade held that registering the colour purple as 'applied to the packaging of the goods' was not sufficiently clear and precise and could not be registered. But the colour purple with no description could be registered.[4]

Issue and Procedure

Nestlé appealed to the High Court on various grounds where they were unsuccessful. They subsequently appealed to the Court of Appeal. Their appeal was upheld.

SIR JOHN MUMMERY

At the end of all the argument below and in this court the outcome of the appeal turns on quite a narrow point on which the Hearing Officer and the judge erred in principle.

The crucial point stems from the misinterpretation of the verbal description of the graphic representation of the mark for which application is made. The description refers not only to the colour purple as applied to the whole visible surface of the packaging of the goods, but also to an alternative i.e. 'or being the predominant colour applied to the whole visible surface...' The use of the word 'predominant' opens the door to a multitude of different visual forms as a result of its implied reference to other colours and other visual material not displayed or described in the application and over which the colour purple may predominate. It is an application for the registration of a shade of colour 'plus' other material, not just of an unchanging application of a single colour, as in *Libertel.*

In my judgment, that description, properly interpreted, does not constitute 'a sign' that is 'graphically represented' within Article 2. If the colour purple is less than total, as would be the case if the colour is only 'predominant', the application would cover other matter in combination with the colour, but not graphically represented or verbally described in the specific, certain, self-contained and precise manner required. The result would not be an application to register 'a sign', in the accepted sense of a single sign conveying a message, but to register multiple signs with different permutations, presentations and appearances, which are neither graphically represented nor described with any certainty or precision, or at all.

The appearance and number of such other signs would be unknown both to the Registrar, who is responsible for the proper functioning of the registration system and is faced with the decision whether or not to register it on a public register, and to competitors, who would not be able to tell from inspecting the register the full scope and extent of the registration. To allow a registration so lacking in specificity, clarity and precision of visual appearance would offend against the principle of certainty. It would also offend against the principle of fairness by giving a competitive advantage to Cadbury and by putting Nestlé and its other competitors at a disadvantage.

(paras 49–52)

13.1.3 Capable of Distinguishing

The final requirement in section 1 is that the sign be 'capable of distinguishing goods or services of one undertaking from those of other undertakings'. However, this requirement has nearly faded into irrelevance since 2002.

Section 3(1)(b) of the TMA states that trade marks which are 'devoid of any distinctive character' will not be registered. For some time, this caused conceptual difficulties for courts as they tried to work out the relationship between section 1(1)(b) and section 3(1)(b).[5] But, in 2002 in *Philips v Remington* (see Case 13.11), the CJEU simplified the law by declaring section 1(1)(b) does not represent a ground for refusal separate from that of section 3(1)(b). In simple terms, what matters is not whether a sign has a 'capacity' to distinguish; what matters is whether it actually does distinguish the goods and services in the market under section 3(1)(b).[6]

Taking a step back, one can see how few applications will be refused on section 1 grounds. Nearly anything can be a sign; the representation requirement has been relaxed; and the capacity to distinguish requirement is now obsolete.

ACTIVITY 13.1

How do the section 1 requirements relate to the functionalist metaphysics of trade mark law?

13.2 CONDITIONALLY REGISTRABLE SIGNS

Not all signs that satisfy the section 1(1) requirements can be owned. Some signs can only be registered on the condition that they have acquired a distinctive character. Other signs can never be registered, regardless of whether they have acquired a distinctive character or not. The former conditionally registrable signs are discussed in this section, and the latter excluded signs are discussed in the next section.

The TMD 2015 contains the same list in article 4(1)(b)–(d), and the acquired distinctive condition appears in article 4(4).

Section 3(1) of the TMA provides a list of conditionally registrable signs;

---

(1) The following shall not be registered –
 (b) trade marks which are devoid of any distinctive character,
 (c) trade marks which consist exclusively of signs or indications which may serve, in trade, to designate the kind, quality, quantity, intended purpose, value, geographical origin, the time of production of goods or of rendering of services, or other characteristics of goods or services,
 (d) trade marks which consist exclusively of signs or indications which have become customary in the current language or in the *bona fide* and established practices of the trade:
Provided that, a trade mark shall not be refused registration by virtue of paragraph (b), (c) or (d) above if, before the date of application for registration, it has in fact acquired a distinctive character as a result of the use made of it.

Subsection (1) (b)–(d) lists signs which normally cannot be registered as a trade mark. Those are signs that lack a 'distinctive character', that designate certain properties about the goods or services (known commonly as 'descriptive' signs), or that have become 'customary' in the language.

Whether a sign lacks distinctiveness, is descriptive or customary is assessed through the eyes of the 'average consumer'. Much like the PSITA in patent law, the average consumer is a legal fiction rather than a real person. The average consumer is defined in countless cases as someone who is 'reasonably well-informed and reasonably observant and circumspect'.[7] The amount of care and attention that fictional person will expend when making purchasing decisions will vary depending on the sector: average consumers buying cars will, for example, pay more attention than when buying toothpaste.

Underlying this fictional legal analysis is an important normative point. Recall the utilitarian argument discussed in Section 11.3.1. According to that argument, trade mark protections have both anti-competitive and pro-competitive effects. The good news is that in some cases, the pro-competitive effects of trade mark protection outweigh the anti-competitive effects. But this is not true in relation to non-distinctive, descriptive or customary signs. As Activity 13.2 illustrates, legal protection of these signs merely causes anti-competitive effects without any offsetting pro-competitive effects.

ACTIVITY 13.2

Consider a seller of laptops. The seller is debating which sign to use to help sell the goods: (i) the word LAPTOP; or (ii) POTPAL. Now consider the following questions:
  (1) what would be the effects on competition if the seller owns the word LAPTOP?
  (2) what would be the effects on competition if the seller owns the word POTPAL?

Finally, at the end, the section introduces an important condition. That is, if a business's sign falls into one of the (b)–(d) subsections, it can nevertheless still be protected if the sign has '**acquired a distinctive character**'. This section first examines the (b)–(d) subsections in order, before turning to the all-important condition.

13.2.1 Devoid of a Distinctive Character

The most fundamental requirement of trade mark law is that signs have a '**distinctive character**'. Normally, signs composed of single letters,[8] numbers[9] or geometric shapes (e.g. a circle or a square),[10] will be considered as insufficiently distinctive. The same is true of simple slogans (e.g. HAVE A BREAK for chocolate biscuits)[11] and names (e.g. ELVIS).[12] Granting protection in such cases would simply deny competitors the opportunity to use these signs while producing few pro-competitive effects because the average consumer rarely relies on such signs as badges of origin.

Trade Marks II: Absolute Grounds for Refusal

Prior to the TMA 1994, surnames could not be registered. The current law permits registration if they are distinctive.

The difficult question is where to draw the line between unprotectable non-distinctive and protectable distinctive signs? This is particularly problematic in relation to 'non-traditional' signs such as colours, shapes and positions. Consider, for example, the *Libertel* case introduced in Section 13.1. Not only did the CJEU consider whether the colour could be represented graphically, they also concluded that under normal circumstances, a single colour lacks a distinctive character.

COURT OF JUSTICE

It is appropriate first of all to examine the third question, by which the national court is asking whether, in assessing the potential distinctiveness of a specific colour as a trade mark, it is necessary to consider whether there is a general interest in that colour remaining available to all, as is the case with respect to signs which designate a geographical origin.

As regards the registration as trade marks of colours per se, not spatially delimited, the fact that the number of colours actually available is limited means that a small number of trade mark registrations for certain services or goods could exhaust the entire range of the colours available. Such an extensive monopoly would be incompatible with a system of undistorted competition, in particular because it could have the effect of creating an unjustified competitive advantage for a single business. Nor would it be conducive to economic development or the fostering of the spirit of enterprise for established businesses to be able to register the entire range of colours that is in fact available for their own benefit, to the detriment of new businesses.

It must therefore be acknowledged that there is, in Community trademark law, a public interest in not unduly restricting the availability of colours for the other operators who offer for sale goods or services of the same type as those in respect of which registration is sought.

The first question and Question 2(a)

By its first question and Question 2(a), the national court is essentially asking whether and, if so, in what circumstances a colour per se may be held to be distinctive within the meaning of Article 3(1)(b) and Article 3(3) of the Directive.

The perception of the relevant public is not necessarily the same in the case of a sign consisting of a colour per se as it is in the case of a word or figurative mark consisting of a sign that bears no relation to the appearance of the goods it denotes. While the public is accustomed to perceiving word or figurative marks instantly as signs identifying the commercial origin of the goods, the same is not necessarily true where the sign forms part of the look of the goods in respect of which registration of the sign as a trade mark is sought. Consumers are not in the habit of making assumptions about the origin of goods based on their colour or the colour of their packaging, in the absence of any graphic or word element, because as a rule a colour per se is not, in current commercial practice, used as a means of identification. A colour per se is not normally inherently capable of distinguishing the goods of a particular undertaking.

In the case of a colour per se, distinctiveness without any prior use is inconceivable save in exceptional circumstances, and particularly where the number of goods or services for which the mark is claimed is very restricted and the relevant market very specific.

(paras 44, 54–55, 61, 65–66)

Article 3(1)(b) TMD 1988 mentioned here corresponds to article 4(1)(b) TMD 2015.

Note the use of the word 'inherently'. The CJEU found that colours are not *inherently* distinctive. There is nothing intrinsically unique or distinctive about the Coca-Cola red colour, for example. As examined later, the colour can become distinctive through use. But without evidence of acquired distinctiveness, applications to register single colours will be refused because the anti-competitive effects are greater than their pro-competitive ones.

Broadly similar considerations are applicable in relation to shapes. One doctrinal rule courts have developed to help divide non-distinctive from distinctive ones is to consider how significantly the shape differs from the normal and customary shapes in the sector.

Case 13.5 *London Taxi Corp v Frazer-Nash Research Ltd* [2017] EWCA Civ 1729

Facts

The London Taxi Corporation (LTC) (claimant–appellant) owned a trade mark on the shape of their model of London taxi car (Figure 13.1). Frazer-Nash Research (defendant–respondent) allegedly wished to introduce a new type of London taxi. LTC claimed that the Frazer-Nash taxi would infringe their shape trade mark.

Issue and Procedure

At trial in the High Court, Frazer-Nash successfully argued that the trade mark on the shape was invalid because it lacked a distinctive character. The LTC appealed to the Court of Appeal.

Figure 13.1 London Taxi Corp trade mark registration

FLOYD LJ

The judge approached the issue of inherent distinctive character on the basis that a necessary, but not a sufficient, condition for registration in the case of a mark consisting of the shape of a product was that the registered shape must be one that departs significantly from the norm or customs of the sector for products of that kind.

In my judgment, drawing on the CJEU's jurisprudence, there are three steps in deciding whether the mark differs significantly from the norms and customs of the sector. The first step in the exercise is to determine what the sector is. Then it is necessary to identify common norms and customs, if any, of that sector. Thirdly it is necessary to decide whether the mark departs significantly from those norms and customs.

Mr Campbell did not suggest that the sector was limited to London licensed taxi cabs. Even if the marks were limited to taxis, which they are not, it would have to include private hire taxis, which can be any model of saloon car within reason. In my judgment it must include not just models in production at the date of application, but those on the road and those which the average consumer can be expected to have seen.

The norms and customs of the car sector are not difficult to establish. Typical cars have a superstructure carried on four wheels, the superstructure having a bonnet, headlamps and sidelights or parking lights, a front grille and no doubt other features. The public will have experienced taxis with sharp linear features like the old Metrocab, and more rounded ones like LTC's taxis. They will have experienced both modern cars and more old fashioned ones. They will know that if the car is a taxi it will often have a light or other sign bearing the word TAXI on its roof.

When the LTC features are compared with these basic design features of the car sector, each is, to my mind, no more than a variant on the standard design features of a car. A windscreen has a slope, a bonnet has a height and a grille has a shape. It is obvious that none of the LTC features is so different to anything which had gone before that it could be described as departing significantly from the norms and customs of the sector. Whether considered individually or as a whole the LTC features are simply minor variants on those norms and customs.

Mr Campbell submitted that it was not clear what specific existing models the judge had in mind in deciding what were the norms and customs of the sector. He submitted that at the relevant dates the only non-LTC taxi was the old Metrocab, and that looked very different to the marks. Mr Campbell is entirely right that the marks applied for look different to the Metrocab, but that is not the correct test. As I have said, it is necessary to widen the perspective to all the different designs of vehicle and the range of variations of each of their features. When the matter is looked at in that way, the marks do not differ significantly from the norms and customs.

Accordingly I think the judge was right to hold that the marks in question did not have inherent distinctive character. If they are to be held to have distinctive character, they must have acquired it by use.

(paras 36, 45–50)

The 'departure from the norms and customs of the sector' analysis has cropped up in a range of other types of signs as well. In the area of product packaging, an application was refused when it related to the twisted wrapper of a sweet as twisted wrappers are normal and customary in that sector.[13]

Product packaging is sometimes called 'get-up and trade dress' in other jurisdictions.

13.2.2 Descriptive

The second type of conditionally registrable sign are those signs that consist 'exclusively' of signs that designate certain properties of the goods or services (e.g. their kind, quality or purpose). Although the term does not appear in the legislation, these are commonly known as 'descriptive' signs, on the grounds that the signs are in a sense **descriptive** of the goods or services.

There is substantial overlap between non-distinctive signs and descriptive signs. As the LAPTOP example demonstrates in Section 13.2.1, a sign will often be non-distinctive precisely because it is descriptive. Furthermore, the argument underlying the exclusion is the same: granting protection to descriptive signs has more anti-competitive effects than pro-competitive effects. And, just as with non-distinctive signs, the challenge for courts is to draw the line between ownable and unownable signs, as the next two cases demonstrate.

Case 13.6 *Windsurfing Chiemsee Produktions und Vertriebs GmbH v Boots und Segelzubehör Walter Huber*, Joined Cases C-108/97 and C-109/97, EU:C:1999:230, [1999] ECR I-2779

Facts

The Chiemsee is the largest lake in Bavaria, Germany. It is a tourist destination and surfing is one of the activities carried on there.

Windsurfing Chiemsee (claimant–appellant), which is based near the shores of the Chiemsee, sells sports fashion clothing, shoes and other sports goods which are designed by a sister company based in the same place, but are manufactured elsewhere. The goods bear the designation 'Chiemsee'. Between 1992 and 1994, Windsurfing Chiemsee registered that designation in Germany as a picture trade mark in the form of various graphic designs, in some cases with additional features or words such as 'Chiemsee Jeans' and 'Windsurfing – Chiemsee – Active Wear'.

Previously the German Patent and Trade Mark Office had denied applications for the word CHIEMSEE as a designation of geographical origin. But they permitted registration for graphic representations of the word 'Chiemsee' such as the one used by Windsurfing Chiemsee (Figure 13.2).

Figure 13.2 Windsurfing Chiemsee trade mark registration

Issue and Procedure

Huber was also selling sports clothing near the shore of Chiemsee. Huber (defendant–respondent) challenged Windsurfing Chiemsee's trade mark on the grounds that it described the geographic origin of the goods.

The German courts referred questions to the CJEU for preliminary ruling. German law at the time would only find such marks to be invalid if there existed a 'real, current, or serious need' to leave the mark free for other competitors to use. The CJEU explains below that a mark may be refused on descriptiveness grounds even if there is not a 'real, current, or serious' need to do so. It is sufficient that the name may, in the future, become associated with a particular geographical origin.

COURT OF JUSTICE

Windsurfing Chiemsee claims that Article 3(1)(c) of the Directive precludes registration of an indication of geographical origin as a trade mark only where the indication in fact designates a specified place, several undertakings manufacture the goods in respect of which protection is applied for in that place, and the place name is habitually used to designate the geographical origin of those goods.

Huber and Mr Attenberger contend that the fact that there is a serious possibility that a name may in future be used to designate geographical origin in the sector of the goods in question is sufficient to preclude registration of that name as a trade mark under Article 3(1)(c) of the Directive. That provision is not, in their view, directed exclusively at indications of origin which relate to manufacture of the goods.

Article 3(1)(c) of the Directive pursues an aim which is in the public interest, namely that descriptive signs or indications relating to the categories of goods or services in respect of which registration is applied for may be freely used by all, including as collective marks or as part of complex or graphic marks. Article 3(1)(c) therefore prevents such signs and indications from being reserved to one undertaking alone because they have been registered as trade marks.

As regards, more particularly, signs or indications which may serve to designate the geographical origin of the categories of goods in relation to which registration of the mark is applied for, especially geographical names, it is in the public interest that they remain available, not least because they may be an indication of the quality and other characteristics of the categories of goods concerned, and may also, in various ways, influence consumer tastes by, for instance,

Article 3(1)(c) TMD 1988 mentioned here corresponds to article 4(1)(c) TMD 2015.

associating the goods with a place that may give rise to a favourable response.

Article 3(1)(c) of the Directive is not confined to prohibiting the registration of geographical names as trade marks solely where they designate specified geographical locations which are already famous, or are known for the category of goods concerned, and which are therefore associated with those goods in the mind of the relevant class of persons, that is to say in the trade and amongst average consumers of that category of goods in the territory in respect of which registration is applied for.

Indeed, it is clear from the actual wording of Article 3(1)(c), which refers to 'indications which may serve . . . to designate . . . geographical origin', that geographical names which are liable to be used by undertakings must remain available to such undertakings as indications of the geographical origin of the category of goods concerned.

However, it cannot be ruled out that the name of a lake may serve to designate geographical origin within the meaning of Article 3(1)(c), even for goods such as those in the main proceedings, provided that the name could be understood by the relevant class of persons to include the shores of the lake or the surrounding area.

It follows from the foregoing that the application of Article 3(1)(c) of the Directive does not depend on there being a real, current or serious need to leave a sign or indication free ('Freihaltebedürfnis') under German case-law, as outlined in the third indent of paragraph 16 of this judgment.

(paras 20–21, 25–26, 29–30, 34–35)

Case 13.7 *Proctor & Gamble Co v Office for Harmonization in the Internal Market (Trade Marks and Designs) (OHIM)*, Case C-383/99 P

Facts

Proctor & Gamble (applicant–appellant) sells, among other things, nappies. On 3 April 1996, Procter & Gamble filed an application with the OHIM for registration of 'BABY-DRY' as an EU trade mark (then called a community trade mark) in respect to nappies. The Office for Harmonization in the Internal Market (OHIM) (respondent) refused the application on the grounds that the sign consisted exclusively of words that designated the intended purpose of the goods.

Issue and Procedure

The Court of First Instance upheld OHIM's decision. The decision was appealed to the CJEU. In the next extract, the court explains why the sign was not descriptive.

COURT OF JUSTICE

As regards trade marks composed of words, such as the mark at issue here, descriptiveness must be determined not only in relation to each word taken separately but also in relation to the whole which they form. Any perceptible difference between the combination of words submitted for registration and the terms used in the common parlance of the relevant class of consumers to designate the goods or services or their essential characteristics is apt to confer distinctive character on the word combination enabling it to be registered as a trade mark.

As it is, that word combination, whilst it does unquestionably allude to the function which the goods are supposed to fulfil, still does not satisfy the disqualifying criteria set forth in paragraphs 39 to 42 of this judgment. Whilst each of the two words in the combination may form part of expressions used in everyday speech to designate the function of babies' nappies, their syntactically unusual juxtaposition is not a familiar expression in the English language, either for designating babies' nappies or for describing their essential characteristics.

Word combinations like 'BABY-DRY' cannot therefore be regarded as exhibiting, as a whole, descriptive character; they are lexical inventions bestowing distinctive power on the mark so formed and may not be refused registration under Article 7(1)(c) of Regulation No 40/94.

The Court of First Instance therefore erred in law in holding that the OHIM'S First Board of Appeal was right to find that 'BABY-DRY' was not capable of constituting a Community trade mark on the basis of that provision.

(paras 40, 43–45)

The *Proctor & Gamble* case illustrates the importance of the word 'exclusively' in subsection (c): the sign BABY DRY was not exclusively descriptive because there was something distinctive about the juxtaposition of the words. Nevertheless, the *Proctor & Gamble* case may represent the most relaxed interpretation of subsection (c). Subsequently the court has rejected BIOMILD for natural yoghurt[14] and DOUBLEMINT for chewing gum,[15] concluding that there needs to be

Trade Marks II: Absolute Grounds for Refusal

something more than a mere combination of words to avoid the exclusion; there need be some 'unusual variation, in particular to syntax or meaning'.[16]

13.2.3 Customary

Many signs start out as distinctive but become '**customary**' (or '**generic**') with time. A classic example is ASPIRIN. The word ASPIRIN was adopted in 1899 as a sign when the pharmaceutical company Bayer started selling acetylsalicylic acid for pain relief. But, over time, the word ASPIRIN lost its association with Bayer and became associated in the minds of consumers with the product acetylsalicylic acid.[17] Today, if someone asks for an 'Aspirin' they are likely not asking for the acetylsalicylic acid produced by Bayer, but acetylsalicylic acid produced by anyone. It has therefore lost its distinctiveness. Other examples include CELLOPHANE and YO-YO.

> Similarly, a trade mark granted on a sign which, after grant, has become customary, will be revoked (see Section 12.4).

13.2.4 Acquired Distinctiveness

While signs that are inherently non-distinctive, descriptive or customary will normally be refused, there is one important exception. Such signs may nevertheless be registered if they have acquired a distinctive character through use. For example, while the average consumer might not naturally see the Coca-Cola red colour as a badge of origin, they may over time come to associate that colour with Coca-Cola. If Coca-Cola can prove that the sign has acquired a distinctive character, it can then be registered. The presence of an acquired distinctive character means that the pro-competitive effects of registration now outweigh the anti-competitive effects.

Once again, courts are tasked with defining the boundaries of this rule. If courts too readily accept claims of acquired distinctiveness, then they may allow businesses to own signs in cases where the consequences of ownership are a net negative for competition and utility. To help draw this line, the CJEU in *Windsurfing* (see Case 13.6) set out a range of factors which may be considered by courts:

> In assessing the distinctive character of a mark in respect of which registration has been applied for, the following may also be taken into account: the market share held by the mark; how intensive, geographically widespread and long-standing use of the mark has been; the amount invested by the undertaking in promoting the mark; the proportion of the relevant class of persons who, because of the mark, identify goods as originating from a particular undertaking; and statements from chambers of commerce and industry or other trade and professional associations.
>
> (para 51)

Those factors, however, say little about what acquired distinctiveness actually is. Case 13.8 illustrates how, factors notwithstanding, ambiguity remains about the underlying concept.

Case 13.8 *Société des Produits Nestlé SA v Cadbury UK Ltd* [2017] EWCA Civ 358

Facts

Nestlé (applicant–appellant) sells chocolates, including the famous Kit Kat. On 8 July 2010, Nestlé applied for a UK trade mark on the four-finger shape of the Kit Kat (Figure 13.3). The application was opposed by Cadbury (opponent–respondent). The application was refused on the grounds that the shape lacked inherent distinctive character and had not acquired a distinctive character through use.

Issue and Procedure

The decision was appealed to the High Court. The litigation centred around what it means to acquire a distinctive character. Mr Justice Arnold (as he then was) outlined two possible approaches: either a sign acquires a distinctive character when consumers 'recognise'

Figure 13.3 Kit Kat shape

the sign, or the sign acquires a distinctive character when consumers 'rely' on the sign as a badge of origin. That is, is it enough that consumers recognised the four-finger shape as a Nestlé Kit Kat? Or does there need to be some proof that consumers in the supermarket would see the shape, and buy the good on the grounds that such a shape must be a Kit Kat? The difference was important in this litigation because Kit Kats are not sold 'naked' but in wrappers. The result is that no consumer relies on the shape when making purchasing decisions. Even if they recognise the shape as a Kit Kat, when it comes to making purchases, they rely on alternative signs (like the Kit Kat logo on the wrapper).

Mr Justice Arnold referred questions to the CJEU for preliminary ruling. The CJEU concluded that to acquire a distinctive character, consumers must 'perceive the goods or services designated exclusively by [the sign], as opposed to any other mark which might also be present, as originating from a particular company'. When the case returned to Mr Justice Arnold, he interpreted the CJEU's decision as requiring reliance, and not mere recognition. The decision was then appealed to the Court of Appeal where Kitchin LJ upheld Arnold's decision and dismissed the appeal.

KITCHIN LJ

Before assessing these rival submissions, I think it may be helpful to say a little more about a concept which is woven into the decisions of the CJEU, including the decision of the CJEU in this case, concerning the acquisition of distinctive character by an inherently non-distinctive three-dimensional shape mark such as the Trade Mark. As we have seen, the CJEU has held that it is not sufficient for the applicant to show that a significant proportion of the relevant class of persons recognise and associate the mark with the applicant's goods. However, to a non-trade mark lawyer, the distinction between, on the one hand, such recognition and association and, on the other hand, a perception that the goods designated by the mark originate from a particular undertaking may be a rather elusive one. Nevertheless, there is a distinction between the two and, as I shall explain in a moment, it is an important one.

The distinction is this. We are concerned here with a mark, the three-dimensional shape of a chocolate product, that has no inherent distinctiveness. A shape of this kind is not inherently such that members of the public are likely to take it as a badge of origin in the way they would a newly coined word or a fancy name. Now assume that products in that shape have been sold on a very large scale under and by reference to a brand name which is inherently highly distinctive. Assume too that the shape has in that way become very well-known. That does not necessarily mean that the public have come to perceive the shape as a badge of origin such that they would rely upon it alone to identify the product as coming from a particular source. They might simply regard the shape as a characteristic of products of that kind or they might find it brings to mind the product and brand name with which they have become familiar. These kinds of recognition and association do not amount to distinctiveness for trade mark purposes, as the CJEU has now confirmed in its decision in this case.

I now turn to the various issues to which the contentions of the parties give rise and begin with the test to be applied in assessing whether a mark which is inherently nondistinctive has acquired distinctive character.

[Nestlé] submits that, for the purpose of establishing the acquisition of distinctive character by an inherently non-distinctive mark, it is not necessary to show that consumers have in fact relied upon the mark in selecting or purchasing the goods or services or that they have used the mark at some point after purchase to verify that they have chosen the right goods or services. In other words, it is not necessary to show that the mark has played any part in consumers'

> purchasing or post-transactional behaviour. Nor is it necessary to show that the mark will play a part in consumer purchasing or post-transactional behaviour in the future. The notion of 'reliance' is, he says, different from 'perception' and is one which has developed through a series of English cases, culminating in Vibe, but it has played no part in the exposition by the CJEU of what is necessary to establish distinctive character under Article 3(3) of the Directive.
>
> I cannot accept the generality of these submissions. I recognise that the CJEU has not used the term 'reliance' in giving the guidance to which I have referred. However, the essential function of a trade mark is to guarantee to consumers the origin of the goods or services in relation to which it is used by enabling them to distinguish those goods or services from others which have a different origin. Perception by consumers that goods or services designated by the mark originate from a particular undertaking means they can rely upon the mark in making or confirming their transactional decisions. In this context, reliance is a behavioural consequence of perception.
>
> (paras 77–78, 80–82)

Article 3(3) TMD 2008 mentioned here corresponds to article 4(4) TMD 2015.

The burden of proving acquired distinctiveness is on the applicant. To that end, the applicant is required to provide the trade mark office with evidence. Case 13.9 illustrates the type of evidence which is normally accepted.

Case 13.9 *The Coca-Cola Corporation v Office for Harmonization in the Internal Market (Trade Marks and Designs) (OHIM)*, Case T-411/14, EU:T:2016:94

Facts

The Coca-Cola Company (applicant–appellant) sells cola in bottles. The most famous bottle contains 'fluting' and appears in Figure 12.2. In 2011, the Coca-Cola Company sought to register an EU TM over the shape of the bottle without fluting, as it appears in Figure 13.4. The Coca-Cola Company claimed this shape without fluting had acquired a distinctive character. The OHIM examiner rejected that claim.

Issue and Procedure

The decision was appealed to the OHIM Board of Appeal which upheld the examiner's decision. Coca-Cola had submitted consumer surveys seeking to establish acquired distinctiveness, information regarding the company's sales and

Figure 13.4 Coca-Cola bottle shape without fluting

turnover and examples of their advertising materials. But this evidence was insufficient in the Board of Appeal's view. They expressed particular doubts on the reliability of the surveys on the grounds that they had not been carried out by a recognised market research company, but rather a former director of the company who had become an independent market consultant. The case was appealed to the CJEU. The CJEU upheld the Board of Appeal decision.

COURT OF JUSTICE

[I]n assessing, in a particular case, whether a mark has become distinctive through use, account must be taken of factors such as the market share held by the mark; how intensive, geographically widespread and long-standing use of the mark has been; the significance of the investments by the undertaking to promote it; the proportion of the relevant class of persons who, because of the mark, identify the goods as originating from a particular undertaking and statements from chambers of commerce and industry or other trade and professional associations. If, on the basis of those factors, the relevant class of persons, or at least a significant proportion thereof, identifies goods as originating from a particular undertaking because of the mark, it must be concluded that the requirement for registering the mark laid down in Article 7(3) of Regulation No 207/2009 is satisfied.

It is therefore necessary to ascertain whether, in the light of the case-law referred to in paragraphs 66 to 68 above, the applicant has been able to establish that the sign in question had, before the application for registration was filed, acquired distinctive character through use throughout the European Union in respect of a significant part of the relevant public. To that end, the applicant was given the opportunity to submit before OHIM various types of evidence, including those set out in paragraph 58 above.

First, as regards the surveys relied on by the applicant, it must be held that the Board of Appeal was correct to find, in paragraph 51 of the contested decision, that those surveys were not capable of proving that the mark applied for had acquired distinctive character throughout the European Union in respect of a significant part of the relevant public. The surveys were conducted in 10 EU Member States, namely Denmark, Germany, Estonia, Greece, Spain, France, Italy, Poland, Portugal and the United Kingdom, even though the European Union had 27 Member States at the date on which the application for registration was lodged. It is true that the surveys in question concluded that the mark applied for had acquired a distinctive character in the 10 Member States where they were carried out, with the recognition rate being between 48% (Poland) and 79% (Spain); however, they did not establish that that was also the case in the other 17 Member States. The results of those surveys cannot be extrapolated to the 17 Member States in which no surveys were conducted. In that regard, it must be pointed out that, particularly in respect of the countries that became members of the European Union after 2004, the surveys provide almost no information regarding the perception of the relevant public in those Member States. Even though surveys were conducted in Poland and Estonia, there is no justification for extrapolating the conclusions relating to those two countries to the other states which became members of the European Union after 2004. Furthermore, the applicant has not demonstrated that certain Member State markets covered by the surveys are comparable to others and that the results of those surveys could be extrapolated to them. It is not for the Court to make assumptions in that regard.

In the light of the foregoing, it must be concluded that the surveys are not sufficient, in themselves, to prove to the requisite standard that the mark applied for has acquired distinctive character through use, throughout the European Union, in respect of a significant part of the relevant public.

Secondly, as regards the investments which have been made in advertising and communication, it is clear from the case-law that the amount invested by the undertaking in promoting a mark may be taken into account for the purposes of considering whether that mark has acquired distinctive character through use. However, in the present case, it should be noted that the figures provided in that regard do not specifically relate to the mark applied for. According to the sworn statement made by the marketing counsel of the applicant's subsidiary in France, the figures provided refer only to the Coca-Cola, Coca-Cola Light and Coca-Cola Zero beverages without specifying which packaging is being referred to. Therefore it is not possible to draw conclusions from those figures with regard to the relevant public's perception of the mark applied for.

Thirdly, as regards the sales figures and the advertising material, it must be pointed out, first of all, that they constitute only secondary evidence which may support, where relevant, direct evidence of distinctive character acquired through use, such as provided by the surveys submitted by the applicant.

The sales figures and advertising material as such do not show that the public targeted by the goods in question perceives the mark applied

> for as an indication of commercial origin. In respect of the Member States for which no survey has been conducted, proof of distinctive character acquired through use cannot, as a rule, be furnished by the mere production of sales figures and advertising material. That particularly applies in the circumstances of the present case since it is apparent that the sales figures provided are not reliable.
>
> Thus, the Board of Appeal was correct in finding, in paragraph 57 of the contested decision, that the evidence was insufficient and unconvincing as regards the actual perception of the mark applied for.
>
> (paras 79–84, 87)

13.3 UNREGISTRABLE SIGNS

Section 3(1) lists signs that normally cannot be registered, but nevertheless can be registered if they have acquired a distinctive character through use. Subsections (2)–(6) of section 3 then list signs which can never be registered, even if they have acquired a distinctive character through use. The provisions appear below.

The TMD 2015 contains the same list in article 4(1)(e)–(h) and article 4(2).

> (2) A sign shall not be registered as a trade mark if it consists exclusively of –
>   (a) the shape or another characteristic, which results from the nature of the goods themselves,
>   (b) the shape or another characteristic, of goods which is necessary to obtain a technical result, or
>   (c) the shape or another characteristic, which gives substantial value to the goods.
> (3) A trade mark shall not be registered if it is –
>   (a) contrary to public policy or to accepted principles of morality, or
>   (b) of such a nature as to deceive the public (for instance as to the nature, quality or geographical origin of the goods or service).
> (5) A trade mark shall not be registered in the cases specified, or referred to, in section 4 (specially protected emblems).
> (6) A trade mark shall not be registered if or to the extent that the application is made in bad faith.

The rest of this section considers these exclusions in turn.

13.3.1 Shapes with Excluded Functionality

As demonstrated in Section 13.3.1, shapes can be protected by trade mark rights when they perform the sign functions explained in Section 12.1. However, there is an important exception to these principles: if the shape performs certain functions, then the shape cannot be protected even if it has acquired a distinctive character. To illustrate why, consider Activity 13.3.

ACTIVITY 13.3

Consider a rugby ball sold by a seller of sporting goods. Imagine that over time, consumers have come to recognise and rely on this shape as a badge of origin; it has accordingly acquired a distinctive character. Why should the shape not be protected as a trade mark? Hint: think about the anti- and pro-competitive consequences of protection in such a case.

Section 2(a)–(c) and associated case law explain the excluded functions.

13.3.1.1 NATURE OF THE GOODS

The trade mark application will be refused if the shape results from the 'nature of the goods themselves'. Broadly, this occurs in three situations. First, the shape may be dictated by nature: for example, the shape of a banana cannot be protected because the shape results from nature. Second, the shape may be necessary to conform to certain human-made regulations: for example, for a ball to be used in the game of rugby, it must conform to certain standards laid down by the Rugby Football Union. Third, the shape may result from 'generic features' of the goods: for example, a kettle must have a spout, a pot must have a lid. This last exclusion has been interpreted broadly by the CJEU, as Case 13.10 demonstrates.

Case 13.10 *Hauck GmbH & Co KG v Stokke A/S*, Case C-205/13, EU:C:2014:322

Facts

Mr Opsvik designed a children's chair called 'Tripp Trapp'. The chair consists of sloping uprights, to which all elements of the chair are attached, and of an L-shaped frame of uprights and gliders (sliding plates). The design of the chair won a number of prizes, was highly praised and was displayed in museums. Since 1972, 'Tripp Trapp' chairs have been marketed by Stokke and others (claimant–respondent).

Trade Marks II: Absolute Grounds for Refusal

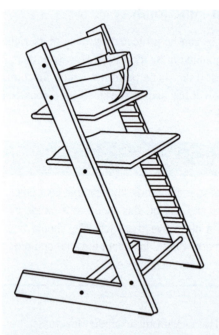

Figure 13.5 Tripp Trapp trade mark registration

On 8 May 1998, Stokke A/S filed an application with the Benelux Office for Intellectual Property for the registration of a three-dimensional trade mark resembling the 'Tripp Trapp' children's chair. The trade mark was registered in the name of Stokke A/S for 'chairs, especially high chairs for children' (Figure 13.5).

Hauck (defendant–appellant) manufactures, distributes and sells children's articles, including two chairs which it has named 'Alpha' and 'Beta'.

Issue and Procedure

Stokke brought a trade mark infringement action against Hauck in the Netherlands. Haucke counterclaimed that the trade mark registration was invalid. The trial court upheld Haucke's claim that the mark was invalid. The Netherlands Court of Appeal agreed that the trade mark was invalid on the grounds that the shape was determined by the nature of the product itself and because the shape gave the product substantial value. The Court of Appeal decision was itself appealed, and the Supreme Court of the Netherlands referred questions to the CJEU. In the next extract, the CJEU interprets the 'nature of the goods' exclusion broadly.

COURT OF JUSTICE (SECOND CHAMBER)

Consequently, in order to apply the first indent of Article 3(1)(e) of the trade marks directive correctly, it is necessary to identify the essential characteristics – that is, the most important elements – of the sign concerned on a case-by-case basis, that assessment being based either on the overall impression produced by the sign or on an examination of each the components of that sign in turn (see, to that effect, judgment in Lego Juris v OHIM, EU:C:2010:516, paragraphs 68 to 70).

In that regard, it must be emphasised that the ground for refusal of registration set out in the first indent of Article 3(1)(e) of the trade

Article 3(1)(e) TMD 2008 mentioned here corresponds to article 4(1)(e) TMD 2015.

marks directive cannot be applicable where the trade mark application relates to a shape of goods in which another element, such as a decorative or imaginative element, which is not inherent to the generic function of the goods, plays an important or essential role (see, to that effect, judgment in Lego Juris v OHIM, EU:C:2010:516, paragraphs 52 and 72).

Thus, an interpretation of the first indent of that provision whereby that indent is to apply only to signs which consist exclusively of shapes which are indispensable to the function of the goods in question, leaving the producer of those goods no leeway to make a personal essential contribution, would not allow the objective of the ground for refusal set out therein to be fully realised.

Indeed, an interpretation to that effect would result in limiting the products to which that ground for refusal could apply to (i) 'natural' products (which have no substitute) and (ii) 'regulated' products (the shape of which is prescribed by legal standards), even though signs consisting of the shapes formed by such products could not be registered in any event because of their lack of distinctive character.

Instead, when applying the ground for refusal set out in the first indent of Article 3(1)(e) of the trade marks directive, account should be taken of the fact that the concept of a 'shape which results from the nature of the goods themselves' means that shapes with essential characteristics which are inherent to the generic function or functions of such goods must, in principle, also be denied registration.

As the Advocate General indicated in point 58 of his Opinion, reserving such characteristics to a single economic operator would make it difficult for competing undertakings to give their goods a shape which would be suited to the use for which those goods are intended. Moreover, it is clear that those are essential characteristics which consumers will be looking for in the products of competitors, given that they are intended to perform an identical or similar function.

(paras 21–26)

13.3.1.2 TECHNICAL RESULT

Shapes which are necessary to obtain a 'technical' result are also denied protection. This is sometimes known as **utilitarian functionality**.

The concept of 'technical' character was covered in Part II in the discussion of patents. That Part explained how there is a plausible argument granting an inventor a twenty-year monopoly over their inventions (knowledge with technical character) will result in good consequences for society overall (e.g. more invention, more disclosure). However, there is no plausible argument that inventors should perpetually own their inventions: the costs of such protection clearly outweigh the benefits.

Granting trade marks on signs that produce a technical result would amount to a perpetual monopoly over the technical result. This occurs because, unlike patents, trade marks can be renewed an infinite number of times. It is accordingly important for trade mark law to prevent perpetual monopoly over inventions, as Case 13.11 illustrates.

Case 13.11 *Koninklijke Philips v Remington*, Case 299/99 [2002] ECR I–5475

Facts

In 1966, Philips (claimant–appellant) developed a new type of three-headed rotary electric shaver. The shaver was protected by various patents. In 1985, after the expiry of the relevant patents, Philips filed an application to register a trade mark consisting of a graphic representation of the shape and configuration of the head of such a shaver, comprising three circular heads with rotating blades in the shape of an equilateral triangle (Figure 13.6). The mark was granted.

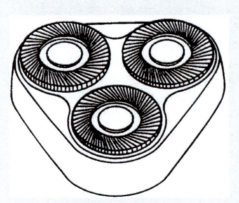

Figure 13.6 Philips trade mark registration

In 1995, Remington (defendant–respondent), a competing company, began to manufacture and sell in the United Kingdom the DT 55, which is a shaver with three rotating heads forming an equilateral triangle, shaped similarly to that used by Philips.

Issue and Procedure

Philips sued Remington for infringement of its trade mark. Remington counterclaimed for revocation of the trade mark registered by Philips. Among other findings, the High Court of Justice of England and Wales, Chancery Division (Patents Court) (United Kingdom), revoked the trade mark on the grounds that it consisted exclusively of a shape which was necessary to obtain a technical result (that is, better shaving function). Philips appealed to the Court of Appeal. Philips argued that a shape should only be denied protection if there are no other available shapes which could also perform the technical function. The Court of Appeal referred several questions for preliminary ruling to the CJEU. Below the CJEU explain why the exclusion applies even if there are other shapes capable of performing the function.

COURT OF JUSTICE

As regards, in particular, signs consisting exclusively of the shape of the product necessary to obtain a technical result, listed in Article 3(1)(e), second indent, of the Directive, that provision is intended to preclude the registration of shapes whose essential characteristics perform a technical function, with the result that the exclusivity inherent in the trade mark right would limit the possibility of competitors supplying a product incorporating such a function or at least limit their freedom of choice in regard to the technical solution they wish to adopt in order to incorporate such a function in their product.

As Article 3(1)(e) of the Directive pursues an aim which is in the public interest, namely that a shape whose essential characteristics perform a technical function and were chosen to fulfil that function may be freely used by all, that provision prevents such signs and indications from being reserved to one undertaking alone because they have been registered as trade marks (see, to that effect, Windsurfing Chiemsee, paragraph 25).

As to the question whether the establishment that there are other shapes which could achieve the same technical result can overcome the ground for refusal or invalidity contained in Article 3(1)(e), second indent, there is nothing in the wording of that provision to allow such a conclusion

In refusing registration of such signs, Article 3(1)(e), second indent, of the Directive reflects the legitimate aim of not allowing individuals to use registration of a mark in order to acquire or perpetuate exclusive rights relating to technical solutions.

Where the essential functional characteristics of the shape of a product are attributable solely to the technical result, Article 3(1)(e), second indent, precludes registration of a sign consisting of that shape, even if that technical result can be achieved by other shapes.

(paras 79–83)

Subsequent to the *Philips* case, the CJEU has concluded that the characteristics of the Christiansen Toy Building Brick (illustrated in Figure 6.1) (e.g. the studs on top, and the tubes inside) are functional, and therefore the shape of the brick cannot be a registered trade mark.[18] However, the shape of the Lego mini-figures (illustrated in Figure 6.6) were not functional by this standard, and could be registered.[19]

13.3.1.3 SUBSTANTIAL VALUE

The shape also will be denied protection if it gives '**substantial value**' to the goods. For some time, 'substantial value' was interpreted as aesthetic value. For example, the Trip Trapp chair in *Hauck* was denied protection not only because the shape was necessary to achieve a technical result, but also because it was aesthetically attractive. The shape had not only technical functionality but also *aesthetic* functionality. The chair's aesthetic qualities should be protected, if at all, by copyright and/or industrial designs.

But more recently the CJEU has widened the scope of this rule beyond aesthetic functionality, as Case 13.12 demonstrates.

Case 13.12 *Gömböc Kutató, Szolgáltató és Kereskedelmi Kft. v Szellemi Tulajdon Nemzeti Hivatala*, Case C-237/19, EU: C:2020:296

Facts

The Gömböc is a three-dimensional shape. It has only one point of stable equilibrium. As a result, if someone places the shape on a flat surface (like a table), the shape will naturally return to its upright position – as depicted in Figure 13.7. The shape was first conjectured by Russian mathematician Vladimir Arnold in 1995. In 2006, Hungarian scientists Gábor Domokos and Péter Várkonyi made the first real-world model of the shape. Together the achievements of Arnold, Domokos and Várkonyi represent a modern mathematical breakthrough.

Figure 13.7 Gömböc.
Author: Domokos. Dedicated to the public domain. From Wikimedia Commons

The Hungarian company Gömböc Kutató (applicant–appellant) applied to the Hungarian trade mark office for trade mark protection over the three-dimensional sign in relation to 'decorative crystalware and chinaware' and 'toys'.

Issue and Procedure

The trade mark application was rejected on the grounds that the shape was necessary to achieve a technical result and because its striking and attractive shape gave it substantial value. Gömböc Kutató appealed the decision and the appellate court referred questions to the CJEU. In this case, part of the value provided by the shape was not aesthetic, but also how the shape had 'become the tangible symbol of a mathematical discovery which addresses questions raised in the history of science'. The CJEU below explains that this feature of the good also gives the shape substantial value, even though that is not connected to any aesthetic functionality.

COURT OF JUSTICE (FIFTH CHAMBER)

In the present case, it is apparent from the order for reference that, as regards the goods coming within the category of 'decorative items' and 'decorative crystalware and chinaware' in Classes 14 and 21 of the Nice Agreement, the perception and knowledge of the product by the relevant public were taken into consideration at first instance in finding, as regards the application of the ground for refusal provided for in Article 3(1)(e)(iii) of Directive 2008/95, that, whatever assessment that product merits from an aesthetic point of view, the substantial value of that product was conferred on it by the fact that that shape, which alone forms the sign at issue, has become the tangible symbol of a mathematical discovery.

In that regard, it must be borne in mind that, although the presumed perception of the sign at issue by the average consumer is not, in itself, a decisive element when applying the ground for refusal set out in Article 3(1)(e)(iii) of Directive 2008/95, it may, nevertheless, be a useful criterion of assessment for the competent authority in identifying the essential characteristics of that sign (see, by analogy, judgment of 18 September 2014, Hauck, C 205/13, EU:C:2014:2233, paragraph 34).

It follows that, in a situation such as that at issue in the main proceedings, Article 3(1)(e)(iii) of Directive 2008/95 allows the competent authority to find, in the light of the perception of the sign at issue by the relevant public and the knowledge of that public, that the shape which alone forms the sign is the tangible symbol of a mathematic discovery. Since it took the view that that fact makes that shape special and striking, the competent authority was entitled to conclude that it is an essential characteristic, within the meaning of the case-law referred to in paragraph 44 above, and that it was necessary to assess whether, as a result of that fact, the shape which alone forms the sign at issue gives substantial value to the goods.

The fact that such a characteristic does not, in itself, concern the aesthetic merits of the shape does not exclude the application of Article 3(1)(e)(iii) of Directive 2008/95. It should be borne in mind, in this regard, that the concept of a 'shape which gives substantial value to the goods' is not limited to the shape of goods having an exclusively artistic or ornamental value. The question as to whether the shape gives substantial value to the goods may be examined on the basis of other relevant factors, including, inter alia, whether the shape is dissimilar from other shapes in common use on the market concerned (see, by analogy, judgment of 18 September 2014, Hauck, C 205/13, EU:C:2014:2233, paragraphs 32 and 35).

(paras 43–46)

ACTIVITY 13.4

Chapter 12 explained how signs are not goods, and thus trade mark law does not grant monopolies over goods. Is that characterisation true when one takes into account how frequently shapes can be protected by trade mark law?

13.3.2 Public Policy or Morality

Applications will also be refused if the sign contravenes public policy or accepted principles of morality. Trade mark applications relating to the words LA MAFIA and CANNABIS STORE AMSTERDAM have been rejected on grounds of public policy because of the sign's connection to illegal activities.[20] Applications on words such as JESUS, TINY PENIS and PAKI have been rejected on the grounds of morality.[21]

As Richard Arnold QC (as he then was) in *French Connection UK* wrote, the rationale behind the public policy or morality absolute ground of refusal is far from clear.[22] Unlike other areas of trade mark law, this provision does not seem connected to promoting competition between sellers in any meaningful way. Indeed, the section even creates a paradox: if the trade mark is refused on the ground that it is immoral, then more people can actually use the sign in commerce. Furthermore, as Case 13.13 demonstrates, creating objective standards for assessing morality is at best difficult.

Case 13.13 *Constantin Film Produktion v EUIPO*, Case C-240/18, EU:C:2020:118

Facts

Constantin Film Produktion (applicant–appellant) produced a German-language comedy film called *Fack Ju Göhte*. The title is a play on the words 'Fuck You Göthe'; (where Göthe is deliberately misspelled). On 21 April 2015, Constantin filed an application for registration of an EU trade mark with EUIPO on the sign *Fack Ju Göhte*. The application was rejected on the grounds of that the sign was against accepted principles of morality.

Issue and Procedure

The EUIPO Board of Appeal rejected Constantin's appeal. Thereafter the decision was appealed to the General Court of the CJEU where the appeal was again dismissed. In the following extract, the Court of Justice of the CJEU overturned the EU IPO and General Court's decisions finding that the sign could be registered.

Article 7(1)(f) Regulation No 207/2009 mentioned here contains the same rule as the current article (4)(1)(f) TMD 2015.

COURT OF JUSTICE (FIFTH CHAMBER)

In order to establish whether that is the case, the examination is to be based on the perception of a reasonable person with average thresholds of sensitivity and tolerance, taking into account the context in which the mark may be encountered and, where appropriate, the particular circumstances of the part of the Union concerned. To that end, elements such as legislation and administrative practices, public opinion and, where appropriate, the way in which the relevant public has reacted in the past to that sign or similar signs, as well as any other factor which may make it possible to assess the perception of that public, are relevant.

The examination to be carried out cannot be confined to an abstract assessment of the mark applied for, or even of certain components of it, but it must be established, in particular where an applicant has relied on factors that are liable to cast doubt on the fact that that mark is perceived by the relevant public as contrary to accepted principles of morality, that the use of that mark in the concrete and current social context would indeed be perceived by that public as being contrary to the fundamental moral values and standards of society.

It is in the light of those principles that the merits of the first ground of appeal, alleging that the General Court erred in its interpretation and application of Article 7(1)(f) of Regulation No 207/2009, must be examined.

[The General Court] concluded in paragraph 20 of the judgment under appeal that, in those circumstances, the Board of Appeal had rightly found that the English expression 'Fuck you' – and, therefore, the mark applied for as a whole – were inherently vulgar and liable to offend the relevant public. Consequently, the Board had been right to infer that the mark applied for had to be refused registration on the basis of Article 7(1)(f) of Regulation No 207/2009.

In that connection, it must be held that the examination carried out by the General Court does not meet the standards required by Article 7(1)(f) of Regulation No 207/2009, as set out in paragraphs 39 to 43 of this judgment.

In fact, having regard to the social context and the factors relied on in that regard by the appellant – and in particular the fact that the word sign 'Fack Ju Göhte' corresponds, as the General Court noted in paragraphs 2 and 19 of the judgment under appeal, to a German cinematic comedy produced by the appellant, having been one of the greatest film successes of 2013 in Germany and having been seen by several million people when it was released in cinemas – the General Court, in order to establish to the requisite legal standard that the mark applied for is perceived by the German-speaking public at large as contrary to accepted principles of morality, could not confine itself to an abstract assessment of that mark and of the English expression to which the first part of it is assimilated by that public.

Thus, the fact that it is that mark itself which is to be examined does not mean that, in the course of that examination, contextual elements capable of shedding light on how the relevant public perceives that mark could be disregarded.

As the Advocate General observes in point 94 of his Opinion, those factors include the great success of the comedy of the same name amongst the German-speaking public at large and the fact that its title does not appear to have caused controversy, as well as the fact that access to it by young people had been authorised and that the Goethe Institute – which is the cultural institute of the Federal Republic of Germany, active worldwide and tasked, inter alia, with promoting knowledge of the German language – uses it for educational purposes.

In so far as those factors are, a priori, capable of constituting an indication that, notwithstanding the assimilation of the first part of the mark applied for to the English phrase 'Fuck you', the German-speaking public at large does not perceive the word sign 'Fack Ju Göhte' as morally unacceptable, the General Court, in concluding that that sign is incompatible with accepted principles of morality, could not rely solely on the intrinsically vulgar character of that English phrase without examining those factors or setting out conclusively the reasons why it considered, despite those factors, that the German-speaking public at large perceives that sign as running counter to the fundamental moral values and standards of society when it is used as a trade mark.

Lastly, it should also be added that, contrary to the General Court's finding in paragraph 29 of the judgment under appeal, that 'there is, in the field of art, culture and literature, a constant concern to preserve freedom of expression which does not exist in the field of trade marks', freedom of expression, enshrined in Article 11 of the Charter of Fundamental Rights of the European Union, must, as EUIPO acknowledged at the hearing and as the Advocate General states in points 47 to 57 of his Opinion, be taken into account when applying Article 7(1)(f) of Regulation No 207/2009. Such a finding is

> corroborated, moreover, by recital 21 of Regulation No 2015/2424, which amended Regulation No 207/2009 and recital 21 of Regulation 2017/1001, both of which expressly emphasise the need to apply those regulations in such a way as to ensure full respect for fundamental rights and freedoms, in particular freedom of expression.
>
> It follows from all of the foregoing considerations that the interpretation and application of Article 7(1)(f) of Regulation No 207/2009, as carried out by the General Court in the judgment under appeal, are vitiated by errors of law, which are sufficient in themselves for the Court of Justice to allow the first ground of appeal, without it being necessary to examine the other arguments relied on by the appellant in support of that ground of appeal.
>
> (paras 42–44, 48–53, 56–57)

ACTIVITY 13.5

Do you see any good reason for refusing trade marks for immoral signs?

13.3.3 Deceptive Marks

Applications shall also be denied if the sign may deceive consumers as to the nature of the goods or services. For example, the word mark CAFFÈ NERO (which means 'black coffee') would be deceptive if used in relation to tea;[23] TITAN (which means 'titanium' in German) would be deceptive if used on non-titanium building materials;[24] WINE OH! would be deceptive if used on non-alcoholic beverages.[25]

The CJEU has confirmed that the risk of deception must be a real and serious one. In the *Elizabeth Emmanuel* case, the wedding dress designer, Elizabeth Emmanuel, assigned her business and the trade mark in the words ELIZABETH EMMANUEL to a third party. Later Emmanuel then opposed the third-party's registration of the ELIZABETH EMMANUEL sign on the grounds that the use of the sign would deceive the public (i.e. they would think the dresses were designed by her). The opposition was denied and the CJEU held there must be some 'actual deceit' or a 'sufficiently serious risk' of deception before the registration will be denied.[26] The result is that a relatively small number of marks will be denied on this ground.

Similarly, a trade mark which is granted on a sign which, after grant, has been used in a deceptive way, will be revoked (see Section 12.4).

13.3.4 Specially Protected Emblems

Section 3(5) prevents protection of 'specially protected emblems'. Section 4 of the TMA lists what those 'specially protected emblems' are. They include emblems related to the crown, such as the royal arms or royal crown. Also prohibited are

Trade Marks II: Absolute Grounds for Refusal

trade marks on national flags, like the Union Jack, and signs associated with the Olympics and Paralympics (such as the five rings).

13.3.5 Bad Faith

Last, but not least, section 3(6) states that marks will be refused if the application is made in bad faith. In Case 13.14, the CJEU clarifies when such a refusal is appropriate.

Case 13.14 *Sky v SkyKick*, Case C-371/18, EU:C:2020:45

Facts

Sky (appellant–claimant) sells television broadcasting, telephony and broadband. Sky owns trade marks in relation to the word SKY. These trade marks were registered in respect to a large class of goods and services including computer software. SkyKick (respondent–defendant) provides cloud management services.

Issue and Procedure

Sky brought a trade mark infringement action against SkyKick. SkyKick brought a counterclaim seeking a declaration that Sky's trade marks were invalid. SkyKick raised various grounds for refusal, including bad faith. SkyKick argued that the marks were registered in bad faith because Sky had no intention of using the SKY mark in relation to computer software. The High Court of Justice (England & Wales) referred questions on the scope of the bad faith provision to the Court of Justice.

COURT OF JUSTICE (FOURTH CHAMBER)

Consequently, the absolute ground for invalidity referred to in Article 51 (1)(b) of Regulation No 40/94 and Article 3(2)(d) of First Directive 89/104 applies where it is apparent from relevant and consistent indicia that the proprietor of a trade mark has filed the application for registration of that mark not with the aim of engaging fairly in competition but with the intention of undermining, in a manner inconsistent with honest practices, the interests of third parties, or with the intention of obtaining, without even targeting a specific third party, an exclusive right for purposes other than those falling within the functions of a trade mark, in particular the essential function of indicating origin recalled in the previous paragraph of the present judgment (judgment of 13 September 2019, *Koton Mağazacilik Tekstil Sanayi ve Ticaret* v *EUIPO*, C-104/18 P, EU:C:2019:724, paragraph 46).

Admittedly, the applicant for a trade mark is not required to indicate or even to know precisely, on the date on which his or her

> application for registration of a mark is filed or of the examination of that application, the use he or she will make of the mark applied for and he or she has a period of 5 years for beginning actual use consistent with the essential function of that trade mark (see, to that effect, judgment of 13 September 2019, *Deutsches Patent- und Markenamt (#darferdas?)*, C-541/18, EU:C:2019:725, paragraph 22).
>
> However, as the Advocate General observed in point 109 of his Opinion, the registration of a trade mark by an applicant without any intention to use it in relation to the goods and services covered by that registration may constitute bad faith, where there is no rationale for the application for registration in the light of the aims referred to in Regulation No 40/94 and First Directive 89/104. Such bad faith may, however, be established only if there is objective, relevant and consistent indicia tending to show that, when the application for a trade mark was filed, the trade mark applicant had the intention either of undermining, in a manner inconsistent with honest practices, the interests of third parties, or of obtaining, without even targeting a specific third party, an exclusive right for purposes other than those falling within the functions of a trade mark.
>
> The bad faith of the trade mark applicant cannot, therefore, be presumed on the basis of the mere finding that, at the time of filing his or her application, that applicant had no economic activity corresponding to the goods and services referred to in that application.
>
> (paras 75–78)

There are broadly two situations where an application will be considered to have been filed with the intention of undermining the interests of third parties. The first situation is the type presented in the *Sky* case. When the case was returned to the High Court, Sky's trade marks in relation to computer software were declared invalid on the ground that there was an intention to undermine the interests of other businesses rather than obtain a trade mark to help the sign perform the sign functions explained in Section 12.1. Subsequently the case was overturned by the Court of Appeal finding that Sky's intention to use was 'implicit'.[27]

At the time of writing, however, the *SkyKick* case is being further appealed to the UK Supreme Court.

The second case type of situation occurs where the business applies for a trade mark to deliberately disadvantage a specific and known competitor. For example, in the Austrian *Lindt & Sprüngli v Hauswirth* case, both Lindt and Hauswirth sold chocolate bunny rabbits wrapped in gold foil complete with a red bow around its neck. Lindt applied for a trade mark on the shape of the bunny and it was alleged that the application was made to disadvantage other businesses, like Hauswirth.[28] As with the *SkyKick* case, the CJEU emphasised the need for an intention to prevent third parties from continuing to use the sign. When the case was returned to the Austrian courts, Lindt's application was upheld as having not been made in bad faith.

13.4 SUMMARY

What type of phenomena can be protected by trade mark law? Broadly, the answer is: nearly anything that performs the sign functions, and particularly, the origin function. In most cases, granting protection to such signs will result in relatively modest anti-competitive effects, and quite significant pro-competitive effects.

There are two departures from the basic principle that nearly anything can be a trade mark. First, in some cases, such as certain types of shapes, the anti-competitive effects of protection are so great that trade mark protection should be avoided even if the sign in question can perform the sign functions. Second, in some cases, some trade marks will be rejected on grounds which have nothing to do with competition. In cases where the sign contravenes public policy or morality, or even where registration occurs in bad faith, concerns of competition give way in favour of broader ethical concerns.

13.5 SELF-ASSESSMENT

Before moving on, try to answer the following questions to consolidate your learning. Answers are provided in the section below.

1. The following four trade mark applications have been made to the UK IPO. Which application is most likely to be rejected?
   a. A 'green-gold' colour (Pantone 15-0636) for a telecommunications company (shown below) with evidence of acquired distinctive character.

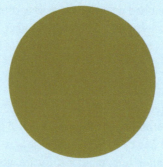

   b. The word 'bananas' for a computer technology company.
   c. The word 'strawberries' for a company selling strawberries.
   d. The following symbol for a rock band:

Figure 13.8 Rock icon.
Image: Flaticon.com

2. Which of the following is true regarding the acquisition of a distinctive character?

   a. Evidence of acquired distinctive character can include the extent and duration of use of the trade mark, as well as marketing and advertising efforts.

   b. A sign can only have acquired a distinctive character if it has been used for at least five years.

   c. A sign can only be registered if it is inherently distinctive.

   d. A sign acquires a distinctive character when consumers recognise it.

3. In *Société des Produits Nestlé SA v Cadbury UK Ltd* [2013] EWCA Civ 1174, Cadbury tried to trade mark the following: 'The colour purple (Pantone 2685C)... applied to the whole visible surface, or being the predominant colour applied to the whole visible surface, of the packaging of [chocolate] goods'. Which of the following best describes the court's decision regarding the application?

   a. The application was rejected because it was not accompanied by a sample.

   b. The application was rejected because it did not constitute a sign capable of representation.

   c. The application was accepted because it was accompanied by an international colour code.

   d. The application was accepted because it had acquired distinctiveness.

4. In Section 12.3.1, Nicolas Economides argued that trade marks do not create monopolies in goods. Using the material presented in this chapter, evaluate this argument.

ACTIVITY DISCUSSION

Activity 13.1 The way the courts have interpreted the section 1 requirements illustrates the functionalist metaphysical approach to signs. Although there are some very minimal limits – as discussed in *Dyson* – almost anything can be a sign, providing it can be represented with sufficient clarity and precision on the register. The crucial question is whether the phenomenon (whether it is a word, a smell, a hologram, etc.), performs the core function of a sign, that is, to indicate origin of the goods or services.

Activity 13.2 (1) Allowing the seller to register the word LAPTOP would have bad effects on competition. Other laptop sellers would find it hard to sell their goods without using the word 'laptop'. The result would be a depressing effect on competition. At the same time, there is no pro-competitive effects offsetting the anti-competitive effects. The word LAPTOP is not distinctive to the seller. The result is the word could hardly be expected to serve as a good badge of origin, thus facilitating consumer choice and competition between sellers.

   (2) The answer is different in the case of POTPAL. Granting the trade mark would not seem to limit the ability of other businesses in a significant way. On the other hand, POTPAL, being quite an unusual word, might well be distinctive in the minds of consumers. The overall effect therefore may be to encourage consumer choice and competition between sellers.

Activity 13.3 Allowing a seller to register the shape of the rugby ball would have clearly negative effects on competition as it would restrict the ability of other sellers to sell rugby balls. The result would be a monopoly and higher prices for consumers. Even if the sign somehow acquired a distinctive character, it seems that the anti-competitive effects would be so great that consumers would lose out overall.

Activity 13.4 The absolute grounds for refusal listed in section 3 prevent parties from using trade marks to acquire perpetual monopolies in goods. One good consequence of cases like *Hauck* and

Gömböc is that the courts apply the exceptions quite robustly. However, potentially these exceptions provide only a modest safeguard against monopolies in goods, given how flexible and open section 1 is interpreted.

Activity 13.5 There may be no clear answer to this question. As Mr Justice Arnold's judgment suggests, the problem flummoxes even the best IP law minds.

For my part, however, it makes sense when one considers the philosophical underpinnings of trade marks. No business has a natural right to a sign used in commerce. Instead, the trade mark is a privilege granted to the business by the state. The state arguably should not award businesses with privileges for using signs which are clearly against society's values. Of course, the state should not prevent the business from using the sign, but nor should the state show any particular favour to that business.

SELF-ASSESSMENT ANSWERS

1. **Correct answer: c.** 'Strawberries' for strawberries is descriptive. A green-gold colour for telecommunications also may also lack an inherent distinctive character, but the evidence of acquired distinctive character may save it.
2. **Correct answer: a.** These factors are referenced in *Coca-Cola Corporation v Office for Harmonization in the Internal Market (Trade Marks and Designs) (OHIM)*, Case T-411/14, EU:T:2016:94.
3. **Correct answer: b**. The term 'predominantly' meant that the sign could not be registered in a manner that would enable the relevant authorities and the public to determine the clear and precise subject matter protected by the proprietor.

Notes

1 TMA 1994, s 47.

2 First Council Directive 89/104/EEC of 21 December 1988 to approximate the laws of the Member States relating to trade marks, art 2.

3 See Pantone Colours <https://www.pantone-colours.com/> (accessed April 2023).

4 [2022] EWHC 1671 (Ch).

5 See *Dyson v Registrar of Trade Marks* [2003] EWHC 1062 (Ch).

6 But see *Fromageries Bel SA v J Sainsbury plc* [2019] EWHC 3454 (Ch).

7 See eg *Linde A*, *Winward Industries*, *Rado Watch*, Cases C-53/01, C-54/01 and C-55/01 [2003] ECR I–3161, [41]; *Société des Produits Nestlé v Mars ('Have a Break')* [2004] FSR (2) 16 [23]. See also Ilanah Fhima and Dev S Gangjee, *The Confusion Test in European Trade Mark Law* (OUP 2019) 134–59.

8 UK IPO, *Letter and Numeral Marks* (May 2006) PAN 10/06.

9 ibid.

10 *Cain Cellars v OHIM*, Case T-304/05 [2007] ECR II–113*, [22].

11 *Nestlé v Mars* [2003] EWCA Civ 1072, [2003] ETMR (101) 1335.

12 *Elvis Presley Trade Marks* [1997] RPC 543, 558.

13 *Storck v OHIM*, Case C25/05 P [2006] ECR I-5719 [30]–[33].

14 *Campina Melkunie v Benelux-Merkenbureau*, Case C-265/00 [2004] ECR I–1699.

15 *Wrigley (Doublemint)*, Case C-191/01P [2003] ECR I–13447.

16 *Campina Melkunie* (n 14) [39].

17 *Bayer Co v United Drug Co*, 272 F 505 (SDNY 1921) (US).

18 *Lego Juris A/S v OHIM*, Case C-48/09P [2010] ECR I–8403 (Grand Chamber).

19 *Best-Lock (Europe) Ltd v OHIM, Lego Juris A/S*, Case T-395/14, EU:T:2015:380, affd Case C-451/15P, EU:C:2016:269.

20 *La Mafia Franchises v EUIPO*, Case T-1/17, EU:T:2018:146.

21 Basic Trademark [2005] RPC 611. *Ghazilian's Application* [2002] RPC 628. *PAKI Logistics v OHIM*, Case C-526/09.

22 *FCUK* [2007] RPC 1 [54].

23 *Caffè Nero*, Case T-29/16, EU:T:2016:635.

24 *Portakabin*, R 789/2001–3.

25 *Wine Oh!'s Application*, R 1074/2005–4 [2006] ETMR (95) 1319.

26 *Elizabeth Florence Emanuel v Continental Shelf 138*, Case C-259/04 [2006] ECR I–3089.

27 *Sky Ltd (formerly Sky plc) v Skykick UK Ltd* [2021] EWCA Civ 1131.

28 *Lindt*, Case C-529/07 [2009] ECR I–4893.

FIGURE ACKNOWLEDGEMENTS

13.1 EU trade mark number 000951871. Owner name London EV Company Limited. *London Taxi Corp v Frazer-Nash Research Ltd* [2017] EWCA Civ 1729

13.2 German trade mark Registernummer 2069767. Owner WSC Windsurfing Chiemsee AG & Co KG, 83355 Grabenstätt, DE

13.3 From *Société des Produits Nestlé SA Appellant v Cadbury UK Ltd* [2017] EWCA Civ 358. Nestlé UK trade mark application 8 July 2010.

13.4 EU trade mark number 010532687. Application withdrawn.

13.5 Benelux trade mark number 915680. Owner: STOKKE AS. Date of registration: 01-06-1999. As reproduced in *Hauck GmbH & Co KG v Stokke A/S*, Case C-205/13, EU:C:2014:322

13.6 Trade mark number UK00001533452. Trade mark cancelled

13.7 Author: Domokos. Dedicated to the public domain. From Wikimedia Commons <https://commons.wikimedia.org/wiki/File:Gomboc2.jpg>

14

Trade Marks III: Scope

When Lord Langdale decided the case of *Croft v Day*, businesses had no rights –
let alone property rights – in their signs. Their right was in the goodwill or reputation
of their business. But that is not the law today. Section 2 of the TMA states that trade
marks are not only rights, but property rights. The question for this chapter is whether
that is true. While it is certainly true that the trade mark is a right in a sign, is it a
property right? Is it a right to exclusively control how the sign is used? Should it be?

It is helpful to split the chapter into three sections. The first section considers the
relative grounds for refusal. In certain situations, a trade mark owner can use their
registered trade mark to prevent later businesses from acquiring trade mark rights. The
second section considers infringement actions. This section discusses the situations
wherein a trade mark owner can prevent other businesses using the sign in the course
of trade. As the relative grounds for refusal and the law on infringement involve a
similar set of concepts, the case law in these two sections is highly interchangeable.
Finally, the chapter turns to defences to infringement before summarising.

14.1   RELATIVE GROUNDS FOR REFUSAL

*Frequently ownership of an
earlier trade mark will form the
basis of an opposition
proceedings.*

Section 5 of the TMA 1995 lists three situations wherein a trade mark application
will be refused due to the presence of an earlier mark. These situations can be
called 'double identity', 'confusing similarity' and 'free riding or dilution'. This
section considers each in turn.

14.1.1   Double Identity

A trade mark application will be refused under section 5(2)(a) of the TMA when it
is 'identical with an earlier trade mark and is to be registered for goods or services

This chapter contains public sector information licensed under the Open Government Licence v3.0.

similar to those for which the earlier trade mark is protected'. This is known as **'double identity'** because it requires identity of signs and identity of goods or services.

Applying the double identity provision is rarely problematic for courts. Whether signs are identical depends on whether the average consumer (introduced in Section 13.2) would perceive them as such. The CJEU has decided that while the provision should be interpreted strictly, the average consumer would not notice 'insignificant differences' between signs.[1] As a result, WEBSPHERE and WEB-SPHERE were held to be identical – both in relation to computer software.[2] Although KCS HERR VOSS and HERR-VOSS were considered not to be identical.[3]

The rationale for the double identity is straightforward. Consider the *Websphere* case. The earlier mark – WEBSPHERE – was granted because doing so would lead to pro-competitive effects: it would allow consumers to recognise providers of computer software, to compare them, and thus facilitate competition between them (see Section 12.3.1). But the pro-competitive effects of the trade mark would be severely harmed if WEB-SPHERE was later granted. Consumers surely would be confused about the origin of their computer software with both WEBSPHERE and WEB-SPHERE operating in the market.

> The same rules can be found in article 5 TMD 2015, in relation to EU trade marks. Under the old Trade Mark Directive 2008 the relevant provision was article 4.

14.1.2 Confusing Similarity

Most trade mark applications do not involve situations of double identity. More often, a trade mark application will be refused under section 5(2)(b) of the TMA for confusing similarity. The later sign will be confusingly similar to a prior sign when the following three conditions are met:

i. the sign is similar or identical to an earlier registered trademark; and
ii. the sign is to be used on similar or identical goods or services as the earlier registered trade mark; and
iii. because of the similarities there exists a likelihood of confusion on the part of the public.

Whether two signs are confusingly similar is subject to the **'global appreciation'** analysis. The global appreciation analysis is introduced in the following cases of *Sabel v Puma* and *Cannon Kabushiki Kaisha v Metro-Goldwyn-Mayer Inc*.

Case 14.1 *Sabel BV v Puma, Rudolf Dassler Sport*, Case C-251/95 [1997] ECR I–6191

Facts

Puma (opponent–respondent) owned a German trade mark for the silhouette of a moving puma (Figure 14.1) in relation to leather bags and clothes. Sabel (applicant–appellant) applied for a German trade mark on a sign which combined the image of a jumping cat and the word 'sabel' to be used in relation to clothes. Puma opposed the registration of Sabel's mark.

Figure 14.1 Puma sign ((a)); Sabel sign ((b))

Issue and Procedure

Initially the German Patent Office rejected the opposition on the grounds that the two signs were dissimilar. Puma appealed to the German Federal Patents Court and won. Sabel appealed to the Federal Court of Justice. The Federal Court of Justice provisionally concluded that there was a risk of confusion because of the similarity of the signs' 'semantic content' i.e. both represented bounding felines.

The court paused proceedings to ask whether similarity of semantic content was sufficient to find the marks to be confusingly similar. In the next extract, the CJEU explains the 'global appreciation' test for confusing similarity.

COURT OF JUSTICE

Article 4(1)(b) TMD 1988 mentioned here corresponds to article 5(1)(b) TMD 2015.

As pointed out in paragraph 18 of this judgment, Article 4(1)(b) of the Directive does not apply where there is no likelihood of confusion on the part of the public. In that respect, it is clear from the tenth recital in the preamble to the Directive that the appreciation of the likelihood of confusion 'depends on numerous elements and, in particular, on the recognition of the trade mark on the market, of the association which can be made with the used or registered sign, of the degree of similarity between the trade mark and the sign and between the goods or services identified'. The likelihood of confusion must therefore be appreciated globally, taking into account all factors relevant to the circumstances of the case.

That global appreciation of the visual, aural or conceptual similarity of the marks in question, must be based on the overall impression given by the marks, bearing in mind, in particular, their distinctive and dominant components. The wording of Article 4(1)(b) of the

Directive – 'there exists a likelihood of confusion on the part of the public' – shows that the perception of marks in the mind of the average consumer of the type of goods or services in question plays a decisive role in the global appreciation of the likelihood of confusion. The average consumer normally perceives a mark as a whole and does not proceed to analyse its various details.

In that perspective, the more distinctive the earlier mark, the greater will be the likelihood of confusion. It is therefore not impossible that the conceptual similarity resulting from the fact that two marks use images with analogous semantic content may give rise to a likelihood of confusion where the earlier mark has a particularly distinctive character, either *per se* or because of the reputation it enjoys with the public.

However, in circumstances such as those in point in the main proceedings, where the earlier mark is not especially well known to the public and consists of an image with little imaginative content, the mere fact that the two marks are conceptually similar is not sufficient to give rise to a likelihood of confusion.

(paras 22–25)

ACTIVITY 14.1

Should 'well-known' signs enjoy broader protection?

Points (i), (ii) and (iii) are all necessary conditions. As a result, two signs are only confusingly similar under a global appreciation analysis if each condition is satisfied. Nevertheless, there is some 'interdependence' between the three steps, as Case 14.2 illustrates.

Case 14.2 *Canon Kabushiki Kaisha v Metro-Goldwyn-Mayer Inc* [1999] 1 CMLR 77

Facts

Canon Kabushiki Kaisha (CKK) (opponent) owned a German trade mark for the word 'CANON' in respect of cameras. In 1986, the predecessor company to Metro-Goldwyn-Mayer Inc (MGM) (applicant) applied for a German trade mark for the word CANNON to be used in relation to 'films recorded on video cassettes'. CKK opposed the registration on the relative ground of confusing similarity.

Issue and Procedure

The German Patent Office granted the MGM trade mark. The Federal Patent Court dismissed CKK's appeal against that decision. CKK appealed to the German Federal Court of Justice, which referred questions for preliminary ruling to the CJEU. Previously, the CJEU in *Sabel* had decided that the distinctiveness of the earlier mark was relevant in the global appreciation analysis. The referring court asked whether the earlier mark's distinctiveness was relevant to the determination of the similarity of the goods and services. In the next extract, the CJEU argues that distinctiveness is relevant to that determination. Equally important, however, is the CJEU's recognition of 'interdependence' between the steps of the analysis.

COURT OF JUSTICE

Second, the Court has held that the likelihood of confusion on the part of the public, in the absence of which Article 4(1)(b) of the Directive does not apply, must be appreciated globally, taking into account all factors relevant to the circumstances of the case (Case C-251/95 *SABEL* v *Puma* [1997] ECR I-6191, paragraph 22).

A global assessment of the likelihood of confusion implies some interdependence between the relevant factors, and in particular a similarity between the trade marks and between these goods or services. Accordingly, a lesser degree of similarity between these goods or services may be offset by a greater degree of similarity between the marks, and vice versa. The interdependence of these factors is expressly mentioned in the tenth recital of the preamble to the Directive, which states that it is indispensable to give an interpretation of the concept of similarity in relation to the likelihood of confusion, the appreciation of which depends, in particular, on the recognition of the trade mark on the market and the degree of similarity between the mark and the sign and between the goods or services identified.

Furthermore, according to the case-law of the Court, the more distinctive the earlier mark, the greater the risk of confusion (*SABEL*, paragraph 24). Since protection of a trade mark depends, in accordance with Article 4(1)(b) of the Directive, on there being a likelihood of confusion, marks with a highly distinctive character, either *per se* or because of the reputation they possess on the market, enjoy broader protection than marks with a less distinctive character.

It follows that, for the purposes of Article 4(1)(b) of the Directive, registration of a trade mark may have to be refused, despite a lesser

> degree of similarity between the goods or services covered, where the marks are very similar and the earlier mark, in particular its reputation, is highly distinctive.
>
> (paras 16–19)

The interdependence of the relevant factors makes it difficult to analyse the conditions atomistically. Under an 'atomistic' approach, one would first consider whether the two signs are similar, then ask whether the goods and services are similar, before moving onto the question of confusion. However, in embracing interdependence, the CJEU has made it clear that the analysis must be holistic, not atomistic. It is incoherent to simply ask 'are signs X and Y similar?' because the answer to that question depends partly on whether consumers would be confused. Similarly, it is incoherent to simply ask whether 'would consumers be confused?' because the answer depends in part on whether the signs and goods or services are similar. While each condition needs to be individually satisfied, to some degree, whether confusing similarity exists must be considered in the round and overall.

The result is that the global appreciation analysis produces highly fact-specific conclusions which have only little precedential value. One can say that the following things have been deemed confusingly similar: the words FIFTIES and MISS FIFTIES in the context of denim clothing;[4] the words MATRATZEN and MATRATZEN MARKT in the context of mattresses;[5] the words BALMORAL in relation to both wine and whisky.[6] Furthermore, the words BETTY BOOP were deemed to be confusingly similar to the 1930s Betty Boop cartoon character on the grounds of the conceptual similarity between the signs.[7] On the other hand, the word TREAT was not confusingly similar when used in relation to both syrup and spread,[8] and the word ALIGATOR on clothing was not confusingly similar to Lacoste's crocodile logo.[9] A similar outcome was reached in the borderline case of *Specsavers v Asda* (Case 14.3).

Case 14.3 *Specsavers Intl Healthcare v Asda Stores* [2010] EWHC 2035 (Ch), affirmed in part in [2012] EWCA Civ 24

Facts

Specsavers (claimant) is an optician's. Specsavers owned the registered trade mark on their logo, as illustrated in Figure 14.2. Asda (defendant) is a supermarket that also offers optician services. Asda used in the course of trade the logo presented in Figure 14.2. Both logos were based on the shape of two ovals complete with wording in the centre.

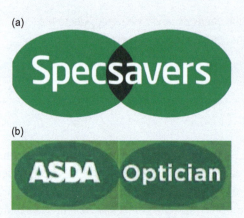

Figure 14.2 Specsavers sign ((a)); Asda sign ((b)).
Reproduced in Specsavers Intl Healthcare v Asda Stores [2012] EWCA Civ 24

Issue and Procedure

Specsavers sued Asda for infringement of their trade mark. Below, Mr Justice Mann dismisses the infringement suit on the grounds that, while there is some similarity between the two signs, this does not amount to a confusing similarity.

MANN J

I find that Specsavers fails in this claim... There is a degree of similarity in that both logos have ovals with text inside, though that degree is significantly lessened by the fact that the Specsavers ovals overlap in a very characteristic fashion and Asda's touch. That introduces a significant area of visual difference. However, while the ovals are an important part of the Specsavers sign they do not dominate so as to subordinate the wording as a matter of overall appearance. The wording is equally significant. That being the case, a different form of wording (in the form of the Asda wording) introduces a very significant difference. In my view a very different overall impression is given. Taking that comparison by itself, I do not see how the reasonably circumspect consumer would be confused by the only real element in common, namely the presence of ovals, and thereby think that the two marks connote the same trade origin. Asda is itself a well-known name, and I do not readily understand how its name expressly spelled out, in prominent letters, could leave a reasonably circumspect consumer thinking that the mark is, or even might be, Specsavers'.

This conclusion is reinforced, not lessened, by the context of most of the actual use of the sign. It is primarily used in the optical section [of] Asda stores, and online. If the circumspect consumer is in an Asda store already, he will hardly make an association with Specsavers by virtue of two ovals with Asda written in one of them. In that context

> I think there is hardly an argument in favour of confusion. The same applies to the online use. By the time that a consumer encounters the logo online he or she will have entered an Asda site already. As I have observed, Asda has its own strong reputation associated with its name, and the non-overlapping logos, with Asda's name in one of them, will not cause any form of confusion with Specsavers.
>
> Further reinforcement for this conclusion comes from the colouration of the Asda logo thus used. It is darker text on a lighter background. The Specsavers logo as registered, and certainly as used, is the other way round. This further distances the Asda logo.
>
> (paras 146–48)

A final complexity to the global appreciation analysis concerns the nature of 'confusion'. On first blush, the nature of confusion would seem to offer few problems. The central sign function is the origin function. A likelihood of confusion will exist if, because of the similarities, the public would mistakenly think the goods of one seller are the goods of another seller: if, for example, Pepsi were to use the sign COKE on their cola, some substantial number of consumers would surely buy Pepsi cola thinking it was Coca-Cola.

However, the wording of article 5(2) of the TMA defines 'confusion' in a particular way. Subsection 2 states that two signs will be confusingly similar if there exists a 'likelihood of confusion on the part of the public, *which includes the likelihood of association*'. In *Sabel v Puma* the CJEU concluded that 'likelihood of association' was not an alternative to a 'likelihood of confusion' but instead served to 'define its scope'. That somewhat cryptic finding was made clearer in the *Canon* case, where the CJEU concluded that 'the risk that the public might believe that the goods or services in question come from the same undertaking or, as the case may be, *from economically linked undertakings*, constitutes a likelihood of confusion'.[10] Thus, even if the public are not confused about the origin of the goods and services, two signs may be confusingly similar if they are likely to believe that the two sellers must have some economic connection, such as a franchise or licensing arrangement.

14.1.3 Free Riding or Dilution

Lastly, some applications will be denied even when the sign is not confusingly similar to a prior sign. Such applications will be refused under section 5(3) of the TMA when the following three conditions are met:

   i. the earlier trade mark has a reputation in the United Kingdom, and
   ii. the sign is identical with or similar to an earlier trade mark, and

iii. the use of the later sign would take unfair advantage of, or be detrimental to, the distinctive character or the repute of the earlier trade mark, and

iv. the use of the later sign is without due cause.

This highly controversial provision is the legacy of Frank Schechter's 'Rational Basis of Trade Mark Protection' argument considered in Section 12.2.3. That article argued that signs perform functions other than indicate origin. Schechter focused on the sign's ability to indicate quality, but Section 12.1 identified a range of other sign functions, including the advertising and identity-building functions. Schechter argued that because signs could perform these other functions, then the law ought to help sellers to use their signs in these ways. Section 12.2.3 questioned the logic of that argument. Schechter offered no reason why the law should protect the sign's other functions; meanwhile, the leading possible answer – the prevention of free riding – is fraught with philosophical problems (Section 12.3.2).

But this provision is not merely the result of Schechter's argument. In many ways, something even more startling is taking place. Chapter 12 started out by saying that signs are not *goods* because they have no value – at best they are instrumentally valuable because they provide information which is valuable (e.g. about the origin or quality of the good). Schechter broadly agreed with that view: he did not argue that signs are actually valuable things. While they may have a broader range of functions than previously acknowledged, that did not mean that signs themselves were *goods*. And yet, in recent years, lawyers have started to conceive of signs as valuable things: goods in themselves. The next extract from Advocate-General Jääskinen in the case of *Interflora v Marks & Spencer* is illustrative.[11]

JÄÄSKINEN AG

Trade mark dilution relates to the idea that the proper purpose of trade mark law should be to protect the efforts and investments made by the trade mark proprietor and the independent value (good will) of the trade mark. This 'property-based' approach to trade marks differs from the 'deception-based' idea that trade mark law primarily protects the origin function with a view to preventing consumers and other end users from erring as to the commercial origin of goods and services. The property-based approach also protects the communication, advertising and investment functions of trade marks with a view of creating a brand with a positive image and independent economic value (brand equity or good will). Consequently, the trade mark ... can be used for various goods and services having nothing in common apart from being under the control of the trade mark proprietor.

(para 50)

ACTIVITY 14.2

Chapter 1 introduced two understandings of 'property': property as exclusive control, and property as a bundle of rights. What kind of 'property' do you understand Advocate General Jääskinen to have in mind in this extract?

Therefore, this protection is doubly controversial. First, it is questionable whether trade mark law should protect functions other than the origin function at all. And, second, even if we agree as a normative matter that trade mark law should protect those functions, why does that as a metaphysical matter mean that signs themselves are valuable things? The following subsections discuss points i–iv in turn, while highlighting these broader points of controversy.

14.1.3.1 REPUTATION

Only signs which have acquired a 'reputation' within the relevant territory (the UK in the case of the UK trade mark system) enjoys enhanced protection. These signs are also known as 'well-known' or 'famous' signs. Examples include COCA-COLA for cola, and APPLE for laptops and mobile phones. But what is a 'reputation'? And how much of a reputation is required? Case 14.4 – *General Motors* – discusses.

Case 14.4 *General Motors Corporation v Yplon*, Case C-375/97 [1999] ECR I–5421

Facts

General Motors (claimant–appellant) is a US corporation that sells cars. General Motors owned a trade mark in the Benelux region for the word 'CHEVY' in relation to cars. General Motors brought an action against Yplon (defendant–respondent) to prevent them from using the word 'CHEVY' in relation to cleaning products and detergents.

Issue and Procedure

While cars and cleaning products are certainly not similar goods, General Motors argued that their trade mark had a 'reputation' in the Benelux region and therefore was entitled to broader protection. Yplon argued in response that the mark 'CHEVY' had not acquired a reputation throughout the entire Benelux region. The Tribunal de Commerce referred questions to the CJEU on the meaning of 'reputation' and whether it was sufficient for a sign to have acquired a reputation within only a part of the territory. The CJEU agreed that a part of the territory was sufficient under certain circumstances.

> ### COURT OF JUSTICE
>
> Such a requirement is also indicated by the general scheme and purpose of the Directive. In so far as [the TMD 1998] protects trade marks registered for non-similar products or services, its first condition implies a certain degree of knowledge of the earlier trade mark among the public. It is only where there is a sufficient degree of knowledge of that mark that the public, when confronted by the later trade mark, may possibly make an association between the two trade marks, even when used for non-similar products or services, and that the earlier trade mark may consequently be damaged.
>
> The public amongst which the earlier trade mark must have acquired a reputation is that concerned by that trade mark, that is to say, depending on the product or service marketed, either the public at large or a more specialised public, for example traders in a specific sector.
>
> It cannot be inferred from either the letter or the spirit of Article 5(2) of the Directive that the trade mark must be known by a given percentage of the public so defined.
>
> The degree of knowledge required must be considered to be reached when the earlier mark is known by a significant part of the public concerned by the products or services covered by that trade mark.
>
> In examining whether this condition is fulfilled, the national court must take into consideration all the relevant facts of the case, in particular the market share held by the trade mark, the intensity, geographical extent and duration of its use, and the size of the investment made by the undertaking in promoting it.
>
> Territorially, the condition is fulfilled when, in the terms of Article 5 (2) of the Directive, the trade mark has a reputation 'in the Member State'. In the absence of any definition of the Community provision in this respect, a trade mark cannot be required to have a reputation 'throughout' the territory of the Member State. It is sufficient for it to exist in a substantial part of it.
>
> (paras 23–28)

14.1.3.2 SIMILARITY

If the sign has acquired a reputation, then the trade mark owner can prevent other sellers from acquiring trade mark rights in 'similar' signs. Section 14.1.2 considered the issue of 'confusing similarity'. However, the 'similarity' has a different meaning in section 5(2) to section 5(3). Under section 5(2) and the global appreciation analysis, the trade mark owner can only prevent the registration of confusingly similar signs. Under section 5(3), the trade mark owner can prevent signs which are similar, but not necessarily so similar as to cause confusion. In *Adidas-Salomon* the CJEU established that two marks are sufficiently similar when consumers would establish a 'link' between them in their minds.[12] Case 14.5 – *Intel* – elaborates on what that link is.

Case 14.5 *Intel Corp v CPM UK*, Case C-252/07 [2008] ECR I–8823

Facts

Intel Corporation (claimant) owned trade mark protection on the word 'INTEL' in relation to computer products. CPM United Kingdom (CPM) (defendant) owned the trade mark for the word INTELMARK in relation to multimedia and business software. Intel Corp brought an action against CPM UK claiming that the INTELMARK trade mark was invalid. Intel Corp argued that their sign had a reputation and that CPM UK's similar mark was taking unfair advantage of, or was otherwise detrimental to, the distinctive character or repute of that earlier sign.

Issue and Procedure

Intel's suit was initially dismissed by the High Court of Justice. Intel appealed to the Court of Appeal referred questions to the CJEU to establish the conditions under which a 'link' would be formed.

COURT OF JUSTICE (FIRST CHAMBER)

As regards, in particular, detriment to the distinctive character of the earlier mark, also referred to as 'dilution', 'whittling away' or 'blurring', such detriment is caused when that mark's ability to identify the goods or services for which it is registered and used as coming from the proprietor of that mark is weakened, since use of the later mark leads to dispersion of the identity and hold upon the public mind of the earlier mark. That is notably the case when the earlier mark, which used to arouse immediate association with the goods and services for which it is registered, is no longer capable of doing so.

The types of injury referred to ... are the consequence of a certain degree of similarity between the earlier and later marks, by virtue of which the relevant section of the public makes a connection between those two marks, that is to say, establishes a link between them even though it does not confuse them (see, in relation to Article 5(2) of the Directive, *General Motors*, paragraph 23; *Adidas-Salomon and Adidas Benelux*, paragraph 29, and *adidas and adidas Benelux*, paragraph 41).

In the absence of such a link in the mind of the public, the use of the later mark is not likely to take unfair advantage of, or be detrimental to, the distinctive character or the repute of the earlier mark.

The existence of such a link must be assessed globally, taking into account all factors relevant to the circumstances of the case (see, in respect of Article 5(2) of the Directive, *Adidas-Salomon and Adidas Benelux*, paragraph 30, and *adidas and adidas Benelux*, paragraph 42). Those factors include:

– the degree of similarity between the conflicting marks;
– the nature of the goods or services for which the conflicting marks were registered, including the degree of closeness or dissimilarity between those goods or services, and the relevant section of the public;
– the strength of the earlier mark's reputation;
– the degree of the earlier mark's distinctive character, whether inherent or acquired through use;
– the existence of the likelihood of confusion on the part of the public.

Finally, a link between the conflicting marks is necessarily established when there is a likelihood of confusion, that is to say, when the relevant public believes or might believe that the goods or services marketed under the earlier mark and those marketed under the later mark come from the same undertaking or from economically-linked undertakings (see to that effect, inter alia, Case C-342/97 *Lloyd Schuhfabrik Meyer* [1999] ECR I-3819, paragraph 17, and Case C-533/06 *O2 Holdings and O2 (UK)* [2008] ECR I-0000, paragraph 59).

However, as is apparent from paragraphs 27 to 31 of the judgment in *Adidas-Salomon and Adidas Benelux*, implementation of the protection introduced by Article 4(4)(a) of the Directive does not require the existence of a likelihood of confusion.

(paras 29–31, 41–42, 57–58)

The result is that in some cases, two signs will be similar enough to establish a 'link' in the minds of consumers, but not sufficiently similar to be 'confusingly similar'. An example of this outcome can be found in the *Specsavers* case. While Mr Justice Mann decided that the signs were not similar enough to confuse consumers, he did find the marks to be similar enough to establish a 'link' in the minds of consumers.

14.1.3.3 UNFAIR ADVANTAGE, DETRIMENTAL TO DISTINCTIVE CHARACTER OR REPUTE

While it need not confuse consumers, the trade mark application will only be denied if the use of the later sign would 'take unfair advantage of, or be detrimental to, the distinctive character or the repute of the earlier trade mark'. Arguably the most controversial aspect of the section 5(3) provision has related to what qualifies as an unfair advantage (or free riding) or dilution. The *L'Oréal* case illustrates the controversial nature of the 'unfair advantage' definition.

Case 14.6 *L'Oréal v Bellure*, Case C-487/07 [2009] ECR I–5185, [2010] EWCA Civ 535

Facts

L'Oréal and others (claimants–appellants) sold high-end fragrances, including the perfume 'Miracle'. L'Oréal and others owned several trade marks in relation to these fragrances. They owned the word 'MIRACLE' and they also owned trade marks in relation to the shape of the Miracle bottle and a figurative mark composed of the words miracle and Lancôme against a pink background (see Figure 14.3).

Bellure (defendant-respondent) manufactured 'smell-alike perfumes'. In particular, they manufactured a perfume called 'Pink Wonder' which they advertised as smelling like Miracle. Bellure sold Pink Wonder in bottles and packaging that resembled the Miracle bottle and packaging. Pink Wonder was marketed in the UK through Malaika and Starion.

Issue and Procedure

L'Oréal and others sued Bellure for trade mark infringement. L'Oréal initially won the case in the High Court. Lord Justice Jacob then proceeded to refer questions about the scope of unfair advantage to the CJEU.

COURT OF JUSTICE (FIRST CHAMBER)

As regards the concept of 'taking unfair advantage of the distinctive character or the repute of the trade mark', also referred to as 'parasitism' or 'free-riding', that concept relates not to the detriment caused to the mark but to the advantage taken by the third party as a result of the use of the identical or similar sign. It covers, in particular, cases where, by reason of a transfer of the image of the mark or of the characteristics which it projects to the goods identified by the identical or similar sign, there is clear exploitation on the coat-tails of the mark with a reputation.

(a)

(b)

Figure 14.3 Lancôme Miracle signs ((a)); Bellure Pink Wonder ((b)).
Photograph of Pink Wonder by Patrick Goold

Just one of those three types of injury suffices for Article 5(2) of Directive 89/104 to apply (see, to that effect, *Intel Corporation*, paragraph 28).

It follows that an advantage taken by a third party of the distinctive character or the repute of the mark may be unfair, even if the use of the identical or similar sign is not detrimental either to the distinctive character or to the repute of the mark or, more generally, to its proprietor.

In order to determine whether the use of a sign takes unfair advantage of the distinctive character or the repute of the mark, it is necessary to undertake a global assessment, taking into account all factors relevant to the circumstances of the case, which include the strength of the mark's reputation and the degree of distinctive character of the mark, the degree of similarity between the marks at issue and the nature and degree of proximity of the goods or services concerned. As regards the strength of the reputation and the degree of distinctive character of the mark, the Court has already held that, the stronger that mark's distinctive character and reputation are, the easier it will be to accept that detriment has been caused to it. It is also clear from the case-law that, the more immediately and strongly the mark is brought to mind by the sign, the greater the likelihood that the current or future use of the sign is taking, or will take, unfair advantage of the distinctive character or the repute of the mark or is, or will be, detrimental to them (see, to that effect, *Intel Corporation*, paragraphs 67 to 69).

In addition, it must be stated that any such global assessment may also take into account, where necessary, the fact that there is a likelihood of dilution or tarnishment of the mark.

In the present case, it is a matter of agreement that Malaika and Starion use packaging and bottles similar to the marks with a reputation registered by L'Oréal and Others in order to market perfumes which constitute 'downmarket' imitations of the luxury fragrances for which those marks are registered and used.

In that regard, the referring court has held that there is a link between certain packaging used by Malaika and Starion, on the one hand, and certain marks relating to packaging and bottles belonging to L'Oréal and Others, on the other. In addition, it is apparent from the order for reference that that link confers a commercial advantage on the defendants in the main proceedings. It is also apparent from the order for reference that the similarity between those marks and the products marketed by Malaika and Starion was created intentionally in order to create an association in the mind of the public between fine fragrances and their imitations, with the aim of facilitating the marketing of those imitations.

In the general assessment which the referring court will have to undertake in order to determine whether, in those circumstances, it can be held that unfair advantage is being taken of the distinctive character or the repute of the mark, that court will, in particular, have to take account of the fact that the use of packaging and bottles similar to those of the fragrances that are being imitated is intended to take advantage, for promotional purposes, of the distinctive character and the repute of the marks under which those fragrances are marketed.

In that regard, where a third party attempts, through the use of a sign similar to a mark with a reputation, to ride on the coat-tails of that mark in order to benefit from its power of attraction, its reputation and its prestige, and to exploit, without paying any financial compensation and without being required to make efforts of his own in that regard, the marketing effort expended by the proprietor of that mark in order to create and maintain the image of that mark, the advantage resulting from such use must be considered to be an advantage that has been unfairly taken of the distinctive character or the repute of that mark.

(paras 41–49)

When the decision returned to the Court of Appeal for final judgment, Lord Justice Jacob held that Bellure's use of similar marks did confer upon them an unfair advantage.[13] As he argues in the next extract, this was regrettable.

JACOB LJ

I have come to the conclusion that the ECJ's ruling is that the defendants are indeed muzzled. My duty as a national judge is to follow EU law as interpreted by the ECJ. I think, with regret, that the answers we have received from the ECJ require us so to hold.

My own strong predilection, free from the opinion of the ECJ, would be to hold that trade mark law did not prevent traders from making honest statements about their products where those products are themselves lawful.

I have a number of reasons for that predilection. First and most generally is that I am in favour of free speech – and most particularly where someone wishes to tell the truth. There is no good reason to dilute the predilection in cases where the speaker's motive for telling the truth is his own commercial gain. Truth in the market place matters – even if it does not attract quite the strong emotions as the right of a journalist or politician to speak the truth.

Moreover there is no harm to the trade mark owner – other than possibly a 'harm' which, to be fair, L'Oréal has never asserted. That 'harm' would be letting the truth out – that it is possible to produce cheap perfumes which smell somewhat like a famous original. I can understand that a purveyor of a product sold at a very high price as an exclusive luxury item would not like the public to know that it can be imitated, albeit not to the same quality, cheaply – there is a bit of a message that the price of the real thing may be excessive and that the 'luxury image' may be a bit of a delusion. But an uncomfortable (from the point of view of the trade mark owner) truth is still the truth: it surely needs a strong reason to suppress it.

My second reason is more specific. It is about freedom to trade – indeed, potentially in other cases, to compete honestly. (This case is a fortiori for the parties' respective products are not in competition with each other). If a trader cannot (when it is truly the case) say: 'my goods are the same as Brand X (a famous registered mark) but half the price', I think there is a real danger that important areas of trade will not be open to proper competition.

(paras 7–9, 15–16)

Detriment to distinctive character is also known as '**dilution** by blurring' on the grounds that use of the sign may 'blur' the origin of the goods associated with the sign.

Similar troubles have existed with respect to the idea of 'detriment' to a distinctive character. One can plausibly claim that *any* use of a sign is detrimental to a distinctive character. If, as Schechter implied, distinctiveness is the same as 'uniqueness', then it follows by definition that any use of the sign will lessen the uniqueness of the sign and thus the distinctiveness. The CJEU in *Intel*, however, was not willing to go quite so far. If a distinctive character is not merely uniqueness, but is instead the ability of a sign to indicate origin, then it follows that even if a 'link' exists, there must be some evidence that the later sign will damage the ability of the earlier sign to fulfil an origin function.

COURT OF JUSTICE (FIRST CHAMBER)

Article 4(4)(a) TMD 2008 mentioned here corresponds to article 5(1)(b) TMD 2015.

So far as concerns, in particular, the fact referred to in point (d) of that question, as follows from paragraph 32 of this judgment, the existence of a link between the conflicting marks does not dispense the proprietor of the earlier trade mark from having to prove actual and present injury to its mark, for the purposes of Article 4(4)(a) of the Directive, or a serious likelihood that such an injury will occur in the future.

Lastly, as regards, more particularly, detriment to the distinctive character of the earlier mark, the answer to the second part of the third question must be that, first, it is not necessary for the earlier mark to be unique in order to establish such injury or a serious likelihood that it will occur in the future.

A trade mark with a reputation necessarily has distinctive character, at the very least acquired through use. Therefore, even if an earlier mark with a reputation is not unique, the use of a later identical or similar mark may be such as to weaken the distinctive character of that earlier mark.

However, the more 'unique' the earlier mark appears, the greater the likelihood that the use of a later identical or similar mark will be detrimental to its distinctive character.

Secondly, a first use of an identical or similar mark may suffice, in some circumstances, to cause actual and present detriment to the distinctive character of the earlier mark or to give rise to a serious likelihood that such detriment will occur in the future.

Thirdly, as was stated on paragraph 29 of this judgment, detriment to the distinctive character of the earlier mark is caused when that mark's ability to identify the goods or services for which it is registered and used as coming from the proprietor of that mark is weakened, since use of the later mark leads to dispersion of the identity and hold upon the public mind of the earlier mark.

It follows that proof that the use of the later mark is or would be detrimental to the distinctive character of the earlier mark requires evidence of a change in the economic behaviour of the average consumer of the goods or services for which the earlier mark was registered consequent on the use of the later mark, or a serious likelihood that such a change will occur in the future.

It is immaterial, however, for the purposes of assessing whether the use of the later mark is or would be detrimental to the distinctive character of the earlier mark, whether or not the proprietor of the later mark draws real commercial benefit from the distinctive character of the earlier mark.

The answer to point (ii) of Question 1 and to Question 3 must therefore be that Article 4(4)(a) of the Directive is to be interpreted as meaning that whether a use of the later mark takes or would take unfair advantage of, or is or would be detrimental to, the distinctive character or the repute of the earlier mark must be assessed globally, taking into account all factors relevant to the circumstances of the case.

(paras 71–79)

474 *Trade Marks III: Scope*

At first blush, the requirement that the latter sign must in some way damage the ability of the earlier sign to perform the origin function would seem to limit the scope and reach of this provision. This is particularly true when one considers the type of argument delivered by Rebecca Tushnet (Box 12.10) that suggests that such damage is unlikely to occur at all.

The last sentence of paragraph 77, however, weakens that potential limiting mechanism. Trade mark owners cannot prove a change in consumer behaviour if their claim is that such a change will occur in the future. Judges are therefore required to consider probabilistically whether such a change is likely to occur. One might, following Tushnet, question whether such a change is ever likely to occur as a result of dilution.

Finally, an application will also be denied if it causes detriment to a mark's reputation, rather than its distinctive character. In *L'Oréal*, the CJEU wrote that such detriment would occur if 'the goods or services offered by the third party possess a characteristic or a quality which is liable to have a negative impact on the image of the mark'. Such a characteristic may be possessed in broadly two situations. In the first situation, the later mark parodies or mocks the earlier sign and associated business. For example, the UK Trade Mark registry denied an application for a figurative sign including the word 'FRAUD' that parodied the Ford Motor Company's famous logo.[14]

> Detriment to repute is also known as 'dilution by **tarnishment**'.

Second, the later sign may damage the earlier sign's reputation when there is some negative association between goods and services. For example, in *Azumi Ltd v Zuma's Choice Pet Products Ltd,* the claimants owned a trade mark on the word ZUMA, which was used in relation to a high-end Japanese restaurant in London. The defendant meanwhile sold specialist dog and cat food under the sign ZUMA. The UK High Court found use of the latter sign would damage the reputation of the earlier sign, because of the negative association made when consumers link the idea of food for humans with food for dogs and cats.[15]

14.1.3.4 WITHOUT DUE CAUSE

While the trade mark owner of well-known marks can oppose later registrations on grounds of unfair advantage, detriment to distinctive character or repute, there exists one important limitation. A later sign may be registered if there is 'due cause' for doing so. The following case explores the nature of the 'due cause' provision.

Case 14.7 *Interflora v Marks & Spencer*, Case C-323/09 [2011] ECR I–8625

Facts

When an Internet user performs a search on the Google search engine, the search engine displays websites which best correspond to the search terms in decreasing order of relevance. These are referred to as the 'natural' results of the search. Google also offered a paid service called 'Adwords'. Under this service, a trader could select one or more 'keywords'. When a user then searched for the keywords, an advertisement linking to the seller's website would be displayed prominently in the search results before the natural results.

Interflora Inc (claimant–appellant) is a worldwide flower-delivery network. Interflora delivers flowers to customers when they place orders over the Internet. Interflora own a trade mark on the word 'INTERFLORA'.

Marks & Spencer (M&S) (defendant–respondent) is one of the main retailers in the United Kingdom. It retails a wide range of goods and supplies services through its network of shops and via its website www.marksandspencer.com. One of those services is the sale and delivery of flowers. Marks & Spencer competes with Interflora in the flower delivery market.

Using the 'AdWords' referencing service, M&S selected as keywords the word 'Interflora', as well as variants made up of that word with minor errors and expressions containing the word 'Interflora' ('Interflora Flowers', 'Interflora Delivery', 'Interflora.com', 'interflora co uk' and so forth). Consequently, when Internet users entered the term 'Interflora', or one of the variants, in the Google search engine, an M&S advertisement appeared under the heading 'sponsored links'.

Issue and Procedure

Interflora brought a trade mark infringement action against M&S in the High Court. The High Court referred questions to the CJEU. In the following extract, the CJEU develops the meaning of 'due cause'.

COURT OF JUSTICE (FIRST CHAMBER)

It is clear from those particular aspects of the selection as internet keywords of signs corresponding to trade marks with a reputation which belong to other persons that such a selection can, in the absence of any 'due cause' as referred to in Article 5(2) of Directive 89/104 and Article 9(1)(c) of Regulation No 40/94, be construed as a use whereby the advertiser rides on the coat-tails of a trade mark with a reputation in order to benefit from its power of attraction, its reputation and its prestige, and to exploit, without paying any financial compensation and without being required to make efforts of its own in that regard, the marketing effort expended by the proprietor of that mark in order to create and maintain the image of that mark. If that is the case, the advantage thus obtained by the third party must be considered to be unfair (Case C-487/07 *L'Oréal and Others*, paragraph 49).

> As the Court has already stated, that is particularly likely to be the conclusion in cases in which internet advertisers offer for sale, by means of the selection of keywords corresponding to trade marks with a reputation, goods which are imitations of the goods of the proprietor of those marks (*Google France and Google*, paragraphs 102 and 103).
>
> By contrast, where the advertisement displayed on the internet on the basis of a keyword corresponding to a trade mark with a reputation puts forward – without offering a mere imitation of the goods or services of the proprietor of that trade mark, without causing dilution or tarnishment and without, moreover, adversely affecting the functions of the trade mark concerned – an alternative to the goods or services of the proprietor of the trade mark with a reputation, it must be concluded that such use falls, as a rule, within the ambit of fair competition in the sector for the goods or services concerned and is thus not without 'due cause' for the purposes of Article 5(2) of Directive 89/104 and Article 9(1)(c) of Regulation No 40/94.
>
> It is for the referring court to determine, in the light of the foregoing interpretative guidance, whether, on the particular facts of the dispute in the main proceedings, there is use of the sign without due cause which takes unfair advantage of the distinctive character of the repute of the trade mark INTERFLORA.
>
> (paras 89–92)

Subsequently, the High Court did not decide whether M&S's use was conducted with 'due cause'. Mr Justice Arnold (as he then was) ruled that M&S was not taking unfair advantage of, or acting a way detrimental to the distinctive character or repute of, the INTERFLORA sign. The due cause issue was accordingly moot.

Focusing on 'fair competition' within the sector means that due cause may address some of the concerns raised by Lord Justice Jacob regarding the free riding or dilution provision. However, protecting competition is not the only role of the due cause proviso. The due cause proviso also provides some protection to other sellers who use the sign in good faith for subjective ends, as illustrated by the *Leidseplein Beheer v Red Bull* case.[16] In that case, the defendant had operated a bar in Amsterdam since the 1970s called 'The Bull Dog'. Later, the energy drink manufacturer Red Bull trade-marked the RED BULL sign. Subsequently, the defendant registered the sign THE BULL DOG for hotel, restaurant and café services. Finally, the defendant branched out and began to sell their own energy drinks under the same name. While the CJEU left it to the national courts to decide whether the particular use was made with due cause, it concluded that the due cause proviso could be applied to protect the defendant's legitimate subjective interests.

14.2 INFRINGEMENT

Section 14.1 introduced three situations where a trade mark application will be refused because of the presence of an earlier registered trade mark, that is, double identity, confusing similarity and free riding or dilution. These categories are also relevant to the issue of infringement. If a defendant uses a sign which falls into one of the three categories (double identity, confusing similarity, free riding or dilution) in the course of trade, they will infringe the earlier trade mark, according to section 10 of the TMA 1994.

It follows that when assessing whether a defendant has committed a trade mark infringement, the first and foundational question is whether they have adopted a sign which corresponds to one of the three aforementioned categories (double identity, confusing similarity, free riding or dilution). As we have already discussed those concepts at length in Section 14.1, we need not do so again here.

The question to consider in this section is what qualifies as 'use in the course of trade'? The 'in the course of trade' language is relatively straightforward: courts have routinely held that the use must be made in a commercial context rather than a non-commercial or private context. But what qualifies as 'use' of the sign? This question has caused significant trouble for courts in the past twenty years.

At first glance, the issue of what qualifies as 'use' is fairly straightforward. Section 10(4) says that the 'use' of the sign occurs when the defendant does any of the following:

> (a) affixes it to goods or the packaging thereof;
> (b) offers or exposes goods for sale, puts them on the market or stocks them for those purposes under the sign, or offers or supplies services under the sign;
> (c) imports or exports goods under the sign;
> (ca) uses the sign as a trade or company name or part of a trade or company name;
> (d) uses the sign on business papers and in advertising; or
> (e) uses the sign in comparative advertising in a manner that is contrary to the Business Protection from Misleading Marketing Regulations 2008.

However, the case law has complicated what otherwise might appear a simple issue. The problem is illustrated in the foundational *Arsenal v Reed* case.

Case 14.8 *Arsenal v Reed*, Case C-206/01 [2002] ECR I–10273

Facts

Arsenal FC (claimant) is a well-known football club in the English Premier League. It is nicknamed 'the Gunners' and has for a long time been associated with two emblems, a cannon device and a shield device.

In 1989 Arsenal FC had inter alia the words 'ARSENAL' and 'ARSENAL GUNNERS' and the cannon and shield emblems registered as trade marks for a class of goods comprising articles of outer clothing, articles of sports clothing and footwear. Arsenal FC designs and supplies its own 'official' products.

Since 1970 Mr Reed (defendant) sold football souvenirs and memorabilia, almost all marked with signs referring to Arsenal FC, from several stalls located outside the grounds of Arsenal FC's stadium. The majority of these products were unofficial and not supplied by Arsenal FC. Mr Reed's stalls clearly indicated which products were unofficial and not supplied by Arsenal FC through the use of the following sign:

> The word or logo(s) on the goods offered for sale, are used solely to adorn the product and does not imply or indicate any affiliation or relationship with the manufacturers or distributors of any other product, only goods with official Arsenal merchandise tags are official Arsenal merchandise.

Issue and Procedure

Arsenal FC brought a trade mark infringement action against Mr Reed on the grounds of double identity: Mr Reed was unquestionably selling the same goods and services (clothing, etc.) adorned with the same signs (ARSENAL, ARSENAL GUNNERS and the emblems). But was Mr Reed 'using' the registered trade mark? Of course, the goods he sold had the Arsenal signs *on* them. But the presence of the sign on the goods does not necessarily mean that Mr Reed was 'using' the registered trade mark.

When the case was brought before the High Court Mr Justice Laddie did not consider Mr Reed's acts to be 'use' of the trade mark. In essence, Mr Reed was not using the sign *in a trade mark way*. The signs were not being used to indicate the origin of the goods. When looking at the goods in the stall, the public would not think that the unofficial goods were produced by Arsenal FC because of the presence of the sign. Instead, consumers would merely perceive the signs as 'badges of support, loyalty or affiliation'. The High Court referred questions to the CJEU on the question of 'use'. In the next extract, the CJEU outlines that a defendant uses the sign if they adopt a sign in such a way that might affect *any* of the sign functions (discussed in Section 12.1), and not merely the origin function.

COURT OF JUSTICE

> To answer the High Court's questions, it must be determined whether Article 5(1)(a) of the Directive entitles the trade mark proprietor to prohibit any use by a third party in the course of trade of a sign

identical to the trade mark for goods identical to those for which the mark is registered, or whether that right of prohibition presupposes the existence of a specific interest of the proprietor as trade mark proprietor, in that use of the sign in question by a third party must affect or be liable to affect one of the functions of the mark.

In that context, the essential function of a trade mark is to guarantee the identity of origin of the marked goods or services to the consumer or end user by enabling him, without any possibility of confusion, to distinguish the goods or services from others which have another origin. For the trade mark to be able to fulfil its essential role in the system of undistorted competition which the Treaty seeks to establish and maintain, it must offer a guarantee that all the goods or services bearing it have been manufactured or supplied under the control of a single undertaking which is responsible for their quality (see, inter alia, Case 102/77 Hoffman-La Roche [1978] ECR 1149, paragraph 7, and Case C-299/99 Philips [2002] ECR I-5475, paragraph 30).

For that guarantee of origin, which constitutes the essential function of a trade mark, to be ensured, the proprietor must be protected against competitors wishing to take unfair advantage of the status and reputation of the trade mark by selling products illegally bearing it (see, inter alia, Hoffmann-La Roche, paragraph 7, and Case C-349/95 Loendersloot [1997] ECR I-6227, paragraph 22). In this respect, the 10th recital of the preamble to the Directive points out the absolute nature of the protection afforded by the trade mark in the case of identity between the mark and the sign and between the goods or services concerned and those for which the mark is registered. It states that the aim of that protection is in particular to guarantee the trade mark as an indication of origin.

It follows that the exclusive right under Article 5(1)(a) of the Directive was conferred in order to enable the trade mark proprietor to protect his specific interests as proprietor, that is, to ensure that the trade mark can fulfil its functions. The exercise of that right must therefore be reserved to cases in which a third party's use of the sign affects or is liable to affect the functions of the trade mark, in particular its essential function of guaranteeing to consumers the origin of the goods.

(paras 42, 48, 50–51)

This idea is now known as '**trade mark use**'. The essential point is that a defendant only 'uses' a trade mark in the course of trade if they use the sign in a

Trade Marks III: Scope

What counts as 'use' of a sign is also significant in relation to revocation. If a registered trade mark is not used in the five-year period following registration, it is liable to revocation (see Section 12.4).

way that will make it harder for the earlier sign to perform any of the sign functions (Section 12.1). Thus, affixing the sign to goods or packaging (as referenced in section 10(4)(a)) is only 'use' of the trade mark if it impairs any of the sign functions.

The most important part in this extract is the use of functions (plural), rather than function (singular). A defendant who uses the sign in a way that impairs the ability of the earlier mark to perform an origin function will engage in trade mark use. Similarly, a defendant who uses the sign in a way that impairs the ability of the earlier sign to indicate quality, to serve as an advert, or to build an identity, will also be 'using' the sign. Furthermore, as the list of sign functions is not closed, but remains ambiguously open-ended, there is the potential for use to occur in other situations.

> ## ACTIVITY 14.3
>
> What implications does the doctrine of trade mark use have for the status of trade mark rights as 'property'? In particular, if one considers property to be the exclusive control over a thing, does the trade mark use doctrine make trade mark rights more, or less, a right of property?

Nevertheless, although the CJEU expanded the concept of trade mark use, it also ultimately indicated that Mr Reed's use of the sign was likely to affect the origin function of the Arsenal trade marks. In the next extract, the CJEU outlines what has come to be known as '**post-sale confusion**'.

> Having regard to the presentation of the word 'Arsenal' on the goods at issue in the main proceedings and the other secondary markings on them (see paragraph 39 above), the use of that sign is such as to create the impression that there is a material link in the course of trade between the goods concerned and the trade mark proprietor.
>
> That conclusion is not affected by the presence on Mr Reed's stall of the notice stating that the goods at issue in the main proceedings are not official Arsenal FC products (see paragraph 17 above). Even on the assumption that such a notice may be relied on by a third party as a defence to an action for trade mark infringement, there is a clear possibility in the present case that some consumers, in particular if they come across the goods after they have been sold by Mr Reed and taken away from the stall where the notice appears, may interpret the sign as designating Arsenal FC as the undertaking of origin of the goods.
>
> In those circumstances, the use of a sign which is identical to the trade mark at issue in the main proceedings is liable to jeopardise the

> guarantee of origin which constitutes the essential function of the mark, as is apparent from the Court's case-law cited in paragraph 48 above. It is consequently a use which the trade mark proprietor may prevent in accordance with Article 5(1) of the Directive.
>
> (paras 56–57, 60)

When the case returned to the High Court, Mr Justice Laddie initially refused to apply the CJEU's ruling as relating to post-sale confusion.[17] He concluded that the CJEU had overstepped its powers by essentially making a finding of fact, rather than confining itself to interpretation of the legal sources. Nevertheless, the Court of Appeal later agreed that the CJEU had not made a factual finding, and that Mr Reed had indeed used the registered trade marks in a way that would affect the origin function.[18]

Although the courts in *Arsenal* concluded that Mr Reed's use of the sign affected the origin function, later cases have focused on whether the defendant's use affects the other sign functions. In the *L'Oréal* case, the CJEU held that trade mark use will occur if the defendant's use affects the 'communications, investment or advertising' functions. When the case was then returned to the Court of Appeal, Lord Justice Jacob had the following, rather scathing, remarks to say:

JACOB LJ

In [56] it appears to be explicitly saying that the use we have to consider is indeed within Art. 5(1)(a); 'Such use falls within the scope of application of Art. 5(1)(a)'. One might have thought that was an end of the point. But then the Court then goes on to refer back to us, the question in [63]. We are to consider whether the functions of communication, investment or advertising are liable to be affected, even though the use 'is not capable of jeopardising the essential function of the mark which is to indicate the origin of the goods' [65].

I am bound to say that I have real difficulty with these functions when divorced from the origin function. There is nothing in the legislation about them. Conceptually they are vague and ill-defined. Take for instance the advertising and investment functions. Trade mark owners of famous marks will have spent a lot of money creating them and need to continue to spend to maintain them. But all advertisements for rival products will impinge on the owner's efforts and affect the advertising and investment function of the brand in question. No-one would say such jostling for fame and image in the market should be stopped. Similarly all comparative advertising (for instance that in O2 v

> Hutchinson [2008] ECR I-04231, said to be acceptable by the Court) is likely to affect the value of the trade mark owner's investment.
>
> I confess I do not know where [the] line is [between use not affecting functions and use affecting functions], but this case falls the wrong side of it. Why? Because the Court has said so. It regards the use as affecting the communication, advertising and investment functions of the mark.
>
> (paras 29–31)

Lord Justice Jacob's points are clear and forceful. The wording of the legislation does not say that a defendant only infringes a trade mark if they use the sign in a way that affects the functions. Furthermore, the nature of the functions remains highly ambiguous. What the CJEU seems to call the 'communication' function is, in Section 12.1 called an 'identity function'; similarly the ability of the sign to 'sell the good', as Schechter put it, might be thought of as a quality function or as an advertising function. As a result, one might be tempted to scrap the entire concept of 'trade mark use' entirely.[19]

In the past twenty years, courts have tried to pin down the meaning of the 'functions' with greater precision. It is likely that fixing a sign to poorly constructed goods will impair the trade mark's ability to guarantee quality. In *Interflora*, Mr Justice Arnold (as he then was) suggested that the 'investment function' would be damaged if the use of the sign impairs the reputation of the sign. The meaning of the investment and advertising function has been further developed in the following two cases.

Case 14.9 *Google France v Louis Vuitton*, Cases C-236/08–238/08 [2010] ECR I–2417

Facts

The *Interflora* case discussed in Section 14.1.3.4 introduced the Google AdWords service. A range of claimants brought trade mark infringement actions against Google for selling AdWords which corresponded to registered trade marks. Many of these cases referred questions to the CJEU. This case concerned the case brought by luxury fashion house, Louis Vuitton.

Issue and Procedure

In the extract below, the CJEU explains why Google is not engaged in trade mark use when selling AdWords which correspond to registered trade marks. The extract begins by outlining why Google, as the seller of the AdWords, is not 'using' the trade mark, and then proceeds to explain why the AdWords do not damage the advertising function of the registered trade marks.

In that regard, suffice it to note that the use, by a third party, of a sign identical with, or similar to, the proprietor's trade mark implies, at the very least, that that third party uses the sign in its own commercial communication. A referencing service provider allows its clients to use signs which are identical with, or similar to, trade marks, without itself using those signs.

(ii) Adverse effect on the advertising function

Since the course of trade provides a varied offer of goods and services, the proprietor of a trade mark may have not only the objective of indicating, by means of that mark, the origin of its goods or services, but also that of using its mark for advertising purposes designed to inform and persuade consumers.

Accordingly, the proprietor of a trade mark is entitled to prohibit a third party from using, without the proprietor's consent, a sign identical with its trade mark in relation to goods or services which are identical with those for which that trade mark is registered, in the case where that use adversely affects the proprietor's use of its mark as a factor in sales promotion or as an instrument of commercial strategy.

Nevertheless, those repercussions of use by third parties of a sign identical with the trade mark do not of themselves constitute an adverse effect on the advertising function of the trade mark.

In accordance with the Cour de cassation's own findings, the situation covered in the questions referred is that of the display of advertising links following the entry by internet users of a search term corresponding to the trade mark selected as a keyword. It is also common ground, in these cases, that those advertising links are displayed beside or above the list of the natural results of the search. Finally, it is not in dispute that the order in which the natural results are set out results from the relevance of the respective sites to the search term entered by the internet user and that the search engine operator does not claim any remuneration for displaying those results.

It follows from those factors that, when internet users enter the name of a trade mark as a search term, the home and advertising page of the proprietor of that mark will appear in the list of the natural results, usually in one of the highest positions on that list. That display, which is, moreover, free of charge, means that the visibility to internet users of the goods or services of the proprietor of the trade mark is guaranteed, irrespective of whether or not that proprietor is successful in also securing the display, in one of the highest positions, of an ad under the heading 'sponsored links'.

(paras 56, 91–92, 95–97)

Despite the desire to make trade mark use more predictable, much uncertainty remains. Case 14.10 illustrates the problem in relation to the practices of 'debranding' and 'rebranding'.

Case 14.10 *Mitsubishi v Duma Forklifts*, Case C-129/17, EU: C:2018:594

Facts

Mitsubishi (claimant) sells, among other things, forklift vehicles. Mitsubishi also owns trade marks for various signs, including their logo and the word mark 'MITSUBISHI'. Duma Forklifts and GS International BVBA (defendants) bought Mitsubishi forklifts outside of the European Economic Area (EEA) and modified them to bring them into EU standards. The MITSUBISHI signs were then removed from the forklifts. The forklifts were subsequently rebranded with Duma Forklifts and GS International signs. The forklifts were then imported into the EEA and sold.

Issue and Procedure

Mitsubishi brought a trade mark infringement action against Duma Forklifts and GS International BVBA in Belgium. The Belgian Court of Appeal referred questions to the CJEU concerning the scope of trade mark use. Below, the CJEU emphasises the harm that such debranding does to the functions of the Mitsubishi trade mark.

COURT OF JUSTICE (SECOND CHAMBER)

[I]t must be observed, first, that the removal of signs identical to the mark prevents the goods for which that mark is registered from bearing that mark the first time that they are placed on the market in the EEA and, hence, deprives the proprietor of that trade mark of the benefit of the essential right, which is conferred on him by the case-law recalled in paragraph 31 above, to control the initial marketing in the EEA of goods bearing that mark.

Secondly, the removal of the signs identical to the mark and the affixing of new signs on the goods with a view to their first placing on the market in the EEA adversely affects the functions of the mark.

As regards the function of the indication of origin, it suffices to recall that, in paragraph 48 of the judgment of 16 July 2015, *TOP Logistics and Others* (C 379/14, EU:C:2015:497), the Court has already held that any act by a third party preventing the proprietor of a registered trade mark in one or more Member States from exercising his right to control the first placing of goods bearing that mark on the market in the EEA, by its very nature undermines that essential function of the trade mark.

The referring court wonders whether it makes any difference that goods thus imported or placed on the market can still be identified by the relevant average consumer as originating from the trade mark proprietor, on the basis of their outward appearance or model. It suggests, in effect, that despite the removal of the signs identical to the mark and the affixing of new signs on the forklift trucks, the relevant consumers continue to recognise them as Mitsubishi forklift trucks. In that regard, it must be observed that, while the essential function of the mark may be harmed irrespective of that fact, that fact is likely to accentuate the effects of such harm.

Moreover, the removal of the signs identical to the mark and the affixing of new signs on the goods precludes the trade mark proprietor from being able to retain customers by virtue of the quality of its goods and affects the functions of investment and advertising of the mark where, as in the present case, the product in question is not still marketed under the trade mark of the proprietor on that market by him or with his consent. The fact that the trade mark proprietor's goods are placed on the market before that proprietor has placed them on that market bearing that trade mark, with the result that consumers will know those goods before being able to associate them with that trade mark, is likely substantially to impede the use of that mark, by the proprietor, in order to acquire a reputation likely to attract and retain consumers, and to serve as a factor in sales promotion or as an instrument of commercial strategy. In addition, such actions deprive the proprietor of the possibility of obtaining, by putting the goods on the EEA market first, the economic value of the product bearing that mark and, therefore, of its investment.

(paras 42–46)

14.3 DEFENCES

Whether trade marks are property in the exclusive control sense depends on the number and scope of exceptions to the trade mark right. As discussed here, a range of defences exist to trade mark infringement actions. These are primarily, although not exclusively, contained in sections 11–12 of the TMA 1994.

14.3.1 Use of Registered Mark

Section 11(1) TMA states that no infringement will occur in using 'a later registered trade mark where that later registered trade mark would not be declared invalid'. Therefore, if the defendant has successfully acquired a trade mark on the sign, they will only be liable for infringement if that trade mark was erroneously granted. However, it is quite likely that if a claimant can make out a case of infringement, then the later sign ought to have been denied protection on relative grounds. The number of cases where this defence is applicable is accordingly relatively small.

Similarly, under section 11(1B) the later registered trade mark is not infringed by the use of the earlier sign, even though the earlier sign may no longer be invoked against the later registered trade mark.

14.3.2 Uses in Accordance with Honest Practices

Section 11(2) TMA states that the following uses of the sign will not infringe the trade mark providing the uses are 'in accordance with honest practices in industrial or commercial matters':

> (a) the use by an individual of his own name or address,
> (b) the use of signs or indications which are not distinctive or which concern the kind, quality, quantity, intended purpose, value, geographical origin, the time of production of goods or of rendering of services, or other characteristics of goods or services, or
> (c) the use of the trade mark for the purpose of identifying or referring to goods or services as those of the proprietor of that trade mark, in particular where that use is necessary to indicate the intended purpose of a product or service (in particular, as accessories or spare parts)

This subsection considers the content of (a)–(c) before turning to the notion of 'honest practices'.

14.3.2.1 NAME OR ADDRESS

Subsection (2)(a) applies only to the names of natural persons. Prior to the Trade Mark Directive 2015, the defence also applied to trade or company names. As a result, in *Hotel Cipriani v Cipriani (Grosvenor Street)*, the defendant was permitted to use the name 'Cipriani (London)' without infringing the claimant's trade mark on the sign 'CIPRIANI'.[20]

14.3.2.2 DESCRIPTIVE USE

Section 14.2 introduced the controversy around 'trade mark use'. That controversy extends into subsection (2)(b). It is not a trade mark use for a defendant to use a sign merely to describe the attributes of their goods or services. For example, although Proctor & Gamble own the BABY-DRY sign, a competitor is permitted to sell their products with the advertising line 'guaranteed to keep your baby dry'. Such use is understood not to interfere with the ability of the trade mark to perform the sign functions, as demonstrated in the *Hölterhoff* case.

Case 14.11 *Hölterhoff v Freiesleben*, Case C-2/00 [2002] ECR I–4187

Facts

Mr Freiesleben (claimant) was the proprietor of two trade marks, 'SPIRIT SUN' and 'CONTEXT CUT', registered in Germany and covering, respectively, 'diamonds for further processing as jewellery' and 'precious stones for further processing as jewellery'.

Both types of products marketed under those trade marks are distinguished by particular cuts. The Spirit Sun trade mark is used for a round cut with facets radiating from the centre and the Context Cut trade mark is used for a square cut with a tapering diagonal cross.

Mr Hölterhoff (defendant) deals in precious stones of all kinds, which he cuts himself or which he purchases from other dealers. He markets both stones which he has produced himself and products acquired from third parties.

On 3 July 1997, in the course of commercial negotiations, Mr Hölterhoff offered for sale to a goldsmith/jeweller some semi-precious and ornamental stones which he described by the names 'Spirit Sun' and 'Context Cut'. The goldsmith/jeweller ordered two garnet stones 'in the Spirit Sun cut' from Mr Hölterhoff. There is no reference on the delivery note or the sales invoice to the trademarks Spirit Sun and Context Cut; the goods are described as 'rhodolites'.

Issue and Procedure

Mr Freiesleben brought an action against Mr Hölterhoff before the Regional Court, Düsseldorf (Germany) on the basis of Paragraph 14 of the German trade mark law, claiming there had been an infringement of his registered trade marks. The German court granted the application. Mr Hölterhoff appealed against that judgment. The appellate court referred questions on the scope of descriptive use to the CJEU.

COURT OF JUSTICE

Consequently, the question for the Court is whether a use of the trade mark such as that at issue in the main proceedings constitutes one of the uses which, according to Article 5(1) of the directive, infringe the exclusive right of the proprietor of the trade mark.

> In that regard, it is sufficient to state that, in a situation such as that described by the national court, the use of the trade mark does not infringe any of the interests which Article 5(1) is intended to protect. Those interests are not affected by a situation in which:
> - the third party refers to the trade mark in the course of commercial negotiations with a potential customer, who is a professional jeweller,
> - the reference is made for purely descriptive purposes, namely in order to reveal the characteristics of the product offered for sale to the potential customer, who is familiar with the characteristics of the products covered by the trade mark concerned,
> - the reference to the trade mark cannot be interpreted by the potential customer as indicating the origin of the product.
>
> In those circumstances, without its being necessary, in the present case, to discuss further what constitutes the use of a trade mark within the meaning of Article 5(1)(a) and (b) of the directive, the answer to the question referred to the Court must be that Article 5(1) of the directive is to be interpreted as meaning that the proprietor of a trade mark cannot rely on his exclusive right where a third party, in the course of commercial negotiations, reveals the origin of goods which he has produced himself and uses the sign in question solely to denote the particular characteristics of the goods he is offering for sale so that there can be no question of the trade mark used being perceived as a sign indicative of the undertaking of origin.
>
> (paras 15–17)

The *Adam Opel* case however, provides a counterpoint. In that case, the car manufacturer, Opel, sued Autec for producing model Opel toy cars. On the Autec toy cars the Opel trade-marked logo appeared. The CJEU decided that this was not merely a descriptive use. By placing the Opel logo on the toy car, the defendant was not attempting to describe the characteristics of the car.[21]

14.3.2.3 NOMINATIVE OR REFERENTIAL USE

Prior to 2018, section 11(2)(c) permitted only the use of the sign where it was 'necessary to indicate the intended purpose of a product or service (in particular, as accessories or spare parts). Unlike the descriptive use provision, which permits a defendant to use the sign to describe the defendant's goods or services, this provision permitted the defendant to use the sign to describe certain features (the intended purpose) of the claimant's goods.

The old provision was particularly important in relation to spare parts. For example, in *BMW v Deenik*, the defendant ran a garage that repaired and maintained BMW cars. BMW brought a trade mark action against the use of their BMW sign. The CJEU held that in such circumstances it was 'necessary' for the defendant to use the BMW sign because there was no other way for the defendant to indicate his repair services to consumers.[22] Similarly, in *Gillette v LA-Laboratories*, a Finnish razor blade manufacturer was permitted to use the sign GILLETTE to indicate the compatibility between the razor blades and Gillette razors.[23]

In 2018, the provision was broadened to include any use 'for the purpose of identifying or referring to goods or services as those of the proprietor of the trade mark'. This is more generally known as '**nominative**' or '**referential**' use. So far, the provision has not been subject to significant judicial interpretation. But an interesting example of how it may apply comes from US law, from which the idea of 'nominative' use originates.

Case 14.12 *New Kids on the Block v News America Publishing, Inc* 971 F.2d 302 (1992) (US)

Facts

The New Kids on the Block (claimant–appellant) were a popular boy band. They owned the trade mark for the sign 'THE NEW KIDS ON THE BLOCK'. The newspaper, *USA Today*, owned by News America Publishing (defendants–respondents), ran an opinion poll that read: 'New Kids on the Block are pop's hottest group. Which of the five is your fave?'

Issue and Procedure

The New Kids on the Block brought a trade mark infringement action against News America Publishing. At trial, the action was dismissed on constitutional grounds. It was held that permitting the trade mark infringement action would interfere with the defendant's freedom of speech rights. The decision was upheld on appeal, but on different grounds. Below Circuit Judge Kozinski holds that nominative use is not trade mark use.

KOZINSKI, CIRCUIT JUDGE

Cases like these are best understood as involving a non-trademark use of a mark – a use to which the infringement laws simply do not apply, just as videotaping television shows for private home use does not implicate the copyright holder's exclusive right to reproduction. ... Indeed, we may generalize a class of cases where the use of the trademark does not attempt to capitalize on consumer confusion or to appropriate the cachet of one product for a different one. Such nominative use of a mark – where the only word

US trade mark law refers to both descriptive use as 'descriptive fair use' and nominative/referential use as 'nominative fair use'. This doctrine is quite different, however, from the fair use doctrine encountered in Section 5.1.1.

> reasonably available to describe a particular thing is pressed into service – lies outside the strictures of trademark law: Because it does not implicate the source-identification function that is the purpose of trademark, it does not constitute unfair competition; such use is fair because it does not imply sponsorship or endorsement by the trademark holder.
>
> (pp. 307–08)

14.3.2.4 HONEST PRACTICES

In order to claim any of the preceding defences, the defendant must act 'in accordance with honest practices in industrial or commercial matters'. What qualifies as honest use was explained by the CJEU in *Gillette*:

COURT OF JUSTICE

> Having regard to the above considerations, the answer to the fourth question must be that the condition of 'honest use' within the meaning of Article 6(1)(c) of Directive 89/104, constitutes in substance the expression of a duty to act fairly in relation to the legitimate interests of the trade mark owner.
>
> Use of the trade mark will not be in accordance with honest practices in industrial and commercial matters if, for example:
> – it is done in such a manner as to give the impression that there is a commercial connection between the third party and the trade mark owner;
> – it affects the value of the trade mark by taking unfair advantage of its distinctive character or repute;
> – it entails the discrediting or denigration of that mark;
> – or where the third party presents its product as an imitation or replica of the product bearing the trade mark of which it is not the owner.
>
> (para 49)

ACTIVITY 14.4

> Does section 11(2) TMA make trade mark rights more like a right of exclusive control or more like a bundle of rights?

14.3.3 Exhaustion

Section 12(1) of the TMA 1994 states that a registered trade mark is not infringed by the use of the trade mark in relation to goods which have been 'put on the market in the United Kingdom or the EEA under that trade mark by the proprietor or with his consent'. Notably, this allows individuals to import goods bearing trade-marked signs into the UK from the EEA, even following the UK's withdrawal from the European Union. This situation is not, however, symmetrical. A trader who owns an EU trade mark may use that trade mark to prevent importation of goods from the UK.

Section 12(2) contains an exception to the section 12(1) rule. Subsection 2 states that the exhaustion rule does not apply 'where there exist legitimate reasons for the proprietor to oppose further dealings in the goods (in particular, where the condition of the goods has been changed or impaired after they have been put on the market)'. The following CJEU case discusses what counts as a 'legitimate reason' to prevent further dealings, as well as the requirement that goods be put on the market by the proprietor.

Case 14.13 *L'Oréal v eBay International*, Case C-324/09 [2011] ECR I–6011

Facts

L'Oréal (claimant) is a manufacturer and supplier of perfumes, cosmetics and hair-care products. In the United Kingdom, L'Oréal is the proprietor of several national trade marks. It is also the proprietor of several Community trade marks. L'Oréal produces 'tester' and 'dramming' (samples) of their products which are not intended for sale and instead distributed to retailers for free.

eBay (defendant) operates an electronic marketplace on which are displayed listings of goods offered for sale by persons who have registered for that purpose with eBay and have created a seller's account with it. eBay charges a percentage fee on completed transactions.

On 22 May 2007, L'Oréal sent eBay a letter expressing its concerns about the widespread infringement of its intellectual property rights on eBay's European websites. L'Oréal complained about the sale of their tester and dramming products. Furthermore, some of the items were sold without packaging.

Issue and Procedure

L'Oréal was not satisfied with the response it received and brought actions against eBay in various member states, including an action before the High Court of Justice (England & Wales), Chancery Division. The High Court referred various questions to the CJEU. Below, the CJEU concludes that L'Oréal had not put the goods on the market.

> **CJEU**
>
> By its first question, the referring court asks, in essence, whether the supply by the proprietor of a trade mark of items bearing that mark, intended for demonstration to consumers in authorised retail outlets, and of bottles also bearing the mark from which small quantities can be taken for supply to consumers as free samples amounts to those goods being put on the market within the meaning of Directive 89/104 and Regulation No 40/94.
>
> The referring court found in that regard that L'Oréal had clearly indicated to its authorised distributors that they could not sell such items and bottles, which in any case were often marked 'not for sale'.
>
> As the Court has already held, where the proprietor of a trade mark affixes that mark to items that it gives away, free of charge, in order to promote the sale of its goods, those items are not distributed in any way with the aim of them penetrating the market (see Case C-495/07 *Silberquelle* [2009] ECR I-147, paragraphs 20 to 22). Where such items are supplied free of charge, they thus cannot, as a rule, be regarded as being put on the market by the trade mark proprietor.
>
> The Court has also stated that when a trade mark proprietor marks items such as perfume testers with the words 'demonstration' or 'not for sale', that precludes, in the absence of any evidence to the contrary, a finding that that proprietor impliedly consented to those items being put on the market (see *Coty Prestige Lancaster Group*, paragraphs 43, 46 and 48).
>
> (paras 69–72)

Furthermore, as the court continues, L'Oréal had legitimate reasons to prevent the further resale of the products.

> In the first place, having regard to the wide variety of perfumes and cosmetics, the question whether the removal of the packaging of such goods harms their image – and thus the reputation of the trade mark that they bear – must be examined on a case-by-case basis. As the Advocate General observed at points 71 to 74 of his Opinion, where perfumes or cosmetics are displayed without packaging, that may sometimes effectively convey the image of the product as a prestige or luxury product, whilst, in other cases, removing the packaging has precisely the effect of harming that image.
>
> Such damage may occur when the packaging is as important as, or more important than, the bottle or the container in the presentation of

> the image of the product created by the trade mark proprietor and his authorised distributors. It may also be the case that the absence of some or all the information required by Article 6(1) of Directive 76/768 harms the product's image. It is for the trade mark proprietor to establish the existence of the constituent elements of such harm.
>
> In the second place, a trade mark, the essential function of which is to provide the consumer with an assurance as to the identity of the product's origin, serves in particular to guarantee that all the goods bearing the mark have been manufactured or supplied under the control of a single undertaking which is responsible for their quality (see, inter alia, Case C-206/01 *Arsenal Football Club* [2002] ECR I-10273, paragraph 48, and Case C-59/08 *Copad* [2009] ECR I-3421, paragraph 45).
>
> When certain information, which is required as a matter of law, such as information relating to the identity of the manufacturer or the person responsible for marketing the cosmetic product, is missing, the trade mark's function of indicating origin is impaired in that the mark is denied its essential function of guaranteeing that the goods that it designates are supplied under the control of a single undertaking which is responsible for their quality.
>
> (paras 78–81)

The CJEU has also held that the trade mark owner may have legitimate reasons to prevent the further sale of goods when the goods have been altered. For example, in *Viking Gas v Kosan Gas*, the claimants sold gas in bottles. The claimants owned a trade mark in the shape of the bottles.[24] The defendants bought the bottles and refilled them with gas from an alternative source. The CJEU agreed that in circumstances such as this, the claimant had legitimate reason to prevent resale. Similar concerns have been raised in relation to repacking and rebranding.

14.4 SUMMARY

This chapter has considered the scope of trade mark rights. As highlighted by Jääskinen, trade marks have evolved away from a 'deception-based' model and become a species of property. Yet conceptual questions remain about what kind of property trade marks are.

In one respect, trade marks clearly do not amount to rights of exclusive control. The trade mark owner can only use their trade mark to prevent registration or use of their sign in certain circumstances. While the trade mark can prevent confusing uses, free riding and dilutive uses, they cannot prevent non-trade mark uses, like descriptive use or referential use.

On the other hand, the list of uses that may infringe the trade mark is steadily growing. It is reasonable to assume that Langdale MR (section 12.2.1) would be quite shocked at the modern trade mark system. Confusing similarity is defined broadly to include not only actual confusion, but also likelihood of association. It is an infringement to put signs on completely dissimilar goods even when that would not confuse the public. It may even be an infringement of a trade mark to *not* use the sign at all, in the case of debranding. These developments certainly push trade marks in the direction of exclusive control, even if they do not get them all the way there.

14.5 SELF-ASSESSMENT

Before moving on, try to answer the following questions to consolidate your learning. Answers are provided in the section below.

1. Which of the following is typically considered when assessing confusing similarity?
   a. Similarity of the signs.
   b. The level of distinctiveness of the claimant's mark.
   c. Consumers' level of awareness.
   d. All of the above.
2. Trade marks which have a 'reputation' receive a higher level of trade mark protection than regular marks. Which of the following can the owner of a trade mark *not* prevent?
   a. Uses of a similar sign on dissimilar goods which would cause dilution.
   b. Uses of a similar sign on similar goods which would cause dilution.
   c. Uses of a similar sign on similar goods which would cause unfair advantage.
   d. Uses of a dissimilar sign on similar goods which would cause unfair advantage.
3. STARBUCKS is a registered trade mark owned by Starbucks Inc for coffee drinks. Peqoud Starbucks lives in London and would like to open a local café called Starbuck's Café. How could Peqoud best argue that his use of the word 'Starbucks' is not an infringement of Starbucks Inc's trade marks?
   a. Pequod can use 'Starbucks' because it is his name and he is using the sign in accordance with honest practices.
   b. Pequod can use 'Starbucks' because he is using the sign to describe his goods and he is using the sign in accordance with honest practices.
   c. Pequod can use 'Starbucks' because he is using the sign to refer to the goods or services of Starbucks Inc, and he is using the sign in accordance with honest practices.

ACTIVITY DISCUSSION

Activity 14.1 On one hand, it may be the case that when a sign is better known to the public, the easier it becomes for two signs to be confusingly similar. If trade mark law aims to prevent confusing similarity, then granting broader protection to more well-known marks is justifiable. The implication is, however, that companies with larger marketing budgets and who can invest in making their signs well known, will enjoy broader protection than other traders.

Activity 14.2 On one hand, Jääskinen does not say that the owner has exclusive control over the use of the sign. The trade mark owner merely has the right to prevent uses which interfere with certain sign functions. On one level, this suggests that the trade mark is merely a bundle of rights – just a rather large bundle containing lots of rights (i.e. the right to prevent confusing uses, the right to prevent uses that interfere with the advertising function, the right to prevent uses that interfere with identity, etc.).

   On the other hand, there are hints of a broader conceptual understanding of trade marks. There is a clear evolution away from trade marks as merely a right to prevent deception, to a much broader and more powerful legal entitlement of 'property', as Jääskinen puts it. Much like the discussion in activity 5.1, one might see trade marks as a right to control any economically valuable use of the sign. This 'propertization' of trade marks has been criticised.[25]

Activity 14.3 Despite the problems clearly indicated by Jacob LJ, trade mark use is arguably one of the doctrines preventing trade marks from becoming much more clearly a right of exclusive control. By limiting trade mark infringement actions only to those uses which interfere with functions, the doctrine puts some limits on the trade mark owner's entitlement. Although one might find those limits trivial, if the list of protected functions is long and ambiguous.

Activity 14.4 Much like the doctrine of trade mark use, the defences – particularly of descriptive and referential use – push trade mark rights away from the exclusive control model, and back towards the bundle of rights model of property, to a certain extent.

SELF-ASSESSMENT ANSWERS

1. **Correct answer: d.** All of these are relevant. Similarity of mark is a basic requirement to consider. The level of distinctiveness is taken account following *Sabel v Puma*. Normally courts will consider the average consumer's attention. In the case of some goods (e.g. cars), it may be assumed that the average consumer pays more attention than in relation to other goods (e.g. toothpaste).

2. **Correct answer: d.** There can be no unfair advantage when the sign is dissimilar. All of the other uses would amount to infringement.

3. **Correct answer: a.** Answer **b.** is not a good fit because the word 'Starbucks' does not describe what Pequod sells (coffee). Answer **c.** is not a good fit because he is not using the sign to refer to Starbucks Inc. Answer **d.** is not a good fit because this is not merely advertising but use in trade. But answer **a.** is a good fit because it is his own name.

Notes

1 *Portakabin v Primakabin*, Case C-558/08 [2010] ECR I–6963, [47]–[49].
2 *Websphere Trade Mark* [2004] EWHC 529 (Ch), [2004] FSR (39) 796.
3 *Blue IP v KCS Herr-Voss* [2004] EWHC 97 (Ch), [49].
4 *Claudia Oberhauser v OHIM*, Case T-6/01 [2002] ECR II–4335.
5 *Matratzen Concord GmbH v OHIM*, Case T-6/01 [2002] ECR II–4335.
6 *Balmoral* [1999] RPC 297.
7 *Hearst Holdings v AVELA* [2014] EWHC 439 (Ch).
8 *British Sugar v Robertson* [1996] RPC 281.
9 *La Chemise Lacoste v Baker Street Clothing* [2011] RPC (5) 165(AP).
10 *Canon Kabushiki Kaisha v Metro-Goldwyn-Mayer Inc*, Case C-39/97 [1998] ECR I–5507, [29].
11 *Interflora v Marks & Spencer*, Case C-323/09 [2011] ECR I–8625 (AG Jääskinen) [50].
12 *Adidas-Salomon AG and Adidas Benelux BV v Fitnessworld*, Case C-408/01 [2003] ECR I–12537, [2004] 1 CMLR (4) 448 [31].
13 *L'Oréal SA v Bellure NV* [2010] EWCA Civ 535.
14 *Fraud Music Company v Ford Motor Company*, BL O/504/13.
15 *Azumi Ltd v Zuma's Choice Pet Products Ltd* [2017] EWHC 609 (IPEC).
16 Case C-65/12, EU:C:2014:49.
17 *Arsenal Football Club plc v Matthew Reed* [2002] EWHC 2695 (Ch).
18 [2003] EWCA Civ 696.
19 Some academic commentary has leant in this direction. See Max Planck Institute, *Study on the Overall Functioning of the Community Trade Mark System* (2010), [2.184].
20 [2010] ECWA Civ 110.
21 *Adam Opel v Autec*, Case C-48/05 [2007] ECR I–1017.
22 *Bayerische Motorenwerke v Ronald Karel Deenik*, Case C-63/97 [1999] ECR I–905.
23 Case C-228/03 [2005] ECR I–2337.
24 Case C-46/10 (2011).
25 For the USA, see Mark A Lemley, 'The Modern Lanham Act and the Death of Common Sense' (1999) 108 Yale LJ 1687.

FIGURE ACKNOWLEDGEMENTS

14.1 Puma mark: German trade mark register number: 540894. Owner: Puma AG Rudolf Dassler Sport, 91074 Herzogenaurach, DE. Date of entry into the register 13 May 1987; Sabel Mark: German trade mark register number: 1106066. Owner: Sabel VOF, Raadhuislaan 20 NL-3271 BT MIJNSHEERENLAND, NL. Date of entry into the register 10 October 1989. Reproduced in *Sabel BV v Puma, Rudolf Dassler Sport*, Case C-251/95 [1997] ECR I–6191.

14.2 Specsavers mark: EU trade mark registration number 018116956. Owner: SPECSAVERS. Registration date 08/01/2020. Reproduced in *Specsavers Intl Healthcare v Asda Stores* [2012] EWCA Civ 24. Asda mark reproduced in *Specsavers Intl Healthcare v Asda Stores* [2012] EWCA Civ 24

14.3 Lancôme marks: International trade mark No 748499. Owner name L'OREAL. Registration date 18 December 2000, and EU trade mark number 001776970. Owner name L'OREAL. Registration date 18/10/2002. Reproduced in *L'Oreal v Bellure NV* [2007] EWCA Civ 968. Photograph of Pink Wonder by Patrick Goold

15

Passing Off

During the late nineteenth and early twentieth centuries, the law protecting businesses gradually split in two directions (as explained in Section 12.2.2). On one hand, businesses were granted property rights in their *signs* (as discussed in Chapters 13 and 14). On the other hand, businesses were also granted property rights in something else: *goodwill*. Activity 12.2 introduced students briefly to goodwill. In Lord Macnaghten's definition, goodwill is the 'attractive force which brings in custom' and the 'benefit and advantage of a good name'.[1] The common law tort of passing off redresses violations of this property right. This chapter considers the latter development.

The law of passing off raises serious metaphysical questions. Is goodwill a thing that can be owned? Like the other phenomena discussed in this book, goodwill is an intangible: one can no more touch and feel goodwill than one can touch and feel the *Starry Night*. But, to many, the idea of goodwill as a *thing* feels intuitively odd.

Passing off also raises serious conceptual questions. Even if goodwill is a thing that can be owned, does anyone really own it? It is often said that there are three elements to a successful passing off action: goodwill, misrepresentation and damage. That is, if someone can prove their business has goodwill, then they can bring a passing off action if someone else damages that goodwill by making some misrepresentation. This raises the question: does anyone have a right of exclusive control over goodwill?

> These elements are sometimes known as the 'classic trinity' of passing off and were established in *Reckitt & Coleman* (see Case 15.2 and related discussion in Section 15.2).

This chapter is structured around the three elements of a passing off action. Section 15.1 introduces the idea of goodwill and the metaphysical question it presents. Sections 15.2 and 15.3 introduce the concepts of misrepresentation and damage, and questions whether the form of protection offered to businesses is truly a type of ownership and property.

This chapter contains public sector information licensed under the Open Government Licence v3.0.

15.1 GOODWILL

What is 'goodwill'? To Lord Macnaghten, goodwill was 'a thing very easy to describe, very difficult to define'.[2] However, recently, the UK Supreme Court has made some progress in clarifying the thing: goodwill is a customer base in the UK.

Case 15.1 *Starbucks (HK) Limited and another (Appellants) v British Sky Broadcasting Group plc and others (Respondents)* [2015] UKSC 31

Facts

Internet protocol television (IPTV) is a way of delivering TV or video content over the Internet. There are two main types of IPTV, 'closed circuit' and 'over the top' (OTT). Closed-circuit IPTV requires the subscriber to have a set top box to receive the service, the signal for which is encrypted. In many respects, closed-circuit IPTV services are akin to traditional cable broadcasts. OTT IPTV involves the signal being delivered via a standard broadband connection. OTT IPTV can be viewed (with appropriate software applications) on any device with a broadband connection.

Starbucks (HK) Ltd and PCCW Media Ltd (claimants–appellants), collectively referred to as 'PCCM', are members of a substantial group based in Hong Kong headed by PCCW Ltd. Since 2003, PCCM has provided a closed-circuit IPTV service in Hong Kong. The service was launched under the name NOW BROADBAND TV, but in March 2006 the name was changed to NOW TV, under which it has operated ever since. By 2012, NOW TV had become the largest pay TV operator in Hong Kong, with around 1.2m subscribers. All PCCM's programmes are in Mandarin or Cantonese, but the channel also carries some English-language programmes. Ninety per cent of PCCM's pay TV revenue comes from subscriptions.

People in the United Kingdom cannot receive PCCM's closed-circuit service. No set top boxes for it have been supplied in the UK, no subscription has been registered to a subscriber with a UK billing address, and there is no evidence of any subscriptions having been paid for with credit or debit cards with billing addresses in the UK. Consistently with this, PCCM has never held an Ofcom licence for broadcasting in the UK. However, a number of Chinese speakers permanently or temporarily resident in the UK in 2012 were aware of the NOW TV service through exposure to it when residing in or visiting Hong Kong. Furthermore, a number of Chinese-speaking members of the UK came to know of NOW TV through PCCM'S YouTube channel, or through taking international flights in which PCCM programming was provided as in-flight entertainment.

On 21 March 2012, Sky Broadcasting Group plc, British Sky Broadcasting Ltd and Sky IP International Ltd (respondents–defendants), who are all part of the British Sky Broadcasting Group, announced that they intended to launch a new IPTV service under the name NOW TV, as an OTT service.

Issue and Procedure

PCCM sued BskyB for trade mark passing off. At trial, Mr Justice Arnold found for the defendants because PCCM had no subscribing customers within the UK. He accepted that some people in the UK were aware of PCCM and therefore that PCCM had a modest reputation within the jurisdiction. But the absence of subscribing customers in the UK amounted to a lack of goodwill within the UK.

The decision was appealed to the Court of Appeal where it was upheld. Subsequently, the decision was further appealed to the UK Supreme Court. The issue presented was whether a claimant in a passing off action only need establish a reputation within a jurisdiction. Below Lord Neuberger upholds the trial court decision of Mr Justice Arnold finding that goodwill requires customers in the jurisdiction. In doing so, he reviews the key cases elaborating on the nature of goodwill.

LORD NEUBERGER

Nonetheless, it does appear that the courts in the United Kingdom have consistently held that it is necessary for a claimant to have goodwill, in the sense of a customer base, in this jurisdiction, before it can satisfy the first element identified by Lord Oliver. That this has been the consistent theme in the cases can be well established by reference to a series of House of Lords decisions, and a decision of the Judicial Committee of the Privy Council, over the past century.

In *AG Spalding & Bros v AW Gamage Ltd* (1915) 32 RPC 273, 284, Lord Parker of Waddington said that 'the nature of the right the invasion of which is the subject of [a] passing-off action' was 'a right of property . . . in the business or goodwill likely to be injured by the misrepresentation', and, at least unless the concept of goodwill is given a significantly wider meaning than that which it naturally has, it would not extend to a mere reputation. Thus, in *Inland Revenue Commissioners v Muller & Co's Margarine Ltd* [1901] AC 217, 235, Lord Lindley explained that goodwill 'is inseparable from the business to which it adds value, and, in my opinion, exists where the business is carried on'. As he went on to explain, goodwill can have 'a distinct locality' even within a particular jurisdiction. Observations of Lord Macnaghten, Lord James of Hereford and Lord Brampton at pp 224, 228 and 231–233 respectively were to much the same effect. Although the observations were made in the context of a revenue case, they purported to be general statements about the meaning of 'goodwill'.

We will see Lord Parker's decision from *AG Spalding* in Section 15.2.2. His pronouncement in this case that goodwill is property has been subject to interesting historical analysis.[3]

In *T Oertli AG v EJ Bowman (London) Ltd* [1959] RPC 1, the House of Lords unanimously upheld a decision of the Court of Appeal, where Jenkins LJ had said that it was 'of course essential to the success of any claim in respect of passing-off based on the use of a given mark or get-up that the plaintiff should be able to show that the disputed mark or get-up has become by user in this country distinctive of the plaintiff's goods' – see at [1957] RPC 388, 397.

In another passing off case, *Star Industrial Co Ltd v Yap Kwee Kor* [1976] FSR 256, 269, Lord Diplock, giving the advice of the Privy Council, referred to and relied on the observations of Lord Parker in *Spalding*. Lord Diplock explained that '[g]oodwill, as the subject of proprietary rights, is incapable of subsisting by itself', having 'no independent existence apart from the business to which it is attached'. He went on to explain that it 'is local in character and divisible', so that 'if the business is carried on in several countries a separate goodwill attaches to it in each'.

In *Erven Warnink BV v J Townend & Sons (Hull) Ltd* [1979] AC 731, 752, Lord Fraser of Tullybelton quoted Lord Diplock's observations in *Star Industrial* with approval. At pp 755–756, he went on to identify five 'facts' which it was 'essential' for a plaintiff to establish in a passing off action, of which the first was that 'his business consists of, or includes, selling in England a class of goods to which a particular trade name applies'. In the same case, Lord Diplock at p 742, citing *Spalding*, identified 'five characteristics which must be present in order to create a valid cause of action for passing off', which included 'caus[ing] actual damage to a business or goodwill of the [plaintiff]'. Viscount Dilhorne, Lord Salmon and Lord Scarman agreed with both speeches.

In the passage in his speech in *Reckitt & Colman*, quoted in para 15 above, Lord Oliver referred to 'a goodwill or reputation . . . in the mind of the purchasing public', and at p 510, Lord Jauncey of Tullichettle referred to a requirement that 'the plaintiff's goods have acquired a reputation in the market and are known by some distinguishing feature'. Lord Bridge of Harwich (with 'undisguised reluctance', albeit not in connection with the point at issue), Lord Brandon of Oakbrook and Lord Goff of Chieveley agreed with both speeches.

The ratio of the decision of the Court of Appeal in *Anheuser-Busch* was indisputably that, in order to support a passing off claim, the claimant must establish goodwill in the form of customers for its goods or services within the jurisdiction. In that case the importation from the United States of bottled beer under the plaintiff's BUDWEISER mark for use and sale in US military and diplomatic establishments within the UK and other European countries did not entitle the plaintiff to establish what Lord Oliver later stated was the first element of a passing off claim in relation to the UK, at any rate outside those establishments. Oliver LJ (later of course Lord Oliver) said at p 470 that the sales of 5,000,000 cases of bottles over 12 years in US diplomatic and military establishments in European countries were 'sales for a very special market having no connection with the market in the countries in which the consumption actually took place'; having said that, he accepted that there could well be 'a localised goodwill' within the diplomatic and military establishments. He also emphasised that the fact that the BUDWEISER mark may have had a reputation among a significant number of people in the UK did not assist the plaintiff as it involved 'confus[ing] goodwill, which cannot exist in a vacuum, with mere reputation', adding that 'reputation which may, no doubt, and frequently does, exist without any supporting local business ... does not by itself constitute a property which the law protects'. O'Connor and Dillon LJJ expressed similar views at pp 471–472 and 476 respectively.

On behalf of PCCM, Mr Silverleaf contended that the notion that goodwill should be limited to jurisdictions where the claimant had business is wrong in principle: the question of where the claimant had goodwill was a matter of fact and evidence, not a matter of law. Further, in the present age of 'international travel and the presence of the internet', he argued that it would be anachronistic and unjust if there was no right to bring passing off proceedings, particularly in relation to an electronically communicated service, in a jurisdiction where, as a matter of fact, the plaintiff's mark had acquired a reputation. He suggested that the mere fact that the customers are in Hong Kong when they enjoy the service should not undermine PCCM's case that they have such a reputation here which deserves to be protected. He also submitted that the law would be arbitrary if PCCM had no right to bring passing off proceedings despite having a reputation in this country simply because users did not pay when they viewed PCCM's programmes free on the websites.

It is of course open to this court to develop or even to change the law in relation to a common law principle, when it has become archaic or unsuited to current practices or beliefs. Indeed it is one of the great virtues of the common law that it can adapt itself to practical and commercial realities, which is particularly important in a world which is fast changing in terms of electronic processes, travel and societal values. Nonetheless, we should bear in mind that changing the common law sometimes risks undermining legal certainty, both because a change in itself can sometimes generate uncertainty and because change can sometimes lead to other actual or suggested consequential changes.

In addition to domestic cases, it is both important and helpful to consider how the law has developed in other common law jurisdictions – important because it is desirable that the common law jurisdictions have a consistent approach, and helpful because every national common law judiciary can benefit from the experiences and thoughts of other common law judges. In the present instance, the Singapore courts follow the approach of the UK courts, whereas the courts of Australia (subject to the High Court holding otherwise) and South Africa seem to favour the approach supported by PCCM. The position is less clear in other Commonwealth jurisdictions. In the United States of America, the approach appears to be consistent with that of the courts below in this case. Thus in *Grupo Gigante SA De CV v Dallo & Co Inc* (2004) 391 F 3d 1088 the Court of Appeals for the 9th circuit said at p 1093 that 'priority of trademark rights in the United States depends solely upon priority of use in the United States, not on priority of use anywhere in the world. Earlier use in another country usually just does not count'. Accordingly it does not appear to me that there is anything like a clear trend in the common law courts outside the UK away from the 'hard line' approach manifested in the UK cases discussed in paras 21–26 and 32–36 above.

(paras 20–26, 28, 48–49)

ACTIVITY 15.1

Lord Macnaghten wrote that goodwill is '*a thing* very easy to describe, very difficult to define'. Lord Neuberger has made some progress in defining goodwill – it is some customer base in the UK. But is a customer base a thing?

To help you think about this, you might want to return to the extract from Hegel in Box 2.12.

Goodwill, however, cannot be transferred on *its own* (so called in gross transfers). It can only be transferred alongside the business.

As goodwill is considered a thing that can be owned, the property right in goodwill can also be transferred.[4] When someone sells a business, the seller will not only sell things like the businesses premises, but also the goodwill in the business. If this were not the case, then there would be a risk that the buyer, in carrying on the business, would interfere with the seller's goodwill.

15.2 MISREPRESENTATION

The tort of passing off protects goodwill from damage caused by '**misrepresentations**'. But what is a misrepresentation? This section considers two leading forms of misrepresentation: misrepresentation of source and misrepresentation of quality. As a creation of common law, the list of actionable misrepresentations is not fixed. It is possible for other forms of misrepresentation to be actionable, if they cause damage.

15.2.1 Misrepresentation of Origin

According to Lord Oliver in *Reckitt & Coleman*: 'The law of passing off can be summarised in one short general proposition – no man may pass off his goods as those of another.' As such, the classic form of passing off occurs where a defendant misrepresents the *origin* of the goods through imitating one of the claimant's signs. In turn, this has the potential to damage the claimant's goodwill: the claimant's customers will be 'stolen' away from them by the defendant.

But what qualifies as a misrepresentation of origin? The issue was addressed in the dramatic – and somewhat misogynistic – case of *Reckitt & Coleman*. In this spectacular case, the House of Lords sets a low bar for misrepresentation of origin. Indeed, the bar was set so low that one judge refers to his 'undisguised reluctance' at the outcome.

Case 15.2 *Reckitt & Colman Products Ltd v Borden Inc (No 3)* [1990] 1 WLR 491 (1990)

Facts

Reckitt & Colman (claimants–respondents) sold lemon juice in yellow plastic squeeze packs since 1956. Each pack held 55 ml of juice and resembled in size, shape and colour, a natural lemon and had a removable yellow cap at one end covering the nozzle (see Figure 15.1). The word 'Jif' was embossed on it and a loose green triangular paper label with the word Jif printed in yellow, slipped over the nozzle and was held by the cap. The product came to be known as 'Jif lemon'. The Jif lemon was also sold with a paper label of triangular shape on which the word 'Jif' appeared (Figure 15.1).

In 1977, the claimants adopted a policy of threatening to bring legal proceedings against any other business that intended to adopt a similarly shaped bottle, but the claimants did allow some other third parties to supply lemon juice in much larger lemon juice bottles (known as the 'LazyLemon' and 'Supercook').

In 1985, Borden (defendants–appellants) produced lemon-shaped containers for selling lemon juice containing 75 ml. of lemon juice and having a green cap and a flat portion on one side which they offered for sale to certain supermarkets. The bottle was sold with a leaf-shaped label on which the words 'ReaLemon' appeared ('ReaLemon' Mark I). On 4 December 1985, the plaintiffs issued a writ seeking, inter alia, an injunction restraining the defendants from passing off lemon juice not being the plaintiffs' as and for such lemon juice by the use of a get-up deceptively similar to that used by the plaintiffs. See Figure 15.1.

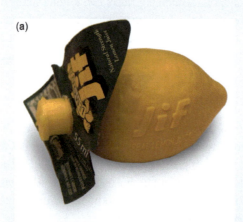

Figure 15.1 Jiff Lemon ((a)); ReaLemon ((b)). *Paul Hurst, A Jiff Lemon, CC-By-SA-2.5, 2.0. ReaLemon photograph by Patrick Goold*

Upon receiving the writ, Borden gave an undertaking not to supply the lemon juice in the Mark I container and not to offer juice in any other lemon-resembling container without giving twenty-eight days' prior notice of submitting samples. Borden redesigned the product in various ways, including fitting it with a red cap (Mark II) and making the bottle slightly larger (Mark III). Upon receipt of the samples for the Mark II and III, Reckitt & Coleman began a second action on 21 May 1986. The result was that at the time of trial, no ReaLemons had been sold.

Issue and Procedure

At trial, Mr Justice Walton held that any of the three versions of the ReaLemon would constitute passing off, and he accordingly granted permanent injunctions in both actions restraining the appellants from selling lemon juice either in packaging corresponding to the Mark I, Mark II or Mark III versions. Mr Justice Walton also found as a fact, although this was strictly irrelevant to the result, that the appellants were fraudulently intending to pass off their goods as the respondents' goods. The appellants appealed to the Court of Appeal which, on 21 April 1988, although reversing the trial judge's findings of fraud, nevertheless affirmed his decision that what was proposed by the appellants would constitute an actionable passing off. This decision was then appealed to the House of Lords.

LORD OLIVER OF AYLMERTON

Your Lordships have been able, as was Walton J. and as were the judges of the Court of Appeal, to see the appellants' and the respondents' products and, indeed, a number of other not wholly dissimilar products, including the 'Lazy Lemon' and the 'Supercook', side by side so as to make a direct comparison. I confess that it came as something of a surprise to me, as indeed I believe it did to others of your Lordships, that a housewife presented with a display of these products in close juxtaposition would be likely to pick up at least the Mark II or Mark III versions of the appellants' product in the belief that what she was buying was the respondents' Jif lemon juice. But it has to be borne in mind that, as the evidence at the trial established, the primary retail outlets for these products are supermarkets. They are not displayed in the supermarket in the way in which they have been shown to your Lordships. In the ordinary way, supermarkets do not carry a selection of different brands of preserved lemon juice, but would be likely to stock only one brand plus possibly one other sold under their own brand name or get-up. So that the goods are not ordinarily offered for sale in the artificial conditions in which they have been displayed in the court room or in the Committee Room of your Lordships' House, and the purchasing member of the public is reliant upon his own perception or recollection, unassisted by the opportunity of side-by-side comparison.

It is this, I think, which accounts for what at first may seem surprising findings of fact by Walton J., and it is, I think, material to say a few words about these findings which, it must be stressed, have not been attacked by the appellants and in respect of which it cannot be suggested that the judge did not have sufficient material to make them. Because of the quia timet nature of the proceedings there was, in the nature of things, little opportunity for either side to observe the reaction of the public to the appellants' products in normal market conditions and the evidence before the court was, inevitably, in the main the result of surveys carried out under somewhat artificial conditions. Judges accustomed to trying cases of this nature are rightly somewhat suspicious of evidence obtained in this way, for so much can depend upon the conditions in which surveys are conducted, the format of the questions posed and the manner in which they are asked. It is clear, however, that Walton J., who was a very experienced judge in this field, had well in mind the limitations and possible defects of such evidence, and he had before him not just the results of surveys conducted by market researchers on both sides but

'Quia timet' is Latin for 'because he fears'. A case is 'quia timet' when a claimant brings the case *before* any damage has actually occurred. This action was 'quia timet' because no ReaLemons had been sold and accordingly there was not yet any harm to goodwill.

the vive voce evidence of a substantial number of the members of the public interviewed which he was able to observe tested in cross-examination. In particular, he had the evidence of the reaction of shoppers to the appellants' products when they were displayed experimentally in a co-operating supermarket. His findings, therefore, although they may appear at first sight a little surprising in the light of a close comparison and inspection of the products with their labels, are quite unassailable.

(pp. 500–01)

LORD BRIDGE OF HARWICH

The idea of selling preserved lemon juice in a plastic container designed to look as nearly as possible like the real thing is such a simple, obvious and inherently attractive way of marketing the product that it seems to me utterly repugnant to the law's philosophy with respect to commercial monopolies to permit any trader to acquire a de jure monopoly in the container as such. But, as Mr. [Robin] Jacob [as he then was], for the respondents, quite rightly pointed out, the order made by the trial judge in this case does not confer any such de jure monopoly because the injunction restrains the appellants from marketing their product 'in any container so nearly resembling the plaintiffs' Jif lemon-shaped container as to be likely to deceive *without making it clear to the ultimate purchaser that it is not of the goods of the plaintiff* ' [emphasis added]. How then are the appellants, if they wish to sell their product in plastic containers of the shape, colour and size of natural lemons, to ensure that the buyer is not deceived? The answer, one would suppose, is by attaching a suitably distinctive label to the container. Yet here is the paradox: the trial judge found that a buyer reading the labels proposed to be attached to the appellants' Mark I, II or III containers would know at once that they did not contain Jif lemon juice and would not be deceived; but he also enjoined the appellants from selling their product in those containers because he found, to put it shortly, that housewives buying plastic lemons in supermarkets do not read the labels but assume that whatever they buy must be Jif. The result seems to be to give the respondents a de facto monopoly of the container as such which is just as effective as de jure monopoly. A trader selling plastic lemon juice would never be permitted to register a lemon as his trade mark, but the respondents have achieved the result indirectly that a container designed to look like a real lemon is to be treated, per se, as distinctive of their goods.

If I could find a way of avoiding this result, I would. But the difficulty is that the trial judge's findings of fact, however surprising they may seem,

> are not open to challenge. Given those findings, I am constrained by the reasoning in the speeches of my noble and learned friends, Lord Oliver of Aylmerton and Lord Jauncey of Tullichettle to accept that the judge's conclusion cannot be faulted in law.
>
> With undisguised reluctance I agree with my noble and learned friends that the appeal should be dismissed.
>
> (p. 495)

In addition to passing off one's goods as those of another, misrepresentation of origin can also occur when one misrepresents the goods of another as one's own. This is so-called **reverse passing off**.

15.2.2 Misrepresentation of Quality

But misrepresentation is not limited to origin. In the following two cases, the House of Lords widened the concept in two ways. First, misrepresentation as to the *quality* of goods can, in some instances, damage a claimant's goodwill. Second, the misrepresentation need not be intentional or deliberate. One might damage the goodwill of another business even as the result of a 'stupid mistake' as the *AG Spalding* case illustrates.

Case 15.3 *AG Spalding Brothers v AW Gamage, Ltd* [1915] All ER Rep 147

Facts

From 1907 to 1910 Spalding (claimants) advertised and sold a novel kind of football under the name of the 'Orb' or 'Improved Orb' football, the outer cover of which was moulded instead of sewn. In 1910, Spalding discovered defects in the balls. The defective balls were sold to a waste rubber firm. The waste rubber firm resold the balls to AW Gamage (defendants) who operated a well-known shop in Holborn, London. In 1912 the claimants brought out a new ball, which they advertised as the 'Improved Sewn Orb', 'Improved Orb' or 'Specially Tested Orb', 'patent 15,168', at 10s 6d each.

The fact that the original balls had been sold under the name 'improved orb' complicated matters further at trial.

In August 1912, the defendants advertised the old balls for sale at 4s 9d each, under the description of 'Improved Orb' footballs and 'Patent No 15,168'. Subsequently, the claimants issued a writ of passing off on the grounds that the defendants were attempting to pass off the old defective balls as the new ones. Thereafter, the defendants wrote to the claimants offering an apology and stated their advertisements were due to a 'stupid mistake'. The claimant proceeded with the action.

Apparently, the mistake occurred because it was prepared by a person – Robert Glasspole – while he was on holiday and was not paying attention.[5]

Issue and Procedure

At trial, Mr Justice Sargent granted the claimants an injunction and damages. The decision was reversed on appeal by the Court of Appeal. The Court of Appeal decision was appealed to the House of Lords. Below, Lord Parker concludes that passing off may occur not only when the defendant misrepresents the source of the goods, but also their quality. He also finds that the fact the misrepresentation was the result of a mistake was immaterial because even a mistaken representation may damage the claimant's goodwill.

LORD PARKER OF WADDINGTON

The proposition that no one has a right to represent his goods as the goods of somebody else must, I think, as has been assumed in this case, involve as a corollary the further proposition that no one who has in his hands the goods of another of a particular class or quality has a right to represent these goods to be the goods of that other of a different quality or belonging to a different class. Possibly, therefore, the principle ought to be restated as follows: 'A cannot, without infringing the rights of B, represent goods which are not B's goods or B's goods of a particular class or quality to be B's goods or B's goods of that particular class or quality.' The wrong for which the relief is sought in a passing-off action consists in every case of a representation of this nature. The basis of a passing-off action being a false representation by the defendant ... It would, however, be impossible to enumerate or classify all the possible ways in which a man may make the false representation relied on.

[T]he really pertinent question is whether the advertisements as a whole were calculated to deceive, and it seems to me that they were so calculated.

If, however, any evidence is required, your Lordships have in this case the evidence of Mr Ritson, who was actually misled by the advertisement in question into thinking that the balls advertised were the 'Improved Sewn Orbs' mentioned in the appellants' 1912 catalogue. Mr Ritson was a retail dealer, and had already stocked some of the appellants' 1912 balls, and was in possession of this catalogue. Seeing one of the respondents' advertisements, he thought they were selling the same ball for 4s 9d., and as he had given the appellants their wholesale price of 8s 4d for the balls stocked by him, and, therefore, could not afford to sell below this price, he was naturally alarmed, and wrote a letter of complaint to them.

> In my opinion, therefore, the misrepresentation on which the appellants rely may be taken as fully established. Further, the misrepresentation so established was, in my opinion, of such a nature as to give rise to a strong probability of actual damage to the appellants in both their retail and wholesale trade. I refrain, however, from amplifying this point so as not to prejudice any question which may arise on any inquiry as to damages which your Lordships may direct. It is sufficient to say that the misrepresentation being established, and being in its nature calculated to produce damage, the appellants are prima facie entitled both to an injunction and to an inquiry as to damage, the inquiry, of course, being at their own risk in respect of costs.
>
> (pp. 149, 152)

In some cases, misrepresentation of origin and misrepresentation of quality seem to overlap. This occurs where a business sells wine as 'champagne' when it does not come from the Champagne region in France, or whisky as 'Scotch' when it does not come from Scotland. These cases have come to be known, following Lord Diplock's judgment in Case 15.4, as '**extended passing off**'.

Case 15.4 *Erven Warnink BV v J Townend & Sons (Hull) Ltd* [1979] AC 731 (1979)

Facts

Warnink (claimant–appellant) was a manufacturer in Holland of an alcoholic drink known as 'advocaat'. Its principal ingredients were eggs and spirits without any admixture of wine. The second claimants were the distributors in England of advocaat manufactured by Warnink. Warnink's advocaat and advocaat made in Holland by a small number of other Dutch manufacturers had been marketed in England for many years prior to the events which gave rise to this action; but the lion's share of the market, some 75 per cent., was held by Warnink.

Keeling (defendants) were an English company and a partnership firm who, acting in association, prior to 1974 manufactured a drink called an 'egg flip'. Its principal ingredients were eggs and a fortified wine. In 1974, however, they produced an alcoholic egg drink from a mixture of dried eggs and a Cyprus sherry. This they put on the market as 'Keeling's Old English Advocaat'. Due to the lower excise duty on wine relative to spirits, Keeling were able to sell their drink cheaper than Warnink. 'Keeling's Old English Advocaat' captured an appreciable share of the English market for advocaat.

Issue and Procedure

At trial, Mr Justice Goulding found actionable passing off. The trial court decision was reversed by the Court of Appeal. Below, Lord Diplock reinstates the trial court decision for extended passing off.

LORD DIPLOCK

My Lords, this is an action for 'passing off', not in its classic form of a trader representing his own goods as the goods of somebody else, but in an extended form first recognised and applied by Danckwerts J. in the champagne case *(J. Bollinger v. Costa Brava Wine Co. Ltd.* [1960] Ch. 262).

The champagne case came before Danckwerts J. in two stages: the first, *J. Bollinger v. Costa Brava Wine Co. Ltd.* [1960] Ch. 262 on a preliminary point of law, the second, *J. Bollinger v. Costa Brava Wine Co. Ltd. (No. 2)* [1961] 1 W.L.R. 277 on the trial of the action. The assumptions of fact on which the legal argument at the first stage was based were stated by the judge to be [1960] Ch. 262, 273:

'(1) The plaintiffs carry on business in a geographical area in France known as Champagne; (2) the plaintiffs' wine is produced in Champagne and from grapes grown in Champagne; (3) the plaintiffs' wine has been known in the trade for a long time as 'champagne' with a high reputation; (4) members of the public or in the trade ordering or seeing wine advertised as 'champagne' would expect to get wine produced in Champagne from grapes grown there; and (5) the defendants are producing a wine not produced in that geographical area and are selling it under the name of 'Spanish champagne'.

These findings disclose a factual situation (assuming that damage was thereby caused to the plaintiff's business) which contains each of the five characteristics which I have suggested must be present in order to create a valid cause of action for passing off. The features that distinguished it from all previous cases were (a) that the element in the goodwill of each of the individual plaintiffs that was represented by his ability to use without deception (in addition to his individual house mark) the word 'champagne' to distinguish his wines from sparkling wines not made by the champenois process from grapes produced in the Champagne district of France, was not exclusive to himself but was shared with every other shipper of sparkling wine to England whose wines could satisfy the same condition and (b) that the

Notably these cases were decided before the development of geographic indications, discussed in Activity 12.2.

class of traders entitled to a proprietary right in 'the attractive force that brings in custom' represented by the ability without deception to call one's wines 'champagne' was capable of continuing expansion, since it might be joined by any future shipper of wine who was able to satisfy that condition.

My Lords, in the champagne case the class of traders between whom the goodwill attaching to the ability to use the word 'champagne' as descriptive of their wines was a large one, 150 at least and probably considerably more, whereas in the previous English cases of shared goodwill the number of traders between whom the goodwill protected by a passing off action was shared had been two, although in the United States in 1898 there had been a case, *Pillsbury-Washburn Flour Mills Co. v. Eagle* (1898) 86 Fed. R. 608, in which the successful complainants to the number of seven established their several proprietary rights in the goodwill attaching to the use of a particular geographical description to distinguish their wares from those of other manufacturers.

It seems to me, however, as it seemed to Danckwerts J., that the principle must be the same whether the class of which each member is severally entitled to the goodwill which attaches to a particular term as descriptive of his goods, is large or small. The larger it is the broader must be the range and quality of products to which the descriptive term used by the members of the class has been applied, and the more difficult it must be to show that the term has acquired a public reputation and goodwill as denoting a product endowed with recognisable qualities which distinguish it from others of inferior reputation that compete with it in the same market. The larger the class the more difficult it must also be for an individual member of it to show that the goodwill of his own business has sustained more than minimal damage as a result of deceptive use by another trader of the widely-shared descriptive term. As respects subsequent additions to the class, mere entry into the market would not give any right of action for passing off; the new entrant must have himself used the descriptive term long enough on the market in connection with his own goods and have traded successfully enough to have built up a goodwill for his business.

For these reasons the familiar argument that to extend the ambit of an actionable wrong beyond that to which effect has demonstrably been given in the previous cases would open the floodgates or, more ominously, a Pandora's box of litigation leaves me unmoved when it is sought to be applied to the actionable wrong of passing off.

So, on the findings of fact by Goulding J. to which I referred at the beginning of this speech, the type of product that has gained for the name 'advocaat' on the English market the reputation and goodwill of which Keelings are seeking to take advantage by misrepresenting that their own product is of that type, is defined by reference to the nature of its ingredients irrespective of their origin. The class of traders of whose respective businesses the right to describe their products as advocaat forms a valuable part of their goodwill are those who have supplied and are supplying on the English market an egg and spirit drink in broad conformity with an identifiable recipe. The members of that class are easily identified and very much fewer in number than in the champagne, sherry or Scotch whisky cases. Warnink with 75 per cent of the trade have a very substantial stake in the goodwill of the name 'advocaat' and their business has been showed to have suffered serious injury as a result of Keelings putting on the English market in competition with Warnink and at a cheaper price an egg and wine based drink which they miscall 'advocaat' instead of egg flip which is its proper name.

(pp. 739, 743–44, 748)

ACTIVITY 15.2

What does the misrepresentation element mean for goodwill as a property right? Does the fact that goodwill will only be protected against certain types of use (i.e. misrepresentations) fit more naturally the 'exclusive control' or 'bundle of rights' idea of property?

15.3 DAMAGE

The final element of a successful passing off is damage. Passing off only occurs if the misrepresentation actually damages the claimant's goodwill. The most obvious way such damage occurs is through lost sales. If consumers buy the defendant's goods, rather than the claimant's because of the misrepresentation, then damage to goodwill has occurred. But damage can occur through other mechanisms. In *Spalding*, the damage caused to the claimant's reputation by the defendant's act of supplying substandard footballs was an actionable form of damage.

Some argue, however, that damage can occur through other mechanisms. The following *Lego* case presents the idea that loss of *potential* trade, or even loss of licensing revenue, is actionable.

15.3 Damage 513

Case 15.5 *Lego v Lemelstrich* [1983] FSR 155

Facts

The Lego Company (claimant) sells children's toys in the form of construction kits the parts of which were made of moulded coloured plastic materials and were marketed under the trade mark LEGO in many countries, including the United Kingdom.

Lemelstrich Ltd (defendants) were an old-established Israeli company which manufactured irrigation equipment, including garden sprays and sprinklers constructed wholly or substantially of coloured plastic material. These they marketed under the trade mark LEGO. This mark had been devised so as to include the initial two letters of the names of the partners who had founded the defendants in 1927. The defendants sold their products in some forty countries but prior to 1979 had not been concerned with the United Kingdom market. In 1979, Lemelstrich applied for a trade mark on the LEGO sign in relation to installations for water supply; installations and apparatus included in Class 11, all for irrigation, and parts and fittings included in Class 11 for the aforesaid goods.

Issue and Procedure

The Lego company brought a passing off action against Lemelstrich. At the time of the action, Lemelstrich had made no sales in the UK. The action was accordingly *quia timet*. At trial, Mr Justice Falconer decided that the Lego company had goodwill in the UK, and that sale of installations for water supply under the LEGO sign would amount to a misrepresentation. But, given that no sales had occurred in the UK, the Lego Company could not prove actual loss of customers. Nevertheless, Mr Justice Falconer said that the damage could exist in the loss of potential sales or of licensing revenue.

FALCONER J

Applying his general proposition to the present case, it is plain, as Mr. Aldous submitted, that the plaintiffs' mark LEGO with its reputation is a very valuable asset – the plaintiffs' evidence, not challenged in cross-Group examination, was that it is the most valuable single asset of the Lego Group. The plaintiffs' goodwill is, of course, attached to that mark with its reputation (cf. essential numbered (3) in Lord Fraser's formulation in the Advocaat case), indeed the reputation in the mark is such that it is probably the most important element in the plaintiffs' goodwill. Mr. Aldous submitted that this is a case where the reputation of the plaintiffs' mark is so wide – the mark is, as he

One historical problem in the law of passing off has been whether the law protects goodwill or signs. In *Spalding*, Parker decided it protected the former, not the latter. But is there a possible slippage in this extract where the law is starting to protect a business's property in signs, rather than the goodwill?

submitted and as I have held, a household word – that the reputation, and hence the plaintiffs' goodwill to which it is attached, extends beyond the field of toys and construction kits. That that reputation extends beyond that field and that it is wide enough to extend, in particular, to goods such as garden irrigation sprinklers made of coloured plastics materials, is, it seems to me, demonstrated by the fact, as I have found, that the defendants' use of LEGO on or in relation to such articles would mislead a very substantial number of the adult persons of the population into thinking those goods were products of the plaintiffs or of a company or concern associated or connected with the plaintiffs. Mr. Aldous submitted that, as the plaintiffs own the property in the goodwill of their business, the extent to which the reputation of their mark LEGO and the goodwill to which it is attached extends beyond their present field of toys and construction kits is part of that property in their goodwill and an asset of the plaintiffs' business. In my judgment, that submission must be right.

As I am satisfied, for the reason I have given, that the reputation of the plaintiffs' mark LEGO and their goodwill is wide enough to extend to goods such as garden sprinklers made of coloured plastics material, for the defendants to market their garden sprinklers and other irrigation equipment products would cause damage to the plaintiffs. The plaintiffs now have the potentiality of using the mark and the attractive force of its reputation themselves to market their own goods in the garden equipment field or to license or franchise another trader to use it in that field. As to using it themselves, the evidence of both Mr. Skovmose and Mr. Powell was to the effect that the plaintiffs would be prevented from entering that field if the defendants are allowed to continue to use the trade mark LEGO in this country on their products. Another course open to the plaintiffs would be to license or franchise another trader to use the mark LEGO in that field. The evidence of the plaintiffs' expert witness, Mr. Weisz, was important in this respect. He is a marketing expert with very wide and successful experience in advertising and marketing, particularly in the launching of new products and new enterprises in this country, and in franchising operations; he is now Managing Director of A.T.V. Licensing Limited which is concerned with the commercial exploitation by franchising of characters associated with television programmes. The effect of his evidence was that, because of the reputation of Lego (meaning the plaintiffs' toy construction products), there would be an opportunity for licensing or franchising the mark LEGO in other fields, that, because of the nature of the Lego products, primarily plastic bricks, the plastics area would be a likely one to exploit and that garden implements would be an ideal market for franchising LEGO, because the purchasers of Lego toys are parents and grandparents; as he put it, the very same people who are likely to be purchasers of garden equipment. Obviously, the possibility of licensing or franchising another trader to use LEGO in the gardening equipment area would be lost if the defendants are allowed to continue using LEGO in this country in relation to their products. The effect, therefore, of the defendants continuing to use LEGO in this country in relation to their products would be to destroy that part of the plaintiffs' reputation in their mark LEGO and goodwill attached to it which extends to such goods. In view of the nature and extent of the reputation in the plaintiffs' mark LEGO, as I have held it to be, it seems to me that the defendants' use of the mark LEGO in this country in respect of their goods is calculated to injure the plaintiffs' business goodwill in that way, in the sense that it is a reasonably foreseeable consequence that it will do so, and further that such damage must result if that use is allowed to continue.

(pp. 193–94)

ACTIVITY 15.3

Pay close attention to Mr Justice Falconer's statement that one 'course open to the plaintiffs would be to license or franchise another trader to use the mark LEGO in that field'. Here, Mr Justice Falconer suggests that the 'damage' caused by the defendant was denying the Lego Company the ability to make money by licensing this sort of use of their sign.

To some, this reasoning is worrisome. What might be the problem here? And what does this say about the nature of goodwill as a form of property? Activity 5.2's discussion of circular reasoning may assist here.

15.4 SUMMARY

If intellectual property is property in intellectual things, then the law of passing off has a rather strained claim to being intellectual property. The idea that goodwill is a thing at all is curious. Furthermore, to those who view property as being some sort of exclusive control, one might question whether protecting goodwill against damage caused by misrepresentation is really property at all.

Nevertheless, there are similarities with other areas of IP. Not only do courts view goodwill as a thing which can be owned and even transferred, but the control businesses are granted over that goodwill has expanded in various directions. It is not only the case that one may not pass one's goods off as another and thereby cause damage to a consumer base. Modern law enables the property owner to control a wide range of 'misrepresentations', and to protect their goodwill from an increasingly amorphous notion of 'damage'.

15.5 SELF-ASSESSMENT

Before moving on, try to answer the following questions to consolidate your learning. Answers are provided in the section below.

1. Which of the following best defines 'goodwill'?
   a. The reputation and positive association that a business has built with its customers.
   b. The physical assets and inventory owned by a business.
   c. The legal rights granted to a business for exclusive use of a particular sign.
   d. The financial value of a business based on its profitability and market share.
2. Jan is from the Netherlands. He owns a successful bakery in London called 'Danish Delights' where he specialises in selling Danish pastries. Jan's pastries use traditional Danish ingredients and follow traditional Danish recipes. His business has become the most popular place for Danish pastries in London.

   Recently, Delilah has opened a new bakery called 'Tasty Danish'. Tasty Danish also sells Danish pastries, among other things. Delilah's pastries do not use traditional ingredients and do not follow traditional Danish recipes. She claims that her pastries have won numerous awards in the Netherlands – which is untrue. The logo and packaging used by Tasty Treats closely resembles those used by Jan's bakery. Sometimes, Delilah will go to Danish Delights at the end of the day, buy their left-over pastries, and sell them in Tasty Danish the next day at a cheap price.

   Which of the following statements are likely to be true? Select one or more.
   a. Jan cannot bring a passing off action because there is no goodwill in his business.
   b. Delilah's use of a similar logo and packaging is a misrepresentation.
   c. Selling Jan's pastries the next day qualifies as reverse passing off.
   d. In selling Danish pastries that do not conform to the traditional ingredient list and recipe, Delilah has misrepresented the quality of her goods.
3. When should lost licence fees be a form of actionable damage in passing off, if ever?

ACTIVITY DISCUSSION

Activity 15.1 Perhaps obviously *consumers* are not things which can be owned. Consumers are people and ownership of people is slavery. Instead, Lord Neuberger seems to say that goodwill is akin to customer loyalty: the fact that customers recognise and repeatedly return to the business to make purchases.

But is the habit and attitudes of consumers a thing? Hegel refers to certain phenomena like 'abilities, attainments, aptitudes' that, while capable of being 'subject of business dealings' is too 'inward and mental' to be a thing (see Box 2.12).

Activity 15.2   The misrepresentation standard seems to fit the bundle-of-rights picture of property. On this account, the business does not have 'exclusive control' over how their goodwill is used. They only have a more limited right to prevent certain activities – misrepresentations – that might adversely affect the goodwill. Once again, however, some might find that account naive. Some might think the issue depends on how broadly 'misrepresentation' is defined by courts. If the list of actionable misrepresentations is very long, and if unintentional misrepresentations are also actionable, the passing off action can grant businesses quite powerful levels of control over their goodwill.

Activity 15.3   There are potentially quite a few objectionable points here. A preliminary point is that Mr Justice Falconer is protecting the *sign's selling power* from damage (as Frank Schechter advocated in Box 12.7). If so, the case is suddenly not about goodwill at all anymore. It has, in effect, become a trade mark case.

But putting that point to one side, there is a more substantial problem. If damage to licensing opportunities is a form of actionable damage, then potentially *all uses* of the sign can damage goodwill. Any time that a defendant has used a claimant's sign in a way that qualifies as a misrepresentation, the claimant will be able to plead that they *could have* licensed this use. The fact that they have not, means they have been damaged in some way. If so, then goodwill starts to look like property of the exclusive control kind. Passing off becomes a tool to exclusively control how others use a business's goodwill.

Again, there is potential for circular reasoning here. Why does use of the Lego sign on sprinklers damage the Lego Company's goodwill? Answer: because the Lego company could have licensed the use of the Lego sign on sprinklers if they desired. But why could Lego license use of the Lego sign on sprinklers? Answer: because use of the Lego sign on sprinklers would be considered damage to goodwill and therefore actionable in passing off.

SELF-ASSESSMENT ANSWERS

1. **Correct answer: a.** Answer **c.** is a good definition of a trade mark. Answer **b.** refers to tangible business assets. Answer **d.** refers to other forms of intangible business assets.

2. **Correct answers: b., c., d.** Answer **a.** seems unlikely to be true, given that Jan's business has become popular. It is likely that the use of a similar logo and packaging is a form of misrepresentation. There is no need to prove the misrepresentation is intentional or deliberate here. By selling Jan's pastries the next day for a cheaper price, Delilah is arguably trying to pass off Jan's goods as her own. It is also likely that Delilah has misrepresented the quality of her goods in a way similar to that of *Advocaat*.

Notes

1 [1901] AC 217, 223–24.

2 ibid.

3 Christopher Wadlow, 'Goodwill in Passing-off: NOW, Then, and for How Much Longer?' (2021) 2 IPQ 80; I Tregoning, 'What's in a Name? Goodwill in Early Passing Off Cases' (2008) 34 Monash U L Rev 75.

4 *Artistic Upholstery v Art Forma (Furniture)* [1999] 4 All ER 277, 286; *Barnsley Brewery Co v RBNB* [1997] FSR 462, 469.

5 Centre for Intellectual Property and Information Law, *AG Spalding and Brothers v AW Gamage (Ltd) and Benetfink and Co* (1915) 32 RPC 273, (1915) LJ Ch 339 <https://www.cipil.law.cam.ac.uk/virtual-museum/g-spalding-and-brothers-v-w-gamage-ltd-and-benetfink-and-co-1915-32-rpc-273-1915-lj> (accessed 22 December 2023).

FIGURE ACKNOWLEDGMENT

15.1 Paul Hurst, A Jiff Lemon, CC-By-SA-2.5, 2.0 <https://commons.wikimedia.org/wiki/File:Jif_Lemon.jpg>; ReaLemon photograph by Patrick Goold

Part V

Remedies and Litigation

An industry has developed in which firms use patents not as a basis for producing and selling goods but, instead, primarily for obtaining licensing fees. For these firms, an injunction, and the potentially serious sanctions arising from its violation, can be employed as a bargaining tool to charge exorbitant fees to companies that seek to buy licenses to practice the patent.

—Justice Anthony Kennedy in *eBay v MercExchange LLC* 547 US 388 (2006) (US) 396

16

Remedies and Litigation

Chapter 1 introduced the conceptual question: are intellectual property rights really property? The preceding Parts have considered that question; most notably Chapters 4, 5, 9 and 14. But the answer is necessarily incomplete without an understanding of remedies and litigation practices. For a common remedy in cases of property violation is the award of an injunction. If IP rights are property rights, then does it follow that IP owners should be empowered through injunctive relief to prevent infringements of their property? Alternatively, are there situations where IP owners should not be so empowered?

This chapter considers the topic of remedies and litigation in five sections. The first three sections consider the remedies an IP owner may be granted after a finding of infringement. Section 16.4 considers pretrial relief. Section 16.5 turns to an area of law that may be understood as providing counter-remedies: actions for unjustified threats.

16.1 FINAL INJUNCTIONS

An **injunction** is an order from a court instructing a person to do, or refrain from doing, something. It is a discretionary equitable remedy. If an IP owner's rights are infringed, courts will commonly order the infringer to refrain from continuing their infringing activities. The purpose of the injunction is to prevent future infringement.

Yet, injunctive relief in IP is frequently a source of controversy. A famous example of the controversy is provided by the American case of *NTP v Research in Motion*.[1] Research in Motion (RIM) produced the Blackberry mobile phone. The Blackberry was one of the first generations of smart phones. It was popular among politicians and businesspeople because it enabled users to access and send emails.

This chapter contains public sector information licensed under the Open Government Licence v3.0.

Remedies and Litigation

NTP was an obscure two-person American company. NTP did not produce or sell any goods, but it did own a patent on wireless technology and made money through licensing that technology; this is known as a non-practising entity (or, pejoratively, a **patent troll**). NTP sued RIM in 2001 and successfully argued that RIM had infringed their patents. The US courts awarded an injunction to prevent RIM selling Blackberries in the USA. This created a hold-up situation: armed with an injunction, NTP could effectively shut down the RIM business, unless RIM settled the case for an exorbitant fee. Eventually, RIM did settle the case for US$612.5 million in 2006.

The concerns about injunctive relief are found in the following US Supreme Court case of *eBay v MercExchange*. This case is instructive because the justices of the Supreme Court all express different opinions about the role that injunctive relief ought to play in IP law. It is helpful to air these arguments before turning to recent UK law.

Case 16.1 *eBay v MercExchange LLC*, 547 US 388 (2006) (US)

Facts

eBay (defendant–appellant) operates an Internet auction website. MercExchange (claimant–respondent) owned several patents, including a business method patent for an electronic market designed to facilitate the sale of goods between private individuals by establishing a central authority to promote trust among participants. MercExchange sought to license its patent to eBay, as it had previously done with other companies, but the parties failed to reach an agreement.

Issue and Procedure

MercExchange successfully sued eBay for patent infringement. The trial court denied MercExchange's motion for permanent injunctive relief. The Court of Appeals for the Federal Circuit reversed, applying a general rule that courts will issue permanent injunctions against patent infringement absent exceptional circumstances. The US Supreme Court disagreed and held there was no such general rule. As an equitable remedy, courts should consider the circumstances of the case before granting an injunction. However, the justices of the court adopted slightly distinct positions on the appropriate role that injunctions ought to play in the IP system.

JUSTICE THOMAS

The decision to grant or deny permanent injunctive relief is an act of equitable discretion by the district court, reviewable on appeal for abuse of discretion.

These familiar principles apply with equal force to disputes arising under the Patent Act. As this Court has long recognized, 'a major departure from the long tradition of equity practice should not be lightly implied.'

To be sure, the Patent Act also declares that 'patents shall have the attributes of personal property', including 'the right to exclude others from making, using, offering for sale, or selling the invention'. According to the Court of Appeals, this statutory right to exclude alone justifies its general rule in favor of permanent injunctive relief. But the creation of a right is distinct from the provision of remedies for violations of that right. Indeed, the Patent Act itself indicates that patents shall have the attributes of personal property '[s]ubject to the provisions of this title', including, presumably, the provision that injunctive relief 'may' issue only 'in accordance with the principles of equity'.

[W]e vacate the judgment of the Court of Appeals, so that the District Court may apply that framework in the first instance. In doing so, we take no position on whether permanent injunctive relief should or should not issue in this particular case, or indeed in any number of other disputes arising under the Patent Act. We hold only that the decision whether to grant or deny injunctive relief rests within the equitable discretion of the district courts, and that such discretion must be exercised consistent with traditional principles of equity, in patent disputes no less than in other cases governed by such standards.

CHIEF JUSTICE ROBERTS

From at least the early 19th century, courts have granted injunctive relief upon a finding of infringement in the vast majority of patent cases. This 'long tradition of equity practice' is not surprising, given the difficulty of protecting a right to exclude through monetary remedies that allow an infringer to use an invention against the patentee's wishes... This historical practice, as the Court holds, does not entitle a patentee to a permanent injunction or justify a general rule that such injunctions should issue... At the same time, there is a difference between exercising equitable discretion pursuant to the established four-factor test and writing on an entirely clean slate. 'Discretion is not whim, and limiting discretion according to legal standards helps promote the basic principle of justice that like cases should be decided alike.' When it comes to discerning and applying those standards, in this area as others, 'a page of history is worth a volume of logic'.

JUSTICE KENNEDY

In cases now arising trial courts should bear in mind that in many instances the nature of the patent being enforced and the economic function of the patent holder present considerations quite unlike earlier cases. An industry has developed in which firms use patents not as a basis for producing and selling goods but, instead, primarily for obtaining licensing fees. For these firms, an injunction, and the potentially serious sanctions arising from its violation, can be employed as a bargaining tool to charge exorbitant fees to companies that seek to buy licenses to practice the patent. When the patented invention is but a small component of the product the companies seek to produce and the threat of an injunction is employed simply for undue leverage in negotiations, legal damages may well be sufficient to compensate for the infringement and an injunction may not serve the public interest.

(pp. 391–92, 394–97)

ACTIVITY 16.1

The judges in *eBay* agreed on some things: they all agreed that patents are 'property' and also that patentees should not automatically enjoy injunctive relief. Nevertheless, there are also important and interesting differences as well. Which of the judgments fits best with an 'exclusive control' model of property, and which with a 'bundle of rights' model?

Similar tensions appear in UK law. The CDPA 1988, PA 1977, the RDA 1949 and TMA 1994 state that copyrights, patents and trade marks are property rights, and that injunctions should be available to the owner.

That does not, however, mean that injunctions must automatically be granted in every case. Section 37(1) of the Senior Courts Act 1981 gives courts the power to grant injunctions when it is 'just and convenient to do so'. Section 50 of the Act also states that damages may be granted 'in addition to, or in substitution for, an injunction' – known as **damages in lieu** of an injunction. Unlike the monetary damages discussed in Section 16.2, which compensate for *past* infringement, damages in lieu are a remedy for *future* infringement. Damages in lieu are essentially a court imposed compulsory licensing regime that permits the defendant to continue infringing the IP rights providing they pay ongoing damages.

The circumstances under which a court will grant damages in lieu were traditionally narrow. The 1895 case of *Shelfer v City of London Electric Lighting Co* concluded that such damages would only be appropriate when: (1) the injury to the claimant's rights is small; and (2) is capable of being estimated in money; and (3) can be adequately compensated by a small money payment; and (4) it would be oppressive to the defendant to grant an injunction.[2] However, in *Coventry v Lawrence* in 2014 the UK Supreme Court signalled that a more flexible approach to injunctions is now appropriate.[3]

The UK provisions on injunctions also must be viewed in light of the EU Enforcement Directive 2004. While no longer directly enforceable in the UK following Brexit, the Directive has shaped judicial attitudes towards the role of injunctive relief in the 21st century. Article 3 of the Directive requires that:

> Member States shall provide for the measures, procedures and remedies necessary to ensure the enforcement of the intellectual property rights covered by this Directive. Those measures, procedures and remedies shall be fair and equitable and shall not be unnecessarily complicated or costly, or entail unreasonable time-limits or unwarranted delays.
>
> Those measures, procedures and remedies shall also be effective, proportionate and dissuasive and shall be applied in such a manner as to avoid the creation of barriers to legitimate trade and to provide for safeguards against their abuse.

How these general principles apply in IP cases is illustrated in the following case of *Evalve v Edwards Lifescience*.

Case 16.2 *Evalve Inc v Edwards Lifescience* [2020] EWHC 513 (Pat)

Facts

Mitral valve regurgitation is a heart condition where the mitral valve does not properly close, allowing blood to 'leak' out of the valve. The only treatment available for many years was open heart surgery. Many patients, particularly elderly ones, are however not strong enough to undergo open heart surgery.

Evalve Inc (claimants) owned a patent on medical devices used to treat mitral valve regurgitation. Evalve produced a device called the MitraClip, which essentially clipped the valve together preventing leakage. Edwards Lifescience produced their own device – the Edwards' PSCAL – which performed the same function. Evalve sued for patent infringement.

Issue and Procedure

In the main proceedings, Mr Justice Birss held that the Edwards PASCAL infringed the Evalve patents. Edwards Lifescience argued that no injunction ought to be granted in this case. They argued that in some circumstances, clinicians had a reason to prefer the PASCAL over the MitraClip. If the court were to award an injunction preventing sales of the PASCAL, this would harm patients. Such an injunction would not be in the public interest, they claimed.

Mr Justice Birss started his judgment by summarising the voluminous case law on IP injunctions. From this summary, he distilled the following principles.

BIRSS J

Drawing all this together, I attempt to summarise the applicable principles as follows:

(i) A general injunction to restrain future infringements is the normal remedy for the patentee.

(ii) The burden is on the defendant to give reasons why such an injunction should not be granted.

(iii) All the circumstances should be considered. The public interest, such as the impact on third parties, is a relevant consideration. This applies under domestic law (Coventry v Lawrence) and under Art 3 of the Enforcement Directive.

(iv) In a proper case the public interest may justify refusal of or carve out from injunction, and an award of damages in lieu. Smallness of the damages in lieu is not determinative. Even if the damages were a large sum of money and/or one which was difficult to calculate, it might still be in the public interest to refuse an injunction or carve scope out of it.

(v) The starting point of any consideration of the public interest in relation to a remedy after a patent trial is that the patent system as a whole is already crisscrossed with provisions which strike balances between different public interests.

(vi) The availability of an exclusionary injunction is an important manifestation of the monopolistic nature of a patent right. While monopolies in general are against the public interest, once a patent has been found valid and infringed, the patent monopoly is something which it is in the public interest to protect by an injunction in order to further the purposes of the system as a whole, such as to promote investment in innovation.

(vii) Therefore when, as here, various public interests are engaged and pull in different directions, one should have in mind that the

> legislator is better equipped than the courts to examine these issues and draw the appropriate broad balance. The jurisdiction to refuse or qualify a patent injunction on public interest grounds is not there to redraw the broad balance of public interests set by Parliament in the patent system. The power should be used sparingly and in limited circumstances.
>
> (para 73)

With the principles in place, Mr Justice Birss turned to the question of whether the public interest required denying the claim for injunctive relief; he decided it did not.

> When a doctor chooses a treatment for a patient they are exercising their clinical judgment in the best interests of that patient. Patents do not cover methods of treatment, in order not to interfere with those decisions, but patent law does certainly place restrictions on those decisions by limiting the available options – in the form of patents for drugs and devices. Stated at this level of generality, as being applicable to any reasonable clinical decision about any medical condition, the fact that reasonable doctors would choose the defendant's drug or device in preference to the patentee's product cannot on its own be sufficient to invoke the public interest as a ground for refusing or putting a carve out into a patent injunction.
>
> For this kind of public interest to begin to be relevant, it must be concerned with treatments for serious medical conditions, and perhaps only for life saving treatments. That does not have to mean only for treating clinical emergencies. It will include treatments of the kind in this case. For many patients these [mitral valve] devices are lifesaving therapies. However even then things can be complicated. The true balance of risk will differ between individual patients.
>
> However there are many life-saving drugs and medical devices. If the legislator had thought the balance of public interests justified it then patent law could but does not contain an express limitation preventing injunctions in that sphere or providing for compulsory licences to any competitor in every such case. And indeed it is not hard to think of reasons why the legislator did not institute a broad exception like that, after all society no doubt most of all wishes to have incentives to invest the vast sums necessary to make and develop life-saving drugs and devices.

Note the importance of the utilitarian argument here. Recall also the potential problems with that argument.

> Another factor must be the nature of the competitive product. I doubt a generic version of a life-saving drug would usually engage the public interest in this way at all. I say 'usually' because one can think of special cases, such as a novel pandemic disease; but if that happened then the Government could invoke Crown use.
>
> The public interest I have identified which would justify refusal or a carve out is not far from the test for a compulsory licence (market demand not met) but as Edwards pointed out the three year period in section 48 of the 1977 Act means they cannot obtain such a licence at this stage at least under patent EP 810. It would justify a carve out pending an application for a compulsory licence. That is not because the three year period should just be overridden. The period itself reflects a decision by the legislator balancing various public interests. It would allow the patentee three years to meet market demand. An example here is the introduction of the independent grasping feature of the MitraClip G4, one reason for which was the spur of PASCAL. It could operate pending an application because on the relevant hypothesis, in the meantime there was no other option to save the lives of patients.
>
> (paras 74–77, 90)

In the judgment, Mr Justice Birss refers to a 'carve-out'. A carve-out is where the injunction is granted, but the defendant can still perform some actions in relation to the property. In this case, a narrow carve-out was adopted. While the injunction was granted, doctors were permitted to install the PASCAL devices in cases where they had previously unsuccessfully tried to install the MitraClip into a patient. The defendants were therefore permitted to continue to supply the PASCAL for this very limited reason.

ACTIVITY 16.2

In the USA, the Supreme Court in *eBay* decided there was no 'general rule' that an injunction should be granted upon a finding of infringement. After reading Mr Justice Birss's decision in *Evalve*, does the UK have a 'general rule' that injunctions ought to be awarded?

16.2 MONETARY REMEDIES

Upon winning an IP infringement action, the claimant can elect either to recover **damages** for their losses or, alternatively, the defendant's profits. Unlike damages in lieu (which are forward looking), monetary damages and account of profits remedy past infringement.

Given the hold-up problem that can accompany injunctions, some might conclude that it is generally preferable for IP owners to make do with monetary remedies only. However, as this section demonstrates, monetary remedies are hardly the easy option. The complexity associated with calculating monetary remedies may lead some to appreciate the comparative simplicity of the injunction.

16.2.1 Monetary Damages

The purpose of monetary damages is to correct the infringement, and thereby put the claimant into the position they would have been in were it not for the infringement. But determining what corrective measures are required is metaphysically difficult. Not only must courts identify the value of what the claimant has 'lost', but they must also decide whether that loss was 'caused' by the defendant's infringement.

The foundational principles on monetary damages are found in the House of Lords decision of *General Tire*.

Case 16.3 *General Tire v Firestone* [1975] 1 WLR 819

Facts

General Tire (claimants–respondents) invented a method of producing 'oil-extended rubber' (or OER) – a mixture of synthetic rubber and mineral oil. The OER could then be compounded with other materials and made into a separate material called 'tyre tread stock' (or TTS) that was used to make tyres. Tyres made in this way were more durable and performed better than previous tyres.

Firestone (defendants–appellants) infringed the patent over a period from 1958 to 1970.

Issue and Procedure

General Tire sued Firestone successfully for infringement. During the litigation, the parties put forward different ways to calculate the damages.

General Tire argued, initially, that the judge should award them 5 per cent of the money Firestone made (revenue) on sales of tyres. This would amount to £7,500,00. This was, in their view, a 'fair and reasonable royalty' – where a royalty is a fee for each infringing act. Later in the litigation, General Tire changed their position and argued instead the judge ought to award 2 US cents per pound weight of all tyre tread stock produced by Firestone.

Firestone put forward different methods of calculating damages. Two methods of calculating damages were particularly important. The first method – the 'OER basis' – would give General Tire three-eighths of a US cent per pound of OER produced. This would amount to £215,000. The second method – the 'TTS basis' – would give General Tire three-eighths of a US cent per pound of TTS produced. This would amount to £486,500.

The trial judge accepted none of the calculations put forward. Instead, the judge ordered Firestone to pay 1 US cent per pound on the first 100,000,000 pounds produced; and thereafter half a US cent per pound. This amounted to £930,000.

Firestone appealed. The Court of Appeal upheld the award. Firestone appealed to the House of Lords. In the extract below, Lord Wilberforce begins by setting out the general principles of damages, as well as three appropriate methods for calculation.

WILBERFORCE L

One who infringes the patent of another commits a tort, the foundation of which is made clear by the terms of the grant. This, after conferring the monopoly of profit and advantage upon the patentee, concludes by declaring infringers 'answerable to the patentee according to the law for damages thereby occasioned'.

As in the case of any other tort (leaving aside cases where exemplary damages can be given) the object of damages is to compensate for loss or injury. The general rule at any rate in relation to 'economic' torts is that the measure of damages is to be, so far as possible, that sum of money which will put the injured party in the same position as he would have been in if he had not sustained the wrong (*Livingstone* v. *Rawyards Coal Co.* (1880) 5 App.Cas. 25, *per* Lord Blackburn, at p. 39).

The respondents did not elect to claim an account of profits: their claim was only for damages. There are two essential principles in valuing that claim: first, that the plaintiffs have the burden of proving their loss: second, that, the defendants being wrongdoers, damages should be liberally assessed but that the object is to compensate the plaintiffs and not punish the defendants (*Pneumatic Tyre Co. Ltd.* v. *Puncture Proof Pneumatic Tyre Co. Ltd.* (1899) 16 R.P.C. 209, 215).

I think it useful to refer to some of the main groups of reported cases which exemplify the approaches of courts to typical situations.

1. Many patents of inventions belong to manufacturers, who exploit the invention to make articles or products which they sell at a profit. The benefit of the invention in such cases is realised through the sale of the article or product. In these cases, if the invention is infringed, the effect of the infringement will be to divert sales from the

owner of the patent to the infringer. The measure of damages will then normally be the profit which would have been realised by the owner of the patent if the sales had been made by him (see *United Horse-shoe and Nail Co. Ltd. v. John Stewart & Co.* (1888) 13 App. Cas. 401). An example of this is *Boyd* v. *Tootal, Broadhurst Lee Co. Ltd.* (1894) 11 R.P.C. 175 where the plaintiff manufacturers proved that a profit of 7s. per spindle would have been made, and settlements of litigation for lesser rates were discarded.

2. Other patents of inventions are exploited through the granting of licences for royalty payments. In these cases, if an infringer uses the invention without a licence, the measure of the damages he must pay will be the sums which he would have paid by way of royalty if, instead of acting illegally, he had acted legally. The problem, which is that of the present case – the respondents not being manufacturers in the United Kingdom – is to establish the amount of such royalty. The solution to this problem is essentially and exclusively one of evidence, and as the facts capable of being adduced in evidence are necessarily individual, from case to case, the danger is obvious in referring to a particular case and transferring its conclusions to other situations.

These are very useful guidelines, but the principle of them must not be misapplied. Before a 'going rate' of royalty can be taken as the basis on which an infringer should be held liable, it must be shown that the circumstances in which the going rate was paid are the same as or at least comparable with those in which the patentee and the infringer are assumed to strike their bargain. To refer again to *Boyd* v. *Tootal Broadhurst Lee Co. Ltd.*, 11 R.P.C. 175: when it was argued that because numerous other persons had agreed to pay at the rate of 4s. per spindle the infringer should also pay at the rate (rather than at 7s. per spindle, which represented the normal profit), it was relevant to show that the rate of 4s. was negotiated by way of settlement of litigation in which the validity of the patent was in doubt. This was not the equivalent of that which the court had to assume: for that purpose the patent must be assumed to be valid.

3. In some cases it is not possible to prove either (as in 1) that there is a normal rate of profit, or (as in 2) that there is a normal, or established, licence royalty. Yet clearly damages must be assessed. In such cases it is for the plaintiff to adduce evidence which will guide the court. This evidence may consist of the practice, as regards royalty, in the relevant trade or in analogous trades; perhaps of expert opinion expressed in publications or in the witness box; possibly of the profitability of the invention; and of any other factor on which the judge can decide the measure of loss. Since evidence of this kind is in

> its nature general and also probably hypothetical, it is unlikely to be of relevance, or if relevant of weight, in the face of the more concrete and direct type of evidence referred to under 2. But there is no rule of law which prevents the court, even when it has evidence of licensing practice, from taking these more general considerations into account. The ultimate process is one of judicial estimation of the available indications.
>
> (pp. 824–26)

In this case, where General Tire did not sell any products in the UK, the appropriate basis for damage calculation was number 2. This method of calculation was not properly applied by the trial judge. The trial judge had, in Lord Wilberforce's view, become overly concerned with what Firestone *should* pay according to some conception of fairness. But the appropriate method was to look to the actual licensing deals General Tire had made in the past. This, Wilberforce concluded, would support the appellant's argument for an OER basis, as he explains in the next extract.

> Following upon the management meeting of August 26, 1960, a number of offers of licences were made by the respondents on the basis stated in the memorandum.
>
> (a) On December 13, 1960 (the date of grant), offers were made to 18 major United States tyre manufacturers including Firestone U.S.-parent of the appellants. With these offers there was sent out a model form of licence which conferred world-wide selling rights and contained a most favoured licensee clause. On the same day the respondents started infringement proceedings against Goodyear Tire & Rubber Co. (the largest tyre manufacturing company in the world) and another major United States company. There was evidence that at this time the respondents believed that Firestone U.S. would accept a licence and there can be no doubt that the offer would have been available to them if they had wanted.
>
> (b) In February 1961 offers were made to 17 tyre manufacturers in Europe (including four Firestone subsidiaries) of licences at three-eighths of a cent per pound T.T.S.
>
> (c) On March 15, 1962, the respondents offered licences on 'reasonable terms' to 29 minor tyre manufacturers in the United States. This was in fact also an offer for a royalty of three-eighths of a cent per pound T.T.S.

None of these offers was accepted and no company in the United States or outside the United States accepted a licence at three-eighths of a cent per pound T.T.S.

So far, then, the respondents are shown as indicating willingness to grant licences to use the invention – established as valid in the United States to a large number of rubber manufacturing companies in the United States and elsewhere. The offering price is three-eighths of a cent per pound T.T.S. apart from Australia where it was the lower three-eighths of a cent per pound O.E.R. The comment may be made that this T.T.S. rate would appear to fix a ceiling above which damages could not be awarded, since any company which applied for a licence at this rate of royalty would have obtained one. This makes it surprising that the learned trial judge should have awarded damages at approximately double this rate. But, in any case, the offer was not accepted and it is necessary to consider what licensing bargains were actually made. Three particular sets of bargains or negotiations are of special importance.

I. Japan. In this country a patent was issued on November 21, 1954... Under Japanese law the patent became incontestable after the lapse of five years from grant, i.e., on November 29, 1959. On December 7, 1959 - just after the date mentioned, so the parallel with the 1960 offers is significant the respondents opened negotiations for a licence with Japan Synthetic Rubber Co. Ltd., a producer of O.E.R. No figure was mentioned initially, but at some date (not proved) in 1960–1961 the respondents offered a licence to the same company at a royalty of three-eighths of a cent per pound O.E.R. On November 4, 1963, the respondents entered into licence agreements with five Japanese companies for a royalty of three eighths of a cent per pound O.E.R.

These agreements, in my opinion, constitute highly relevant and important evidence as to the rate of royalty which the respondents were willing to accept and which licensees were willing to pay for a licence *under a valid patent.* The respondents attempted to discount their relevance by pointing to special factors but I do not find any of these significant. The point of paramount importance was the offer and acceptance of three-eighths of a cent per pound O.E.R. at a time when the validity of the Japanese patent was incontestable.

II. In May 1961 the respondents opened negotiations with the Cooper Tire & Rubber Co., a small United States manufacturer, with which the respondents were not in litigation. Substantial agreement seems to have been reached about August 1962, and on

> September 16, 1963, a licence agreement was entered into providing for a royalty rate of three-eighths of a cent per pound O.E.R.
>
> III. In December 1960 the respondents started negotiations with Dunlop Rubber Co. Ltd., a United Kingdom company, putting forward an initial rate of three-eighths of a cent per pound T.T.S. Dunlop's attitude was that it did not intend to dispute the patent but wished to wait for the grant. The evidence tends to show that by September 1962 the respondents would have been willing to conclude an agreement at three-eighths of a cent per pound O.E.R. Dunlop considered that this rate was too high, but, while using the invention, created a reserve based on that figure. Later Dunlop agreed to pay a lump sum.
>
> My Lords, it is obvious from a bare statement of these offers and agreements that a royalty rate of three-eighths of a cent per pound. O.E.R. has strong evidence to support it. Indeed there can be few cases in which so concrete and relevant evidence can have been available.
>
> I would therefore set aside the judge's finding and return the case to the High Court for judgment to be entered for the respondents for a sum which represents a royalty at the rate of three-eighths of a U.S. cent per pound of O.E.R. of infringing use. I understand that this figure is agreed at £215,000.
>
> (pp. 828–30, 835)

The *General Tire* case established the framework for assessing damages which continues broadly to this day. In a case such as this, where the patent owner made money through licensing rather than sales, the appropriate basis for calculation was number 2 from Wilberforce's list of calculation methods. But, in other cases where the patent owner makes money through sales, the appropriate basis may instead be number 1, that is, profit on the lost sales. However, as *Fabio* illustrates (Case 16.4), this method of calculation raises complex questions of causation as well as quantification.

Case 16.4 *Fabio v LPC Group* [2012] EWHC 911 (Ch)

Facts

Fabio Perini SpA ('Perini') (claimants) manufactured 'converting lines'. Converting lines are machines which convert industrial rolls of paper into the rolls of kitchen and toilet paper. Fabio owned several patents relating to their converting lines.

Perini sued Paper Converting Machine Company (PCMC) and LPC Group (defendants) for patent infringement. PCMC had produced a converting line machine called the 'Rotoseal' which infringed the Perini patents. PCMC sold Rotoseal machines to LPC Group and a third party, Georgia-Pacific.

Issue and Procedure

Perini sued PCMC and LPC group successfully for patent infringement. Below, the High Court quantifies the appropriate monetary damages. In this regard, Perini argued that what they had lost was the ability to sell their own patented machine to LPC, or failing that, the chance to have made such a sale. Mr Justice Norris in the next extract starts by clarifying the standard to be applied.

NORRIS J

Addressing these issues requires me to determine of a number of questions of principle that were raised by Counsel for PCMC and LPC.

The first is: what does Perini generally have to prove to show that LPC's infringement (or Georgia-Pacific's infringement) caused the loss claimed by Perini? According to ordinary principles, Perini must adduce evidence to show that it is more than 50% probable that, but for LPC's (or Georgia-Pacific's) infringing use, the loss for which Perini seeks compensation would not have occurred. Perini primarily says that it lost a sale to LPC or to Georgia-Pacific, or the chance of such a sale; its secondary case is that it lost the royalty it could have levied if permission for use had been sought.

The next step is assessment of the damage. The position to which Perini is entitled to be restored is that which would have obtained if PCMC's infringing tail sealer had not been on the market when LPC and Georgia-Pacific were looking for converting lines. The assessment of such damages requires the Court to construct and value hypotheses. As Jacob J put it in Gerber v Lectra Systems [1995] RPC 383 at 395, the Court is 'asked to re-write history' and to form a view about 'what would have been' (rather than its ordinary function in civil actions of determining 'what was'). In that context one cannot expect much in the way of accuracy.

(paras 56–57, 75)

Following the clarification, Mr Justice Norris summarised the facts and considered what loss was caused to Perini by the infringement. The following extract is reasonably lengthy and, while students do not need a fine-grained appreciation of the facts of this case, it serves to illustrate the sort of complex factual analysis courts must consider.

NORRIS J

I must now apply the legal principles outlined above and (so far as necessary) enter the world of 'what would have been'.

LPC's infringement was to use a process or method within claims 16 and 17 of Patent 929. PCMC is liable as joint tortfeasor for that infringement. Did the infringement cause any loss at all to Perini? In my judgment the infringement by use was embedded in the contracts which LPC and PCMC entered. But for their mutual agreement to use the infringing process, Perini would have had the market to itself for tail sealers embodying the invention. They could then deploy the advantages offered by the patented technology against the advantages of price and delivery times that their competitors held.

Causation questions (like assessment questions) have to be approached in a commercially realistic and common sense way and with the ultimate object of yielding compensation that is fair (but no more than fair) for the wrong suffered. That is true whether one is considering causation in fact or causation in law. Looking at what (if any) loss was caused by the infringement, I hold that in this case the loss caused to Perini was the loss of the chance of securing the LPC contract. The loss of the chance of deploying the monopoly of profit and advantage that it was the object of the 929 Patent to grant is in these circumstances in itself compensatable loss. In the world of (what would have been) Perini was not the sole company offering converting lines to LPC, and LPC would not have been compelled to accept what Perini offered. 'What would have been' depends on the hypothetical actions of LPC, or Perini and of Gambini. . .

Having now identified the nature of the chance lost I must turn to quantification. The first step is to value the notional contracts; the second step is to evaluate the chance that such contract would have been obtained. My task is to make a fair assessment without pretending to achieve unattainable precision.

I have found that the chance that Perini lost was the chance to supply a Sincro 65 and a Sincro 55 line in accordance with its October 2005 quotation, together with the additional equipment which LPC ordered from PCMC subsequently, together with the benefit of after sales.

The total for the two lines including the embosser would have been €3.824 million.

It is now necessary to evaluate the chance that Perini would have obtained such contracts and earned such profits. [On this, LPC argued that in absence of the infringement, they would have bought the machines from the alternative providers of Futura or Gambini, and not from Perini]

In my judgment the following factors enter into the assessment of the chance:

(i) In late 2004 Perini had a 70% share of the market for [converting line] machinery.

(ii) During 2005 that market share came under attack from Futura (in relation to higher end machinery) and Gambini (in relation to mid-level machinery) to the extent that PCMC was considered the third choice ... (after Perini and Futura).

(iii) Perini responded to this market pressure by reduction of its margins (rather than by abandonment of market share) and was seeking to restore its margins by making its products more technologically advanced.

(iv) In LPC's case, technological advance which enhanced production speed would never be particularly significant because its immediate demand was for a basic converting line; but technological advance that supported reliability of production would have been attractive. Perini's patented method of tail sealing provided a significant advantage over nozzle- and brush-based systems.

(v) Perini was offering LPC a 40% discount on market leading machinery incorporating the latest tail sealing technology.

(vi) Futura did not represent serious competition for LPC's business because (a) in the UK it was a very new company without any track record (though with a sound European reputation); (b) it would have had to be the subject of further investigations by Mr Dharamshi; and (c) although it had quoted, it had never been successful in selling anything to LPC.

(vii) Gambini did represent a serious competitive threat because (a) it had already supplied equipment to LPC; and (b) it used a wire-based tail sealing technology (the possibility that this might have also infringed Perini's patent being irrelevant for the purposes of this exercise since as a matter of fact the tail sealer was in the market).

(viii) Gambini could only supply new equipment in July 2006 (offering prior to that to provide temporary second hand machinery).

(ix) Perini's scheduled delivery time for the first line was October 2006 but it was prepared to depart from normal delivery times if

> delivery was presented as a 'deal breaker', had a capacity to do so through its use of sub-contractors, and probably would have brought the date forward (if told that it was a 'deal breaker') to July 2006.
>
> (x) The evidence does not establish the actual existence of spare capacity in the critical period but it does establish the existence of arrangements.
>
> (xi) LPC had a preference for Perini machinery and had obtained from Perini detailed specifications for the siting of the machinery in Rothley Lodge (which it had not obtained from PCMC or, so far as the evidence shows, from Gambini).
>
> (xii) If delayed delivery was a real problem, Mr Dharamshi was prepared to consider other options such as using second hand equipment until new machinery could be built and delivered and brought into production.
>
> Balancing these competing considerations I put the chance of Perini's successfully obtaining the contracts at 65%.
>
> ### Conclusion
>
> I find and hold that PCMC and LPC must pay damages for infringement of Patent 929 being loss of profit calculated on the basis that Perini had a 65% chance of selling a Sincro 65 and a Sincro 55 to the specification quoted in the October 2005 quotations at a total price of €3.824 million.
>
> (paras 99–100, 106, 122–24, 126, 132–33, 166)

Where the defendant is neither in the business of making sales or licensing the invention, the appropriate basis for calculation is number 3 on Wilberforce's list. This is called the 'user principle' and involves imaging a hypothetical bargain between the patent owner and infringer using secondary data – such as evidence of fees charged in the relevant market.

While Wilberforce suggested that different methods of calculation may be more or less appropriate, broadly the claimant is permitted to select which type of damage the judge should consider.

Since Wilberforce's judgment, two further developments have occurred. First, some statutes now deny damages in cases of 'innocence'. Damages will not be awarded in patent or registered designs cases will not be liable if, at the date of infringement, they were not aware of the patent and had no reasonable grounds for supposing that one existed. Second, there is now a greater potential for damages to extend to non-monetary injuries. Article 13 of the Enforcement Directive permits damages for 'moral prejudice'.

16.2 Monetary Remedies

Case 16.5 *Henderson v All Around the World* [2014] EWHC 3087 (IPEC)

Facts

Jodie Aysha Henderson (claimant) had performers rights in a song called 'Heartbroken'. The song was released without her consent by All Around the World (defendants).

Issue and Procedure

Henderson successfully sued for infringement of her performer's rights. In addition to economic injury, she claimed damages for moral prejudice. Henderson claimed moral prejudice arose from: (i) mental distress as a result of not being paid for her song for years and not being able as an artist to release any music for years; (ii) loss of opportunity to promote herself with the release of new music so as to enhance her reputation as an artist and to advance her career; (iii) injury to Miss Henderson's feelings at being strung along by All Around the World; (iv) humiliation as a result of her minimal appearance in the music video for 'Heartbroken'. Judge Hacon decided that (ii) was a form of economic injury rather than moral prejudice. He then continued to consider the remaining injuries.

HACON HHJ

The categories of moral prejudice on which Miss Henderson relies are, in summary, (i) mental distress, (ii) loss of promotional opportunity, (iii) injury to feelings and (iv) humiliation. Miss Henderson claims £15,000 for all of these.

Damage for 'moral prejudice' has its roots in continental civil law. In France, the concept of préjudice moral permits the financial compensation for pain and suffering for injury or wrongful death. The civil law tradition has shaped public international law and since at least the early part of the 20th century moral damages have formed part of international awards.

So far as I am aware, damages for moral prejudice under that name are new to English law generally. But the concept of compensation for a non-economic loss is not new, even to intellectual property law. In Nichols Advanced Vehicle Systems Inc. v Rees [1979] RPC 127, Templeman J (as he then was) made an order for additional damages pursuant to section 17(3) of the Copyright Act 1956 on grounds which included the humiliation of the claimant:

'this is a case where the defendants, by stealing a march based on infringement, received benefits and inflicted humiliation and loss

> which are difficult to compensate and difficult to assess in the normal course' (at page 140).
>
> 'Moral prejudice' in the context of art. 13(1)(a) must of course have a single meaning according to Community law which is independent of the various meanings under national laws.
>
> I think I have to assume that art. 13(1)(a) in principle entitles a claimant to recover in relation to three of the categories of non-economic loss on which Miss Henderson relies: mental distress, injury to feelings and humiliation.
>
> In my view the moral prejudice contemplated by art. 13(1)(a) is confined to prejudice arising in limited circumstances, in particular where the claimant suffers little or no financial loss and would either be left with no compensation unless the moral prejudice were taken into account, or the compensation would not be proportionate to the overall damage suffered where this includes significant moral prejudice. For instance, if a defendant were to infringe the copyright in photographs disclosing private grief by publishing them on the internet, that may generate no profit for the defendant and no financial loss for the copyright owner. But the emotional stress caused might be acute. In those circumstances art. 13(1)(a) would allow the court to award appropriate compensation, hitherto unavailable in England to copyright owners.
>
> In my judgment only in unusual circumstances will moral prejudice be sufficiently significant such that damages for economic loss are not proportionate to the overall actual prejudice suffered by the claimant. I do not believe that this case falls into that category and I make no award for moral prejudice.
>
> (paras 85–86, 88–89, 92, 94–95)

Subsequently, however, the CJEU has interpreted the Enforcement Directive as permitting claimants to recover damages for both economic and moral loss.

16.2.2 Account of Profits

As an alternative to monetary damages, claimants may elect to receive the infringer's profits. This is an equitable remedy and can be denied by the court on appropriate facts. It also is unavailable in cases of patents, registered designs, trade marks and passing off actions where the defendant was at the time of infringement unaware of the existence of an IP right and without reasonable grounds for supposing an IP right existed.

As with monetary damages, calculation of profits is a complex task. One method, known as the 'incremental' approach, is to identify what portion of the defendant's profits flow from the infringement. This approach is not commonly followed in the UK, however. Instead, the approach to calculation is illustrated in *Potton v Yorkclose*.

Case 16.6 *Potton v Yorkclose* [1990] FSR 11

Facts

Potton Ltd (claimant) owned copyright in the architectural drawings for a style of house called the 'Grandsen'. Yorkclose Ltd (defendants) infringed the copyright by using the drawings and building houses therefrom.

Issue and Procedure

Yorkclose argued that the court should identify the increment of profit flowing from the use of the drawings. This approach was rejected by Mr Justice Millet.

MILLET J

It is obvious that some apportionment will be required in order to ascertain what part of the total profits made by the defendants has been made by their wrongful acts in infringing the plaintiffs' copyright. Argument has been directed primarily not to the method by which such apportionment ought to be made, but to the nature of the enquiry which is necessary. Mr. Miller [counsel for defendants] submitted that the purpose of the inquiry is to ascertain what advantage, and in particular what saving of costs, the defendants obtained from their use of the plaintiffs' Grandsen drawings, and that accordingly when the account comes to be taken the relevant comparison will be between: (i) the profits which the defendants would have made in respect of the fourteen houses if they had not used the plaintiffs' Grandsen drawings; and (ii) the profits which they did in fact make from those houses. In practice this will come to the cost of commissioning similar drawings from another source. In support of this proposition Mr. Miller relied on *Cartier v. Carlisle* (*supra*) (trade mark); [p 17] *The United Horsenail Company v. Stewart & Co. (1886) 3 R.P.C. 139 at 143* (patent); and *Siddell v. Vickers (1892) 9 R.P.C. 152* (patent).

In my judgment those cases do not assist him. In each of them the need for an apportionment arose because the defendant made improper use of the plaintiff's trade mark or patent during the process of manufacture, but the goods manufactured thereby did not themselves infringe the plaintiff's trade mark or patent. It was necessary therefore to ascertain what part of the profits obtained by the sale of the goods was attributable to the infringement of the plaintiff's rights in the course of manufacturing them. In like manner, a defendant might use a plaintiff's copyright drawings to make machinery, and then use the machinery to manufacture articles for sale. If the machinery reproduced the plaintiff's work in a material form it would infringe the plaintiff's copyright (see section 3(5)(a) of the Copyright Act 1956), but using the machinery to produce the manufactured articles would not. In such a case the plaintiff would be entitled to an account of the profits obtained by the unauthorised use of the machinery, not necessarily the profits obtained by the sale of the articles, and an inquiry of the kind directed in the cited cases would be appropriate.

A similar inquiry will be appropriate in the present case, if the plaintiffs require it, as regards the use made by the defendants of the plaintiffs' Grandsen drawings to obtain planning permission. But the defendants' admitted breaches of copyright did not stop at making use of the plaintiffs' Grandsen drawings to obtain planning permission or to build houses. They admit that the houses themselves constitute a reproduction in a material form of the plaintiffs' Grandsen drawings. Although the houses are part of the realty and outside the scope of section 18 of the Copyright Act 1956, building them was itself an infringement of the plaintiffs' copyright. The plaintiffs are entitled under section 17 of the Copyright Act 1956 to have by way of restitution 'an account of profits in respect of the infringement', that is to say not merely the additional profits obtained by the defendants by their unauthorised use of the plaintiffs' drawings in building the houses, but all the profits obtained by them by their infringing acts of building them. A similar distinction was drawn by Pennycuick J. in a different context but for not dissimilar reasons in *Peter Pan Manufacturing Corporation v. Corsets Silhouette Limited [1963] R.P.C. 45 at 60*, where he held that the plaintiffs were entitled to an account of the profits made by the defendants from the sale of the offending articles, and not merely an account of the additional profits made by them by their use of confidential information in the course of manufacturing them.

In my judgment ... [t]he admitted acts of infringement are not confined to the unauthorised use of the plaintiffs' Grandsen drawings in designing the houses; they include the building of the houses themselves. The plaintiffs are entitled to all the profits obtained by the defendants by building the houses as and where they built them.

It may seem hard that the defendants should have no share of the profits obtained by their skill and efforts in building the houses, but these were the infringing acts complained of and the profits made thereby belong in equity to the plaintiffs. The plaintiffs are entitled to be put in the same position as if they had built the houses. Profits, of course, means net profits, and the defendants are entitled to deduct the costs and expenses of building the houses. Such deductions may include just allowances for time and effort, but just allowances do not include profits: see *Re United Merthyr Collieries Company (1872) 15 L.R. Eq. 46*.

(paras 16–18)

16.3 ADDITIONAL REMEDIES

Although injunctions and damages are the core remedies, two further remedies may be imposed in appropriate cases. These include punitive damages and/or criminal sanctions, destruction of infringing goods (delivery up) and stopping imports.

16.3.1 Punitive Damages and Criminal Sanctions

In setting out the general principles of damages, Lord Wilberforce in *General Tire* wrote that the purpose of damages is to 'compensate the plaintiffs and not punish the defendants'. This rule fits well with the understanding of IP infringement as a private wrong. Awarding the claimant extra damages to 'punish' the defendant risks giving the claimant an excessive and undeserved windfall.

Despite that statement, there have been broader moves towards punishing IP infringers. Courts have the power to award 'exemplary' or 'aggravated' damages to IP owners in appropriate circumstances. In addition, in some areas of IP, statutes provide courts with the power to grant additional damages taking into account the 'flagrancy' of the infringement.

Similarly, with the exception of patents and unregistered designs, statutes provide for criminal sanctions in certain circumstances. Section 107 of the CDPA creates a criminal offence of knowingly infringing copyright and with either intention to gain or knowledge that the infringement will cause loss to the copyright owner. Section 92 of the TMA 1994 creates a criminal offence of using a trade mark with a 'view to gain. . .or with intent to cause loss to another'. Section 35ZA of the RDA 1949 creates a criminal offence of copying a registered design intentionally and with features which are exactly the same as, or differ only immaterially from, the design when such activities are carried out 'in the course of business'. Any of these offenses can result in a fine and/or up to ten years' imprisonment.

In imposing criminal sanctions, courts often use the language of theft or stealing; this is particularly true in relation to property. The following statement from the Court of Appeal in *R v Carter* is illustrative:[4]

> Turning to the suspended sentence of nine months' imprisonment, it has to be borne in mind that counterfeiting of video films is a serious offence. In effect to make and distribute pirate copies of films is to steal from the true owner of the copyright, the property for which he has to expend money in order to possess it. It is an offence really of dishonesty.

ACTIVITY 16.3

Is infringement of copyright similar to 'theft' or 'stealing'? What might be different about infringement or theft?

16.3.2 Delivery Up

A remedy which often accompanies the final injunction is **delivery up**. This is a court order demanding the delivery of the infringing goods for either forfeiture or destruction. As Case 16.7 illustrates, the purpose of the remedy is to ensure compliance with the injunction.

Case 16.7 *Merck Canada v Sigma (No 2)* [2013] EWCA Civ 326

Facts

Merck (claimant–respondent) owned a UK patent and supplementary protection certificate (SPC) relating to a chemical called montelukast sodium. This is the active ingredient of a pharmaceutical product sold by Merck under the name Singulair for the treatment of asthma. The patent expired on 10 October 2011 and the SPC expired on 24 February 2013.

Merck sold Singulair in Poland. Sigma (defendant–appellant) bought Singulair in Poland and imported it into the UK. Under normal circumstances, this would have been permissible under the doctrine of exhaustion. However, in this instance exhaustion did not apply. Poland and a number of other now EU states historically did not permit patenting of pharmaceuticals. When they became EU member states, an exception to the free movement of goods rules was put in place. It was felt that it would unduly harm the pharmaceutical industry's interests if goods sold in Poland, without IP protections and therefore at a cheaper price, could be freely imported into other EU countries.

In 2009, before importation, Sigma contacted Merck's exclusive licensee in the UK asking whether they objected to the importation, but received no response.

Issue and Procedure

In 2011, following expiry of the patent, but while the SPC still applied, Merck brought infringement proceedings against Sigma. On March 2012, Mr Justice Birss held at trial that the defendant's conduct was infringing and ordered the delivery up and destruction of their remaining stock of Singulair (a quantity valued at £2 million). The decision was appealed to the Court of Appeal. By the time of the appeal, both the patent and SPC had expired.

LORD JUSTICE KITCHIN

I can deal with this quite shortly. The judge having found infringement, he made a consequential order that Sigma must destroy the infringing products which it held. The question which arises is whether he fell into error in so doing, on the assumption that his finding of infringement was correct.

The jurisdiction to make an order for the destruction of infringing products is conferred by s.61(1)(b) of the 1977 Act. This is consistent with Article 10 of the Enforcement Directive 2004/48 EC which reads:

'Corrective measures

1. Without prejudice to any damages due to the rightholder by reason of the infringement, and without compensation of any sort, Member States shall ensure that the competent judicial authorities may order, at the request of the applicant, that appropriate measures be taken with regard to goods that they have found to be infringing an intellectual property right and, in appropriate cases, with regard to materials and implements principally used in the creation or manufacture of those goods. Such measures shall include:

(a) recall from the channels of commerce,

(b) definitive removal from the channels of commerce, or

(c) destruction.'

The purpose of such an order was explained by Jacob LJ in Mayne v Pharmacia [2005] EWCA Civ 294:

'4. Furthermore, it is important to remember what the jurisdiction to grant an order for delivery up is for. It is not anything more than a way of making sure that the injunction is obeyed. Einfield J in Rousel Uclaf & Another v Pan Laboratories Limited [1994] 51 FCR 316, in the Federal Court of Australia, on 17th May 1994, dealing with a very similar case, said this:

"In this case the products cannot, while they remain outside the jurisdiction, infringe the Australian patents of the applicants. Nor is there any evidence that, unless ordered to do so by the Court, the respondents intend to re-import them. All that can be said in support of such an order is that while in Australia the products infringed the patents and that the respondents should not be allowed to 'gain a benefit' by 'sneaking' them out of the jurisdiction. But an order for delivery up is not for punishment of the infringer or compensation to the patentee. It is to protect the patentee's rights. As I see it, the presence of the products in Papua New Guinea does not place the rights of the applicants at risk and in need of protection. See further Blanco White, Patents for Inventions 1974 4th ed paras 12–128; Terrell on the Law of Patents 13th ed, paras 14.178–14.180."

5. The order for delivery up therefore being ancillary to the injunction, one always has to ask whether it is necessary to be made. Sometimes the court refuses to make it simply on the basis that a particular machine which has been found to infringe can be modified. In that case the court makes the alternative order of modification upon oath. There is no case for delivery up of material which may have had a temporary presence in this country.'

In this case the judge ordered delivery up for five reasons. First, he thought the best way to ensure compliance with the injunction was to order delivery up. Second, Sigma's retention of unlawfully imported products would give it an unwarranted advantage when the SPC expired because it might well be able to sell those products into the market more quickly than would have been the case had it not infringed. Third, the fact the products were perfectly marketable was neither here nor there; their relevant characteristic was that they were infringing. Fourth, the remedy was proportionate because the products ought never to have been imported. Fifth, there were no third party interests which required consideration.

On this appeal, Sigma contends the judge fell into error. It says that the effect of the order is that the products must be destroyed even though it is now perfectly lawful to sell them in the United Kingdom. This, it says, is senseless and punitive. It continues that it should also be borne in mind that the products were imported and repackaged in good faith and in the belief that Merck did not object; that the products were in fact made by Merck; and that the order has had the effect of preventing the sale of products in the United Kingdom after the expiry of the SPC and so also allowing Merck to maintain price differentials between the market in the United Kingdom and the markets of other Member States.

In considering these submissions I would emphasise at the outset that an order for delivery up is a discretionary remedy and so Sigma must show the judge has erred in principle or that he has exceeded the generous ambit within which reasonable disagreement is possible. It must also be noted that, as Sigma fairly accepted, the question whether the judge has fallen into error must be considered as at the date he made his order.

I turn then to consider the various matters relied upon by Sigma. As for the first point, it is of course true that Merck no longer has any relevant rights but, as I have said, the matter must be judged as at the date of the order, and this was made some nine months before the SPC expired. I also accept that Sigma has acted in good faith and in the belief that Merck did not object. But this is far from determinative; Sigma had been found to infringe and the products it had imported were all infringing goods. So also, the fact that the products were originally made by Merck is beside the point. They were bought in a jurisdiction that did not offer protection at the relevant time and, on the assumption the judge was right, their importation into the United Kingdom amounted to an infringement. Finally, it is true that the effect of the order is to prevent the sale of the products in the United Kingdom after the expiry of the SPC, but this is because the judge found them to be infringing products. As he held, to allow Sigma to sell them after the expiry would have been to confer upon it an unwarranted advantage.

For all these reasons I am satisfied that the judge was entitled to make the order he did, on the assumption his finding of infringement was correct. It cannot be said he erred in principle or made an order which was plainly wrong.

(paras 88–95)

ACTIVITY 16.4

Was destroying perfectly good medicines 'senseless and punitive', as argued by the defendant?

16.3.3 Stopping Imports

Lastly, mechanisms exist to prevent the importation of infringing goods from other jurisdictions. The most significant mechanism is the EU Border Regulation.[5] The regulation allows customs authorities to retain goods which infringe IP rights.

16.4 PRETRIAL RELIEF

Sections 16.1–16.3 considered actions taken by courts following a finding of infringement at trial. This section turns to actions courts can take before the trial begins. This can be split into two subsections: interim injunctions and evidentiary orders.

16.4.1 Interim Injunctions

After an IP owner starts an infringement action, it may be several months before the trial. The gap in time causes a problem. If the defendant's activities infringe upon the IP owner's rights, then permitting the defendant to continue their activities might unduly prejudice the IP owner's interests. To prevent that outcome, courts might award an interim injunction restraining the defendant from their activities until the trial. Such an injunction might, however, unduly prejudice the defendant. If the trial court later finds that the defendant's activities were non-infringing, then the injunction has unnecessarily interfered with their business. Courts therefore need to strike a balance between protecting IP owners against possible infringement, and not unnecessarily restricting activity which is potentially non-infringing. How courts strike the balance is explained in Case 16.8.

Case 16.8 *American Cyanamid Co (No 1) v Ethicon Ltd* [1975] AC 396

Facts

American Cyanamid Co (claimant–appellant) owned a UK patent relating to surgical sutures that disintegrated and absorbed into the body once they served their purpose. Ethicon (defendants–respondents) intended to introduce their own sutures to the market. American Cyanamid considered the Ethicon sutures to infringe the patent.

Issue and Procedure

American Cyanamid brought an infringement action against Ethicon. The trial court awarded an interim injunction.

The interim injunction was overturned by the Court of Appeal. In the Court of Appeal's judgment, a court should consider the witness statements provided by each party (also known as affidavit evidence). There is no opportunity at this stage to cross-examine those witnesses. If on the basis of this evidence, the court is satisfied that the claimant would win their case at trial, the court should then – and only then – consider the 'balance of conveniences' and decide whether to award an interim injunction. In this particular case, the Court of Appeal judged that the witness statements did not support a finding of infringement. Therefore, the interim injunction should not be awarded.

In the extract below, the House of Lords overturned the Court of Appeal and set out principles governing the award of interim injunctions. The House of Lords disagreed with the Court of Appeal that, as a matter of rule, the witness statements must support a finding of infringement; instead, all that is necessary before considering the 'balance of conveniences' is that there exists a serious question to be tried.

LORD DIPLOCK

Your Lordships should in my view take this opportunity of declaring that there is no such rule. The use of such expressions as 'a probability', 'a prima facie case', or 'a strong prima facie case' in the context of the exercise of a discretionary power to grant an interlocutory injunction leads to confusion as to the object sought to be achieved by this form of temporary relief. The court no doubt must be satisfied that the claim is not frivolous or vexatious, in other words, that there is a serious question to be tried.

It is no part of the court's function at this stage of the litigation to try to resolve conflicts of evidence on affidavit as to facts on which the claims of either party may ultimately depend nor to decide difficult questions of law which call for detailed argument and mature considerations. These are matters to be dealt with at the trial. One of the reasons for the introduction of the practice of requiring an undertaking as to damages upon the grant of an interlocutory injunction was that 'it aided the court in doing that which was its great object, viz. abstaining from expressing any opinion upon the merits of the case until the hearing': *Wakefield v. Duke of Buccleugh (1865) 12 L.T. 628, 629*. So unless the material available to the court at the hearing of the application for an interlocutory injunction fails to disclose that the plaintiff has any real prospect of succeeding in his claim for a permanent injunction at the trial, the court should go on to consider whether the balance of convenience lies in favour of granting or refusing the interlocutory relief that is sought.

As to that, the governing principle is that the court should first consider whether, if the plaintiff were to succeed at the trial in establishing his right to a permanent injunction, he would be adequately compensated by an award of damages for the loss he would have sustained as a result of the defendant's continuing to do what was sought to be enjoined between the time of the application and the time of the trial. If damages in the measure recoverable at common law would be adequate remedy and the defendant would be in a financial position to pay them, no interlocutory injunction should normally be granted, however strong the plaintiff's claim appeared to be at that stage. If, on the other hand, damages would not provide an adequate remedy for the plaintiff in the event of his succeeding at the trial, the court should then consider whether, on the contrary hypothesis that the defendant were to succeed at the trial in establishing his right to do that which was sought to be enjoined, he would be adequately compensated under the plaintiff's undertaking as to damages for the loss he would have sustained by being prevented from doing so between the time of the application and the time of the trial. If damages in the measure recoverable under such an undertaking would be an adequate remedy and the plaintiff would be in a financial position to pay them, there would be no reason upon this ground to refuse an interlocutory injunction.

It is where there is doubt as to the adequacy of the respective remedies in damages available to either party or to both, that the question of balance of convenience arises. It would be unwise to attempt even to list all the various matters which may need to be taken into consideration in deciding where the balance lies, let alone to suggest the relative weight to be attached to them. These will vary from case to case.

Where other factors appear to be evenly balanced it is a counsel of prudence to take such measures as are calculated to preserve the status quo. If the defendant is enjoined temporarily from doing something that he has not done before, the only effect of the interlocutory injunction in the event of his succeeding at the trial is to postpone the date at which he is able to embark upon a course of action which he has not previously found it necessary to undertake; whereas to interrupt him in the conduct of an established enterprise would cause much greater inconvenience to him since he would have to start again to establish it in the event of his succeeding at the trial.

Save in the simplest cases, the decision to grant or to refuse an interlocutory injunction will cause to whichever party is unsuccessful on the application some disadvantages which his ultimate success at the trial may show he ought to have been spared and the disadvantages may be such that the recovery of damages to which he would then be entitled either in the action or under the plaintiff's undertaking would not be sufficient to compensate him fully for all of them. The extent to which the disadvantages to each party would be incapable of being compensated in damages in the event of his succeeding at the trial is always a significant factor in assessing where the balance of convenience lies, and if the extent of the uncompensatable disadvantage to each party would not differ widely, it may not be improper to take into account in tipping the balance the relative strength of each party's case as revealed by the affidavit evidence adduced on the hearing of the application. This, however, should be done only where it is apparent upon the facts disclosed by evidence as to which there is no credible dispute that the strength of one party's case is disproportionate to that of the other party. The court is not justified in embarking upon anything resembling a trial of the action upon conflicting affidavits in order to evaluate the strength of either party's case.

I would reiterate that, in addition to those to which I have referred, there may be many other special factors to be taken into consideration in the particular circumstances of individual cases. The instant appeal affords one example of this.

(pp. 407–09)

On the facts of the case, the House of Lords saw no reason to interfere with the trial court judgment. There was a serious question to be tried, in their view, and the trial court judge had established that, on the balance of conveniences, an interim injunction should be issued. Various factors were put forward in support of that conclusion, including the fact that Ethicon's sutures were not yet on the market, and so they had no business which could be stopped by the interim injunction.

Today, the interim injunction procedure has to be viewed in the light of the Enforcement Directive and the requirement of proportionality. Whether an interim injunction is proportional may be considered under the balance of convenience analysis.

16.4.2 Evidentiary Orders

In addition to interim injunctions, courts may award any of the following orders: **search orders**, freezing orders and *Norwich Pharmaceutical* orders. Broadly,

Remedies and Litigation

these orders are designed to preserve and reveal evidence that may later be important at trial.

The most famous of these orders is the **search order**, formerly known as the *Anton Piller* order on the grounds that it was first employed in *Anton Piller KG v Manufacturing Processes Ltd*. Despite centuries-old precedents stating that courts cannot award search warrants, this is arguably what the *Anton Piller* order does.

Case 16.9 *Anton Piller KG v Manufacturing Processes Ltd* [1976] Ch 55

Facts

Anton Piller (claimants) was a German manufacturer of computer converters, among other things. Manufacturing Processes Ltd (MPL) (defendants) were the agents of Piller in the UK. Anton Piller became aware that MPL were supplying confidential information, including Piller's copyright protected drawings, to their competitors in Germany. Anton Piller began legal proceedings against MPL but were concerned that if MPL were given notice of the proceedings, they would take steps to destroy documents or evidence which may later be used against them.

Issue and Procedure

On 26 November 1975, Anton Piller asked the High Court to issue an interim injunction and an order permitting them to enter the premises of MPL to search for documents and, if necessary, remove the documents from the premises. This process took place *ex parte*, that is, without the presence of MPL. Initially, Mr Justice Brightman granted the interim injunction, but refused the search order. In the view of Mr Justice Brightman, such a search order might 'become an instrument of oppression, particularly in a case where a plaintiff of big standing and deep pocket is ranged against a small man who is alleged on the evidence of one side only to have infringed the plaintiffs' rights'. However, Lord Denning in the Court of Appeal subsequently granted the search order.

DENNING MR

During the last 18 months the judges of the Chancery Division have been making orders of a kind not known before. They have some resemblance to search warrants. Under these orders, the plaintiff and his solicitors are authorised to enter the defendant's premises so as to inspect papers, provided the defendant gives permission.

Now this is the important point: The court orders the defendant to give them permission. The judges have been making these orders on ex parte applications without prior notice to the defendant. None of the cases have been reported except the one before Templeman J. on December 3, 1974, *E.M.I. Ltd. v. Pandit* [1975] 1 W.L.R. 302. But in the present case Brightman J. refused to make such an order.

On appeal to us, Mr. Laddie appears for the plaintiffs. He has appeared in most of these cases, and can claim the credit – or the responsibility – for them. He represented to us that in this case it was in the interests of justice that the application should not be made public at the time it was made. So we heard it in camera. It was last Tuesday. After hearing his submissions, we made the order. We now come to give our reasons in public. But at the outset I must state the facts, for it is obvious that such an order can only be justified in the most exceptional circumstances.

Let me say at once that no court in this land has any power to issue a search warrant to enter a man's house so as to see if there are papers or documents there which are of an incriminating nature, whether libels or infringements of copyright or anything else of the kind. No constable or bailiff can knock at the door and demand entry so as to inspect papers or documents. The householder can shut the door in his face and say 'Get out'. That was established in the leading case of Entick v. Carrington (1765) 2 Wils.K.B. 275. None of us would wish to whittle down that principle in the slightest. But the order sought in this case is not a search warrant. It does not authorise the plaintiffs' solicitors or anyone else to enter the defendants' premises against their will. It does not authorise the breaking down of any doors, nor the slipping in by a back door, nor getting in by an open door or window. It only authorises entry and inspection by the permission of the defendants. The plaintiffs must get the defendants' permission. But it does do this: It brings pressure on the defendants to give permission. It does more. It actually orders them to give permission – with, I suppose, the result that if they do not give permission, they are guilty of contempt of court.

Accepting such to be the case, the question is in what circumstances ought such an order be made... It seems to me that such an order can be made by a judge ex parte, but it should only be made where it is essential that the plaintiff should have inspection so that justice can be done between the parties: and when, if the defendant were forewarned, there is a grave danger that vital evidence will be destroyed, that papers will be burnt or lost or hidden, or taken beyond the jurisdiction, and so the ends of justice be defeated: and when the inspection would do no real harm to the defendant or his case.

(pp. 58, 60–61)

Hugh Laddie was later appointed a High Court judge. He later became the Chair of Intellectual Property at UCL. After his death, the chair was renamed the Sir Hugh Laddie Chair in Intellectual Property, and is currently held by Sir Robin Jacob. It is reported that later in life, he criticised the *Anton Piller* order as a 'Frankenstein's monster'.[6]

> ### ACTIVITY 16.5
>
> The search order pits property owner against property owner. On one side, we have an intellectual property owner who fears their rights are being infringed. On the other side, we find a land (or real property) owner who has the right to 'shut the door' and tell people to 'get out'. Can anyone have 'exclusive control' over their property when property rights often come into conflict in this way?

In addition to search orders, courts can award freezing orders (formerly known as *Mareva* injunctions) and *Norwich Pharmaceutical* orders. A freezing order requires a party to retain and not dispose of property prior to trial. The *Norwich Pharmaceutical* order requires parties to reveal information relevant to the action, such as names and addresses of relevant parties.

16.5 UNJUSTIFIED THREATS

Last, but not least, the Intellectual Property (Unjustified Threats) Act 2017 provides counter-remedies. The principles contained in the Act permit parties to receive remedies for '**unjustified threats**' of infringement proceedings. If a person receives a threat of an infringement action, the burden then shifts to the IP owner to show that the threat is 'justified', that is, by showing that an IP right exists and the defendant's actions constitute infringement. If the threat is unjustified, the defendant may receive remedies, including: declarations that the threats were unjustified, injunctions against the continuance of threats, and damages for any losses caused by the threats.

The Act provides some protection against over-zealous enforcement of IP rights. However, in practice the provisions are limited in scope in three important ways.

First, the provisions only apply in cases of patent, trade mark or registered design infringement. There are no statutory unjustified threats provisions in relation to copyright or passing off. In relation to these latter rights, defendants must rely on common law actions such as injurious falsehood.

Second, the unjustified threats provisions apply only to secondary infringements, and not primary infringements. The consequence is that most of the cases introduced in Parts I–III of this book are outside the scope of the unjustified threats provisions.

Third, even in relation to secondary infringers, IP owners will not be subject to any remedies for so-called permitted communications. Permitted communications are any communications necessary for a 'permitted purpose' such as: requesting a person to cease doing, for commercial purposes, anything in relation to a product or process; requesting a person to deliver up or destroy a product; requesting a person to give an undertaking relating to a product or process.

16.6   SUMMARY

Is intellectual property really property? If one adopts an 'exclusive control' model of property, one might find many property-like features within the topic of IP remedies and litigation. Injunctions, although formally equitable and discretionary, are very frequently granted. Infringement of IP rights may result in not only civil remedies, but criminal punishment. Even the unproven possibility that a defendant has infringed an IP right may result in their premises being searched, and their business temporarily stopped.

On the other hand, there are potential deviations from the exclusive control model of property. The public interest does play some role in the award of injunctive relief. Counter-remedies, like actions for unjustified threats, exist, if in a very limited form. These deviations suggest that the IP owner's control over their things is not perfectly exclusive, but can be narrowly tailored to fit normative values. Perhaps, therefore, IP is still a bundle of narrowly tailored rights. It is ultimately up to students to decide.

16.7   SELF-ASSESSMENT

Before moving on, try to answer the following questions to consolidate your learning. Answers are provided in the section below.

1. When deciding whether to grant a final injunction, which of the following is *not* a general principle, according to Birss J in *Evalve Inc v Edwards Lifescience* [2020] EWHC 513 (Pat)?
   a. A final injunction is the 'normal remedy' for patent owners.
   b. The public interest is a relevant consideration.
   c. The power to deny injunctions should be used sparingly and in limited circumstances.
   d. If damages in lieu are large, it will not be in the public interest to deny the injunction.
2. Company A owns a patent on a method of brewing coffee. Company B has infringed the patent. Which of the following is not relevant to the calculation of damages? Choose one or more answers.
   a. What would be fair in the circumstances for Company B to pay.
   b. Evidence that Company A has offered to license the method to Company C in the past for £10 million. Company C declined the offer.
   c. Evidence that Company A has offered to license the method to Company D in the past for £1 million. Company D accepted the offer.
   d. Whether the circumstances described in c. are comparable to the circumstances in the current case.
3. Which of the following should courts consider when deciding to grant an interim injunction? Choose one or more answers.
   a. Whether there is a serious question to be tried.
   b. Whether the witness affidavits support a finding of infringement.
   c. Whether the claimant can be adequately compensated in damages for any loss suffered before trial.
   d. All of the above.
4. Are there any circumstances where judges should deny permanent injunctive relief. If so, provide examples.

ACTIVITY DISCUSSION

Activity 16.1 The decision of Justice Kennedy is more naturally inclined towards a bundle of rights vision of property. The law should tailor the IP owner's rights and remedies to fit society's social and economic needs. In a world of non-practising entities, those needs may be better served by denying injunctive relief. Society's needs might, therefore, be more important than the IP owner's desire for exclusive control.

By contrast, Chief Justice Roberts says comparatively little about social and economic needs. Unlike Kennedy, Roberts does not explicitly allow such needs to override the IP owner's desire for exclusive control.

Activity 16.2 The UK law does not state clearly that injunctions will follow a finding of infringement as a matter of a general rule. Indeed, as Mr Justice Birss says, the public interest may plausibly override the IP owner's desire for such relief.

On the other hand, there are points of Mr Justice Birss's judgment that suggest a general rule is in operation. Infringements are considered the 'normal' remedy. While defendants can use the public interest to argue against injunctive relief, the circumstances in which they will be successful seem very narrow. After all, Parliament may have been said to have already considered the public interest when defining the scope of the IP owner's rights.

Activity 16.3 One similarity between theft and IP infringement is that, in both cases, the defendant has done something in respect of the property against the wishes of the owner. Both acts disrupt the owner's exclusive control of the thing they own.

On the other hand, metaphysical differences exist between theft and infringement. When I steal your car, you no longer have that car. When I copy your song, you do not lose that song; it has instead been duplicated and shared. This flows from the nature of intellectual phenomena as non-rivalrous.

Does the metaphysical difference matter? If you see property as 'exclusive control', and IP as property, then arguably not. In that case, we may be dealing with a 'distinction without a difference'.

Activity 16.4 Destroying asthma medication, which could have been used by people, seems like a waste; especially so when one considers the IP owner's rights had, at that time, already expired. In this regard, the delivery up may well be seen as senseless. One might disagree, however, if one thinks that the IP owner does deserve exclusive control over their intellectual goods.

Activity 16.5 I am inclined to say no. Cases like *Anton Piller* suggest that property rights cannot be absolute because property rights often conflict with one another. Even if both property owners desire exclusive control over their property, one of them will necessarily lose. To me, this suggests that property must be a bundle of rights. In dealing with cases such as *Anton Piller*, courts ought to shape the owner's rights in a way that best satisfies our normative values.

SELF-ASSESSMENT ANSWERS

1. **Correct answer: d.** Mr Justice Birss agreed that whether damages in lieu are large or small is irrelevant when considering whether to deny the injunction.

2. **Correct answers: a.** and **b.** Judges, according to *General Tire v Firestone*, should calculate damages based on actual licensing practices, and not based on considerations of fairness. It is not enough to demonstrate that licenses have been offered at a certain price; what matters is what license deals have actually been made, providing these are the 'going rate' in the circumstances.

3. **Correct answers: a.** and **c.** Answer **b.** is incorrect, following *American Cyanamid Co (No 1) v Ethicon Ltd* [1975] UKHL 1. Answer **d.** is accordingly also incorrect.

Notes

1 261 F Supp 2d 423 (ED Va 2002) (US).

2 [1895] 1 Ch 287.

3 [2014] UKSC 13.

4 [1983] FSR 303, 304 (CA).

5 608/2013/EU Regulation concerning customs enforcement of intellectual property rights and repealing Council Regulation 1383/2003/EC (Border Measures Regulation (BMR)). Application to the UK via Customs (Enforcement of Intellectual Property Rights) (Amendment) (EU Exit) Regulations 2019 (SI 2019/514).

6 Professor Sir Hugh Laddie, Obituary, *The Telegraph* (3 December 2008) <https://www.telegraph.co.uk/news/obituaries/3546410/Professor-Sir-Hugh-Laddie.html> (accessed 22 December 2023).

17

Epilogue

Peter Smith in Section 1.2 wrote that 'reason-giving arguments are the very stuff of all serious inquiry'. And, so far, this book has presented IP as something that is responsive to reason and argument. We started by introducing three foundational questions (the metaphysical, conceptual and normative questions). The book has introduced students to different arguments in response to those questions. It is for students to evaluate those arguments and form their own conclusions.

However, I want to end on a more worrisome note. Is IP really responsive to reason and argument? Or, to put the question another way, does IP depend on something other than reason? In the following provocative essay, Mark Lemley suggests that, at least for some people, our beliefs about IP do not depend on reason at all, but instead on something else: faith.

For my part, I largely agree with Lemley. Vincent van Gogh, Christiansen and Robert Law, and the businesses they founded, have all made significant contributions to our world and I think they deserve something in return. I think that creators deserve celebration and praise, acknowledgement and even some form of financial reward.

What I find far more controversial, however, is the claim that creators deserve *property* in their intangibles. This is especially true if one thinks of property as exclusive control over a thing. That sort of control seems, in my mind, almost indefensible. Nevertheless, that sort of control is increasingly what IP is in the twenty-first century. That trend, in my opinion, has less to do with reason and argument, and more to do with private interests, the pressures of capitalism, lobbying, emotion and maybe, as Lemley writes, faith.

BOX 17.1 MARK A LEMLEY, 'FAITH-BASED INTELLECTUAL PROPERTY' (2015) 62 UCLA L REV 1328

IP rights are a form of government regulation of the free market designed to serve a useful social end – encouraging innovation and creation.[1] IP rights represent government interventions in the marketplace that seek to achieve that desirable social end by restricting the freedom of some people (consumers, reusers, critics) to do what they want with their own real and personal property in order to improve the lives of other people (inventors and creators). My freedom to make art or build a new phone is constrained by a government requirement that my art or my phone not be too similar to someone else's. In the case of patents, that's true even if I have never heard of the other person or seen their phone or their patent, and indeed even if they never built a phone at all.

The fact that IP is government regulation of the marketplace doesn't mean it is a bad thing. Many regulations are desirable, and I think IP rights of some form are among them. But it does mean that it is not an inherently good thing. In a market-based economy, regulation requires some cost–benefit justification before we accept it.

For a long time, evidence that might support that justification was in short supply. We had a plausible-sounding theory: Rational actors won't spend a lot of money to create something if others can just copy it more cheaply. But we had very little evidence one way or the other to bolster that theory. . . .

That is no longer true. In the past three decades there has been an unprecedented – indeed, astonishing – outpouring of sophisticated empirical work on virtually every aspect of IP law and innovative and creative markets. We now have empirical studies on who obtains IP rights, who enforces them, and who wins. We have studies on how IP rights affect stock performance. We have industry-specific studies that examine what drives creativity in virtually every field imaginable, including those protected by patents, by copyright, and by no IP right at all. We have evidence about how innovation in various industries has fared under changes in IP regimes, the growth of the Internet, internationalization, and various other exogenous shocks. We have experimental evidence that explores how test subjects view the sale of things they have actually created, and iterative-play games that model economies with different IP regimes. We have surveys of creators and inventors that ask about their motivations. And we have psychological studies that explore both why and how people create and how money affects (or does not affect) that creative impulse.

The upshot of all this evidence is something rather less than a complete vindication of the theory of IP regulation. As Lisa Ouellette puts it, 'none of these studies resolves whether patents have a net positive effect on innovation, much less their net welfare effect, or

Mark Lemley is the William H Neukom Professor of Law at Stanford Law School and the Director of the Stanford Program in Law, Science and Technology, USA.

whether alternative innovation incentives such as grants, prizes, and tax credits are inferior'. This doesn't mean that we are no better off than we were in Fritz Machlup's day. The problem isn't that we don't have enough evidence, or the right kind of evidence. The problem is that the picture painted by the evidence is a complicated one...

Instead of questioning the theory of IP in light of this evidence, however, a number of people have instead sought ways to ignore the evidence and keep on doing what they have always been doing.

I call this retreat from evidence faith-based IP, both because adherents are taking the validity of the IP system on faith and because the rationale for doing so is a form of religious belief. The adherents of this new religion believe in IP. They don't believe it is better for the world than other systems, or that it encourages more innovation. Rather, they believe in IP as an end in itself – that IP is some kind of prepolitical right to which inventors and creators are entitled. Because that is a belief, evidence cannot shake it any more than I can persuade someone who believes in the literal truth of the bible that his god didn't create the world in seven days. Sure, there may be geological and archeological evidence that makes the seven-day story implausible. But faith is not just ambivalent about evidentiary support; it is remarkably resistant to evidentiary challenge. Indeed, many proponents of this new religion even tout that as an advantage for their faith, claiming that it 'avoids the need for empirical validation demanded by the utilitarian approach'.

Maybe – hopefully – I have persuaded you that we need to take seriously the evidence we have about how well or poorly the IP system works. That doesn't mean I have persuaded you that we should abandon IP. Indeed, I haven't tried to do so; I don't think the evidence justifies that conclusion.

Rather, the line I hope to draw here is between theories of IP that are responsive to evidence and those that are impervious to it. The evidentiary support for the current IP regime is dubious enough that it should prompt us to have a serious conversation as a society about when IP is serving the goals of encouraging the creation and dissemination of new content and when it isn't. At the very least, one would hope, I could persuade you to look at the evidence.

(pp. 1330–35, 1337–38, 1344–45)

Note

1 Reproduced with permission of author.

Glossary

absolute grounds for refusal a collection of reasons for rejecting a trade mark application, not related to any pre-existing rights.

absolute novelty the rule that material outside of a jurisdiction can form part of the state of the art.

account of profits an equitable remedy wherein the defendant pays the claimant the value of the profits they have obtained as a result of their infringement.

acquired distinctive character a distinctive character acquired through use of the sign in commerce.

aesthetic neutrality the rule that copyright should not grant greater or fewer rights depending on the aesthetic merit of the work.

altered copying the copying of a work where no identifiable section is copied. A paradigmatic case is that of translation.

alternatives objection an objection to the utilitarian argument stating there are better ways of maximising utility than IP rights (primarily through the use of subsidies or prizes).

anticipated an invention which is not new because of an enabling disclosure in the state of the art is said to have been anticipated by the prior art.

any hardware an approach used to define technical character at the EPO. Computer programs and business methods, in particular, will be considered patentable if they are carried out on some form of hardware.

as such a key rule in defining inventions. Some phenomena, like discoveries, are as such not inventions.

attribution the right of the author to be identified as the author.

author's own intellectual creation the rule in EU copyright, and UK copyright in the twenty-first century, that a work must be the author's own intellectual creation (with a personal touch) to be original.

author's rights those granted to authors in continental European countries, including *droit d'auteur* (France) and *Urheberrecht* (Germany).

badge of origin a sign that performs the origin function.

balance the idea that if copyright is not too strong, nor too weak, utility will be maximised.

Blackstonian property A quote from William Blackstone describing property as 'that sole and despotic dominion which one man claims and exercises over the external things of the world, in total exclusion of the right of any other individual in the universe'.

brand an ambitious term, sometimes used to refer to a sign used in commerce.

breach of confidence a common law action that can be used to protect secret information.

bundle of rights (property) a conception of property in which property is composed of multiple different legal rights which may or may not be owned by different persons.

claim construction the process of defining a claim's legal effect.

claims (patent) a section of the patent specification that defines the property rights in an invention.

communication function the ability of signs to communicate non-origin information (e.g. as business values or identity). The definition of communication function is, however, contested.

communication to the public a restricted act in copyright where a person communicates a work to a **new public**.

competition objection an objection to the prospect theory that claims competition is the best way to encourage development of ideas.

complex product a product which is composed of at least two replaceable component parts permitting disassembly and reassembly of the product.

compulsory licence when the state compels an owner to license the use of the intellectual thing.

consumer confusion where consumers are confused about the origin of goods or the economic associations between producers of goods.

copying objection an objection to the personality argument stating that merely copying a work does not harm or impair the special bond between the author and the work.

copyright a property right over works.

Copyright, Designs and Patents Act 1988 the controlling legislation in UK copyright law.

copyright's associated rights non-copyright rights that are nevertheless associated with copyright (e.g. performer's rights or press publishers' rights).

cover page (patent) the first page of a patent specification. It provides information such as the applicant/owner and the name of the inventor.

cumulation acceptance that some IP rights will overlap; particularly relevant in relation to copyright and designs.

cumulative (creativity, innovation) the idea that creating original works and new inventions involves building on pre-existing works and inventions.

customary/generic signs which do not have a distinctive character because they are understood to refer to a class of goods, rather than the goods of a particular business.

damages a legal remedy whereby the defendant pays the claimant monetary compensation for past infringement.

damages in lieu an alternative form of remedy to the injunction. Permits an individual to continue engaging in a particular action or behaviour, subject to them paying ongoing damages.

deadweight loss the reduced consumption of goods produced by a market inefficiency, such as a monopoly (*see also* **problem of monopoly**).

delivery up an equitable remedy in which the court orders infringing goods to be delivered to the court. Commonly the goods will be destroyed.

demarcation an attempt to minimise overlapping IP rights; particularly relevant in relation to copyright and designs.

description (patent) a written description of an invention in the patent specification. The purpose of the description is to set out to the **PSITA** how an invention works.

descriptiveness a sign that designates the kind, quality, quantity, intended purpose, value, geographical origin, the time of production of goods or of rendering of services, or other characteristics of goods or services.

descriptive use the use of a sign to describe one's own goods.

design the subject matter of design rights. Different forms of design rights define designs differently. In registered designs rights, 'designs' refers to the 'appearance' of products. In unregistered design rights, designs refer to the 'shape or configuration' of articles.

Design Directive 1998 EU directive harmonising EU member states' design law.

design drawings those that illustrate the appearance of a product or shape of an article.

Design Regulation 2001 EU regulation creating the community registered design right and community unregistered design right.

dilution uses of signs that reduce the sign's uniqueness.

direct evidence of copying either an admission or first-hand account of copying.

discoveries phenomena which are discovered rather than invented by humans. Examples include the moon and dinosaur fossils.

discrete copying the copying of an identifiable section of a work.

distinctive character a sign has a distinctive character if it performs an origin function.

distribution the issuing of copies of a work to the public. A restricted act.

doctrine of equivalents doctrine which enables patent owners to own inventions outside of the claim language.

double identity a sign that is identical with an earlier sign and is to be registered for, or used in connection with, goods or services similar to those of the earlier sign.

economic rights rights of the copyright owner notionally designed to protect their financial interest in the work.

efficiency a central concept to utilitarian thinking about IP. As used in this book, the concept refers to achieving the best possible good consequences, while minimising any bad consequences.

embodiment a specific and tangible form or implementation of an invention that is described in a patent specification.

empirical objection an objection to the utilitarian argument stating that insufficient evidence supports the claim that IP rights (even when appropriately balanced) maximise utility.

empiricism the idea that knowledge is acquired through the senses, perception and observation.

enabling disclosure the test for determining whether a claimant's invention forms part of the state of the art, or alternatively, is novel.

Enlarged Board of Appeal appellate court in the EPO which considers appeals from the EPO Examining Division. Decides on points of law of fundamental importance referred to it by the Technical or Legal Board of Appeals, or the EPO President.

European patent a bundle of national patents granted by the EPO.

European Patent Convention 1973 multilateral patent treaty creating the European patent.

European Patent Office (EPO) organisation which administers the European patent and unitary patent systems.

European Union trade mark an EU-wide trade mark right.

evergreening an attempt to extend a monopoly by making minor modifications to an original work, invention, or some other IP-protected subject matter.

exceptions a rule that permits a person to perform a restricted act.

excludable the degree to which a good can be limited only to certain persons.

exclusive control (property) a conception of property in which the owner has absolute control over a thing (*see also* **Blackstonian property**)

exclusive licence a licence to use an intellectual thing to the exclusion of all other persons.

exhaustion a rule stating that when an IP owner consensually puts a tangible good on the market, the IP rights in that particular tangible good, exhaust. It accordingly infringes no IP rights for buyers to distribute the good further.

experimental use a defence to patent infringement actions permitting experimental use of an invention.

express licence a licence granted expressly in writing or orally.

extended passing off where goodwill is shared by a group of businesses, any individual member of said group may bring a passing off action against a defendant who through misrepresentation damages that goodwill.

fair dealing an exception in UK copyright permitting persons to perform restricted acts for certain statutorily identified purposes so long as the act is 'fair dealing'.

fair use an exception to US copyright that permits persons to perform restricted acts providing such acts are 'fair use'.

first mover advantage the ability to enjoy monopoly profits by virtue of being the first producer in the market. The first mover advantage only lasts until competitors also enter the market.

fixation the rule that certain works must be recorded in some way before they can be owned.

free riding enjoying a benefit without sharing in the costs required to produce that benefit.

functions (sign) the things that signs do, including indicating origin or quality of goods.

geographic indication a sign used to specify the geographic origin of a good. Famous geographic indications include Champagne and Cornish pasties.

global appreciation the standard by which confusing similarity in trade mark law is assessed. The analysis involves taking into account all factors relevant to the circumstances of the case.

good a phenomenon that is valuable in some way

goodwill an intangible asset sometimes defined as the 'attractive force which brings in custom' or the 'benefit and advantage of a good name'. The metaphysical nature of goodwill is contested.

idea–expression distinction a copyright rule stating that a person cannot own ideas, only the expression of said ideas.

implied licence a licence granted by the owner but implied by a court.

***Improver* questions** a set of questions from the *Improver v Remington* case to help construe claims. Recently modified in *Actavis v Eli Lilly*.

incentive–access tradeoff the dual effects of copyright: stronger copyright increases utility by generating 'incentives' to create, but reduces utility by limiting 'access' to the works (*see* **problem of monopoly**).

independent creation the creation of a work which shares similarities to a prior work. The similarities are due to coincidence and not copying.

indirect evidence of copying evidence of circumstances (primarily access and similarities) from which copying can be inferred.

individual character the overall impression a product's design produces on the informed user.

industrial application the ability of an invention to be made or used in some kind of industry.

industrial copyright an out-of-date term used to refer to copyright in design drawings which could be infringed by the making of products or articles corresponding to said drawings.

industrial policy a country's official strategic effort to encourage economic development and growth.

inherent value/instrumental value as used in this book, something is inherently valuable to the extent people value it for itself (e.g. a beautiful painting). Something is instrumentally valuable to the extent people value it for what it does, such as providing information.

injunction an equitable remedy which orders a person or entity to stop engaging in a particular action or behaviour.

intangible incapable of being touched.

integrity the right of the author to prevent distortion of the work.

Intellectual Property Enterprise Court (IPEC) a part of the High Court of Justice of England and Wales that hears small IP cases.

interpretation–construction difference the distinction between interpretation (i.e. defining the meaning of words) and construction (i.e. defining the words' legal effect).

invention knowledge having a technical character. The subject matter of patents.

inventive step/obviousness the quality of being inventive. One of the patentability requirements.

investment function the ability of signs to encourage investment in the quality of goods. The definition of investment function is, however, contested.

isolation a central concept in separating discoveries from inventions, particularly in relation to biotechnological inventions. The process of isolating some thing from its natural environment may make that thing an invention rather than a discovery.

junior mark when a sign is used by two businesses, the sign which is used second in time is considered the 'junior mark'. (*See also* **senior mark**.)

labour argument the argument that someone who labours to produce an intellectual thing ought to own that intellectual thing.

laissez-faire capitalism an economic philosophy of free market capitalism that opposes government intervention.

Legal Board of Appeals appellate court in the EPO which considers appeals from the EPO Examining Division. Primarily composed of legally qualified members.

legal duty a legal obligation to do or not do some act. Legal duties correlate with legal rights.

legal rights an entitlement provided by the state. It correlates with legal duty.

letters patent an instrument through which the monarch grants a person or organisation some special form of privilege.

liberty/privilege a legal freedom to do something without breaching a legal duty.

licence permission to perform a restricted act (or more broadly to use the intellectual thing) granted by the owner (either voluntarily or compulsorily).

limitation a rule that helps divide restricted from non-restricted acts.

market failure a market that fails to supply the optimal number of goods for consumption.

market power the ability of a seller to increase the price of goods in a market above the price produced in a perfectly competitive market.

minimum standards the minimum level of ownership of intellectual things that a country must provide according to international law.

misrepresentation one of the elements of passing off. Includes misrepresentation of origin or quality of a business's goods.

mixing objection an objection to the labour argument stating that someone who labours to produce an intellectual thing has lost ownership of their labour.

monopolistic competition a type of imperfect market structure where many producers compete against each other, but each has some market power and ability to raise prices above a perfectly competitive level.

monopoly a market structure characterised by several features, the most important of which is the presence of a singular seller.

moral rights rights of the copyright owner notionally designed to protect their personal interest in the work.

national treatment an arrangement under which one country gives foreign citizens the same IP rights as it gives its own nationals.

natural rights those created by nature rather than by humans.

nature objection an objection to the labour argument. It states that the nature of public goods is to be public, and not privately owned.

neighbouring or related rights non-copyright rights granted to non-original works primarily in continental European jurisdictions.

new public a person communicates a work to a 'new public' when they communicate the work to a public not taken into account by the original copyright owner.

nominative/referential use the use of a sign to describe the goods of another.

non-exclusive licence a licence to use an intellectual thing concurrently with other persons.

not copied the rule in UK copyright, primarily prior to the twenty-first century, that to be original a work must not be copied from other sources.

novelty newness. A central requirement in patents and registered design rights.

obscure disclosures disclosures which could not reasonably have become known in the normal course of business to the circles specialised in the sector concerned.

obviousness if an invention would have been obvious to a PSITA, it will not have a sufficiently inventive step to be awarded a patent.

originality a requirement of copyrightable subject matter. Different legal systems define originality in different ways (*see* **skill, labour and/or judgement** and **author's own intellectual creation**).

origin function the ability of a sign to indicate from where goods originate.

orphan works a work for which an owner cannot be found following a diligent search.

overlap the potential for certain intangible phenomena to be protected by various different IP rights simultaneously.

Paris Convention 1883 multilateral patent treaty establishing a union for the protection of 'industrial property' (particularly patents, trade marks and designs).

parody a work that evokes an existing work, while being noticeably different from the existing work, and which constitutes an expression of humour or mockery.

passing off a common law tort that protects a business's property right in goodwill.

patent a property right over inventions.

patentability a set of criteria an applicant must satisfy to receive a patent.

Patents Act 1977 the controlling legislation in UK patent law.

patent bargain a metaphor for patent law in which inventors are granted property monopolies in return for inventive disclosure.

Patent Cooperation Treaty 1970 multilateral patent treaty creating a unified procedure for filing patent applications to protect inventions in each of its contracting states.

patent specification a written document that describes an invention. It serves as the patent application and defines the patent owner's property rights.

patentable subject matter the type of things eligible for patent protection.

perfect competition a market structure characterised by several features, the most important of which is the presence of multiple sellers.

permitted act a restricted act which a person can perform without permission from the owner by virtue of an exception.

personality argument the argument that IP rights protect a special bond that exists between the creator and the intellectual thing.

person having skill in the art (PSITA) a fictional person used for assessing patentability.

plant variety protections a *sui generis* right in plant varieties established after the 1961 International Convention for the Protection of New Varieties of Plants.

pluralist the view that no one argument can justify IP rights, but that a combination of arguments can.

political economy the interaction between politics and economics. In IP, it often is used in the context of lobbying efforts by businesses for greater IP protection.

post-sale confusion confusion among consumers about the origin of goods that occurs after the goods have already been sold.

primary evidence evidence from actual people having skill in the art that an invention was not obvious.

primary liability legal responsibility for infringing an IP right.

priority date the date on which novelty and inventive step in patent law will be assessed. Also the date on which novelty and individual character is assessed in registered design law.

private goods goods that are excludable and rivalrous.

prizes an alternative method of encouraging inventions. Historical examples have included granting large monetary sums to individuals for solving particular problems.

problem of monopoly the fact that monopolies over intellectual things result in higher prices, and therefore less use and enjoyment, of said things.

product differentiation the process of distinguishing one's goods from the goods of a competitor. Product differentiation can be a source of market power and monopolistic competition.

prospect theory the argument that patents are necessary to efficiently coordinate research and development activities.

public domain all intellectual things that are not privately owned.

public goods goods that are non-excludable and non-rivalrous.

purposive construction the practice of constructing claim language in accordance with what the PSITA would take to be the applicant's purpose.

quality function the ability of signs to indicate the quality of goods.

reciprocity an arrangement under which one country gives foreign citizens the same IP rights that the foreign country gives its own nationals.

Registered Designs Act 1949 (RDA 1949) the controlling legislation in UK-registered design rights.

registered design rights design rights that only exist upon successful registration. They include the UK registered design right and the community registered design right.

registered rights IP rights that require registration in order to be enforceable.

relative grounds for refusal rejection of a trade mark application because of a pre-existing trade mark.

reproduction the copying of an intellectual thing. To be distinguished from independent creation. A restricted act in copyright.

restricted acts those in relation to a work that normally require the permission of the owner.

reverse infringement test a test to determine whether a disclosure has occurred in the state of the art. Under this test, a disclosure occurs where the prior art discloses something which, if practised, would infringe the applicant's patent.

reverse passing off misrepresenting the goods of another as one's own.

revival (copyright) where a work has fallen into the public domain, and then later becomes protected by copyright again due to changes in law.

rivalrous the degree to which consumption of a good prevents simultaneous consumption by other persons.

royalty a royalty is a payment made by one party to another in return for the right to use an asset on an ongoing basis.

sampling the discrete copying of a small section from a prior sound recording to be reused in a second sound recording.

scope the level of control over an intellectual thing by an owner defined by the rights minus any relevant exceptions.

search costs the resources (e.g. time or energy) that consumers and producers in a market expend trying to find one another in order to engage in transactions.

search orders (previously *Anton Piller* orders) an interim equitable remedy permitting a claimant to search a defendant's premise for information relevant to the alleged infringement.

secondary evidence evidence from circumstances that may indicate that an invention was not obvious (e.g. its commercial success).

secondary liability legal responsibility for aiding in the infringement of an IP right performed by another person.

secret/inherent use disclosure of an invention to the public prior to the priority date, but in a way that is not obvious to the public.

senior mark when a sign is used by two businesses, the sign which is used first in time is considered the 'senior mark'. (*See also* **junior mark**.)

sign the subject matter of trade mark law. Any phenomenon capable of performing the sign functions.

skill, labour and/or judgement the rule in UK copyright, primarily prior to the twenty-first century, that to be original a work must result from the skill, labour and/or judgement of the author.

state of the art/prior art all matter produced before the priority date of an invention or design.

state of nature a world without governments, laws or organised society.

subconscious copying copying from a prior work without conscious awareness of the copying.

subsidy money granted by the state to authors in return for the generation of creative works.

substantial value a shape that is ineligible for trade mark protection, even if it has a distinctive character, on the grounds that the shape gives the good substantial value.

substitutes one good is a substitute for another when they serve a similar purpose or function and can be used interchangeably by consumers.

sufficiency of disclosure a written description's ability to clearly and completely disclose an invention to the public.

sui generis Latin for 'constituting a class alone' or 'unique'. Various IP rights are described as *sui generis* (e.g. database rights and plant variety protections) in the sense that they are different from more traditional forms of IP protection (e.g. patent and copyright).

supplementary protection certificates (SPCs) a grant of an additional five years of protection to a patent owner to beyond the twenty-year term.

supplementary unregistered design right three years of protection automatically to those who produce a design that is new and has an individual character, so long as that design was first made available to the public within the UK.

tangible capable of being touched.

target parody a parody where the target of the humour or mockery is not the existing work but a third-party individual or object.

tarnishment damage to the reputation of a well-known mark.

Technical Board of Appeals appellate court in the EPO which considers appeals from the EPO Examining Division. Primarily composed of technically qualified members.

technical character a central concept patentable subject matter. Sometimes defined as a human intervention in the material world. Sometimes defined as a contribution to a technical art.

technical drawings (patent) drawings found in a patent specification which illustrate an invention.

temporary copies copies that are not permanent. Temporary copies can exist for fractions of a section. Often such copies appear in digital form in the hard drive of a computer.

term the duration of an IP right.

territoriality the principle that IP rights can only be enforced within the jurisdiction of the state which grants the right.

three-step test a rule of international IP law defining when a state can or cannot provide exceptions to IP rights.

trade mark a property right over signs used in trade.

Trade Mark Act 1994 the controlling legislation of UK trade mark law.

trade mark register a publicly accessible government register of granted trade marks.

trade mark use the use of a sign to perform one of the sign functions protected by trade mark law.

trade secret information enjoyed by a business that is not generally known to the public and which confers economic benefits on the business.

transaction costs the cost of creating a transaction (e.g. the cost of bargaining over a good's price or search costs). Transaction costs can prevent otherwise desirable transactions from taking place. Without IP rights, transaction costs would be zero as consumers could use the underlying assets without the need to obtain permission.

trumps (rights as trumps) the idea that in a conflict between an individual's rights (whether legal or natural) and other considerations (e.g. maximisation of utility), rights always win.

unitary patent a singular EU-wide patent granted by the EPO.

unjustified threats an action against an IP owner for unjustified threats of legal proceedings.

unregistered design rights design rights that are automatic and do not require registration to be enforceable. Includes the UK unregistered design right, the UK supplementary design right, and the community unregistered design right.

unregistered rights IP rights that are automatic and do not require registration to be enforceable.

use objection an objection to the labour argument stating that IP rights, unlike tangible property rights, are not necessary to ensure things are used as God intended.

user rights rights in a work held by persons other than the author, their assignees or successors.

utilitarian argument the argument that the state ought to grant IP to maximise utility.

utilitarian functionality a shape that is ineligible for trade mark protection, even if it has a distinctive character, on the grounds that the shape is necessary to achieve a technical result.

utility the happiness created by, or the preferences satisfied by, an act or law.

variant a variation on a patented invention. Typically discussed in the context of patent litigation when discussing whether the defendant has practised the patent.

voluntary licence the voluntary issue of a licence by an owner.

work the subject matter of copyright.

Index

Arnold, Richard, 80, 105, 146–47, 151, 202, 301, 344, 347, 349, 351, 355–56, 359, 361, 446, 476, 482, 499
artificial intelligence, 159–60, 201

Bentham, Jeremy, 1, 32
Bently, Lionel, 50, 325, 327, 329–30, 332, 363, 369, 388
Birss, Colin, 80, 105, 110, 229–31, 265, 526, 545
Blackstone, William, 5
Boldrin, Michele, 186
Boyle, James, 131
Bracha, Oren, 33, 131
brand, 379
breach of confidence, 189
Brexit and UK–EU relationship, 10
Breyer, Stephen, 37

Cage, John, 65
Christiansen, Godtfred Kirk, 169
Coke, Edward, 175
colonialism, 327, 365
copying
    in copyright: *see* copyright, rights
    in patents: *see* patents, infringing acts
    In registered design right: *see* designs, registered design right
    In unregistered design right: *see* designs, unregistered design right
copyright, exceptions
    computer programs, 132
    databases, 132
    designs, 368–71
    disclosure in the public interest, 157–59
    educational establishments, 132
    exceptions, overview, 131
    fair dealing, criticism or review, 144
    fair dealing, fairness analysis, 147–50

fair dealing, overview, 133
fair dealing, parody caricature pastiche, 143
fair dealing, quotation, 144–46
fair dealing, reporting current events, 146–47
fair dealing, research and private study, 147
fair dealing, statutory purposes, 133
fair dealing, sufficient acknowledgement, 151
fair use, 136
incidental use, 132
libraries, archives and museums, 132
people with disabilities, 132
permitted acts, 131
personal copying for private use, 155–64
public administration, 132
target parody, 140
temporary copies, 151–55
text and data analysis, 159–62
user rights, 131
works in electronic form, 132
copyright, history
    censorship, 18
    common law copyright, 24
    licensing order, 19
    precursors to copyright, 18–20
    Stationers' Company, 19
    Statute of Anne, 20–24
copyright, licensing, 124–25
    compulsory licences, 124
    exclusive licences, 124
    express licences, 124
    implied licences, 124
    non-exclusive licences, 124
    orphan works, 124
    voluntary licences, 124
copyright, neighbouring rights, 81
copyright, ownership, 123
    assignment, 123
    authors as owners, 123

duration, 120–22
employees, 123
formalities, 81
joint authorship, joint ownership, 123
copyright, related rights, 81
copyright, rights
    adaptation, 113–14
    any material form, 98–130
    communication right, new public, 109
    communication to public, 104–13
    copying versus independent creation, 88
    copying, altered versus discreet, 95–130
    copying, evidence of, 88–130
    copying, subconscious, 91
    digital exhaustion, 100
    distribution, 99–103
    economic rights, overview, 86–87
    e-lending, 103
    exhaustion of distribution right, 99
    limitation, 99
    performance, 103–4
    rental and lending, 103
    reproduction, 87–99
    restricted acts, 87
    secondary liability, 87
    substantial part, 93–98
    temporary copies, 99
copyright, subject matter
    aesthetic neutrality, 60–63
    artistic work, 69–74
    author's own intellectual creation, 78
    broadcasts, 74
    closed list, 59
    computer programs, 63
    computer-generated works, 123
    databases, 63
    designs, 363–68
    dramatic work, 63–65
    entrepreneurial/non-original works, 74, 81

films, 74
fixation, UK, 59
functionality, 74
idea–expression distinction, 52
literary work, 60–63
musical work, 65–69
open list, 80
originality as origination, 55
originality, European influence, 80
originality, UK circa twentieth
    century, 59
personal touch, 78
silence, 65
single words, 61
skill, labour and/or judgement, 55
sound recordings, 74
TV show format, 64
typographical arrangements, 74
work, European influences, 76–78
work, UK circa twentieth century,
    50–53
Cornish, William, 323

Defoe, Daniel, 21
design drawings, 333
designs, continuing unregistered
    community design right, 363
designs, history, 327–35
    cumulation, policy of, 332–35
    demarcation, policy of, 329–32
    Designs Registration Act, 327
    early history, 327–29
designs, registered design right, 342–53
    absolute novelty, 347
    appearance, 343–45
    citation or teaching exception, 353
    complex product, 345
    disclosures in breach of confidence,
    349
    duration, 342
    experimental use, 353
    grounds for invalidity, 346
    individual character, 349–50
    novelty, 347–49
    obscure disclosures, 347
    private non-commercial use
    exception, 353
    product, 345
    registration, 342
    representations, 342
    scope, 350–53
    subject matter, 342–46

technical function exclusion, 346
written disclaimers, 342
designs, supplementary unregistered
    design right, 362–63
designs, unregistered community design
    right, 363
designs, unregistered design right,
    353–62
    article, 355
    assignment, 353
    citation or teaching exception, 362
    commonplace designs, 360
    experimental use exception, 362
    licensing, 353
    method or principle of construction
    exclusion, 356–57
    must fit, must match, exclusion,
    357–58
    originality, 359–61
    private non-commercial use
    exception, 362
    scope, 361–62
    shape or configuration, 354
    subject matter, 354–59
    surface decorations, 358–59
designs, works of applied art, 330
Diplock, Kenneth, 292, 297, 301, 500,
    510, 549
Drassinower, Abraham, 3
Drescher, Thomas, 379
droit d'auteur/author's rights, 41

economic concepts, 33
    deadweight loss, 7
    efficiency, 190
    excludability, 3
    first mover advantage, 339
    free rider problem, 403
    goods, 3, 377
    growth, 134
    laissez-faire, 179
    market failure, 33, 163
    market power, 6
    markets, 6
    monopolistic competition, 397–99
    monopoly, 6–8
    perfect competition, 6
    preferences, 33
    private goods, 3
    problem of monopoly, 8
    product differentiation, 399
    public goods, 3, 33, 375, 400

rivalry, 3
search costs, 400, 402
subsidies, 38
substitutes, 381
welfare, 33
Edison, Thomas, 191, 276
epistemological concepts
    empiricism, 36
    empiricism in copyright, 36
    empiricism in trade marks, 394
    faith, 558
    reason, 8
equity
    account of profits, 540
    injunctions, 521
    role in trade marks, 388
ethical concepts, 33
    free riding, in trade marks, 402–5, 469
    hedonism, 33
    hedonism, quantitative versus
    qualitative, 339
    preferences, 33
    supererogatory acts, 404
    utility maximisation, 32
    value, inherent versus instrumental,
    378
    welfare, 33
European Union IP
    Biotechnology Directive, 205, 233
    Design Directive, 342
    Design Regulation, 342
    Directive on Copyright in the Digital
    Single Market, 104
    Enforcement Directive, 525
    European Union Intellectual Property
    Office, 407
    European Union Trade Mark, 407
    Information Society Directive,
    75–76, 136, 155
    Rental and Lending Directive, 103
    Term Directive, 368
    Trade Mark Directive, 407, 416
    Trade Mark Regulation, 407
    unitary patent, 206

geographic indication, 410
Gutenberg, Johannes, 18

Hargreaves Report, 134
Hegel, Georg WF, 39
Hoffmann, Leonard, 253, 255, 266–67,
    296–97, 300–1, 304

Hudson, Emily, 140
Hugo, Victor, 81

industrial copyright, 333
industrial property, 203
Intellectual Property Enterprise Court, 137
International Convention for the Protection of New Varieties of Plants, 241
international copyright law, 41–44
  Berne Convention, 43
  World Intellectual Property Organization Copyright Treaty, 43
international designs law
  Hague Agreement concerning International Registration of Industrial Designs, 342
international IP law concepts
  minimum standards, 43, 204–5, 407–8
  national treatment, 43
  reciprocity, 43
  territoriality, 42
  three-step test, 136
  TRIPS Agreement, 205
international patent law, 203–7
  European patent, 204
  European Patent Convention, 204–5
  European Patent Office, 204
  European Patent Office, Boards of Appeal (technical, legal, enlarged), 205
  Paris Convention, 203–4
  Paris Cooperation Treaty, 204–5
international trade mark law, 407–9
  Madrid system, 407
  Paris Convention, 407

Jacob, Robin, 72, 182, 216, 231, 253, 266–67, 366, 469, 471, 476, 481, 506, 535, 546, 553

Kant, Immanuel, 41

labour argument
  copyright, 25–32
  mixing objection, 29
  nature objection, 32, 183
  patents, 182–84
  problems with, 29–38
  trade marks, 405

use objection, 29
Laddie, Hugh, 73, 95, 117, 268, 366, 478, 553
Landes, William M, 400
Law, Robert, 325
Lemley Mark A, 36, 559
Levine, David K, 186
Locke, John, 19, 47
logic concepts
  arguments, 8
  circular reasoning, 150, 163, 515
  inferences, valid versus invalid, 9
  is–ought fallacy, 385
  objections, 29
  premises, 9
  premises, true versus false, 9
Lovelace, Ada, 222

Macauly, Thomas, 15
Machlup, Fritz, 167, 179, 188
MacLeod, Christine, 171, 173, 176
Merges, Robert, 28, 36, 157, 182, 190
metaphysical concepts
  functionalism, 396
  tangibility versus intangibility, 2
  things versus acts, 3, 75
  things versus knowledge, 213
  things versus non-things, 40, 50
  things, intellectual, 3
Mill, John Stuart, 339
moral rights
  attribution, 119–20
  duration, 120
  false attribution, 120
  integrity, 116–30
  integrity, objective versus subjective standard, 116–30
  overview, 114–16
  waiver, 125
Moser, Petra, 187

Neuberger, David, 225, 272, 294, 301–2, 353, 499
Newton, Isaac, 185
non-practising entity, 522
Nozick, Robert, 30, 403

online platforms, 105
overlaps, 326
  cumulation, 332
  demarcation, 330
  designs, unity of art, 330

Page, Hillary, 169
passing off
  classic trinity, 497
  damage, 512–15
  damage, lost licensing revenue, 512–15
  extended passing off, 509
  goodwill, 498–503
  in gross transfers, 502
  misrepresentation, 503–12
  misrepresentation of quality, 507–12
  misrepresentation, of origin, 503–7
patent troll, 522
patent, ownership
  evergreening, 254
patent, registration
  grace periods, 250
  revocation, 200
patent, specification
  claims, 199
  cover page, 199
  description, 199
  drawings, 199
  embodiments, 277
patents, claim construction, 288–304
  Actavis v Eli Lilly, 300–4
  doctrine of equivalents, 297–300
  European Patent Convention, article 203, 204, 295
  European Patent Convention, protocol on the interpretation of article 203, 204, 300
  Improver questions, 295–97
  interpretation versus construction, 290
  purposive construction, 290–95
  variants, 294
patents, claims
  purpose, 199
  requirements, 280–82
  types, 199
patents, compulsory licensing, 308–17
  crown use, 315–17
  failure to work, 309
  international law, 308–14
  UK law, 314–17
patents, exceptions, 304–8
  exhaustion, 288
  experimental use, 305–8
  prior use, 308
  private non-commercial use, 308

patents, history
  first-to-invent, 201
  hostility to monopolies, 173–75
  industrial policy, 171–73
  letters patent, 170
  nineteenth-century controversy,
    178–80
  Statute of Monopolies, 175–78
  Venice Senate Act, 172
patents, industrial application, 271–74
patents, infringing acts, 287
patents, inventive step, 260–71
  analysis, 267–83
  mosaicking, 261
  obviousness, 260
  obvious to try, 265
  person having ordinary skill in the art
    (PSITA), 260
  primary evidence, 267
  problem-and-solution approach,
    264
  secondary evidence, 267–70
  state of the art, 260
patents, novelty, 249–60
  absolute novelty, 249, 561
  anticipation, 252, 561
  disclosures at international
    exhibitions, 251
  disclosures in breach of confidence,
    251
  enabling disclosure, 252–57
  mosaicking, 261
  novelty of purpose, 257–60
  person having ordinary skill in the art
    (PSITA), 251–52
  prior art: *see* state of the art
  reverse infringement test, 253
  right to work doctrine, 254
  secret use, 254
  state of the art, 249–51
patents, ownership
  assignment, 288
  duration, 288
  exhaustion, 288
  licensing, 288
patents, registration
  entitlement, 201–3
  first-to-file, 201
  grant procedure, 200–1
  priority, 204
  specification, 193–200
patents, right to repair, 288

patents, subject matter
  any hardware, 223, 561
  as such, 216
  business methods, 226–28
  computer programs, 222–26
  discoveries, 217–22
  genes, 217
  invention, nature of, 212–15
  isolation, 220
  mental acts, 230–32
  methods of treatment, 243
  plant and animal varieties, 240–43
  presentation of information, 228–30
  products of nature, 217
  public policy and morality, 232–40
  technical character, 214–15
patents, sufficiency of disclosure,
    275–80
  biogen sufficiency, 277
  classical insufficiency, 275
  enabling disclosure, 275
  excessive breadth, 275
Penrose, Edith, 179
personality argument
  copying objection, 41
  copyright, 38–40
  inventor as genius, 181
  patents, 181
  problems with, 40–41
  romantic author, 39
  trade marks, 405
Pila, Justine, 214
piracy, 43
plant variety protection, 318
political economy concepts
  lobbying, 22, 69, 122, 325, 338, 369,
    558
  political economy, 184, 186, 332
political philosophy concepts, 19
  autonomy, 39
  equality, 25
  freedom of expression, 19, 104, 471
  legitimacy, 25
  liberalism, 5, 44, 179, 339
  liberty (freedom), 27
  natural rights, 25
  pluralism, 44
  rights as trumps, 159
  self-determination, 39
  social contract, 27
  state of nature, 25
  utilitarianism, consequentialism, 32

Posner, Richard A, 400
property concepts, 4–6
  appurtenance, 393
  Blackstonian property, 5
  bundle of rights, 4
  designs as property, 350, 353
  exclusive control, 4
  goodwill as property, 497
  in gross transfers, 502
  inventions as property, 286
  'property-based' approach to trade
    marks, 464
  public domain, 24
  restraint on alienation, 99
  rights versus privileges, 86, 180
  signs as property, 388, 456
  works as property, 50

Raustiala, Kal, 336
remedies
  account of profits, 540–43
  account of profits, apportionment,
    541
  account of profits, incremental
    approach, 540–43
  Anton Piller orders, 551–54
  criminal sanctions, 543
  damages in lieu of injunction, 524
  delivery up, 544–48
  freezing orders, 554
  going rate, 531
  hold-up, 522
  imports, 548
  injunctions, carve outs, 528
  injunctions, final, 521–28
  injunctions, interim, proportionality,
    551
  injunctions, *Mareva*, 554
  injunctions, preliminary, 548–51
  monetary damages, 529–40
  monetary damages, causation
    principles, 534
  monetary damages, innocent
    infringement, 538
  monetary damages, moral prejudice,
    538
  monetary damages, quantification
    principles, 532
  Norwich Pharmaceutical orders, 554
  punitive damages, 543
  quia timet action, 505
  search orders, 551–54

rights associated to copyright, 162
   database rights, 162
   droit de suite, 162
   performers' rights, 162
   press publishers' right, 162
   technological protection measures, 162
royalties, 67

sampling, 97
Saw, Cheng Lim, 65
Schechter, Frank, 391
Sheeran, Ed, 89–130
Sherman, Brad, 50
Shiffrin, Seanna, 47
Shikbbu, Murasaki, 25
Smith, Adam, 179
Smith, Peter, 8–9
Sprigman, Christopher, 336
sui generis rights, 241
supplementary protection certificates (SPCs), 318
Syed, Talha, 33, 213

Towse, Ruth, 6
trade marks, absolute grounds for refusal
   acquired distinctive character, 432–38
   acquired distinctive character, evidence, 435
   acquired distinctive character, reliance versus recognition, 435
   bad faith, 450–52
   customary, 432
   deceptive marks, 449
   descriptive of goods or services, 428–32
   devoid of distinctive character, 423–28
   distinctive character, inherent, 425
   generic, 432
   lack of subject matter, 413–22
   public policy or morality, 446–49
   shapes necessary to achieve technical result, 441–43
   shapes resulting from the nature of the goods, 439–41
   shapes that give substantial value, 443–45
   shapes with excluded functionality, 439–46

shapes, aesthetic functionality, 444
shapes, utilitarian functionality, 441
specially protected emblems, 449
trade marks, average consumer, 423
trade marks, defences, 485–94
   descriptive use, 486–88
   exhaustion, 491–94
   honest practices, 490
   nominative or referential use, 488–90
   spare parts, 488
   use of own name or address, 486
   use of registered mark, 485–86
trade marks, duration, 405
trade marks, history, 385–97
   action of deceit, 385–88
   dilution, 394
   functionalism, 396–97
   protecting functions beyond origin, 390–96
   register, 388
   trade marks as property, 388–90
trade marks, infringement, 477–85
   confusing similarity, 457–63
   confusing similarity, interdependent versus atomistic analysis, 461
   confusing similarity, likelihood of association, 463
   consumer confusion, 390
   debranding, 484
   dilution, 472
   double identity, 456–57
   global appreciation, 457
   in the course of trade, 477
   marks with reputation, 463–77
   marks with reputation, detrimental to distinctive character, 469–74
   marks with reputation, detrimental to reputation, 469–74
   marks with reputation, establishing a link, 467
   marks with reputation, reputation, 465–66
   marks with reputation, similarity, 466–69
   marks with reputation, unfair advantage, 469–74
   marks with reputation, without due cause, 474–77
   post-sale confusion, 480
   rebranding, 493
   repackaging, 493
   senior versus junior marks, 395

tarnishment, 474
trade mark use, 477–83
trade marks, registration, 406
   invalidity, 406
   revocation, 406
trade marks, relative grounds for refusal, 456–77
   confusing similarity, 457–63
   confusing similarity, interdependent versus atomistic analysis, 461
   confusing similarity, likelihood of association, 463
   dilution, 472
   double identity, 456–57
   global appreciation, 457
   marks with reputation, 463–77
   marks with reputation, detrimental to distinctive character, 469–74
   marks with reputation, detrimental to reputation, 469–74
   marks with reputation, establishing a link, 467
   marks with reputation, reputation, 465–66
   marks with reputation, similarity, 466–69
   marks with reputation, unfair advantage, 469–74
   marks with reputation, without due cause, 474–77
   post-sale confusion, 480
   senior versus junior marks, 395
   tarnishment, 474
trade marks, sign functions, 378–85
   advertising, 380–82
   badges of origin, 379–80
   communication, 385
   identity, 383–85
   investment function, 383
   quality, 382–83
   warranty, 382–83
trade marks, subject matter, 413–22
   abstract concepts, 415
   colour codes, 418
   colours, 414, 418
   graphic representation, 416
   scents, 417
   shapes, 414, 420
   Sieckmann criteria, 417
   signs, 414–16
   signs, capable of distinguishing goods or services, 421–22

signs, capable of representation on
register, 421
sounds, 414
trade secret, 188
Tushnet, Rebecca, 395

unjustified threats, 554–55
utilitarian argument
alternatives objection, 35, 37–38,
185, 561
balance concept, 35
competition objection, 190

copyright, 35–38, 80, 134, 157
cumulative creativity, 34
cumulative innovation, 207
designs, 335–37
empirical objection, 35
formal statement thereof, 35
incentive–access tradeoff, 35
patents, 184–93
patents, incentives to disclose, 187–90
patents, incentives to invent, 184–88
patents, patent bargain, 207, 317–18
patents, prospect theory, 192

piracy paradox, fashion, 336
prizes, 209
problems with, 35–38
prospect theory, 190
quid pro quo, 189
subsidies, 38
trade marks, 397–402
Van Gogh, Vincent, 1

World Intellectual Property
Organization, 43
World Trade Organization, 43